Finding Aids to the Microfilmed Manuscript Collection of the Genealogical Society of Utah

PRELIMINARY SURVEY OF THE GERMAN COLLECTION

For abreviations see "IV"

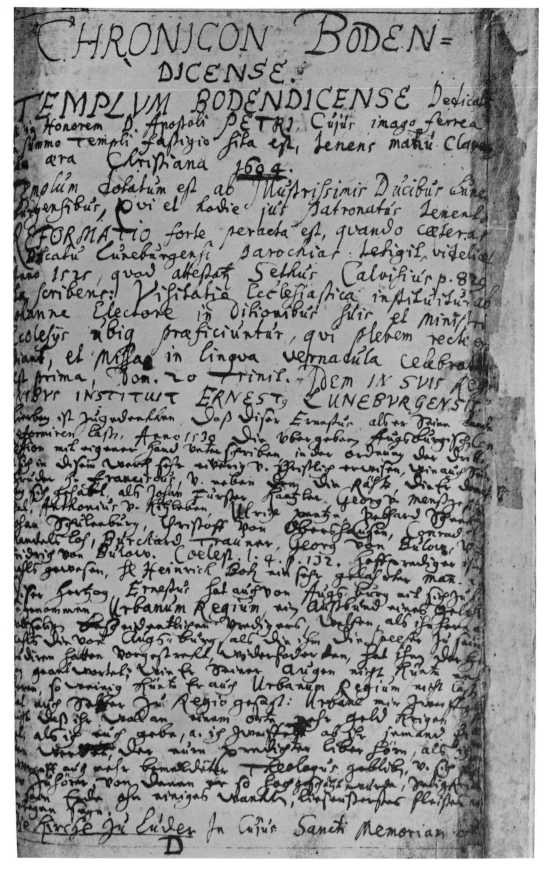

Title page of the town chronicle of Brysach (now Breisach), Chronicon Bodendicense, a document spanning most of the seventeenth century. Repository of original document unknown.

NUMBER 2

FINDING AIDS
TO THE MICROFILMED MANUSCRIPT COLLECTION
OF THE GENEALOGICAL SOCIETY OF UTAH

ROGER M. HAIGH, EDITOR

PRELIMINARY SURVEY
OF
THE GERMAN COLLECTION

BY

RONALD SMELSER

WITH THOMAS DULLIEN AND HERIBERT HINRICHS

UNIVERSITY OF UTAH PRESS
SALT LAKE CITY
1979

The series <u>Finding Aids to the Microfilmed Manuscript Collection</u> <u>of the Genealogical Society of Utah</u> is funded in part by grants from the National Endowment for the Humanities and the University of Utah. Number 1 in the series is the <u>Preliminary Survey of the</u> <u>Mexican Collection</u>, published December 1978.

CONTENTS

SURVEY OF THE GERMAN COLLECTION

Territories Now Part of the Federal Republic of Germany (West Germany)

Territories Now Part of the German Democratic Republic (East Germany)

Territories Formerly Part of the German Empire, Now Within the Borders of France, Poland, or the Soviet Union

Prepared with the assistance of the Center for Historical

Population Studies, University of Utah

Dean May, Acting Director

Anne Mette Haigh, Associate Editor

ACKNOWLEDGMENTS

The author wishes to express his gratitude to the staff of the Genealogical Society of Utah, especially Mr. George Fudge, Dr. Ray Wright, Mr. Norm Storrer, and Ms. Marta Hall, for their generous cooperation in making this publication possible. I am grateful to the Institutional Funds Committee of the University of Utah and its chairman, Dr. William Partridge, for financing the project; and I am indebted to Ms. Cheryl Willey for typing the manuscript.

R.S.

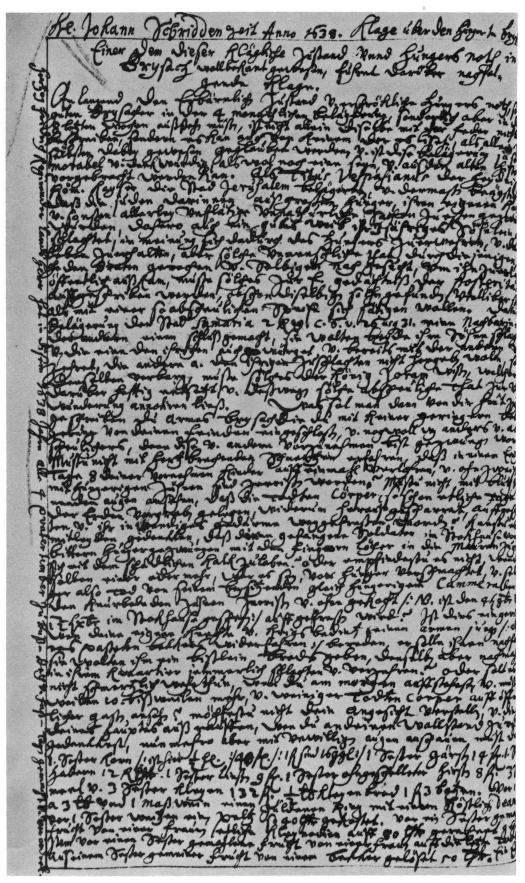

Pages from the town chronicle of Brysach. The most dramatic
passages illustrate the destructive impact of the Thirty Years' War

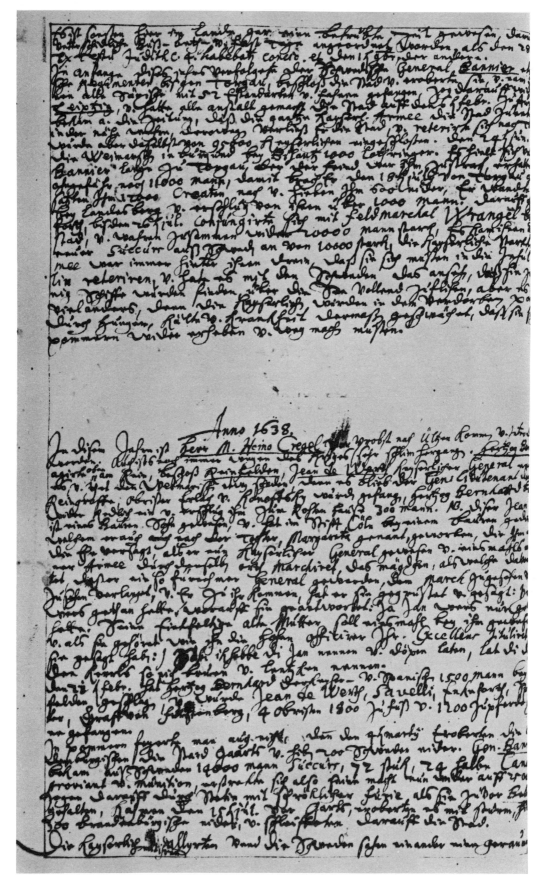

on the town, which, like so many other communities in Germany, was
besieged and looted in 1638. Repository of original document unknown.

PREFACE

The largest collection of filmed manuscripts in the world, more than a million 100-foot rolls, is used only sparingly by the world's academic community and other genealogical researchers. This problem is a result of misinformation or lack of information about the Genealogical Society of Utah's collection. It is precisely this situation that the series <u>Finding Aids to the Microfilmed Manuscript Collection of the Genealogical Society of Utah</u> is designed to correct.

The scope of the collection is truly international. The declared intention of the Society is "to gather records on everyone who has ever lived." As astonishing as this statement may appear, this is the Society's goal. At the present time significant collections of microfilmed manuscripts exist for the United States, Europe, Latin America, and the Far East.

The bulk of this awesome collection is comprised of civil and parish registers of births, marriages, deaths, and whatever other kinds of information records of this type may contain. However, the remaining rolls of film alone constitute the largest collection of non-parish or non-civil register in the world! Included here is an amazing variety of types of materials--letters, maps, factory records, guild records, immigration material, to name a few. Whereas the parish and civil registers are usually adequately cataloged, these other kinds of records are not. The primary aim of the <u>Finding Aids</u> is to acquaint scholars with the nature and location of these historical manuscripts.

Three types of aids will be offered through the series: preliminary surveys, descriptive inventories, and bibliographic guides.

The <u>preliminary survey</u> is planned to give the researcher rather precise information about the holdings of parish and civil registers in large national collections. Designed as much to indicate regions within a national area where records are missing as those for which there are extensive holdings, the survey attempts to insure that those coming to use the collection are not disappointed, and that the library

can have requested rolls available for the researcher upon arrival.
The surveys also provide a general idea of the types of other
materials that, for a variety of reasons, are a part of the Society's
holdings in a given national area. Finally, the surveys identify
sections for which existing cataloging is reliable and those for
which it is not.

The descriptive inventory is a more precise bibliographic
instrument. Aimed at collections less than 50 percent complete (as
estimated by the Society), the inventories classify and record
manuscripts and indicate film footage. The material is cross-
referenced to give an interested researcher quite an accurate picture
of holdings of particular types of records, holdings in given time
periods, and holdings of various types of records within given
geographic regions.

The bibliographic guide is the most detailed of the aids. It is
designed to focus on smaller collections of previously uncataloged
material. The bibliographic guide requires the reading of each roll
of film in the collection and a precise description of its contents.
The rolls are then cross-referenced by manuscript type, time span,
region, etc. Bibliographic guides are planned only for collections
the Society regards as complete.

The Finding Aids series represents the response of the University
of Utah to needs expressed by the international community of scholars.
This process began in 1976, when the University Institutional Funds
Committee generously granted funds to the Department of History to
bring in a team of social scientists to evaluate the scholarly
potential of the collection and to make recommendations to facilitate
its use. Jerome Clubb, Samuel Hays, and Jackson Turner Main
represented researchers with an interest in holdings for the United
States; and Louise Tilly, Lewis Hanke, and Richard Wall, the latter
representing the Cambridge Population Studies program, investigated
the potential of the international holdings. Their recommendations
varied, but they were in complete agreement on two points: (1) The
collection has fantastic potential for many types of scholarly
research; and (2) a series of finding aids is urgently needed to make
the collection more accessible to and more efficiently usable by
scholars and other researchers.

As this book goes to press, a preliminary survey of the Mexican
holdings has been published, and a descriptive inventory of the
English collection is ready for publication. These first three studies

were made possible by additional funds specially allocated by the University of Utah and administered through the newly established Center for Historical Population Studies, Dean May, Acting Director.

Three more finding aids are in preparation, funded by a grant from the National Endowment for the Humanities: a bibliographic guide to a collection filmed in the Casa de Morelos, formerly the library of the Archdiocese of Michoacán, Mexico; a descriptive inventory of the filmed manuscript holdings for the state of New York; and a preliminary survey of the holdings for France.

These aids will be kept current through supplements issued as needed, listing all pertinent, newly cataloged material. Supplements will be made available at cost to purchasers of the books.

If additional funding is available, the next three years will see the completion of a preliminary survey of Denmark; descriptive inventories of New England, Japan, and Louisiana-Georgia; and bibliographic guides for Scotland, Hungary, and Guatemala. Their publication will complete the series' first five years.

The series itself will then be reevaluated. The response of the academic community and researchers of all kinds, the needs of the Society, the availability of funds, and many other factors will be considered. If the results warrant continuation, another publication program will be outlined.

The authors and the publisher want these finding aids to be as effective a tool as possible. With this in mind, we earnestly solicit suggestions for improving their usefulness, which may be addressed to the series editor in care of the University of Utah Press.

Roger M. Haigh

INTRODUCTION

Genesis

The genesis of the German collection held by the Genealogical
Society of the Church of Jesus Christ of Latter-day Saints (LDS)
lies largely in the activities of a very dedicated member of that
church, who was also a civil servant in the Third Reich. The
collapse of Hitler's Germany in 1945 gave this Mormon the oppor-
tunity to secure for his church many valuable records which other-
wise would have been lost or, in later years, closed to access.
During the years immediately following World War II, the Russians
made no effort to control the collection of genealogical material,
so it was possible to gather further large numbers of civil and
church records for the Genealogical Society. Correspondence with
the Society produced funds to establish a copy center at the LDS
East Berlin Mission headquarters; and a great deal of material was
funneled through this center and filmed for the Genealogical Society.
After 1949, when the German Democratic Republic was established, the
far less casual East German authorities made the record gathering
project much more difficult.

The archives of the Genealogical Society are housed in Salt
Lake City, Utah. Here the German collection has continued to grow,
to the point where today it consists of more than 50,000 rolls of
microfilm, a figure being increased at the rate of 90 to 150 rolls
a month. One can gain some idea of the incredible amount of
material involved here from the German section of the card catalog,

which houses over 60,000 cards in 78 drawers. And yet, in the
calculations of the Society, microfilming in Germany is at this
point only 15 percent completed! Although the Länder of Baden-
Württemberg, Rheinland-Pfalz and Nordrhein-Westfalen are well
represented (though by no means complete), the other states are
represented quite sparsely. Moreover, there is practically no
material from the area of the German Democratic Republic, with the
exception of the former Grand Duchy of Mecklenburg, where over 90
percent of the church records have been filmed. Surprisingly, the
former German eastern provinces now part of Poland are well represented due, in part, to Polish cooperation in recent years.

The incomplete nature of the German collection (in contrast,
for example, to the relatively complete Scandinavian and British
collections) naturally gives rise to the question: Why this guide
at this time? Our reasons for beginning the project were fourfold;
and time and the project itself have confirmed our judgment. First,
we felt it important that the scholarly world be made aware of the
existence and magnitude of the collection, now. Awareness of the
collection has not been widespread, and those scholars who have
known of its existence have had only vague ideas of its nature or
scope. Some assumed that it was only a small collection of strictly
genealogical materials. We hope to remedy this impression by pre-
senting as complete an initial inventory as possible.

Second, we undertook our task in order to facilitate, as much
as possible, use of the Society's materials by those who want to do
scholarly research. The survey provides information on parish
and civil records by province and town; it indicates the nature of
other materials available, including where that material was
originally filmed, the time span it covers, and the number of rolls
available. In addition, by explaining in some detail the methods

and specific problems of information retrieval at the Society, we hope to save the researcher time-consuming delays during what might be very brief research stays in Utah.

Third, considering the enormous amount of material in the collection and the rapid rate at which more is acquired, it seemed wise to assert some bibliographic control over the existing collection in a form which would make it most accessible to scholars--and then handle the arriving material in regularly scheduled supplements.

Finally, we found it advisable to undertake the project at this time, because we hope that the project itself will aid in effecting a more complete and efficient acquisitions policy on the part of the Genealogical Society. The primary goal of the Society is, quite naturally, to gather materials for genealogical purposes; and the directors of the Society are quite aware that useful genealogical materials go far beyond collections of names and family histories. To do effective genealogical work demands support materials which are at the same time the very data that scholars, particularly those who are engaged in quantitative studies, need for their own research. There is, thus, a community in which the Society and scholars have been, and can be, of enormous mutual benefit. We hope that this inventory will further that relationship.

We do not purport to have produced a complete guide to the German holdings of the Genealogical Society. Rather, we suggest that this represents 1) a preliminary survey of the collection giving scholars an overview of the kinds of materials to be found there, and 2) a listing by community and province of the parish and civil records now available and cataloged.

Acquisitions

The Society has 100 camera teams worldwide, one third of which are in Europe. There are three active teams in Germany producing 90 to 150 rolls per month. In 1979 there will be five or six teams operating in Germany with an expected monthly production of 150 to 250 rolls per month.

The filming is done according to priorities set by the Acquisitions Planning Committee of the Society. Aiding this committee with information and suggestions are personnel on the scene in Germany, whose job it is to uncover new sources of material and to aid in negotiations with secular and religious authorities for the filming of material.

As one might expect, church records have the highest priority, followed by other materials of genealogical value, including everything from immigration to guild and court records. In procuring the right to film these materials, the Society is wholly dependent on the good will and cooperation of church and civil authorities, both local and regional. The fact that some of these authorities have looked favorably on the filming project while others have been completely uncooperative is reflected in the collection holdings. In some cases (Baden-Württemberg on the Land and Augsburg on the municipal level, for example) ecclesiastical leaders have been very helpful, resulting in fairly complete coverage of those areas. In other cases (Bavaria on the Land and Cologne on the municipal level, for example) the opposite has been the case, resulting in rather meager coverage of these areas.

Moreover, the fact that one authority or another, either religious or secular, may at any moment reverse an earlier decision for or against cooperation with the filming project, results in priorities having to be very flexible. For example, recently the Society gained permission to film the Kriegsarchiv in Vienna and

Linz, an enormous undertaking which will involve several camera teams for the next five years, resulting in an addition to the collection of more than 30,000 reels. This endeavor will possibly necessitate that other projects be held in abeyance.

Cataloging

The microfilmed materials arrive at the Genealogical Society's archives for processing and cataloging. The time lag between filming and cataloging is approximately one year, so that at any given time, approximately 1 to 3 percent of the holdings are not reflected in the catalog. The catalog itself is organized alphabetically and by geographic area. Thus, the names of German localities (parish towns, seats of the local registrars) and provinces can be found first arranged alphabetically in the general catalog, and second, listed under the appropriate province in the German section of the catalog. Munich, then, would be found in the "M" section of the general catalog and under "Bayern" in the German section. In the catalog under "Germany" there is a general section with listings labeled vital records, immigration records, probate records, etc., followed by the various Länder in alphabetical order. Individual localities are listed alphabetically under the appropriate Land. It should be noted that the German section of the catalog must be used with the aid of Meyer's Orts- und Verkehrslexikon des deutschen Reiches and Müller's Grosses deutsches Ortsbuch or many localities will be missed.

In cataloging materials, the Society has adopted a policy of following current political boundaries. Thus, many areas formerly part of Germany are now part of neighboring countries and this is reflected in the catalog. To find these materials, one should consult so-called "see cards" in the German section of the catalog. These are arranged alphabetically under the name of the former

German province and give the former German name of a locality as
well as the province (and occasionally, but not always, the
county) along with the new equivalent. Thus, to find material in
the catalog one may turn to the country of a particular location,
then find the present name of the province of interest, and there
identify the place by its new name. The "see card" sections, however, are incomplete and represent only two-thirds of the former
German localities now listed in the catalog drawers under Poland,
etc. Moreover, only a portion of the older German jurisdictions
will be found in the German section; the rest must be sought in the
general section of the catalog under the local entries.

With respect to local boundaries, the catalog reflects, again
by means of "see cards", the Eingemeindung (urban annexation) process in the post-war period. In order to avoid the necessity of
constant changes in the catalog and the concomitant chaos, the
local boundaries used are those of the 1958 edition of Müller.

Examples of Card Catalog Entries

country ————————————————— GER
                                                Film

film no. —————————————————— 1,054,759

locality (as author) ——————

parish ————————————————————— Gschwend, Germany. Röm.-kath. Kirche,
                                     Schlechtbach.

nature of record & dates ——— Kirchenbuch, 1840-1902. -- Rottenburg,
   (as title)   Diözesanarchiv : Genealogical Society, 1976.

where filmed & when ————————— 1 reel ; 35 mm. : pt. index. hand-
                                     written.

                                        Parish register of baptisms, marriages,
                                 deaths, family registers for Schlechtbach,

description (content notes) — part of Gschwend. Includes Marzellenhof,
                                 part of Gschwend; Mittelbronn and Hohenreusch,

camera team —————————————————— Ger 71 2135 —————— 24 May 1977
                                                 Card 1 of 3   SV

date cataloged —————————————

        GER
        Film
        1,054,759
                Gschwend, Germany. ...

                both part of Frickenhofen; Gschwend, and
                Spraitbach.

description (content notes)— I. Taufregister   1856-1900
                II. Ehe-Register   1840-1901
                III. Todten-Register 1843-1902
                IV. Register (index) & Familienregister 1856

cross-references ————————————— 1. Germany, Baden-Württemberg, Gschwend -
                Vital records. 2. Germany,Baden-Württemberg.

                                    24 May 1977
                                    Card 2 of 3   SV

        GER
        Film
        1,054,759
                Gschwend, Germany. ...

                Frickenhofen - Vital records. 3. Germany,
                Baden-Württemberg, Spraitbach - Vital

cross-references ——————————————records. I. Frickenhofen, Germany, Röm.-
                kath. Kirche. II. Spraitbach, Germany.
                Röm.-kath. Kirche.

                Ger 71 2135   24 May 1977
                                  Card 3 of 3   SV

Special Concerns

Given the staggering task of acquiring and cataloging this immense collection of records, it would be surprising indeed if mistakes were not made--if problem areas did not develop. For the most part the catalog is accurate and systematic, but the researcher should keep in mind the following:

1) Over the past twenty years the cataloging has undergone four phases. During the earliest and most primitive phase, call numbers were assigned on the basis of geographic area and the order in which the material had been filmed (e.g. Germany-12840); older political jurisdictions were used (e.g. Germany under the Kaiserreich); and there were no cross-references. There followed two other phases in which a **red numerical system was** employed-- one without cross-referencing, one with cross-referencing. Today's system, in service since 1968, is arranged according to reel accession number, employs current political jurisdictions, and includes a thorough cross-referencing system. Over 90 percent of the German collection is under the newest system; and although one occasionally finds cards from the third phase, there are apparently none left from the first two phases.

2) Several related problems crop up as a result of multiple listings in the catalog. As previously noted, all locality records appear at least twice in the card catalog: once in the general catalog and once under the Germany section. Often they will appear three times; for example, a military parish register for a specific town will appear in the general catalog alphabetically under that town; in the Germany General section under military records; and once again, alphabetically, under the Land in which that town is located. This system of replication can indeed help the researcher

avoid missing a source. Occasionally, however, such replication produces discrepancies: a) In cases of formerly independent units which have recently been annexed by larger ones, an independent card for the old one should be replaced by a "see card" referring to the larger unit of which it is now a part. Catalogers have not always kept up with these changes. The three villages of Genin, Travemünde, and Schlutup in Schleswig-Holstein were once independent; now they are all part of the city of Lübeck. This is correctly noted in the Germany section of the catalog under Lübeck. However, in the general catalog, where all three should now appear as only a "see card" referring to Lübeck, only Schlutup does. Travemünde still has its own card; and there is no reference to Genin at all. It would be wise, therefore, to consult all sections of the catalog--Germany and general--where a locality might appear. b) Occasionally, bits and pieces of a collection appear in different places in one drawer. Probate court records from various parts of Gross Berlin, for example, appear in different places in the drawer under Berlin, and then again later in that same drawer intact as a unit. The researcher should be aware of this and peruse an entire section to ensure that he has found all the records of a particular sort. c) Sometimes the same material will appear under different reel numbers in different sections of the same drawer. This occurs because camera teams often film the same material twice, either because it was located at more than one archive; because it was moved from one archive to another; or, because teams may have been allowed to film only part of a collection at one point, found the entire collection open at a later date, and filmed it in its entirety in accordance with the filming contract.

3) At times an incorrect provenance will be listed, as the cataloger confuses the agency which originally generated a document with the archive in which it reposes. Incorrect time spans of material have been found on some catalog cards; but one can sometimes check for this, as well as the completeness of a given holding, by comparing the number of rolls with the time span given. If, for example, a given parish record occupies only one roll, yet the time span indicated is several centuries, one can assume that there is an error in the date, or that the material is very fragmentary. A cataloger's ignorance of language or of political changes can also cause confusion. There were, for example, until corrected, two sets of cards for the former Prussian province of East Prussia --one under East Prussia, another under Ostpreussen.

Filming policies sometimes complicate both the cataloging and the retrieval process. For example, microfilmers save on film and processing costs by filling every roll of film, even if it means adding frames of material completely extraneous to the main body of information on a particular roll.

4) One problem arises in connection with parish records. Many of the records dating from 1808 to 1875 are, in fact, not parish records at all, but transcripts of parish records. During those years, clergymen were compelled by the state to submit copies of their annual records. The practice was stopped in 1875 after the introduction of the Zivilstandesamt in Germany. Some of these transcripts are complete, others are not. Sometimes a priest or pastor would submit a separate book for each village in his parish. Until recently, the card catalog did not reflect the difference between the genuine parish record and the transcripts, an oversight which is now being corrected.

5) A special category of problems emerges as a result of the transfer to other nations of what at one time was German territory. Most conspicuous in this regard are the former German eastern provinces now part of Poland or the Soviet Union. It is not surprising that problems and errors have crept in precisely here, for catalogers have to deal with two completely different languages, political systems and forms of administration. At no administrative level do Polish or Russian boundaries coincide exactly with the former German ones. Furthermore, since 1900 several renamings of localities have occurred; the same name often refers to province, county, and municipality (e.g. Szczecin); administrative gerrymandering still happens frequently; and there is plenty of room for error.

In cataloging materials from the former German eastern provinces, the Society, following its usual policy of observing current political boundaries, has arranged such materials under Poland or the Soviet Union. To make the transition from former German to current Polish designation, the catalogers have placed "see cards" in the German part of the catalog under the names of the former provinces, alphabetically listing the older German name of a locality along with the newer Polish or Russian name under which the material can be found. Again, only two-thirds of these places have "see cards." Often, but not always, the counties, former and current, are also part of the listing. Thus, under Westpreussen in the German catalog might be found:

        Germany, Westpreussen, Rheinsberg
          (Briesen)

        SEE

        Poland, Bydgoszcz, Ryńsk (Wąbrzeźno)

The appropriate drawer under Poland would then show:

POL
Film
245,331
    Ryńsk, Poland. ...

      1. Poland, Bydgoszcz, Ryńsk - Vital
records. 2. Poland, Bydgoszcz, Wąbrzeźno
(powiat) - Vital records. 3. Wąbrzeźno
(powiat), Bydgoszcz, Poland - Vital records.

GRMN/G.W. (L)   29 Sep '75 r 9 Aug '77
11   Card 2 of 2   AB

POL
Film
245,331
    Ryńsk, Poland. Evang.-luth. Kirche.
      Kirchenbuch, 1898-1941. -- Lübeck :
Genealogical Society, 1958.
      1 reel ; 35 mm. : handwritten.
      Parish register of Evang. Church of
Rheinsberg (Kreis Strasburg), Westpreussen,
Germany, now Ryńsk and surrounding area in
Wąbrzeźno district, Bydgoszcz, Poland.
      Deaths 1898-1941; births 1898-1913

GRMN/G.W. (L)   29 Sep '75 r 9 Aug '77
11   Card 1 of 2   AB

The process works fairly well, although a few points should be kept in mind. In the Polish section of the catalog is found an additional category not used in the German section. That is, Germany is broken down by Länder, and the various localities are listed alphabetically under the appropriate Land. This is also true in the case of Poland, but here there is a further breakdown by county within each Land. Localities are listed alphabetically under both the province and under the powiat (county). These two are interfiled and in some cases the reference may be duplicated. This dovetailing of two listings interrupts the usual alphabetical flow and can be confusing. Adding to the confusion is the fact that often through cataloging error, the desired community is under one listing, but not under the other. Thus, both province and county should be checked; especially since there are often five or six entries under a given locality (parish records for Lutheran, Catholic, Jewish and Mennonite churches, plus civil records for certain communities in the East). Sampling indicates that entries under powiat tend to be most complete. Often, but by no means always, the former German designations are noted at the bottom of the Polish card; and one Polish name will designate the records of several former German localities by virtue of modern urban annexation procedures. Although the Society is now in the process of checking and recataloging, there are discrepancies (e.g. missing cards, misfilings, etc.) between the "see cards" on the German side and the actual listings on the Polish. Finally, as previously noted the Society generally adheres to its rule of cataloging according to current political boundaries; in the case of Poland, where a great deal of administrative manipulation has occurred in recent years, catalogers have remained with the 1967 changes.

Other Material

In addition to the vital and parish records which form the bulk of the German collection, there is a variety of other kinds of materials, which, although of secondary importance to the genealogist, are of prime interest to the social historian as well as to scholars in other fields. Because this material was not systematically sought by the LDS camera teams, but was acquired, often inadvertently, as part of larger collections of vital or parish records, it tends to be spotty, though nevertheless voluminous.

In some cases such "other material" arrived as a bulk collection (e.g. the guild records of Augsburg) and has been sampled thoroughly. In the case of more scattered data, our sampling has been limited. Generally, though not always, the card catalog entries for vital and parish records indicate when such records contain other kinds of material. Only film for which such additional materials were noted in the card catalog entries was sampled for this part of the survey. The sampling is not statistically viable, since only about 2 percent of the holdings are included. For that reason alone this survey makes no claims to be exhaustive; it is, rather, a preliminary indication of what scholars can expect to find within the microfilm archives of the Genealogical Society of Utah.

For the purposes of this survey, the non-parish records have been grouped under representative headings:

Guild Records	Municipal Records
Migration Records	Provincial Records
Legal Records	Genealogical Records
Medical Records	Jewish Records
Military Records	"Diamonds in the Rough"

I.   Guild Records

    In the microfilm archives of the Genealogical Society, guild records are highly concentrated for several German cities, most notable of which is Augsburg. To give the scholar an idea of the breadth and depth of the holdings of this type of record, there follows a detailed list of the guilds represented and the dates covered, as well as the results of a limited sampling to determine the nature of these records. The collection contains 643 rolls of microfilm which for the most part were obtained at the Stadtpflegeamt in Augsburg. We have followed the Genealogical Society's pattern of listing some occupations in German and others in English. There are also some overlaps in trade designations and time spans which we do not presume to explain at this point.

> Bäcker (1489-1809)
>
> Ballenbinder (1536-1790)
>
> Barettmacher (1585-1735)
>
> Bierringler (1551-1855)
>
> Bierbrauer (1693-1774)
>
> Bortenmacher (1808-1813)
>
> Botenschaffner (1804-1855)
>
> Branntweinbrenner (1537-1858)
>
> Brückler (1779-1848)
>
> Briefmaler, Illuministen und Formschneider
>   (1529-1699)
>
> Friseure (1828-1856)
>
> Fournierschneider (1845-1854)
>
> Gärtner (1568-1863)
>
> Kräutler und Obstler (1638-1860)
>
> Geschmeidemacher (1680-1743)
>
> Glaser (1548-1867)

Glockengiesser (n.d.)

Goldschläger (1556-1751)

Goldschmiede (1657-1670)

Langwarenhändler (1830-1855)

Laubsägenmacher (1837)

Metzger (1510-1757)

Milchleute und Schweizer (1779-1813)

Modelschneider (1722-1783)

Mueller (1511-1583)

Pallierer (1550-1736)

Schmiede (1594-1799)

Schneider (1443-1705)

Schuhmacher (1604-1808)

Weber (1549-1811)

Armourers (1541-1811)

Bakers (1489-1747)

Basket Makers (1830-1854)

Bellfounders (1526-1854)

Blacksmiths and Coppersmiths (1549-1688)

Bladesmiths (1554-1699)

Brickmakers (1617-1806)

Butchers (1417-1856)

Button Makers (1722-1856)

Carpenters (1548-1838)

Cartwrights (1548-1847)

Clockmakers (1544-1859)

Coachmen (1716-1856)

Coopers (1564-1872)

Cutlers (1490-1736)

Dry Goods Dealers (1836-1846)

Engravers (1530-1802)

Frame Makers (1700-1800)

Fruit Dealers (1530-1855)

Furriers (1472-1669)

Goldsmiths (1664-1864)

Grinders (1548-1776)

Harness Makers (1548-1826)

Lace Makers (1583-1811)

Leatherworkers (1548-1858)

Lithographers (1803-1813)

Locksmiths (1550-1855)

Manglers (1675-1854)

Masons (1549-1804)

Mead Dispensers (1590-1640)

Millers (1636-1821)

Nailsmiths (1549-1850)

Needle Makers (1549-1845)

Organ Builders (1576-1726)

Painters (1727-1804)

Papermakers (1583-1835)

Pastry Bakers (1559-1860)

Potters (1508-1856)

Poulterers (1802-1811)

Purse Makers (1550-1851)

Ribbon Weavers (1830-1856)

Rope Makers (1454-1812)

Saddlers (1722-1859)

Salters (1275-1613)

Sausage Makers (1696-1813)

Sawyers (1524-1799)

Scissor Makers (1709-1756)

Sculptors (1509-1851)

Shoemakers (1548-1903)

Silkweavers (1579-1813)

Soapmakers (1551-1836)

Spurmakers (1549-1810)

Stocking Weavers (1616-1852)

String Makers (1534-1794)

Swordsmiths (1548-1808)

Tailors (1706-1845)

Tanners (1548-1854)

Tavern Owners (1520-1860)

Tin Founders (1549-1780)

Tobacconists (1744-1813)

Type Founders (1764-1813)

Umbrella Makers (1783-1835)

Upholsterers (1815-1861)

Venison Dealers (1740-1849)

Watchmakers (1751-1798)

Wigmakers (1708-1822)

Windlass Makers (1624-1881)

Yarn Dealers (1539-1674)

The guild records are for the most part membership lists and financial records, but a great deal of other material does appear throughout. The following small sampling, done where "other material" was noted on catalog cards, will give some indication of the variety of such content.

Film No. 476,281: Pflegschaftskassabuch 1690-1695

    1st Item
-Verzeichnis der Kreditoren 1690.
-Bilanzkonten von 1690.
-Abrechnung und Richtlinien des Oberpflegeamtes mit Anmerkungenen der Zinsdaten Georgi und Michaelis.
-Dokumente über Schuldschriften für Pflegekinder 1685.
-Richtlinien und dokumentierte Fälle für Kapitalausgaben und Verzinsung.

    2nd Item
-Protokolle der Verträge 1578-1584 bezüglich der Kreditgewährung und der Geldausleihe.

Film No. 476,282: Personen- und Berufregister zum Steuerbuch des gemeinen Pfennigs (Bd. IVI b).

-A listing of names of individuals who were reported for taxation. Only names and the amount of taxes are indicated. In the second part of the film is a listing of the various guilds for the year 1497.

Film No. 576,283: Register zur Hussiten-Steuer 1428.

-Names and the amount of taxes are recorded.

Film No. 476,284: Register zu den Nachsteuer-Einträgen 1500-1600

-Names of all occupations related to art and artistic craftsmanship--continuation of list from 1601-1633.

Film No. 563,145: Handwerkerakten Weberhaus, Notstandshilfe, Brotverteilung, Weberzählung 1501, 1552, 1601.

-List of names of people who received financial or material help.

Film No. 561,221: Handwerkerakten: Hereinbringen Fremder Cottone 1594-1794

-Order from Josef II concerning the import and transport of cotton.
-Publication: Instructions and orders concerning the import and the sale of East Indian cotton.
-Instructions and orders for cotton manufacturers.
-Instruction and duties of the "Roh-Geschaumeister," the inspector responsible for the import and manufacturing of cotton.
-Instructions for the manufacturing of cotton 1666.
-New guidelines and instructions for weavers.
    October 11, 1785
    August 23, 1792
    November 3, 1792
    March 1, 1794

Film No. 581,168: Handwerkerakten Fischer (Vol 16, 1st item on
                    film) Dates: 1751-1817

        -Geschäftserlaubnis von der königlichen
         Polizeidirektion.
        -Allgemeine Korrespondenz und Widerrufe von
         Erlassen.
        -Protokolle von Sitzungen der Handwerkskammer.
        -Korrespondenz zwischen dem Landgericht
         Friedberg und der Polizeidirektion Augsburg.
        -Aufnahme in die Gilde, Gewerbeverleihung und
         Streitigkeiten bezüglich der Fischer 1779-
         1806.
        -Verordnungen und Artikel von 1657.
        -Venedig und Hochgebiet.
        -Auszug von der Fischer und hohen Obrigkeit-
         liche Marktordnung zur Veneration.

        Fischer-Ordnung
        -Neue Handwerkerordnung und Artikel 1672.
        -Ordnungen und Artikel des ehrbaren Handwerks
         von deren Fischer Meisteren.
        -Verordnungen und Erlasse den Fischmarkt
         betreffend.
        -Erneuerte Marktordnung, Augsburg 1738.

Film No. 476,282: Personen- und Berufsregister zum Steuerbuch des
                   gemeinen Pfennigs 1497

        -Tax records listed according to the different
         parishes--six volumes (Vol. VI has a,b) which
         mention names and amount of taxes.

Film No. 580,428: -Birth register 1870-1875.
        -Marriage register 1869-1875.
        -Death register 1869-1875.
        -Register of the members of the catholic-
         apostolic community.
        -Alphabetical register of persons living out-
         side the community who were married in a
         church within the community.
        -Söldnerbuch (register of mercenaries) 1360-
         1381 written in Latin and Old German.
        -Söldnerbuch: Mercenaries in the fight against
         the Hussiten 1427-1430, Latin.
        -Landfriedbuch.
        -Söldnerbuch 1447-1449, 1465-1504, Mercenaries
         in the fight against the Hussiten 1427-1431.
        -Fussgesellenbuch 1450.
        -Büchsenmeisterbuch 1463.
        -Ausrüstung fur Kriegszüge 1492.

Film No. 559,724: Handwerkerakten Weberhaus-Cottondrucker 1795-
                   1811

        -Protokolle, Verordnungen, Korrespondenz
        -Erlass des Königs (filmed document)
        Handwerkerakten Weberhaus, Kattunfabrikanten
        1707-1787
        -Erlasse (acta).

-Verordnungen.
-Verwaltungskorrespondenz.

Film No. 559,729: Handwerkerakten Weberhaus, Cottonfabrikanten
1650-1760

-Dokumente, Verordnungen und Korrespondenz.

Film No. 559,737: Streit der Weber, Cottondrucker und Fabrikanten
1794

-Erlass und Verordnungen des Rathes (Senat),
Strafandrohung, Dokumente hierzu.
-Diesbezügliche Korrespondenz zwischen Webern
und Senat.

Film No. 558,554: Handwerkerakten Weberhaus, Verwaltung 1733-1788

-Verordnungen des Senats und der Deputierten
als auch ihre Korrespondenz.

Film No. 558,564: Handwerkerakten Weberhaus, Varia insbesondere
Gesellen, verschiedenes

-Senats erlass 1684; 1705; 1730.
-Protokolle der Senatssitzungen 1732-1790.
-Abgabegelder.
-Einnahmegelder.
-Verordnungen des Bürgermeisters.
-Bürgschaften.
-Verzinsungen.

Film No. 558,579: Handwerkerakten Weberhaus, Cottondrucker 1793-
1794

-Appellationssachen gegen die Weber-
hausdeputierten.

II.   Migration Records

    Among the more useful and valuable records in the Genealogical

Society collection are those concerning migration, both within

Germany and to and from Germany. Such records appear, in part, in

the Rathaus files of several German cities particularly Hamburg and

Kaiserslautern under Reisepasskontrolle, Reisepass-Protokolle,

Fremdenmeldeprotokolle, Dienstboten-Meldeprotokolle, Auswanderung-

sakten, etc.

    Two collections stand out as particularly voluminous and useful:

The migration records of Baden-Württemberg and the Hamburg passenger

lists.

The migration records of the Königlich-Württembergische Regierung are the most extensive of the Society's collection. The bulk of these cover the nineteenth and early twentieth centuries, although there is some material going back to the fifteenth century. The documents, stemming from the various Oberämter, deal with both internal and external migration. They represent for the most part requests for permission to migrate, the disposition of such requests and Bürgerrechts-Verzichts-Urkunden. Information provided usually includes the individual's destination, place and date of birth, as well as identification of parents. The collection consists of approximately 800 rolls; the following overview gives some idea of its scope.

Site	Dates Covered	Destination
Backnang	1807-1800	U.S.-Switzerland
Balingen	1806-1882	
Besigheim	1811-1915	
Biberach	1806-1923	U.S.-Europe
Blaubeuren	1813-1869	
Böblingen	1831-1933	
Brackenheim	1806-1887	U.S.-Europe
Burgau	1422-1878	U.S.-Russia-Switzerland
Calw	1815-1920	
Cannstatt	1815-1922	U.S.-Europe
Creilsheim	1811-1891	
Ellwangen	1803-1863	
Ellwangen	1881-1899	U.S.-South America-Austria
Esslingen	1806-1859	U.S.-Austria-Rumania
Geislingen	1852-1884	U.S.-France
Gerabronn	1818-1874	U.S.-Switzerland-England-France

Site	Dates Covered	Destination
Göppingen	1817-1917	
Heilbronn	1854-1887	Prussia Poland-U.S.-South America
Herrenberg	1853-1927	
Herrenberg	1780-1920	U.S.-Switzerland
Horb	1780-1924	U.S.-Switzerland
Kirchheim	1829-1910	Prussia Poland-U.S.-France-Switzerland
Künzelsau	1807-1855, 1859-1913	
Laupheim	1811-1892	
Leonberg	1806-1891	Prussia-U.S.-Switzerland
Leutkirch	1807-1871	Prussia-U.S.-Hungary
Ludwigsburg	1806-1900	
Marbach	1811-1869	
Maulbronn	1852-1910	
Münsingen	1804-1889	
Münsingen	1807-1880	
Nagold	1833-1895	Prussia-Australia-U.S.-Switzerland-Internal-Hungary
Neckarsulm	1868-1870	Prussia-U.S.-Switzerland-England
Neckarsulm	1846-1867	
Neuenburg	1861-1879	Prussia-U.S.-Africa-Internal-Switzerland
Nürtingen	1806-1863	Russia-U.S.-Switzerland
Nürtingen	1863-1899	France-Hessen-Palestine-Switzerland-U.S.
Oberndorf	1811-1881	Switzerland-U.S.
Oberndorf	1814-1870	U.S.-England-Internal
Öhringen	1851-1890	U.S.-England-Austria-Internal

Site	Dates Covered	Destination
Ravensburg	1807-1930	U.S.-South America-Switzerland-Internal
Reutlingen	1807-1892	Bavaria-Switzerland-U.S.
Reutlingen	1847-1869	Bavaria-Switzerland-U.S.
Riedlingin	1807-1892	U.S.
Rottenburg	1811-1923	Prussia-U.S.-England
Rottweil	1821-1896	Prussia-France-U.S.-Switzerland
Saulgau	1813-1842, 1806-1910	Prussia-France-U.S.-Switzerland
Schorndorf	1808-1909	Russia-France-Switzerland-U.S.-Internal
Schwäbisch Hall	1803-1870	
Schwäbisch Gmünd	1819-1872	Austria-France-Switzerland-Internal
Spaichingen	1806-1869	U.S.-Switzerland
Stuttgart	1869-1919	
Stuttgart	1806-1915	U.S.-Switzerland
Stuttgart	1915-1918	
Sulz	1807-1897	U.S.-Russian Poland-Internal
Tettnang	1836-1871	Austria-U.S.-Switzerland-Internal
Tübingen	1806-1900	France-Switzerland-U.S.-England-Internal
Tuttlingen	1806-1891	Switzerland-U.S.-France-Internal
Tuttlingen	1842-1879	Switzerland-U.S.-France-Internal
Ulm	1843-1872	France-Switzerland-U.S.-Internal
Urach	1854-1873	Prussia-U.S.-Internal
Vaihingen	1811-1918	Russia-France-Switzerland-U.S.-Internal
Waiblingen	1815-1911	Prussia-Russia-Palestine-U.S.-Internal

Site	Dates Covered	Destination
Waldsee	1833-1893	Bavaria-U.S.-Switzerland-Internal
Wangen	1827-1932	Africa-U.S.-Switzerland-Internal
Weinsberg	1812-1858	Australia-U.S.-Prussia-Internal
Welzheim	1818-1892	Switzerland-U.S.-England-Internal

The Hamburg Passenger Lists represent an extremely valuable part of the Society's collection. Along with Bremen (whose records were destroyed during World War II), Hamburg was the most important continental port of embarcation for European emigrants in the nineteenth century. In fact, between 1859 and 1891, 30 percent of all European emigrants passed through Hamburg on their way to a new homeland, usually the United States of America.

The Hamburg Passenger Lists cover all persons who embarked from that port between 1850 and 1934. The lists are arranged chronologically by date of departure of the ship--revealing the name of the captain and of the ship, the flag under which it sailed and the destination. With respect to the passengers, the lists give name, sex, age, place of origin, occupation, number of accompanying family members (broken down by those over ten, under ten and under one year of age), and destination.

The lists are separated into two sections. The "direct" lists cover the period 1850-1934 and deal with passengers traveling directly from Hamburg to the port of final destination. The "indirect" lists cover the years 1854-1910 and deal with passengers who were going to stop at one or more intermediate ports, often to change ships, before going on to the final destination. Reflecting the fact that most emigrants went directly to their new homeland, the "direct" lists are more extensive (256 rolls) than the "indirect" lists (81 rolls).

Several indexes available on microfilm at the Genealogical Society will aid the researcher in dealing with this rather large collection:

1) A partially alphabetized index was compiled by the German authorities covering the period 1855-1934 (126 rolls) for the "direct" lists and 1855-1910 (12 rolls) for the "indirect" lists. This index is arranged by the first letter of the surname of the head of the family. Dependents are included but not indexed separately.

2) The other index was created by Mormons living in Germany and is a fully alphabetized card index of the "direct" lists. It includes name, occupation, age, place of origin, accompanying family members and their ages, the year, whether the family intended to travel directly or indirectly, as well as the page of entry for the family in the original passenger list. Unfortunately this very valuable aid covers only the period 1856-1871 (10 rolls).

Of special value to social and demographic scholars is the Hamburg material dealing with workers, artisans and servants as they move into and about the city during the second half of the nineteenth century. This material has as its provenance the allgemeine Fremdenpolizei and reflects name, age, place of birth, occupation, last residence and a continuing record of change of address or of placement (in the case of servants). These records have been broken down in the Genealogical Society in the following manner:

Nature of Material	Time Covered	No. of rolls
Allgemeine Fremdenmelde-protokolle (weibliche)	1868-1890	37
Allgemeine Fremdenmelde-protokolle (männliche)	1868-1889	253
Fremdenmeldeprotokolle männlicher und weiblicher Gesinde	1834-1840	17
Meldeprotokolle für Gesinde und Handwerker	1834-1867	32
Meldeprotokolle für männliche fremde Arbeiter und Dienstboten	1851-1890	13
Fremdenmeldeprotokolle weiblicher Dienstboten	1843-1890	82
Dienstbotenmelde-protokolle	1880-1890	12
Dienstbotenmelde-protokolle (weibliche)	1880-1889	41
Fremdenmeldeprotokolle männlicher Arbeiter Handwerker und Dienstboten	1861-1890	47
Gesellenprotokolle	1850-1867	25
		559

III.   Legal Records

The predominant legal material appearing in the Genealogical Society's German collection consists of probate court and guardianship records. These are scattered throughout the collection and are noted in the catalog under the pertinent town or city. By far the largest collection of probate records relate to Berlin and its environs. The collection consists of over 1700 rolls of Testamentsakten covering the period 1616-1932. The collection is broken down in the following manner:

Berlin proper	1686-1929	208 rolls
Charlottenburg	1685-1932	406
Spandau	1685-1920	409
Gross-Lichterfelde	1685-1732	545
Tempelhof	1906-1920	131
Königliches Stadtgericht (indexes and calendars of wills for various Berlin courts)	1616-1849	76
Testamentsakten	1616-1849	30
Innenministerium (Adresse-Kalender)	c.1704-1918	75
Juden- und Dissentenregister	1812-1874	31

IV.   Medical Records

Increasingly, vital records are becoming an important tool for medical research, as investigators attempt to trace disease patterns over several generations. The immense collection of vital records in the archives of the Genealogical Society is a rich vein for such studies. The collection also has useful material for the scholar in the fields of medical history and the history of medical administration. The hospital records of the city of Speyer are all excellent examples. These records cover a number of hospitals and almshouses in that city during the late medieval and early modern period and shed light on the financial aspects of such institutions

in a period when church and municipality were locked in struggle
over their control.

Elendherberg-Almosen	Rechnungen der Pfleger Einnahmen und Ausgaben Lagerbuch	1558-1798	12 rolls
Platter- und Stockal-mosen	Rechnung aller Einnahmen und Ausgaben	1547-1658	4
Neu-Almosen	Salbuch, Lagerbuch, Zinsbuch, Kapitalbuch, Rechnungen der Pfleger	1585-1807	11
Lazarett-Almosen Lazarett zum heiligen Grab	Rechnungen aller Einnahmen und Ausgaben	1594-1689	6
Heilig-Geist Almosen	Rechnungen aller Einnahmen und Ausgaben, Lagerbuch, Gülten, Pfennig- Heller- und Koppenzinsen. Geld- Frucht- und Ölzinsen	1528-1784 1584, 1600-1812	13 2
Stockalmosen	Rechnungen aller Einnahmen und Ausgaben	1698-1798	7
Sondersiechenhaus	Rechnungen der Pfleger, Einnahmen und Ausgaben, Lagerbuch	1555-1798	15
Sankt Georgen-Hospital	Rechnungen der Pfleger	1514-1700	32
Sankt Georgen-Hospital	Seelbuch, Zinsbuch, Sal- und Lagerbuch Kontraktenbuch, Pfründnerbuch, Amstsprotokolle	1310-1798	43
Beguinenhaus zum Roten Schild	Gült-und Zinsbuch, Inventar und Aufnahme von Beguinensch-western	1524-1571	1
Heilig-Kreuz-Kopelle	Rechnungen der Pfleger	1549-1616	1

V.   Military Records

The military records in the German collection of the
Genealogical Society consist largely of military parish registers
of various Prussian regiments as they were stationed throughout the
land. These records are reflected in scattered fashion geographi-
cally under the various towns. Catalog cards for a given

community will note when a given parish register is from a military unit. But these records are also cataloged together in the Germany General part of the catalog under vital records, Königliche Preussische Armee, as well as Berlin, Military Records. The card will usually note the name of the regiment(s), the town in which it was stationed, and the date span covered. This collection is in excess of 150 rolls and covers the time period 1719-1918, with some records continuing to 1944. Other miscellaneous records of a military nature scattered through the holdings of the Genealogical Society include those of several Hessian regiments serving in America during the Revolutionary War, diaries of officers, records of the reactions in western German towns to French invasions during the Napoleonic Period, as well as a good collection of casualty lists from the First World War.

VI.   Municipal Records

In a number of cases, the records of German towns, back as early as the thirteenth century, have been filmed rather extensively, thus offering the urban historian, for example, a rich lode of material on German towns back to the time of their flowering as independent political units. These records include such materials as registry office records, charnel house lists, notarial documents, citizenship rolls, tax rolls, city council minutes, and guild records, as well as the usual parish registers. Two of the best collections of municipal records at the Genealogical Society's archives are those from Augsburg and Speyer. The variety of these records is reflected in the following brief summary:

Augsburg:	Type of Material	Time Covered	No. of Rolls
Notarialarchiv	Notariatsakten	1567-1600	34
Rathaus	Bürgerbuch und Zunftbuch	1288-1680	5
Rathaus	Musterregister	1520-1583 1610-1645	5
Rathaus	Bürgerrechts-Aufgabe und Austritte	1550-1813	8
Rathaus	Geburtsscheine	1811-1932	541
Rathaus	Bürger-und Zunftbuch	1288-1680, 1721-1804	5
Stadtamt	Besitzaufnahme (petitions to become freemen)	1548-1810	56
Stadtamt	Bürgeraufnahmeakten	1507-1812	64
Stadtamt	Bürgerrechts-Aufnahme und Austritte	1550-1813	8
Standesamt	Pflegschaftsbuch mit Register	1435-1780	37
Standesamt	Steuerbuch mit Register	1346-1717	70
Standesamt	Hochzeitsamtsprotokolle und Namenregister	1563-1813	23

In addition, see section under "guild records" for Augsburg.

Speyer:

	Type of Material	Time Covered	No. of Rolls
Stadtrat	Ratsprotokolle und Rechnungen	1549-1798	177
Bürgermeisteramt	Bürgermeisterliche Audienzprotokolle	1750-1798	17
Rechenkammer	Rechnungen	1657-1798	23
Bürgermeisteramt	Personalakten der Stadt- und Ratschreiber, Archivare, Rechnungsrevisoren und Kanzlisten	1614-1796	12
Bürgermeisteramt	Kontraktenbuch fremder Personen	1584-1629	10
Kammergericht	Kammergerichtsprotokolle	1521-1524	1
Amtsgericht	Gerichtsakten	1582-1698	2
Standesamt	Belege	1876-1908	230

Speyer: (cont.)	Type of Material	Covered	No. of Rolls
Polizei-Meldeamt	Gesinderegister der Männlichen Personen	1875-1914	6
Polizei-Meldeamt	Gesinderegister der weiblichen Personen	1875-1914	6

VII.   Provincial Records

The German collection is not yet sufficiently complete to boast extensive holdings at the provincial level. One conspicuous exception, however, is the former German province of Westpreussen (West Prussia). Today, this area consists largely of the Polish provinces of Bydgoszcz and Gdansk and it is under these designations that the records described below are to be found. Filmed for the most part in the Geheimes Preussisches Staatsarchiv at Berlin/ Dahlem, the provincial administrative records of Westpreussen offer a variegated cross-section of official concerns and activities in this part of Prussia from the late eighteenth to the early twentieth century, ranging in subject matter from the school system, to religious organizations and settlement problems. The following sample illustrates the nature and scope of one rather voluminous set of provincial records. Most of this material has its origin in the innere Verwaltung of the districts of Marienwerder and Grenzmark.

Type of Material	Dates Covered	No. of Rolls
Verwaltungsakten, allgemeine	1808-1885	14
Verleihung des Grundeigentums	1772-1892	42
Verwaltungsakten über Juden	1812-1854	7
Verwaltungsakten über Adlige	1819-1835	7
Judenwesen in den Städten	1848-1919	13
Welfare, farm officials, pensions, land and property, new settlers	1789-1920	59
General statistics, supervision of clergy	1808-1885	14
Kreis records, complaints to Landratsamt, personnel, sales of government farms, land exchanges and sales, rental contracts, forest records and deeds	1778-1920	164
Grundsätze für die Andiedlung deutscher Arbeiter in den Provinzen Westpreussen und Posen	1910-1919	1
Verwaltung--Catholic priests and teachers	1816-1921	41
Jewish community records	1847-1865	16
Foreigners, exiles, staff, elections, army, school, police, domestic servants, hospitals, settlements, legislation, nobility, scholarships, school inspections	1774-1895	188
Jüdisches Schulwesen	1812-1856	9
Entlassung der Schulkinder	1884-1900	27
Anstellung und Versorgung der Lehrer, Prüfungen, Zeugnisse und Atteste der Lehrer	1806-1894	49
Schülerverzeichnisse und Stundenpläne	1832	1
Briefe an das Privatschulwesen Wespreussens und Verzeichnis der Privatlehrer	1820-1865	10

VIII.   Genealogical Records

The Genealogical Society of the Church of Jesus Christ of
Latter-day Saints does, of course, specialize in genealogical
records. One special collection, however, deserves mention here,
first because it contains valuable material for the genealogist,
but mainly because it represents, graphically, one of the less
salubrious uses to which genealogical study can be put.

The Brenner Collection, named for a German official represented in the correspondence, consists of 671 rolls of microfilm
containing the lineages (Ahnentafel) of families in the area of
Mittelfranken, as well as voluminous correspondence among a number
of Nazi and governmental offices, including the Reichsbauernschaft.
The purpose of the collection was to establish proof of non-Jewish
lineage in order to receive the certificate of genuine German blood
(Ariernachweis). A close look at the collection reveals the purpose, method, and extent of this "genealogical" research in one area
of Germany during the Third Reich.

The collection is in nine parts:

1) An alphabetical listing (A-We) by surname of families along
with vital record information.

2) Records from the Reichsbauernschaft and other agencies
indicating where background research was done.

3) Miscellaneous family information not integrated into the
bulk of the collection (part 1).

4) Marriage records from the 18th and 19th century of soldiers
stationed in the area.

5) Directory of locations in Mittelfranken where research was
done.

6) "Erbhofliste"--a pedigree of families living in the area
for 200 years or more--an interesting example of the Nazi combina-
tion of "blood and soil."

7) Verification material including vital and parish records dating back to the sixteenth century as well as pertinent correspondence.

8) Pedigree of Heinrich Himmler's family.

9) A file of genealogists who were appointed to do research. Correspondence between various genealogists and the Reichsbauernschaft dealing with their employment and the results of their work.

A rough sampling of 35 rolls revealed that the family information provides names, dates of birth and death, place of residence, occupation as well as names and occupations of parents, and a confirmation of whether the person in question was considered an "Arier" or a "Jude." The sampling also revealed a sprinkling of other materials including genealogical journals, local newspapers, essays and pedigrees of a number of famous Germans, including Schiller, Moerike, Uhland and Schelling.

IX.   Jewish Records

The holocaust has made the history and fate of Jews in Germany a subject of continuing fascination for scholars and laymen alike. Scattered throughout the enormous collection of parish and civil records are the remains of the documentation of many of the Jewish communities in Germany. In the card catalog these are usually noted variously as Judenmatrikel, Judenregister, Synagogenbuch or Judengemeinde or the Zivilstandsregister where it will be noted when Jewish records are included.

Many of the records of the Jewish community, especially the synagogue ones, were destroyed during the Nazi period, particularly with the burning of the synagogues in 1938. Thus, such records are fragmentary in the Genealogical Society collection. In most German states, however, from the early nineteenth century on, Jews were required to register births, marriages and deaths with the civil authorities, with the result that much of this material survived the Nazi period.

A rather complete catalog of the German Jewish holdings of the
Society may be found in Toledot: The Journal of Jewish Genealogy,
Vol. 2, Number 1 (summer, 1978), pp. 16-25. This listing is
arranged alphabetically by town and includes province, record type,
date span and microfilm reel numbers.

X.   "Diamonds in the Rough"

The vast bulk of this inventory is an alphabetical listing by
Land of those communities from which the Genealogical Society has
material, along with information showing what kind of material,
where filmed, date span and numbers of rolls in each case.

It is apparent that most--but by no means all--of this material
is composed of parish and vital records. Scattered throughout these
vital records is a wealth of material of various kinds and
provenances. It ranges from official records to early city histories to diaries to correspondence. A small sampling, about 1 percent of the towns represented, will give some indication of the
"diamonds in the rough" which the scholar might find in the collection. The following list was taken selectively from Rheinland-
Pfalz, Nordrhein-Westfalen, and Baden-Württemberg. The list
excludes vital and parish records present in all cases.

RHEINLAND-PFALZ

Bacharach: Irrungen zwischen Kurpfalz und Kurköln im Oberamt.
                    (1612-1699)
                    Documents: 1399-Frederico minore
                                1454-Theodorio majore
                                1455
                                1495
                                1644-Churfürst, Carl Ludwig Pfalzgraf
                                     Maximillian, Herzog von Bayern
                    Anklagen, Bittschriften, Korrespondenz, Zollab-
                    kommen 1688.

Bad Kreuznach: Verstorbene der rheinisch-schwäbischen Augustiner-
                    provinz und der neuen deutschen Ordensprovinz
                    (1650).
                    Bürgerbuch der Stadt Kreuznach 1509-1620.
                    Urkundenbücher Diepolz
                    Stiftungen der württemberger Familien

Barweiler: Geldgeschäfte, Geldverleih, Zinsrückzahlung.

Battweiler: Chronik der Stadt (1761-1786).

Berschweiler: Historisch-meteorologisches.

Bitburg: Auswanderung, alphabetisches Namensverzeichnis, mahnende Worte als Einleitung, Erlaubnis, Richtlinien und Durchführung von legalen Auswanderungen, illegale Auswanderungen; Fallstudien und Korrespondenz.

Dierdorf: Wechsel zur katholischen Kirche.

Ebernburg: Protestversammlung gegen Einführung der neuen Landverteilung.

Erfenbach: Abschrift einer Urkunde von 1600. Der kompetenzbereich des Pfarrers von Erfenbach 1558, Status der Kirche Hohenecken, Abgabeliste.

Feilbingert: Kirchenzucht.

Frankenthal: Zum Gedächtnis des Grafen Ludwig von Leiningen-Dachsburg.

Glanmüchweiler: Breitenborner Codex, Urkunden (1288-1439).

Herxheim: Anniversary requiem ab. (1677-1680).

Sehlem: Indulgencies (1484).

Trippstadt: Biblische Texte auf der Rückseite von "Tableau General de L'Histoire."

Zweibrücken: "Hauptstück und summa des ganzen Evangeliums und was innen ein christlichem Leben steht."

NORDRHEIN-WESTPHALEN

Ahsen: Acta der Königlichen Kriegsduputation zu Recklinghausen (1861-1875).

Bad-Salzufflen: Kirchenkontobuch für die Armen 1656
Register der Kirchenstühle 1705
Gästeliste zur Konfirmation 1775

Berleburg: Bericht über das erste Abendmahl der Prinzen Albrecht, Franz und Georg (1795).

Bielefeld: Churbrandenburgische monatliche Interimsverpfleg- ung. Acta militaria, Bilanzen, Ordinantz, Gestze zur Unterbringung von Soldaten.

Bonn: Bestimmungen über die Verwendung von Stempel- marken, Kriegsschauplatzbericht (Kölner Zeitung). n.d.

NORDRHEIN-WESTPHALEN (cont.)

Brilon:
Protokoll über Versammlungen: Abrechnungen Überprüfugen, Landvermessung und Verteilung, Kirchenfonds.

Burbach:
Pfarrer Register Notizen: Über lutherische und reformierte.
Prediger; ihr Leben und ihre Arbeit Dokumente von 1558 und Früher.
Altes Kirchenbuch mit handgeschriebenen Sprüchen in Latein, Alt-hochdeutsch und Hebräisch.

BADEN WÜRTTEMBERG

Achstetten:
Schulordnung, Besoldungsliste (1792).

Aitrach:
List of pastors, Bericht über Kirchweihe.

Almannshofen:
Verzeichnis von Spenden für Jahresmessen; Kirchliche Verordnungen.

Andelfingen:
Report of a spiritual play, church accounts, report of visitation, financial accounts, letters pertaining to jurisdiction of monastery.

Angeltürn:
Public statements of conversion, heretics recanting, Jahrestage.

Bad Rappenau:
Church accounts, document of conversion, description of donations and church property, extract of protocol of Wormser Synode, report of acquisitions.

Baind:
Beschreibung der Pfarrei, Kirchlicher Handlungen, Prozessionen.

Baldringen:
Letters about the French invasions and other catastrophies.

Occasionally one will find an incredible variety of material in an unexpected place. A sampling of the town of Alfhausen in Niedersachsen brought to light the following documents:

-Tax records for Kettenkamp, Hannover, Prussia, 1721-1722.

-Extract from the records of Osnabrück pertaining to the cloister of Bersenbrück.

-Various records from the town of Fallingbostel, 1528.

-Tax list for Winsen/Aller, 1521.

-Tax list for Winsen/Aller, 1628.

-Militia muster roll for Beedenbostel, 1606.

-Tax list for Bergen, 1511.

-List of Nortrum Laxten citizens, 1659.

-History of the town of Alfhausen, from 1717.

-Militia muster roll for Bergen, 1606.

-Militia muster roll for Flotwedel, 1606.

-Cattle tax records for Winsen/Aller and Flotwedel, 1589.

-Confirmations in the parish of Bippen, 1728-1731.

-List of house owners in Celle, 1664.

-List of Neuenkirchen citizens, n.d.

-Beiträge zur älteren Geschichte der Neumärkischen Ritterschaft by H.F.P. von Wedel, Leipzig, 1886.

-Die Regenten, Oberbefehlshaber und Oberbeamten des Estlandes by Julius Pancker, Reval, 1855.

Finds like this are by no means atypical, and they do show the need for a complete and thorough guide to the entire German collection.

What follows is an alphabetical listing of municipalities by Land showing the kind of record represented from the particular locality, where that record was filmed, date span covered by the material, and the number of microfilm rolls represented. In the case of areas now part of West and East Germany, the material is organized according to present jurisdiction. With other territories formerly part of Germany, we have used terms in effect in Imperial Germany (1871-1918).

These records are primarily Zivilstandsregister (civil registers) and Kirchenbücher (parish registers). The civil registers cover the period 1876 to the present, except for those from the west bank of the Rhine occupied by the French, where civil registers go back to 1798. For the most part, the parish registers cover the period since the sixteenth century. In both cases, birth (or christening), marriage, and death information is given, usually with

names, dates, places, and occupations. In the case of parish
registers, early records are usually in Latin with a transitional
period around the eighteenth century when both Latin and German were
used. Prior to the eighteenth century, records were kept in prose,
with information given varying widely according to the relative
thoroughness of the recorder and the prominence of the person being
described. By the late eighteenth century most listings were
written in German; and as forms were introduced, the information
became more and more standardized. Although these two kinds of
registers dominate the collection, they do not exhaust it. Volks-
zählumgslisten (census materials), Bürgerbücher (citizenship rolls),
Grundbücher, Kaufbücher, Überschreibungen (land records, etc.)
appear throughout.

As previously noted, this list is not complete, the German
collection will soon be growing at the rate of 150-250 rolls per
month, and future addenda will be necessary to keep the collection
current. This survey reflects the material present in the German
collection as of summer, 1977. The column headed "Nature of
Material" indicates the kind of record and/or provenance of the
record, depending on which is reflected in the catalog. The column
"Where Filmed" tells where the material was microfilmed. In many
cases there were several archives in a given city; the "List of
Archives," also part of this section, gives the names of the major
archives in each city. For some provinces, most notably Alsace-
Lorraine (Elsass-Lothringen), a number of smaller communities, not
included in the above list, do appear. In these cases, filming was
not done in major repositories but rather in the local Standesamt.

The researcher should be aware that in this survey listing many
entries are out of exact alphabetical order. Entries do, however,
reflect the exact order found in the archive catalog.

Abbreviations Used

AG	Amtsgericht	Local Court
Archives		Ancient Papers
BA	Bischöfliches Archiv	Bishop's Archive
BGM or BM	Bürgermeisteramt	Mayor's Office
BZG	Bezirksgericht	District Court
EA	Erzbischöfliches Archiv	Archbishop's Archive
evKB	Evangelisches Kirchenbuch	Evangelical Parish Record
evLutKB	Evangelisches lutheranisches Kirchenbuch	Evangelical Lutheran Parish Register
franz.refKB	Französisch-reformiertes Kirchenbuch	French Reformed Church Parish Register
Gem.A	Gemeindeamt	Communal Center
Heer		Military Record
HzB	Hochzeitsbuch	Marriage Record
JüdGem	Jüdische Gemeinde	Jewish Record
KB	Kirchenbuch	Parish Register
KBA	Kirchenbuchamt	Parish Register Office
KG	Kreisgericht	County Court
Kirchen		Misc. Church Records
LDS		Latter-day Saints
LG	Landgericht	State Court
LKA	Landeskirchenamt	State Church Office
LRA	Landratsamt	County Administrator's Office
MKB or MilKB	Militärkirchenbuch	Military Parish Register
OBGM	Oberbürgermeisteramt	Lord Mayor's Office
PSA	Personenstandsarchiv	Legal Status Archive
rkKB	Römisch-katholisches Kirchenbuch	Roman Catholic Parish Register

Abbreviations (continued)

Secretaire	Secretaire de la Mairie	
STA	Standesamt	Civil Registry Office
StGer	Stadtgericht	City Court
STRA	Stadtratsamt	City Council Office
ZSR	Zivilstandsregister	Civil Registry

Archives Filmed for the German Collection

AUGSBURG

    Katholisches Matrikelamt
    Stadtarchiv
    Bischöfliches Ordinariatsarchiv

BAMBERG

    Standesamt

BERLIN

    Evangelische Kirche der Union
    Landesarchiv

BERLIN-CHARLOTTENBURG

    Landesarchiv

BERLIN-DAHLEM

    East German Mission (LDS Church)
    North German Mission (LDS Church)
    Hauptarchiv
    Standesamt I
    Preussisches Geheimes Staatsarchiv

BIELEFELD

    Evangelisches Landeskirchenamt

BRAUNSCHWEIG

    Stadtarchiv

BREMEN

    Evangelisches lutheranisches Kirchenamt

BRESLAU

    Erzbischöfliches Archiv

BRÜHL (Schloss)

    Personenstandsarchiv

COLMAR (France)

    Archives Departmentales
      du Haut-Rhin

DARMSTADT

    Staatsarchiv

DETMOLD

    Staatsarchiv
    Personenstandsarchiv

DÜSSELDORF

    Evangelisches Kirchenarchiv

EIBENSTOCK

    Militärisches Kirchenarchiv

FRANKFURT

    Stadtarchiv

FREIBURG

    Stadtarchiv
    Erzbischöfliches Archiv

GOSLAR

    Zentrales Archivlager

HAGUE (THE)

    Rijksarchief

HAMBURG

    Staatsarchiv

HANNOVER

    Staatsarchiv
    Stadtarchiv
    Landeskirchenamt
    Kirchenbuchamt

KAISERSLAUTERN

    Stadtarchiv
    Landratsamt
    Oberbürgermeisteramt

KASSEL

    Stadtarchiv
    Landeskirchliches Archiv

KOBLENZ

    Landesarchiv

KUSEL

    Stadtarchiv

LUDWIGSBURG

    Staatsarchiv
    Stadtarchiv
    Volksbüro

LÜBECK

    Kirchliches Archiv
    Stadtarchiv

MAINZ

    Stadtarchiv
    Erzbischöfliches Archiv
    Diözesanarchiv

MARBURG

    Staatsarchiv

METTLACH

    Personenstandsregister
    Amtsgericht

MÜNSTER

    Staatsarchiv
    Bistumsarchiv

PADERBORN

    Erzbistumsarchiv
    Stadtarchiv

POZNAN

    Archivum Panstwowe

ROTTENBURG

    Diözesanarchiv
    Stadtarchiv

SPEYER

    Staatsarchiv
    Landesarchiv
    Stadtarchiv
    Bistumsarchiv

STRASBOURG (France)

    Archives Departmentales
      du Bas-Rhin

STUTTGART

    Evangelisches Landeskirchenamt
    Hauptstaatsarchiv

TRIER

    Stadtarchiv
    Bistumsarchiv

UELZEN

    Stadtarchiv

VELZEN

    Stadtarchiv

WARSAW

    Archivum Panstwowe

ZIELONA GORA

    Archivum Panstwowe

TERRITORIES NOW PART
OF THE FEDERAL REPUBLIC OF GERMANY
(WEST GERMANY)

BADEN-WÜRTTEMBERG

Location	Nature of Material	Where Filmed	Dates Covered	No. of Rolls
Aach-Linz	rkKB	Freiburg	1653-1897	5
Aach-Stockach	rkKB	Freiburg	1629-1899	3
Aalen	rkKB	Rottenburg	1868-1919	2
Aasen	rkKB	Freiburg	1682-1900	4
Ablach	rkKB	Freiburg	1784-1900	2
Abtsgemünd	rkKB	Ludwigsburg Rottenburg	1808-1876 1664-1914	10
Achern	rkKB	Freiburg	1727-1900	4
Achkarren	rkKB	Freiburg	1785-1900	2
Achstetten	rkKB	Rottenburg	1651-1900	3
Adelhausen	rkKB	Freiburg	1735-1900	2
Adelsreute	rkKB	Rottenburg	1672-1900	3
Adolzhausen	evKB	Augsburg	1579-1820	2
Affaltrach	rkKB	Ludwigsburg	1671-1941	2
Afftersteg	rkKB	Freiburg	1689-1900	8
Ahausen	rkKB	Freiburg	1849-1900	2
Ahlen -Kr. Biberach-	rkKB	Ludwigsburg Rottenburg	1808-1876 1663-1902	3 3
Aichelau	rkKB	Rottenburg	1680-1901	2
Aichelberg -Esslingen-	LDS members	Historian's Office, Salt Lake City	1863-1874	
Aichelberg -Göppingen-	evKB	Stuttgart	1555-1734	1
Aichen -Waltshut-	rkKB rkKB	Freiburg Freiburg	1681-1900 1621-1900	7

Location	Nature of Material	Where Filmed	Dates Covered	No. of Rolls
Aichalden -Rottweil-*	rkKB	Rottenburg Ludwigsburg	1642-1934	11
Aichstetten -Wangen-	rkKB Hzb	Rottenburg Ludwigsburg Augsburg	1638-1900	8
Ailingen	rkKB	Rottenburg Ludwigsburg	1659-1900	7
Ailringen	rkKB	Ludwigsburg	1700-1886	4
Aitern	rkKB	Freiburg	1638-1900	15
Aitrach	rkKB	Rottenburg	1633-1900	5
Aixheim	rkKB	Rottenburg	1708-1975	5
Albbruck	rkKB	Freiburg	1670-1947	4
Alberweiler	rkKB	Rottenburg	1666-1901	2
Aldingen	evKB	Augsburg	1577-1807	1
Allensbach	rkKB	Freiburg	1681-1900	4
Alleshausen	rkKB	Rottenburg	1659-1901	5
Allfeld	rkKB	Freiburg	1653-1907	3
Allmannsweiler	rkKB	Rottenburg	1647-1907	6
Allmendingen	rkKB	Rottenburg Ludwigsburg	1663-1905	5
Allmendshofen	rkKB	Freiburg	1594-1894	11
Altbieslingen	rkKB	Rottenburg	1657-1901	7
Altdorf	rkKB	Freiburg	1740-1900	3
Altenbach	rkKB	Freiburg	1699-1901	4
Altenburg	rkKB	Freiburg	1700-1900	2
Altenschwang	rkKB	Freiburg	1788-1900	1
Altglashütten	rkKB	Freiburg	1799-1900	3
Althausen	rkKB	Ludwigsburg	1808-1879	1
Altheim -Buchen-	rkKB	Freiburg	1613-1900	3
Altheim -Kr. Ehingen-	rkKB	Rottenburg	1577-1900	2

----
*See last paragraph of Introduction

Location	Nature of Material	Where Filmed	Dates Covered	No. of Rolls
Altheim -Kr. Biberach-	rkKB	Rottenburg	1687-1901	5
Altheim -Ehingen-	rkKB	Ludwigsburg	1808-1876	2
Altheim -Kr. Saulgau-	rkKB	Rottenburg	1682-1901	4
Altheim -Stockach-	rkKB	Freiburg	1721-1900	2
Altheim -Überlingen-	rkKB	Freiburg	1665-1900	2
Altingen	rkKB	Rottenburg Ludwigsburg	1643-1900	3
Altkrautheim	rkKB	Ludwigsburg	1770-1888	3
Altmannshofen	rkKB	Rottenburg Ludwigsburg	1639-1900	9
Altneudorf	rkKB	Freiburg	1699-1901	4
Altschweier	rkKB	Freiburg	1810-1900	2
Altshausen	rkKB	Rottenburg	1589-1900	7
Altsteusslingen	rkKB	Rottenburg Ludwigsburg	1690-1905	2
Amoltern	rkKB	Freiburg	1785-1900	2
Amrichshausen	rkKB	Ludwigsburg	1595-1900	3
Amrigschwand	rkKB	Freiburg	1670-1900	9
Amtzell	rkKB	Rottenburg Ludwigsburg	1596-1900	6
Andelfingen	rkKB	Rottenburg Ludwigsburg	1612-1900	8
Angeltürn	rkKB	Freiburg	1687-1920	7
Anhausen	rkKB	Rottenburg	1642-1893	5
Apfelbach	rkKB	Ludwigsburg	1808-1887	3
Äpfingen	rkKB	Rottenburg	1605-1901	4
Appenweier	rkKB	Freiburg	1654-1900	6
Arnach	rkKB	Rottenburg	1646-1900	8
Aschhausen	rkKB	Ludwigsburg	1675-1903	8

Location	Nature of Material	Where Filmed	Dates Covered	No. of Rolls
Assamstadt	rkKB	Freiburg	1669-1900	4
Assmannshardt	rkKB	Rottenburg Ludwigsburg	1679-1901	3
Attenweiler	rkKB	Rottenburg Ludwigsburg	1604-1874	2
Au -Rastatt-	rkKB	Freiburg	1580-1966	11
Auerbach -Mosbach-	rkKB	Freiburg	1699-1900	5
Aufen	rkKB	Freiburg	1594-1894	11
Aufhausen -Aalen-	rkKB	Ludwigsburg	1824-1872	1
Aufhofen	rkKB	Rottenburg	1666-1905	5
Aulendorf	rkKB	Rottenburg Ludwigsburg	1638-1900	16
Aulfingen	rkKB	Freiburg	1749-1900	1
Aurich	evKB	Augsburg	1562-1920	1
Bach -Kr. Ehingen-	rkKB	Rottenburg	1664-1921	4
Bachenau	rkKB	Ludwigsburg	1765-1967	3
Bachheim	rkKB	Freiburg	1700-1900	2
Bad Buchau	rkKB	Rottenburg	1613-1925	6
Bad Ditzenbach	rkKB	Rottenburg Ludwigsburg	1624-1900	3
Bad Dürrheim	rkKB	Freiburg	1644-1900	5
Bad Friedrichshall	rkKB	Ludwigsburg	1643-1884	2
Bad Janau	rkKB	Freiburg	1769-1900	2
Bad Krozingen	rkKB	Freiburg	1648-1882	4
Bad Liebenzell	evKB	Augsburg	1678-1760	3
Bad Mergentheim	rkKB	Ludwigsburg	1600-1924	2
Bad Niedernau	rkKB	Rottenburg	1586-1900	3
Bad Peterstal	rkKB	Freiburg	1801-1900	3
Bad Rappenau	rkKB	Freiburg	1704-1900	2

Location	Nature of Material	Where Filmed	Dates Covered	No. of Rolls
Bad Rippoldsau	rkKB	Freiburg	1658-1899	2
Bad Waldsee	rkKB	Rottenburg	1609-1896	10
Bad Wimpfen	evKB	Augsburg	1590-1856	4
Bad Wurzach	rkKB	Rottenburg	1660-1900	6
Baden-Baden			1689-1970	33
Baienfurt	rkKB	Rottenburg	1597-1900	17
Baiertal	rkKB	Freiburg	1757-1900	1
Baindt	rkKB	Rottenburg Ludwigsburg	1597-1900	24
Baldern	rkKB	Rottenburg	1826-1876	1
Balgheim	rkKB	Ludwigsburg Rottenburg	1652-1875	2
Ballenberg	rkKB	Freiburg	1584-1901	6
Ballmertshofen	rkKB	Ludwigsburg	1808-1874	1
Ballrechten	rkKB	Freiburg	1670-1900	2
Balsbach	rkKB	Freiburg	1649-1898	5
Baltersweil	rkKB	Freiburg	1621-1900	1
Baltringen	rkKB	Rottenburg Ludwigsburg	1705-1901	3
Bambergen	rkKB	Freiburg	1664-1900	3
Bamlach	rkKB	Freiburg	1640-1900	3
Banmental	rkKB	Freiburg	1810-1900	1
Bannholz	rkKB	Freiburg	1593-1900	7
Bargau	rkKB	Ludwigsburg	1808-1876	1
Bargen -Konstanz-	rkKB	Freiburg	1859-1900	1
Bargen -Sinsheim-	rkKB	Freiburg	1705-1884	2
Bartenstein	rkKB	Ludwigsburg	1690-1900	4
Bartholomä	rkKB	Ludwigsburg	1807-1875	1
Baustetten	rkKB	Rottenburg Ludwigsburg	1654-1900	3

Location	Nature of Material	Where Filmed	Dates Covered	No. of Rolls
Bechingen	rkKB	Rottenburg	1615-1906	1
Bechtersbohl	rkKB	Freiburg	1844-1899	1
Beckstein	rkKB	Freiburg	1833-1889	1
Beersbach	rkKB	Ludwigsburg	1808-1878	1
Beffendorf	rkKB	Ludwigsburg	1808-1876	1
Behla	rkKB	Freiburg	1836-1895	1
Beihingen -Neckar-	evKB	Stuttgart		1
Beilstein	evKB	Augsburg	1558-1810	1
Bellamont	evKB	Rottenburg Ludwigsburg	1622-1904	6
Bellingen -Kr. Müllheim-	evKB	Freiburg	1669-1899	2
Benningen	evKB	Stuttgart	1808-1963	1
Benningen -Kr. Ludwigsburg-	evKB	Stuttgart	1624-1966	2
Benzingen	rkKB	Freiburg	1733-1900	2
Berau	rkKB	Freiburg	1705-1899	2
Berg -K. Ehingen-	rkKB	Rottenburg	1657-1901	7
Berg -Ravensburg-	rkKB	Ludwigsburg	1805-1876	1
Berg -Tettnang-	rkKB	Ludwigsburg	1808-1875	1
Bergalingen	rkKB	Freiburg	1784-1900	3
Bergatrente	rkKB	Rottenburg Ludwigsburg	1597-1900	20
Berghaupten	rkKB	Freiburg	1736-1900	4
Bergöschingen	rkKB	Freiburg	1810-1871	1
Berkheim	rkKB	Rottenburg Ludwigsburg	1661-1905	4
Berlichingen	rkKB	Ludwigsburg	1600-1887	5
Bermatingen	rkKB	Freiburg	1647-1900	3

Location	Nature of Material	Where Filmed	Dates Covered	No. of Rolls
Bermersbach	rkKB	Freiburg	1587-1889	14
Bermersstadt -Rastadt-	rkKB	Freiburg	1621-1909	6
Bernau	rkKB	Freiburg	1605-1900	4
Bernsfelden	rkKB	Freiburg Ludwigsburg	1606-1904	5
Berolzheim	rkKB	Freiburg	1690-1904	2
Betra	rkKB	Freiburg	1753-1900	4
Bettmaringen	rkKB	Freiburg	1647-1900	6
Betzenweiler	rkKB	Rottenburg Ludwigsburg	1669-1906	4
Beuren -Kr. Wangen-	rkKB	Rottenburg	1672-1900	2
Beuren -Stockach-	rkKB	Freiburg	1650-1900	2
Beuren -Überlingen-	rkKB	Freiburg	1799-1900	3
Beuren -Wangen-	rkKB	Rottenburg Ludwigsburg	1672-1900	3
Beuren am Ried	rkKB	Freiburg	1645-1900	4
Beuron	rkKB	Freiburg	1706-1900	1
Biberach an der Riss	rkKB	Rottenburg	1623-1901	23
Biberach -Biberach-	rkKB	Ludwigsburg	1822-1827	1
Biberach -Heilbronn-	rkKB	Ludwigsburg	1702-1879	2
Biberach -Wolfach-	rkKB	Freiburg	1715-1900	5
Bichiushausen	rkKB	Rottenburg Ludwigsburg	1631-1905	4
Biederbach	rkKB	Freiburg	1716-1912	3
Biengen	rkKB	Freiburg	1588-1899	2
Bierbronnen	rkKB	Freiburg	1847-1870	2
Bieringen -Horb-	rkKB	Ludwigsburg	1808-1889	2

Location	Nature of Material	Where Filmed	Dates Covered	No. of Rolls
Bieringen -Künzelsau-	KB	Ludwigsburg	1599-1904	6
Bierlingen	rkKB	Ludwigsburg	1808-1891	1
Bierstetten	rkKB	Rottenburg	1661-1884	2
Biesingen	rkKB	Ludwigsburg	1841-1876	1
Bietigheim	rkKB	Ludwigsburg	1808-1888	1
Bietingen -Stockach-	rkKB	Freiburg	1832-1900	2
Bietingen -Konstanz-	rkKB	Freiburg	1683-1900	2
Bihlafingen	rkKB	Rottenburg	1593-1900	2
Bilfingen	rkKB	Freiburg	1625-1936	7
Billafingen	rkKB	Freiburg Rottenburg	1618-1903	6
Billigheim	rkKB	Freiburg	1650-1900	3
Bilsbach	evKB	Augsburg	1655-1731	1
Bingen	rkKB	Freiburg	1625-1899	5
Binningen	rkKB	Freiburg	1658-1900	2
Binsdorf	rkKB	Rottenburg Ludwigsburg	1711-1963	4
Binswangen	rkKB	Ludwigsburg	1808-1875	1
Binzwangen	rkKB	Rottenburg Ludwigsburg	1650-1902	5
Birkendorf	rkKB	Freiburg	1789-1952	3
Birkenhard				19
Birkingen	rkKB	Freiburg	1613-1900	6
Birndorf	rkKB	Freiburg		6
Bisingen	rkKB	Freiburg	1660-1900	3
Bissingen ob Lontal	rkKB	Rottenburg	1628-1917	5
Bittelbronn -Hechingen-	rkKB	Freiburg	1680-1900	3

Location	Nature of Material	Where Filmed	Dates Covered	No. of Rolls
Bittelbronn -Horb-	rkKB	Rottenburg	1802-1937	1
Blasiwald	rkKB	Freiburg	1606-1900	9
Blaufelden	evKB	Augsburg	1533-1812	2
Bleibach	rkKB	Freiburg	1633-1909	4
Blitzenreute	rkKB	Rottenburg	1597-1900	19
Blochingen	rkKB	Rottenburg Ludwigsburg	1579-1901	10
Blönried	rkKB	Rottenburg	1638-1900	16
Blumberg	rkKB	Freiburg	1653-1900	9
Blumegg	rkKB	Freiburg	1604-1900	1
Blumenfeld	rkKB	Freiburg	1646-1900	2
Bochingen	rkKB	Rottenburg Ludwigsburg	1808-1875	2
Bodman	rkKB	Freiburg	1612-1900	5
Bodneg	rkKB	Rottenburg	1611-1900	5
Bofsheim	rkKB	Freiburg	1698-1898	3
Bohlingen	rkKB	Freiburg	1690-1900	4
Bohlsbach	rkKB	Freiburg	1608-1900	17
Böhmenkirch	rkKB	Ludwigsburg	1808-1878	3
Böhringen -Konstanz-	rkKB	Freiburg	1700-1900	2
Böhringen -Rottweil-	rkKB	Rottenburg	1734-1969	3
Boll -Hechingen-	rkKB	Freiburg	1727-1900	3
Boll -Hochschwarzwald-	rkKD	Freiburg	1640-1900	3
Boll -Stockach-	rkKB	Freiburg	1848-1900	1
Böllen	rkKB	Freiburg	1638-1900	16
Bollingen	rkKB	Rottenburg	1691-1906	2
Bollschwell	rkKB	Freiburg	1646-1904	5

Location	Nature of Material	Where Filmed	Dates Covered	No. of Rolls
Bolstern	rkKB	Rottenburg	1661-1905	3
Bombach	rkKB	Freiburg	1737-1900	2
Boms	rkKB	Rottenburg Ludwigsburg	1308-1905	14
Bondorf	rkKB	Rottenburg	1308-1900	12
Bonfeld	evKB	Augsburg	1607-1921	1
Bonndorf -Überlingen-	rkKB	Freiburg	1625-1900	5
Boonegg	rkKB	Ludwigsburg	1808-1876	1
Boos -Saulgau-	rkKB	Ludwigsburg	1808-1865	1
Bopfingen	rkKB	Rottenburg	1739-1878	2
Börstingen	rkKB	Rottenburg	1751-1878	1
Bösingen -Rottweil-	rkKB	Rottenburg Ludwigsburg	1658-1975	5
Bottenau	rkKB	Freiburg	1637-1900	3
Böttingen	rkKB	Ludwigsburg	1842-1875	1
Bötzingen	rkKB	Freiburg	1660-1903	8
Boxberg -Tauberb.-	rkKB	Freiburg	1687-1920	6
Boxtal	rkKB	Freiburg	1709-1952	2
Braunenweiler	rkKB	Rottenburg	1633-1907	8
Bräunlingen	rkKB	Freiburg	1681-1900	6
Braunsbach	evKB	Augsburg	1595-1860	2
Braunsbach	rkKB	Rottenburg	1727-1905	1
Brehmen	rkKB	Freiburg	1726-1901	3
Breisach	rkKB	Freiburg	1606-1900	15
Breitenbronn	rkKB	Freiburg	1699-1905	2
Breitenfeld	rkKB	Freiburg	1621-1900	6
Breitman	rkKB	Freiburg	1684-1900	5
Bremelau	rkKB	Rottenburg	1655-1900	2
Bremgarten	rkKB	Freiburg	1650-1870	3

Location	Nature of Material	Where Filmed	Dates Covered	No. of Rolls
Brenden -Waldshut-	rkKB	Freiburg	1789-1952	2
Bretten	rkKB	Freiburg	1698-1900	4
Bretzingen	rkKB	Freiburg	1577-1929	2
Bronnacker	rkKB	Freiburg	1698-1898	3
Bronnen -Kr. Biberach-	rkKB	Rottenburg Ludwigsburg	1742-1900	2
Bronnen -Reutlingen-	rkKB	Freiburg	1657-1900	7
Bruchsal	evKB	Hannover	1872-1918	1
Bruchsal	rkKB	Freiburg	1730-1904	12
Brühl -Kr. Mannheim-	rkKB	Freiburg	1699-1900	5
Brunnadern -Hochschwarzwald-	rkKB	Freiburg	1745-1893	1
Bubenbach	rkKB	Freiburg	1790-1901	2
Bubsheim	rkKB	Rottenburg	1635-1975	4
Buch -Waldshut-	rkKB	Freiburg	1613-1900	6
Buchau	rkKB	Ludwigsburg	1808-1866	1
Buchen	rkKB	Freiburg	1598-1904	8
Büchenau	rkKB	Freiburg	1696-1900	6
Buchenbach	rkKB	Freiburg	1764-1900	5
Buchenbach	evKB	Augsburg	1574-1716	1
Buchheim	rkKB	Freiburg	1708-1907	6
Buchholz	rkKB	Freiburg	1700-1900	3
Büchig b. Bretten	rkKB	Freiburg	1725-1887	3
Buggensegel	rkKB	Freiburg	1861-1900	1
Bühl -Tübingen-	rkKB	Rottenburg	1700-1900	3
Bühl -Bühl-	rkKB	Freiburg	1666-1900	20
Bühl -Kr. Biberach-	rkKB	Rottenburg	1627-1900	5

Location	Nature of Material	Where Filmed	Dates Covered	No. of Rolls
Bühl -Kr. Offenburg-	rkKB	Freiburg	1608-1900	7
Bühl -Rottenburg-	rkKB	Ludwigsburg	1834-1882	1
Bühl -Waldshut-	rkKB	Freiburg	1619-1900	7
Bühlertal	rkKB	Freiburg	1763-1900	9
Bühlertann	rkKB	Ludwigsburg Rottenburg	1637-1900	6
Bühlerzell	rkKB	Rottenburg	1719-1900	2
Burbach	rkKB	Freiburg	1726-1901	4
Burgberg -Kr. Heidenheim-	rkKB	Rottenburg	1739-1900	6
Burgrieden	rkKB	Rottenburg Ludwigsburg	1762-1900	2
Burgweiler	rkKB	Freiburg	1639-1895	4
Burkheim -Freib.-	rkKB	Freiburg	1600-1900	2
Burladingen	rkKB	Freiburg	1685-1904	6
Busenbach	rkKB	Freiburg	1646-1900	4
Busslingen	rkKB	Freiburg	1645-1900	4
Bussmannshausen	rkKB	Rottenburg Ludwigsburg	1650-1900	2
Butschbach	rkKB	Freiburg	1811-1900	1
Calw	evKB	Augsburg	1595-1775	2
Christazhofen	rkKB	Rottenburg Ludwigsburg	1510-1900	8
Crailsheim	rkKB	Ludwigsburg	1855-1900	1
Dächingen	rkKB	Rottenburg	1690-1905	2
Dahenfeld	rkKB	Ludwigsburg	1600-1913	3
Dainbach	rkKB	Freiburg	1713-1923	2
Dalkingen	rkKB	Ludwigsburg	1579-1875	2
Dallau	rkKB	Freiburg	1699-1900	2
Dangstetten	rkKB	Freiburg	1811-1899	1

Location	Nature of Material	Where Filmed	Dates Covered	No. of Rolls
Dätzingen	rkKB	Ludwigsburg	1652-1900	3
Dauchingen	rkKB	Freiburg	1799-1900	5
Daugendorf	rkKB	Rottenburg	1614-1902	2
Dautmergen	rkKB	Rottenburg	1651-1876	1
Degerfelden	rkKB	Freiburg	1784-1900	2
Degernau	rkKB	Freiburg	1593-1915	3
Deggingen	rkKB	Ludwigsburg	1822-1877	2
Degmarn	rkKB	Ludwigsburg	1607-1938	2
Deilingen	rkKB	Rottenburg	1753-1898	4
Deisslingen	rkKB	Rottenburg Ludwigsburg	1685-1951	5
Dellmensingen	rkKB	Rottenburg Ludwigsburg	1662-1877	3
Demmingen	rkKB	Ludwigsburg	1812-1887	1
Denkinken -Tuttlingen-	rkKB	Rottenburg Ludwigsburg	1673-1942	6
Denkingen -Überlingen-	rkKB	Freiburg	1736-1900	4
Dettensee	rkKB	Freiburg	1790-1900	1
Dettighofen	rkKB	Freiburg	1619-1900	7
Dettingen -Hechingen-	rkKB	Freiburg	1581-1900	4
Dettingen -Konstanz-	rkKB	Freiburg	1711-1900	2
Dettingen -Nurtingen-	evKB	Augsburg	1571-1577	1
Dettingen -Tübingen-	rkKB	Rottenburg	1648-1905	4
Dettlingen	rkKB	Freiburg	1800-1900	1
Deubach	rkKB	Ludwigsburg	1800-1900	2
Deuchelried	rkKB	Rottenburg Ludwigsburg	1729-1889	5
Dewangen	rkKB	Rottenburg Ludwigsburg	1594-1902	12

Location	Nature of Material	Where Filmed	Dates Covered	No. of Rolls
Diebach	rkKB	Ludwigsburg	1756-1874	1
Diedelsheim	rkKB	Freiburg	1698-1900	4
Diedelsheim	evKB	Frankfurt	1797-1959	2
Diedesheim	rkKB	Freiburg	1699-1899	3
Dielheim	rkKB	Freiburg	1757-1890	4
Dienstadt	rkKB	Freiburg	1671-1900	1
Diepoldshofen	rkKB	Ludwigsburg Rottenburg	1663-1900	3
Diersburg	rkKB	Freiburg	1810-1900	1
Diessen	rkKB	Freiburg	1655-1900	2
Dietelhofen	rkKB	Ludwigsburg Rottenburg	1664-1905	7
Dietenheim	rkKB	Ludwigsburg	1811-1876	1
Dietershausen	rkKB	Rottenburg	1647-1901	3
Dietershofen	rkKB	Freiburg	1662-1900	5
Dieterskirch	rkKB	Rottenburg Ludwigsburg	1647-1901	4
Dietingen -Rottweil-	rkKB	Ludwigsburg	1808-1876	1
Dietmanns -Biberach-	rkKB	Rottenburg	1662-1906	2
Dillendorf	rkKB	Freiburg	1745-1893	1
Dilsberg	rkKB	Freiburg	1732-1926	3
Dingelsdorf	rkKB	Freiburg	1642-1900	2
Dirgenheim	rkKB	Rottenburg Ludwigsburg	1588-1875	3
Dischingen	rkKB	Ludwigsburg	1811-1878	1
Distelhausen	rkKB	Freiburg	1670-1906	3
Dittigheim	rkKB	Freiburg	1585-1902	3
Dittishausen	rkKB	Freiburg	1624-1900	4
Dittwar	rkKB	Freiburg	1702-1931	2
Dogern	rkKB	Freiburg	1620-1947	4

Location	Nature of Material	Where Filmed	Dates Covered	No. of Rolls
Döggingen	rkKB	Freiburg	1694-1900	3
Donaueschingen	rkKB	Freiburg	1594-1894	11
Donaurieden	rkKB	Ludwigsburg Rottenburg	1752-1960	2
Donaustetten	rkKB	Ludwigsburg Rottenburg	1711-1902	3
Donebach	rkKB	Freiburg	1660-1903	8
Donzdorf	rkKB	Rottenburg	1597-1900	7
Dörlesberg	rkKB	Freiburg	1674-1922	3
Dormettingen	rkKB	Ludwigsburg Rottenburg	1662-1974	4
Dornberg -Buchen-	rkKB	Freiburg	1692-1951	1
Dorndorf -Kr. Ulm-	rkKB	Rottenburg	1666-1874	1
Dorndorf	rkKB	Ludwigsburg	1800-1875	1
Dornstadt	rkKB	Ludwigsburg	1800-1875	1
Dörrenzimmern	evKB	Augsburg	1665-1711	2
Dörzbach	evKB	Augsburg	1596-1835	1
Dossenheim	KB	Freiburg	1820-1869	1
Dossenheim	rkKB	Freiburg	1650-1900	3
Dotternhausen	rkKB	Ludwigsburg Rottenburg	1651-1974	4
Drackenstein	rkKB	Ludwigsburg	1800-1875	1
Dühren	rkKB	Freiburg	1719-1899	2
Dundenheim	rkKB	Freiburg	1793-1900	1
Dunningen	rkKB	Ludwigsburg Rottenburg	1643-1965	6
Dunstelklingen	rkKB	Ludwigsburg	1808-1876	1
Durbach	rkKB	Freiburg	1608-1900	21
Dürbheim	rkKB	Ludwigsburg Rottenburg	1646-1935	4

Location	Nature of Material	Where Filmed	Dates Covered	No. of Rolls
Durchhausen	rkKB	Ludwigsburg Rottenburg	1625-1900	3
Dürmentingen	rkKB	Ludwigsburg Rottenburg	1600-1902	6
Durmersheim	rkKB	Freiburg	1660-1900	8
Dürnau -Kr. Göppingen-	evKB	Stuttgart	1596-1967	2
Dürnau -Kr. Saulgau-	rkKB	Rottenburg	1662-1905	1
Dürrenwaldstetten	rkKB	Ludwigsburg Rottenburg	1611-1901	4
Duttenberg	rkKB	Ludwigsburg	1610-1927	5
Ebenheid	rkKB	Freiburg	1709-1900	1
Ebenweiler	rkKB	Rottenburg	1668-1900	3
Eberbach -Kr. Heidelberg-	rkKB	Freiburg	1668-1900	3
Eberfingen	rkKB	Freiburg	1799-1900	1
Eberhardzell	rkKB	Ludwigsburg	1628-1901	7
Ebersbach -Saulgau-	rkKB	Ludwigsburg Rottenburg	1638-1900	4
Ebersberg	rkKB	Ludwigsburg	1654-1900	5
Ebersberg -Saulgau-	rkKB	Ludwigsburg	1808-1876	1
Eberstal	rkKB	Ludwigsburg Ludwigsburg	1561-1900	3
Ebnat	rkKB	Rottenburg	1660-1915	7
Ebnet -Freiburg-	rkKB	Freiburg	1645-1900	2
Ebringen -Freiburg-	rkKB	Freiburg	1645-1927	5
Ebringen -Konstanz-	rkKB	Freiburg	1784-1900	8
Eckartshausen	rkKB	Ludwigsburg	1696-1900	1
Edelfingen	rkKB	Freiburg	1656-1900	4

Location	Nature of Material	Where Filmed	Dates Covered	No. of Rolls
Edingen -Kr. Mannheim-	rkKB	Freiburg	1729-1900	2
Egelfingen	rkKB	Rottenburg	1745-1904	1
Egenhausen	evKB	Augsburg	1668-1775	1
Egesheim	rkKB	Rottenburg	1649-1975	7
Eggingen	rkKB	Rottenburg Ludwigsburg	1603-1901	4
Eglingen	rkKB	Ludwigsburg Rottenburg	1666-1900	3
Eglofs	rkKB	Rottenburg Ludwigsburg	1615-1913	4
Ehestetten	rkKB	Rottenburg	1666-1901	3
Ehingen -Konstanz-	rkKB	Freiburg	1693-1900	2
Ehingen -Donau-	rkKB	Rottenburg	1600-1921	13
Ehrestein	rkKB	Rottenburg	1603-1901	3
Eichelberg	rkKB	Freiburg	1655-1894	3
Eichsel	rkKB	Freiburg	1735-1900	2
Eichstegen	rkKB	Rottenburg	1589-1900	7
Eichstetten	rkKB	Rottenburg	1650-1900	2
Eichtersheim	KB	Freiburg	1811-1869	1
Eichtersheim	rkKB	Freiburg	1719-1899	2
Eigeltingen	rkKB	Freiburg	1650-1900	4
Eiersheim	rkKB	Freiburg	1609-1931	3
Einbach	rkKB	Freiburg	1649-1909	6
Einhart	rkKB	Freiburg	1672-1900	1
Einsingen	rkKB	Rottenburg	1776-1960	1
Eintürnen	rkKB	Rottenburg	1655-1900	2
Eintürnenberg	rkKB	Ludwigsburg	1808-1876	1
Einzingen	rkKB	Ludwigsburg	1808-1875	1
Eisenbach	rkKB	Freiburg	1846-1870	1

Location	Nature of Material	Where Filmed	Dates Covered	No. of Rolls
Eisenharz	rkKB	Rottenburg	1748-1907	3
Eisental	rkKB	Freiburg	1810-1900	3
Elgersweiler	rkKB	Freiburg	1608-1900	17
Ellenberg	rkKB	Ludwigsburg	1598-1900	5
Ellwangen		Ludwigsburg	1923-1924	1
Ellwangen -Aalen-	rkKB	Ludwigsburg	1563-1900	28
Ellwangen -Kr. Biberach-	rkKB	Rottenburg	1675-1886	3
Elsenz	rkKB	Freiburg	1699-1900	4
Elzach	rkKB	Freiburg	1697-1900	8
Emerfeld	rkKB	Rottenburg	1680-1905	2
Emerkingen	rkKB	Rottenburg	1637-1974	5
Emmendingen	rkKB	Freiburg	1857-1900	1
Empfingen	rkKB	Freiburg	1597-1900	6
Endingen -Emmendingen-	rkKB	Freiburg	1586-1900	7
Engelschwand	rkKB	Freiburg	1837-1877	1
Engelswies	rkKB	Freiburg	1717-1900	2
Engen	rkKB	Freiburg	1611-1900	11
Ennabeuren	rkKB	Rottenburg	1733-1908	1
Ennetach	rkKB	Rottenburg	1579-1900	8
Epfenbach	rkKB	Freiburg	1734-1924	4
Eppingen	rkKB	Freiburg	1698-1900	4
Eppligen	rkKB	Freiburg	1687-1920	6
Erbach	rkKB	Rottenburg	1639-1900	4
Erbstetten -Kr. Ehingen-	rkKB	Rottenburg	1777-1905	1
Erfeld	rkKB	Freiburg	1577-1929	2
Erisdorf	rkKB	Rottenburg	1628-1927	4
Eriskirch	rkKB	Rottenburg	1614-1975	3

Location	Nature of Material	Where Filmed	Dates Covered	No. of Rolls
Erlach	rkKB	Freiburg	1811-1889	1
Erlaheim	rkKB	Rottenburg	1648-1895	2
Erlenbach -Heilbronn-	rkKB	Ludwigsburg	1654-1961	8
Ermingen	rkKB	Rottenburg	1603-1901	3
Ermingen	rkKB	Rottenburg	1801-1900	1
Erolzheim	rkKB	Rottenburg	1686-1900	2
Ersingen	rkKB	Freiburg	1625-1909	5
Ertingen	rkKB	Rottenburg	1671-1900	5
Erzingen -Waldshut-	rkKB	Freiburg	1600-1900	3
Eschach -Ravensburg-	rkKB	Rottenburg	1611-1900	9
Eschbach	rkKB	Freiburg	1620-1947	4
Eschbach -Freiburg-	rkKB	Freiburg	1620-1900	3
Eschbach -Müllheim-	rkKB	Freiburg	1615-1893	2
Eschbach -Waldshut-	rkKB	Freiburg	1786-1900	1
Eschelbach -Sinsheim-	rkKB	Freiburg	1836-1898	1
Esenhausen	rkKB	Rottenburg	1623-1904	3
Espasingen	rkKB	Freiburg	1657-1900	3
Esslingen -Donaueschingen-	rkKB	Freiburg	1595-1900	1
Esslingen -Esslingen-	LDS records	Salt Lake City	1900-1931	1
Esslingen -Esslingen-	rkKB	Ludwigsburg	1695-1900	6
Ettenhausen	evKB	Augsburg	1470-1808	2
Ettenheim	rkKB	Freiburg	1583-1907	10
Ettenheimmünster	rkKB	Freiburg	1564-1900	8
Ettenkirch	rkKB	Rottenburg	1672-1900	5

Location	Nature of Material	Where Filmed	Dates Covered	No. of Rolls
Ettlingen	evKB	Hannover	1872-1919	1
Ettlingen	rkKB	Freiburg	1689-1931	9
Ettlingenweier	rkKB	Freiburg	1646-1900	4
Etzenrot	rkKB	Freiburg	1646-1900	4
Eubigheim	rkKB	Freiburg	1612-1898	4
Ewattingen	rkKB	Freiburg	1668-1900	3
Eybach	rkKB	Rottenburg	1598-1909	2
Fahrenbach	rkKB	Freiburg	1810-1904	1
Falkensteig	rkKB	Freiburg	1764-1900	5
Faulenfürst	rkKB	Freiburg	1700-1900	4
Fautenbach	rkKB	Freiburg	1724-1900	4
Feckenhausen	rkKB	Rottenburg	1803-1883	2
Feldberg -Hochschwarzwald-	rkKB	Freiburg	1706-1900	5
Feldhausen	rkKB	Freiburg	1706-1854	2
Feldkirch	rkKB	Freiburg	1654-1889	4
Felldorf	rkKB	Rottenburg	1801-1968	2
Fessenbach	rkKB	Freiburg	1608-1900	15
Feuerbach -Stuttgart-	LDS records	Salt Lake City	1924-1948	
Fischbach -Kr. Biberach-	rkKB	Rottenburg	1663-1901	5
Fischbach -Villingen-	rkKB	Freiburg	1736-1900	2
Fischerbach	rkKB	Freiburg	1696-1900	5
Fischingen -Hechingen-	rkKB	Freiburg	1790-1900	1
Flehingen	rkKB	Freiburg	1657-1900	2
Flein	evKB	Augsburg	1574-1824	2
Fleinswangen	rkKB	Rottenburg	1646-1903	2
Forbach	rkKB	Freiburg	1621-1909	8

Location	Nature of Material	Where Filmed	Dates Covered	No. of Rolls
Forchheim -Emmendingen-	rkKB	Freiburg	1689-1900	3
Forchheim -Karlsruhe-	rkKB	Freiburg	1708-1900	8
Forchtenberg	evKB	Augsburg	1576-1809	1
Forst -Kr. Bruchsal-	rkKB	Freiburg	1700-1899	7
Frankenhofen -Kr. Ehingen-	rkKB	Rottenburg	1655-1900	2
Freiamt -Emmendingen-	rkKB	Rottenburg	1650-1852	1
Freiburg	LDS records	Salt Lake City	1950-1951	1
Freiburg	evKB	Hannover	1872-1900	2
Freiburg	rkKB	Freiburg	1572-1907	27
Freiburg	rkKB	Freiburg	1646-1918	4
Freiburg	rkKB	Freiburg	1649-1938	3
Freiburg	rkKB	Freiburg	1582-1900	4
Freiburg	rkKB	Freiburg	1648-1907	5
Freiburg	rkKB	Freiburg	1730-1900	3
Freiburg	rkKB	Freiburg	1650-1907	9
Freiburg	rkKB	Freiburg	1810-1870	7
Freiburg	LDS records	Salt Lake City	1928-1948	1
Freiolsheim	rkKB	Freiburg	1686-1900	6
Freisenheim	rkKB	Freiburg	1676-1900	3
Freudenbach	evKB	Augsburg	1565-1922	1
Freudenberg -Tauberbischofsheim-	rkKB	Freiburg	1631-1907	7
Freudenstadt	evKB	Augsburg	1603-1808	1
Freudenstadt	rkKB	Augsburg	1860-1900	1
Frickenweiler	rkKB	Freiburg	1650-1900	3
Frickingen	rkKB	Freiburg	1650-1900	6

Location	Nature of Material	Where Filmed	Dates Covered	No. of Rolls
Fridingen	rkKB	Rottenburg	1651-1900	4
Friedberg -Saulgau-	rkKB	Rottenburg	1661-1901	1
Friedenweiler	rkKB	Freiburg	1668-1900	3
Friedingen -Konstanz-	rkKB	Freiburg	1693-1900	2
Friedingen -Saulgau-	rkKB	Rottenburg	1651-1900	2
Friedrichsdorf -Heidelberg-	rkKB	Freiburg	1688-1900	3
Friedrichshafen	rkKB	Rottenburg	1660-1903	2
Friesenhofen	rkKB	Rottenburg	1611-1900	6
Frittlingen	rkKB	Rottenburg	1635-1898	3
Fröhnd	rkKB	Freiburg	1638-1900	16
Frohnstetten	rkKB	Freiburg	1700-1900	2
Frommenhausen	rkKB	Rottenburg	1732-1900	2
Fronhofen	rkKB	Rottenburg	1673-1885	4
Fulgenstadt	rkKB	Rottenburg	1706-1901	2
Füramoos	rkKB	Rottenburg	1622-1904	2
Furschenbach	rkKB	Freiburg	1824-1900	3
Fürstenberg	rkKB	Freiburg	1621-1899	1
Furtwangen	rkKB	Freiburg	1609-1891	7
Fützen	rkKB	Freiburg	1670-1900	5
Gaggenau	rkKB	Freiburg	1614-1930	13
Gaiberg	rkKB	Freiburg	1688-1901	3
Gaienhofen	rkKB	Freiburg	1846-1900	1
Gaildorf	rkKB	Rottenburg	1869-1900	1
Gailingen	rkKB	Freiburg	1706-1900	3
Gaisbeuren	rkKB	Rottenburg	1609-1900	16
Gallmannsweil	rkKB	Freiburg	1643-1900	1
Gamburg	rkKB	Freiburg	1609-1921	3

Location	Nature of Material	Where Filmed	Dates Covered	No. of Rolls
Gamerschwang	rkKB	Rottenburg	1660-1893	5
Gammertingen	rkKB	Freiburg	1657-1900	5
Gammesfeld	evKB	Augsburg	1634-1774	1
Gamshurst	rkKB	Freiburg	1663-1900	6
Gauangelloch	rkKB	Freiburg	1779-1901	3
Gauingen	rkKB	Rottenburg	1631-1900	6
Gausbach	rkKB	Freiburg	1621-1909	6
Gauselfingen	rkKB	Freiburg	1685-1904	2
Gebrazhofen	rkKB	Rottenburg	1510-1900	7
Geislingen	rkKB	Rottenburg	1613-1909	3
Gechingen	evKB	Augsburg	1563-1808	1
Geislingen -Aalen-	rkKB	Ludwigsburg	1613-1900	4
Geisingen -Donaneschingen-	rkKB	Freiburg	1653-1900	4
Geisingen -Kr. Münsin.-	rkKB	Rottenburg	1631-1900	7
Geisslingen	rkKB	Freiburg	1815-1900	1
Gengenbach	rkKB	Freiburg	1587-1900	36
Gerabronn -Crailsheim-	OBA	Ludwigsburg	1844-1870	7
Gerchsheim	rkKB	Freiburg	1643-1942	6
Gerichtsstetten	rkKB	Freiburg	1577-1929	4
Gerlachsheim	rkKB	Freiburg	1726-1900	4
Gerlingen	evKB	Augsburg	1561-1794	1
Gernsbach	rkKB	Freiburg	1744-1889	4
Gerolzahn	rkKB	Freiburg	1613-1902	4
Geschwend	rkKB	Freiburg	1638-1900	14
Gessen	rkKB	Manz	1632-1876	3
Gissingheim	rkKB	Freiburg	1612-	4
Glashofen -Buchen-	rkKB	Freiburg	1613-1902	5

Location	Nature of Material	Where Filmed	Dates Covered	No. of Rolls
Glatt	rkKB	Freiburg	1561-1900	2
Glottertal	rkKB	Freiburg	1714-1905	5
Göbrichen	evKB		1564-1756	1
Gochsen	evKB	Augsburg	1556-1780	1
Göffingen	rkKB	Rottenburg	1622-1904	1
Gögglingen	rkKB	Rottenburg	1611-1902	2
Gögglingen	rkKB	Rottenburg	1721-1900	1
Göggingen	rkKB	Freiburg	1663-1900	4
Göhringen	rkKB	Freiburg	1700-1900	2
Goldscheuer	rkKB	Freiburg	1785-1900	6
Göllsdorf	rkKB	Rottenburg	1808-1974	2
Gölshausen	rkKB	Freiburg	1698-1900	4
Gommersdorf	rkKB	Freiburg	1598-1900	3
Göppingen	LDS records	Salt Lake City	1927-1948	1
Göppingen	evKB	Stuttgart	1596-1967	2
Görwihl	rkKB	Freiburg	1648-1900	4
Göschweiler	rkKB	Freiburg	1781-1900	2
Gosheim	rkKB	Rottenburg	1650-1955	1
Gospoldshofen	rkKB	Rottenburg	1660-1900	8
Göttelfingen -Horb-	rkKB	Rottenburg	1627-1876	1
Gottenheim	rkKB	Freiburg	1741-1926	5
Gottmadingen	rkKB	Freiburg	1701-1900	3
Götzingen	rkKB	Freiburg	1613-1900	6
Grafenhausen -Hochschwarzwald-	rkKB	Freiburg	1639-1900	3
Grafenhausen -Lahr-	rkKB	Freiburg	1680-1900	6
Granheim	rkKB	Rottenburg	1680-1901	2
Greffern	rkKB	Freiburg	1613-1889	12

Location	Nature of Material	Where Filmed	Dates Covered	No. of Rolls
Gremmelsbach	rkKB	Freiburg	1791-1900	4
Griesheim	rkKB	Freiburg	1726-1899	3
Griesingen	rkKB	Rottenburg	1597-1901	2
Griessen	rkKB	Freiburg	1647-1900	3
Grimmelshofen	rkKB	Freiburg	1640-1900	5
Grissheim	rkKB	Freiburg	1683-1908	8
Grombach	rkKB	Freiburg	1640-1900	3
Gronau	evKB	Augsburg	1640-1804	1
Gross-Sachsenheim	evKB	Augsburg	1564-1647	1
Grossbettlingen	evKB	Augsburg	1578-1773	1
Grosschönach	rkKB	Freiburg	1720-1900	2
Grosseicholzheim	rkKB	Freiburg	1699-1900	5
Grosselfingen	rkKB	Freiburg	1814-1900	1
Grossengstingen	rkKB	Ludwigsburg	1615-1900	4
Grossglattbach	evKB	Augsburg	1647-1808	1
Grossherrischwand	rkKB	Freiburg	1851-1900	1
Grossholzleute	rkKB	Rottenburg	1690-1875	1
Grosskuchen	rkKB	Rottenburg	1662-1973	2
Grossrinderfeld	rkKB	Freiburg	1596-1900	3
Grossachsen	rkKB	Freiburg	1701-1900	4
Grosschaffhausen	rkKB	Rottenburg	1652-1900	2
Grosschönach	rkKB	Freiburg	1824-1900	3
Grosstissen	rkKB	Rottenburg	1633-1900	5
Grossweier	rkKB	Freiburg	1677-1901	9
Grundsheim	rkKB	Rottenburg	1663-1910	5
Grunern	rkKB	Freiburg	1648-1900	1
Grüningen -Donaneschingen-	rkKB	Freiburg	1743-1900	1
Grüningen -Kr. Saulgau-	rkKB	Rottenburg	1633-1903	3

Location	Nature of Material	Where Filmed	Dates Covered	No. of Rolls
Grünkraut	rkKB	Rottenburg	1597-1900	23
Grünsfeld	rkKB	Freiburg	1643-1901	7
Grünsfeldhausen	rkKB	Freiburg	1643-1901	7
Gruol	rkKB	Freiburg	1607-1900	3
Geschwend	rkKB	Freiburg	1854-1899	1
Gundelfingen	rkKB	Rottenburg	1631-1905	3
Gundelsheim	rkKB	Ludwigsburg	1740-1877	1
Gündelwangen	rkKB	Freiburg	1640-1900	3
Gundershofen	rkKB	Rottenburg	1646-1901	2
Gundholzen	rkKB	Freiburg	1846-1900	1
Günzkofen	rkKB	Rottenburg	1664-1900	12
Gurtweil	rkKB	Freiburg	1738-1951	1
Gussenstadt	evKB	Augsburg	1564-1787	2
Gütenbach	rkKB	Freiburg	1614-1900	5
Gutenstein	rkKB	Freiburg	1677-1885	2
Gutenzell	rkKB	Rottenburg	1618-1900	3
Gutmadingen	rkKB	Freiburg	1651-1900	2
Guttenbach	rkKB	Freiburg	1686-1901	3
Güttingen	rkKB	Freiburg	1747-1900	1
Habsthal	rkKB	Freiburg	1609-1900	1
Hachtel	rkKB	Ludwigsburg	1863-1900	1
Hagnau	rkKB	Freiburg	1571-1928	5
Haid -Saulgau-	rkKB	Rottenburg	1308-1905	13
Haidgau	rkKB	Rottenburg	1758-1900	2
Haigerloch	rkKB	Freiburg	1683-1900	3
Hailfingen	rkKB	Rottenburg	1784-1900	3
Hailtingen	rkKB	Rottenburg	1672-1902	2
Hainstadt	rkKB	Freiburg	1608-1899	4

Location	Nature of Material	Where Filmed	Dates Covered	No. of Rolls
Haisterkirch	rkKB	Rottenburg	1680-1907	4
Hambrücken	rkKB	Freiburg	1686-1922	4
Hammereisenbach-Bregenbach	rkKB	Freiburg	1818-1900	2
Hänner	rkKB	Freiburg	1672-1900	3
Hart	rkKB	Freiburg	1668-1900	2
Harthausen -Mergentheim-	rkKB	Ludwigsburg	1808-1900	1
Harthausen -Sigmaringen-	rkKB	Freiburg	1656-1900	4
Hartheim -Stockach-	rkKB	Freiburg	1785-1900	2
Hartschwand	rkKB	Freiburg	1837-1877	1
Hasenweiler	rkKB	Rottenburg Ludwigsburg	1623-1904	8
Haslach -Kr. Biberach-	rkKB	Rottenburg	1670-1900	1
Haslach -Wolfach-	rkKB	Freiburg	1596-1943	14
Hattenweiler	rkKB	Freiburg	1835-1900	1
Hattingen	rkKB	Freiburg	1680-1900	4
Hauenstein	rkKB	Freiburg	1643-1900	6
Hauerz	rkKB	Rottenburg	1462-1963	3
Hausach	rkKB	Freiburg	1651-1945	6
Hausen -am Bussen-	rkKB	Rottenburg	1716-1898	1
Hausen -Balingen-	rkKB	Rottenburg	1676-1887	2
Hausen -Crailsheim-	evKB	Augsburg	1545-1750	1
Hausen -Hechingen-	rkKB	Freiburg	1609-1900	5
Hausen ob Urspring	rkKB	Rottenburg	1602-1900	7
Hausen -Rottweil-	rkKB	Rottenburg	1808-1966	1

Location	Nature of Material	Where Filmed	Dates Covered	No. of Rolls
Hausen -Sigmaringen-	rkKB	Freiburg	1700-1900	2
Hausen -Stockach-	rkKB	Freiburg	1718-1904	3
Häusern	rkKB	Freiburg	1606-1900	9
Hausen vor Wald	rkKB	Freiburg	1693-1900	1
Häusern -Hochschwarzwald-	rkKB	Freiburg	1670-1900	9
Hayingen	rkKB	Rottenburg	1642-1893	5
Hecheln	rkKB	Freiburg	1664-1900	3
Hechingen	rkKB	Freiburg	1663-1900	4
Heckfeld	rkKB	Freiburg	1727-1895	2
Hecklingen	rkKB	Freiburg	1656-1900	2
Heddesheim	rkKB	Freiburg	1698-1900	3
Hegne	rkKB	Freiburg	1681-1900	4
Heidelberg	rkKB	Freiburg	1622-1907	11
Heidelsheim	rkKB	Freiburg	1699-1904	2
Heidenhofen	rkKB	Freiburg	1682-1900	4
Heidersbach	rkKB	Freiburg	1694-1909	6
Heilbronn	Rathaus	Heilbronn	1200-1931	850
Heilbronn	evKB	Heilbronn	1538-1953	99
Heiligenberg	rkKB	Freiburg	1846-1896	1
Heiligenzell	rkKB	Freiburg	1845-1900	1
Heiligenzimmern	rkKB	Freiburg	1800	1
Heiligkreuzsteinach	rkKB	Freiburg	1699-1901	4
Heiligkreuztal	rkKB	Rottenburg	1612-1900	7
Heimbach -Emmendingen-	rkKB	Freiburg	1677-1900	2
Heinsheim	rkKB	Freiburg	1704-1900	2
Heinstetten	rkKB	Freiburg	1813-1913	3
Heitersheim	rkKB	Freiburg	1612-1951	7

Location	Nature of Material	Where Filmed	Dates Covered	No. of Rolls
Helmsheim	rkKB	Freiburg	1699-1900	2
Helmstadt	rkKB	Freiburg	1705-1884	2
Hemmendorf	rkKB	Rottenburg	1674-1900	2
Hemmenhofen	rkKB	Freiburg	1627-1900	2
Hemmingen	evKB	Augsburg	1560-1807	1
Hemsbach -Buchen-	rkKB	Freiburg	1668-1900	5
Hemsbach -Mannheim-	rkKB	Freiburg Mannheim	1649-1900	8
Hengen	evKB	Augsburg	1608-1807	1
Hengstfeld	evKB	Augsburg	1486-1750	1
Herbertingen	rkKB	Rottenburg	1673-1877	4
Herbertshofen -Ehingen-	rkKB	Rottenburg	1600-1921	13
Herboldsheim -Emmendingen-	rkKB		1598-1900	8
Herbolzheim -Jagst- -Kr. Mosbach-	rkKB	Freiburg	1595-1907	2
Herbrechtingen	evKB	Augsburg	1558-1800	1
Herbsthansen	evKB	Augsburg	1645-1808	1
Herdwangen	rkKB	Freiburg	1667-1900	3
Hermentingen	rkKB	Freiburg	1730-1876	1
Herlazhofen	rkKB	Rottenburg	1600-1900	16
Herrentierbach	evKB	Augsburg	1673-1800	1
Herrenzimmern -Rottweil-	rkKB	Rottenburg	1657-1924	2
Herrischried	rkKB	Freiburg	1695-1900	5
Herzogenweiler	rkKB	Freiburg	1585-1930	8
Heslach	evKB	Augsburg	1662-1790	1
Hettigenbeuren	rkKB	Freiburg	1650-1901	1
Hettingen -Buchen-	rkKB	Freiburg	1639-1900	2

Location	Nature of Material	Where Filmed	Dates Covered	No. of Rolls
Hettingen -Sigmaringen-	rkKB	Freiburg	1611-1900	3
Heuchlingen -Schw. Gmünd-	rkKB	Rottenburg	1591-1900	3
Heudorf am Bussen	rkKB	Rottenburg	1672-1902	3
Heudorf -Saulgau, b. Mengen-	rkKB	Rottenburg	1668-1900	2
Heudorf -Stockach-	rkKB	Freiburg	1586-1970	5
Heufelden	rkKB	Rottenburg	1600-1921	13
Heuweiler	rkKB	Freiburg	1687-1900	2
Hilsbach -Sinsheim-	rkKB	Freiburg	1699-1900	3
Hilzingen	rkKB	Freiburg	1784-1900	8
Hindelwangen	rkKB	Freiburg	1673-1900	5
Hinterzarten	rkKB	Freiburg	1610-1900	4
Hintschingen	rkKB	Freiburg	1810-1900	1
Hirrlingen	rkKB	Rottenburg	1605-1900	6
Hirschau	rkKB	Rottenburg	1635-1900	4
Hochberg -Saulgau-	rkKB	Rottenburg	1648-1896	1
Hochdorf -Freiburg-	rkKB	Freiburg	1791-1900	2
Hochdorf -Kr. Biberach-	rkKB	Rottenburg	1660-1900	1
Hochemmingen	rkKB	Freiburg	1659-1900	1
Höchenschwand	rkKB	Freiburg	1670-1900	9
Hochhausen -Kr. Mosbach-	rkKB	Freiburg	1750-1910	2
Hochhausen -Tauberbischofsheim-	rkKB	Freiburg	1618-1900	3
Höchstberg	rkKB	Ludwigsburg	1713-1887	2
Hockenheim	rkKB	Freiburg	1726-1900	4

Location	Nature of Material	Where Filmed	Dates Covered	No. of Rolls
Hödingen	rkKB	Freiburg	1807-1900	1
Höfen -Aalen-	rkKB	Rottenburg	1639-1914	5
Höfen -Kr. Biberach-	rkKB	Rottenburg	1605-1901	4
Höfen -Ludwigsburg-	evKB	Augsburg	1579-1927	1
Höfendorf	rkKB	Freiburg	1731-1900	1
Hofsgrund	rkKB	Freiburg	1855-1900	1
Hofweier	rkKB	Freiburg	1642-1899	4
Hogschür	rkKB	Freiburg	1857-1900	1
Hohebach	evKB	Augsburg	1525-1927	2
Hohenberg	rkKB	Ludwigsburg	1655-1900	5
Hohensachsen	rkKB	Freiburg	1701-1900	2
Hohenstadt	rkKB	Freiburg	1612-1878	1
Hohenstadt -Aalen-	rkKB	Rottenburg	1580-1920	9
Hohenstadt -Buchen-	rkKB	Freiburg	1698-1898	3
Hohenstadt -Kr. Göppingen-	rkKB	Rottenburg	1637-1901	2
Hohentengen	rkKB	Freiburg	1810-1870	1
Hohentengen -Waldshut-	rkKB	Freiburg	1627-1900	6
Hohentengen -Saulgau-	rkKB	Rottenburg	1664-1900	12
Hollenbach	evKB	Augsburg	1230-1937	3
Hollerbach	rkKB	Freiburg	1604-1901	1
Höllstein	rkKB	Freiburg	1845-1899	2
Holzhausen -Freiburg-	rkKB	Freiburg	1654-1900	2
Holzschlag	rkKB	Freiburg	1640-1900	4
Homberg -Überlingen-	rkKB	Freiburg	1622-1900	3

Location	Nature of Material	Where Filmed	Dates Covered	No. of Rolls
Honau -Kr. Kehl-	rkKB	Freiburg	1721-1902	2
Hondingen	rkKB	Freiburg	1636-1900	2
Honstetten	rkKB	Freiburg	1716-1900	3
Höpfingen	rkKB	Freiburg	1650-1936	3
Hoppentenzel	rkKB	Freiburg	1673-1900	3
Horb -Horb-	land and tax record	Berlin-Dahlem	1697	1
Horb	rkKB	Rottenburg	1731-1956	7
Horben	rkKB	Freiburg	1870-1900	1
Hörden	rkKB	Freiburg	1786-1917	7
Horn	rkKB	Freiburg	1627-1900	3
Hornbach -Buchen-	rkKB	Freiburg	1810-1902	2
Hornberg -Säckingen-	rkKB	Freiburg	1780-1900	4
Horrenbach	rkKB	Freiburg	1603-1900	10
Horrenberg	rkKB	Freiburg	1703-1894	3
Hosskirch	rkKB	Rottenburg	1629-1900	2
Hüffenhardt	rkKB	Freiburg	1704-1900	2
Hüfingen	rkKB	Freiburg	1577-1900	9
Hügelsheim	rkKB	Freiburg	1707-1900	4
Hugstetten	rkKB	Freiburg	1708-1907	6
Huldstetten	rkKB	Rottenburg	1631-1926	7
Hulen	rkKB	Rottenburg	1808-1887	1
Hundersingen -Kr. Ehingen-	rkKB	Rottenburg	1627-1901	5
Hundheim	rkKB	Freiburg	1860-1907	1
Hüngheim	rkKB	Freiburg	1701-1900	2
Hürbel	rkKB	Rottenburg	1605-1902	7
Hütten -Säckingen-	rkKB	Freiburg	1788-1900	1

Location	Nature of Material	Where Filmed	Dates Covered	No. of Rolls
Huttenheim	rkKB	Freiburg	1692-1900	3
Huttingen	rkKB	Freiburg	1586-1900	5
Hüttisheim	rkKB	Rottenburg	1592-1900	4
Hüttlingen	rkKB	Rottenburg	1644-1900	6
Ibach -Offenburg-	rkKB	Freiburg	1843-1871	1
Ichenheim	rkKB	Freiburg	1727-1900	3
Iffezheim	rkKB	Freiburg	1679-1900	6
Igelswies	rkKB	Freiburg	1619-1900	8
Igersheim	rkKB	Ludwigsburg	1625-1934	5
Illerrieden	rkKB	Rottenburg	1667-1901	2
Illmensee	rkKB	Freiburg	1716-1900	2
Illwangen	rkKB	Rottenburg	1652-1900	2
Ilmspan	rkKB	Freiburg	1825-1890	1
Ilsfeld	evKB	Augsburg	1660-1808	1
Ilvesheim	rkKB	Freiburg	1734-1900	2
Immendingen	rkKB	Freiburg	1650-1900	5
Immenried	rkKB	Rottenburg	1857-1900	1
Immenstaad	rkKB	Freiburg	1812-1901	2
Impfingen	rkKB	Freiburg	1657-1900	3
Indelhausen	rkKB	Rottenburg	1642-1893	5
Indlekofen	rkKB	Freiburg	1847-1870	2
Ingerkingen	rkKB	Rottenburg	1667-1901	2
Ingoldingen	rkKB	Rottenburg	1670-1897	3
Ingstetten	rkKB	Rottenburg	1703-1900	5
Inneringen	rkKB	Freiburg	1588-1900	4
Inzigkofen	rkKB	Freiburg	1600-1900	3
Inzlingen	rkKB	Freiburg	1618-1900	5
Ippingen	rkKB	Freiburg	1672-1900	1
Irrendorf	rkKB	Rottenburg	1760-1900	2

Location	Nature of Material	Where Filmed	Dates Covered	No. of Rolls
Irslingen	rkKB	Rottenburg	1756-1918	2
Isny	rkKB	Rottenburg	1635-1900	6
Istein	rkKB	Freiburg	1586-1900	5
Ittendorf	rkKB	Freiburg	1655-1904	4
Ittenhausen -Saulgau-	rkKB	Rottenburg	1611-1901	3
Iznang	rkKB	Freiburg	1760-1881	2
Jagstberg	rkKB	Ludwigsburg	1610-1900	5
Jastzell	rkKB	Ludwigsburg	1667-1900	5
Jechtingen	rkKB	Freiburg	1620-1900	3
Jestetten	rkKB	Freiburg	1602-1900	4
Jettenhansen	rkKB	Rottenburg	1700-1900	2
Jöhlingen	rkKB	Freiburg	1640-1900	7
Jungingen -Hechingen-	rkKB	Freiburg	1684-1900	2
Jungnau	rkKB	Freiburg	1764-1900	2
Justingen	rkKB	Rottenburg	1703-1900	5
Kaltbrunn -Wolfach-	rkKB	Freiburg	1651-1900	3
Kaltenbrunn -Buchen-	rkKB	Freiburg	1810-1910	1
Kaltenbrunn -Konstanz-	rkKB	Freiburg	1681-1900	4
Kandern	rkKB	Freiburg	1818-1893	1
Kanzach	rkKB	Rottenburg	1671-1905	1
Kappel -Freiburg-	rkKB	Freiburg	1643-1900	4
Kappel -Hochschwarzwald-	rkKB	Freiburg	1628-1900	2
Kappel -Kr. Saulgau-	rkKB	Rottenburg	1613-1925	6
Kappel -Lahr-	rkKB	Freiburg	1700-1900	4

Location	Nature of Material	Where Filmed	Dates Covered	No. of Rolls
Kappel -Ravensburg-	rkKB	Rottenburg	1662-1902	2
Kappelrodeck	rkKB	Freiburg	1665-1900	9
Karlsdorf	rkKB	Freiburg	1707-1894	3
Karlsruhe	LDS records		1927-1951	7
Karlsruhe	LDS records		1927-1951	7
Karlsruhe	rkKB	Freiburg	1796-1901	2
Karlsruhe	LDS records	Salt Lake City	1861-1948	
Karlsruhe	evKB	Hannover	1872-1920	2
Karsau	rkKB	Freiburg	1636-1900	1
Karsee	rkKB	Rottenburg	1686-1900	3
Katzenmoos	rkKB	Freiburg	1639-1900	12
Katzental	rkKB	Freiburg	1650-1900	4
Kehl	evKB	Hannover	1717-1918	1
Kehl	rkKB	Freiburg	1747-1901	3
Kehlen -Ravensburg-	rkKB	Rottenburg	1682-1900	5
Kehlen -Tettnang-	rkKB	Rottenburg	1618-1900	3
Kenzingen	rkKB	Freiburg	1678-1900	7
Kerchenhausen	rkKB	Freiburg	1653-1900	3
Kerkingen	rkKB	Rottenburg	1658-1879	6
Ketsch	rkKB	Freiburg	1785-1900	3
Kettenacker	rkKB	Freiburg	1794-1900	1
Kiebingen	rkKB	Rottenburg	1622-1902	3
Kiechlinsbergen	rkKB	Freiburg	1646-1901	3
Kilchberg	rkKB	Rottenburg	1700-1900	3
Killer	rkKB	Freiburg	1609-1900	5
Kinzigtal	rkKB	Freiburg	1784-1889	3

Location	Nature of Material	Where Filmed	Dates Covered	No. of Rolls
Kippenheim	rkKB	Freiburg	1652-1900	6
Kirchardt	rkKB	Freiburg	1699-1900	2
Kirchberg an der Iller	rkKB	Rottenburg	1613-1900	3
Kirchbierlingen	rkKB	Rottenburg	1657-1901	7
Kirchdorf -Villingen-	rkKB	Freiburg	1604-1899	5
Kirchdorf an der Iller	rkKB	Rottenburg	1661-1905	5
Kirchentellinsfurt	evKB	Augsburg	1594-1829	1
Kirchhausen	rkKB	Ludwigsburg	1693-1940	5
Kirchen	rkKB	Rottenburg	1640-1901	3
Kirchhausen	rkKB	Ludwigsburg	1693-1818	2
Kirchheim -Aalen-	rkKB	Rottenburg	1612-1876	3
Kirchheim -Ludwigsburg-	evKB	Augsburg	1694-1789	1
Kirchheim -Nürtingen-		Stadtarchiv	1572-1943	1462
Kirchheim unter Teck		Stadtarchiv	1731-1872	120
Kirchhofen	rkKB	Freiburg	1642-1900	7
Kirchzarten	rkKB	Freiburg	1609-1907	12
Kirrlach	rkKB	Freiburg	1669-1888	3
Kisslegg	rkKB	Rottenburg	1663-1900	2
Kleineichholzheim	rkKB	Freiburg	1688-1899	2
Klepsau	rkKB	Freiburg	1625-1901	2
Kluftern	rkKB	Freiburg	1629-1900	1
Kocherstetten	evKB	Augsburg	1653-1824	1
Kochertürn	rkKB	Ludwigsburg	1685-1892	5
Kolbingen	rkKB	Rottenburg	1676-1900	2
Kollnau	rkKB	Freiburg	1784-1907	2

Location	Nature of Material	Where Filmed	Dates Covered	No. of Rolls
Kommingen	rkKB	Freiburg	1640-1900	3
Königsheim	rkKB	Freiburg	1630-1900	8
Königseggwald	rkKB	Rottenburg	1731-1929	2
Königsheim	rkKB	Rottenburg	1635-1949	10
Königshofen	rkKB	Freiburg	1611-1889	4
Konstanz	evKB	Hannover	1872-1943	1
Konstanz		Freiburg	1863-1869	1
Konstanz	rkKB	Freiburg	1576-1901	34
Krauchenwies	rkKB	Freiburg	1619-1900	3
Krautheim	rkKB	Freiburg	1603-1900	7
Krenhainstetten	rkKB	Freiburg	1618-1902	3
Krenkingen	rkKB	Freiburg	1645-1900	1
Krensheim	rkKB	Freiburg	1643-1975	8
Kressbronn -Tettnang-	rkKB	Rottenburg	1639-1928	5
Kronau	rkKB	Freiburg	1678-1900	5
Krumbach -Mosbach-	rkKB	Freiburg	1649-1902	5
Krumbach -Stockach-	rkKB	Freiburg	1657-1900	2
Külsheim	rkKB	Freiburg	1623-1900	4
Küntelsau	evKB	Augsburg	1622-1808	1
Küntelsau	rkKB	Ludwigsburg	1626-1901	2
Kupferzell	rkKB	Rottenburg	1727-1867	1
Kuppenheim	rkKB	Freiburg	1694-1902	6
Kupprichshausen	rkKB	Freiburg	1689-1915	3
Kürzell	rkKB	Freiburg	1650-1900	3
Küssnach	rkKB	Freiburg	1810-1870	1
Kützbrunn	rkKB	Freiburg	1810-1903	1
Lackendorf	rkKB	Rottenburg	1662-1967	3

Location	Nature of Material	Where Filmed	Dates Covered	No. of Rolls
Ladenburg	rkKB	Freiburg	1646-1900	5
Lahr	evKB	Hannover	1898-1920	1
Lahr	rkKB	Freiburg	1849-1890	2
Laiz	rkKB	Freiburg	1600-1900	3
Lampenhain	rkKB	Freiburg	1699-1901	4
Lampertsweiler	rkKB	Rottenburg	1308-1900	14
Landshausen	rkKB	Freiburg	1650-1915	3
Lang-n-au	rkKB	Rottenburg	1627-1900	4
Langenargen	rkKB	Rottenburg	1600-1900	6
Langenbach	rkKB	Freiburg	1585-1930	8
Langenbrandt -Rastatt-	rkKB	Freiburg	1580-1960	7
Langenbrücken	rkKB	Freiburg	1712-1900	4
Langenbrunn	rkKB	Freiburg	1718-1904	3
Langenburg	evKB	Augsburg	1587-1829	1
Langenelz	rkKB	Freiburg	1660-1903	8
Langenschemmern	rkKB	Rottenburg	1666-1905	5
Langenenslingen	rkKB	Freiburg	1651-1900	2
Langenhart	rkKB	Freiburg	1794-1900	1
Langenordnach	rkKB	Freiburg	1846-1870	1
Langnau	rkKB	Rottenburg	1621-1900	3
Lauchheim	rkKB	Ludwigsburg	1677-1807	2
Lauda	rkKB	Freiburg	1624-1900	4
Laudenbach -Kr. Mannheim-	rkKB	Freiburg	1649-1900	7
Laudenbach -Mergentheim-	rkKB	Ludwigsburg	1655-1900	6
Laudenberg	rkKB	Freiburg	1649-1900	5
Lauf	rkKB	Freiburg	1697-1899	2
Laufenburg	rkKB	Freiburg	1601-1900	2

Location	Nature of Material	Where Filmed	Dates Covered	No. of Rolls
Lauffen -Heilbronn-	evKB	Augsburg	1565-1788	6
Lauffen -Rottweil-	rkKB	Rottenburg	1669-1973	3
Laupertshausen	rkKB	Rottenburg	1636-1901	7
Laupheim	rkKB	Rottenburg	1652-1902	14
Lausheim	rkKB	Freiburg	1604-1900	1
Lautenbach -Offenburg-	rkKB	Freiburg	1647-1900	11
Lautenbach -Rastatt-	rkKB	Freiburg	1795-1913	3
Lauterach	rkKB	Rottenburg	1600-1905	4
Lauterbach	rkKB	Rottenburg	1647-1912	5
Lautlingen	rkKB	Rottenburg	1609-1933	2
Lehen	rkKB	Freiburg	1659-1900	4
Leibertingen	rkKB	Freiburg	1678-1919	3
Leiberstung	rkKB	Freiburg	1613-1889	12
Leimen -Kr. Heidelberg-	rkKB	Freiburg	1698-1896	2
Leingarten	rkKB	Ludwigsburg	1778-1900	1
Leinheim	rkKB	Freiburg	1700-1900	2
Leipferdingen	rkKB	Freiburg	1650-1900	3
Lembach	rkKB	Freiburg	1750-1900	1
Lengenreiden	rkKB	Freiburg	1669-1915	3
Lenzkirch	rkKB	Freiburg	1729-1900	5
Leonberg	evKB	Augsburg	1651-1807	1
Leupolz	rkKB	Rottenburg	1700-1886	2
Leustetten	rkKB	Freiburg	1805-1900	1
Leutershansen -Kr. Mannheim-	rkKB	Freiburg	1710-1900	2
Leutkirch -Wangen-	rkKB	Rottenburg	1617-1900	7

Location	Nature of Material	Where Filmed	Dates Covered	No. of Rolls
Leuzendorf	evKB	Augsburg	1577-1677	1
Levertsweiler	rkKB	Freiburg	1683-1900	1
Liebenzell	evKB	Augsburg	1678-1760	1
Liel	rkKB	Freiburg	1714-1900	2
Lierbach	rkKB	Freiburg	1843-1871	1
Liggersdorf	rkKB	Freiburg	1659-1900	3
Limbach	rkKB	Freiburg	1649-1898	4
Linach	rkKB	Freiburg	1535-1930	12
Lindach	rkKB	Freiburg	1686-1901	3
Lippach	rkKB	Ludwigsburg	1822-1900	1
Lippertsreuthe	rkKB	Freiburg	1653-1900	3
Liptingen	rkKB	Freiburg	1600-1900	5
Litzelstetten	rkKB	Freiburg	1827-1900	1
Lobenfeld	rkKB	Freiburg	1734-1924	5
Locherhof -Rottweil-	rkKB	Rottenburg	1643-1965	5
Löffelstelzen	rkKB	Ludwigsburg	1780-1900	1
Löffingen	rkKB	Freiburg	1624-1900	6
Lörrach	rkKB	Freiburg	1630-1900	4
Lottstetten	rkKB	Freiburg	1663-1900	3
Ludwigsburg	LDS records	Salt Lake City	1927-1930	1
Ludwigsburg		Ludwigsburg	1806-1918	41
Ludwigsburg	MKB	Hannover	1775-1852	1
Ludwigsburg	rkKB	Ludwigsburg	1800-1905	5
Ludwigsburg	krKB	Ludwigsburg	1567-1920	2
Ludwigshafen	rkKB	Freiburg	1611-1900	4
Lützelsachsen	rkKB	Freiburg	1701-1900	2
Lützenhardt	rkKB	Ludwigsburg	1808-1900	4
Machtolsheim	rkKB	Rottenburg	1637-1901	2

Location	Nature of Material	Where Filmed	Dates Covered	No. of Rolls
Magenbuch	rkKB	Freiburg	1683-1900	1
Magolsheim	rkKB	Rottenburg	1672-1889	2
Mahlberg	rkKB	Freiburg	1722-1900	3
Mahlspüren	rkKB	Freiburg	1601-1900	6
Mahlstetten	rkKB	Rottenburg	1671-1891	1
Mainhardt	evKB	Augsburg	1571-1816	1
Mainwangen	rkKB	Freiburg	1650-1900	2
Maisach	rkKB	Freiburg	1843-1871	1
Maisach	rkKB	Freiburg	1843-1871	1
Malsch -Karlsruhe-	rkKB	Freiburg	1730-1900	12
Malsch -Kr. Heidelberg-		Freiburg	1811-1870	1
Malsch	krKB	Freiburg	1682-1900	7
Malschenberg	rkKB	Freiburg	1785-1900	2
Mannheim	evMKB	Hannover	1936-1943	1
Mannheim	rkMKB	Freiburg	1685-1912	5
Mannheim	rkKB	Freiburg	1651-1973	26
Marbach -Ludwigsburg-		Ludwigsburg	1811-1869	18
Marbach -Saulgau-	rkKB	Rottenburg	1672-1901	2
Marburg -Tauberbischofsheim-	rkKB	Freiburg	1833-1889	1
Margrethausen	rkKB	Rottenburg	1609-1975	3
Mariazell	rkKB	Rottenburg	1675-1974	3
Markbronn	rkKB	Ludwigsburg	1808-1876	1
Markdorf	rkKB	Freiburg	1606-1912	10
Markelfingen	rkKB	Freiburg	1717-1900	2
Markelsheim	rkKB	Ludwigsburg	1593-1900	8
Marktlustenau	rkKB	Ludwigsburg	1653-1900	4
Marlach	rkKB	Ludwigsburg	1659-1884	2

Location	Nature of Material	Where Filmed	Dates Covered	No. of Rolls
Maselheim	rkKB	Rottenburg	1613-1905	3
Massenbachhausen	rkKB	Ludwigsburg	1694-1878	5
Mauchen -Kr. Müllheim-	rkKB	Freiburg	1614-1917	7
Mauchen -Waldshut-	rkKB	Freiburg	1647-1900	6
Mauenheim	rkKB	Freiburg	1680-1900	3
Mauer -Heidelberg-	rkKB	Freiburg	1779-1901	3
Maulbronn		Ludwigsburg	1832-1926	24
Meckenbeuren	rkKB	Rottenburg Ludwigsburg	1682-1900	9
Meckesheim	rkKB	Freiburg	1779-1901	3
Meersburg	rkKB	Freiburg	1586-1920	9
Meimsheim	evKB	Augsburg	1662-1808	1
Melchingen	rkKB	Freiburg	1615-1900	2
Mengen -Saulgau-	rkKB	Rottenburg	1579-1901	8
Menningen	rkKB	Freiburg	1692-1900	3
Menzenschwand	rkKB	Freiburg	1670-1900	1
Merdingen	rkKB	Freiburg	1671-1899	4
Merklingen -Kr. Ulm-	rkKB	Rottenburg	1637-1901	2
Merklingen -Leonberg-	evKB	Augsburg	1578-1784	1
Merzhausen	rkKB	Freiburg	1604-1908	4
Messbach	rkKB	Ludwigsburg	1771-1876	1
Messelhausen	rkKB	Freiburg	1665-1901	2
Messkirch	rkKB	Freiburg	1619-1900	8
Mettenberg -Kr. Biberach-	rkKB	Rottenburg	1587-1903	5
Michelbach -Crailsheim-	evKB	Augsburg	1646-1742	1

Location	Nature of Material	Where Filmed	Dates Covered	No. of Rolls
Michelbach -Öhringen-	evKB	Augsburg	1555-1789	1
Michelbach -Rastatt-	rkKB	Freiburg	1730-1926	4
Michelfeld -Schwäbisch. Hall-	evKB	Augsburg	1572-1721	1
Michelwinnaden	rkKB	Rottenburg	1846-1901	1
Mieterkingen	rkKB	Rottenburg	1596-1901	2
Mietingen	rkKB	Rottenburg	1705-1901	5
Mindersdorf	rkKB	Freiburg	1661-1900	4
Mingolsheim	rkKB	Freiburg	1693-1915	7
Minseln	rkKB	Freiburg	1679-1900	4
Mittelbuch	rkKB	Rottenburg	1628-1925	6
Mittelschefflenz	rkKB	Freiburg	1688-1899	2
Mittelsteinweiler	rkKB	Freiburg	1861-1900	1
Mittelurbach	rkKB	Rottenburg	1609-1896	10
Möggingen	rkKB	Freiburg	1641-1900	2
Möhringen -Donaueschingen-	rkKB	Freiburg	1621-1900	4
Möhringen -Kr. Saulgau-	rkKB	Rottenburg	1698-1901	6
Monakam	evKB	Augsburg		1
Mönchzel	rkKB	Freiburg	1734-1924	5
Mondfeld	rkKB	Freiburg	1700-1952	2
Moos -Bühl-	rkKB	Freiburg	1613-1889	13
Moos -Konstanz-	rkKB	Freiburg	1842-1877	1
Moosbeuren	rkKB	Rottenburg	1627-1902	8
Moosbrunn	rkKB	Freiburg	1699-1905	2
Moosheim	rkKB	Rottenburg	1308-1900	17
Mörsch	rkKB	Freiburg	1708-1900	5

Location	Nature of Material	Where Filmed	Dates Covered	No. of Rolls
Mörschenhardt	rkKB	Freiburg	1660-1903	8
Mörsingen	rkKB	Rottenburg	1631-1901	8
Mörtelstein	rkKB	Freiburg	1699-1910	4
Mosbach	rkKB	Freiburg	1847-1890	1
Mösbach	rkKB	Freiburg	1811-1900	2
Mosbach	rkKB	Freiburg	1688-1900	6
Mössingen	rkKB	Rottenburg	1700-1900	3
Mückenloch	rkKB	Freiburg	1732-1926	3
Muckental	rkKB	Freiburg	1699-1900	4
Mudau	rkKB	Freiburg	1660-1903	8
Muddeldingen	rkKB	Rottenburg	1627-1891	4
Muggensturm	rkKB	Freiburg	1654-1900	4
Mühlbach	rkKB	Freiburg	1698-1900	4
Mühlenbach	rkKB	Freiburg	1643-1900	6
Mühlhausen -Kr. Heidelberg-	rkKB	Freiburg	1671-1900	4
Mühlhausen -Rottweil-	rkKB	Rottenburg	1651-1965	1
Mühlingen	rkKB	Freiburg	1664-1907	3
Mülben	rkKB	Freiburg	1660-1906	11
Mühlhausen -Konstanz-	rkKB	Freiburg	1667-1900	4
Mühlingen	rkKB	Freiburg	1664-1900	3
Mulfingen	rkKB	Ludwigsburg	1606-1900	10
Müllen	rkKB	Freiburg	1728-1966	1
Müllheim	rkKB	Freiburg	1850-1900	1
Münchhof	rkKB	Freiburg	1812-1882	1
Münchingen -Hochschwarzwald-	rkKB	Freiburg	1811-1900	1
Müchweier	rkKB	Freiburg	1564-1900	8
Mundelfingen	rkKB	Freiburg	1712-1900	2

Location	Nature of Material	Where Filmed	Dates Covered	No. of Rolls
Munderkingen	rkKB	Rottenburg	1594-1905	10
Münsingen		Ludwigsburg	1804-1889	10
Münsingen	evKB	Augsburg	1574-1785	1
Münzdorf	rkKB	Rottenburg	1642-1893	5
Murg	rkKB	Freiburg	1620-1900	6
Musbach	rkKB	Rottenburg	1638-1901	7
Muttensweiler	rkKB	Rottenburg	1611-1877	1
Nagold	rkKB	Ludwigsburg	-1900	2
Nasgenstadt	rkKB	Rottenburg	1664-1889	2
Neckargemünd	rkKB	Freiburg	1688-1901	3
Neckarsulm		Ludwigsburg	1846-1867	6
Neckarsulm	rkKB	Ludwigsburg	1600-1905	15
Neckarbischofsheim	rkKB	Freiburg	1704-1904	4
Neckarbucken	rkKB	Freiburg	1810-1909	1
Neckarelz	rkKB	Freiburg	1699-1899	2
Neckargemünd	rkKB	Freiburg	1622-1648	1
Neckargerach	rkKB	Freiburg	1686-1901	3
Neckarhausen	rkKB	Freiburg	1766-1900	2
Neckarkatzenbach	rkKB	Freiburg	1699-1905	2
Neibsheim	rkKB	Freiburg	1654-1900	5
Neidingen	rkKB	Freiburg	1718-1904	3
Neidlingen	evKB	Augsburg Stuttgart	1596-1967	3
Nellingen	rkKB	Rottenburg	1637-1901	2
Nendingen	rkKB	Rottenburg	1654-1900	3
Nenningen	rkKB	Rottenburg	1601-1901	4
Nenzingen	rkKB	Freiburg	1683-1900	3
Nesselried	rkKB	Freiburg	1815-1900	1
Nesselwangen	rkKB	Freiburg	1667-1900	1

Location	Nature of Material	Where Filmed	Dates Covered	No. of Rolls
Neuburgweier	rkKB	Freiburg	1708-1900	5
Neudenau	rkKB	Freiburg	1652-1902	3
Neudingen	rkKB	Freiburg	1627-1900	3
Neudorf	rkKB	Freiburg	1714-1900	4
Neuenburg	rkKB	Freiburg	1810-1916	5
Neuenburg -Kr. Bruchsal-	rkKB	Freiburg	1691-1900	3
Neuenburg -Kr. Müllheim-	rkKB	Freiburg	1640-1916	4
Neuershausen	rkKB	Freiburg	1679-1899	3
Neufra -Kr. Saulgau-	rkKB	Rottenburg	1628-1927	4
Neufra -Sigmaringen-	rkKB	Freiburg	1609-1900	5
Neufrach	rkKB	Freiburg	1600-1900	3
Neuhaus -Villingen-	rkKB	Freiburg	1674-1900	4
Neuhausen -Esslingen-	rkKB	Ludwigsburg	1606-1900	5
Neukirch -Donaneschingen-	rkKB	Freiburg	1621-1900	3
Neukirch -Rottweil-	rkKB	Rottenburg	1663-1975	2
Neukirch -Tettnang-	rkKB	Rottenburg	1663-1900	5
Neuler	rkKB	Ludwigsburg	1711-1900	5
Neunkirchen -Kr. Mosbach-	rkKB	Freiburg	1699-1905	2
Neuravensburg	rkKB	Rottenburg	1647-1900	4
Neuses	rkKB	Ludwigsburg	1830-1900	1
Neustadt -Hochschwarzwald-	rkKB	Freiburg	1619-1900	9
Neuthard	rkKB	Freiburg	1696-1900	4
Neutrauchburg	rkKB	Rottenburg	1611-1900	3

Location	Nature of Material	Where Filmed	Dates Covered	No. of Rolls
Neuweier	rkKB	Freiburg	1810-1900	2
Niederhausen -Emmendingen-	rkKB	Freiburg	1784-1900	2
Niederbühl	rkKB	Freiburg	1697-1900	3
Niedereschach	rkKB	Freiburg	1650-1900	3
Niedergebisbach	rkKB	Freiburg	1784-1900	3
Niederhausen -Kr. Emmendingen-	rkKB	Freiburg	1784-1900	2
Niederhofen -Kr. Ehingen-	rkKB	Rottenburg	1767-1900	1
Niederrimsingen	rkKB	Freiburg	1685-1899	2
Niederschopfheim	rkKB	Freiburg	1690-1901	4
Niederstetten	evKB	Augsburg	1551-1808	2
Niederstetten	rkKB	Ludwigsburg	1682-1900	1
Niederstotzingen	rkKB	Rottenburg	1672-1900	4
Niederwangen	rkKB	Rottenburg	1598-1900	4
Niederwasser	rkKB	Freiburg	1788-1900	3
Niederwihl	rkKB	Freiburg	1700-1889	3
Niederwinden	rkKB	Freiburg	1652-1900	2
Nöggenschwiel	rkKB	Freiburg	1674-1900	1
Nordhalden	rkKB	Freiburg	1640-1900	3
Nordhausen	rkKB	Ludwigsburg	1600-1900	3
Nordrach	rkKB	Freiburg	1608-1900	5
Nordschwaben	rkKB	Freiburg	1679-1900	4
Nuhlingen	rkKB	Freiburg	1664-1900	3
Nürtingen	LDS records	Salt Lake City	1949	
Nürtingen	evKB	Augsburg	1559-1828	2
Nusplingen	rkKB	Rottenburg	1662-1881	3
Nussbach -Offenburg-	rkKB	Freiburg	1637-1900	3

Location	Nature of Material	Where Filmed	Dates Covered	No. of Rolls
Nussbach -Villingen-	rkKB	Freiburg	1705-1900	5
Nussloch	rkKB	Freiburg	1752-1900	4
Ober-Beerbach	rkKB	Ludwigsburg	1589-1900	1
Oberachern	rkKB	Freiburg	1602-1900	4
Oberalpfen	rkKB	Freiburg	1593-1900	7
Oberbalbach	rkKB	Freiburg	1655-1901	2
Oberbränd	rkKB	Freiburg	1790-1901	2
Oberbruch	rkKB	Freiburg	1809-1900	2
Oberdielbach	rkKB	Freiburg	1699-1906	3
Oberdischingen	rkKB	Rottenburg	1645-1902	4
Oberdorf -Tettnang-	rkKB	Rottenburg	1811-1900	1
Obereggingen	rkKB	Freiburg	1765-1900	2
Oberentersbach	rkKB	Freiburg	1849-1900	2
Oberessendorf	rkKB	Rottenburg	1784-1900	2
Oberflacht	rkKB	Rottenburg	1602-1901	4
Oberflokenbach	rkKB	Freiburg	1710-1900	2
Obergimpern	rkKB	Freiburg	1704-1904	4
Oberginsbach	rkKB	Ludwigsburg	1653-1900	2
Obergriesheim	rkKB	Ludwigsburg	1602-1929	2
Obergrombach	rkKB	Freiburg	1785-1893	2
Oberharmersbach	rkKB	Freiburg	1643-1900	8
Oberhausen -Emmendingen-	rkKB	Freiburg	1688-1900	3
Oberhausen -Bruchsal-	rkKB	Freiburg	1727-1901	6
Oberhof -Säckingen-	rkKB	Freiburg	1672-1900	3
Oberkessach	rkKB	Ludwigsburg	1688-1903	6
Oberkirch	rkKB	Ludwigsburg	1647-1900	11

Location	Nature of Material	Where Filmed	Dates Covered	No. of Rolls
Oberkirchberg	rkKB	Rottenburg	1608-1914	11
Oberkochen	rkKB	Rottenburg	1658-1911	4
Oberlauchringen	rkKB	Freiburg	1810-1900	1
Oberlauda	rkKB	Freiburg	1625-1900	2
Obermarchtal	rkKB	Rottenburg	1600-1951	11
Obermettingen	rkKB	Freiburg	1810-1900	1
Obermünstertal	rkKB	Freiburg	1650-1900	7
Obernau	rkKB	Rottenburg	1621-1900	2
Oberndorf -Buchen-	rkKB	Freiburg	1603-1900	7
Oberndorf -Tübingen-	rkKB	Rottenburg	1791-1900	3
Oberneudorf	rkKB	Freiburg	1604-1901	1
Oberheim	rkKB	Rottenburg	1606-1899	2
Oberopfingen	rkKB	Rottenburg	1792-1904	1
Oberöwisheim	rkKB	Freiburg	1691-1900	2
Oberried	rkKB	Freiburg	1787-1907	4
Oberrimsingen	rkKB	Freiburg	1784-1899	2
Oberrot	rkKB	Rottenburg	1698-1904	2
Oberrotweil	rkKB	Freiburg	1653-1900	6
Oberschefflenz	rkKB	Freiburg	1688-1899	2
Oberschopfheim	rkKB	Freiburg	1698-1900	6
Oberschüpf	rkKB	Freiburg	1713-1923	2
Oberschwarzach -Kr. Mosbach-	rkKB	Freiburg	1699-1905	2
Obersimonwald	rkKB	Freiburg	1614-1900	5
Obersimonswald	rkKB	Freiburg	1789-1918	2
Oberstadion	rkKB	Rottenburg	1627-1891	4
Obersteinfeld	evKB	Augsburg	1685-1807	1
Obersteinweiler	rkKB	Freiburg	1861-1900	1

Location	Nature of Material	Where Filmed	Dates Covered	No. of Rolls
Oberstetten	rkKB	Rottenburg	1668-1900	2
Oberstotzingen	rkKB	Rottenburg	1672-1900	4
Obersulmetingen	rkKB	Rottenburg	1650-1900	2
Obertalheim	rkKB	Rottenburg	1819-1932	2
Obertbergen	rkKB	Freiburg	1700-1900	4
Oberteuringen	rkKB	Rottenburg	1658-1895	4
Obertsrot	rkKB	Freiburg	1795-1913	3
Oberuhldingen	rkKB	Freiburg	1647-1900	6
Oberwachingen	rkKB	Rottenburg	1647-1901	3
Oberwangen	rkKB	Freiburg	1647-1952	8
Oberweier -Lahr-	rkKB	Freiburg	1699-1952	5
Oberwihl	rkKB	Freiburg	1826-1889	1
Oberwinden	rkKB	Freiburg	1639-1900	3
Oberwinden -Emmendingen-	rkKB	Freiburg	1784-1900	2
Oberwittinghausen	rkKB	Freiburg	1677-1900	3
Oberwittstadt	rkKB	Freiburg	1576-1899	2
Oberwolfach	rkKB	Freiburg	1661-1900	5
Obrigheim -Kr. Mosbach-	rkKB	Freiburg	1699-1910	4
Ochsenhausen	rkKB	Rottenburg	1527-1900	8
Odenheim	rkKB	Freiburg	1695-1900	7
Ödheim	rkKB	Ludwigsburg	1600-1900	4
Ödsbach	rkKB	Freiburg	1811-1900	2
Offenau	rkKB	Ludwigsburg	1634-1919	3
Offenburg	evMKB	Hannover	1901-1917	1
Offenburg	rkKB	Freiburg	1608-1900	15
Offingen -Kr. Saulgau-	rkKB	Rottenburg	1698-1899	5
Ofteringen	rkKB	Freiburg	1593-1915	3

Location	Nature of Material	Where Filmed	Dates Covered	No. of Rolls
Oftersheim	rkKB	Freiburg	1622-1900	6
Oggelsbeuren	rkKB	Rottenburg	1663-1902	4
Oggelshausen	rkKB	Rottenburg	1651-1890	2
Öhringen	evKB	Augsburg	1584-1921	2
Ölligen	rkKB	Rottenburg	1740-1900	2
Önsbach	rkKB	Freiburg	1792-1900	4
Öpfingen	rkKB	Rottenburg	1660-1893	3
Oppenau	rkKB	Freiburg	1628-1900	9
Oppenweiler	rkKB	Ludwigsburg	1807-1900	2
Orschweier	rkKB	Freiburg	1810-1873	1
Orsenhausen	rkKB	Rottenburg	1607-1900	2
Orsingen	rkKB	Freiburg	1783-1900	2
Ortenberg -Kr. Offenburg-	rkKB	Freiburg	1608-1900	18
Öschingen	rkKB	Rottenburg	1700-1900	3
Osterburken	rkKB	Freiburg	1634-1893	4
Ostrach	rkKB	Freiburg	1639-1900	5
Östringen	rkKB	Freiburg	1596-1891	7
Otigheim	rkKB	Freiburg	1691-1914	6
Ottenheim	rkKB	Freiburg	1686-1899	2
Ottenhöfen	rkKB	Freiburg	1824-1900	3
Ottersdorf	rkKB	Freiburg	1700-1913	3
Otterswang -Biberach-	rkKB	Rottenburg	1638-1900	5
Ottersweier	rkKB	Freiburg	1641-1900	9
Owen	evKB	Augsburg	1563-1807	1
Owingen -Überlingen-	rkKB	Freiburg	1664-1900	3
Owingen -Hechingen-	rkKB	Freiburg	1668-1900	3
Paimar	rkKB	Freiburg	1643-1901	7

Location	Nature of Material	Where Filmed	Dates Covered	No. of Rolls
Pfaffenrot	rkKB	Freiburg	1726-1901	4
Pfaffenweiler -Freiburg-	rkKB	Freiburg	1515-1909	6
Pfaffenweiler -Villingen-	rkKB	Freiburg	1633-1898	3
Pfahlheim	rkKB	Ludwigsburg	1776-1900	3
Pfedelbach	evKB	Augsburg	1585-1788	2
Pfedelbach	rkKB	Ludwigsburg	1808-1904	4
Pfitzingen	evKB	Augsburg	1696-1806	1
Pfohren	rkKB	Freiburg	1671-1900	3
Pforzheim	LDS records	Salt Lake City	1920-1930	
Pfronstetten	rkKB	Rottenburg	1769-1900	1
Pfrungen	rkKB	Rottenburg	1652-1900	2
Pfullendorf	rkKB	Freiburg	1613-1900	8
Plankstadt	rkKB	Freiburg	1699-1900	6
Pleutersbach	rkKB	Freiburg	1688-1900	3
Plittersdorf	rkKB	Freiburg	1717-1913	4
Polringen	rkKB	Rottenburg	1614-1900	5
Pommertsweiler	rkKB	Ludwigsburg	1838-1900	2
Poppenhausen	rkKB	Freiburg	1558-1919	1
Präg	rkKB	Freiburg	1638-1900	16
Prechtal	rkKB	Freiburg	1760-1909	2
Prinzbach	rkKB	Freiburg	1651-1900	4
Pülfringen	rkKB	Freiburg	1726-1901	3
Radolfzell	rkKB	Freiburg	1597-1900	14
Raitenbuch	rkKB	Freiburg	1729-1900	5
Raithaslach	rkKB	Freiburg	1682-1900	4
Rammersweier	rkKB	Freiburg	1608-1900	15
Rammingen	rkKB	Rottenburg	1628-1917	5

Location	Nature of Material	Where Filmed	Dates Covered	No. of Rolls
Ramsbach -Offenburg-	rkKB	Freiburg	1843-1871	1
Randegg	rkKB	Freiburg	1779-1900	2
Rangendingen	rkKB	Freiburg	1602-1900	2
Rast	rkKB	Freiburg	1668-1900	2
Rastatt	rkKB	Freiburg	1648-1916	22
Rastatt	evMKB	Hannover Eibenstock	1839-1920	4
Ratshausen	rkKB	Rottenburg	1609-1930	7
Ratzenried	rkKB	Rottenburg	1610-1907	2
Rauenberg -Heidelberg-	rkKB	Freiburg	1721-1900	4
Rauenberg -Tanberbischofsheim-	rkKB	Freiburg	1800-1900	2
Rauental	rkKB	Freiburg	1786-1902	1
Ravensburg	rkKB	Rottenburg	1610-1902	15
Rechberg -Kr. Schwäbisch Gmünd-	rkKB	Rottenburg	1597-1900	7
Rechberg -Waldshut-	rkKB	Freiburg	1600-1900	3
Rechtenstein	rkKB	Rottenburg	1630-1951	5
Reckingen	rkKB	Freiburg	1811-1872	1
Regglisweiler	rkKB	Rottenburg	1713-1906	2
Richenau	rkKB	Freiburg	1594-1907	12
Reichenbach b. Biberach Riss	rkKB	Rottenburg	1636-1901	4
Reichenbach b. Schussenried	rkKB	Rottenburg	1647-1907	3
Reichenbach -Karlsruhe-	rkKB	Freiburg	1646-1900	5
Reichenbach -Lahr-	rkKB	Freiburg	1831-1900	2
Reichenbach -Saulgau-	rkKB	Rottenburg	1647-1907	3

Location	Nature of Material	Where Filmed	Dates Covered	No. of Rolls
Reichenbach -Tuttlingen-	rkKB	Rottenburg	1649-1974	2
Reichenbuch	rkKB	Freiburg	1686-1901	3
Reichenhofen	rkKB	Rottenburg	1667-1900	3
Reichental	rkKB	Freiburg	1580-1966	11
Reicholzheim	rkKB	Freiburg	1641-1931	5
Reihen	rkKB	Freiburg	1699-1900	5
Reilingen	rkKB	Freiburg	1744-1900	2
Reinhardsachsen	rkKB	Freiburg	1810-1900	1
Reinstetten	rkKB	Rottenburg	1713-1888	4
Reiselfingen	rkKB	Freiburg	1726-1900	2
Reisenbach	rkKB	Freiburg	1660-1903	8
Remetschwiel	rkKB	Freiburg	1593-1900	7
Renchen	rkKB	Freiburg	1650-1900	9
Rengershansen	rkKB	Ludwigsburg	1590-1908	5
Renhardsweiler	rkKB	Rottenburg	1661-1884	2
Renguishausen	rkKB	Rottenburg	1690-1900	2
Rettigheim	rkKB	Freiburg	1682-1900	2
Reubach	evKB	Augsburg	1586-1769	2
Reute -Emmendingen-	rkKB	Freiburg	1594-1947	4
Reute -Kr. Biberach-	rkKB	Rottenburg	1623-1901	15
Reute -Kr. Stockach-	rkKB	Freiburg	1716-1900	3
Reute -Ravensburg-	rkKB	Rottenburg	1609-1900	16
Reutlingen	LDS records	Salt Lake City	1927-1930	
Reutlingen		Ludwigsburg	1818-1870	12
Reutlingen	evKB	Augsburg	1574-1749	1
Reutlingen	KB	Berlin-Dahlem	1599-1631	1

Location	Nature of Material	Where Filmed	Dates Covered	No. of Rolls
Reutlingen	rkKB	Ludwigsburg	1824-1900	1
Reutlingendorf	rkKB	Rottenburg	1605-1906	2
Rheinfelden	rkKB	Freiburg	1659-1900	4
Rheinhausen -Emmendingen-	rkKB	Freiburg	1784-1900	2
Rheinhausen -Kr. Bruchsal-	rkKB	Freiburg	1785-1901	2
Rheinheim	rkKB	Freiburg	1649-1889	2
Rheinsheim	rkKB	Freiburg	1692-1901	3
Rheinweiler	rkKB	Freiburg	1640-1900	3
Richen	rkKB	Freiburg	1699-1899	1
Rickenbach -Säckingen-	rkKB	Freiburg	1683-1900	3
Rickenbach -Überlingen-	rkKB	Freiburg	1650-1900	6
Riechenhofen	rkKB	Rottenburg	1663-1900	2
Riedbach	evKB	Augsburg	1632-1807	1
Riedböhringen	rkKB	Freiburg	1700-1900	2
Riedern -Waldshut-	rkKB	Freiburg	1619-1900	7
Riedhausen	rkKB	Rottenburg	1666-1907	2
Riedheim -Konstanz-	rkKB	Freiburg	1640-1900	2
Riedheim -Überlingen-	rkKB	Freiburg	1822-1900	1
Riedlingen -Kr. Saulgau-	rkKB	Rottenburg	1594-1901	7
Riedöschingen	rkKB	Freiburg	1677-1900	3
Riegel -Emmendingen-	rkKB	Freiburg	1650-1900	7
Rielasingen	rkKB	Freiburg	1665-1900	3
Rinderfeld	evKB	Augsburg	1650-1710	1
Ringelbach	rkKB	Freiburg	1840-1900	1

Location	Nature of Material	Where Filmed	Dates Covered	No. of Rolls
Ringgenbach	rkKB	Freiburg	1692-1900	3
Ringingen -Hechingen-	rkKB	Freiburg	1652-1943	5
Ringingen -Kr. Ehingen-	rkKB	Rottenburg	1664-1904	3
Ringschnait	rkKB	Rottenburg	1636-1901	7
Ringsheim	rkKB	Freiburg	1679-1900	4
Rinklingen	rkKB	Freiburg	1698-1900	4
Rinschheim	rkKB	Freiburg	1806-1900	1
Rippberg	rkKB	Freiburg	1810-1902	2
Rippenweier	rkKB	Freiburg	1710-1900	2
Rippolingen	rkKB	Freiburg	1697-1900	5
Rissegg	rkKB	Rottenburg	1623-1901	14
Risstissen	rkKB	Rottenburg	1570-1900	3
Ritschweier	rkKB	Freiburg	1701-1900	2
Rittersbach -Kr. Mosbach-	rkKB	Freiburg	1699-1900	4
Robern	rkKB	Freiburg	1649-1898	5
Rockenau	rkKB	Freiburg	1688-1900	3
Roggenbeuren	rkKB	Freiburg	1585-1915	1
Rohlingen	rkKB	Ludwigsburg	1688-1873	3
Rohrbach am Gieshübel	rkKB	Freiburg	1661-1900	4
Rohrbach -Donaueschingen-	rkKB	Freiburg	1639-1900	7
Rohrbach i. Schwarzwald	rkKB	Freiburg	1585-1930	8
Rohrbach -Sinsheim-	rkKB	Freiburg	1722-1900	2
Rohrdorf -Horb-	rkKB	Rottenburg	1684-1877	2
Rohrdorf -Stockach-	rkKB	Freiburg	1727-1900	4

Location	Nature of Material	Where Filmed	Dates Covered	No. of Rolls
Rohrdorf -Wangen-	rkKB	Rottenburg	1602-1900	2
Rorgenwies	rkKB	Freiburg	1832-1915	1
Rosenberg -Buchau-	rkKB	Freiburg	1698-1898	3
Rosenfeld	evKB	Augsburg	1558-1833	1
Rosna	rkKB	Rottenburg	1579-1900	6
Rosswangen	rkKB	Rottenburg	1645-1952	3
Rot an der Rot	rkKB	Rottenburg	1670-1901	5
Rot bei Laupheim	rkKB	Rottenburg	1778-1900	2
Rot -Kr. Heidelberg-	rkKB	Freiburg	1696-1900	4
Rot -Mergentheim-	rkKB	Ludwigsburg	1667-1900	2
Rötenbach -Hochschwarzwald-	rkKB	Freiburg	1781-1900	2
Rotenberg	rkKB	Freiburg	1662-1901	1
Rottenburg	rkKB	Rottenburg	1580-1912	19
Röttingen	rkKB	Rottenburg	1598-1876	2
Rottum -Kr. Biberach-	rkKB	Rottenburg	1750-1900	1
Rottweil	rkKB	Rottenburg Ludwigsburg	1564-1933	15
Rotzingen	rkKB	Freiburg	1837-1877	2
Rudenberg	rkKB	Freiburg	1846-1870	1
Rulfingen	rkKB	Freiburg Rottenburg	1579-1900	8
Rumpfen	rkKB	Freiburg	1602-1903	2
Ruppertshofen	rkKB	Rottenburg	1788-1901	2
Rüsswihl	rkKB	Freiburg	1826-1889	3
Rust	rkKB	Freiburg	1652-1900	5
Rütschdorf	rkKB	Freiburg	1692-1951	1
Rütte -Säckingen-	rkKB	Freiburg	1784-1900	3

Location	Nature of Material	Where Filmed	Dates Covered	No. of Rolls
Sachsenflur	rkKB	Freiburg	1713-1923	2
Säckingen	rkKB	Freiburg	1592-1900	10
Saig	rkKB	Freiburg	1713-1900	2
Salem	rkKB	Freiburg	1668-1900	1
Salmendingen	rkKB	Freiburg	1700-1901	3
Sandhansen -Kr. Heidelberg-	rkKB	Freiburg	1810-1928	1
Sandweier	rkKB	Freiburg	1679-1920	3
Sankt Blasien	rkKB	Freiburg	1606-1900	9
Sankt Leon	rkKB	Freiburg	1695-1900	5
Sankt Märgen	rkKB	Freiburg	1605-1879	2
Sankt Peter	rkKB	Freiburg	1630-1901	14
Sankt Ulrich	rkKB	Freiburg	1641-1900	3
Sasbach	rkKB	Freiburg	1657-1900	4
Sasbach -Bühl-	rkKB	Freiburg	1697-1930	10
Sasbachwalden	rkKB	Freiburg	1804-1900	3
Sauggart	rkKB	Rottenburg	1652-1904	1
Sauldorf	rkKB	Freiburg	1650-1900	3
Saulgau	rkKB	Rottenburg	1308-1901	18
Schaiblishausen	rkKB	Rottenburg	1657-1901	7
Schapbach	rkKB	Freiburg	1646-1900	6
Schalthausen	rkKB	Freiburg	1779-1901	3
Schechingen	rkKB	Rottenburg	1658-1904	5
Scheer	rkKB	Rottenburg	1562-1900	8
Schelingen	rkKB	Freiburg	1700-1900	2
Schelklingen	rkKB	Rottenburg	1602-1901	5
Schemmerberg	rkKB	Rottenburg	1687-1901	3
Schenkenzell	rkKB	Freiburg	1706-1900	3
Scheringen	rkKB	Freiburg	1649-1898	4

Location	Nature of Material	Where Filmed	Dates Covered	No. of Rolls
Scherzingen	rkKB	Freiburg	1648-1786	1
Schielberg	rkKB	Freiburg	1672-1901	6
Schienen	rkKB	Freiburg	1463-1900	2
Schielingstadt	rkKB	Freiburg	1745-1900	2
Schlatt -Freiburg-	rkKB	Freiburg	1606-1952	2
Schlatt -Hechingen-	rkKB	Freiburg	1683-1900	1
Schlatt -Konstanz-	rkKB	Freiburg	1667-1900	4
Schlatt unter Krähen -Konstanz-	rkKB	Freiburg	1645-1900	4
Schliengen	rkKB	Freiburg	1614-1917	7
Schlier	rkKB	Rottenburg	1597-1900	17
Schlierstadt	rkKB	Freiburg	1668-1900	4
Schlossau	rkKB	Freiburg	1660-1903	8
Schluchsee	rkKB	Freiburg	1700-1900	4
Schluchtern	evKB	Augsburg	1726-1822	1
Schmalegg	rkKB	Rottenburg	1657-1900	2
Schmalfelden	evKB	Augsburg	1596-1717	1
Schmerbach	evKB	Augsburg	1608-1810	1
Schmiechen -Kr. Ehingen-	rkKB	Rottenburg	1660-1901	2
Schmittlingen	rkKB	Rottenburg	1601-1901	8
Schnürpflingen	rkKB	Rottenburg	1666-1902	3
Schollach	rkKB	Freiburg	1818-1900	1
Schöllbronn	rkKB	Freiburg	1663-1900	3
Schollbrunn	rkKB	Freiburg	1668-1906	6
Schömberg -Balingen-	rkKB	Rottenburg	1609-1930	5
Schomburg	rkKB	Rottenburg	1642-1901	6

Location	Nature of Material	Where Filmed	Dates Covered	No. of Rolls
Schonach	rkKB	Freiburg	1605-1900	8
Schönau i. Schwarzwald	rkKB	Freiburg	1638-1900	14
Schönau Kr. Heidelberg	rkKB	Freiburg	1739-1900	2
Schönau -Lörrach-	rkKB	Freiburg	1638-1900	5
Schönau -Distrikt-	rkKB	Freiburg	1865-1900	2
Schönberg -Lahr-	rkKB	Freiburg	1651-1900	4
Schöneburg	rkKB	Rottenburg	1666-1900	2
Schönenbach -Donaueschingen-	rkKB	Freiburg	1639-1900	4
Schönenbach -Hochschwarzwold-	rkKB	Freiburg	1639-1900	3
Schönenberg	rkKB	Freiburg	1854-1899	1
Schönenberg -Kr. Lörrach-	rkKB	Freiburg	1638-1900	14
Schönfeld	rkKB	Freiburg	1640-1900	1
Schöntal	rkKB	Ludwigsburg	1683-1901	3
Schörzingen	rkKB	Rottenburg	1650-1907	2
Schramberg	rkKB	Rottenburg	1639-1934	9
Schriesheim	rkKB	Freiburg	1700-1900	2
Schrozberg	evKB	Augsburg	1646-1808	1
Schussenried	rkKB	Rottenburg	1647-1907	8
Schuttern	rkKB	Freiburg	1650-1907	8
Schuttertal	rkKB	Freiburg	1695-1893	3
Schutterwald	rkKB	Freiburg	1676-1900	4
Schutterzell	rkKB	Freiburg	1817-1972	1
Schwabhausen	rkKB	Freiburg	1745-1800	1
Schwäbish Gmünd		Ludwigsburg	1811-1872	6
Schwäbisch Hall	evKB	Augsburg	1596-1756	2

Location	Nature of Material	Where Filmed	Dates Covered	No. of Rolls
Schwäbisch Hall	rkKB	Rottenburg	1671-1900	5
Schwabsberg	rkKB	Ludwigsburg	1732-1900	2
Schwackenreute	rkKB	Freiburg	1664-1907	3
Schwaibach	rkKB	Freiburg	1587-1889	14
Schwäblishausen	rkKB	Freiburg	1758-1900	2
Schwalldorf	rkKB	Rottenburg	1718-1903	2
Schwandorf	rkKB	Freiburg	1848-1900	3
Schwaningen	rkKB	Freiburg	1870-1900	1
Schwarzach -Bühl-	rkKB	Freiburg	1613-1889	12
Schwärzenbach	rkKB	Freiburg	1846-1870	1
Schweigern	rkKB	Freiburg Ludwigsburg	1687-1920	7
Schweighausen	rkKB	Freiburg	1646-1900	5
Schweinberg -Buchen-	rkKB	Freiburg	1663-1921	3
Schweinhausen	rkKB	Rottenburg	1660-1901	7
Schwendi	rkKB	Rottenburg	1642-1888	2
Schwenningen	rkKB	Freiburg	1626-1950	3
Schwetzingen	rkKB	Freiburg	1622-1899	5
Schwörstadt	rkKB	Freiburg	1679-1920	5
Seckach	rkKB	Freiburg	1668-1900	2
Seebach	rkKB	Freiburg	1828-1900	2
Seebronn	rkKB	Rottenburg	1736-1876	2
Seekirch	rkKB	Rottenburg	1659-1901	5
Seelbach	rkKB	Freiburg	1739-1900	8
Segeten	rkKB	Freiburg	1837-1877	1
Seibranz	rkKB	Rottenburg	1674-1900	2
Seitingen	rkKB	Rottenburg	1602-1901	4
Sersheim	evKB	Augsburg	1534-1925	2

Location	Nature of Material	Where Filmed	Dates Covered	No. of Rolls
Scheringen	rkKB	Freiburg	1826-1909	2
Siegelau	rkKB	Freiburg	1697-1900	8
Siegelsbach	rkKB	Freiburg	1704-1900	2
Siessen	rkKB	Rottenburg	1737-1900	2
Siggen -Wangen-	rkKB	Rottenburg	1693-1900	2
Sigmaringen	rkKB	Freiburg	1597-1900	16
Simmringen	rkKB	Ludwigsburg	1808-1900	1
Simprechtshausen	rkKB	Ludwigsburg	1830-1900	1
Sindeldorf	rkKB	Ludwigsburg	1590-1895	2
Singen -Konstanz-	rkKB	Freiburg	1645-1900	6
Sinningen	rkKB	Rottenburg	1613-1900	3
Sinsheim	rkKB	Freiburg	1699-1900	5
Sinzheim	rkKB	Freiburg	1623-1909	12
Sipplingen	rkKB	Freiburg	1685-1900	3
Sölden	rkKB	Freiburg	1641-1900	3
Söllingen	rkKB	Freiburg	1629-1900	5
Söllingen -Kr. Rastatt-	rkKB	Freiburg	1717-1900	2
Sonderbuch -Kr. Münsingen-	rkKB	Rottenburg	1631-1900	6
Spaichingen	rkKB	Rottenburg	1644-1880	9
Spechbach	rkKB	Freiburg	1734-1924	4
Spessart	rkKB	Freiburg	1663-1900	3
Spielbach	evKB	Augsburg	1546-1938	2
Spielberg -Calw-	evKB	Augsburg	1595-1775	1
Spindelwag	rkKB	Rottenburg	1670-1901	5
Stadelhofen	rkKB	Freiburg	1738-1974	3
Stafflangen	rkKB	Rottenburg	1673-1902	3

Location	Nature of Material	Where Filmed	Dates Covered	No. of Rolls
Strahringen	rkKB	Freiburg	1767-1905	2
Starnberg -Bayen-	rkKB	Augsburg	1674-1897	3
Starzeln	rkKB	Freiburg	1609-1900	5
Staufen -Müllheim-	rkKB	Freiburg	1676-1899	10
Staufen -Waldshut-	rkKB	Freiburg	1789-1952	2
Stein am Kocher	rkKB	Freiburg	1810-1900	3
Stein -Hechingen-	rkKB	Freiburg	1675-1900	3
Steinbach -Kr. Buchen-	rkKB	Freiburg	1604-1901	1
Steinbach -Bühl-	rkKB	Freiburg	1683-1907	11
Steinbach -Buchen-	rkKB	Freiburg	1810-1900	1
Steinberg -Ulm-	rkKB	Rottenburg	1582-1818	1
Steinbach -Tauberbischofsheim-	rkKB	Freiburg	1860-1907	2
Steinberg -Kr. Ulm-	rkKB	Rottenburg	1582-1867	2
Steinenstadt	rkKB	Freiburg	1614-1917	7
Steinfurt -Tauberbischofsheim-	rkKB	Freiburg	1892-1951	1
Steinhausen a.d. Rottum	rkKB	Rottenburg	1608-1901	2
Steinhausen b. Schussenied	rkKB	Rottenburg	1611-1877	1
Steinhilben	rkKB	Freiburg	1842-1900	1
Steinmauern -Rastatt-	rkKB	Freiburg	1727-1901	6
Steinsfurt	rkKB	Freiburg	1699-1900	7
Steisslingen	rkKB	Freiburg	1607-1957	5
Stetten -Donaueschingen-	rkKB	Freiburg	1810-1900	1

Location	Nature of Material	Where Filmed	Dates Covered	No. of Rolls
Stetten -Kr. Biberach-	rkKB	Rottenburg	1725-1900	2
Stetten -Kr. Tuttlingen-	rkKB	Rottenburg	1808-1900	1
Stetten -Kr. Waldshut-	rkKB	Freiburg	1810-1871	2
Stetten ob bontal	rkKB	Rottenburg	1628-1917	3
Stetten -Rottweil-	rkKB	Rottenburg	1662-1967	2
Stetten -Stockach-	rkKB	Freiburg	1621-1900	6
Stetten bei Haigerloch -Hechingen-	rkKB	Freiburg	1667-1886	2
Stetten unter Holstein -Kr. Waldshut-	rkKB	Freiburg	1694-1900	3
Stetten -Waldshut-	rkKB	Freiburg	1810-1870	1
Stettfeld -Kr. Bruchsal-	rkKB	Freiburg	1699-1900	4
Stimpfach	rkKB	Ludwigsburg	1605-1900	5
Stockach -Stockach-	rkKB	Freiburg	1690-1925	6
Stockheim	rkKB	Ludwigsburg	1600-1882	2
Stödtlen	rkKB	Ludwigsburg	1662-1900	3
Stollhofen	rkKB	Freiburg	1629-1900	5
Storzingen	rkKB	Freiburg	1763-1900	1
Strittmatt	rkKB	Freiburg	1837-1877	2
Strümpfelbrunn	rkKB	Freiburg	1699-1906	3
Stühlingen	rkKB	Freiburg	1664-1947	3
Stupferich	rkKB	Freiburg	1646-1900	4
Stuppach	rkKB	Ludwigsburg	1658-1875	5
Stürzenhardt	rkKB	Freiburg	1598-1904	8

Location	Nature of Material	Where Filmed	Dates Covered	No. of Rolls
Stuttgart	LDS records	Salt Lake City	1907-1951	11
Stuttgart	Passports	Ludwigsburg	1845-1918	1
Stuttgart	evKB	Augsburg Stuttgart	1533-1945	169
Stuttgart	MilKB	Ludwigsburg	1813-1900	1
Stuttgart	rkKB	Ludwigsburg Ludwigsburg	1634-1900	22
Sulmingen	rkKB	Rottenburg	1605-1887	2
Sulzbach -Kr. Mannheim-	rkKB	Freiburg	1649-1900	7
Sulzbach -Kr. Mosbach-	rkKB	Freiburg	1809-1901	1
Sulzbach -Rastatt-	rkKB	Freiburg	1811-1942	3
Sunthausen	rkKB	Freiburg	1648-1900	1
Tafertsweiler	rkKB	Freiburg	1667-1900	2
Taisersdorf	rkKB	Freiburg	1835-1900	1
Taldorf	rkKB	Rottenburg Ludwigsburg	1609-1900	12
Tannau	rkKB	Rottenburg	1644-1975	6
Tannhausen -Aalen-	rkKB	Ludwigsburg	1623-1899	11
Tannhausen -Ravensburg-	rkKB	Rottenburg	1684-1897	13
Tannheim -Donaueschingen-	rkKB	Freiburg	1806-1900	2
Tannheim -Kr. Biberach-	rkKB	Rottenburg	1598-1904	3
Tauberbischof- sheim	rkKB	Freiburg	1597-1936	8
Tengen	rkKB	Freiburg	1640-1895	4
Tettnang	rkKB	Rottenburg	1635-1896	11
Thalheim	rkKB	Rottenburg Freiburg	1700-1900	5
Thanheim	rkKB	Freiburg	1739-1900	1

Location	Nature of Material	Where Filmed	Dates Covered	No. of Rolls
Tiefenbach -Heilbronn-	rkKB	Ludwigsburg	1770-1955	3
Tiefenbach -Kr. Saulgau-	rkKB	Rottenburg	1659-1901	5
Tiefenbach -Kr. Sinsheim-	rkKB	Freiburg	1655-1894	3
Tiefenbronn	rkKB	Freiburg	1650-1902	3
Tiefenhäusern	rkKB	Freiburg	1670-1900	9
Tiengen -Waldshut-	rkKB	Freiburg	1621-1900	6
Tiergarten -Offenburg-	rkKB	Freiburg	1811-1900	2
Tigerfeld	rkKB	Rottenburg	1650-1900	2
Todtmoos	rkKB	Freiburg	1710-1900	5
Todtnau	rkKB	Freiburg	1689-1900	8
Todtnauberg	rkKB	Freiburg	1744-1900	2
Tomerdingen	rkKB	Rottenburg	1684-1900	2
Treffelhausen	rkKB	Rottenburg	1601-1901	8
Triberg	rkKB	Freiburg	1605-1923	9
Trienz	rkKB	Freiburg	1649-1900	5
Trillfingen	rkKB	Freiburg	1720-1900	3
Trochtelfingen -Sigmaringen-	rkKB	Freiburg	1602-1900	5
Tübingen	rkKB	Rottenburg	1792-1900	3
Tunau	rkKB	Freiburg	1639-1900	15
Tunsel	rkKB	Freiburg	1703-1950	3
Überlingen	rkKB	Freiburg	1597-1901	11
Ubstadt	rkKB	Freiburg	1698-1915	4
Uiffingen	rkKB	Freiburg	1669-1915	3
Uigendorf	rkKB	Rottenburg	1664-1902	7
Uissigheim	rkKB	Freiburg	1730-1975	4
Ulm -Donau-	rkKB	Rottenburg	1608-1902	17

Location	Nature of Material	Where Filmed	Dates Covered	No. of Rolls
Ulm -Donau-	evKB	Stuttgart	1596-1967	2
Ulm -Kr. Bühl-	rkKB	Freiburg	1613-1963	15
Ulm -Kr. Offenburg-	rkKB	Freiburg	1655-1903	16
Umkirch	rkKB	Freiburg	1784-1900	3
Ummendorf -Kr. Biberach-	rkKB	Rottenburg	1636-1901	4
Unadingen	rkKB	Freiburg	1659-1900	3
Unlingen	rkKB	Rottenburg	1656-1872	5
Unteralpfen	rkKB	Freiburg	1709-1900	4
Unterbalbach	rkKB	Freiburg	1656-1909	4
Unterbaldingen	rkKB	Freiburg	1651-1900	1
Unterbiederbach	rkKB	Freiburg	1697-1900	8
Unterdenfstetten	rkKB	Ludwigsburg	1736-1883	5
Unterdigisheim	rkKB	Rottenburg	1753-1952	2
Untereggingen	rkKB	Freiburg	1765-1900	2
Untereutersbach	rkKB	Freiburg	1849-1900	2
Unteressendorf	rkKB	Rottenburg	1671-1874	1
Untergimpern	rkKB	Freiburg	1704-1904	4
Unterglottertal	rkKB	Freiburg	1714-1905	5
Untergriesheim	rkKB	Ludwigsburg	1649-1905	3
Untergrombach	rkKB	Freiburg	1683-1900	5
Untergröningen	rkKB	Rottenburg	1777-1926	2
Untergruppernbach	evKB	Augsburg	1600-1794	2
Unterharmersbach	rkKB	Freiburg	1849-1898	2
Unteribach	rkKB	Freiburg	1606-1900	3
Unteribental	rkKB	Freiburg	1764-1900	5
Unterkirchberg	rkKB	Rottenburg	1583-1902	11
Unterkirnach	rkKB	Freiburg	1784-1900	3

Location	Nature of Material	Where Filmed	Dates Covered	No. of Rolls
Unterkochen	rkKB	Rottenburg	1674-1904	7
Unterlanchingen	rkKB	Freiburg	1812-1900	1
Untermarchtal	rkKB	Rottenburg	1600-1905	5
Untermettingen	rkKB	Freiburg	1688-1900	4
Unterneudorf	rkKB	Freiburg	1598-1904	9
Unterprechtal	rkKB	Freiburg	1697-1900	8
Unterschefflenz	rkKB	Freiburg	1688-1899	2
Unterschweidheim	rkKB	Ludwigsburg	1603-1900	5
Unterschüpf	rkKB	Freiburg	1713-1923	2
Unterschwarzach -Biberach-	rkKB	Rottenburg	1700-1900	4
Untersiggingen	rkKB	Freiburg	1784-1900	2
Untersimonswald	rkKB	Freiburg	1635-1910	7
Unterstadion	rkKB	Rottenburg	1627-1891	4
Untersulmetingen	rkKB	Rottenburg	1650-1900	2
Unterwachingen	rkKB	Rottenburg	1637-1974	5
Unterwaldhausen	rkKB	Rottenburg	1662-1906	1
Unterwangen	rkKB	Freiburg	1647-1900	6
Unterweiler	rkKB	Rottenburg	1608-1900	4
Unterwilfingen	rkKB	Ludwigsburg	1769-1900	4
Unterwittighansen	rkKB	Freiburg	1677-1900	3
Unterwittstadt	rkKB	Freiburg	1584-1901	6
Unzhurst	rkKB	Freiburg	1613-1889	12
Upflamör	rkKB	Rottenburg	1631-1901	8
Urach -Reutlingen-	rkKB	Freiburg	1619-1876	2
Urloffen	rkKB	Freiburg	1657-1900	6
Uruau	rkKB	Freiburg	1666-1900	1
Ursenbach	rkKB	Freiburg	1710-1900	2
Ursendorf	rkKB	Rottenburg	1664-1900	12

Location	Nature of Material	Where Filmed	Dates Covered	No. of Rolls
Uttenhofen -Konstanz-	rkKB	Freiburg	1640-1900	3
Uttenweiler	rkKB	Rottenburg	1623-1915	4
Utzenfeld	rkKB	Freiburg	1638-1900	15
Vaihingen	evKB	Augsburg	1609-1791	2
Varnhalt	rkKB	Freiburg	1810-1907	2
Vilchband	rkKB	Freiburg	1606-1904	2
Villingen	rkKB	Freiburg	1576-1900	13
Villingendorf	rkKB	Rottenburg	1572-1897	2
Vilsingen	rkKB	Freiburg	1740-1900	4
Vimbuch	rkKB	Freiburg	1613-1889	12
Vogt	rkKB	Rottenburg	1778-1900	4
Vöhrenbach	rkKB	Freiburg	1585-1930	15
Völkersbach	rkKB	Freiburg	1686-1900	3
Volkersheim	rkKB	Rottenburg	1657-1901	7
Volkertshausen	rkKB	Freiburg	1630-1900	2
Völlkofen	rkKB	Rottenburg	1664-1900	12
Vollmersdorf	rkKB	Freiburg	1692-1951	1
Wachbach	evKB	Augsburg	1633-1807	1
Wachbach	rkKB	Ludwigsburg	1734-1900	1
Wachendorf	rkKB	Rottenburg	1635-1876	2
Wagenschwend	rkKB	Freiburg	1649-1898	5
Wagenstadt	rkKB	Freiburg	1684-1900	2
Wagensteig	rkKB	Freiburg	1764-1900	6
Waghurst	rkKB	Freiburg	1780-1900	3
Wahlwies	rkKB	Freiburg	1735-1964	3
Waiblingen	evKB	Augsburg	1535-1892	1
Waibstadt	rkKB	Freiburg	1598-1900	5
Walbertsweiler	rkKB	Freiburg	1669-1900	2
Wald	rkKB	Freiburg	1706-1900	4

Location	Nature of Material	Where Filmed	Dates Covered	No. of Rolls
Waldburg	rkKB	Rottenburg	1597-1900	20
Waldenbuch	evKB	Augsburg	1558-1808	1
Waldenburg	evKB	Augsburg	1593-1808	1
Waldenburg	rkKB	Rottenburg	1771-1882	1
Waldhausen -Aalen-	rkKB	Rottenburg	1762-1900	5
Waldhausen -Buchen-	rkKB	Freiburg	1649-1909	6
Waldhausen -Saulgau-	rkKB	Rottenburg	1682-1901	4
Waldhilsbach	rkKB	Freiburg	1688-1901	3
Waldkatzenbach	rkKB	Freiburg	1699-1906	3
Waldkirch -Emmendingen-	rkKB	Freiburg	1643-1900	17
Waldkirch -Waldshut-	rkKB	Freiburg	1593-1900	7
Waldmössingen	rkKB	Rottenburg	1656-1923	3
Waldmühlbach	rkKB	Freiburg	1650-1900	4
Waldprechtsweier	rkKB	Freiburg	1730-1900	12
Waldshut	rkKB	Freiburg	1578-1900	3
Waldstetten -Buchen-	rkKB	Freiburg	1577-1929	5
Waldulm	rkKB	Freiburg	1610-1900	5
Waldwimmersbach	rkKB	Freiburg	1734-1924	5
Wallbach	rkKB	Freiburg	1784-1900	1
Wallburg	rkKB	Freiburg	1564-1900	8
Walldorf -Kr. Heidelberg-	rkKB	Freiburg	1697-1895	3
Walldürn	rkKB	Freiburg	1587-1900	12
Walpertshofen	rkKB	Rottenburg	1651-1900	1
Waltershofen -Freiburg-	rkKB	Freiburg	1602-1898	3
Waltershofen -Wangen-	rkKB	Rottenburg	1602-1888	2

Location	Nature of Material	Where Filmed	Dates Covered	No. of Rolls
Waltersweier	rkKB	Freiburg	1608-1900	17
Wangen -Kr. Ulm-	rkKB	Rottenburg	1713-1906	2
Wangen -Sigmaringen-	rkKB	Freiburg	1603-1900	2
Wangen -Wangen-	rkKB	Rottenburg	1591-1900	10
Warthausen	rkKB	Rottenburg	1659-1901	7
Wasenweiler	rkKB	Freiburg	1650-1900	3
Wasser -Stockach-	rkKB	Freiburg	1619-1900	8
Wasseralfingen	rkKB	Rottenburg	1834-1902	2
Watterdingen	rkKB	Freiburg	1708-1900	2
Wehingen	rkKB	Rottenburg	1649-1900	7
Wehr	rkKB	Freiburg	1643-1900	6
Wehrhalden	rkKB	Freiburg	1851-1900	2
Weier	rkKB	Freiburg	1608-1900	3
Weigheim	rkKB	Rottenburg	1655-1962	2
Weiher -Kr. Bruchsal-	rkKB	Freiburg	1696-1900	5
Weihwang	rkKB	Freiburg	1758-1900	2
Weikersheim	evKB	Augsburg	1556-1808	5
Weil -Konstanz-	rkKB	Freiburg	1646-1900	2
Weil -Stuttgart-	evKB	Augsburg	1553-1807	1
Weil der stadt	rkKB	Ludwigsburg	1649-1920	9
Weildorf -Hechingen-	rkKB	Freiburg	1680-1889	2
Weildorf -Überlingen-	rkKB	Freiburg	1605-1900	3
Weilen	rkKB	Rottenburg	1726-1930	1
Weiler -Sinsheim-	rkKB	Freiburg	1699-1900	3

Location	Nature of Material	Where Filmed	Dates Covered	No. of Rolls
Weiler -Konstanz-	rkKB	Freiburg	1760-1881	2
Weiler -Tübingen-	rkKB	Rottenburg	1808-1900	2
Weilheim -Hechingen-	rkKB	Freiburg	1655-1900	4
Weilheim -Nürtingen-	evKB	Augsburg	1566-1834	1
Weilheim -Waldshut-	rkKB	Freiburg	1608-1900	6
Weingarten -Kr. Ravensburg-	rkKB	Rottenburg	1597-1900	16
Weinheim -Kr. Mannheim-	rkKB	Freiburg	1722-1900	3
Weinsberg	evKB	Augsburg	1571-1783	1
Weinstetten	rkKB	Rottenburg	1520-1878	2
Weisbach	rkKB	Freiburg	1699-1906	3
Weisenbach -Rastatt-	rkKB	Freiburg	1580-1966	8
Weissach	evKB	Augsburg	1564-1768	1
Weissenstein	rkKB	Rottenburg	1601-1901	4
Weissweil -Waldshut-	rkKB	Freiburg	1600-1900	3
Weiterdingen	rkKB	Freiburg	1657-1900	3
Weizen	rkKB	Freiburg	1728-1900	1
Wellendingen -Hochschwarzwald-	rkKB	Freiburg	1625-1900	4
Wellendingen -Rottweil-	rkKB	Rottenburg	1624-1930	4
Welschensteinach	rkKB	Freiburg	1682-1902	5
Wembach	rkKB	Freiburg	1829-1899	1
Wembach -Kr. Lörrach-	rkKB	Freiburg	1638-1900	14
Wendelsheim	rkKB	Rottenburg	1636-1900	3
Wenkheim	rkKB	Freiburg	1666-1900	2

Location	Nature of Material	Where Filmed	Dates Covered	No. of Rolls
Werbach	rkKB	Freiburg	1597-1900	4
Wernau	rkKB	Ludwigsburg	1646-1900	4
Wessental	rkKB	Freiburg	1813-1900	1
Westerheim -Kr. Münsingen-	rkKB	Rottenburg	1708-1900	3
Westernhausen	rkKB	Ludwigsburg	1590-1900	7
Westerstetten	rkKB	Rottenburg	1589-1900	2
Westhausen	rkKB	Freiburg	1572-1876	4
Wettelbrunn	rkKB	Freiburg	1639-1900	2
Wettersdorf -Buchen-	rkKB	Freiburg	1613-1951	4
Widdern	evKB	Augsburg	1593-1600	1
Wiechs -Konstanz-	rkKB	Freiburg	1694-1900	2
Wiechs -Stockach-	rkKB	Freiburg	1775-1957	1
Wieden	rkKB	Freiburg	1811-1900	2
Wiesenbach, Crailsheim	evKB	Augsburg	1670-1811	1
Wiesenbach -Kr. Heidelberg-	rkKB	Freiburg	1810-1900	1
Wiesloch	rkKB	Freiburg	1715-1904	3
Wildbad	rkKB	Ludwigsburg	1868-1900	1
Wildgutach	rkKB	Freiburg	1787-1879	1
Wildtal	rkKB	Freiburg	1811-1920	3
Wilfingen -Kr. Saulgau-	rkKB	Rottenburg	1618-1903	2
Wilfingen -Rottweil-	rkKB	Rottenburg	1796-1899	2
Wilhelmsfeld	rkKB	Freiburg	1699-1901	4
Willaringen	rkKB	Freiburg	1784-1900	1
Willsbach	evKB	Augsburg	1655-1731	1
Wilschingen	rkKB	Freiburg	1651-1900	3

Location	Nature of Material	Where Filmed	Dates Covered	No. of Rolls
Wilsingen	rkKB	Rottenburg	1700-1901	1
Wimmental	rkKB	Ludwigsburg	1629-1938	2
Wimpfen	evKB	Augsburg	1700-1756	1
Windischbuch	rkKB	Freiburg	1745-1900	1
Wintersdorf	rkKB	Freiburg	1717-1900	3
Winterspüren	rkKB	Freiburg	1650-1899	3
Winterstetten	rkKB	Rottenburg	1733-1900	4
Winterstettendorf	rkKB	Rottenburg	1846-1901	1
Wintersulgen	rkKB	Rottenburg	1611-1900	4
Winzenhofen	rkKB	Freiburg	1590-1900	1
Winzingen	rkKB	Speyer	1791-1957	9
Wissgoldingen	rkKB	Rottenburg	1618-1900	3
Wittelbach	rkKB	Freiburg	1739-1900	8
Wittenschwand	rkKB	Freiburg	1749-1850	1
Wittlekofen	rkKB	Freiburg	1647-1900	6
Wittnau	rkKB	Freiburg	1784-1912	2
Wölchingen	rkKB	Freiburg	1687-1920	6
Wolfach	rkKB	Freiburg	1595-1900	6
Wolfartsweiler	rkKB	Rottenburg	1308-1900	13
Wolfegg	rkKB	Rottenburg Ludwigsburg	1618-1900	8
Wolketsweiler	rkKB	Rottenburg	1657-1901	4
Wolpertswende	rkKB	Rottenburg	1689-1915	5
Wolterdingen	rkKB	Freiburg	1594-1900	6
Worblingen	rkKB	Freiburg	1715-1860	1
Worndorf	rkKB	Freiburg	1675-1901	2
Wört	rkKB	Ludwigsburg	1744-1844	2
Wuchtenhofen	rkKB	Rottenburg	1617-1900	8
Wullenstetten	rkKB	Rottenburg	1666-1902	3

Location	Nature of Material	Where Filmed	Dates Covered	No. of Rolls
Würmersheim	rkKB	Freiburg	1660-1900	8
Wurmlingen -Kr. Tuttlingen-	rkKB	Rottenburg	1599-1895	4
Würmlingen -Tübingen-	rkKB	Rottenburg	1674-1913	3
Wyhl	rkKB	Freiburg	1649-1900	5
Wyhlen	rkKB	Freiburg	1605-1900	3
Yach	rkKB	Freiburg	1697-1904	11
Zaisenhausen -Kr. Sinsheim-	rkKB	Freiburg	1657-1900	2
Zaisenhausen -Künzelsau-	rkKB	Ludwigsburg	1808-1900	1
Zell -Überlingen-	rkKB	Freiburg	1758-1900	2
Zell unter Aichelberg	rkKB	Stuttgart	1555-1734	1
Zell -Wolfach-	rkKB	Freiburg	1654-1899	9
Zell District -Lörrach-	rkKB	Freiburg	1768-1900	11
Zell Weierbach	rkKB	Freiburg	1608-1900	15
Zepfenhau	rkKB	Rottenburg	1803-1951	1
Ziegelhausen	rkKB	Freiburg	1622-1901	5
Zimmerholz	rkKB	Freiburg	1866-1900	1
Zimmern -Balingen-	rkKB	Rottenburg	1808-1974	2
Zimmern -Buchen-	rkKB	Freiburg	1668-1900	2
Zimmern -Hechingen-	rkKB	Freiburg	1819-1900	1
Zimmern -Rottweil-	rkKB	Rottenburg	1748-1954	2
Zimmern -Tauerbischofsheim-	rkKB	Freiburg	1643-1901	7
Zipplingen	rkKB	Ludwigsburg	1713-1900	6

Location	Nature of Material	Where Filmed	Dates Covered	No. of Rolls
Zizenhausen	rkKB	Freiburg	1812-1900	4
Zöbingen	rkKB	Ludwigsburg	1650-1900	2
Zogenseiler	rkKB	Rottenburg	1625-1901	2
Zogenweiler	rkKB	Rottenburg	1656-1901	4
Zollenreute	rkKB	Rottenburg	1684-1897	13
Zoznegg	rkKB	Freiburg	1812-1900	1
Zusenhofen	rkKB	Freiburg	1637-1900	3
Zussdorf	rkKB	Rottenburg	1652-1900	2
Zuzenhausen	rkKB	Freiburg	1699-1900	2
Zwiefalten	rkKB	Rottenburg	1631-1900	6
Zwiefaltendorf	rkKB	Rottenburg	1650-1901	2
Zwingenberg	rkKB	Freiburg	1686-1901	3

BAYERN

Location	Nature of Material	Where Filmed	Dates Covered	No. of Rolls
Baar	rkKB evKB	Augsburg	1568-1933	3
Babenhausen	rkKB	Augsburg	1594-1892	7
Bachen	rkKB	Augsburg	1620-1880	2
Bachhazel	rkKB	Augsburg	1690-1915	2
Bach Heilbrunn	rkKB	Augsburg	1788-1936	1
Bad Wörishofen	rkKB	Augsburg	1639-1829	4
Baierhofe	rkKB	Augsburg	1637-1817	2
Baindlkirch	rkKB	Augsburg	1636-1945	3
Baisweil	rkKB	Augsburg	1751-1895	3
Balderschway	rkKB	Augsburg	1797-1970	1
Balhhausen	rkKB	Augsburg	1635-1962	4
Balshausen	rkKB	Augsburg	1629-1878	2
Bamberg	LDS records	Salt Lake City	1945-1948	1
Bamberg	Hospital	Frankfurt	1820-1835	1
Bamberg	rkKB	Frankfurt Bamberg	1607-1959	13
Bamberg	STA	Bamberg Frankfurt	1599-1961	60
Bamberg	misc.	Bamberg Frankfurt	1599-1805	3
Batzeshofe	rkKB	Augsburg	1627-1957	6
Bayerchillig	rkKB	Augsburg	1671-1926	2
Bayernicherhofe	rkKB	Augsburg	1628-1881	2
Bayersreid	rkKB	Augsburg	1814-1878	1
Bayreuth	evKB MKB	Hannover	1792-1807	1
Beckstetten	rkKB	Augsburg	1663-1912	1
Bedernau	rkKB	Augsburg	1665-1884	2

Location	Nature of Material	Where Filmed	Dates Covered	No. of Rolls
Behlingen	rkKB	Augsburg	1613-1808	4
Belsheim	rkKB	Augsburg	1659-1909	2
Benediktbeuren	rkKB	Augsburg	1620-1883	3
Benniaze	rkKB	Augsburg	1632-1879	2
Berg -Donauwörth-	rkKB	Augsburg	1665-1877	2
Berg -Schrobenhausen-	rkKB	Augsburg	1646-1889	3
Bergheim -Augsburg-	rkKB	Augsburg	1726-1964	4
Bergheim -Dillingen-	rkKB	Augsburg	1707-1836	3
Bernbach	rkKB	Augsburg	1659-1902	2
Bernbeuren	rkKB	Augsburg	1692-1893	3
Bernreich	rkKB	Augsburg	1653-1878	1
Bertholdshofe	rkKB	Augsburg	1682-1873	2
Bertoldsheim	rkKB	Augsburg	1658-1880	3
Betsigau	rkKB	Augsburg	1812-1883	2
Beuren	rkKB	Augsburg	1637-1947	3
Biberachsell	rkKB	Augsburg	1705-1948	2
Biberbach	rkKB	Augsburg Trier	1528-1937	5
Biberach	rkKB	Augsburg	1662-1968	2
Biberberg	rkKB	Augsburg	1663-1970	3
Biburg	rkKB STA	Augsburg	1650-1894	2
Bichingen	rkKB	Augsburg	1746-1934	3
Bittenhausen	rkKB	Augsburg	1748-1946	2
Binswangen	rkKB	Augsburg	1637-1876	3
Bissingen	rkKB	Augsburg	1610-1963	3
Blaichach	rkKB	Augsburg	1615-1877	2
Bliensbach	rkKB	Augsburg	1625-1881	2

Location	Nature of Material	Where Filmed	Dates Covered	No. of Rolls
Blindheim	rkKB	Augsburg	1658-1946	6
Blöcktach	rkKB	Augsburg	1755-1918	1
Bobingen	rkKB	Augsburg	1673-1905	9
Böhen	rkKB	Augsburg	1690-1968	4
Bonstetten	rkKB	Augsburg	1637-1875	1
Boos	rkKB	Augsburg	1595-1880	2
Brackenlohr	evKB	Augsburg	1576-1950	1
Breitenbronn	rkKB	Augsburg	1650-1877	2
Breitenbrunn	rkKB	Augsburg	1626-1885	2
Breitenthal	rkKB	Augsburg	1636-1960	2
Brunnen	rkKB	Augsburg	1659-1879	2
Bubenhausen	rkKB	Augsburg	1745-1968	2
Bubenreuth		Buch		
Bubesheim	rkKB	Augsburg	1650-1954	2
Buchenberg	rkKB	Augsburg	1620-1939	7
Buchloe	rkKB	Augsburg	1688-1898	4
Bühl	rkKB	Augsburg	1633-1953	2
Bullenheim	evKB	Augsburg	1675-1953	1
Burg	rkKB	Augsburg	1788-1878	1
Burgau	rkKB	Augsburg	1686-1886	6
Burgbernheim	evKB	Frankfurt	1830-1895	2
Burghazel	rkKB	Augsburg	1670-1866	1
Burgheim	rkKB	Augsburg	1629-1877	3
Burlafingen	rkKB	Augsburg	1613-1897	2
Buttenwiesen	rkKB	Augsburg	1700-1879	1
Burheim	rkKB	Augsburg	1634-1879	2
Chiemsee	LG	Innsbruck	1739-1806	6
Coburg	LDS records	Salt Lake City	1931-1948	1

Location	Nature of Material	Where Filmed	Dates Covered	No. of Rolls
Daiting	rkKB	Augsburg Berlin-Dahlem	1665-1886	3
Dasing	rkKB	Augsburg	1726-1950	2
Deffingen	rkKB	Augsburg	1570-1881	1
Deggingen	rkKB	Augsburg	1652-1943	2
Deimhausen	rkKB	Augsburg	1672-1885	2
Deimingen	rkKB	Augsburg	1826-1880	2
Deisenhausen	rkKB	Augsburg	1645-1880	3
Deisenhofen	rkKB	Augsburg	19th-20th LG	1
Demharthofe	rkKB	Augsburg	1636-1935	4
Derching	rkKB	Augsburg	1632-1969	1
Dettenschwarz	rkKB	Augsburg	1636-1886	2
Deubach -Gimsberg-	rkKB	Augsburg	1670-1901	3
Deubach -Augsburg-	rkKB	Augsburg	1655-1937	2
Diedorf	rkKB STA	Augsburg	1692-1968	2
Diemantstein	rkKB	Augsburg	1740-1877	2
Diepols	rkKB	Augsburg	1816-1970	1
Diessen	rkKB	Augsburg	1621-1893	4
Dietenhofen	rkKB	Augsburg	1618-1885	2
Dietkirch	rkKB STA	Augsburg	1601-1954	6
Dietmannsreich	rkKB	Augsburg	1595-1885	7
Dillingen	rkKB Km	Augsburg Frankfurt	1551-1960	12
Dillishausen	Km	Frankfurt	1655-1898	1
Dinkelsbühl	Km	Frankfurt	1568-1883	8
Dinkelscherben	Km	Frankfurt	1657-1876	3
Dirlewang	rkKB	Augsburg	1605-1950	3
Donaualtheim	rkKB	Augsburg	1602-1877	3

Location	Nature of Material	Where Filmed	Dates Covered	No. of Rolls
Donaumünster	rkKB	Augsburg	1813-1876	1
Donauwörth	rkKB	Augsburg	1579-1928	9
Dornhofen	STA	Augsburg	1680-1948	1
Dorschhausen	rkKB	Augsburg	1752-1934	1
Dösingen	rkKB	Augsburg	1722-1878	2
Drösslingen	rkKB	Augsburg	1719-1874	2
Droisheim	rkKB	Augsburg	1638-1916	2
Dünselbach	rkKB	Augsburg	1630-1953	1
Durach	rkKB	Augsburg	1638-1889	2
Dürrlauningen	rkKB	Augsburg	1616-1887	3
Ebenhausen	rkKB	Marburg	1805-1885	1
Ebenhofen	rkKB	Augsburg	1729-1902	1
Ebenried	rkKB	Augsburg	1709-1873	1
Ebenbach	rkKB	Augsburg	1622-1877	3
Ebenshausen	rkKB	Augsburg	1650-1942	3
Ebratshofe	rkKB	Augsburg	1707-1970	2
Echenbrunn	rkKB	Augsburg	1574-1965	3
Eching	rkKB	Augsburg	1725-1873	1
Eckarts	rkKB	Augsburg	1664-1938	3
Ecknach	rkKB	Augsburg	1648-1945	2
Edelhausen	rkKB	Augsburg	1687-1898	1
Edelsfeld	evKB	Augsburg	1756-1884	1
Edelstetten	rkKB	Augsburg	1637-1898	4
Edenhausen	rkKB	Augsburg	1665-1878	3
Edenreich	rkKB	Trier	1637-1969	3
Egelhofen	rkKB	Augsburg	1665-1884	1
Egg	rkKB	Augsburg	1616-1887	3
Eggenthal	rkKB	Augsburg	1637-1968	3
Eglfing	rkKB	Augsburg	1629-1915	1

Location	Nature of Material	Where Filmed	Dates Covered	No. of Rolls
Egling	rkKB	Augsburg	1628-1879	2
Egloffstein	evKB	Augsburg	1612-1627	1
Ehingen	rkKB	Augsburg	1610-1957	4
Ehrenberg	rkKB	Augsburg	1659-1963	2
Eisenbach	rkKB	Augsburg	1803-1970	2
Ellerbach	rkKB	Augsburg	1677-1900	1
Ellgau	rkKB	Trier	1827-1919	1
Ellhofen	rkKB	Augsburg	1632-1954	1
Ellsee	rkKB	Augsburg	1787-1881	1
Emersacker	rkKB	Augsburg	1670-1874	2
Emershofen	rkKB	Augsburg	1590-1970	4
Emmerhausen	rkKB	Augsburg Berlin-Dahlem	1641-1887	3
Engetreich	rkKB	Augsburg	1662-1890	4
Engishausen	rkKB	Augsburg	1816-1924	1
Enheim	evLutKB	Augsburg	1655-1936	1
Entraching	rkKB	Augsburg	1607-1837	1
Epfach	rkKB	Augsburg	1605-1900	2
Eppisburg	rkKB	Augsburg	1636-1935	5
Eppishausen	rkKB	Augsburg	1613-1886	2
Eresing	rkKB	Augsburg	1617-1882	3
Eresreich	rkKB	Augsburg	1656-1860	1
Erisreich	rkKB	Augsburg	1653-1887	1
Erkheim	rkKB	Augsburg	1603-1946	3
Erling-Andechs	rkKB	Augsburg	1627-1909	3
Erlingshofen	rkKB	Augsburg	1813-1876	1
Ernhüll	evLutKB	Augsburg	1833-1878	1
Erpfting	rkKB	Augsburg	1580-1921	2
Eschenfelden	evLutKB	Augsburg	1857-1900	1

Location	Nature of Material	Where Filmed	Dates Covered	No. of Rolls
Ettelreich	rkKB	Augsburg	1845-1876	1
Ettenbrunen	rkKB	Augsburg	1721-1883	4
Ettringen	rkKB	Augsburg	1802-1914	2
Etschwang	evLutKB	Augsburg	1613-1878	1
Eurasburg	rkKB	Augsburg	1824-1935	1
Eurishofen	rkKB	Augsburg	1748-1946	1
Eutenhausen	rkKB	Augsburg	1632-1892	2
Eutenhofen	rkKB	Augsburg	1659-1963	2
Fahlenbach	rkKB	Augsburg	1732-1872	2
Faimingen	rkKB	Augsburg	1574-1965	3
Feldafing	rkKB	Augsburg	1651-1880	1
Feldheim	rkKB	Augsburg	1661-1918	1
Finmingen	rkKB	Augsburg	1703-1935	1
Fischach	rkKB	Augsburg	1681-1957	3
Fischen	rkKB	Augsburg	1635-1936	6
Fleinhausen	rkKB	Augsburg	1802-1870	1
Forst -Weilheim-	rkKB	Augsburg	1752-1878	2
Frankenhofen	rkKB	Augsburg	1663-1903	2
Frankenreich	rkKB	Augsburg	1666-1968	1
Frauenreichhausen	rkKB	Augsburg	1619-1877	1
Frauenstetten	rkKB	Augsburg	1722-1883	1
Frauensell	rkKB	Augsburg	1619-1956	2
Frechenreich	rkKB	Augsburg	1645-1947	2
Freihalden	rkKB	Augsburg	1675-1950	2
Freinhausen	rkKB	Augsburg	1671-1884	3
Fremdingen	rkKB	Augsburg	1666-1880	2
Freidberg	rkKB	Augsburg	1635-1913	8
Freiding	rkKB	Augsburg	1630-1878	2

Location	Nature of Material	Where Filmed	Dates Covered	No. of Rolls
Friesenreich	rkKB	Augsburg	1692-1879	2
Fristingen	rkKB	Augsburg	1650-1877	3
Fürnreich	evKB	Augsburg	1649-1956	6
Fürth	LDS records	Salt Lake City	1922-1923	1
Füssen	rkKB	Augsburg	1596-1897	9
Gabelbach	rkKB	Augsburg	1634-1900	2
Gablingen	rkKB HzB.	Augsburg	1612-1968	9
Gambach	rkKB	Augsburg	1804-1885	3
Gansheim	rkKB	Augsburg	1838-1949	1
Gebenhofen	rkKB	Augsburg	1704-1876	1
Geisenreich	rkKB	Augsburg	1713-1912	1
Geisslingen	evLutKB	Augsburg	1615-1937	1
Geltendorf	rkKB	Augsburg	1637-1873	2
Gempfing	rkKB	Augsburg	1678-1908	4
Gennach	rkKB	Augsburg	1610-1876	1
Gerlenhofen	rkKB	Rottenburg	1583-1883	4
Gersthofen	rkKB HzB.	Augsburg	1639-1943	4
Gestratz	rkKB	Augsburg	1684-1880	3
Glött	rkKB	Augsburg	1643-1877	2
Grodstadt	evLutKB	Augsburg	1533-1950	1
Göggingen	rkKB HzB.	Augsburg	1633-1941	9
Goresreich	rkKB	Augsburg	1658-1890	2
Graben	rkKB	Augsburg	1647-1920	2
Grisbeckersell	rkKB	Augsburg	1593-1876	2
Grimoldsried	rkKB	Augsburg	1650-1850	1
Grimolshausen	rkKB	Augsburg	1711-1893	1
Grönenbach	rkKB	Augsburg	1615-1888	4

Location	Nature of Material	Where Filmed	Dates Covered	No. of Rolls
Grossaifingen	rkKB	Augsburg	1618-1925	5
Grosskissendorf	rkKB	Augsburg	1604-1914	4
Grosskätz	rkKB	Augsburg	1626-1942	4
Grossohrenbronn	rkKB	Augsburg	1855-1877	1
Grünenbach	rkKB	Augsburg	1667-1942	3
Grünenbaindt	rkKB	Augsburg	1668-1876	2
Gumdamsreid	rkKB	Augsburg	1742-1943	3
Gundelfingen	rkKB	Augsburg	1632-1938	7
Gundelsdorf	rkKB	Augsburg	1583-1879	3
Gundremmingen	rkKB	Augsburg	1639-1876	3
Güns	rkKB	Augsburg	1740-1878	2
Günsburg	rkKB	Augsburg	1585-1895	15
Habach	rkKB	Augsburg	1608-1899	1
Haberskirch	rkKB	Augsburg	1632-1969	2
Häder	rkKB	Augsburg	1657-1968	2
Hafenhofen	rkKB	Augsburg	1656-1875	1
Hagenheim	rkKB	Augsburg	1613-1848	1
Hamhofen	rkKB	Augsburg	1658-1969	5
Haldenwang	rkKB	Augsburg	1646-1881	7
Halsbach -Dinkelsbühl-	rkKB	Augsburg	1596-1968	4
Hammel	HzB.	Augsburg	1683-1875	1
Handsell	rkKB	Augsburg	1656-1944	2
Happurg	evLutKB	Augsburg	1379-1878	6
Harburg	Einw. Buch	Frankfurt	1926	1
Harberg	rkKB	Augsburg	1592-1881	2
Haselbach -Mindelheim-	rkKB	Augsburg	1624-1928	2
Haselbach -Newburg-	rkKB	Augsburg	1600-1879	1

Location	Nature of Material	Where Filmed	Dates Covered	No. of Rolls
Haunshofen	rkKB	Augsburg	1686-1942	1
Haunstetten	rkKB HzB.	Augsburg	1636-1923	5
Haunswier	rkKB	Trier	1688-1888	1
Hausen -Dillingen-	rkKB	Augsburg	1617-1929	1
Hausen -Fürstenfeldbruch-	rkKB	Augsburg	1691-1886	2
Hausen -Karlstadt-			1674-1945	1
Hausen -Krumbach-	rkKB	Augsburg	1822-1876	1
Hausen -Mindelheim-	rkKB	Augsburg	1837-1872	1
Hausen -Nördlingen-	rkKB	Augsburg	1760-1876	1
Hawangen	rkKB	Augsburg	1607-1880	5
Hechendorf	rkKB	Berlin-Dahlem	1742-1876	1
Hegelhofen	rkKB	Augsburg	1797-1912	2
Hegnenbach	rkKB	Augsburg	1640-1950	1
Heimenkirch	rkKB	Augsburg	1616-1891	4
Heimertingen	rkKB	Augsburg	1735-1884	3
Hellengerst	rkKB	Augsburg	1654-1882	2
Herbertshofen	rkKB	Trier	1652-1921	2
Herchsried	rkKB	Augsburg	1636-1828	1
Hergensweiler	rkKB	Augsburg	1720-1884	1
Herrenstetten	rkKB	Augsburg	1674-1881	1
Herrberchtheim	evKB	Augsburg	1562-1800	1
Hendorf	rkKB	Augsburg	1636-1935	4
Hilgertshausen	rkKB	Augsburg	1685-1894	2
Hiltenfingen	rkKB	Augsburg	1649-1899	3
Hindelang	rkKB	Augsburg	1621-1953	7
Hisblingen	rkKB	Augsburg	1639-1963	2

Location	Nature of Material	Where Filmed	Dates Covered	No. of Rolls
Hirschbach -Wertingen-	rkKB HzB.	Augsburg	1685-1883	1
Hirschbrunn	rkKB	Augsburg	1706-1904	1
Hirschsell	rkKB	Augsburg	1687-1883	1
Hochaltingen	rkKB	Augsburg	1591-1931	5
Hochdorf -Friedberg-	rkKB	Augsburg	1810-1881	1
Hochgreut	rkKB	Augsburg	1810-1853	1
Höchstädt -Dillingen-	rkKB	Augsburg	1580-1969	11
Hochwang	rkKB	Augsburg	1662-1848	1
Hofbegnenberg	rkKB	Augsburg		1
Hofstetten	rkKB	Augsburg	1686-1897	1
Hohenwart	rkKB	Augsburg	1593-1886	5
Hohensell	rkKB	Augsburg	1802-1890	1
Hollenbach	rkKB	Augsburg	1625-1876	2
Holsen -Wertingen-	rkKB	Augsburg	1852-1877	1
Holshausen -Landsberg-	rkKB	Augsburg	1568-1886	1
Holsheim -Dillingen-	rkKB	Augsburg	1636-1935	4
Holsheim -Neuberg-	rkKB	Augsburg	1617-1891	3
Holsheim -Uffenheim-	evLutKB	Augsburg	1566-1934	1
Holsheim -Neu-Ulm-	rkKB	Augsburg	1651-1903	3
Holsgums	rkKB	Augsburg	1613-1878	3
Holskirchen	rkKB	Augsburg	1641-1967	2
Hopfen -Füssen-	rkKB	Augsburg	1632-1885	4
Hopfen a. See	rkKB	Augsburg	1632-1885	4
Hoppingen	rkKB	Augsburg	1652-1943	1

Location	Nature of Material	Where Filmed	Dates Covered	No. of Rolls
Horgan	rkKB HzB.	Augsburg	1637-1966	6
Hörstein	rkKB	Mainz	1816	1
Hörshausen	rkKB	Augsburg	1661-1878	2
Haglfingen	rkKB	Augsburg	1618-1961	4
Hurlach	rkKB	Augsburg	1694-1894	1
Huttenwang	rkKB	Augsburg	1666-1882	1
Hütting	rkKB	Augsburg	1678-1893	1
Ichenhausen	rkKB	Augsburg	1596-1900	7
Iffeldorf	rkKB	Augsburg	1656-1941	4
Igenhausen	rkKB	Trier	1684-1969	2
Illerberg	rkKB	Augsburg	1590-1970	4
Illerbeuren	rkKB	Augsburg Marburg	1669-1880	4
Illereichen -Altenstadt-	rkKB	Augsburg	1606-1887	2
Illertirsen	rkKB	Augsburg	1682-1876	3
Illersell	rkKB	Augsburg	1668-1910	2
Illschwang	evLutKB	Augsburg	1590-1963	6
Immelstetten	rkKB	Augsburg	1730-1966	1
Immenstadt	rkKB	Augsburg	1613-1948	9
Inchenhofen	rkKB	Augsburg	1686-1915	3
Ingenreich	rkKB	Augsburg	1665-1968	1
Inming	rkKB	Augsburg	1664-1873	3
Inmingen	rkKB	Augsburg	1666-1949	3
Ippsheim	evLutKB	Augsburg	1653-1933	1
Irsee	rkKB	Augsburg	1673-1968	3
Issing	rkKB	Augsburg	1657-1876	1
Jachenau	rkKB	Augsburg	1662-1933	2
Jedesheim	rkKB	Augsburg	1726-1834	1
Jettingen	rkKB	Augsburg	1655-1888	8

Location	Nature of Material	Where Filmed	Dates Covered	No. of Rolls
Kadelthofen	rkKB	Augsburg	1787-1968	1
Kallmünz	rkKB	Augsburg	1684-1878	2
Karlskron	rkKB	Augsburg	1791-1951	3
Kaufbeuren	rkKB	Augsburg	1733-1936	8
Kaufering	rkKB	Augsburg	1650-1892	2
Kemnat -Gimsberg-	rkKB	Augsburg	1678-1880	5
Kempten	rkKB	Augsburg	1651-1906	22
Kettershausen	rkKB	Augsburg	1772-1903	3
Kichlingen	rkKB	Augsburg	1647-1879	2
Kimrathshofen	rkKB	Augsburg	1659-1960	6
Kirchhaslach	rkKB	Augsburg	1615-1948	6
Kirchenreinbach	evLutKB	Augsburg	1833-1878	1
Kirchensittenbach	evLutKB	Augsburg	1554-1904	10
Kirchheim	rkKB	Augsburg	1652-1878	4
Kissing	rkKB	Augsburg	1615-1888	4
Kleinaiting	rkKB	Augsburg	1649-1953	1
Kleinerdlingen	rkKB	Augsburg	1638-1874	3
Kleinkemnat	rkKB	Augsburg	1670-1890	1
Kleinkötz	rkKB	Augsburg	1834-1937	1
Kleinweiler	rkKB	Augsburg	1715-1908	1
Klenau	rkKB	Augsburg	1641-1911	2
Klimmach	rkKB	Augsburg	1701-1882	2
Klingen	rkKB	Augsburg	1835-1893	1
Klosterbanes	rkKB	Augsburg	1715-1966	1
Klosterholsen		--see Holsen--		
Knottenreid	rkKB	Augsburg	1864-1970	1
Kochel	rkKB	Augsburg	1662-1970	1
Körgetreid	rkKB	Augsburg	1638-1879	2

Location	Nature of Material	Where Filmed	Dates Covered	No. of Rolls
Könghausen	rkKB	Augsburg	1658-1881	1
Königsbrunn	rkKB	Augsburg	1839-1969	3
Konradshofen	rkKB	Augsburg	1618-1884	3
Konsenberg	rkKB	Augsburg	1658-1880	1
Kreusthal -Kempten-	rkKB	Augsburg	1803-1970	2
Krugsell	rkKB	Augsburg	1637-1912	2
Krambach	rkKB	Augsburg	1676-1912	4
Kichbach -Aichad-	rkKB	Augsburg	1680-1897	4
Kühlenthal	rkKB	Trier	1870-1949	1
Kutsenhausen	rkKB	Augsburg	1639-1960	2
Lachen -Memmingen-	rkKB	Augsburg	1701-1876	1
Laimering	rkKB	Augsburg	1721-1911	1
Lanelsberg	rkKB	Augsburg	1647-1905	1
Landshausen -Dillingen-	rkKB	Augsburg	1690-1915	3
Langenmosen	rkKB	Augsburg	1583-1876	3
Langenneufach	rkKB	Augsburg	1662-1882	9
Langerringen	rkKB	Augsburg	1667-1942	3
Langweich	rkKB HzB.	Augsburg Trier	1662-1937	2
Lauben	rkKB	Augsburg	1701-1897	1
Lauchdorf	rkKB	Augsburg	1595-1880	2
Lauf	rkKB	Heilbronn	1643-1920	1
Laugnee	rkKB	Augsburg	1671-1877	2
Lauingen	rkKB	Augsburg	1560-1838	15
Lauterbach -Wertingen-	rkKB	Augsburg	1612-1880	1
Lauterbrunn	rkKB	Augsburg	1663-1877	1
Lautrach	rkKB	Augsburg	1695-1877	1

Location	Nature of Material	Where Filmed	Dates Covered	No. of Rolls
Lechbruck	rkKB	Augsburg	1722-1894	2
Lechhausen	rkKB	Augsburg	1635-1944	21
Lechsend	rkKB	Augsburg	1672-1799	1
Legau	rkKB	Augsburg	1626-1885	6
Lehrberg	evLutKB	Frankfurt Mainz	1722-1915	1
Leichling	rkKB	Augsburg	1675-1891	1
Leinheim	rkKB	Augsburg	1853-1937	1
Leitershofen	rkKB	Augsburg	1636-1964	2
Leitheim	rkKB	Augsburg	1593-1944	2
Lengenfeld -Lech-	rkKB	Augsburg	1650-1874	2
Lengenwang	rkKB	Augsburg	1830-1879	1
Lenzfried	rkKB	Augsburg	1638-1952	4
Lenterschach	rkKB	Augsburg	1650-1937	1
Lindan	rkKB	Augsburg	1618-1917	6
Lindenberg -Kaufbeuren-	rkKB	Augsburg	1650-1967	1
Lindenberg -Lindau-	rkKB	Augsburg	1636-1892	3
Loppeshausen	rkKB	Augsburg	1620-1942	2
Luchenhausen	rkKB	Augsburg	1628-1860	1
Lütselburg	rkKB HzB.	Augsburg	1651-1875	1
Lutsinge	rkKB	Augsburg	1704-1883	2
Machtlfing	rkKB	Augsburg	1641-1878	1
Magnetreich	rkKB	Augsburg	1618-1947	1
Maierhofen	rkKB	Augsburg	1811-1876	3
Maihingen	rkKB	Augsburg	1616-1883	3
Mainbernheim	rkKB	Augsburg	1648-1950	1
Manching	rkKB	Augsburg	1676-1941	6

Location	Nature of Material	Where Filmed	Dates Covered	No. of Rolls
Margerlshausen	rkKB	Augsburg	1680-1911	2
Maria Steinbach	HzB.	Augsburg	1672-1902	2
Marieaweiler	rkKB	Augsburg	1839-1875	1
Markt Rettenbach	rkKB	Augsburg	1629-1880	5
Markt Wald	rkKB	Augsburg	1649-1882	4
Marktaberdorf	rkKB	Augsburg	1633-1969	5
Marktoffingen	rkKB	Augsburg	1728-1956	2
Martinsheim	evLutKB	Augsburg	1655-1875	1
Martinssell	rkKB	Augsburg	1674-1879	3
Marscheim	rkKB	Augsburg	1638-1878	4
Massbach	rkKB	Augsburg	1595-1940	6
Mattsier	rkKB	Augsburg	1712-1955	3
Mauern	rkKB	Augsburg	1606-1838	1
Mauerstetten	rkKB	Augsburg	1637-1938	1
Memhölz	rkKB	Augsburg	1667-1968	2
Memmenhausen	rkKB	Augsburg	1587-1884	2
Memmingen	rkKB	Augsburg	1680-1893	5
Memmingerberg	rkKB	Augsburg	1620-1875	1
Merching	rkKB	Augsburg	1635-1878	3
Mering	rkKB	Augsburg	1700-1878	1
Michelfeld	evKB	Augsburg	1642-1959	1
Michhausen	rkKB	Augsburg	1648-1861	4
Mindelheim	rkKB	Augsburg	1611-1888	6
Mindelsell	rkKB	Augsburg	1626-1945	3
Minderoffinge	rkKB	Augsburg	1728-1884	1
Missen	rkKB	Augsburg	1653-1802	3
Mittelberg	rkKB	Augsburg	1718-1890	4
Mittelfranken -Nürnberg-		Salt Lake City	-Filmed 1969-	-

Location	Nature of Material	Where Filmed	Dates Covered	No. of Rolls
Mittelneufnach	rkKB	Augsburg	1652-1880	2
Mittelsimm	Synagogen-Gem.		1826-1855	1
Mittelstetten -Fürse-	rkKB	Augsburg	1641-1959	1
Mordelshausen	rkKB HzB.	Augsburg	1681-1931	2
Mödingen	rkKB	Augsburg	1589-1876	2
Modishofen	rkKB	Augsburg	1684-1856	1
Mohrenhausen	rkKB	Augsburg	1802-1942	1
Mönchsdeggingen	rkKB	Augsburg	1652-1943	2
Mönchsondheim	evLutKB	Augsburg	1606-1960	1
Moorenweis	rkKB	Augsburg	1798-1886	2
Moosbad -Kempten-	rkKB	Augsburg	1623-1885	4
Mörgen	rkKB	Augsburg	1735-1884	1
Mörslingen	rkKB	Augsburg	1712-1903	3
München	LDS records	Salt Lake City	1926-1951	8
Mummingen	rkKB	Augsburg	1677-1938	2
Münster -Neuburg-	rkKB	Augsburg	1704-1895	2
Münsterhausen	rkKB	Augsburg	1675-1952	5
Muman -Weitheim-	rkKB	Augsburg	1702-1894	4
Muthmannshofen	rkKB	Augsburg	1669-1904	2
Nassenbeuren	rkKB	Augsburg	1642-1877	2
Nattenhausen	rkKB	Augsburg	1663-1895	4
Neuschwang	rkKB	Augsburg	1676-1878	2
Neu-Ulm	rkKB	Augsburg	1860-1878	1
Neuburg -Krumbach-	rkKB	Augsburg	1664-1937	4

Location	Nature of Material	Where Filmed	Dates Covered	No. of Rolls
Neukirchen -Neuburg-	rkKB	Augsburg	1673-1958	2
Neukirchen -Sulsbad-Rosanberg-	evLutKB	Augsburg	1734-1891	1
Neusänn	HzB.	Augsburg	1667-1875	1
Niecherdorf -Memmingen-	rkKB	Augsburg	1643-1928	3
Niederraunau	rkKB	Augsburg	1597-1968	4
Niederriechen	rkKB	Augsburg	1644-1887	3
Niederschönenfeld	rkKB	Augsburg	1686-1879	1
Niedersonthofen	rkKB	Augsburg	1658-1892	3
Nördlingen	rkKB HzB.	Augsburg	1782-1961	6
Nürnberg	Stadtmagistral	Berlin	1904	1
Obenhausen	rkKB	Augsburg	1649-1949	2
Oberalting	rkKB	Augsburg	1641-1876	4
Oberauerbach	rkKB	Augsburg	1646-1967	3
Oberbach	rkKB	Augsburg	1685-1882	2
Oberbergen	rkKB	Augsburg	1692-1878	1
Oberbembach	rkKB	Augsburg	1678-1901	2
Oberbechingen	rkKB	Augsburg	1777-1885	1
Oberbeuren	rkKB	Augsburg	1633-1885	2
Oberdissen	rkKB	Augsburg	1649-1947	1
Oberelchingen	rkKB	Augsburg	1621-1902	2
Oberfahlheim	rkKB	Augsburg	1618-1888	3
Oberfinning	rkKB	Augsburg	1641-1911	3
Obergermasingen	rkKB	Augsburg	1643-1880	2
Obergessertshausen	rkKB	Augsburg	1619-1880	2
Obergnisbach	rkKB	Augsburg	1689-1805	1
Obergünsburg	rkKB	Augsburg	1628-1955	6

Location	Nature of Material	Where Filmed	Dates Covered	No. of Rolls
Oberhausen -Neu-Ulm Neusäss-	STA rkKB	Augsburg	1667-1970	4
Oberigling	rkKB	Augsburg	1609-1882	1
Oberkammbach	rkKB	Augsburg	1647-1968	4
Oberkrembach	evLutKB	Augsburg	1591-1932	2
Oberlauterbach	rkKB	Augsburg	1713-1887	3
Oberliesheim	rkKB	Augsburg	1666-1889	1
Obermaischstein	rkKB	Augsburg	1666-1875	1
Obermeldinge	rkKB	Augsburg	1651-1900	7
Oberostendorf	rkKB	Augsburg	1611-1914	3
Oberathmarshausen	rkKB	Augsburg	1659-1958	1
Oberpeiching	rkKB	Augsburg	1766-1907	1
Oberpfaffenhofen	rkKB	Augsburg	1675-1884	2
Oberrammingen	rkKB	Augsburg	1739-1880	2
Oberreichenbach	rkKB	Augsburg	1677-1896	2
Oberreitnau	rkKB	Augsburg	1829-1970	2
Oberrente	rkKB	Augsburg	1797-1883	2
Oberricher	rkKB	Augsburg	1714-1914	1
Oberrath	rkKB HzB.	Augsburg	1725-1957	2
Oberschöneberg	rkKB	Augsburg	1668-1876	3
Oberstaufen	rkKB	Augsburg Berlin-Dahlem	1681-1882	7
Oberstdorf	rkKB	Augsburg	1615-1938	9
Oberstimm	rkKB	Augsburg	1677-1883	1
Oberthingan	rkKB	Augsburg	1710-1881	1
Obertierheim	rkKB	Augsburg	1839-1876	1
Oberwaldbad	rkKB	Augsburg	1667-1879	2
Oberwiesenbad	rkKB	Augsburg	1660-1892	5
Oettingen	rkKB	Augsburg	1590-1970	6

Location	Nature of Material	Where Filmed	Dates Covered	No. of Rolls
Offingen	rkKB	Augsburg	1776-1964	2
Ofterschwang	rkKB	Augsburg	1683-1968	2
Ollarsried	rkKB	Augsburg	1732-1890	1
Opfenbach	rkKB	Augsburg	1647-1936	2
Ortefing	rkKB	Augsburg	1636-1877	1
Ostendorf	rkKB	Trier	1669-1950	5
Osterberg	rkKB	Augsburg	1666-1940	4
Osterbuch	rkKB	Augsburg	1729-1915	3
Ostersell	rkKB	Augsburg	1641-1874	2
Ostershausen	rkKB	Augsburg	1704-1851	1
Ottacher	rkKB	Augsburg	1663-1860	1
Öttingen	rkKB	Augsburg	1857-1878	1
Ottmaring	rkKB	Augsburg	1707-1909	1
Ottmarshausen	rkKB HzB.	Augsburg	1683-1969	4
Ottobeuren	rkKB	Augsburg	1663-1950	10
Oxenbronn	rkKB	Augsburg	1655-1842	1
Paar -Friedberg-	rkKB	Augsburg	1825-1876	1
Päll	rkKB	Augsburg	1590-1911	3
Passenburg	rkKB	Augsburg	1704-1880	3
Pensberg	rkKB	Augsburg	1808-1877	1
Pensing	rkKB	Augsburg	1804-1881	1
Perchting	rkKB	Augsburg	1613-1878	2
Petersthal	rkKB HzB.	Augsburg	1617-1885	4
Peterswörth	rkKB	Augsburg	1574-1965	6
Pfaffenhausen	rkKB	Augsburg	1636-1894	6
Pfaffenhofen	rkKB	Augsburg	1597-1940	20
Pfarsen	rkKB	Augsburg	1616-1968	2
Pfronten	rkKB	Augsburg	1636-1895	5

Location	Nature Material	Where Filmed	Dates Covered	No. of Rolls
Pipinsried	rkKB	Augsburg	1698-1849	1
Plen	rkKB	Augsburg	1677-1896	2
Pobenhausen	rkKB	Augsburg	1775-1956	1
Pöcking	rkKB	Augsburg	1644-1877	2
Pommelsbrun	evLutKB	Augsburg	1559-1945	9
Poppenricht	evLutKB	Augsburg	1574-1905	1
Pornbach	rkKB	Augsburg	1720-1921	3
Pöttmes	rkKB	Augsburg	1704-1879	2
Prettelshofen	rkKB	Augsburg	1651-1877	2
Prittriching	rkKB	Augsburg	1675-1906	3
Probstried	rkKB	Augsburg	1675-1906	4
Pullenrath	rkKB	Berlin-Dahlem	1591-1770	3
Pürgen	rkKB	Augsburg	1662-1893	2
Purk	rkKB	Augsburg	1850-1970	1
Rain	rkKB	Augsburg	1636-1966	6
Randelsriech	rkKB	Augsburg	1792-1955	1
Rauhensell	rkKB	Augsburg	1703-1936	1
Rechbergreuthen	rkKB	Augsburg	1652-1952	1
Rechtis	rkKB	Augsburg	1750-1916	1
Regensburg	LDS records	Salt Lake City	1927-1929 1946-1948	1
Regensburg	Adressbuch	Frankfurt	1912	1
Regensburg	Einw Buch	München	1939-1940	1
Relling	rkKB	Trier	1642-1896	2
Rehrosbach	rkKB	Augsburg	1686-1876	1
Reichau	rkKB	Augsburg	1797-1885	1
Reichestschofen	rkKB	Augsburg	1581-1892	6
Reilling	rkKB	Augsburg	1580-1878	3
Reicholsried	rkKB	Augsburg	1707-1891	2

Location	Nature of Material	Where Filmed	Dates Covered	No. of Rolls
Reimlingen	rkKB	Augsburg	1642-1878	2
Reisensburg	rkKB	Augsburg	1877-1920	1
Reisfingen	rkKB	Augsburg	1634-1908	2
Remnatsried	rkKB	Augsburg	1686-1939	2
Remshart	rkKB	Augsburg	1806-1907	1
Rennertshofen	rkKB	Augsburg	1571-1931	3
Rettenbad	rkKB	Augsburg	1591-1959	4
Rettenberg	rkKB	Augsburg	1612-1878	3
Rentern	rkKB	Augsburg	1800-1950	1
Rheinhartshausen	rkKB	Augsburg	1661-1879	3
Reich -Augsburg-	rkKB	Augsburg	1594-1876	2
Reich -Freiburg-	rkKB	Augsburg	1834-1896	1
Reich -Ginsburg-	rkKB	Augsburg	1759-1880	1
Reichen -Freidburg-	rkKB	Augsburg	1663-1896	1
Reichen -Ginsburg-	rkKB	Augsburg	1802-1914	2
Reichhausen -Ginsburg-	rkKB	Augsburg	1806-1964	1
Riedlingen	rkKB HzB.	Augsburg	1665-1895	3
Riegsee	rkKB	Augsburg	1612-1881	2
Rimpar	rkKB	Augsburg	1642-1948	1
Röfingen	rkKB	Augsburg	1643-1950	2
Roggenburg	rkKB	Augsburg	1596-1871	3
Rohr -Pfaffenhofen-	rkKB	Augsburg	1804-1885	3
Rohrbach -Pfaffenhofen-	rkKB	Augsburg	1637-1882	4
Rommetsried	rkKB	Augsburg	1650-1936	1

Location	Nature of Material	Where Filmed	Dates Covered	No. of Rolls
Ronsberg	rkKB	Augsburg	1787-1968	2
Rosenheim	Stadt	Frankfurt	1939	1
Rosshaupten -Füssen-	rkKB	Augsburg	1634-1949	3
Rosstal	Heimatbuch			
Röthenbach -Lindau-	rkKB	Rottenburg Augsburg	1615-1946	6
Rott -Landsberg-	rkKB	Augsburg	1631-1880	2
Rottach	rkKB	Augsburg		1
Rothenburg	Beckh Hermann	Neustadt Aisch	Die dehmus aus Rothenburg - Tauber Nach- fahrentafel	1
Rückensdorf	evLutKB	Augsburg	1750-1875	1
Ruderatshofen	rkKB HzB.	Augsburg	1613-1878	3
Sainbach	rkKB	Augsburg	1648-1878	3
Sandisell	rkKB	Augsburg	1671-1895	2
Schabringen	rkKB	Augsburg	1707-1882	1
Scheffan -Lindau-	rkKB	Augsburg	1697-1959	1
Scheidegg	rkKB	Augsburg	1618-1800	2
Scheppach	rkKB	Augsburg	1613-1880	7
Schernau	evLutKB	Augsburg	1587-1886	1
Scherstetten	rkKB	Augsburg	1662-1883	2
Schiessen	rkKB	Augsburg	1672-1924	2
Schiltberg	rkKB	Augsburg	1606-1967	3
Schlingen	rkKB	Augsburg	1700-1926	1
Schmichen	rkKB	Augsburg	1648-1880	2
Schnellmannsbreuth	rkKB	Augsburg	1822-1968	1
Schöffelding	rkKB	Augsburg	1609-1884	1
Schöllang	rkKB HzB.	Augsburg	1620-1936	2

Location	Nature of Material	Where Filmed	Dates Covered	No. of Rolls
Schönebad	rkKB	Augsburg	1821-1882	1
Schönenberg	rkKB	Augsburg	1855-1883	1
Schönesberg	rkKB	Augsburg	1843-1969	1
Schopflohe	rkKB	Augsburg	1740-1963	1
Schom -Neuburg-	rkKB	Augsburg	1706-1911	1
Schretzheim	rkKB	Augsburg	1665-1906	2
Schrobenhausen	rkKB	Augsburg	1656-1961	10
Schwabegg	rkKB	Augsburg	1835-1880	1
Schwabhausen -Landsberg-	rkKB	Augsburg	1638-1900	2
Schwabmünden	rkKB	Augsburg	1658-1885	5
Schwenningen	rkKB	Augsburg	1696-1838	2
Schwennenbad	rkKB	Augsburg	1705-1897	1
Schwifting	rkKB	Augsburg	1609-1963	2
Seeg	rkKB	Augsburg	1637-1891	9
Seehausen -Weilheim-	rkKB	Augsburg	1636-1887	1
Seeshaupt	rkKB	Augsburg	1696-1890	1
Segnitz	evLutKB	Augsburg	1609-1952	1
Senden	rkKB	Augsburg	1750-1888	1
Sichershausen	evLutKB	Augsburg	1673-1954	1
Siebnach	rkKB	Augsburg	1652-1897	3
Siegertshofen	rkKB	Augsburg	1663-1882	1
Sigmarsell	rkKB	Augsburg	1845-1877	1
Simmershofen	evKB	Augsburg	1566-1934	1
Sindelsdorf	rkKB	Augsburg	1675-1879	2
Singenbad	rkKB	Augsburg	1609-1947	1
Sonderheim	rkKB	Augsburg	1658-1881	2
Sontheim	rkKB	Augsburg	1658-1888	2

Location	Nature of Material	Where Filmed	Dates Covered	No. of Rolls
Sonthofen	rkKB HzB.	Augsburg	1610-1826	3
Spatzenhause	HzB.	Augsburg	1621-1884	1
Stadl	rkKB	Augsburg	1750-1932	3
Stadtbergen	rkKB HzB.	Augsburg	1607-1938	8
Statzling	rkKB	Augsburg	1689-1838	1
Standheim	rkKB	Augsburg	1709-1960	2
Stanfen	rkKB	Augsburg	1635-1962	4
Stegaurad	rkKB	Bamberg Frankfurt	1762-1961	3
Steibis	rkKB	Augsburg	1782-1882	1
Stein -Sonthofen-	rkKB	Augsburg	1612-1920	3
Steindorf -Fürstenfeldbruck-	rkKB	Augsburg	1641-1896	3
Steinekirch -Augsburg-	rkKB HzB.	Augsburg	1660-1875	2
Steinheim -Dillingen-	rkKB	Augsburg	1583-1886	3
Steppoch -Augsburg-	rkKB HzB.	Augsburg	1693-1942	3
Steppeg	rkKB	Augsburg	1647-1883	2
Stetten -Mindelheim-	rkKB	Augsburg	1646-1967	3
Steifenhofen	rkKB	Augsburg	1721-1879	3
Stillnau	rkKB	Augsburg	1848-1955	1
Stockheim	rkKB	Augsburg	1751-1962	2
Stoffen	rkKB	Augsburg	1650-1874	2
Stoffenried	rkKB	Augsburg	1652-1952	2
Stötten	rkKB	Augsburg	1693-1900	2
Stöttwang	rkKB HzB.	Augsburg	1621-1958	5
Stotzard	rkKB	Augsburg	1666-1876	1

Location	Nature of Material	Where Filmed	Dates Covered	No. of Rolls
Strass	rkKB	Augsburg	1638-1881	1
Strassberg	rkKB	Augsburg	1785-1941	2
Streitheim	HzB.	Augsburg	1640-1930	1
Sulsbach -Aichach-	rkKB	Augsburg	1802-1882	1
Sulsberg -Kempten-	rkKB	Augsburg	1619-1942	6
Sulsschneid	rkKB	Augsburg	1658-1962	2
Täfertingen	rkKB	Augsburg	1657-1957	5
Taiting	rkKB	Augsburg	1802-1876	1
Tandern	rkKB	Augsburg	1608-1929	4
Tapfheim	rkKB	Augsburg	1669-1883	2
Thaining	rkKB	Augsburg	1617-1878	4
Thal	rkKB	Augsburg	1590-1970	4
Thalfingen	rkKB	Augsburg	1620-1880	2
Thalhausen	rkKB	Augsburg	1835-1893	1
Thalhofen	rkKB	Augsburg	1663-1903	1
Thalkirchdorf	rkKB	Augsburg	1644-1889	2
Thannhausen -Krumbach-	rkKB	Augsburg	1753-1895	3
Thierhaupten	rkKB	Augsburg	1585-1891	3
Thundorf -Billissig-	rkKB evKB	Augsburg	1566-1942	2
Tiefenbach -Illertissen-	rkKB	Augsburg	1622-1875	2
Todlenreid	rkKB	Augsburg	1601-1875	1
Todtemweis	rkKB	Augsburg	1650-1913	2
Traubing	rkKB	Augsburg	1728-1879	1
Trauchgau	rkKB	Augsburg	1700-1879	3
Traunstein	LDS records	Salt Lake City	1940-1948	1
Trugenhofen	rkKB	Augsburg	1481-1922	2

Location	Nature of Material	Where Filmed	Dates Covered	No. of Rolls
Türkenfeld	rkKB	Augsburg	1612-1881	3
Türkheim	rkKB	Augsburg	1610-1943	4
Tussenhausen	rkKB	Augsburg	1636-1886	3
Tutsing	rkKB	Augsburg	1661-1858	1
Uffenheim	evLutKB	Augsburg	1670-1830	1
Uffing	rkKB	Augsburg	1615-1946	3
Ungerhausen	rkKB	Augsburg	1648-1825	1
Unterbechingen	rkKB	Augsburg	1671-1861	1
Unterbergen	rkKB	Augsburg		1
Unterbleichen	rkKB	Augsburg	1638-1952	4
Unterbrunn -Starnberg-	rkKB	Augsburg	1652-1882	2
Unterdiessen	rkKB	Augsburg	1649-1967	2
Unteregg -Mindelheim-	rkKB	Augsburg	1645-1952	1
Untereichen	rkKB	Augsburg	1691-1877	2
Unterelchingen	rkKB	Augsburg	1645-1926	2
Unterfinnig	rkKB	Augsburg	1813-1860	1
Unterfinnigen -Dillingen-	rkKB	Augsburg	1664-1902	2
Untergernaringen	rkKB	Augsburg	1744-1926	1
Unterglauheim	rkKB	Augsburg	1858-1876	1
Unterhausen	rkKB	Augsburg	1802-1879	1
Unterigling	rkKB	Augsburg	1654-1941	1
Unterkammlach	rkKB	Augsburg	1647-1968	4
Unterköringen	rkKB	Augsburg	1705-1882	2
Unterliesheim	rkKB	Augsburg	1650-1845	2
Untermaiselstein	rkKB	Augsburg	1720-1850	2
Untermedlingen	rkKB	Augsburg Berlin-Dahlem	1684-1877	3
Untermeitingen	rkKB	Augsburg	1587-1879	4

Location	Nature of Material	Where Filmed	Dates Covered	No. of Rolls
Untermeillhausen	rkKB	Augsburg	1640-1927	1
Unterammingen	rkKB	Augsburg	1739-1880	2
Unterreitnau	rkKB	Augsburg	1784-1970	3
Unterriden	rkKB	Augsburg	1817-1964	1
Unterröchering	rkKB	Augsburg	1618-1878	2
Unterthingau	rkKB	Augsburg	1660-1969	4
Unterthürheim	rkKB	Augsburg	1839-1890	1
Untrasried	rkKB	Augsburg	1568-1948	2
Ursberg	rkKB	Augsburg	1608-1901	6
Ustersbach	rkKB	Augsburg	1671-1963	2
Uttenhofen	rkKB	Augsburg	1846-1970	1
Utting -Landsberg-	rkKB	Augsburg	1613-1948	2
Utswingen	rkKB	Augsburg	1350-1883	2
Veitriedhausen	rkKB	Augsburg	1619-1877	1
Villenbach	rkKB	Augsburg	1927-	1
Violau -Wertingen-	rkKB	Augsburg	1820-1951	1
Vöhringen	rkKB	Augsburg	1699-1876	3
Vorderburg	rkKB	Augsburg	1661-1938	2
Waal -Kaufbueren-	rkKB	Augsburg	1651-1915	3
Waal -Pfaffenhofen-	rkKB	Augsburg	1637-1882	4
Waalhaupten	rkKB	Augsburg	1652-1968	1
Waidhofen	rkKB	Augsburg	1620-1967	4
Walchstadt -Starnberg-	rkKB	Augsburg	1667-1884	1
Wald -Marktoberndorf-			1610-1883	2
Walda	rkKB	Augsburg	1672-1877	1
Waldberg -Augsburg-	rkKB	Augsburg	1663-1940	2

Location	Nature of Material	Where Filmed	Dates Covered	No. of Rolls
Waldkirch -Ginsberg-	rkKB	Augsburg	1653-1880	3
Waldstetten -Ginsberg-	rkKB	Augsburg	1631-1968	3
Walkertshofen -Schwabmünd-	rkKB	Augsburg	1725-1905	2
Walleshause	rkKB	Augsburg	1637-1885	3
Wallenhausen	rkKB	Augsburg	1663-1970	3
Wallerstein	rkKB	Augsburg	1611-1752	1
Waltenhausen	rkKB	Augsburg	1627-1968	3
Waltenhofen -Füssen-	rkKB	Augsburg	1627-1963	3
Walterhofen -Kampten-	rkKB	Augsburg	1640-1922	3
Warmisreid	rkKB	Augsburg	1640-1889	1
Warnerburg -Lindau-	rkKB	Augsburg	1664-1891	5
Wassertrüdingen	Einwohner- buch	Frankfurt	1926	1
Wattenweilen	rkKB	Augsburg	1712-1896	2
Wahringen	rkKB	Augsburg	1671-1919	3
Weichering	rkKB	Augsburg	1638-1878	3
Weicht	rkKB	Augsburg	1664-1881	2
Weiden	Adressbuch	München	1938	1
Weil -Landsberg-	rkKB	Augsburg	1637-1844	2
Weilach	rkKB	Augsburg	1748-1941	3
Weiler -Lindau-	rkKB	Augsburg	1640-1877	4
Weilheim	rkKB	Augsburg	1633-1967	9
Weinhausen	rkKB	Augsburg	1664-1881	2
Weinried	rkKB	Augsburg	1714-1880	1
Weisingen	rkKB	Augsburg	1636-1935	6
Weissenhorn	rkKB	Augsburg	1661-1904	9

Location	Nature of Material	Where Filmed	Dates Covered	No. of Rolls
Weissensee	rkKB	Augsburg	1597-1878	2
Weitnau	rkKB	Augsburg	1633-1891	5
Welbhausen	evLutKB	Augsburg	1533-1950	1
Wending	Einwohner-buch	Frankfurt	1926	1
Wessling	rkKB	Augsburg	1689-1745	1
Westendorf -Kaufbeuren-	rkKB	Augsburg	1665-1949	2
Westerheim	rkKB	Augsburg	1595-1879	2
Welden -Augsburg-	rkKB	Augsburg	1693-1875	3
Wellheim	rkKB	Augsburg	1640-1910	5
Wengen -Kempten-	rkKB	Augsburg	1607-1884	1
Wertrach	rkKB	Augsburg	1638-1960	4
Wertingen	rkKB	Augsburg	1612-1950	9
Wessling	rkKB	Augsburg	1746-1886	1
Wessobrunn	rkKB	Augsburg	1630-1885	4
Wertendorf -Kaufbeuren-	rkKB		1616-1796	1
Wertendorf -Wertingen-	rkKB	Trier	1669-1950	5
Westernach -Mindelheim-	rkKB	Augsburg	1618-1887	2
Wertheim -Augsburg-	rkKB	Augsburg	Chronik	1
Wettenhausen	rkKB	Augsburg	1587-1966	4
Wiedergeltingen	rkKB	Augsburg	1626-1898	2
Wiesenbad	rkKB	Augsburg	1317-1963	3
Wiggensbad	rkKB	Augsburg	1696-1952	5
Wilbergstetten	rkKB	Augsburg	1680-1877	3
Willishausen	rkKB	Augsburg	1655-1937	4
Willmatshofen	rkKB	Augsburg	1665-1882	2

Location	Nature of Material	Where Filmed	Dates Covered	No. of Rolls
Willprechtssell	rkKB	Augsburg	1704-1890	1
Wilpoldsried	rkKB	Augsburg	1613-1879	3
Winkl -Landsberg-	rkKB	Augsburg	1660-1937	2
Winterbad	rkKB	Augsburg	1668-1876	1
Winterüden	rkKB	Augsburg	1635-1883	2
Winser -Kranbach-	rkKB	Augsburg	1643-1947	1
Wittislingen	rkKB	Augsburg	1649-1876	4
Witzighausen	rkKB	Augsburg	1789-1875	1
Wohmbrechts	rkKB	Augsburg	1804-1900	1
Wolfertschwerden	rkKB	Augsburg	1666-1906	3
Wollbad	rkKB	Augsburg	1603-1932	2
Wollmetshofen	rkKB	Augsburg	1813-1857	1
Woringen	rkKB	Augsburg	1750-1875	1
Wörteschwang	rkKB	Augsburg	1638-1875	2
Wörnitsstein	rkKB	Augsburg	1668-1813	1
Wullenstetten	rkKB	Augsburg	1590-1878	2
Zahling	rkKB	Augsburg	1843-1875	1
Zaiertshofen	rkKB	Augsburg	1647-1881	3
Zarkerhausen	rkKB	Augsburg	1591-1900	1
Zell -Füssen-	rkKB	Augsburg	1647-1878	3
Zell -Memmingen-	rkKB	Augsburg	1585-1908	3
Ziemetshausen	rkKB	Augsburg	1600-1968	9
Ziertheim	rkKB	Augsburg	1639-1908	3
Zöschingen	rkKB	Augsburg	1624-1935	2
Zucheringen	rkKB	Augsburg	1663-1884	3
Zusamaltheim	rkKB	Augsburg	1637-1878	5

Location	Nature of Material	Where Filmed	Dates Covered	No. of Rolls
Zusamsell	rkKB	Augsburg	1661-1878	1
Zusmarschsell	rkKB	Augsburg	1612-1888	4

BERLIN -WEST-

Location	Nature of Material	Where Filmed	Dates Covered	No. of Rolls
Berlin	evKB -various churches-	Berlin	1677-1920	549
Berlin	evMKB	Berlin	1671-1944	213
Berlin	JüdGem	Berlin	1812-1874	31
Berlin	LDS records	Berlin	1907-1937	8
Berlin	Steueramt- Steuerheberrolle	Berlin	1887	1

For further Berlin records see sections on Probate and Military Records in Introduction.

BREMEN

Location	Nature of Material	Where Filmed	Dates Covered	No. of Rolls
Bremen	evKB -Various churches-	Hamburg	1650-1970	179
Bremen	evMKB	Hamburg	1867-1939	4
Bremen	ZSR	Bremen	1648-1939	28

HAMBURG

Location	Nature of Material	Where Filmed	Dates Covered	No. of Rolls
Hamburg	Bürgermilitär-Umschreibungslisten	Hamburg	1831-1867	229
Hamburg	Land- und Schutz-bürger Protokolle	Hamburg	1769-1865	23
Hamburg	Heimatscheine	Hamburg	1826-1849	2
Hamburg	Heimatsbücher	Hamburg	1837-1857	2
Hamburg	Bürgerbuch	Hamburg	1748-1871	1
Hamburg	Bürgerzulassungs-Protokolle	Hamburg	1843-1846	5
Hamburg	Schutzverwandten-Protokolle	Hamburg	1698-1853	29
Hamburg	evMKB	Hannover	1667-1939	10
Hamburg	Verhairatungs-Protokolle	Hamburg	1816-1865	118
Hamburg	STA	Hamburg	1821-1874	69

For further material on Hamburg see Migration Records in the Introduction.

HESSEN

Location	Nature of Material	Where Filmed	Dates Covered	No. of Rolls
Abterode	AG STA evKB	Marburg Abterode	1630-1968	15
Achenbach	AG	Marburg	1838-1869	2
Adorf	AG	Marburg	1838-1863	2
Ahlersbach	AG	Marburg	1718-1797	1
Albach	Gem.A	Darmstadt	1808-1875	3
Allendorf -Giessen-	JüdGem AG	Darmstadt Marburg	1808-1875	6
Allendorf -Biedenkopf-	AG	Marburg	1829-1866	1
Alleringshausen	Justizamt	Marburg	-1852	1
Allertshofen	evKB	Darmstadt	1808-1875	7
Almendorf	Justizamt	Marburg	-1813	1
Alraft	Justizamt	Marburg	-1820	1
Alsbach	evKB	Darmstadt	1808-1875	2
Alsberg	STA	Marburg	1874-1875	1
Alsfeld	rkKB evKB	Mainz Darmstadt	1798-1876	9
Alten-Buseck	JüdGem evKB	Darmstadt	1808-1875	10
Altenburg -Alsfeld-	evKB	Darmstadt	1808-1875	2
Altengronau	Justizamt AG	Marburg	1718-1824	9
Altenhasslan	AG STA	Marburg	1744-1875	4
Altenhasungen	STA	Marburg	1809-1875	2
Altenmittlau	STA	Marburg	1811	1
Altenschlirf	evKB	Darmstadt	1808-1875	7
Altenstadt	evKB rkKB JüdGem	Darmstadt Mainz	1744-1875	10

Location	Nature of Material	Where Filmed	Dates Covered	No. of Rolls
Altenstein	AG	Marburg	1724-1766	1
Altheim	evKB	Darmstadt	1788-1855	6
Altmorschen	evKB STA	Hamborn Marburg	1647-1875	4
Alsenau	AG	Marburg	1730, 1736	2
Amönau	STA	Marburg	1808-1812	1
Amöneburg	Justizamt AG	Marburg	1697-1874	19
Angersbach	evKB	Darmstadt	1808-1875	5
Annerod	evKB	Darmstadt	1808-1875	4
Ansefahr	rkKB	Marburg	1766-1810	1
Appenhain	Justizamt	Marburg	1806-1843	1
Arenborn	STA	Marburg	1808-1810	1
Arnsburg	evKB	Darmstadt	1836-1875	1
Arnshain	evKB	Darmstadt	1836-1875	1
Arolsen	evKB MKB	Hannover	1869-1919	1
Assenheim	JüdGem evKB rkKB	Darmstadt Mainz	1646-1876	8
Assmannshausen	rkKB	Mainz	1756-1791	1
Asterode	STA	Marburg	1874-1875	1
Astheim	rkKB evKB	Mainz Darmstadt	1661-1875	9
Atzelrode	evKB	Braach	1830-1964	2
Aufenan	STA	Marburg	1874-1875	1
Bebenhausen	evKB MKB	Darmstadt Hannover	1811-1941	8
Bad Hersfeld	AG STA	Marburg	1817-1897	23
Bad Homburg	rkKB MKB	Mainz Eibenstock	1756-1885	3
Bad König		Darmstadt	1808-1875	7

Location	Nature of Material	Where Filmed	Dates Covered	No. of Rolls
Bad Neuheim	LDS records evKB	Salt Lake City Darmstadt	1832-1948	2
Bad Orb	Justizamt STA MKB	Marburg Hannover	1777-1919	5
Bad Schwalbach	rkKB	Mainz	1756-1791	1
Bad Soden -Main Taunus-	evKB	Düsseldorf	1818-1874	3
Bad Soden -Schlüchtern-	Justizamt	Marburg	-1861	1
Bad Sooden- Allendorf	AG Justizamt Heer	Marburg Bad Sooden	1735-1876	28
Bad Vilbel	evKB rkKB	Darmstadt Mainz	1655-1876	12
Balhorn	STA	Marburg	1808-1875	2
Balkhausen	evKB	Darmstadt	1812-1875	3
Batten	LG	Marburg	1834-1882	1
Battenberg	STA	Marburg	1811-1874	7
Battenfeld	Justizamt STA	Marburg	1808-1874	13
Battenhausen	Justizamt	Marburg	1809-1811	1
Bauerbach	Justizamt	Marburg	1808-1828	1
Bauernheim	evKB	Darmstadt	1808-1875	2
Baumbach	evKB	Oberchlenbach	1658-1964	5
Bauschheim	evKBq	Darmstadt	1808-1875	4
Beberbeck	Justizamt	Marburg	1759-1837	4
Bebra	STA	Marburg	1874-1875	1
Beedenkirchen	evKB	Darmstadt	1808-1875	2
Beenhausen	STA	Marburg	1874-1875	1
Beerfelden	evKB JüdGem	Darmstadt Berlin-Dahlem	1810-1875	32
Beienheim	evKB	Düsseldorf Darmstadt	1701-1899	3

Location	Nature of Material	Where Filmed	Dates Covered	No. of Rolls
Beiseforth	STA	Marburg	1826-1852	1
Bellersheim	evKB	Darmstadt	1808-1875	4
Bellings	AG	Marburg	1701-1821	1
Bellnhausen -Marburg-	STA	Marburg	1861-1873	1
Beltershausen	STA	Marburg	1857-1859	1
Benstein	evKB rkKB	Darmstadt Mainz	1568-1875	39
Berger-Enkheim	AG Justizamt	Marburg	1740-1874	67
Bergheim -Büdingen-	evKB	Darmstadt	1819-1875	3
Berkach	evKB	Darmstadt	1858-1875	1
Bernbach -Gelnhausen-	Justizamt	Marburg	-1811	1
Berneburg	STA	Marburg	1808-1875	2
Bernsburg	evKB	Darmstadt	1808-1875	4
Bersrod	evKB	Darmstadt	1861-1875	1
Berstadt	JüdGem evKB	Darmstadt	1811-1875	2
Besse	evKB Justizamt STA	Hamborn Marburg	1574-1875	4
Bettenhausen	Justizamt evKB	Marburg Darmstadt	1808-1875	5
Betziesdorf	Justizamt JüdGem	Marburg	1808-1849	4
Beuren	evKB JüdGem	Darmstadt	1808-1849	6
Biblis	rkKB	Mainz Darmstadt	1580-1886	16
Bickenbach	evKB	Darmstadt	1808-1875	4
Bieben	evKB	Darmstadt	1808-1875	8
Bieber	AG Justizamt STA	Marburg	1729-1875	6

Location	Nature of Material	Where Filmed	Dates Covered	No. of Rolls
Bieberstein	AG	Marburg	1671-1807	7
Biebesheim	evKB	Darmstadt	1808-1875	6
Biedenkopf	LG AG STA	Darmstadt	1808-1876	48
Billertshausen	evKB STA	Darmstadt	1808-1876	6
Billings	evKB	Darmstadt	1808-1876	13
Bindsachsen	STA	Darmstadt	1818-1875	2
Bingenheim	STA	Darmstadt	1808-1875	4
Birkenau	rkKB evKB	Mainz Darmstadt	1808-1876	10
Birkenau -Bergstrasse-	evKB	Darmstadt	1808-1875	3
Birklar	evKB JüdGem	Darmstadt	1827-1875	4
Birstein	Justizamt STA AG	Marburg	1821-1875	18
Bischhausen -Eschwege-	Justizamt STA	Marburg	1686-1878	11
Bischofsheim -Hanau-	Justizamt AG	Marburg	1686-1878	12
Bisses	evKB	Darmstadt	1808-1875	3
Blasbach	evKB	Düsseldorf	1691-1738	1
Blauberg	evKB	Darmstadt	1808-1875	4
Bleichenbach	evKB	Darmstadt	1820-1875	4
Bleidenstadt	rkKB	Mainz	1765-1791	1
Blofeld	evKB	Darmstadt	1808-1875	2
Bobenhausen -Alsfeld-	evKB	Darmstadt	1808-1875	9
Böckels	Justizamt	Marburg	1812-1813	1
Böddiger	AG STA	Marburg	1808-1875	3
Böminghausen	Justizamt	Marburg	1872-1884	1

Location	Nature of Material	Where Filmed	Dates Covered	No. of Rolls
Bönstadt	evKB	Darmstadt	1823-1875	1
Borken	Justizamt	Marburg	1772-1874	6
Böss Gesäss -Büdingen-	evKB	Darmstadt	1841-1875	2
Bosserode	STA	Marburg	1808-1812	1
Bottendorf	Justizamt	Marburg	1808-1812	1
Braach	evKB STA Justizamt	Oberchlenbad Braach Marburg	1658-1964	12
Bracht	Justizamt	Marburg	1808-1811	1
Brandau	evKB	Darmstadt	1808-1875	7
Brandenstein	AG Justizamt	Marburg	1784-1832	16
Brauerschwend	evKB	Darmstadt	1808-1875	3
Braunfels	evKB MKB	Hannover	1856-1870	1
Breidenbach	STA AG	Marburg	1791-1875	18
Breitau	STA	Marburg	1808-1875	2
Breitenbach -Kassel-	STA	Marburg	1849-1867	1
Breitenbach -Rotenburg-	STA	Marburg	1874-1875	1
Breitenbach -Schlüchtern-	STA	Marburg	1685-1823	2
Breitenbach -Ziegenhain-	STA	Marburg	1797-1875	4
Brensbach	evKB	Darmstadt	1808-1875	6
Breuna -Bosserode-	STA	Marburg	1808-1812	1
Breungeshain	evKB	Darmstadt	1808-1875	4
Briedel	evKB	Darmstadt	1808-1854	3
Bromskirchen	evKB Justizamt	Marburg	1808-1874	7
Bronnsell	STA	Marburg	1812	1

Location	Nature of Material	Where Filmed	Dates Covered	No. Rolls
Brotterode	STA	Marburg	1808-1812	2
Bruchenbrüchen	evKB	Darmstadt	1823-1875	3
Bründersen -Wolfhagen-	STA	Marburg	1808-1810	1
Buchenau -Biedenkopf-	AG evKB	Marburg	1808-1881	6
Buchenau -Hünfeld-	STA	Marburg	1874-1875	1
Budesheim -Friedberg-	evKB	Darmstadt	1808-1875	4
Büdingen	evKB	Darmstadt	1818-1875	6
Burg-Gemünden	evKB	Darmstadt	1807-1875	4
Burg-Gräfenrode	evKB JüdGem	Darmstadt	1821-1875	4
Bürgeln	Polizeiamt	Marburg	1808-1867	1
Burghaum	AG STA Justizamt	Marburg	1745-1875	21
Burgholz	AG	Marburg	1745-1821	1
Burgholzhausen	evKB rkKB	Darmstadt Mainz	1718-1876	5
Burgjoss	AG	Marburg	1802-1814	2
Burguffeln	Justizamt	Marburg	1828-1864	1
Burkhards	evKB	Darmstadt	1808-1876	5
Burkhardsfelden	evKB JüdGem	Darmstadt	1808-1875	5
Bürstadt	rkKB	Mainz Darmstadt	1715-1875	17
Butzbach -Friedberg-	evKB	Darmstadt	1808-1875	13
Busenborn	evKB	Darmstadt	1808-1875	3
Büttelborn	evKB	Darmstadt	1808-1875	6
Calden	AG STA	Marburg	1787-1866	3

Location	Nature of Material	Where Filmed	Dates Covered	No. of Rolls
Caldern	AG Justizamt	Marburg	1781-1867	5
Cappel -Marburg-	AG STA	Marburg	1808-1812	2
Carlsdorf	Justizamt STA	Marburg	1762-1877	2
Cölbe	LG	Marburg	1723-1849	1
Crainfeld	evKB	Darmstadt	1808-1875	5
Crumstadt	evKB	Darmstadt	1808-1875	6
Cuxhagen	STA	Marburg	1808-1875	2
Dagobertshausen -Melsungen-	STA	Marburg	1808-1812	1
Daisbach	rkKB	Mainz	1756-1796	1
Dalherda	LG	Marburg	1858-1860	1
Damm -Marburg-	Polizeiamt	Marburg	1865	1
Damshausen	LG	Marburg	1867	1
Darmstadt	Bürger- Aufnahme Adressbuch	Darmstadt Berlin-Dahlem	1716-1883 1935	35
Darmstadt	evKB MKB	Darmstadt Hannover	1808-1918	19
Darmstadt -Bessungen-	evKB	Darmstadt	1810-1831	7
Darmstadt	evKB	Darmstadt	1808-1875	32
Darmstadt -Arheiligen Eberstadt-	KB	Darmstadt	1808-1875	15
Darmstadt	rkKB	Darmstadt	1808-1875	8
Darmstadt	LDS records	Salt Lake City	1947	1
Darmstadt	refKB	Darmstadt	1808-1826	1
Datterode	AG STA Rentkammer	Marburg	1796-1886	3
Dauernhein	evKB	Darmstadt	1808-1875	4

Location	Nature of Material	Where Filmed	Dates Covered	No. of Rolls
Dautphe	AG	Marburg	1808-1874	11
Deisfeld	AG	Marburg	1799-1854	1
Densberg	Finanz-kammer Kreisamt	Marburg	1808-1836	4
Dexbach	LG STA	Marburg	1808-1874	6
Dieburg	evKB rkKB	Darmstadt Mainz	1603-1876	23
Diedenhausen	AG	Marburg	1849	1
Diemerode	STA	Marburg	1808-1812	1
Dietzenbach	evKB	Darmstadt	1788-1875	9
Dilschhausen	Polizeiamt	Marburg	1849-1869	1
Dodenau	Gemeindeamt	Marburg	1808-1874	8
Dohrenbach	STA	Marburg	1808-1812	2
Dorf Gull	Kirchen	Darmstadt	1808-1875	3
Dorfitter	AG	Marburg	1845-1861	1
Dörmbach -Fulda-	AG	Marburg	1812	1
Dorn-Assenheim	rkKB	Mainz	1654-1876	3
Dörnberg	STA	Marburg	1874-1875	1
Dorndiel -Mosbach-	rkKB	Darmstadt	1811, 1819-1875	2
Dörnhagen	STA	Marburg	1808-1812	1
Dornheim	Kirchen	Darmstadt	1808-1875	7
Dornholzhausen -B. Hamburg-	Walloon Church	Den Haag	1755-1790	1
Dörningheim	Justizamt STA	Marburg	1811, 1812	2
Dreieichenheim	evKB	Darmstadt	1819-1875	4
Dreihausen	STA	Marburg	1849-1869	1
Düdelsheim	Kirchen	Darmstadt	1818-1875	5
Dudenhofen	evKB	Darmstadt	1811-1875	4

Location	Nature of Material	Where Filmed	Dates Covered	No. of Rolls
Dudenrode	AG STA	Marburg	1808-1875	3
Eberschütz	AG STA	Marburg	1748-1872	2
Ebsdorf	LRA Polizeiamt	Marburg	1723-1872	6
Echzell	Kirchen	Darmstadt	1808-1875	6
Eckardroft	LRA	Marburg	1826-1875	1
Eckartshausen	evKB	Darmstadt	1818-1875	9
Eckelshausen	AG STA	Marburg	1808-1882	7
Eddersheim	rkKB	Mainz	1756-1791	1
Edelzell	STA	Marburg	1812	1
Ederbringhausen	STA	Marburg	1808-1813	1
Effolderbach	evKB	Darmstadt	1808-1875	3
Egelsbach	evKB	Darmstadt	1808-1875	6
Ehlen	STA	Marburg	1808-1875	3
Ehringen	STA	Marburg	1808-1874	2
Ehringshausen -Alsfeld-	evKB	Darmstadt	1808-1875	3
Ehrsten	STA	Marburg	1808-1810	1
Eich	evKB	Darmstadt	1808-1875	4
Eichelsdorf	evKB	Darmstadt	1808-1875	5
Eichenzell	STA	Marburg	1812-1813	1
Eifen -Alsfeld-	evKB	Darmstadt	1808-1875	6
Eifen -Frankenberg-	STA	Marburg	1808-1874	5
Einhartshausen	evKB	Darmstadt	1808-1875	2
Einhausen	rkKB	Darmstadt	1808-1875	3
Eiterfeld	Justizamt STA	Marburg	1788-1875	10
Eiterhagen	STA	Marburg	1808-1812	2

Location	Nature of Material	Where Filmed	Dates Covered	No. of Rolls
Elben	STA	Marburg	1808-1875	3
Elgershausen -Kassel-	STA	Marburg	1808-1812	1
Ellenbach	rkKB	Darmstadt	1808-1813	1
Ellershausen -Witzenhausen-	AG STA	Marburg	1808-1875	2
Elmshausen -Biedenkopf-	LG	Marburg	1837-1872	1
Elmshage	AG	Marburg	1849-1867	1
Elnhausen	STA	Marburg	1808-1812	2
Eltville	rkKB	Mainz	1756-1791	1
Emsdorf	STA	Marburg	1808-1811	1
Engelbach -Biedenkopf-	AG	Marburg	1803-1871	2
Engelthal	rkKB	Darmstadt	1822-1875	2
Enzheim	evKB	Darmstadt	1817-1875	2
Eppe	AG	Marburg	1838-1899	1
Eppertshausen	rkKB	Mainz	1740-1876	7
Epterode	STA	Marburg	1808-1811	1
Erbach -Bergstr.-	rkKB	Darmstadt	1810-1875	13
Erbach	evKB rkKB	Darmstadt	1808-1875	7
Erbach -Rheingau-	rkKB	Mainz	1756-1876	3
Erbenhausen -Alsfeld-	Kirchen	Darmstadt	1808-1875	4
Erbenhausen -Marburg-	STA	Marburg	1814-1818	1
Erbstadt	Synagogen	Marburg	1852	1
Erdenfelden	evKB	Darmstadt	1808-1875	3
Erdpenhausen	evKB	Hergeishause	1718-1968	2
Erfurtshausen	STA AG	Marburg	1759-1809	2

Location	Nature of Material	Where Filmed	Dates Covered	No. of Rolls
Erksdorf	STA	Marburg	1808-1874	2
Ermenrod	evKB	Darmstadt	1808-1875	1
Ermetheis	STA	Marburg	1808-1812	1
Ermschwerd	STA	Marburg	1808-1810	1
Ernsthausen -Frk.berg-	STA	Marburg	1808-1873	1
Ersen	AG	Marburg	1818-1864	1
Ersrode	AG	Marburg	1824-1829	1
Ershausen	evKB	Darmstadt	1808-1875	5
Eschenrod	evKB	Darmstadt	1808-1875	2
Eschollbrücke	evKB	Darmstadt	1808-1875	2
Eschwege	AG STA Justizamt	Marburg	1799-1874	12
Essentruth	STA	Marburg	1808-1812	1
Ettingshausen	evKB	Darmstadt	1808-1875	3
Eudorf	evKB	Darmstadt	1808-1875	2
Eulersdorf	evKB	Darmstadt	1808-1875	8
Falkenberg	Justizamt	Marburg	1787-1804	1
Fauerbach -Burdingen-	evKB	Darmstadt	1830-1875	1
Fauerbach -Friedberg-	evKB	Darmstadt	1808-1875	3
Feldkrücken	evKB	Darmstadt	1826-1875	2
Felsberg -Melsungen-	AG STA	Marburg	1808-1884	4
Findlos	STA	Marburg	1811	1
Fischbach -M. Taunus-	rkKB	Mainz	1756-1791	1
Florshain	STA	Marburg	1828-1840	1
Flörsheim	rkKB evKB	Darmstadt Mainz	1757-1875	3
Frankenau	STA	Marburg	1808-1813	1

Location	Nature of Material	Where Filmed	Dates Covered	No. of Rolls
Frankenberg	STA	Marburg	1808-1813	3
Frankenhain -Ziegenhain-	Justizamt	Marburg	1792-1874	1
Frankenhausen -Darmstadt-	evKB	Darmstadt	1809-1875	2
Frankershausen	STA	Marburg	1808-1810	1
Frankfurt Main	LDS records	Salt Lake City	1907-1951	10
Frankfurt Main	franz. refKB	Frankfurt	1685-1825	19
Frankfurt Main	rkKB	Frankfurt	1525-1791	5
Frankfurt Main	evKB MKB	Frankfurt Hannover	1851-1919	4
Frankfurt Main	evKB KB	Frankfurt	1533-1850	232
Frankfurt Main	STA	Frankfurt	1851-1938	475
Frankfurt Main	Justizamt	Marburg	1721-1901	45
Frankfurt Main	STA	Frankfurt	1811-1949	235
Frankfurt Main	AG	Marburg	1815-1831	4
Fränkisch Crumbach	evKB	Darmstadt	1808-1875	8
Frauenborn	STA	Marburg	1808-1812	1
Fraurombach	evKB	Darmstadt	1808-1875	6
Frechenhausen	STA	Marburg	1874-1875	1
Freienhagen -Waldeck-	Justizamt	Marburg	1809-1896	3
Freinseen	evKB	Darmstadt	1808-1875	3
Freiensteinau	evKB	Darmstadt	1808-1875	7
Frieda	STA	Marburg	1808-1812	1
Friedberg	evKB rkKB	Darmstadt Mainz	1808-1876	14

Location	Nature of Material	Where Filmed	Dates Covered	No. of Rolls
Friedensdorf	Ortsgericht	Marburg	1816-1861	1
Friedewald	STA Justizamt	Marburg	1749-1875	22
Friedrichsdorf -Hofgeismar-	Justizamt	Marburg	1831-1849	1
Friedrichshausen	STA	Marburg	1808-1812	1
Friedricksthal -Hofgeismar-	Justizamt	Marburg	1845-1861	1
Frielendorf	Justizamt	Marburg	1792-1796	1
Frielingen	STA	Marburg	1874-1875	1
Frisenhausen	STA	Marburg	1811	1
Frischborn	evKB	Darmstadt	1808-1875	4
Fritzlar	MKB STA evKB	Marburg Hannover	1808-1888	3
Fronhausen	AG Justizamt Kirchen	Marburg	1750-1874	22
Froschhausen	rkKB evKB	Darmstadt	1774-1876	5
Fulda	AG	Marburg	1735-1848	36
Fulda	Justizamt	Marburg	1764-1887	25
Fulda	evKB MKB	Marburg	1867-1906	3
Fulda	Heer	Marburg	1793-1831	1
Fulda	STA LG	Marburg	1818-1875	15
Fürstenwald	Justizamt	Marburg	1813-1871	1
Fürth	rkKB	Mainz Darmstadt	1663-1876	15
Gadernheim	LDS records	Salt Lake City	1947-1948	1
Gambach	evKB	Darmstadt	1808-1875	6
Garbenteich	evKB	Darmstadt	1808-1875	3
Gedern	evKB	Darmstadt	1808-1875	7

Location	Nature of Material	Where Filmed	Dates Covered	No. of Rolls
Geinsheim	evKB rkKB	Darmstadt Mainz	1820-1875	5
Geisenheim	rkKB	Mainz	1756-1791	1
Geislitz	STA	Marburg	1811-1812	1
Geismar	STA Kirchen	Marburg	1808-1874	4
Geiss-Nidda	evKB	Darmstadt	1808-1875	2
Gelnhaar	evKB	Darmstadt	1819-1875	4
Gelnhausen	AG Justizamt Freigericht	Marburg	1596-1874	26
Gemünden -Frankenberg-	STA Justizamt	Marburg	1808-1884	6
Gensungen	evKB STA	Marburg Hamborn	1661-1875	4
Georgenhausen	evKB	Darmstadt	1808-1875	3
Germerode	Kirchen	Marburg	1808-1810	1
Gernsheim	rkKB evKB	Darmstadt Mainz	1652-1875	17
Gersfeld	LG	Marburg	1786-1862	4
Gessen	rkKB	Mainz	1797-1876	4
Gethsemane	STA	Marburg	1808	1
Gettenau	evKB	Darmstadt	1808-1875	2
Gewissenruh	STA	Marburg	1808-1812	1
Giebringhause	AG	Marburg	1839-1899	1
Gieselwerder	STA	Marburg	1808-1812	1
Giessen	rkKB AG MKB evKB	Darmstadt Mainz Hannover	1797-1931	46
Gilserberg	Justizamt	Marburg	1791-1845	2
Ginseldorf	STA	Marburg	1808-1828	1
Gisselberg	AG	Marburg	1835-1873	1
Gittersdorf	Justizamt	Marburg	1840-1875	1

Location	Nature of Material	Where Filmed	Dates Covered	No. of Rolls
Gladenbach	AG STA	Marburg	1718-1875	44
Glashütten -Büdingen-	evKB	Darmstadt	1830-1875	2
Gleichen	STA	Marburg	1808-1812	1
Goddellau	evKB	Darmstadt	1808-1875	5
Goddelsheim	AG KG	Marburg	1857-1891	2
Gombeth	STA	Marburg	1808-1812	1
Gonterskirchen	evKB	Darmstadt	1808-1875	3
Gossfelden	STA	Marburg	1808-1883	2
Gottsbüren	STA	Marburg	1808-1812	1
Gottstreu	STA	Marburg	1808-1812	1
Götzenhain	evKB	Darmstadt	1819-1875	4
Gräfenhausen	evKB	Darmstadt	1808-1875	4
Grandenborn	STA	Marburg	1808-1812	1
Grebenau -Alsfeld-	evKB	Darmstadt	1808-1875	8
Grebenau -Melsungen-	STA	Marburg	1808-1813	1
Grebenstein	Justizamt	Marburg	1798-1906	19
Grebenstein	AG	Marburg	1754-1909	11
Grebenstein	STA	Marburg	1808-1812	4
Griesheim	evKB	Darmstadt	1808-1875	11
Grifte	STA	Marburg	1808-1812	1
Grimelsheim	Justizamt	Marburg	1821-1873	1
Gronau -Bergstrasse-	rkKB STA	Darmstadt Marburg	1740-1819	28
Gross-Bieberau	evKB	Darmstadt	1808-1875	13
Gross-Buseck	Kirchen	Darmstadt	1808-1875	8
Gross-Eichen	Kirchen	Darmstadt	1808-1875	3
Gross-Felda	evKB	Darmstadt	1808-1875	5

Location	Nature of Material	Where Filmed	Dates Covered	No. of Rolls
Gross-Gerau	evKB	Darmstadt	1808-1875	10
Gross-Karben	evKB	Darmstadt	1808-1875	3
Gross-Rohrhein	STA	Darmstadt	1808-1875	3
Gross-Sielheim	AG	Marburg	1737-1834	3
Gross-Umstadt	evKB rkKB	Darmstadt Mainz	1756-1876	11
Gross-Zimmern	evKB rkKB	Darmstadt Mainz	1718-1876	11
Grossalmerode	Justizamt STA	Marburg	1795-1868	13
Grossen-Linden	Kirchen	Darmstadt	1808-1875	4
Grossenenglis	STA	Marburg	1808-1812	1
Grossenhausen	STA	Marburg	1811-1812	1
Grossenlüder	Justizamt	Marburg	1818-1858	24
Grossenritte	STA	Marburg	1808-1812	1
Grossentaft	STA	Marburg	1874-1875	1
Grossrechten-bach	evKB	Düsseldorf	1655-1758	2
Grünberg	evKB	Darmstadt	1817-1875	12
Grüningen	evKB	Darmstadt	1810-1875	3
Grusen	STA	Marburg	1808-1812	2
Gudensberg	STA AG Justizamt	Marburg	1808-1874	15
Gundernhausen	evKB	Darmstadt	1808-1875	3
Günsterode	STA	Marburg	1808-1812	1
Güttersbach	evKB	Darmstadt	1808-1875	8
Guschagen	Justizamt	Marburg	1848-1849	1
Habitzheim	evKB rkKB	Darmstadt Mainz	1681-1876	1
Habitzheim	evKB rkKB	Darmstadt Mainz	1681-1876	7
Hahn	evKB	Darmstadt	1808-1875	4

Location	Nature of Material	Where Filmed	Dates Covered	No. of Rolls
Hähnlein	evKB	Darmstadt	1808-1875	4
Hailer	AG	Marburg	1770-1782	1
Haina	AG STA	Marburg	1722-1826	6
Hainchen	Kirchen	Darmstadt	1820-1875	4
Hainhausen	rkKB	Darmstadt Mainz	1808-1875	4
Hainstadt	rkKB	Darmstadt Mainz	1836-1876	4
Hallgarten	rkKB	Mainz	1756-1791	1
Hambach -Bergstr.-	rkKB	Darmstadt	1810-1875	13
Hammelbach	evKB	Darmstadt	1808-1875	5
Hanau	AG	Marburg	1750-1832	17
Hanau	evKB MKB Prussian Army	Eibenstock Hannover	1867-1920	2
Hanau	STA	Marburg	1744-1875	12
Hanau	Justizamt	Marburg	1717-1869	10
Harheim	rkKB	Mainz	1663-1876	3
Harle	Justizamt STA	Marburg	1808-1889	3
Harmathsachsen	AG STA	Marburg	1804-1812	3
Harpertshausen	evKB	Darmstadt	1788-1855	6
Harreshausen	evKB	Darmstadt	1811-1875	3
Hartenrod -Buchenkopf-	STA	Marburg	1874-1875	1
Hartershausen	Kirchen	Darmstadt	1808-1875	5
Hassenhausen	AG	Marburg	1808-1821	1
Hassenroth	evKB	Darmstadt	1808-1875	7
Hattenheim	rkKB	Mainz	1756-1791	1
Hattenrod	Kirchen	Darmstadt	1808-1875	2
Hattersheim	rkKB	Mainz	1756-1751	1

Location	Nature of Material	Where Filmed	Dates Covered	No. of Rolls
Hatzbach	STA	Marburg	1808-1874	1
Haueda	AG STA	Marburg	1808-1874	2
Hauheim -Gr. Ger.-	evKB	Darmstadt	1808-1875	3
Hausen -Friedberg-	Kirchen	Darmstadt	1808-1875	2
Hausen -Giessen-	Kirchen	Darmstadt	1808-1875	2
Hausen -Offenbach-	Kirchen	Darmstadt	1819-1875	2
Hausen -Witzenhausen-	evKB	Hamborn	1717-1875	1
Hebstahl	rkKB	Freiburg	1688-1900	3
Hechershausen	STA	Marburg	1808-1812	1
Heegheim	Kirchen	Darmstadt	1859-1875	1
Heenes	AG	Marburg	1823-1875	1
Heidelbach	Kirchen	Darmstadt	1808-1875	3
Heiligenrode	STA	Marburg	1808-1812	1
Heimanshausen	STA	Marburg	1808-1812	1
Heimbach	AG	Marburg	1808-1844	1
Heimboldshausen	AG	Marburg	1808-1844	1
Heinebach	Justizamt	Marburg	1659-1968	14
Heldra	STA	Marburg	1809-1812	1
Hellstein	STA	Marburg	1874-1875	1
Helmarshausen	STA	Marburg	1803-1889	1
Helmscheid	AG	Marburg	1839-1883	1
Helsa	STA	Marburg	1808-1812	1
Hemmen	Kirchen	Darmstadt	1808-1817	1
Heppenheim	rkKB	Darmstadt	1810-1875	13
Herlstein	evKB rkKB	Darmstadt Mainz	1647-1875	12
Herchenhain	Kirchen	Darmstadt	1808-1875	4

Location	Nature of Material	Where Filmed	Dates Covered	No. of Rolls
Herchenrode	evKB	Darmstadt	1808-1875	7
Hergershausen	evKB	Darmstadt Aeigers Heinbach	1672-1968	5
Hering	rkKB	Darmstadt Mainz	1702-1876	11
Heringen -Hersfeld-	AG STA	Marsburg	1809-1875	2
Heringhausen	STA	Marburg	1839-1861	1
Herlefeld	STA	Marburg	1808-1878	2
Herleshausen	AG STA	Marburg	1786-1884	2
Herzfeld	evKB MKB	Hannover	1867-1890	1
Herzhausen -Biedenkopf-	AG	Marburg	1844-1862	1
Hesken	AG	Marburg	1775-1865	2
Hesselbach	rkKB	Mainz Darmstadt Freiburg	1660-1903	12
Hesserode	AG	Marburg	1875-1883	1
Hessisch- Lichtenau	AG Justizamt	Marburg	1755-1874	7
Hesslar	AG	Marburg	1874-1887	1
Hessbach	rkKB STA	Darmstadt Marburg	1808-1875	6
Heuchelhein -Beichige-	evKB	Darmstadt	1816-1875	1
Heuchelheim -Giessen-	evKB	Darmstadt	1808-1875	6
Heusenstamm	evKB rkKB	Darmstadt Mainz	1700-1876	7
Hilders	LG AG	Marburg	1674-1918	14
Hilgershausen -Melsunge-	AG STA	Marburg	1808-1896	5
Hillertshausen	AG	Marburg	1826-1855	1

Location	Nature of Material	Where Filmed	Dates Covered	No. of Rolls
Hintersteinau	AG	Marburg	1693-1874	7
Hinschhorn	rkKB STA	Darmstadt Mainz	1636-1876	11
Hirzenhain	evKB	Darmstadt	1808-1875	3
Hitzkirchen	evKB	Darmstadt	1818-1875	5
Hochheim	rkKB	Mainz	1756-1795	1
Höchst -Büdingen-	evKB	Darmstadt	1817-1875	4
Höchst -Erbach-	evKB	Darmstadt	1808-1875	8
Hochstadt	STA	Marburg	1811-1873	1
Hofaschenbach	STA	Marburg	1874-1875	1
Hofbieber	STA	Marburg	1810-1811	1
Hofgeismar	AG STA	Marburg	1795-1904	18
Hofgeismar	Justizamt evKB MKB	Marburg Hannover	1806-1919	16
Hofheim -Bergstr.-	rkKB STA	Mainz Darmstadt	1698-1876	13
Hofheim -Taunus-	rkKB	Mainz	1756-1795	1
Hohenkirchen	STA AG	Marburg	1807-1892	2
Hohenzell	STA AG	Marburg	1721-1875	2
Höhlerbach	evKB	Darmstadt	1843-1875	1
Hohlstein	STA	Marburg	1808-1812	1
Holzburg	STA	Marburg	1808-1813	1
Holzhausen -Biedenkopf-	STA	Marburg	1874-1875	1
Holzhausen -Hofgeismar-	STA	Marburg	1808-1812	1
Holzhausen -Marburg-	Justizamt	Marburg	1756-1809	1

Location	Nature of Material	Where Filmed	Dates Covered	No. of Rolls
Holzheim	Kirchen	Darmstadt	1808-1875	5
Holzheim -Hersfeld-	LG	Marburg	1819-1835	1
Homberg -Alsfeld-	Kirchen	Darmstadt	1808-1875	7
Homberg -Kassel-	Justizamt	Marburg	1816-1867	23
Homberg -Fritslar-	Justizamt LG	Marburg	1733-1880	36
Hombressen	STA	Marburg	1808-1812	2
Homburg	MKB LDS records	Hannover Salt Lake City	1867-1920	2
Hommershausen	AG	Marburg	1809-1813	1
Hommertshausen	STA	Marburg	1874-1875	1
Hoof	AG	Marburg	1849-1860	1
Hopfelde	STA	Marburg	1808-1812	1
Hopfgarten	Kirchen	Darmstadt	1808-1875	5
Hopfmannsfeld	Kirchen	Darmstadt	1808-1875	3
Horbach	AG	Marburg	1811	1
Hordheim -Bergstr.-	STA	Darmstadt	1808-1875	9
Hoxhohl	evKB	Darmstadt	1808-1875	7
Hümrne	AG STA	Marburg	1806-1872	5
Hundelshuasen	STA Gericht	Marburg	1808-1816	3
Hundshausen	Landesamt	Marburg	1809	1
Hünfeld	AG Justizamt	Marburg	1707-1874	19
Hungen	evKB	Darmstadt	1808-1875	6
Hüttenberg	JüdGem	Darmstadt	1809-1822	1
Hüttengesäss	Landesamt	Marburg	1840-1877	1
Hutzdorf	evKB	Darmstadt	1808-1875	5

Location	Nature of Material	Where Filmed	Dates Covered	No. of Rolls
Iba	STA	Marburg	1808-1875	2
Illnhausen	evKB	Darmstadt	1841-1875	2
Ilschhausen	Landesamt	Marburg	1815-1820	1
Ilsdorf	evKB	Darmstadt	1857-1875	1
Immenhausen	Justizamt STA	Marburg	1808-1870	2
Immickenhain	Justizamt STA	Marburg	1809-1875	2
Immighausen	Justizamt	Marburg	1838-1885	1
Ippinghausen	STA	Marburg	1808-1810	1
Itzenhain	AG	Marburg	1833-1842	1
Jesberg	Justizamt	Marburg	1734-1875	41
Jesberg	evKB KBA STA LG	Marburg Hamborn	1801-1875	18
Johannesberg	rkKB AG	Marburg Mainz	1756-1803	2
Josbach	STA	Marburg	1808-1874	1
Jugenheim	evKB	Darmstadt	1808-1875	3
Jügesheim	rkKB	Darmstadt Mainz	1808-1875	6
Kaichen	evKB	Darmstadt	1808-1875	1
Kailbach	rkKB	Freiburg	1660-1903	8
Kammerbach	STA	Marburg	1808-1812	1
Kämmerzell	STA	Marburg	1812	1
Karben	rkKB evKB	Darmstadt	1808-1876	11
Karlshafen	Justizamt STA Franz.KB	Marburg	1751-1860	4
Kassel	LDS records	Salt Lake City	1927-1951	4
Kassel	evKB MKB	Hannover	1866-1940	5

Location	Nature of Material	Where Filmed	Dates Covered	No. of Rolls
Kassel	Döll Phillipp	Kassel	1894, 1903	2
Kassel	AG STA Hofgericht	Kassel Marburg	1735-1874	167
Kassel	STA evKB Hofgericht	Marburg	1755-1812	31
Kelsterbach	Kirchen	Darmstadt	1808-1875	6
Kelze	AG	Marburg	1840-1876	1
Kempfenbach	STA	Marburg	1874-1875	1
Kerspenhausen	STA	Marburg	1874-1875	2
Kesselstadt	STA	Marburg	1811	1
Kiedrich	rkKB	Mainz	1756-1791	1
Kilianstädten	STA	Marburg	1811	1
Kirch-Beerfurth	evKB	Darmstadt	1841-1875	1
Kirchbracht	STA	Marburg	1874-1875	1
Kirch-Brombach	evKB	Darmstadt	1808-1875	15
Kirch-Göns	evKB	Darmstadt	1808-1875	3
Kirchhain	Justizamt STA	Marburg	1723-1876	33
Kirchhasel	STA	Marburg	1874-1875	1
Kirschhausen	rkKB	Darmstadt	1810-1875	13
Kirstorf	Kirchen	Darmstadt	1808-1875	5
Klaestadt	Kirchen	Darmstadt	1811-1875	3
Klein-Auheim	Kirchen	Darmstadt	1836-1875	3
Klein-Eicher	Kirchen	Darmstadt	1808-1875	4
Klein-Gerau	Kirchen	Darmstadt	1858-1875	1
Klein-Gumpen	evKB	Darmstadt	1808-1875	7
Klein-Karben	evKB	Darmstadt	1808-1875	4
Klein-Krotzen-burg	rkKB Kirchen	Mainz Darmstadt	1605-1876	8
Klein-Umstadt	evKB	Darmstadt	1808-1875	3

Location	Nature of Material	Where Filmed	Dates Covered	No. of Rolls
Klein-Welzheim	rkKB Kirchen	Mainz Darmstadt	1808-1875	4
Kleinensee	STA	Marburg	1808-1812	1
Kleinrechtenbach	evLutKB	Düsseldorf	1655-1758	2
Kleinseelheim	STA	Marburg	1808-1809	1
Kleinrach	AG	Marburg	1808-1876	1
Klosterhofe	AG	Marburg	1702-1817	1
Knoden	Kirchen	Darmstadt	1821-1874	1
Kohlhausen	AG	Marburg	1874	1
Königstein	rkKB	Mainz	1756-1791	1
Königswald	STA	Marburg	1808-1812	1
Korbach	Oberjustiz-amt	Marburg	1780-1875	13
Körle	STA	Marburg	1874-1875	1
Kransberg	rkKB	Mainz	1756-1791	1
Kressenbach	AG	Marburg	1628-1824	1
Kreftel	rkKB	Mainz	1756-1795	1
Kronberg	rkKB	Mainz	1756-1791	1
Kruspis	STA	Marburg	1874-1875	1
Laisa	STA	Marburg	1811-1874	5
Lamerden	Justizamt	Marburg	1815-1876	2
Lämmerpeie	rkKB	Mainz Darmstadt	1705-1879	5
Lampertsheim	evKB rkKB	Mainz Darmstadt	1689-1876	23
Landau	evLutKB	Hamborn	1647-1875	3
Landeck	Justizamt	Marburg	1784-1799	1
Landenhausen	Kirchen	Darmstadt	1808-1875	4
Langel	Kirchen	Darmstadt	1808-1875	3
Langen	evKB	Darmstadt	1808-1875	10
Langenbieber	STA	Marburg	1811-1814	1

Location	Nature of Material	Where Filmed	Dates Covered	No. of Rolls
Langendiebach	Justizamt	Marburg	1826-1881	3
Langendorf	Justizamt	Marburg	1808-1811	1
Langenhain -Eschwege-	STA	Marburg	1808-1812	1
Langenhain -Friedberg-	Kirchen	Darmstadt	1808-1875	3
Langenschwarz	Reichs- gericht STA Justizamt	Marburg	1771-1875	3
Langenschbold	Landesamt	Marburg	1826-1877	1
Langenstein	Justizamt	Marburg	1793-1842	2
Langenthal	Justizamt STA	Marburg Darmstadt	1814-1875	3
Lang Göns	evKB STA	Darmstadt	1808-1875	6
Langsdorf	evKB	Darmstadt	1808-1875	3
Langstadt	evKB	Darmstadt	1811-1875	2
Langwaden	STA	Darmstadt	1808-1875	4
Lanzenhain	evKB	Darmstadt	1860-1875	1
Lardenbach	evKB	Darmstadt	1808-1875	2
Laubach -Giessen-	evKB	Darmstadt	1808-1875	6
Laudenau	evKB	Darmstadt	1808-1875	7
Lautenbach	evKB	Hamborn	1717-1875	2
Lautenhausen	AG	Marburg	1810-1812	1
Lauterbach	evKB	Darmstadt	1808-1875	10
Leckringhausen	AG	Marburg	1769-1796	1
Leeheim	Kirchen	Darmstadt	1808-1875	5
Lehrbach	Kirchen	Darmstadt	1808-1875	4
Leidenhofen	LRA	Marburg	1850-1873	1
Leidhecken	evKB	Darmstadt	1808-1875	2
Leighestern	evKB	Darmstadt	1808-1875	5

Location	Nature of Material	Where Filmed	Dates Covered	No. of Rolls
Lelbach	AG	Marburg	1838-1873	1
Lengefeld	AG	Marburg	1839-1869	1
Lengers	AG	Marburg	1811-1812	1
Lengfeld	evLutKB	Darmstadt	1808-1875	5
Lettgenbrunn	STA	Marburg	1874-1875	1
Leusel	evLutKB	Darmstadt	1808-1875	2
Lich	evLutKB	Darmstadt	1808-1875	6
Lichenroth	STA	Marburg	1874-1875	1
Lichtenberg	evLutKB	Darmstadt	1808-1875	13
Lichterode	Justizamt	Marburg	1854-1876	1
Liebenau	Landesamt STA	Marburg	1811-1888	3
Lindenfels	rkKB refKB	Mainz Darmstadt	1728-1876	10
Lindheim	evKB	Darmstadt	1826-1875	3
Lingelbach	STA	Marburg	1874-1875	1
Lippoldsberg	Obergericht STA	Marburg	1808-1824	2
Lischeid	Obergericht	Marburg	1816-1846	1
Lissberg	evLutKB	Darmstadt	1808-1875	4
Lixfeld	LRA	Marburg	1853-1866	1
Lohfelden	STA	Marburg	1780-1810	1
Löhlbach	AG	Marburg	1782-1812	1
Lohne	Kirchen STA	Marburg Hamborn	1633-1875	4
Lohra	AG	Marburg	1808-1869	1
Lohre	STA	Marburg	1874-1875	1
Lohrhaupten	STA	Marburg	1874-1875	1
Londorf	evLutKB	Darmstadt	1808-1875	13
Lorbach	evKB	Darmstadt	1818-1875	4
Lorch	rkKB	Mainz	1756-1791	1

Location	Nature of Material	Where Filmed	Dates Covered	No. of Rolls
Lorchhausen	rkKB	Mainz	1756-1791	1
Lorsch	rkKB	Mainz Darmstadt	1679-1875	22
Louisendorf	AG	Marburg	1808-1813	1
Lüderbach	STA	Marburg	1808-1812	1
Ludwigseck	AG	Marburg	1801-1809	1
Ludwigstein	AG	Marburg	1814-1848	5
Lützelbach	evKB	Darmstadt	1808-1875	7
Lützelhausen	AG	Marburg	1811-1812	1
Maar	Kirchen	Darmstadt	1808-1875	5
Mackenzell	AG	Marburg	1703-1805	27
Maden	STA	Marburg	1808-1812	1
Mahlerts	AG	Marburg	1812-1876	1
Mainflingen	rkKB	Mainz Darmstadt	1682-1876	8
Malchen	evLutKB	Darmstadt	1858-1875	1
Malsfeld	STA AG	Marburg	1754-1812	2
Mansbach	STA LRA	Marburg	1825-1875	2
Marburg	AG LG	Marburg	1698-1890	86
Marburg	Kirchen KB Sippenbuch	Marburg	1500-1850	17
Marburg	STA Justizamt	Marburg	1808-1883	9
Mardorf	AG	Marburg	1761-1823	2
Mariendorf	STA Justizamt	Marburg	1806-1861	2
Marjoss	AG STA	Marburg	1622-1875	2
Markershausen	STA	Marburg	1808-1812	1
Marköbel	JüdGem	Marburg	1849-1866	1

Location	Nature of Material	Where Filmed	Dates Covered	No. of Rolls
Martinhagen	STA	Marburg	1808-1812	1
Massenheim -Friedberg-	Justizamt	Marburg	1739-1843	9
Maulbach	evKB	Darmstadt	1808-1875	5
Mauloff	evKB	Salt Lake City	1641-1818	1
Meckbad	AG	Marburg	1839-1874	1
Mecklar	STA	Marburg	1874-1875	1
Meerholz	STA AG Justizamt	Marburg	1759-1875	10
Meiches	evKB	Darmstadt	1808-1875	3
Meimbressen	AG STA LG JüdGem	Marburg	1808-1889	4
Meineringhausen	KG	Marburg	1820-1878	2
Melbach	evKB	Darmstadt	1808-1875	3
Mellnau	STA	Marburg	1808-1813	1
Melsfeld	STA	Marburg	1874-1875	1
Melsungen	STA AG Justizamt JüdGem	Marburg	1723-1875	41
Mengsberg	Justizamt	Marburg	1828-1845	1
Merlau	evKB	Darmstadt	1808-1875	5
Mersehausen -Wolfhagen-	STA	Marburg	1808-1875	2
Merzhausen -Ziegenhain-	AG JüdGem	Marburg	1808-1866	3
Messel	evKB	Darmstadt	1808-1875	3
Metze	Gericht STA	Marburg	1808-1821	2
Metzebach	Vormund-schafts ger.	Marburg	1824-1875	1
Michelau	evKB	Darmstadt	1818-1875	2

Location	Nature of Material	Where Filmed	Dates Covered	No. of Rolls
Michelbach -Marburg-	STA	Marburg	1808-1813	1
Michelsrombach	STA	Marburg	1874-1875	1
Michelstadt	LDS records evKB	Salt Lake City Darmstadt	1808-1875 1931-1947	31
Mittel-Grünau	evKB	Darmstadt	1818-1875	4
Mittelbuchen	STA	Marburg	1811-1812	1
Mittelseemen	evKB	Darmstadt	1808-1875	3
Mitterode	STA	Marburg	1808-1812	1
Moischeid	Justizamt	Marburg	1828-1845	1
Momberg	AG Synag.	Marburg	1856-1889	3
Mörfleden	evKB	Darmstadt	1808-1875	1
Mörfelden	evKB	Darmstadt	1808-1875	3
Mörhenbach	rkKB	Darmstadt Mainz	1653-1876	11
Mornshausen -Biedenkopf-	LG	Marburg	1816-1866	1
Mörshausen -Melsungen-	STA	Marburg	1808-1875	2
Mosbach -Dieburg-	rkKB	Mainz Darmstadt	1692-1876	5
Motzfeld	STA	Marburg	1874-1875	1
Mühlhausen -Waldeck-	AG KG	Marburg	1850-1885	2
Mühlheim	rkKB	Darmstadt Mainz	1650-1876	15
Munchhausen -Marburg-	STA	Marburg	1808-1813	2
Mündershausen	AG	Marburg	1824-1876	1
Münster -Dieburg-	rkKB	Mainz	1756-1876	6
Münster -Friedberg-	evKB	Darmstadt	1808-1875	8
Münzenberg	evKB	Darmstadt	1818-1875	3

Location	Nature of Material	Where Filmed	Dates Covered	No. of Rolls
Muschenheim	Kirchen	Darmstadt	1808-1875	4
Nans-Willers-hausen	BGM Amt	Marburg	1849-1864	1
Nassenerfruth	Vormund-schafts-gericht	Marburg	1822-1875	1
Naumburg -Wolfhagen-	Justizamt STA	Marburg	1808-1875	3
Neckar-Steinach	evKB rkKB	Darmstadt Mainz	1662-1876	10
Neerda	AG	Marburg	1840	1
Nieder-Eschbach	JüdGem	Darmstadt	1827-1875	1
Niederklein	AG	Marburg	1809-1889	1
Nieder-Mockstadt	JüdGem	Darmstadt	1823-1866	1
Neutershausen	AG STA	Marburg	1723-1875	15
Nesselbrunn	Justizamt	Marburg	1834-1860	1
Nesselröden	STA	Marburg	1808-1812	1
Netra	Justizamt STA	Marburg	1808-1897	5
Neu-Isenburg	Kirchen	Darmstadt	1837-1875	5
Neuenberg	AG	Marburg	1727-1735	1
Neuenstein	Justizamt	Marburg	1733-1819	3
Neukirchen -Hünfeld-	STA	Marburg	1874-1875	1
Neukirchen -Zeigenhain-	STA Justizamt	Marburg	1768-1875	6
Neumorschen	STA	Marburg	1798-1897	2
Neunkirchen	evKB	Darmstadt	1808-1849	1
Neunkirchen -Darmstadt-	evKB	Darmstadt	1808-1875	13
Neuseesen	evKB	Bielefeld	1668-1907	2
Neuses	STA	Marburg	1811	1

Location	Nature of Material	Where Filmed	Dates Covered	No. of Rolls
Neustadt -Erbach-	rkKB	Darmstadt Mainz	1821-1876	13
Neustadt -Fulda-	AG	Marburg	1789-1874	3
Neuwort	AG	Marburg	1675-1853	1
Nidda	evKB	Darmstadt	1808-1875	8
Niddatal	rkKB	Mainz	1647-1927	5
Niddawitzhausen	STA	Marburg	1808-1812	1
Nidderau	rkKB	Mainz Darmstadt	1684-1875	9
Niedenstein	STA	Marburg	1808-1812	1
Nieder-Beerbach	evKB	Darmstadt	1808-1875	4
Nieder-Euse	Justizamt	Marburg	1840-1886	1
Nieder-Eschbach	refKB	Darmstadt	1812-1875	3
Nieder-Florstadt	evKB	Darmstadt	1808-1875	7
Nieder-Gemünden	Kirchen	Darmstadt	1808-1875	4
Nieder-Kaimsbach	Kirchen	Darmstadt	1863-1875	1
Nieder-Mockstadt	evKB	Darmstadt	1819-1875	5
Nieder-Modau	evKB	Darmstadt	1808-1875	7
Nieder-Moos	evKB	Darmstadt	1808-1875	7
Nieder-Mörlen	rkKB	Mainz Darmstadt	1734-1876	4
Nieder-Ohmen	evKB	Darmstadt	1808-1874	5
Nieder-Ramstadt	evKB	Darmstadt	1808-1875	9
Nieder-Roden	rkKB	Mainz	1649-1875	4
Nieder-Rossbach	evKB	Darmstadt	1808-1875	1
Nieder-Schleidern	AG	Marburg	1839-1879	1
Nieder-Seemen	STA	Darmstadt	1808-1875	3
Nieder-Weisch	STA	Darmstadt	1808-1875	6
Nieder-Wöllstadt	Kirchen	Darmstadt	1808-1875	2

Location	Nature of Material	Where Filmed	Dates Covered	No. of Rolls
Nieder-Asphe	STA	Marburg	1808-1811	1
Nieder-Aula	Justizamt	Marburg	1777-1896	27
Niederbessingen	evKB	Darmstadt	1808-1875	2
Niederdieten	Justizamt	Marburg	1837-1850	1
Niederdienz-bach	STA	Marburg	1808-1812	2
Niedereisen-hausen	Justizamt	Marburg	1823-1852	1
Niederellen-bach	evKB	Oberchlenbach	1717-1875	2
Niederelsungen	STA	Marburg	1808-1812	1
Niedergrünau	STA	Marburg	1874-1875	1
Niedergude	STA	Marburg	1874-1875	1
Niederhone	STA	Marburg	1808-1810	1
Niederissigheim	STA	Marburg	1811-1812	1
Niederkaufungen	STA evKB	Marburg Düsseldorf	1573-1955	10
Niederklein	AG Synag.	Marburg	1809-1889	2
Niederlistigen	STA	Marburg	1809-1812	1
Niedermeister	Justizamt STA	Marburg	1808-1869	2
Niedermittlau	Justizamt STA	Marburg	1841-1875	11
Niedermöllrich	AG STA	Marburg	1808-1875	2
Niedernhausen -Dieburg-	evKB	Darmstadt	1808-1875	13
Niederrodenbach	STA	Marburg	1811-1867	1
Niederrurff	STA	Marburg	1919-1921	1
Niederwald	STA	Marburg	1808-1810	1
Niederwalgern	Justizamt	Marburg	1808-1812	1
Niederweidbach	STA	Marburg	1874-1875	1

Location	Nature of Material	Where Filmed	Dates Covered	No. of Rolls
Niederweimar	Vormund- schaftsamt	Marburg	1815-1840	1
Niederzell	Justizamt	Marburg	1718-1832	1
Neisig	STA	Marburg	1811	1
Nonnenrath	evKB	Darmstadt	1808-1875	8
Nonrod	evKB	Darmstadt	1808-1875	13
Nordeck	Polizeiamt Justizamt	Marburg	1807-1869	2
Nordeneck	Justizamt	Marburg	1839-1871	1
Nordheim	rkKB	Mainz	1676-1886	2
Nothfelden	STA	Marburg	1809-1812	1
Obbornhofen	Kirchen	Darmstadt	1808-1852	3
Ober-Absteinach	rkKB	Mainz Darmstadt	1716-1875	18
Ober-Beerbach	evKB	Darmstadt	1808-1875	7
Ober-Bessingen	Kirchen	Darmstadt	1850-1875	1
Ober- Breidenbach	Kirchen	Darmstadt	1808-1875	4
Ober-Ense	Justizamt	Marburg	1841-1885	1
Ober-Erlenbach	rkKB KB	Darmstadt Mainz	1677-1889	5
Ober-Eschbad	evKB	Darmstadt	1816-1875	2
Ober-Florstadt	evKB	Darmstadt	1808-1875	4
Ober-Hörgern	Kirchen	Darmstadt	1808-1875	2
Ober-Klingen	evKB	Darmstadt	1830-1875	5
Ober-Lais	Kirchen	Darmstadt	1830-1875	2
Ober-Melsungen	STA	Marburg	1808-1812	1
Ober-Mochstadt	evKB	Darmstadt	1819-1875	5
Ober-Mörlen	rkKB	Darmstadt Mainz	1716-1876	11
Ober-Mossau	evKB	Darmstadt	1849-1875	2
Ober-Ofleichen	Kirchen	Darmstadt	1808-1875	8

Location	Nature of Material	Where Filmed	Dates Covered	No. of Rolls
Ober-Ohmen	evKB	Darmstadt	1808-1874	5
Ober-Ramstadt	Kirchen	Darmstadt	1808-1875	7
Ober-Roden	rkKB	Mainz	1720-1876	7
Ober-Rossbach	evKB	Darmstadt	1808-1875	5
Ober-Seemen	Kirchen	Darmstadt	1808-1875	5
Ober-Wegfurth	Kirchen	Darmstadt	1808-1832	1
Ober-Werbe	Justizamt	Marburg	1820-1884	1
Ober-Widdersheim	evKB	Darmstadt	1808-1875	4
Ober-Wöllstadt	rkKB Kirchen	Darmstadt Mainz	1660-1884	10
Ober-Asphe	BGM Amt.	Marburg	1750-1847	2
Oberau	Kirchen	Darmstadt	1808-1860	4
Oberaula	evKB STA Justizamt	Hamborn Marburg	1694-1932	23
Oberdieten	STA	Marburg	1874-1875	1
Oberdünzebach	STA	Marburg	1808-1812	2
Obereisenhausen	Justizamt STA	Marburg	1801-1875	10
Oberellenbach	STA evKB	Marburg Oberellenbach	1659-1876	5
Oberelsungen	STA	Marburg	1808-1875	2
Obergeis	Vormund-schafts-gericht STA	Marburg	1834-1875	2
Obergladbach -Unter-Taunus-	rkKB	Mainz	1756-1791	1
Obergude	STA	Marburg	1808-1812	1
Oberhausen -Hersfeld-	Vormund-schafts-gericht	Marburg	1820-1875	1
Oberhone	STA	Marburg	1808-1810	1
Oberhörlen	Justizamt evKB	Marburg	1808-1874	5

Location	Nature of Material	Where Filmed	Dates Covered	No. of Rolls
Oberissingheim	Justizamt	Marburg	1808-1812	1
Oberkaufungen	Justizamt STA evKB	Marburg Düsseldorf	1573-1955	11
Oberlistingen	Justizamt STA	Marburg	1765-1875	3
Obermeiser	Justizamt	Marburg	1808-1872	2
Obermelsungen	STA	Marburg	1808-1812	3
Obermöllnich	STA	Marburg	1808-1812	1
Oberndorf -Gelnhausen-	LG	Marburg	1835-1875	2
Oberndorf -Marburg-	STA	Marburg	1808-1812	1
Oberorke	Justizamt	Marburg	1808-1813	1
Oberreifenberg	OBM Amt.	Niederrn Juberg	1925	1
Oberrieden	STA	Marburg	1808-1812	1
Oberrosphe	Justizamt	Marburg	1808-1812	1
Oberschönau -Witzenhausen-	STA	Marburg	1808-1811	1
Obersetzbach	Justizamt	Marburg	1865-1882	1
Obersuhl	STA	Marburg	1808-1875	2
Obertshausen	rkKB	Darmstadt	1819-1876	4
Oberursel	rkKB	Darmstadt	1756-1791	1
Obervellmar	STA	Marburg	1808-1812	1
Obervorschütz	STA	Marburg	1808-1812	1
Oberwalgern	Justizamt	Marburg	1869	1
Oberweidbach	LG	Marburg	1822-1859	1
Oberwiemar	Justizamt	Marburg	1808-1882	1
Oberwöllstadt	rkKB	Mainz	1660-1884	6
Oberzell	Kreisamt	Marburg	1826-1875	1
Ockstadt	rkKB	Darmstadt Mainz	1650-1876	5

Location	Nature of Material	Where Filmed	Dates Covered	No. of Rolls
Oedelsheim	STA Justizamt	Marburg	1808-1812	2
Oes -Friedberg-	Kirchen	Darmstadt	1808-1875	2
Oetmannshausen	STA	Marburg	1808-1809	1
Offenbach	rkKB LDS records	Mainz Darmstadt Salt Lake City	1646-1948	30
Offenthal	evLutKB	Darmstadt	1819-1875	3
Ohmes	rkKB	Mainz	1731-1876	4
Oppenrod	evKB	Darmstadt	1853-1875	1
Oppenhofen	rkKB	Mainz Darmstadt	1733-1876	6
Orferode	Justizamt STA	Marburg	1808-1855	2
Ortenberg	evKB	Darmstadt	1808-1875	5
Ossenheim	evKB	Darmstadt	1808-1875	3
Ostheim -Friedberg-	evKB	Darmstadt	1808-1875	2
Ostheim -Hofgeismar-	STA	Marburg	1811-1812	1
Ostheim -Melsungen-	Justizamt	Marburg	1747-1857	1
Ottrau	Landesamt STA	Marburg	1808-1900	2
Obergleen	Kirchen	Darmstadt	1808-1875	4
Petersberg -Hersfeld-	LG	Marburg	1815-1822	1
Petterweil	Kirchen	Darmstadt	1808-1875	2
Pfaffen- Bierfurth	JüdGem	Darmstadt	1868-1874	1
Pfaffenhausen -Gelnhausen-	LG	Marburg	1846-1869	1
Pfieffe	AG STA	Marburg	1808-1886	3
Pfordt	Kirchen	Darmstadt	1808-1817	1

Location	Nature of Material	Where Filmed	Dates Covered	No. of Rolls
Pfungstadt	Kirchen	Darmstadt	1808-1875	9
Pfillippsthal	STA AG	Marburg	1774-1875	2
Pohl Göns	evKB	Darmstadt	1808-1875	3
Queck	evKB	Darmstadt	1808-1875	8
Quentel	STA	Marburg	1808-1812	1
Quotshausen	Justizamt	Marburg	1836-1846	1
Rabertshausen	Kirchen	Darmstadt	1853-1875	1
Raboldshausen	Justizamt	Marburg	1756-1867	5
Radheim	rkKB KB	Darmstadt	1811-1875	4
Reubach	evLutKB	Darmstadt	1808-1875	2
Reunrod -Alsfeld-	evKB	Darmstadt	1837-1875	1
Reunrod -Büdingen-	Kirchen	Darmstadt	1808-1875	4
Rambach -Eschwege-	STA	Marburg	1808-1810	1
Ramholz	Justizamt	Marburg	1782-1848	3
Ransbach	STA	Marburg	1874-1875	1
Ranstadt	evKB	Darmstadt	1808-1875	4
Rasdorf	STA	Marburg	1874-1875	1
Rassdorf	rkKB	Berlin-Dahlem	1604-1661	1
Rattlar	Justizamt	Marburg	1839-1890	1
Rauischholz- hausen	Justizamt	Marburg	1809-1871	1
Raunheim	evKB	Darmstadt	1808-1875	3
Rauschenberg	Justizamt	Marburg	1783-1874	16
Rebgeshain	evKB	Darmstadt	1856-1875	1
Rechtebach	STA	Marburg	1808-1811	1
Reddehausen	Justizamt	Marburg	1822-1875	1
Relna	AG	Marburg	1862-1898	1

Location	Nature of Material	Where Filmed	Dates Covered	No. of Rolls
Reichelsheim -Erbach-	evKB STA	Darmstadt	1808-1875	18
Reichenbach -Witsenhausen-	evKB STA	Darmstadt Marburg	1808-1875	7
Reichensachsen	STA	Marburg	1808-1812	1
Reilos	Justizamt	Marburg	1835-1877	1
Reimenrod	evKB	Darmstadt	1808-1875	8
Reinhards -Schliechten-	Justizamt	Marburg	1808-1821	1
Reinheim	evKB	Darmstadt	1809-1875	5
Reiskirchen -Giessen-	evKB	Darmstadt	1808-1823	4
Reitzberg	Justizamt	Marburg	1781-1820	4
Rembrücke	Kirchen	Darmstadt	1822-1875	1
Renda	Justizamt STA evKB	Marburg Hamborn	1676-1875	3
Rendel	evKB Kirchen	Darmstadt	1808-1875	3
Rangershausen -FUB-	Justizamt	Marburg	1802-1846	1
Rengshausen	STA	Marburg	1874-1875	1
Rennertehausen	LG	Marburg	1768-1846	1
Rhenegge	Justizamt	Marburg	1839-1880	1
Rhienda	STA	Marburg	1808-1812	1
Richelsdorf	STA	Marburg	1808-1812	1
Richen	Kirchen	Darmstadt	1808-1875	2
Rimbad -Bergstr.-	evKB JüdGem	Darmstadt	1808-1875	13
Rimbad -Lauterbach-	Kirchen	Darmstadt	1808-1832	1
Rimhorn	evKB	Darmstadt	1808-1875	3
Rinderbügen	evKB	Darmstadt	1818-1875	1
Rixfeld	evKB	Darmstadt	1808-1875	2

Location	Nature of Material	Where Filmed	Dates Covered	No. of Rolls
Rochenberg	KB rkKB	Darmstadt Mainz	1610-1876	7
Rockensüss	STA	Marburg	1808-1875	2
Rodan -Bergstr.-	STA	Darmstadt	1808-1875	4
Rodan -Dieberg-	evKB	Darmstadt	1808-1875	13
Röddenau	Justizamt	Marburg	1808-1873	1
Rodenbach -Büdingen-	Kirchen	Darmstadt	1808-1875	3
Rödgen -Giessen-	Kirchen	Darmstadt	1808-1875	3
Rodheim -Friedberg-	evKB	Darmstadt	1811-1875	4
Rodheim -Giessen-	Kirchen	Darmstadt	1808-1875	4
Rohrach -Büdingen-	evKB	Darmstadt	1818-1875	3
Rohrbad -Darmstadt-	Huguenothen- Kirchen	Darmstadt	1808-1875	4
Röhrda	STA	Marburg	1808-1812	1
Röhrenfurt	STA	Marburg	1808-1812	3
Röllshausen	Justizamt STA	Marburg	1809-1935	3
Römersberg	Justizamt	Marburg	1838-1844	1
Rommerode	STA	Marburg	1808-1812	1
Rommershausen	Gericht	Marburg	1789-1886	2
Rommersrain	Gericht	Marburg	1776	1
Romrod	evKB	Darmstadt	1808-1875	6
Ronhausen	STA	Marburg	1808-1812	1
Rönshausen	STA	Marburg	1812-1875	2
Rosenthal -FUB-	Justizamt	Marburg	1752-1874	20
Rossberg	Justizamt	Marburg	1812-1882	1

Location	Nature of Material	Where Filmed	Dates Covered	No. of Rolls
Rondorf -Darmstadt-	evKB	Darmstadt	1808-1875	7
Rondorf -Hanau-	STA	Marburg	1811-1812	1
Rondorf -Marburg-	AG	Marburg	1753-1807	1
Rotenburg	STA AG evKB	Marburg Braach	1729-1964	36
Rotensee	AG	Marburg	1839-1876	1
Rott -Biedenkopf-	LG	Marburg	1754-1874	3
Rothenberg	evKB	Darmstadt	1810-1875	5
Rothenkirchen	STA	Marburg	1811-1812	1
Röthges	Kirchen	Darmstadt	1808-1875	2
Rüdesheim	rkKB	Mainz	1756-1791	1
Rüdigheim -Hanau-	AG	Marburg	1759-1808	1
Rudlos	evKB	Darmstadt	1820-1875	1
Ruhlkirchen	KB rkKB	Darmstadt Mainz	1731-1876	6
Rumpenheim -Offenb.-	STA	Marburg	1811-1812	1
Ruppertsburg	Kirchen	Darmstadt	1808-1875	3
Rüsselsheim	evKB rkKB	Darmstadt Mainz	1600-1930	15
Ruttershausen	evKB	Darmstadt	1808-1875	11
Saasen -Fritzlar-	AG	Marburg	1764-1807	1
Saasen -Giessen-	evKB	Darmstadt	1808-1875	8
Sachsenberg	KG	Marburg	1807-1895	1
Sachsenhausen -Waldeck-	Justizamt	Marburg	1815-1881	2
Salmünster	Justizamt LRA	Marburg	1718-1869	1

Location	Nature of Material	Where Filmed	Dates Covered	No. of Rolls
Sand	STA	Marburg	1808-1812	1
Sandbach	evLutKB	Darmstadt	1808-1875	11
Sandlofs	KB evKB	Darmstadt	1808-1875	3
Sannerz	Justizamt	Marburg	1806-1832	3
Sarnau	Justizamt	Marburg	1822-1883	1
Schaafheim	Kirchen	Darmstadt	1788-1875	7
Schachten	Justizamt	Marburg	1815-1874	1
Schachau	Justizamt	Marburg	1792-1898	4
Schemmern	STA	Marburg	1808-1812	1
Scheklengsfeld	Justizamt STA	Marburg	1784-1875	12
Schiffelbach	Justizamt	Marburg	1808-1874	1
Schlierbach -Bergstr.-	Kirchen	Darmstadt	1808-1875	9
Schlierbach -Dieburg-	Kirchen	Darmstadt	1788-1875	7
Schlitz	Kirchen	Darmstadt	1808-1875	9
Schlüchtern	Justizamt	Marburg	1659-1875	55
Schnellrode	AG	Marburg	1837-1880	1
Schneppenhausen	evLutKB	Darmstadt	1808-1875	4
Schöllenbach	rkKB	Freiburg	1660-1903	8
Schönau	Justizamt	Marburg	1800-1845	2
Schöneberg	Justizamt	Marburg	1835-1871	1
Schöneck	Justizamt	Marburg	1811-1812	1
Schönstadt	STA AG	Marburg	1808-1830	3
Schotten	Kirchen	Darmstadt	1808-1875	13
Schrecksbach	STA	Marburg	1824-1883	2
Schreufa	STA	Marburg	1808-1813	1
Schröck	Justizamt	Marburg	1756-1809	1

Location	Nature of Material	Where Filmed	Dates Covered	No. of Rolls
Schwabendorf	STA	Marburg	1808-1809	1
Schwalefeld	AG	Marburg	1839-1893	2
Schwalheim	evKB Kirchen	Darmstadt	1833-1875	2
Schwanheim -Bergstr.-	STA	Darmstadt	1808-1875	4
Schwarz	Kirchen	Darmstadt	1808-1875	4
Schwarzbach	Justizamt	Marburg	1805-1875	2
Schwarzenberg	STA	Marburg	1808-1812	3
Schwarzenborn	Justizamt STA	Marburg	1737-1875	3
Schwarzenfels	Justizamt	Marburg	1723-1873	13
Schwarzenkasel	Justizamt	Marburg	1815-1875	2
Schweinsberg	Justizamt	Marburg	1783-1874	4
Schweinsbühl	Justizamt	Marburg	1835-1895	2
Schwicharts-hausen	Kirchen	Darmstadt	1808-1875	8
Sebbeterode	Justizamt	Marburg	1828-1845	1
Seckmauern	evKB	Darmstadt	1808-1875	11
Seeheim	evKB	Darmstadt	1808-1875	3
Seibeldorf	rkKB	Mainz	1731-1876	4
Seidenroth	STA	Marburg	1730-1821	1
Seifertshausen	STA	Marburg	1874-1875	1
Seligenstadt	evKB rkKB	Darmstadt Mainz	1590-1875	23
Sellnrod	evKB	Darmstadt	1808-1875	6
Selters	evKB	Darmstadt	1820-1875	2
Semd	evKB	Darmstadt	1808-1875	4
Sichertshausen	Justizamt	Marburg	1800-1821	1
Sieglos	Justizamt	Marburg	1827-1875	1
Sielen	Justizamt	Marburg	1814-1876	1
Sickenhofen	evKB	Darmstadt	1811-1875	2

Location	Nature of Material	Where Filmed	Dates Covered	No. of Rolls
Silberg	Justizamt	Marburg	1845-1870	2
Simmersbach	Justizamt STA	Marburg	1822-1875	4
Simmershausen -Kassel-	STA	Marburg	1808-1813	2
Sindersfeld	STA	Marburg	1808	1
Sippenshausen	STA	Marburg	1808-1812	1
Södel	evKB	Darmstadt	1808-1875	4
Solz	STA	Marburg	1808-1875	2
Somborn	STA	Marburg	1749-1875	2
Sondenbach	rkKB	Darmstadt	1810-1875	13
Sontra	Justizamt STA	Marburg	1722-1875	4
Sorga	STA	Marburg	1874-1875	1
Sprachbrücken	evKB	Darmstadt	1808-1875	4
Spangenberg	AG STA	Marburg	1756-1882	42
Speckswinkel	STA	Marburg	1808-1861	1
Spielberg	STA	Marburg	1874-1875	1
Sprendlingen	evKB	Darmstadt	1819-1875	6
Stachen	Kirchen	Darmstadt	1808-1875	3
Stammheim	STA	Darmstadt	1808-1875	4
Starkenburg	Diehl/ Wilhelm	Darmstadt	1928	1
Stammen	STA	Marburg	1808-1812	1
Stausebach	STA	Marburg	1808-1811	1
Steinau -Schleichten-	Justizamt	Marburg	1659-1879	23
Steinau -Dieberg-	evKB	Darmstadt	1808-1875	13
Steinbach -Giessen-	STA	Darmstadt	1808-1875	5
Steinfurth -Friedberg-	evKB STA	Darmstadt	1808-1875	4

Location	Nature of Material	Where Filmed	Dates Covered	No. of Rolls
Steinheim -Giessen-	STA	Darmstadt	1855-1875	1
Steinheim -Offenbach-	evKB rkKB	Darmstadt Mainz	1657-1876	20
Steinperf	AG	Marburg	1834-1870	2
Sterkelshausen	evKB	Frankfurt Oberellebach	1658-1964	9
Sterzhausen	STA	Marburg	1808-1871	1
Stockhausen -Lauterbach-	STA	Marburg	1808-1875	5
Stockheim -Büdingen-	STA	Marburg	1853-1875	1
Stockstadt	STA	Darmstadt	1808-1875	5
Stornbruch	AG	Marburg	1839-1898	1
Storndorf	STA	Darmstadt	1808-1875	5
Strebendorf	Kirchen	Darmstadt	1808-1875	4
Strothe	Justizamt	Marburg	1820-1899	2
Stumpertenrod	evKB	Darmstadt	1808-1875	7
Sudeck	Justizamt	Marburg	1839-1889	1
Sulzbach	evKB	Düsseldorf	1818-1874	3
Süss	STA	Marburg	1808-1812	1
Tann -Fulda-	Justizamt Gericht	Marburg	1664-1889	22
Thurnhosbach	STA	Marburg	1808-1812	1
Trais-Horloft	evKB	Darmstadt	1808-1875	5
Trais-Münzenberg	evKB	Darmstadt	1818-1875	2
Trebur	Kirchen	Darmstadt	1808-1875	7
Tries	Justizamt Kirchen	Marburg Darmstadt	1872-1881	8
Treisbach	STA	Marburg	1809-1811	1
Trendelberg	AG Justizamt	Marburg	1747-1824	4
Treysa	evKB Justizamt	Marburg Hamborn	1567-1902	32

Location	Nature of Material	Where Filmed	Dates Covered	No. of Rolls
Udenhausen	evLutKB	Darmstadt	1808-1875	8
Ueberau	evKB Kirchen	Darmstadt	1809-1875	8
Uensterode	STA	Marburg	1808-1811	1
Ulfen	Kirchen	Darmstadt	1808-1875	6
Ulfen	STA	Marburg	1808-1875	2
Ullershausen	Kirchen	Darmstadt	1808-1817	1
Ulrichstein	Kirchen	Darmstadt	1808-1875	4
Ungedenken	STA	Marburg	1808-1812	1
Unshausen	STA	Marburg	1808-1812	1
Unter-Morsau	evKB	Darmstadt	1849-1875	2
Unter-Schönmattenwang	rkKB KB	Darmstadt Mainz	1743-1875	10
Unter-Seibertenrod	Kirchen	Darmstadt	1856-1875	1
Unter-Wegfurth	Kirchen	Darmstadt	1808-1832	1
Untertraun	STA	Marburg	1874-1875	1
Unterreichen-bach	STA	Marburg	1874-1875	1
Unterrosphe	Justizamt	Marburg	1787-1796	1
Urberach	Kirchen rkKB	Darmstadt Mainz	1808-1876	8
Usenborn	Kirchen	Darmstadt	1808-1875	3
Usingen	Steinmetr. E.G.	Usingen Its.	1927	1
Usseln	Justizamt	Marburg	1839-1864	1
Uttrichshausen	Synagoguen	Marburg	1837-1873	1
Vaake	STA	Marburg	1808-1818	1
Vadenrod	Kirchen	Darmstadt	1831-1875	1
Veckerhagen	Justizamt	Marburg	1767-1879	26
Velmeden	STA	Marburg	1808-1812	1

Location	Nature of Material	Where Filmed	Dates Covered	No. of Rolls
Vernawahlhansen	STA	Marburg	1808-1812	1
Vielbrunn	Kirchen	Darmstadt	1808-1875	5
Viermünden	Justizamt	Marburg	1734-1813	1
Viernheim	rkKB STA	Mainz Darmstadt	1627-1876	16
Viesebeck	STA	Marburg	1808-1812	1
Villingen	evKB	Darmstadt	1808-1875	6
Vochenrod	rkKB	Mainz	1731-1876	4
Vocherode	evKB AG	Alsterode Marburg	1630-1968	8
Volkartshain	evKB	Darmstadt	1808-1875	2
Volkershausen	Justizamt STA	Marburg	1808-1875	2
Volkmarsen	Justizamt STA rkKB	Marburg Detmold	1808-1879	8
Vollmarshausen	STA	Marburg	1808-1813	1
Wabern	STA	Marburg	1808-1812	1
Wachenbuch	STA	Marburg	1811-1812 1849-1869	1
Wächtersbach	Justizamt STA	Marburg	1774-1875	22
Wahlen -Alsfeld-	Kirchen	Darmstadt	1808-1875	4
Walburg	Justizamt STA	Marburg	1808-1861	2
Wald-Amorbach	evKB	Darmstadt	1808-1875	1
Waldenberg	STA	Marburg	1874-1875	1
Waldkappel	STA	Marburg	1808-1811	1
Wald-Mittelbach	rkKB evKB	Mainz Darmstadt	1698-1881	22
Wahlau	Justizamt	Marburg	1830-1868	3
Walldorf	evKB	Darmstadt	1808-1875	2
Wallenrod	evKB	Darmstadt	1808-1875	4

Location	Nature of Material	Where Filmed	Dates Covered	No. of Rolls
Wallernhausen	evKB	Darmstadt	1830-1875	3
Wallersdorf	evKB	Darmstadt	1808-1875	8
Wallerstädten	evKB	Darmstadt	1808-1875	3
Walroth	Justizamt	Marburg	1692-1822	1
Waltersbrück	Justizamt STA	Marburg	1792-1912	2
Wanfried	STA	Marburg	1754-1833	3
Warzenbach	STA	Marburg	1808-1868	1
Wasenberg	Justizamt	Marburg	1828-1845	1
Wathenheim	rkKB STA	Mainz Darmstadt	1676-1886	4
Watzenborn	STA	Darmstadt	1861	1
Watzen- Steinheim	Kirchen	Darmstadt	1808-1875	5
Wechesheim	evKB	Darmstadt	1808-1875	2
Wehrda -Hünfeld-	Justizamt STA	Marburg	1808-1875	3
Wehrda -Marburg-	Justizamt	Marburg	1814-1882	4
Wehru	STA	Marburg	1808-1812	1
Wehrhausen	Justizamt	Marburg	1831-1881	1
Weidelbach -Dillkreis-	STA	Marburg	1808-1812	1
Weidelbach -Melsungen-	Justizamt	Marburg	1869	1
Weiden	Justizamt	Marburg	1823-1875	1
Weifenbach	Justizamt	Marburg	1832-1869	1
Weilburg	evKB MKB	Hannover	1867-1920	1
Weimar	STA	Marburg	1808-1812	1
Weipoldshausen	AG	Marburg	1862-1873	1
Weiskirchen	Kirchen	Darmstadt	1808-1875	2
Weisskirchen	rkKB	Mainz	1690-1876	3

Location	Nature of Material	Where Filmed	Dates Covered	No. of Rolls
Weissenborn -Eschwege-	STA	Marburg	1808-1810	1
Weitershausen	Justizamt	Marburg	1840	1
Weiterstadt	Kirchen	Darmstadt	1808-1875	4
Weiershausen	Justizamt	Marburg	1837-1869	1
Welkers	AG	Marburg	1812	1
Welleringhausen	AG	Marburg	1840-1899	1
Wellingerode	evKB	Ulsterode	1716-1968	4
Wendershausen	STA	Marburg	1808-1812	1
Wenings	STA	Darmstadt	1818-1875	7
Wenkbach	AG	Marburg	1809-1812	1
Werleshausen	evLutKB	Bielefeld	1668-1907	2
Wermertshausen	Justizamt	Marburg	1814-1844	1
Wernges	evLutKB	Darmstadt	1808-1875	2
Wersau	STA	Darmstadt	1808-1875	4
Wertuffeln	Justizamt STA	Marburg	1806-1874	3
Wetter	Justizamt	Marburg	1627-1874	34
Wetterfeld	STA	Darmstadt	1808-1875	3
Wettertal	evKB	Darmstadt	1808-1875	2
Wettesingen	STa	Marburg	1808-1812	1
Wettges	Justizamt	Marburg	1840-1882	1
Wetzlar	evKB MKB	Berlin-Dahlem Hannover	1741-1945	3
Weyhers	Justizamt	Marburg	1715-1878	53
Wichmannshausen	STA	Marburg	1739-1812	2
Wichte	STA	Marburg	1809-1811	1
Wickerode	STA	Marburg	1808-1811	1
Wickersrode	STA	Marburg	1808-1812	1
Wiera	Justizamt	Marburg	1795-1895	1
Wiesbaden	rkKB	Mainz	1596-1908	4

Location	Nature of Material	Where Filmed	Dates Covered	No. of Rolls
Wiesbaden	Church of England Roy Brung	Eibenstock London	1848-1876	2
Wiesbaden	evKB MKB	Hannover	1867-1919	4
Wiesenbach	Justizamt	Marburg	1803-1874	1
Willingshausen	Synagoguen Justizamt	Marburg	1793-1873	2
Willershausen -Eschu-	STA	Marburg	1808-1812	1
Willingen	Justizamt	Marburg	1838-1875	3
Willofs -Lauterbach-	evKB	Darmstadt	1808-1875	4
Windhausen	evKB	Darmstadt	1842-1875	2
Wingershausen	evKB	Darmstadt	1808-1875	4
Winner	Justizamt	Marburg	1810-1845	1
Winnerod	Kirchen	Darmstadt	1808-1875	2
Winterhasten	evKB	Darmstadt	1808-1875	7
Winterscheid	Justizamt	Marburg	1827-1845	1
Wipperode	STA	Marburg	1808-1809	1
Wippershaim	AG	Marburg	1825-1874	1
Wirminghausen	Justizamt	Marburg	1837-1882	2
Wirtheim	STA	Marburg	1874-1875	1
Wissels	STA	Marburg	1813	1
Wittelsberg	Justizamt	Marburg	1768-1865	4
Witzenhausen	AG STA	Marburg	1761-1874	31
Wixhausen	Kirchen	Darmstadt	1808-1875	4
Wohnbach	evKB	Darmstadt	1808-1875	2
Wohra	STA	Marburg	1808-1813	1
Wolf	Kirchen	Darmstadt	1818-1875	3
Wolferborn	STA	Marburg	1874-1875	1
Wolferode	STA	Marburg	1808-1812	1

Location	Nature of Material	Where Filmed	Dates Covered	No. of Rolls
Wolfershausen	AG evKB STA	Marburg Hamborn	1715-1876	4
Wölfershausen	STA	Marburg	1808-1811	1
Wölfersheim	evKB	Darmstadt	1808-1875	1
Wolfhagen	Justizamt	Marburg	1808-1875	8
Wölfersheim	Kirchen	Darmstadt	1808-1875	2
Wolfshausen	Justizamt	Marburg	1865-1873	1
Wolfshausen	Justizamt	Marburg	1850-1873	1
Wolfskehlen	evKB	Darmstadt	1808-1875	4
Wolfterode	STA	Marburg	1808-1810	1
Wölfterode	STA	Marburg	1808-1812	1
Wolfgruben	LG	Marburg	1828-1853	2
Wollmar	Justizamt	Marburg	1808-1814	1
Wollrode	STA	Marburg	1808-1812	2
Wolzhausen	LRA	Marburg	1839-1866	4
Wommen	Justizamt	Marburg	1865	1
Worfelden	evKB	Darmstadt	1858-1875	1
Zeilhard	Kirchen	Darmstadt	1808-1824	1
Zella	STA	Marburg	1808-1812	1
Zellhausen	rkKB	Darmstadt Mainz	1773-1876	7
Ziegenhagen	STA	Marburg	1808-1812	1
Ziegenhain	Justizamt	Marburg	1794-1866	20
Zeilbach	Kirchen	Darmstadt	1856-1875	1
Zierenberg	Justizamt STA	Marburg	1792-1876	14
Zimmersrode	STA	Marburg	1809-1921	2
Zwerge	Justizamt	Marburg	1819-1874	2
Zwestern	STA	Marburg	1809-1921	2
Zwingenberg	STA	Darmstadt	1808-1875	5

NIEDERSACHSEN

Location	Nature of Material	Where Filmed	Dates Covered	No. of Rolls
Achim -Wolfenbüttel-	ZSR BM	Wolfenbüttel	1809-1813	1
Aderhausen	ZSR BM	Wolfenbüttel	1809-1813	1
Ahlshausen	ZSR BM	Wolfenbüttel	1809-1813	1
Ahlum	ZSR BM	Wolfenbüttel	1808-1814	1
Altenoythe	rkKB	Münster	1669-1802	2
Altenoythe	rkKB	Münster	1749	1
Altgandersheim	ZSR BM	Wolfenbüttel	1809-1813	1
Alversdorf	ZSR BM	Wolfenbüttel	1808-1814	1
Ammensen	ZSR BM	Wolfenbüttel	1809-1813	1
Ampleben	ZSR BM	Wolfenbüttel	1808-1814	1
Anderten -Hannover-	evKB	Hannover	1640-1895	1
Apelnstedt	ZSR BM	Wolfenbüttel	1808-1814	1
Aschendorf	rkKB		1750	1
Astfeld	ZSR BM	Wolfenbüttel	1808-1812	1
Aurich	KB	Berlin-Dahlen	1677-1784	1
Aurich	MilKB	Hannover	1866-1914	1
Bad Gundersheim	ZSR BM	Wolfenbüttel	1808-1813	1
Bad Gundersheim	JüdGem	Wolfenbüttel	1775-1852	1
Bad Harzburg	ZSR BM	Wolfenbüttel	1808-1814	1
Bad Sachsa	evKB	Bielefeld	1637-1952	1
Badenhausen	ZSR BM	Wolfenbüttel	1808-1813	1

Location	Nature of Material	Where Filmed	Dates Covered	No. of Rolls
Bahrdorf	ZSR BM	Wolfenbüttel	1808-1813	1
Bakum	rkKB		1749	1
Bansleben	ZSR BM	Wolfenbüttel	1810-1813	1
Barbecke	ZSR BM	Wolfenbüttel	1808-1813	1
Barmke	ZSR BM	Wolfenbüttel	1808-1812	1
Barnstorf -Wolfenbüttel-	ZSR BM	Wolfenbüttel	1808-1814	
Barssel	rkKB	Münster	1651-1900	2
Bartshausen	ZSR BM	Wolfenbüttel	1810-1813	1
Beckedorf	LDS records	Salt Lake City	1923-1929	1
Beedenbostel	Heer	Salt Lake City	1606	2
Beierstedt	ZSR BM	Wolfenbüttel	1808-1814	1
Bemerode	evKB	Hannover	1546-1904	1
Bentrierode	ZSR BM	Wolfenbüttel	1808-1814	2
Berel	ZSR BM	Wolfenbüttel	1808-1813	1
Bergen -Celle-	Heer	Salt Lake City	1606	2
Bergen -Celle-	Tax list	Salt Lake City	1511	1
Bersenbrück	Kirchen	Salt Lake City	1201-1300	1
Bessingen	ZSR BM	Wolfenbüttel	1810-1811	6
Bettingerode	ZSR BM	Wolfenbüttel	1808-1812	1
Bettmar	ZSR BM	Wolfenbüttel	1808-1813	1
Beulshausen	ZSR BM	Wolfenbüttel	1809-1813	1

Location	Nature of Material	Where Filmed	Dates Covered	No. of Rolls
Bevenrode	ZSR BM	Wolfenbüttel	1808-1914	1
Bevern -Holzminden-	Gericht	Wolfenbüttel	1811-1812	1
Billerbeck -Gandersheim-	ZSR BM	Wolfenbüttel	1809-1813	1
Bippen	evKB	Salt Lake City	1728-1731	1
Bockel -Soltau-	Tax record	Salt Lake City	1598	1
Bodenburg -Hildesheim-	ZSR BM	Wolfenbüttel	1808-1813	2
Bodenstein	ZSR BM	Wolfenbüttel	1808-1812	1
Bodenteich	evLutKB	Uelzen	1604-1963	2
Boimsdorf	ZSR BM	Wolfenbüttel	1808-1814	1
Bokeloh	rkKB		1749	1
Börger	rkKB		1748, 1750	1
Bornhausen	ZSR BM	Wolfenbüttel	1808-1812	1
Bornum -Gandersheim-	ZSR BM	Wolfenbüttel	1808-1813	1
Bornum -Helmstedt-	ZSR BM	Wolfenbüttel	1808-1813	1
Bortfeld	ZSR BM	Wolfenbüttel	1808-1813	1
Bröckeln	ZSR BM	Wolfenbüttel	1809-1810	1
Broistedt	ZSR BM	Wolfenbüttel	1808-1814	1
Bruchhof	ZSR BM	Wolfenbüttel	1809-1813	1
Brunsen	ZSR BM	Wolfenbüttel	1809-1812	1
Bückeburg	evMilKB	Hannover	1816-1926	2
Bündheim	ZSR BM	Wolfenbüttel	1808-1813	1

Location	Nature of Material	Where Filmed	Dates Covered	No. of Rolls
Burgdorf -Wolfenbüttel-	ZSR BM	Wolfenbüttel	1808-1813	1
Cappeln	rkKB	Münster	1660-1900	2
Celle	LDS records	Salt Lake City	1931-1948	1
Celle	MilKB	Hannover	1757-1942	2
Celle	Census	Salt Lake City	1664	1
Cloppenburg	rkKB	Münster	1613-1885	2
Clus	ZSR BM	Wolfenbüttel	1810-1813	1
Cramme	ZSR BM	Wolfenbüttel	1808-1814	1
Cremlingen	ZSR BM	Wolfenbüttel	1808-1814	1
Damme	rkKB	Münster	1560-1910	1
Damme	ZSR STA	Münster	1808-1812	1
Dankelsheim	ZSR BM	Wolfenbüttel	1810-1813	1
Dannhausen	ZSR BM	Wolfenbüttel	1808-1812	1
Dedelsdorf	MilKB	Hannover	1938-1943	1
Delligsen	ZSR BM	Wolfenbüttel	1810-1812	1
Denstorf	ZSR BM	Wolfenbüttel	1808-1813	1
Destedt	ZSR BM	Wolfenbüttel	1808-1812	1
Dettum	ZSR BM	Wolfenbüttel	1808-1814	1
Dielmissen	JüdGem BM	Wolfenbuttel	1810-1813	1
Dinklage	rkKB	Münster	1668-1884	1
Dissen -Kr. Osnabrück-	evKB	Detmold	1814-1839	2
Dobbeln	ZSR BM	Wolfenbüttel	1808-1813	1

Location	Nature of Material	Where Filmed	Dates Covered	No. of Rolls
Eicklingen	Heer	Salt Lake City	1606	1
Eimen	ZSR BM	Wolfenbüttel	1809-1813	1
Einbeck	MilKB	Hannover	1868-1896	1
Eitzum -Wolfenbüttel-	ZSR BM	Wolfenbüttel	1808-1814	1
Ellierode -Gandersheim-	ZSR BM	Wolfenbüttel	1809-1812	1
Emden	LDS records	Salt Lake City	1931-1938	1
Emden	evMilKB	Hannover	1867-1876	1
Emmerstedt	ZSR BM	Wolfenbüttel	1808-1814	1
Emsteck	rkKB	Münster	1630-1908	1
Emtinghausen	ZSR BM	Wolfenbüttel	1811-1812	1
Engelnstedt -Saltzgitter-	ZSR BM	Wolfenbüttel	1808-1813	1
Erkerode	ZSR BM	Wolfenbüttel	1808-1814	1
Erzhausen	ZSR BM	Wolfenbüttel	1809-1813	1
Esbeck	ZSR BM	Wolfenbüttel	1808-1814	1
Eschershausen -Holzminden-	ZSR JüdGem	Wolfenbüttel	1773-1876	3
Essen	rkKB		1749	1
Essen -Cloppenburg-	rkKB	Münster	1758-1900	1
Esterwegen	rkKB		1749	1
Evesen	evKB	Detmold	1809-1874	1
Evessen	ZSR BM	Wolfenbüttel	1808-1813	1
Fallingbostel		Salt Lake City	1528	1
Fintel	KB	Hamburg	1820-1905	2
Freden	ZSR BM	Wolfenbüttel	1808-1814	1

Location	Nature of Material	Where Filmed	Dates Covered	No. of Rolls
Frellstedt	ZSR BM	Wolfenbüttel	1808-1814	1
Frestorf	evKB	Detmold	1808-1813	1
Friesoythe	rkKB	Münster	1675-1900	2
Fümmelsee	ZSR BM	Wolfenbüttel	1808-1814	1
Fürstenau	ZSR BM	Wolfenbüttel	1808-1813	1
Garbsen	evKB	Hannover	1661-1934	1
Garlebsen	ZSR BM	Wolfenbüttel	1809-1813	1
Garrel	rkKB	Münster	1799-1900	1
Gehrde	evKB	Salt Lake City	1713-1808	1
Gehrenrode	ZSR BM	Wolfenbüttel	1809-1813	1
Geitelde	ZSR BM	Wolfenbüttel	1808-1813	1
Gevensleben	ZSR BM	Wolfenbüttel	1808-1813	1
Gilzum	ZSR BM	Wolfenbüttel	1808-1813	1
Gittelde	ZSR BM	Wolfenbüttel	1808-1814	1
Glentorf	evKB	Detmold	1776-1948	1
Goldbeck -K. Schaumburg-	evKB	Bielefeld	1776-1948	3
Godenstedt	rkKB	Münster	1740-1909	3
Goslar	LDS records	Salt Lake City	1946-1949	1
Goslar	MilKB	Hannover	1867-1934	2
Göttingen	LDS records	Salt Lake City	1927-1930	1
Göttingen	MilKB	Hannover	1869-1944	1
Grafhorst	ZSR BM	Wolfenbüttel	1808-1812	1
Grasleben	ZSR BM	Wolfenbüttel	1808-1813	2

Location	Nature of Material	Where Filmed	Dates Covered	No. of Rolls
Greene	ZSR BM	Wolfenbüttel	1808-1813	1
Gremsheim	ZSR BM	Wolfenbüttel	1808-1813	1
Gross Aschen	evKB	Detmold	1808-1874	1
Gross Berssen	rkKB		1749	1
Gross Dahlum	ZSR BM	Wolfenbüttel	1808-1814	1
Gross Denkte	ZSR BM	Wolfenbüttel	1808-1814	1
Gross Gleidingen	ZSR BM	Wolfenbüttel	1808-1813	2
Gross Lobke	evKB	Hannover	1854-1874	1
Gross Steinum	ZSR BM	Wolfenbüttel	1808-1814	1
Gross Twülpstedt	ZSR BM	Wolfenbüttel	1808-1814	1
Gross Vahlberg	ZSR BM	Wolfenbüttel	1814	1
Gross Winnigstedt	ZSR BM	Wolfenbüttel	1808-1814	1
Hachum	ZSR BM	Wolfenbüttel	1808-1813	1
Hahausen	ZSR BM	Wolfenbüttel	1808-1813	1
Haieshausen	ZSR BM	Wolfenbüttel	1809-1813	1
Halle -Holzminden-	ZSR BM	Wolfenbüttel	1808-1812	1
Hallendorf	ZSR BM	Wolfenbüttel	1808-1813	1
Hallensen	ZSR BM	Wolfenbüttel	1808-1813	1
Hameln	LDS records	Salt Lake City	1931-1934	1
Hameln	evLutKB	Hannover	1696-1852	3
Hannover	LDS records		1907-1951	6
Hannover	Heer -casualties-	Hannover	1914-1918	2

Location	Nature of Material	Where Filmed	Dates Covered	No. of Rolls
Hannover	evKB -various churches-	Hannover	1538-1959	462
Hannover	evMKB	Hannover	1690-1945	22
Hannover	ZSR	Hannover	1810-1813	10
Hanstedt	evLutKB	Salt Lake City	1770-1919	1
Harderode	ZSR BM	Wolfenbüttel	1810	1
Haren	rkKB	Münster	1749	1
Harkebrügge	rkKB	Münster	1867-1875	1
Harlingerode	ZSR BM	Wolfenbüttel	1808-1814	1
Harrienstedt	evLutKB	Detmold	1808-1874	2
Harvesse	ZSR BM	Wolfenbüttel	1808-1813	1
Haselünne	rkKB		1749	1
Heckenbeck	ZSR BM	Wolfenbüttel	1808-1813	2
Hedeper	ZSR BM	Wolfenbüttel	1808-1814	1
Helilen	ZSR BM	Wolfenbüttel	1809-1810	2
Helmscherode	ZSR BM	Wolfenbüttel	1809-1813	1
Helmstedt	ZSR BM	Wolfenbüttel	1808-1814	4
Helmstedt	JüdGem	Wolfenbüttel	1847-1874	1
Hemkenrode	ZSR BM		1808-1812	1
Herzlake	rkKB		1749	1
Herseke -Bersenbrüch-	rkKB		1750	1
Hildesheim	LDS records	Salt Lake City	1931-1934	1
Hildesheim	MilKB	Hannover	1803-1921	4

Location	Nature of Material	Where Filmed	Dates Covered	No. of Rolls
Hobe	ZSR BM	Wolfenbüttel	1809	1
Hohenassel	ZSR BM	Wolfenbüttel	1808-1813	1
Hoiersdorf	ZSR BM	Wolfenbüttel	1809-1814	1
Holdenstedt	evLutKB	Uelzen	1708-1962	7
Holdorf	rkKB	Münster	1790-1885	2
Holte-Lastrup	rkKB	Münster	1750	2
Holzminden	JüdGem	Wolfenbüttel	1839-1876	1
Holzminden	ZSR BM	Wolfenbüttel	1808-1814	1
Holzminden	evLutMilKB	Berlin-Dahlem	1913-1919	1
Hordorf	ZSR BM	Wolfenbüttel	1808-1814	1
Hornburg	ZSR BM	Wolfenbüttel	1808-1814	1
Hötzum	ZSR BM	Wolfenbüttel	1808-1812	1
Ildehausen	ZSR BM	Wolfenbüttel	1808-1813	2
Ippensen	ZSR BM	Wolfenbüttel	1809-1813	1
Jemgum	Heer	Groningen	1813	1
Jerxheim	ZSR BM	Wolfenbüttel	1808-1813	1
Jever	rkKB	Münster	1782-1905	2
Kaierde	ZSR BM	Wolfenbüttel	1809-1812	1
Kalme	ZSR BM	Wolfenbüttel	1809-1812	1
Kemnade	ZSR BM	Wolfenbüttel	1809-1812	1
Kettenkamp	Tax records	Salt Lake City	1721-1722	1
Kirchberg	ZSR BM	Wolfenbüttel	1808-1813	1

Location	Nature of Material	Where Filmed	Dates Covered	No. of Rolls
Kirchweyel -Velzen-	evLutKB	Uelzen	1669-1962	3
Kissenbrück	ZSR BM	Wolfenbüttel	1808-1814	1
Klein Berssen	rkKB		1749	1
Klein Dahlum	ZSR BM	Wolfenbüttel	1808-1813	1
Klein Denkte	ZSR BM	Wolfenbüttel	1808-1814	1
Klein Drehle	Census	Salt Lake City	1658-1659	1
Klein Gleidingen	ZSR BM	Wolfenbüttel	1808-1813	1
Klein Lobke	evKB	Hannover	1854-1874	1
Klein Winnigstedt	ZSR BM	Wolfenbüttel	1808-1814	1
Kleinenheerse	evKB	Detmold	1808-1874	2
Kneitlingen	ZSR BM	Wolfenbüttel	1808-1814	1
Königslutter	JüdGem	Wolfenbüttel	1872-1874	2
Kreinsen	ZSR BM	Wolfenbüttel	1809-1813	1
Krückeberg	evLutKB	Detmold	1808-1874	4
Küblingen	ZSR BM	Wolfenbüttel	1808-1814	2
Lamme	ZSR BM	Wolfenbüttel	1808-1813	2
Langelsheim	ZSR BM	Wolfenbüttel	1809-1813	2
Langförden	rkKB	Münster	1652-1900	3
Lastrup -Cloppenburg-	rkKB	Münster	1656-1876	2
Lathen	rkKB		1749	1
Lauingen	ZSR BM	Wolfenbüttel	1808-1814	1
Leerort	KB	The Hague	1654-1744	1

Location	Nature of Material	Where Filmed	Dates Covered	No. of Rolls
Lehmke	evLutKB	Uelzen	1708-1962	2
Lehre	ZSR	Braunschwieg	1808-1812	2
Leinde	ZSR BM	Wolfenbüttel	1808-1814	1
Lelm	ZSR BM	Wolfenbüttel	1813-1814	1
Linden -Saltzgitter-	ZSR BM	Wolfenbüttel	1811	1
Lindern	ZSR BM	Wolfenbüttel	1809-1814	1
Lindern -Kr. Cloppenburg-	rkKB	Münster	1651-1876	1
Lindern -Löningen-	rkKB		1750	1
Lingen	MilKB	Hannover	1800-1902	1
Lohne	rkKB	Münster	1683-1902	1
Löningen	rkKB	Münster	1639-1907	3
Lotup	rkKB		1749	1
Lüneburg	LDS records	Salt Lake City	1931-1948	1
Lüneburg	evMilKB	Hannover	1652-1937	2
Lutten	rkKB	Münster	1674-1905	2
Lutter -Gandersheim-	ZSR BM	Wolfenbüttel	1808-1813	2
Mackendorf	ZSR BM	Wolfenbüttel	1808-1813	1
Mahlum	ZSR BM	Wolfenbüttel	1808-1812	1
Mariental	ZSR BM	Wolfenbüttel	1808-1812	1
Markhausen	rkKB	Münster	1697-1912	2
Mascherode	ZSR	Wolfenbüttel	1808-1812	1
Meerdorf -Braunschweig-	ZSR	Wolfenbüttel	1808-1813	1
Meinkot	ZSR BM	Wolfenbüttel	1808-1813	1

Location	Nature of Material	Where Filmed	Dates Covered	No. of Rolls
Menslage	evLutKB	Salt Lake City	1694-1724	1
Meppen	rkKB		1749	1
Misburg	evLutKB	Hannover	1642-1885	1
Molbergen	rkKB	Münster	1683-1903	2
Molzen	evLutKB	Uelzen	1733-1962	2
Mönchevahlberg	ZSR BM	Wolfenbüttel	1808-1814	2
Münchehagen	LDS records	Salt Lake City	1929-1949	1
Münchehof	ZSR	Wolfenbüttel	1808-1813	1
Münden	evMilKB	Hannover	1901-1920	2
Münster	evMilKB	Hannover	1898-1919	1
Naesen	ZSR BM	Wolfenbüttel	1808-1813	1
Natendorf	evLutKB	Salt Lake City	1770-1919	1
Neindorf	ZSR BM	Wolfenbüttel	1809-1814	1
Nettelhamp	evLutKB	Uelzen	1709-1962	3
Neu Büddenstedt	ZSR BM	Wolfenbüttel	1808-1814	1
Neubruch	ZSR BM	Wolfenbüttel	1809-1812	1
Neuerkirchen -Bersenbrück-	Census	Salt Lake City	1658-1859	1
Neuerkirchen -Vechta-	rkKB	Münster	1651-1900	1
Neuerkirchen -Vechta-	ZSR STA	Münster	1808-1811	1
Neuhof -Blankenburg-	ZSR BM	Wolfenbüttel	1809-1813	1
Nordassel	ZSR BM	Wolfenbüttel	1808-1813	1
Nordsteimke	ZSR BM	Wolfenbüttel	1808-1813	1
Nordheim	evLutKB	Hannover	1867-1941	1

Location	Nature of Material	Where Filmed	Dates Covered	No. of Rolls
Nortrup	Census	Salt Lake City	1659	1
Obeisickle	ZSR BM	Wolfenbüttel	1808-1811	1
Offleben	ZSR BM	Wolfenbüttel	1808-1814	1
Oker	ZSR BM	Wolfenbüttel	1808-1813	1
Ölber Am Weissen Wege	ZSR BM	Wolfenbüttel	1808-1814	1
Oldenburg	rkKB	Münster	1787-1902	1
Oldenburg	evMilKB	Hannover	1868-1938	2
Oldenstadt	evLutKB	Uelzen	1655-1960	2
Olxheim	ZSR BM	Wolfenbüttel	1808-1813	1
Opperhausen	ZSR BM	Wolfenbüttel	1808-1813	1
Oppershausen	ZSR BM	Wolfenbüttel	1809	1
Ortshausen	ZSR BM	Wolfenbüttel	1808-1813	1
Orxhausen	ZSR BM	Wolfenbüttel	1808-1813	1
Osnabrück	Urkunden- buch	Salt Lake City	1201-1300	1
Osnabrück	MilKB	Hannover	1762-1821	1
Ostharingen	ZSR BM	Wolfenbüttel	1808-1813	1
Ottenstein	JüdGem	Wolfenbüttel	1768-1876	1
Ottenstein	ZSR BM	Wolfenbüttel	1809-1813	1
Papenburg	rkKB		1749	1
Parsan	ZSR BM	Wolfenbüttel	1808-1813	1
Pölilde	Historical description	Berlin-Dahlen	publ. 1707	2
Quakenbrück	evLutKB	Salt Lake City	1667-1775	1

Location	Nature of Material	Where Filmed	Dates Covered	No. of Rolls
Räbke	ZSR BM	Wolfenbüttel	1808-1813	1
Ramsloh	rkKB	Münster	1660-1910	3
Rätzlingen	evLutKB	Uelzen	1545-1963	2
Rautheim	ZSR STA	Wolfenbüttel	1808-1814	1
Reinsdorf -Helmstedt	ZSR BM	Wolfenbüttel	1808-1814	2
Remlingen	ZSR	Wolfenbüttel	1808-1814	1
Rickensdorf	ZSR BM	Wolfenbüttel	1808-1813	1
Rieseberg	ZSR BM	Wolfenbüttel	1808-1814	1
Rittierode	ZSR	Wolfenbüttel	1809-1813	1
Rosche	evLutKB accounts	Uelzen	1638-1964	3
Rotenkamp	ZSR STA	Wolfenbüttel	1808-1813	2
Rüningen	ZSR STA	Wolfenbüttel	1808-1812	1
Runstedt	ZSR STA	Wolfenbüttel	1808-1809	1
Saalsdorf	ZSR STA	Wolfenbüttel	1808-1813	1
Salzbergen	rkKB		1749	1
Salzdahlum	ZSR	Wolfenbüttel	1808-1814	1
Salzgitter	ZSR BM	Wolfenbüttel	1808-1814	13
Salzgitter	evKB	Wolfenbüttel	1809-1814	1
Sampleben	ZSR STA	Wolfenbüttel	1808-1814	1
Samingen	ZSR STA	Wolfenbüttel	1808-1813	1
Scharrel -Cloppenburg-	rkKB	Münster	1654-1876	2

Location	Nature of Material	Where Filmed	Dates Covered	No. of Rolls
Scheppau	ZSR STA	Wolfenbüttel	1808-1813	1
Schepsdorf- Sohne	rkKB		1749	1
Schichelsheim -Sandersheim-	ZSR BM	Wolfenbüttel	1813-1814	1
Schlewecke	ZSR BM	Wolfenbüttel	1808-1814	1
Schneverdingen	evLutKB	Hamburg	1642-1877	2
Schoningen	ZSR BM	Wolfenbüttel	1808-1814	2
Schoningen	JüdGem	Wolfenbüttel	1818-1876	1
Schöppenstedt	ZSR STA	Wolfenbüttel	1808-1814	1
Schulenrode	ZSR BM	Wolfenbüttel	1808-1814	1
Seesen	ZSR BM	Wolfenbüttel	1809	1
Seinstedt	ZSR BM	Wolfenbüttel	1809-1814	1
Semmenstedt	ZSR BM	Wolfenbüttel	1808-1814	1
Senlingen	rkKB	Kirchheim	1790-1843	1
Sieboldshausen	ZSR BM	Wolfenbüttel	1809-1813	1
Siersse	ZSR BM	Wolfenbüttel	1808-1813	1
Sögel	rkKB		1749	1
Söllingen	ZSR BM	Wolfenbüttel	1808-1814	1
Sonnenberg	ZSR STA	Braunschweig	1808-1811	1
Sottmar	ZSR BM	Wolfenbüttel	1808-1813	1
Stade	LDS records	Salt Lake City	1931-1948	1
Stade	Swedish military records	Stockholm	1695	2

Location	Nature of Material	Where Filmed	Dates Covered	No. of Rolls
Stade	evMilKB	Hannover	1756-1919	2
Stadthagen	LDS records	Salt Lake City	1931-1948	1
Stadtoldendorf	JüdGem	Wolfenbüttel	1774-1876	1
Stederdorf	evLutKB	Uelzen	1711-1962	2
Steinfeld -Vechta-	rkKB	Münster	1662-1903	3
Stiddien	ZSR BM	Wolfenbüttel	1808-1813	1
Stöcken -Braunschweig-	evLutKB	Hannover	1661-1934	1
Stöckheim	ZSR	Wolfenbüttel	1808-1813	1
Stroit	ZSR BM	Wolfenbüttel	1809-1812	1
Strücklingen	rkKB	Münster	1703-1900	2
Suderburg	evLutKB	Uelzen	1874-1962	1
Suhlendorf	evLutKB	Uelzen	1718-1962	2
Sunderburg	evLutKB	Uelzen	1575-1875	1
Süpplingen	ZSR	Wolfenbüttel	1808-1814	1
Süpplingenburg	ZSR STA	Wolfenbüttel	1808-1814	1
Teichhutte	ZSR BM	Wolfenbüttel	1808-1813	1
Telgte	rkKB		1749	1
Tettenborn	evKB	Bielefeld	1627-1966	1
Thedinghausen	ZSR BM	Wolfenbüttel	1812	1
Timmerlah	ZSR STA	Braunsweig	1808-1811	1
Timmern -Wolfenbüttel-	ZSR BM	Wolfenbüttel	1808-1814	1
Todenmann	evKB	Detmold	1808-1874	1
Twieflingen	ZSR BM	Wolfenbüttel	1808-1814	1
Twistringen	rkKB		1750-	1

Location	Nature of Material	Where Filmed	Dates Covered	No. of Rolls
Uehrde	ZSR BM	Wolfenbüttel	1809-1814	1
Uelzen	evLutKB	Uelzen	1541-1811	4
Uelzen	evLutKB	Uelzen	1529-1963	9
Uelzen	evLutMilKB	Hannover	1868-1903	1
Uelzen	Rathaus	Uelzen	1618-1933	3
Ülzen	LDS records	Salt Lake City	1808-1809	1
Üfingen	ZSR BM	Wolfenbüttel	1917-1930	1
Vechta	MilKB	Münster	1675-1812	2
Vechta	rkKB	Münster	1642-1900	5
Veerssen	evLutKB	Uelzen	1874-1962	1
Velpke	ZSR BM	Wolfenbüttel	1808-1813	1
Veltheim	ZSR STA	Wolfenbüttel	1808-1814	1
Verden	Swedish military records	Stockholm	1620-1723	1
Verden	evMilKB	Hannover	1819-1942	2
Vestrup	rkKB	Münster	1692-1897	1
Visbek	rkKB	Münster	1561-1905	1
Völkenrode	ZSR STA	Wolfenbüttel	1808-1813	1
Volkersheim	ZSR STA	Wolfenbüttel	1808-1812	1
Volkmarsdorf	ZSR STA	Wolfenbüttel	1808-1813	1
Volzum	ZSR STA	Wolfenbüttel	1808-1814	1
Vorsfelde	ZSR STA	Wolfenbüttel	1808-1814	1
Wahle	ZSR STA	Wolfenbüttel	1808-1813	1
Wahrstedt	ZSR BM	Wolfenbüttel	1808-1813	1

Location	Nature of Material	Where Filmed	Dates Covered	No. of Rolls
Walkenriedt	ZSR STA	Wolfenbüttel	1808-1813	1
Warbeig	ZSR STA	Wolfenbüttel	1808-1814	1
Watenstedt	ZSR STA	Wolfenbüttel	1808-1814	1
Watzum	ZSR STA	Wolfenbüttel	1808-1814	1
Weener	Dutch military records	Gioningen	1813	1
Wendeburg	ZSR STA	Braunchweig Wolfenbüttel	1808-1812	2
Wendessen -Braunschweig-	ZSR STA	Wolfenbüttel	1808-1814	1
Wendhausen	ZSR STA	Wolfenbüttel	1808-1813	1
Wenzen	ZSR STA	Wolfenbüttel	1808-1813	1
Werete	rkKB		1750	1
Westerlinde	ZSR STA	Wolfenbüttel	1808-1813	1
Westerode -Wolfenbüttel-	ZSR STA	Wolfenbüttel	1808-1812	1
Wesuwe	rkKB		1749-1750	1
Wetzleben	ZSR BM	Wolfenbüttel	1808-1814	2
Wieda	ZSR STA	Wolfenbüttel	1808-1813	1
Wildeshausen	rkKB	Münster	1678-1875	1
Wilhelushaven	LDS records	Salt Lake City	1931-1948	1
Windhausen	ZSR STA	Wolfenbüttel	1809-1813	
Winsen	Tax records	Salt Lake City	1521-1628	
Wittmar	ZSR STA	Wolfenbüttel	1808-1813	

Location	Nature of Material	Where Filmed	Dates Covered	No. of Rolls
Wobeck	ZSR STA	Wolfenbüttel	1808-1814	
Wolfenbüttel	Chronicle	Salt Lake City	publ. 1747	
Wolfenbüttel	evLutMilKB	Hannover	1815-1935	
Wolfenbüttel	ZSR STA	Wolfenbüttel	1808-1814	
Wolfshagen	ZSR STA	Wolfenbüttel	1808-1813	
Wolperode	ZSR STA	Wolfenbüttel	1809-1812	
Wolsdorf	ZSR STA	Wolfenbüttel	1808-1809	
Woltwiesche	ZSR STA	Wolfenbüttel	1808-1812	
Wrescherode	ZSR STA	Wolfenbüttel	1809-1813	
Wülferode	KB	Hannover	1641-1897	

NORDRHEIN-WESTFALEN

Location	Nature of Material	Where Filmed	Dates Covered	No. of Rolls
Aachen	OBA STA	Schloss Brühl	1798-1878	290
Aachen	evKB	Düsseldorf	1593-1877	10
Aachen	MKB Royal Navy	Hannover Eibenstock London	1583-1944	3
Adendorf	rkKB STA	Schloss Brühl	1643-1875	16
Aegichienberg	rkKB STA	Schloss Brühl	1698-1875	17
Afden	rkKB	Schloss Brühl	1648-1798	1
Ahaus	evKB rkKB STA	Detmold Bielefeld Berlin-Dahlem Münster	1607-1885	9
Ahden	rkKB STA	Detmold Paderborn	1681-1874	5
Ahlen	evKB rkKB STA	Detmold Bielefeld	1634-1884	53
Ahlsen	evKB	Detmold	1809-1874	5
Ahsen	rkKB	Detmold Münster	1715-1901	9
Albachten	rkKB	Detmold Münster	1663-1876	3
Albaxen	evLut	Detmold	1808-1874	3
Albensloh	rkKB	Detmold Münster	1658-1874	4
Aldekerk	rkKB	Münster Brühl	1603-1908	5
Aldendorf	rkKB	Brühl	1702-1738	1
Aldenhoven	STA BA rkKB	Brühl	1594-1875	15
Alfen	rkKB	Detmold Paderborn	1628-1874	4

Location	Nature of Material	Where Filmed	Dates Covered	No. of Rolls
Alfter	rkKB	Brühl	1628-1798	1
Alhausen	rkKB	Detmold	1808-1874	2
Allagen	rkKB	Detmold Paderborn	1692-1874	4
Allendorf	rkKB	Detmold	1808-1874	1
Alme	rkKB	Detmold	1808-1874	10
Almsick	rkKB	Detmold	1815-1874	2
Alpen	STA evKB BA rkKB	Düsseldorf Schloss Brühl Münster	1656-1943	22
Alsdorf	rkKB BA	Schloss Brühl	1724-1875	7
Alstätte	rkKB	Detmold Münster	1660-1925	5
Alswede	evLut	Bielefeld	1646-1929	10
Altahlen	STA rkKB	Detmold	1803-1874	8
Altastenberg	rkKB	Detmold	1792-1874	1
Altena	evKB STA BA	Bielefeld Detmold	1687-1969	38
Altenbeken	rkKB evKB	Detmold Paderborn	1730-1874	4
Altenberge	rkKB	Münster	1666-1875	5
Altenbergen	rkKB	Detmold	1749-1814	2
Altenbögge	evKB	Bielefeld	1694-1933	9
Altenbüren	rkKB	Detmold	1808-1874	8
Altendorf	STA	Schloss Brühl	1799-1875	15
Altengeske	rkKB	Detmold Paderborn	1657-1874	4
Altenharse	rkKB	Detmold	1808-1874	3
Altenmilbrich	rkKB	Paderborn	1683-1874	3
Altenrath	rkKB	Schloss Brühl	1770-1811	1

Location	Nature of Material	Where Filmed	Dates Covered	No. of Rolls
Altenrüthen	rkKB	Detmold Paderborn	1666-1874	6
Altkalhar	rkKB	Münster Schloss Brühl	1688-1843	2
Altbienen	rkKB	Detmold	1749-1874	3
Altschermbeck	BA rkKB STA	Münster Detmold	1681-1884	5
Alverdissen	evKB	Bielefeld Detmold	1693-1969	7
Alvers	rkKB	Detmold Münster	1676-1875	5
Alwede	ev.refKB	Detmold	1815-1874	3
Ameke	rkKB	Detmold	1779-1874	4
Amelsbüren	rkKB	Detmold Münster	1648-1875	5
Amelunsen	evKB rkKB STA	Bielefeld Detmold	1674-1966	10
Amen	rkKB STA	Schloss Brühl	1648-1875	18
Aminghausen	evKB	Detmold	1808-1874	2
Ammelve	rkKB	Münster	1740-1935	2
Angelmodde	rkKB	Detmold Münster	1688-1875	3
Angelsdorf	rkKB	Schloss Brühl	1768-1798	1
Angermund	BA STA rkKB	Schloss Brühl	1756-1875	26
Anholt	rkKB evKB STA	Münster Bielefeld Detmold	1627-1899	6
Anrath	STA rkKB	Schloss Brühl	1664-1875	13
Anreppen	rkKB STA	Detmold Paderborn	1641-1875	7
Anröchte	rkKB	Detmold Pederborn	1648-1874	5

Location	Nature of Material	Where Filmed	Dates Covered	No. of Rolls
Antfeld	rkKB	Paderborn	1614-1874	4
Aphoven	BGM	Schloss Brühl	1797-1875	9
Appeldorn	rkKB	Schloss Brühl Münster	1689-1880	13
Appelhülsen	rkKB	Detmold Münster	1677-1867	3
Arfeld	evKB	Detmold Bielefeld	1676-1961	8
Arloff	rkKB	Schloss Brühl	1779-1799	1
Arnoldsweiler	BGM rkKB STA	Schloss Brühl	1706-1875	10
Arnsberg	rkKB evKB	Detmold Bielefeld Paderborn	1612-1936	23
Arrenkamp	evLutKB	Detmold	1815-1874	3
Arsbeck	rkKB	Schloss Brühl	1653-1791	1
Asbeck	rkKB	Detmold Münster	1680-1885	3
Aschebeck	rkKB	Detmold Münster	1649-1882	6
Aschen	evKB	Bielefeld	1831-1965	1
Asseln	rkKB	Paderborn	1661-1874	1
Assinghausen	rkKB	Paderborn Detmold	1715-1879	8
Atteln	rkKB	Paderborn	1696-1884	4
Attendorn	evKB MKB rkKB STA	Detmold Hannover	1808-1942	9
Auenhausen	rkKB	Detmold	1808-1874	1
Auenheim	rkKB	Schloss Brühl	1725-1801	1
Augustdorf	evKB rkKB	Bielefeld Detmold	1646-1943	22
Avenwedde	rkKB	Detmold	1808-1810	1

Location	Nature of Material	Where Filmed	Dates Covered	No. of Rolls
Bad Driberg	evKB rkKB STA	Detmold Bielefeld	1808-1946	5
Bad Godesberg	rkKB STA	Schloss Brühl	1625-1875	22
Bad Lippspringe	evKB rkKB	Bielefeld Detmold Paderborn	1645-1965	5
Bad Meinberg	evKB	Bielefeld Berlin-Dahlem	1683-1969	8
Bad Münstereifel	BA rkKB	Schloss Brühl	1631-1875	7
Bad Oeynhausen	evKB rkKB	Detmold	1808-1874	10
Bad Salzufflen	AG evKB	Detmold Bielefeld	1624-1969	61
Bad Sassendorf	evKB rkKB	Bielefeld Detmold	1654-1874	30
Bad Westernhotten	rkKB	Detmold	1779-1874	9
Baesweiler	rkKB BA evKB	Schloss Brühl Düsseldorf	1658-1875	13
Bakam	rkKB	Münster	1694-	2
Balve	rkKB	Detmold	1808-1874	5
Bardenberg	BGM rkKB STA	Schloss Brühl	1652-1875	16
Barkhausen	rkKB evKB	Detmold Paderborn Bielefeld	1706-1874	8
Barlo -Borken-	rkKB	Münster Detmold	1682-1941	3
Barmen	rkKB STA	Schloss Brühl	1770-1875	7
Barnhausen	rkKB	Detmold	1808-1874	1
Barntrup	LG AG evKB	Detmold Bielefeld	1661-1875	15

Location	Nature of Material	Where Filmed	Dates Covered	No. of Rolls
Barop	evKB	Bielefeld	1560-1929	6
Batenhorst	rkKB	Detmold	1808-1874	3
Bausenhagen	evKB rkKB	Bielefeld Detmold	1735-1933	5
Bechen	rkKB	Schloss Brühl	1721-1809	1
Beckum	STA rkKB evKB	Detmold Münster	1628-1875	43
Bedburdyk	BGM STA	Schloss Brühl	1799-1877	19
Bedburg	rkKB	Schloss Brühl	1647-1801	2
Bedburg-Hau	rkKB STA	Münster Schloss Brühl	1766-1875	6
Beek	BGM	Schloss Brühl	1802-1872	1
Beelen	rkKB STA	Detmold Münster	1669-1874	7
Bega	evKB	Bielefeld Detmold	1704-1918	7
Beggendorf	rkKB	Schloss Brühl	1654-1798	1
Belecke	evKB rkKB	Detmold Paderborn	1779-1874	6
Bellar	rkKB	Detmold	1808-1874	1
Beller	rkKB	Detmold	1808-1874	2
Bellersen	rkKB	Detmold	1808-1874	2
Benhausen	rkKB	Detmold Paderborn	1776-1874	4
Benninghausen	rkKB	Detmold Paderborn	1748-1879	6
Bensberg	rkKB evKB	Berlin Schloss Brühl	1624-1916	4
Bentfeld	rkKB STA	Detmold Paderborn	1641-1875	7
Berchum	evKB	Bielefeld Detmold	1638-1888	2
Berg -Schleiden-	rkKB	Schloss Brühl	1715-1798	1

Location	Nature of Material	Where Filmed	Dates Covered	No. of Rolls
Berge	rkKB	Paderborn	1641-1882	1
Berghausen	rkKB	Schloss Brühl Detmold	1676-1874	3
Bergheim	rkKB STA	Schloss Brühl Detmold	1770-1874	4
Bergisch-Gladbach	rkKB	Schloss Brühl	1657-1810	2
Bergisch-Neukirchen	BGM STA evKB	Schloss Brühl	1770-1875	6
Bergkamen	evKB	Detmold	1815-1874	6
Bergkirchen	evKB	Bielefeld	1671-1944	16
Bergstein	STA	Schloss Brühl	1802-1872	1
Berg-Thuir	rkKB	Schloss Brühl	1740-1799	1
Beringhause	rkKB evKB	Paderborn Detmold	1653-1874	14
Berk	STA	Schloss Brühl	1799-1875	5
Berkum	rkKB	Schloss Brühl	1673-1798	1
Berleburg	evKB	Bielefeld Detmold	1621-1969	16
Berrendorf	rkKB	Schloss Brühl	1687-1798	1
Bessenich	rkKB	Schloss Brühl	1682-1798	1
Bestwig	evKB	Bielefeld	1855-1948	1
Bettendorf	rkKB	Schloss Brühl	1770-1798	1
Beuel	rkKB	Schloss Brühl	1651-1810	7
Bevergern	rkKB STA	Detmold Münster	1654-1876	6
Beverungen	evKB rkKB	Bielefeld Detmold Düsseldorf	1766-1942	6
Bielefeld	LDS records	Salt Lake City	1923-1951	6
Bielefeld	evKB MB MKB	Bielefeld Hannover	1648-1965	68
Bielefeld	Rathaus STA	Bielefeld	1567-1766	7

Location	Nature of Material	Where Filmed	Dates Covered	No. of Rolls
Bielefeld	STA	Bielefeld	1608-1886	11
Bielefeld	rkKB KBA	Bielefeld Detmold	1667-1853	5
Bielefeld	STA	Bielefeld	1753-1820	5
Bielstein	ev.refKB	Schloss Brühl	1675-1809	1
Biemenhorst	rkKB	Detmold	1815-1874	6
Biemsen-Ahmsen	evLutKB	Detmold	1815-1874	10
Bierde	evKB	Detmold	1808-1874	2
Bieren	evKB	Detmold	1852-1873	1
Bietenhausen	rkKB	Freiburg	1785-1900	1
Bigge	rkKB	Paderborn	1614-1874	4
Bigge-Olsberg	rkKB	Detmold	1808-1874	3
Billerbeck	rkKB	Münster	1622-1889	7
Billing	STA	Schloss Brühl	1798-1875	14
Binsfeld	STA	Schloss Brühl	1802-1872	1
Birgel	BA STA	Schloss Brühl	1798-1875	13
Birgelen	STA BA rkKB	Schloss Brühl	1743-1875	9
Birkelbach	evKB	Detmold	1656-1960	7
Birkesdorf	BGM rkKB	Schloss Brühl	1732-1875	9
Bislich	rkKB	Münster	1649-1875	3
Blankenau	rkKB	Detmold	1808-1874	2
Blankenheim	STA BA rkKB	Schloss Brühl	1669-1875	18
Blankenrode	rkKB STA	Detmold Paderborn	1656-1874	11
Blankenstein	evKB	Bielefeld	1687-1961	3
Blasheim	evKB	Bielefeld Detmold	1661-1910	20

Location	Nature of Material	Where Filmed	Dates Covered	No. of Rolls
Blatzheim	rkKB	Schloss Brühl	1750-1798	1
Bleiwäsche	rkKB	Detmold Paderborn	1713-1874	2
Bliesheim	rkKB	Schloss Brühl	1653-1798	1
Blomberg	evKB	Bielefeld	1667-1969	9
Blomberg -Detmold-	evKB AG St. GER	Bielefeld Detmold	1579-1969	32
Bocholt	rkKB STA evKB	Münster Detmold Bielefeld	1654-1905	53
Bochum	evKB	Bielefeld Detmold Hannover	1583-1944	112
Bochum	AG BGM STA	Detmold	1810-1874	12
Bochum	LDS records rkKB	Salt Lake City Detmold	1931-1948 1815-1874	11
Bockhorst	STA evKB rkKB	Bielefeld Detmold	1727-1965	8
Bochum-Hövel	rkKB	Detmold Münster	1659-1903	6
Bödenfeld	rkKB	Detmold	1805-1874	3
Bodexen	rkKB evKB		1808-1874	4
Bodingen	KBA	Schloss Brühl	1652-1809	2
Boele	evKB	Bielefeld	1847-1935	2
Boisheim	rkKB STA	Schloss Brühl	1644-1875	6
Boke	rkKB STA	Detmold Paderborn	1641-1875	7
Bokel	rkKB STA	Detmold Paderborn	1665-1911	23
Bökenförde	rkKB	Detmold Paderborn	1713-1891	3
Bölhorst	evKB	Detmold	1815-1874	5

Location	Nature of Material	Where Filmed	Dates Covered	No. of Rolls
Bönen	evKB	Detmold Bielefeld	1694-1933	12
Bonenburg	rkKB	Detmold Paderborn	1808-1874	6
Bonn	LG	Schloss Brühl		1
Bonn	evKB MKB	Hannover	1816-1940	2
Bonn	STA	Schloss Brühl	1798-1875	58
Bonn	LDS records	Salt Lake City	1859-1873	1
Bonsdorf	rkKB	Schloss Brühl	1616-1813	1
Bontkirchen	rkKB	Detmold	1808-1874	3
Borchum	MKB	Eibenstock	1869-1907	1
Borgentreich	rkKB evKB STA	Detmold	1809-1874	3
Borgholz	STA rkKB evKB	Detmold	1808-1874	5
Borgholshausen	STA evKB	Detmold Bielefeld	1652-1920	17
Borghorst	rkKB	Münster	1622-1885	5
Bork	rkKB STA	Münster Detmold	1668-1907	8
Borken	rkKB STA evKB MKB	Detmold Bielefeld Münster	1614-1912	51
Borkenwirthe	rkKB	Detmold Münster	1768-1961	5
Borlinghausen	rkKB	Detmold	1808-1874	2
Born -Höxten-	rkKB	Detmold	1808-1874	2
Bornheim	rkKB	Schloss Brühl	1699-1807	2
Bornholte	STA rkKB	Detmold	1809-1874	4
Börninghausen	evKB	Detmold Bielefeld	1689-1962	9

Location	Nature of Material	Where Filmed	Dates Covered	No. of Rolls
Borntosten	rkKB	Paderborn	1685-1874	2
Borr	rkKB	Schloss Brühl	1734-1875	8
Borschemich	rkKB	Schloss Brühl	1770-1798	1
Borth	evKB STA	Düsseldorf Münster Schloss Brühl	1675-1942	12
Bösenzell	rkKB	Detmold Münster	1732-1908	4
Bösingfeld	evKB	Bielefeld Detmold	1652-1948	25
Boslar	rkKB	Schloss Brühl	1714-1800	1
Bosseborn	rkKB STA	Detmold	1808-1874	2
Bottenbroich	KBA	Schloss Brühl	1740-1797	1
Bourheim	rkKB	Schloss Brühl	1723-1738	1
Brachelen	rkKB BA STA	Schloss Brühl	1639-1875	13
Bracht	evKB rkKB	Schloss Brühl	1770-1802	2
Brackwede	evKB STA	Bielefeld Detmold	1712-1959	37
Brake -Bielefeld-	evKB	Detmold	1815-1874	10
Brake -Lippe,Lemgo-	evKB	Bielefeld Detmold	1637-1910	12
Brake -Lemgo-	evKB	Bielefeld	1637-1910	9
Brakel	STA evKB rkKB	Bielefeld Detmold	1808-1892	6
Brand	BA STA	Schloss Brühl	1800-1875	9
Braunsrath	BA rkKB	Schloss Brühl	1696-1875	7
Brauweiler	rkKB	Schloss Brühl	1716-1799	2
Breberen	BA rkKB	Schloss Brühl	1691-1875	4

Location	Nature of Material	Where Filmed	Dates Covered	No. of Rolls
Breckenfeld	BA evKB	Detmold Bielefeld	1674-1931	17
Breckelar	rkKB evKB	Detmold Paderborn	1653-1874	14
Bredenborn	rkKB STA	Detmold	1808-1874	2
Breitenbinden	rkKB STA	Detmold	1808-1875	2
Breitscheid	rkKB STA BA evKB	Schloss Brühl	1682-1875	22
Bremen -Soest-	rkKB	Detmold	1779-1874	5
Bremerberg	rkKB	Detmold	1808-1874	2
Brenken	rkKB evKB	Paderborn Detmold	1681-1874	5
Brenkhausen	rkKB STA evKB	Detmold	1808-1874	5
Breyell	rkKB STA	Schloss Brühl	1631-1875	20
Bricht	rkKB	Detmold	1815-1874	1
Brilon	evKB rkKB	Bielefeld Detmold	1808-1948	9
Brochterbeck	evKB rkKB	Detmold Bielefeld Münster	1694-1909	10
Brockhagen	rkKB evKB STA	Bielefeld Detmold	1666-1965	12
Bröderhausen	evKB	Detmold	1815-1874	3
Broich -Jülich-	rkKB STA	Schloss Brühl	1668-1875	2
Broichweiden	BA evKB rkKB	Schloss Brühl	1611-1875	19
Bruchhausen	rkKB evKB	Detmold Bielefeld Paderborn	1603-1941	13

Location	Nature of Material	Where Filmed	Dates Covered	No. of Rolls
Brüggen -Krefeld-	rkKB BA refKB	Schloss Brühl	1628-1875	24
Brühl -Köln-	rkKB	Schloss Brühl	1655-1803	4
Brünen	rkKB	Münster	1708-1875	2
Brunskappel	rkKB	Detmold Paderborn	1738-1874	5
Buchholz	evKB STA	Detmold Bielefeld	1645-1964	9
Budberg	BA evKB	Schloss Brühl Düsseldorf	1666-1943	9
Büderich -Grevenbroich-	rkKB STA	Münster Schloss Brühl	1668-1875	3
Büderich -Moers- -Grevenbroich-	rkKB BA evKB	Schloss Brühl Münster	1658-1876	13
Büderich -Neuss-	BGM	Schloss Brühl	1798-1875	10
Bühne	evKB rkKB STA	Detmold	1808-1874	3
Buir -Bergheim-	rkKB	Schloss Brühl	1712-1798	1
Buke	evKB rkKB STA	Detmold Paderborn	1730-1874	4
Buldern	rkKB STA	Münster Detmold	1676-1875	6
Bünde	evKB rkKB STA	Detmold Bielefeld	1696-1904	30
Burbach	evKB	Detmold Bielefeld	1548-1889	19
Büren	evKB rkKB STA	Detmold Bielefeld Paderborn	1697-1966	7
Burg	rkKB evKB	Schloss Brühl	1649-1809	2

Location	Nature of Material	Where Filmed	Dates Covered	No. of Rolls
Burgsteinfurt	evKB rkKB STA	Bielefeld Detmold Münster	1652-1903	16
Burscheid	rkKB BA evKB	Schloss Brühl Düsseldorf	1770-1872	10
Bürvenich	BA rkKB	Schloss Brühl	1770-1875	11
Buschhoven	rkKB	Schloss Brühl	1721-1798	1
Bustedt	evKB	Detmold	1808-1874	4
Büttendorf	evKB	Detmold	1815-1874	1
Büttgen	BGM STA rkKB	Schloss Brühl	1646-1875	16
Calenberg	rkKB STA	Detmold	1808-1874	2
Calle -Meschede-	rkKB	Detmold Paderborn	1622-1874	7
Capelle	rkKB	Detmold	1832-1873	1
Cappel	evKB	Bielefeld	1621-1933	6
Cappel -Lippstadt-	rkKB	Paderborn	1860-1880	1
Cappel -Detmold	evKB rkKB	Bielefeld Detmold	1708-1947	8
Cappeln	evKB	Bielefeld	1649-1907	12
Castrop-Rauxel	STA evKB rkKB	Bielefeld Detmold	1676-1902	24
Clarholz	rkKB STA	Detmold	1810-1874	2
Cleve	MKB French church	Eibenstock Den Haag	1583-1944	3
Cobbenroche	rkKB	Detmold	1808-1874	1
Coesfeld	STA rkKB evKB	Bielefeld Münster Detmold	1637-1919	31
Dabringhausen	evKB	Schloss Brühl	1665-1809	2

Location	Nature of Material	Where Filmed	Dates Covered	No. of Rolls
Dahl -Paderborn	rkKB	Paderborn Detmold	1631-1875	2
Dahlem	STA BA	Schloss Brühl	1795-1872	5
Dalhausen	STA rkKB	Detmold	1808-1814	1
Dalheim -Büren-	rkKB evKB	Paderborn Detmold	1656-1874	13
Damscheid	rkKB	Trier	1719-1798	1
Dankersen	evKB	Detmold Bielefeld	1729-1948	3
Dansweiler	rkKB	Schloss Brühl	1632-1798	1
Darfeld	rkKB	Münster	1615-1875	5
Darup	rkKB	Münster	1637-1914	5
Daseburg	STA evKB rkKB	Detmold Berlin-Dahlem	1649-1874	3
Datteln	STA evKB rkKB	Bielefeld Detmold Münster	1643-1953	36
Dechenborn	STA	Schloss Brühl	1798-1836	3
Dedinghausen	rkKB	Detmold	1808-1874	3
Dehme	evKB rkKB STA	Detmold	1808-1874	10
Deilinghofen	evKB	Detmold Bielefeld	1680-1929	9
Delbrück	rkKB STA	Detmold	1808-1874	3
Dellwig	evKB	Bielefeld Detmold	1673-1909	10
Denklingen	evKB STA	Schloss Brühl Düsseldorf	1810-1881	18
Densborn	rkKB	Trier	1683-1807	1
Derichsweiler	rkKB	Schloss Brühl	1770-1803	1
Derne	evKB	Detmold	1815-1874	4
Destel	evKB	Detmold	1808-1874	4

Location	Nature of Material	Where Filmed	Dates Covered	No. of Rolls
Detmold	rkKB evKB AG MKB	Detmold Bielefeld Hannover	1620-1969	58
Dhünn	evKB	Schloss Brühl	1694-1809	2
Diebrock	evKB STA	Detmold	1811-1874	11
Diedenshausen	evKB	Detmold	1808-1874	2
Dielingen	evKB STA	Bielefeld Detmold	1660-1942	19
Diestedde	rkKB STA	Detmold Münster	1654-1875	6
Dingden	rkKB STA	Detmold Münster	1670-1883	5
Dinslaken	rkKB evKB	Hannover Münster Düsseldorf	1612-1891	7
Dirmesheim	rkKB STA	Schloss Brühl	1718-1875	12
Disternich	rkKB	Schloss Brühl	1708-1798	1
Döhren	evKB	Detmold	1808-1873	2
Dolberg	STA rkKB	Detmold Münster	1674-1875	6
Donop	evKB	Bielefeld Detmold	1669-1905	6
Donsbrüggen	STA	Schloss Brühl	1801-1875	9
Dörenhagen	evKB rkKB STA	Detmold Paderborn	1710-1874	4
Dörentrup	evKB	Detmold	1670-1875	2
Dorfbauerschaft -Delbrück-	rkKB	Detmold	1815-1874	2
Dolar	rkKB	Detmold	1808-1874	1
Dormagen	STA BGM	Schloss Brühl	1683-1935	23
Dornberg	evKB STA	Detmold Bielefeld	1666-1952	11
Dornick	rkKB	Münster	1661-1875	1

Location	Nature of Material	Where Filmed	Dates Covered	No. of Rolls
Dorsten	STA evKB rkKB	Münster Bielefeld Detmold	1617-1958	53
Dorstfeld	evKB	Bielefeld	1885-1912	2
Dortmund	evKB	Bielefeld Detmold	1801-1968	145
Dortmund	rkKB	Detmold	1805-1874	22
Dortmund	BGM STA	Detmold	1674-1968	11
Dortmund	LDS records	Salt Lake City	1931-1948	1
Dortmund-Asseln	evKB	Bielefeld	1756-1908	4
Dortmund-Barop	evKB	Bielefeld	1560-1929	6
Dortmund-Derne	evKB	Bielefeld	1674-1932	7
Dortmund-Kirchhörde	evKB	Bielefeld	1891-1951	2
Dortmund-Lütgendortmund	evKB	Bielefeld	1811-1900	4
Dortmund-Marten	evKB	Bielefeld	1881-1899	2
Dortmund-Mengede	evKB	Bielefeld	1658-1906	7
Dortmund-Öspel	evKB	Bielefeld	1896-1931	2
Dortmund-Syburg	evKB	Bielefeld	1879-1968	1
Dortmund-Wickede	evKB	Bielefeld	1729-1880	2
Dössel	rkKB evKB	Detmold Paderborn	1670-1874	3
Doveren	BGM rkKB	Schloss Brühl	1677-1875	14
Drankhausen	rkKB	Detmold	1815-1874	1
Dreiborn	BGM rkKB	Schloss Brühl	1723-1875	16
Dreierwalde	rkKB	Münster Detmold	1666-1875	3
Dremmen	BGM rkKB	Schloss Brühl	1663-1875	16
Drenke	rkKB	Detmold	1808-1874	2

Location	Nature of Material	Where Filmed	Dates Covered	No. of Rolls
Drensteinfurt	rkKB STA	Münster Detmold Berlin	1644-1956	11
Drewer	rkKB	Paderborn	1666-1874	3
Driburg	evKB	Bielefeld	1853-1946	1
Dringenburg	rkKB evKB STA	Detmold	1808-1874	4
Drohne	evKB	Detmold	1815-1874	3
Drolshagen	rkKB	Schloss Brühl Detmold	1737-1874	6
Drove	rkKB	Schloss Brühl	1775-1875	11
Druffel	rkKB	Detmold	1808-1874	7
Duffelward	rkKB	Schloss Brühl	1690-1798	1
Duisburg	LDS records rkKB STA	Salt Lake City Schloss Brühl Hannover	1651-1932	8
Dülken	evKB rkKB STA	Schloss Brühl Düsseldorf	1644-1891	24
Dülmen	evKB rkKB	Münster Bielefeld Detmold	1628-1959	21
Dürboslar	rkKB	Schloss Brühl	1625-1798	1
Düren	MKB BA evKB rkKB	Schloss Brühl Berlin	1618-1873	26
Dürscheid	rkKB	Schloss Brühl	1770-1810	1
Dürten	rkKB	Schloss Brühl	1776-1809	1
Dürwiss	BGM rkKB	Schloss Brühl	1770-1875	13
Düsseldorf	BGM STA	Düsseldorf Schloss Brühl	1799-1875	264
Düsseldorf	evKB MKB	Hannover	1821-1920	18
Düsseldorf	evKB	Schloss Brühl Düsseldorf	1663-1905	18

Location	Nature of Material	Where Filmed	Dates Covered	No. of Rolls
Düsseldorf	rkKB	Schloss Brühl	1622-1810	44
Düsseldorf	LDS records	Salt Lake City Schloss Brühl	1861-1948 1737-1795	3
Düsseldorf	Church of England	London	1861-1868	1
Dützen	STA evKB	Detmold	1815-1874	6
Ebbinghausen	STA rkKB	Detmold Paderborn	1689-1874	3
Echthausen	rkKB	Detmold	1806-1874	1
Echtz-Konzendorf	BGM	Schloss Brühl	1801-1875	10
Eckenhagen	STA evKB rkKB	Schloss Brühl	1769-1875	18
Effeln	evKB rkKB	Detmold Paderborn	1688-1874	2
Eggerode	rkKB	Münster Detmold	1630-1875	3
Eicherscheid	BGM	Schloss Brühl	1798-1875	6
Eichel	evKB	Bielefeld	1747-1908	9
Eickelborn	rkKB	Detmold	1779-1874	4
Eickhoff	rkKB	Detmold	1804-1874	2
Eichhorst	evKB	Detmold	1808-1873	3
Eichum	evKB STA	Detmold	1811-1874	11
Eichinghausen	rkKB evKB STA	Detmold Bielefeld	1756-1932	10
Eikelborn	KBA	Detmold	1839-1842	4
Eikeloh	rkKB	Detmold Paderborn	1661-1874	17
Eilendorf	rkKB	Schloss Brühl	1665-1798	1
Eilhausen	evKB	Detmold	1811-1874	4
Eilshausen	evKB	Detmold	1808-1874	4
Eilversen	rkKB	Detmold	1808-1814	1

Location	Nature of Material	Where Filmed	Dates Covered	No. of Rolls
Einen	rkKB	Detmold Münster	1687-1875	2
Eisbergen	evKB	Detmold Bielefeld	1730-1942	9
Eiserfeld	evKB	Detmold Bielefeld	1826-1943	14
Eissen	rkKB	Detmold	1808-1874	1
Eitorf	rkKB STA	Schloss Brühl	1656-1809	20
Elbrinsen	evKB	Detmold Bielefeld	1706-1969	8
Eldagsen	evKB	Detmold	1808-1874	3
Elgen	rkKB BA	Schloss Brühl	1733-1875	12
Ellen	rkKB	Schloss Brühl	1729-1817	1
Elleringhausen	rkKB	Paderborn	1614-1874	4
Elmpt	BGM rkKB	Schloss Brühl	1619-1875	12
Elsdorf	rkKB	Schloss Brühl	1651-1798	1
Elsen	rkKB	Paderborn Detmold	1705-1874	4
Elsoff	evKB	Detmold Bielefeld	1608-1962	14
Elspe	rkKB	Detmold	1869-1874	1
Elte	rkKB	Detmold Münster	1665-1872	3
Elten	rkKB	Münster	1636-1875	3
Elverdissen	evKB	Detmold	1815-1874	10
Embken	rkKB	Schloss Brühl	1770-1807	1
Emmerich	rkKB Wallvor Church	Den Haag Münster	1620-1875	7
Emsbüren	rkKB		1749-1750	1
Emsdetten	rkKB	Münster	1648-1875	5
Ende	evKB	Bielefeld	1704-1913	6

Location	Nature of Material	Where Filmed	Dates Covered	No. of Rolls
Endorf	rkKB	Detmold	1779-1874	4
Engar	rkKB	Detmold	1808-1874	2
Engelsdorf	rkKB	Schloss Brühl	1638-1798	1
Engelskirchen	rkKB	Schloss Brühl	1647-1809	1
Enger	evKB STA	Bielefeld Detmold	1679-1928	26
Engerhausen	evKB	Detmold	1815-1874	3
Engers	evKB MKB	Hannover	1901-1918	1
Enkhausen	rkKB	Detmold	1779-1874	5
Enneperstrasse	evKB	Bielefeld	1810-1814	6
Ennepethal	evKB	Detmold Bielefeld	1799-1925	18
Enniger	rkKB	Detmold	1671-1874	4
Enningerloh	rkKB	Münster Detmold	1626-1875	6
Enringhausen	rkKB	Detmold	1779-1873	3
Entrup	rkKB	Detmold	1808-1874	1
Ensen	rkKB	Schloss Brühl	1798-1815	7
Epe	rkKB evKB	Detmold Münster	1641-1904	9
Eppenhausen	evKB	Bielefeld	1899-1949	2
Erbschloh	rkKB	Schloss Brühl	1770-1801	1
Erder	evKB	Detmold	1808-1873	1
Ergste	evKB STA	Bielefeld Detmold	1673-1929	6
Eringerfeld	rkKB	Paderborn	1626-1874	2
Erkelenz	BGM rkKB	Schloss Brühl	1604-1872	26
Erkeln	rkKB	Detmold	1808-1874	2
Erkrath	BA rkKB	Schloss Brühl	1664-1875	6
Erle	rkKB	Münster	1678-1891	4

Location	Nature of Material	Where Filmed	Dates Covered	No. of Rolls
Erle -Reckling- hausen-	rkKB	Detmold	1815-1874	1
Erlinghausen	rkKB	Paderborn	1664-1882	3
Ermsinghausen	rkKB	Detmold	1779-1873	3
Erndtebrück	evKB	Detmold	1671-1937	13
Erp	rkKB	Schloss Brühl	1696-1875	10
Erpentrup	rkKB	Detmold	1808-1874	2
Ersdorf	STA rkKB	Schloss Brühl	1615-1875	16
Erwitte	evKB rkKB	Detmold Bielefeld Paderborn	1661-1944	17
Erwitzen	rkKB	Detmold	1808-1874	2
Esbeck	rkKB	Detmold Paderborn	1696-1876	4
Esch -Bergheim-	rkKB	Schloss Brühl	1677-1738	1
Esch -Köln-	rkKB	Schloss Brühl	1736-1799	1
Eschweiler	BGM evKB	Schloss Brühl Düsseldorf	1616-1875	58
Eschweiler -Düren-	rkKB	Schloss Brühl	1680-1800	2
Eschweiler -Euskirchen	evKB rkKB	Düsseldorf Schloss Brühl	1637-1802	2
Eschweiler- über-Feld	rkKB	Schloss Brühl	1650-1800	1
Eslohe	rkKB	Detmold Paderborn	1612-1874	7
Espelkamp	rkKB	Detmold	1842-1874	1
Essen	LDS records STA evKB rkKB	Düsseldorf Detmold Salt Lake City	1652-1891	23
Essentho	rkKB	Detmold Paderborn	1733-1874	2
Estern	rkKB	Detmold	1815-1874	2

Location	Nature of Material	Where Filmed	Dates Covered	No. of Rolls
Etteln	rkKB	Paderborn	1648-1874	2
Euskirchen	rkKB STA	Schloss Brühl	1746-1875	16
Eversberg	rkKB	Detmold Paderborn	1668-1874	7
Eversen	rkKB	Detmold	1808-1874	1
Everswinkel	rkKB	Detmold Münster	1649-1874	6
Eving	evKB	Bielefeld	1895-1921	2
Exter	evKB	Bielefeld Detmold	1667-1966	13
Extertal	evKB	Bielefeld Berlin-Dahlem	1677-1969	13
Falkendiek	evKB	Detmold	1808-1874	6
Falkenhagen	evKB	Bielefeld	1685-1969	9
Falkenhagen -Detmold-	evKB	Detmold	1840-1875	2
Feudingen	evKB	Bielefeld Detmold	1525-1922	22
Finnentrop	rkKB	Detmold	1808-1874	5
Fischelbach	evKB	Bielefeld Detmold	1490-1956	10
Fischeln	BGM	Schloss Brühl	1803-1842	1
Flaesheim	rkKB	Münster	1779-1915	1
Flamersheim	STA evKB rkKB	Schloss Brühl	1659-1875	23
Flersheim	rkKB	Schloss Brühl	1692-1798	1
Flierich	evKB	Bielefeld	1683-1966	6
Floisdorf	rkKB	Schloss Brühl	1722-1800	1
Fölsen	rkKB	Detmold	1808-1874	1
Frechen	evKB rkKB	Schloss Brühl	1645-1799	4
Freckenhorst	rkKB STA	Münster Detmold	1707-1875	8

Location	Nature of Material	Where Filmed	Dates Covered	No. of Rolls
Fredeburg	rkKB	Detmold	1808-1874	3
Freialdenhoven	BGM rkKB	Schloss Brühl	1691-1875	8
Freienoll	rkKB	Detmold	1779-1874	2
Freimersdorf	rkKB	Schloss Brühl	1632-1799	1
Freudenberg	evKB rkKB STA	Dielefeld Detmold	1612-1966	13
Freudenberg -Sügen-	evKB	Detmold	1826-1874	3
Friedewalde	evKB	Detmold Bielefeld	1809-1925	3
Friemersheim	BGM	Schloss Brühl	1803-1842	1
Friesheim	rkKB STA	Schloss Brühl	1705-1875	8
Frille	evKB	Detmold	1808-1874	2
Frimmersdorf	STA BGM rkKB	Schloss Brühl	1692-1875	13
Fritzdorf	STA rkKB	Schloss Brühl	1678-1875	16
Frohnhausen	rkKB	Detmold	1808-1874	1
Frömern	evKB	Bielefeld	1761-1878	3
Fröndenberg	evKB rkKB STA	Bielefeld Detmold	1715-1919	12
Frotheim	evKB	Detmold	1808-1874	7
Füchtorf	BGM rkKB	Detmold Münster	1650-1885	7
Fünfzehnhofe	evKB	STA	1654-1809	1
Fürstenau	rkKB	Detmold	1808-1874	5
Fürstenberg	evKB rkKB	Bielefeld Detmold Paderborn	1727-1966	6
Füssenich	BGM rkKB	Schloss Brühl	1670-1875	10

Location	Nature of Material	Where Filmed	Dates Covered	No. of Rolls
Ganegelt	BGM STA	Schloss Brühl	1725-1875	25
Garenfeld	evKB	Detmold	1819-1874	2
Garfeln	rkKB	Detmold	1808-1874	3
Garsweiler	STA BGM rkKB	Schloss Brühl	1697-1874	18
Gehlenbeck	evKB	Detmold	1811-1874	4
Gehrden	rkKB	Detmold	1808-1874	2
Geisecke	evKB rkKB	Detmold	1819-1874	2
Gelden	rkKB STA	Schloss Brühl Berlin-Dahlem	1710-1878	11
Gelsenkirchen	evKB rkKB	Detmold	1779-1875	7
Gehlensbeck	evKB	Bielefeld	1767-1946	10
Geilenkirchen	rkKB evKB BGM	Schloss Brühl Düsseldorf	1649-1875	23
Geldern	BGM MKB evKB	Eibenstock Hannover Schloss Brühl Münster	1667-1918	23
Gelsenkirchen	evKB STA	Bielefeld Detmold	1716-1940	22
Gemen	rkKB evKB	Münster Detmold Bielefeld	1661-1921	8
Gemünd	evKB rkKB BGM STA	Schloss Brühl	1728-1872	11
Gensberg	evKB	Berlin	1909-1916	1
Gerderath	BGM STA rkKB	Schloss Brühl	1696-1875	7
Germiete	rkKB evKB	Detmold	1808-1874	2
Gescher	rkKB	Münster	1630-1916	8

Location	Nature of Material	Where Filmed	Dates Covered	No. of Rolls
Geseke	evKB rkKB	Paderborn Detmold Bielefeld	1612-1952	23
Getmold	evKB	Detmold	1815-1874	3
Gevelinghausen	BGM rkKB	Schloss Brühl	1658-1874	12
Gevelsberg	evKB rkKB	Detmold Bielefeld	1636-1945	31
Geyen	rkKB	Schloss Brühl	1691-1803	1
Gieshage	rkKB evKB	Detmold Paderborn	1648-1875	7
Gimbke	rkKB		1749	1
Gimborn	evKB rkKB	Schloss Brühl	1683-1809	3
Gimb	rkKB	Münster Detmold	1750-1875	2
Girkhausen	evKB	Bielefeld Detmold	1677-1958	8
Gladbach	BGM rkKB evKB	Schloss Brühl	1739-1852	3
Gladbeck	evKB rkKB	Detmold	1815-1879	3
Glehn	rkKB STA BGM	Schloss Brühl	1617-1815	18
Glimbach	rkKB	Schloss Brühl	1710-1798	1
Goch	STA BGM rkKB	Schloss Brühl Münster	1630-1933	40
Godelsheim	rkKB	Detmold	1808-1874	1
Gohfeld	rkKB evKB	Bielefeld Detmold	1636-1945	23
Golzheim	rkKB	Schloss Brühl	1770-1798	1
Gorspen-Vahlsen	evKB	Detmold	1808-1874	4
Götteswickerhamm	GER evKB	Hamborn	1472-1886	11
Götzenkirchen	rkKB	Schloss Brühl	1770-1798	1

Location	Nature of Material	Where Filmed	Dates Covered	No. of Rolls
Grafschaft -Meschede-	rkKB	Detmold	1800-1874	4
Greffen	rkKB	Münster	1693-1875	4
Grefrath	BGM	Schloss Brühl	1799-1875	11
Gressenich	BGM	Schloss Brühl	1798-1875	15
Greven	rkKB BGM	Münster	1645-1925	10
Grevenbroich	rkKB STA	Schloss Brühl	1660-1872	40
Grevenbrück	evKB rkKB	Detmold	1807-1874	5
Grevenhagen	rkKB	Detmold	1808-1874	2
Grevenstein	rkKB	Detmold Paderborn	1621-1874	3
Grieth	rkKB STA	Münster Schloss Brühl	1647-1876	12
Grimlinghausen	rkKB	Paderborn	1614-1874	4
Gronau	STA evKB rkKB	Bielefeld Münster Detmold	1653-1934	8
Grönebach	rkKB	Detmold	1808-1874	3
Gross-Reken	rkKB STA	Detmold Münster	1660-1935	8
Grossbüllesheim	rkKB	Schloss Brühl	1681-1875	22
Grossenbreden	rkKB	Detmold	1808-1875	2
Grossenecher	rkKB	Detmold Paderborn	1718-1874	3
Grien	evKB rkKB	Düsseldorf Schloss Brühl	1675-1880	4
Grundsteinheim	rkKB	Detmold	1808-1875	1
Grütlohn	rkKB	Detmold	1815-1874	3
Gummersbach	STA evKB	Schloss Brühl	1641-1972	30
Gürenich	rkKB	Schloss Brühl	1684-1799	1
Güsten	rkKB	Schloss Brühl	1754-1798	1

Location	Nature of Material	Where Filmed	Dates Covered	No. of Rolls
Gustdorf	rkKB BA STA	Schloss Brühl	1625-1875	17
Gütersich	evKB rkKB	Bielefeld Detmold Zweibrücken	1675-1951	45
Gymnich	rkKB STA	Schloss Brühl	1632-1875	12
Haan	evKB	Düsseldorf Schloss Brühl	1671-1848	5
Haarbrück	rkKB	Detmold	1808-1874	3
Haaren	rkKB	Schloss Brühl Paderborn	1674-1875	17
Haaren -Selfkantkreis-	BGM STA	Schloss Brühl	1798-1875	8
Haddenhausen	evKB	Detmold	1815-1873	4
Haffen	rkKB	Münster	1702-1875	1
Haffen-Mehr	rkKB	Schloss Brühl Münster	1709-1875	2
Hagedorn	ev.refKB	Detmold	1819-1874	1
Hagen	evKB rkKB	Detmold	1808-1874	2
Hagen	evKB STA BGM rkKB	Detmold Bielefeld	1682-1874	64
Hagen -Boche-	evKB	Bielefeld	1847-1935	2
Hagen -Paderborn-	rkKB STA	Detmold	1808-1874	3
Hahlen	evKB	Detmold Bielefeld	1801-1935	10
Hakenberg	rkKB	Detmold Paderborn	1689-1879	2
Haldern	evKB	Detmold	1815-1874	3
Haldern	evKB	Düsseldorf Münster	1678-1957	3
Halle	evKB rkKB	Bielefeld Detmold	1653-1935	20

Location	Nature of Material	Where Filmed	Dates Covered	No. of Rolls
Hallenberg	rkKB	Detmold	1808-1874	2
Haltern	evKB rkKB STA	Detmold Münster Bielefeld	1639-1959	36
Halver	evKB STA	Bielefeld Detmold	1646-1968	16
Halverde	rkKB evKB	Münster Detmold	1784-1899	6
Hambach	BGM rkKB	Schloss Brühl	1607-1875	13
Hamm	evKB rkKB MKB	Detmold Hannover	1779-1912	3
Hamm -Bossendorf-	rkKB	Münster	1647-1900	2
Hamm -Düsseldorf-	rkKB	Schloss Brühl	1647-1809	3
Hamm -Hannover-	evKB	Detmold Bielefeld	1615-1966	40
Hamm -Hannover-	MKB	Hannover Eibenstock	1583-1944	6
Hamm -Hannover-	rkKB	Münster Detmold	1811-1874	8
Hamm -Hannover-	LDS records	Salt Lake City	1948	1
Hamm -Hannover-	STA	Detmold Schloss Brühl	1809-1814	9
Hamm -Recklinghausen-	rkKB	Detmold	1815-1874	4
Hampenhausen	rkKB	Detmold	1808-1874	2
Handorf	rkKB	Detmold Münster	1650-1862	2
Hanselaer	rkKB	Schloss Brühl	1674-1798	1
Hapenscheid	BGM	Schloss Brühl	1797-1872	
Harhinghausen	evKB	Detmold	1815-1874	3
Harpen	evKB	Bielefeld	1688-1943	7
Harsewinkel	rkKB	Münster Detmold	1683-1874	8

Location	Nature of Material	Where Filmed	Dates Covered	No. of Rolls
Harth	rkKB	Detmold Paderborn	1752-1874	2
Hartum	evKB	Bielefeld Detmold	1661-1946	21
Harsheim	rkKB	Schloss Brühl	1779-1798	1
Hasselweiler	rkKB	Schloss Brühl	1637-1802	1
Hasseim	rkKB	Schloss Brühl	1695-1798	1
Hattingen	evKB	Bielefeld Detmold	1614-1961	41
Hattingen	rkKB STA	Detmold	1818-1874 1810	7 1
Hau	STA	Schloss Brühl	1801-1975	9
Hausberge	evKB	Bielefeld Detmold	1654-1904	5
Hävern	evKB	Detmold	1808-1874	7
Häverstädt	evKB	Detmold	1815-1874	4
Havert	rkKB	Schloss Brühl	1734-1798	1
Havixbeck	rkKB	Münster	1590-1887	5
Heddighausen	rkKB	Paderborn Detmold	1685-1874	6
Heddinghoven	rkKB	Schloss Brühl	1707-1815	1
Heek	rkKB	Detmold Münster	1662-1926	5
Heepen	evKB STA	Bielefeld Detmold	1668-1961	37
Heesen	STA rkKB	Detmold	1641-1874	9
Hegensdorf	rkKB	Paderborn Detmold	1711-1874	2
Heheim	evKB	Bielefeld	1852-1932	1
Heiden -Borker-	rkKB STA	Detmold Münster	1649-1902	5
Heiden -Detmold-	evKB	Bielefeld	1641-1907	15
Heiligenhaus	evLut	Schloss Brühl	1770-1809	2

Location	Nature of Material	Where Filmed	Dates Covered	No. of Rolls
Heiligenkirchen	evKB	Bielefeld Detmold	1680-1900	8
Heimbach	BA rkKB	Schloss Brühl	1726-1875	8
Heimsen	evKB	Detmold Bielefeld	1751-1900	7
Heimsberg	BGM	Schloss Brühl	1798-1875	14
Heimsberg -Selfkantkreis-	evLut rkKB	Schloss Brühl	1584-1798	3
Heinsberg	BGM	Schloss Brühl	1802-1872	1
Hellefeld	rkKB	Detmold	1779-1874	2
Hellenthal	BGM rkKB	Schloss Brühl	1684-1875	21
Hellinghausen	rkKB	Detmold Paderborn	1779-1879	3
Helmeringhausen	rkKB	Paderborn	1614-1874	4
Helmern	rkKB	Detmold	1696-1884	5
Helminghausen	rkKB evKB	Detmold Paderborn	1653-1874	15
Helpegs	evKB	Bielefeld	1906-1963	2
Hembergen	rkKB	Münster	1749-1875	2
Hembsen	rkKB	Detmold	1815-1874	2
Hemden	rkKB	Detmold	1815-1874	7
Hemer	evKB STA	Detmold Bielefeld	1717-1920	15
Hemmerden	evKB STA BA	Schloss Brühl Detmold	1732-1955	19
Hemmerich	rkKB	Schloss Brühl	1674-1801	1
Hemmern	rkKB	Paderborn	1666-1874	3
Hengeler	rkKB	Detmold	1815-1874	2
Henglarn	rkKB	Paderborn	1696-1884	4
Hennef	rkKB STA	Schloss Brühl	1652-1875	22

Location	Nature of Material	Where Filmed	Dates Covered	No. of Rolls
Hennen	ev.refKB rkKB evLutKB	Detmold Bielefeld	1726-1945	11
Henrichenburg	rkKB	Detmold	1780-1874	1
Henrichsburg	rkKB	Münster	1725-1881	2
Heppendorf	rkKB	Schloss Brühl	1623-1798	1
Herbede	rkKB evKB	Detmold Bielefeld	1584-1919	19
Herbern	rkKB	Detmold Münster	1650-1884	5
Herbram	rkKB	Detmold	1808-1813	1
Herchen	STA evLutKB rkKB	Schloss Brühl	1752-1875	16
Herdecke	evKB rkKB	Detmold Bielefeld	1667-1968	19
Herferd	LDS records MKB	Salt Lake City Hannover Eibenstock	1931-1948 1833-1845	1 4
Herferd	rkKB STA	Detmold	1808-1874	4
Herferd	evLutKB	Detmold Bielefeld	1677-1939	84
Hergarten	rkKB	Schloss Brühl	1710-1793	1
Heringhausen	rkKB	Detmold Paderborn	1658-1879	6
Herkenrath	rkKB	Schloss Brühl	1675-1811	2
Herlinghausen	evKB	Detmold Bielefeld	1709-1902	3
Herne	rkKB STA evKB LDS records	Bielefeld Detmold Salt Lake City	1683-1914	20
Herongen	rkKB STA	Schloss Brühl Münster	1630-1875	11
Herringen	evKB	Detmold Bielefeld	1694-1965	13
Herringhausen	evKB STA	Detmold	1811-1874	11

Location	Nature of Material	Where Filmed	Dates Covered	No. of Rolls
Herscheid	BGM evKB	Detmold Bielefeld	1733-1959	20
Hersch	rkKB STA	Schloss Brühl	1680-1875	17
Herste	rkKB	Detmold	1808-1874	2
Herstelle	rkKB	Detmold	1808-1874	1
Herten	STA rkKB	Münster Detmold	1701-1877	7
Hertsfeld	rkKB		1759-1750	1
Hersebocholt	rkKB	Detmold	1815-1874	6
Hersebroch	rkKB evKB	Detmold	1810-1874	6
Hersfeld	rkKB	Münster Detmold	1643-1875	5
Hersagenrath	BA rkKB	Schloss Brühl	1648-1875	15
Hesborn	rkKB	Detmold	1808-1874	2
Hesseln	rkKB	Detmold	1808-1874	1
Hesselteich	STA evKB	Detmold Bielefeld	1614-1938	8
Hiddenhausen	evKB	Detmold Bielefeld	1691-1933	15
Hiddesen	ev.refKB	Bielefeld	1947-1969	1
Hiddingsel	rkKB	Detmold Münster	1815-1876	3
Hilbech	evKB	Detmold	1818-1974	1
Hilberath	rkKB	Schloss Brühl	1687-1798	1
Hilchenbach	STA evKB rkKB	Detmold Bielefeld	1620-1917	20
Hilden	evKB rkKB BA STA	Schloss Brühl Düsseldorf	1682-1875	32
Hille	ev.refKB	Bielefeld Detmold	1725-1929	19
Hillensberg	rkKB	Schloss Brühl	1616-1738	1

Location	Nature of Material	Where Filmed	Dates Covered	No. of Rolls
Hillentrup	evKB	Bielefeld Detmold	1670-1945	10
Hiltrup	rkKB	Münster	1748-1874	3
Himmighausen	rkKB	Detmold	1808-1874	2
Hinsbeck	rkKB STA	Schloss Brühl	1607-1875	12
Hirschberg	rkKB	Detmold Paderborn	1653-1874	4
Hitdorf	STA	Schloss Brühl	1843-1875	6
Hochkirchen	rkKB	Schloss Brühl	1683-1805	2
Hochneukirch	STA BA rkKB	Schloss Brühl	1655-1875	15
Hoengen	BA	Schloss Brühl	1798-1875	11
Hoeningen	BA rkKB	Schloss Brühl	1779-1875	12
Hoetmar	rkKB STA	Detmold Münster	1610-1875	6
Höfen	rkKB BA	Schloss Brühl	1651-1875	9
Hohehaus	rkKB	Detmold	1808-1874	2
Hohenhausen	AG ev.refKB evKB	Detmold Bielefeld	1686-1905	35
Hohenhimburg	evKB STA	Detmold Bielefeld	1624-1935	26
Hohenwepel	rkKB	Detmold	1808-1874	2
Hohkeppel	rkKB	Schloss Brühl	1768-1804	1
Hoinkhausen	rkKB	Detmold Paderborn	1626-1874	4
Holsen	evKB	Detmold	1815-1874	3
Holtfeld	rkKB	Detmold	1808-1874	1
Holtheim	rkKB	Detmold Paderborn	1689-1874	3
Holtrup	evKB	Detmold Bielefeld	1647-1949	6

Location	Nature of Material	Where Filmed	Dates Covered	No. of Rolls
Holtwick	rkKB	Münster Berlin-Dahlem Detmold	1692-1925	11
Holze	evKB	Detmold	1818-1874	5
Holzhausen -a.d. Porta-	evKB	Detmold Bielefeld	1645-1937	10
Holzhausen -Hoxtes-	rkKB	Detmold	1809-1874	1
Holzhausen -Liebkeche-	evKB	Detmold Bielefeld	1674-1951	6
Holzhausen -Minde-	evKB	Detmold Bielefeld	1661-1935	21
Holzhein	BGM STA	Schloss Brühl	1799-1875	10
Holzhein -Goevenbroich-	rkKB STA	Schloss Brühl	1708-1842	2
Holzhein -Schleiche-	rkKB	Schloss Brühl	1692-1805	1
Holzweiler	BGM STA rkKB	Schloss Brühl	1667-1875	5
Holzwichede	evKB rkKB	Detmold	1815-1874	2
Homberg -Moen-	STA evKB rkKB	Schloss Brühl Münster	1669-1900	16
Homer	rkKB	Detmold	1815-1874	3
Höngen -Aachen-		Schloss Brühl	1638-1827	3
Honnef	rkKB STA	Schloss Brühl	1689-1875	21
Hopsten	rkKB	Münster Detmold	1656-1890	7
Horn	evKB	Bielefeld	1657-1905	7
Horn -Detmold-	evKB	Bielefeld Detmold	1657-1969	19
Horn -Millinghausen-	rkKB	Paderborn Detmold	1642-1874	10

Location	Nature of Material	Where Filmed	Dates Covered	No. of Rolls
Horneburg	BGM rkKB	Münster Detmold	1650-1876	3
Horren	rkKB	Schloss Brühl	1707-1798	1
Hörste -Halle-	evLut	Bielefeld	1707-1905	4
Horste -Halle-	rkKB evKB	Detmold Paderborn	1808-1874	10
Hörste -Lippe-	evLut ev.refKB	Bielefeld Detmold Berlin-Dahlem	1646-1908	17
Hörste -Büren-	rkKB	Detmold Paderborn	1644-1874	6
Hörstel	rkKB	Detmold Münster	1875	4
Hörstger		Den Haag	1737-1798	1
Hörstmar	rkKB	Münster	1708-1875	5
Höveldorf	rkKB	Detmold	1808-1874	3
Hovel	LDS records	Salt Lake City	1924-1928	1
Hoxfeld	rkKB	Detmold	1815-1874	3
Höxter	rkKB STA MKB evKB	Hannover Bielefeld Eibenstock Detmold	1649-1920	18
Hubbelrath	STA rkKB	Schloss Brühl	1662-1872	10
Hüchelhoven	rkKB BGM	Schloss Brühl	1734-1852	4
Huchsen	evKB	Detmold	1815-1874	3
Hüchelhoven	BGM rkKB	Schloss Brühl	1590-1875	32
Hücher	evKB	Bielefeld Detmold	1808-1965	7
Hücheswage	rkKB evLutKB ev.refKB	Schloss Brühl	1666-1809	4
Hulleon	rkKB	Münster Detmold	1663-1900	3

Location	Nature of Material	Where Filmed	Dates Covered	No. of Rolls
Hüllhorst	evKB	Bielefeld Detmold	1661-1958	8
Hüls	rkKB	Schloss Brühl	1633-1798	1
Hülscheid	evLutKB	Bielefeld Detmold	1670-1903	5
Hülscheid -Altena-	evKB rkKB	Detmold	1815-1874	3
Humbruck	evKB	Bielefeld	1891-1951	2
Hundewick	rkKB	Detmold	1815-1874	2
Hunxe	evLut	Düsseldorf	1723-1874	6
Hürtgen	rkKB	Schloss Brühl	1744-1819	1
Hürtgenwald	STA BA rkKB	Schloss Brühl	1708-1875	17
Hürth	rkKB	Schloss Brühl	1688-1800	2
Husen	rkKB	Paderborn	1696-1884	4
Hüttertal	STA evKB	Detmold	1811-1874	9
Ibbenbüren	evKB	Detmold Bielefeld	1678-1928	10
Ibbenbüren	rkKB	Detmold Bielefeld	1660-1936	15
Iggenhausen	PSA rkKB	Detmold Paderborn	1716-1874	2
Iivese	evKB	Detmold	1808-1874	2
Ikenhausen	rkKB	Detmold	1808-1874	2
Ilse	evKB	Detmold	1808-1873	2
Ilserheide	evKB	Detmold	1808-1874	4
Imgenbroich	rkKB	Schloss Brühl	1637-1798	1
Imgenbroich	ZSR BGM	Schloss Brühl	1799-1875	15
Immekeppel	rkKB	Schloss Brühl	1645-1810	1
Immendorf -Leileukirchen-	rkKB ZSR BGM	Schloss Brühl	1595-1872	3

Location	Nature of Material	Where Filmed	Dates Covered	No. of Rolls
Immerath	ZSR BGM rkKB	Schloss Brühl	1644-1875	11
Inden	ZSR BGM	Brühl	1799-1875	6
Inger	rkKB	Schloss Brühl	1770-1809	1
Isenstedt	evLutKB	Bielefeld Detmold	1811-1952	11
Iserlohn	evKB	Bielefeld Detmold	1635-1931	33
Iserlohn	MiKB	Bielefeld	1834-1919	1
Iserlohn	rkKB	Bielefeld	1645-1921	4
Iserlohn	rkKB	Detmold	1818-1874	5
Iserlohn	ZSA ZA	Detmold Bielefeld	1810-1813	9
Isingdorf	evKB	Detmold	1808-1874	5
Isselburg	rkKB BGM	Münster	1786-1875	1
Isselhorst	evKB	Detmold Bielefeld	1714-1962	9
Issum	evKB	Düsseldorf Schloss Brühl	1700-1839	2
Issum	rkKB BA	Münster Schloss Brühl	1614-1875	4
Issum	ZSA STA	Brühl	1799-1875	9
Istrup -Detmold-	evKB	Bielefeld	1950-1969	1
Istrup -Kr. Höxke-	rkKB	Detmold	1808-1874	2
Iteil	KB	Detmold	1818-1874	3
Ittenbach	rkKB	Schloss Brühl	1668-1809	1
Ittenbach	ZSA STA	Brühl	1810-1875	15
Iversheim	rkKB	Schloss Brühl	1770-1790	1
Jakobswullesheim	rkKB	Schloss Brühl	1770-1800	1

Location	Nature of Material	Where Filmed	Dates Covered	No. of Rolls
Jakobsberg	rkKB	Detmold	1808-1874	1
Jöllenbeck	evKB	Detmold Bielefeld	1676-1944	16
Jössen	evKB PSA	Detmold	1808-1873	2
Jüchen	ZSA STA BM PSA	Bruhl	1798-1875	21
Jüchen	evLut refKB	Düsseldorf Schloss Brühl	1653-1798	6
Jüchen	rkKB	Schloss Brühl	1641-1798	1
Jülich	ZSR BGM PSA	Brühl Schloss Brühl	1798-1875	38
Jülich	evLut MilKB	Hannover Schloss Brühl	1611-1918	2
Jülich	rkKB MilKB	Schloss Brühl	1635-1801	6
Junkersdorf	rkKB	Schloss Brühl	1670-1826	3
Kaarst	PSA BGM rkKB	Schloss Brühl	1632-1875	15
Kaldenkirchen	ev.refKB rkKB	Schloss Brühl	1705-1805	2
Kalkar	rkKB BA	Schloss Brühl	1654-1878	2
Kalkar -Euskirchen-	rkKB	Schloss Brühl	1770-1809	1
Kalkar	PSA BGM rkKB evLutKB	Brühl Schloss Brühl Münster	1633-1879	15
Kall	PSA BGM	Brühl	1797-1875	15
Kall	rkKB	Schloss Brühl	1642-1798	1
Kallenhardt	rkKB PSA EA	Detmold Paderborn	1715-1874	4

Location	Nature of Material	Where Filmed	Dates Covered	No. of Rolls
Kalletal	ev.refKB PSA	Detmold	1751-1875	3
Kallmuth	rkKB	Schloss Brühl	1804-1858	1
Kalterherberg	PSA BGM rkKB	Schloss Brühl	1651-1875	11
Kamen	evLutKB ev.refKB PSA	Detmold Bielefeld	1621-1930	25
Kamen	PSA STA	Detmold	1810-1813	3
Kamp- Lintfort	rkKB PSA STA BA	Münster Schloss Brühl Brühl	1655-1901	15
Kanstein	rkKB	Paderborn	1658-1874	2
Kapellen	rkKB	Schloss Brühl	1643-1798	1
Kapellen -Geldern-	rkKB BA	Münster Berlin-Dahlem	1667-1878	9
Kapellen -Grevenbroich-	PSA BGM	Brühl	1799-1875	9
Kapellen -Moers-	rkKB	Schloss Brühl	1643-1798	1
Kapellen -Moers-	PSA BGM	Brühl	1799-1875	7
Karken	PSA BGM	Brühl	1799-1875	10
Karken	rkKB	Schloss Brühl	1621-1829	1
Kaster	rkKB	Schloss Brühl	1770-1798	1
Kattenvenne	evKB	Bielefeld	1889-1960	1
Keeken	rkKB BA	Schloss Brühl Bielefeld	1676-1875	8
Keeken	PSA STA	Brühl	1798-1875	7
Keldenich	rkKB	Schloss Brühl	1763-1822	1
Kellinghausen	rkKB BA	Paderborn	1666-1874	3

Location	Nature of Material	Where Filmed	Dates Covered	No. of Rolls
Kempen-Feldrom	rkKB PSA	Detmold	1808-1874	2
Kempen -Heinsberg-	rkKB	Schloss Brühl	1670-1798	1
Kempen -Kempen-	rkKB	Schloss Brühl	1625-1824	5
Kempen -Krefeld-	PSA BGM	Brühl	1798-1875	36
Keppeln	rkKB BA	Münster Schloss Brühl	1683-1875	2
Keppeln	PSA STA	Brühl	1798-1875	6
Kerken	ZSR BM STA	Brühl	1798-1875	19
Kerken	rkKB BA	Münster	1859-1875	1
Kervendonk	PSA STA	Brühl	1798-1875	10
Kervenheim	evKB evKA evLut	Düsseldorf Schloss Brühl	1663-1842	2
Kervenheim	rkKB BA	Münster Schloss Brühl	1703-1882	2
Kervenheim	PSA STA	Brühl	1798-1875	10
Kessel	rkKB	Schloss Brühl	1675-1798	1
Kessel	PSA STA ZSR	Brühl	1798-1875	6
Kesternich	ZSR BGM	Brühl	1798-1875	9
Kesternich	rkKB	Schloss Brühl	1719-1798	1
Kettwig	evKB evKA	Düsseldorf	1641-1928	38
Kevelaer	rkKB	Schloss Brühl Münster	1682-1875	5
Kevelaer	ZSR STA PSA	Brühl	1798-1875	15

Location	Nature of Material	Where Filmed	Dates Covered	No. of Rolls
Keyenberg	ZSR PSA BGM	Brühl	1799-1875	10
Keyenberg	rkKB	Schloss Brühl	1700-1800	2
Kierdorf	rkKB	Schloss Brühl	1732-1798	1
Kierspe	evKB LKA PSA	Bielefeld Detmold	1559-1954	11
Kinzweiler	ZSR BM PSA	Brühl	1802-1872	4
Kinzweiler	rkKB	Schloss Brühl	1714-1808	2
Kirchberg	ZSR BGM PSA	Schloss Brühl	1799-1875	7
Kirchborchen	rkKB EA PSA	Paderborn Detmold	1628-1874	4
Kirchderne	evPB LKA	Bielefeld	1674-1932	7
Kirchdornberg	evPB ZSR STA	Bielefeld	1666-1952	11
Kirchheim	rkKB	Schloss Brühl	1717-1798	1
Kirchheim -Kr. Fuskirchen-	ZSR STA PSA	Brühl	1800-1875	21
Kirchhellen	evKB rkKB PSA BA	Detmold Münster	1688-1932	5
Kirchhellen	ZSR STA BA PSA	Münster Detmold	1809-1814	2
Kirchoven	ZSR BM PSA	Brühl	1799-1875	11
Kirchoven	rkKB	Schloss Brühl	1733-1798	1
Kirchhundem	rkKB PSA	Detmold	1779-1874	5

Location	Nature of Material	Where Filmed	Dates Covered	No. of Rolls
Kirchlengern	evLutKB LKA	Bielefeld	1723-1940	5
Kirchellen	rkKB BA	Münster	1668-1932	3
Kirchhundem	rkKB PSA	Detmold	1779-1874	9
Kirchlengern	evKB PSA	Detmold	1810-1874	3
Kleekamp	evKB ev.refKB	Detmold	1814-1839	4
Klein Büllesheim	rkKB	Schloss Brühl	1690-1798	2
Klein Büllesheim	ZSR STA PSA	Brühl	1800-1875	21
Klein Gladboden	rkKB	Schloss Brühl	1590-1798	1
Klein Königsdorf	rkKB	Schloss Brühl	1632-1799	1
Klein Reeken	rkKB PSA	Detmold	1815-1874	1
Kleinen	ZSR BM PSA	Brühl	1863-1872	1
Kleinenberg -Kr. Büren-	rkKB EA	Paderborn	1652-1874	2
Kleinenbreden	rkKB PSA	Detmold	1808-1874	2
Kleinenbremen	evKB LKA PSA	Bielefeld Detmold	1703-1947	9
Kleinenbroich	ZSR BGM PSA	Brühl	1799-1875	11
Kleingladbach	ZSR BGM PSA	Brühl	1797-1872	1
Kleinich	evLutKB evKB	Düsseldorf	1593-1702	1
Kleinkempen	ZSR BGM PSA	Brühl	1799-1839	4

Location	Nature of Material	Where Filmed	Dates Covered	No. of Rolls
Kleve	ZSR STA BGM PSA	Brühl	1798-1875	45
Kleve	rkKB BA	Schloss Brühl Münster	1653-1875	7
Kleve	evKB evKA	Düsseldorf	1696-1862	4
Kleve	evLutKB	Schloss Brühl	1662-1798	2
Kleve	ev.refKB	Schloss Brühl	1617-1810	5
Kleve	French refKB	Schloss Brühl	1696-1798	1
Kleve	Mennonite KB	Schloss Brühl	1758-1798	1
Kleve	evKB KBA MKB	Hannover	1869-1917	1
Kleve	Eglise Wollonne KB	The Hague	1696-1795	1
Klieve	rkKB EA	Paderborn	1683-1874	3
Klotingen	evKB PSA	Detmold	1819-1874	2
Klüppelberg	evLutKB evKA	Düsseldorf	1798-1890	3
Kneblinghausen	rkKB EA	Paderborn	1679-1875	1
Kobbenrode	rkKB	Paderborn	1701-1874	1
Kohlhagen	rkKB	Paderborn	1656-1944	8
Kohlscheid	ZSR BGM STA PSA	Brühl	1799-1875	27
Kollerbeck	rkKB PSA	Detmold	1808-1874	2
Köln	Inventory of church records	Schloss Brühl		1
Köln	LDS records	Salt Lake City	-1951	17

Location	Nature of Material	Where Filmed	Dates Covered	No. of Rolls
Köln	MilKB KBA	Koblenz Hannover	1745-1943	26
Köln	evLutKB ev.refKB	Schloss Brühl	1593-1803	1
Köln	evLutKB	Schloss Brühl	1796-1809	1
Köln	ev.refKB	Schloss Brühl	1634-1809	2
Köln	French refKB	Schloss Brühl	1600-1802	1
Köln	Holland refKB	Schloss Brühl	1571-1803	1
Köln	rkKB	Schloss Brühl	1591-1810	100
Kommern	rkKB	Schloss Brühl	1710-1804	2
Kommern	ZSR STA PSA	Brühl	1798-1875	6
Königshoven	rkKB	Schloss Brühl	1770-1810	1
Königswinter	rkKB	Schloss Brühl	1716-1809	2
Konzen	rkKB	Schloss Brühl	1637-1798	1
Korbecke -Kr. Warburg-	rkKB PSA	Detmold	1809-1874	1
Körbeckel	evKB	Detmold	1826-1874	1
Kornelimünster	ZSR BM PSA	Brühl	1798-1875	14
Kornelimüster	rkKB	Schloss Brühl	1601-1798	4
Korschenbroich	ZSR BM PSA	Brühl	1799-1875	16
Korschenbroich	rkKB	Schloss Brühl	1657-1811	2
Körrenzig	BGM KB PSA	Brühl	1800-1875	10
Korschenbroich	ZSR STA	Brühl	1803-1842	1
Koslas	ZSR BGM	Brühl	1801-1875	10
Koslas	rkKB	Schloss Brühl	1635-1798	1

Location	Nature of Material	Where Filmed	Dates Covered	No. of Rolls
Kostedt	evKB PSA	Detmold	1809-1874	3
Kranenburg	ZSR BM PSA	Brühl	1799-1875	12
Kranenburg	rkKB BA	Münster Schloss Brühl	1640-1876	5
Krange	evKB LKA	Bielefeld	1745-1833	2
Krefeld	ZSR BM STA PSA	Brühl	1799-1875	192
Krefeld	evKB evKA	Düsseldorf	1846-1873	6
Krefeld	evLutKB	Schloss Brühl	1748-1798	1
Krefeld	ev.refKB	Schloss Brühl	1647-1798	4
Krefeld	Mennoniten KB	Schloss Brühl	1738-1798	1
Krefeld	rkKB	Schloss Brühl	1620-1803	7
Krenzan	ZSR BM PSA	Brühl	1799-1875	9
Krenzan	rkKB	Schloss Brühl	1750-1800	1
Krenztal	evKB LKA ev.refKB PSA	Bielefeld Detmold	1576-1945	50
Kreuzweingarten-Rheder	rkKB	Schloss Brühl	1697-1805	1
Krombach	evKB LKA	Bielefeld	1597-1795	3
Kronenburg	rkKB	Schloss Brühl	1709-1797	1
Kronenburg	ZSR STA PSA	Brühl	1796-1875	8
Kuchenheim	rkKB	Schloss Brühl	1648-1798	1
Kuchenheim	ZSR STA PSA	Brühl	1800-1875	21

Location	Nature of Material	Where Filmed	Dates Covered	No. of Rolls
Kückhoven	SZR BGM	Brühl	1709-1875	3
Kückhoven	rkKB	Schloss Brühl	1698-1798	1
Kühlsen	rkKB PSA	Detmold	1808-1874	2
Künsebeck	evKB	Detmold	1808-1874	3
Kutenhausen	evKB PSA LKA	Detmold Bielefeld	1801-1816	6
Laar -Kr. Herford-	evLutKB PSA	Detmold	1815-1874	10
Laar	ZSR STA	Detmold	1811-1813	1
Laasphe	evKB LKA PSA	Bielefeld Detmold	1654-1953	19
Ladbergen	evKB PSA	Detmold	1803-1874	2
Ladbergen	ZSR STA PSA LKA	Detmold Bielefeld	1810-1814	3
Laer	rkKB BA	Münster	1629-1875	5
Lage	evKB LKA	Bielefeld	1701-1969	34
Lage	evLutKB	Berlin	1701-1809	4
Lage -Detmold-	ev.refKB PSA	Detmold	1839-1875	2
Lage -Detmold-	Court records AG	Detmold	1807-1883	14
Lage -Detmold-	ZSR STA	Detmold	1791-1875	2
Lahed	evKB PSA	Detmold	1808-1874	4
Lahde	evLutKB LKA	Bielefeld	1654-1964	8
Lamersdorf	rkKB	Schloss Brühl	1699-1818	3

Location	Nature of Material	Where Filmed	Dates Covered	No. of Rolls
Lamersdorf	ZSR BM PSA	Brühl	1800-1875	5
Lämershagen-gräfinghagen	ev.refKB PSA	Brühl	1750-1875	5
Lammersdorf	ZSR BGM	Brühl	1801-1875	6
Lammersdorf	rkKB	Schloss Brühl	1705-1818	1
Lank-fatum	rkKB	Schloss Brühl	1690-1798	1
Langeland	rkKB PSA	Detmold	1808-1874	2
Langenberg -Düsseldorf-	evKB KA	Düsseldorf	1740-1900	18
Langenberg	ev.refKB	Schloss Brühl	1675-1809	4
Langenberg	rkKB	Schloss Brühl	1766-1809	1
Langenberg -Dusseldorf- Mettmann-	evKB rkKB PSA	Detmold	1866	1
Langenberg -Kr. Wieden- brück-	rkKB evKB	Detmold	1808-1874	6
Langendorf	rkKB	Schloss Brühl	1674-1798	1
Langendreer	evKB LKA	Bielefeld	1727-1913	10
Langeneicke	rkKB PSA	Detmold	1779-1873	3
Langenfeld	KB	Schloss Brühl	1770-1809	1
Langenholz-hausen	evKB LKA	Bielefeld	1684-1959	12
Langenholz-hausen -Kr. Lemgo-	ev.refKB PSA	Detmold	1776-1875	1
Langenhorst	KB BA	Münster	1670-1875	1
Langenskasse-Heddinghausen	rkKB PSA EA	Detmold Paderborn	1676-1874	5

Location	Nature of Material	Where Filmed	Dates Covered	No. of Rolls
Langerwehe	ZSR BM PSA	Brühl	1802-1876	7
Langerwehe	rkKB	Schloss Brühl	1626-1806	1
Lashorst	evKB PSA	Detmold	1815-1874	3
Laurensberg	ZSR MB PSA	Brühl	1799-1875	9
Laurensberg	rkKB	Schloss Brühl	1706-1875	3
Laurenzberg	rkKB	Schloss Brühl	1685-1805	2
Laurenzberg	ev.refKB	Schloss Brühl	1741-1798	1
Lauthausen	rkKB	Schloss Brühl	1673-1809	1
Lauthausen	ZSR STA PSA	Brühl	1810-1875	12
Lechenich	rkKB	Schloss Brühl	1668-1815	3
Lechenich	ZSR STA PSA	Brühl	1798-1875	9
Ledde	evKB PSA LKA	Detmold Bielefeld	1693-1957	8
Ledde	ZSR STA PSA	Detmold	1811-1812	1
Leeden	ZSR STA	Detmold	1810-1813	3
Leeden	evKB PSA LKA	Detmold Bielefeld	1670-1897	4
Leer	rkKB BA	Münster	1683-1875	2
Leer-Ostendorf	rkKB		1749	1
Legden	rkKB BA PSA	Detmold Münster	1661-1939	9
Leiberg	rkKB PSA EA	Detmold Paderborn	1803-1877	5

Location	Nature of Material	Where Filmed	Dates Covered	No. of Rolls
Leichlingen	ZSR BN STA PSA	Brühl	1810-1875	24
Leinen	evKB LKA	Bielefeld	1711-1837	3
Leitmar	rkKB EA	Paderborn	1685-1874	2
Lembeck	rkKB PSA BA	Detmold Münster	1713-1900	5
Lembeck	ZSR STA PSA	Detmold	1812-1814	1
Lemgo	evKB LKA	Bielefeld	1673-1966	27
Lemgo	ev.refKB PSA	Detmold	1751-1875	6
Lemgo	rkKB	Detmold	1854-1875	1
Lendersdorf- Kranthausen	rkKB	Schloss Brühl	1656-1800	1
Lengerich	evKB LKA PSA	Bielefeld Detmold	1644-1907	25
Lengerich	rkKB BA	Münster	1851-1875	1
Lengerich	ZSR STA PSA	Detmold	1810-1813	2
Lengerich -Tecklehburg-	Church rules LKA	Bielefeld	1588	1
Lenne	rkKB PSA	Detmold	1779-1874	2
Lennestadt	evKB	Detmold	1865-1874	1
Lennestadt	rkKB	Detmold	1779-1874	8
Lenzinghausen	evKB	Detmold	1808-1874	6
Leopoldshöhe	evKB ev.refKB LKA PSA	Bielefeld Detmold	1840-1969	9

Location	Nature of Material	Where Filmed	Dates Covered	No. of Rolls
Lerbeck	evKB evLutKB LKA PSA	Bielefeld Detmold	1656-1959	13
Lerche	evKB ev.refKB PSA	Detmold	1815-1874	5
Lessenich	rkKB	Schloss Brühl	1691-1798	1
Leteln	evKB PSA	Detmold	1808-1874	2
Letmathe	evKB PSA LKA	Detmold Bielefeld	1819-1969	4
Letmathe	rkKB PSA	Detmold	1821-1874	2
Lette	rkKB		1749	1
Lette -Coesfeld-	rkKB BA	Münster	1661-1928	3
Lette -Kr. Wieden- brück-	rkKB PSA BA	Detmold Münster	1672-1875	3
Leuth	rkKB	Schloss Brühl	1616-1798	1
Leuth	ZSR STA PSA	Brühl	1798-1875	5
Leverkusen	ZSR BM PSA	Brühl	1811-1875	25
Leverkusen	JüdGem	Schloss Brühl	1808	1
Leverkusen	rkKB	Schloss Brühl	1750-1810	7
Levern	evKB PSA LKA evLutKB	Detmold Bielefeld	1679-1918	13
Liblar	rkKB	Schloss Brühl	1679-1798	1
Liblar	ZSR STA PSA	Brühl	1800-1880	7
Libus	rkKB	Schloss Brühl	1770-1809	1

Location	Nature of Material	Where Filmed	Dates Covered	No. of Rolls
Lichtenau	evKB PSA	Detmold Bielefeld	1840-1966	2
Lichtenau	rkKB PSA EA	Detmold Paderborn	1689-1874	2
Lichtendorf	evLutKB PSA	Detmold	1818-1874	3
Liedberg	ZSR BM PSA	Brühl	1799-1875	12
Liedberg	rkKB	Schloss Brühl	1784-1794	1
Liedern	rkKB PSA	Detmold	1815-1874	6
Liedern	ZSR STA PSA	Detmold	1812-1814	3
Lieme	evKB LKA	Bielefeld	1727-1957	7
Liemke	ZSR STA PSA	Detmold	1808-1813	1
Liemke	rkKB	Detmold	1815-1874	3
Liener	evKB LKA PSA	Bielefeld Detmold	1711-1908	24
Liener	ZSR STA PSA	Detmold	1810-1814	2
Liesborn	rkKB BA PSA	Münster Detmold	1654-1875	9
Liesborn	ZSR STA PSA	Detmold	1810-1814	2
Limbergen	rkKB	Detmold	1750, 1810-1874	2
Lindlar	rkKB	Schloss Brühl	1716-1809	4
Linich	ZSR BGM PSA	Brühl	1802-1872	1

Location	Nature of Material	Where Filmed	Dates Covered	No. of Rolls
Linnich	ZSR BGM STA PSA	Schloss Brühl	1798-1875	54
Linnich	rkKB	Schloss Brühl	1650-1806	3
Lintel	rkKB PSA	Detmold	1808-1874	8
Lintorf	rkKB	Schloss Brühl	1659-1809	2
Linzenich- Lövenich	rkKB	Schloss Brühl	1750-1793	1
Lippborg	rkKB BA PSA	Münster Detmold	1654-1875	5
Lipperode	evKB LKA ev.refKB PSA	Bielefeld Detmold	1651-1963	5
Lipperode	ZSR STA PSA	Detmold	1754-1785	1
Lipperreihe	rkKB PSA	Detmold	1808-1874	2
Lippetal	rkKB	Detmold	1779-1874	12
Lippinghausen	evKB	Detmold	1808-1874	4
Lippramsdorf	rkKB BA	Münster	1646-1899	1
Lippstadt		Eibenstock Hannover	1833-1890	3
Lippstadt	evKB LKA	Bielefeld	1653-1930	23
Lippstadt	rkKB EA	Paderborn	1807-1906	3
Lippstadt	ZSR BM LKA PSA	Bielefeld Detmold	1810-1814	4
Lobberich	rkKB	Schloss Brühl	1637-1798	2
Lobberich	PSR STA PSA	Brühl	1798-1875	12

Location	Nature of Material	Where Filmed	Dates Covered	No. of Rolls
Lohe -Minden-	rkKB PSA	Detmold	1863-1874	1
Lohe	evKB PSA LKA	Detmold Bielefeld	1808-1960	10
Lohe	rkKB PSA	Detmold	1818-1842	5
Lohfeld	evKB	Detmold	1808-1874	4
Lohmar	rkKB	Schloss Brühl	1738-1809	1
Lohn	rkKB	Schloss Brühl	1644-1801	2
Lohn	ZSR BGM PSA	Brühl	1798-1810	3
Löhne	evKB PSA LKA evLutKB	Detmold Bielefeld	1697-1965	11
Lohne	evKB LKA	Bielefeld	1664-1919	4
Loikum	rkKB BA	Münster	1653-1875	1
Lommersdorf	ZSR BM PSA	Brühl	1799-1875	8
Lommersdorf	rkKB	Schloss Brühl	1680-1798	1
Lomersum	rkKB	Schloss Brühl	1631-1798	2
Lotte	evKB LKA PSA	Bielefeld Detmold	1643-1967	5
Lotte	ZSR STA PSA	Detmold	1811-1814	1
Louisendorf	ZSR STA PSA	Brühl	1798-1875	10
Lövenich -Erkelenz	ZSR BGM PSA	Brühl	1799-1875	11
Lövenich	ev.refKB	Schloss Brühl	1770-1798	1
Lövenich	rkKB	Schloss Brühl	1646-1798	1

Location	Nature of Material	Where Filmed	Dates Covered	No. of Rolls
Lövenich -Köln-	rkKB	Schloss Brühl	1701-1800	1
Löwen	rkKB PSA	Detmold	1808-1874	2
Löwendorf	rkKB	Detmold	1808-1874	2
Lowick	rkKB	Detmold	1815-1874	6
Loxten	evKB PSA LKA	Detmold Bielefeld	1614-1938	7
Loxten	rkKB PSA	Detmold	1863-1874	1
Libbecke	evKB PSA LKA evLutKB	Detmold Bielefeld	1682-1947	15
Libbecke	rkKB PSA	Detmold	1842-1874	1
Lüchtringen	evLutKB	Detmold	1808-1874	3
Lüchtringen	rkKB	Detmold	1813-1874	3
Ludendorf	rkKB	Schloss Brühl	1723-1798	1
Lüdenhausen	evKB PSA LKA ev.refKB	Detmold Bielefeld	1611-1969	9
Lüdenscheid	evKB PSA LKA	Detmold Bielefeld	1719-1962	25
Lüdenscheid	rkKB PSA	Detmold	1833-1874	1
Lüdenscheid	ZSR STA	Detmold	1810-1812	2
Lüdge	rkKB	Detmold	1808-1874	4
Lüdinghausen	evKB PSA	Detmold	1847-1874	1
Lüdinghausen	rkKB	Detmold Berlin	1748, 1750 1832-1874	4
Lüftelberg	rkKB	Schloss Brühl	1691-1798	1

Location	Nature of Material	Where Filmed	Dates Covered	No. of Rolls
Lüftelberg	ZSR STA PSA	Brühl	1799-1875	15
Lüdge	evKB PSA LKA ev.refKB	Detmold Bielefeld	1855-1963	2
Lüdge	rkKB PSA	Detmold	1854-1875	1
Luhden	evKB	Detmold	1808-1872 1808-1872	1
Lülsdorf	rkKB	Schloss Brühl	1729-1809	2
Lunden	rkKB BA	Münster	1602-1897	3
Lünen	rkKB PSA	Detmold	1815-1874	2
Lünen	evKB LKA	Bielefeld	1686-1900	3
Lünen	ZSR STA PSA	Detmold	1810-1813	2
Lünern	evKB LKA	Bielefeld	1680-1897	4
Lussem	rkKB	Schloss Brühl	1657-1805	1
Lütgendorfmund	evKB LKA	Bielefeld	1811-1900	4
Lütgeneder	rkKB PSA EA	Detmold Paderborn	1654-1875	2
Lutmarsen	evLutKB PSA	Detmold	1808-1874	3
Lütmarsen	rkKB	Detmold	1808-1874	2
Lützenkirchen	rkKB	Schloss Brühl	1729-1809	1
Maaslingen	evKB	Detmold	1808-1874	3
Machheim	rkKB	Detmold Paderborn	1667-1874	4
Manheim	rkKB	Schloss Brühl	1656-1798	1
Manrode	STA	Detmold	1808-1874	1

Location	Nature of Material	Where Filmed	Dates Covered	No. of Rolls
Manstedten	rkKB	Schloss Brühl	1632-1798	1
Mantinghausen	rkKB STA	Detmodl Paderborn	1641-1875	7
Marbeck	rkKB	Detmold	1815-1874	3
Marienwirler- hoven	rkKB	Schloss Brühl	1630-1807	1
Marienberg- hausen	rkKB	Schloss Brühl	1749-1809	1
Marienfeld	rkKB	Münster Detmold	1804-1890	2
Marienheile	rkKB	Schloss Brühl	1657-1818	2
Marienhol	rkKB	Paderborn Detmold	1776-1874	4
Mark -Hannover-	evKB	Bielefeld	1700-1950	7
Marl	rkKB STA	Detmold Münster	1643-1875	22
Marsberg	evKB	Bielefeld	1862-1948	1
Marten	evKB	Bielefeld	1881-1899	2
Mastholte	rkKB	Detmold	1808-1874	5
Materborn	rkKB STA	Schloss Brühl	1654-1875	10
Maubach	rkKB	Schloss Brühl	1770-1797	1
Mechenich	BA rkKB	Schloss Brühl	1675-1875	13
Mechenheim	rkKB STA	Schloss Brühl	1638-1875	16
Medebach	rkKB evKB	Detmold Bielefeld	1808-1966	7
Meerbusch	BA rkKB STA	Schloss Brühl	1659-1875	41
Meerhof	rkKB STA	Detmold Paderborn	1656-1874	11
Meinerzhagen	STA evKB rkKB	Bielefeld Detmold	1662-1918	12

Location	Nature of Material	Where Filmed	Dates Covered	No. of Rolls
Meiningsen	evKB	Bielefeld	1692-1901	2
Meinkenbracht	rkKB	Detmold	1779-1874	2
Meissen	evLutKB	Detmold	1815-1874	2
Meiste	rkKB	Detmold Paderborn	1679-1875	2
Mellrich	rkKB	Paderborn Detmold	1683-1874	5
Menelen	evKB rkKB	Detmold Bielefeld Schloss Brühl	1656-1949	11
Mengede	evKB	Bielefeld	1658-1906	7
Menne	rkKB	Detmold	1808-1874	2
Menninghüffen	evKB	Detmold Bielefeld	1695-1928	12
Mensel	rkKB	Paderborn	1666-1879	3
Merchenich	BA	Schloss Brühl	1799-1875	14
Merfeld	rkKB	Detmold	1815-1874	3
Merken	BA rkKB	Schloss Brühl	1675-1875	10
Merkstein	BA rkKB	Schloss Brühl Den Haag	1598-1875	12
Merl	STA	Schloss Brühl	1799-1875	15
Merlsheim	rkKB	Detmold	1808-1874	2
Mersch	BA rkKB	Schloss Brühl	1749-1875	4
Mersenich	BA	Schloss Brühl	1799-1875	10
Mersenich -Düren-	rkKB	Schloss Brühl	1663-1798	1
Mersenich -Euskirche-	rkKB	Schloss Brühl	1609-1798	1
Merschede	MKB evKB rkKB	Bielefeld Detmold Paderborn	1646-1944	22
Messlingen	evKB	Detmold	1808-1874	3
Mesum	rkKB	Münster Detmold	1690-1891	3

Location	Nature of Material	Where Filmed	Dates Covered	No. of Rolls
Metelen	rkKB	Münster Berlin-Dahlem	1624-1875	4
Methler	evKB	Bielefeld	1680-1913	7
Metternich	rkKB	Schloss Brühl	1740-1798	1
Metlingen	evKB rkKB	Münster Bielefeld Detmold	1653-1939	16
Mettmann	evKB rkKB	Schloss Brühl	1636-1809	6
Miel	rkKB	Schloss Brühl	1694-1798	1
Millen	rkKB	Schloss Brühl	1651-1800	1
Millingen	rkKB evKB	Düsseldorf Münster	1697-1940	3
Milte	rkKB	Münster Detmold	1680-1874	4
Minde	LDS records MKB evKB rkKB	Salt Lake City Hannover Paderborn Bielefeld	1652-1939	58
Moers	STA evKB rkKB	Düsseldorf Münster Schloss Brühl	1612-1889	31
Moese	rkKB	Detmold Paderborn	1665-1911	20
Moheim	rkKB	Schloss Brühl	1770-1809	1
Möhnesee	evKB rkKB	Detmold	1779-1874	8
Möllbergen	evKB	Detmold	1809-1874	3
Mönchengladbach	rkKB STA BA evKB	Düsseldorf Schloss Brühl	1611-1904	147
Mondorf	rkKB	Schloss Brühl	1664-1809	1
Monheim	BA evKB	Düsseldorf Schloss Brühl	1803-1880	27
Mönninghausen	rkKB	Paderborn	1733-1874	1

Location	Nature of Material	Where Filmed	Dates Covered	No. of Rolls
Monschau	rkKB BA evKB	Hannover Berlin-Dahlem Schloss Brühl	1651-1918	19
Morenhoven	rkKB	Schloss Brühl	1657-1798	1
Mörs	rkKB MKB	Schloss Brühl Koblenz	1774-1945	2
Morsball	evKB rkKB	Düsseldorf Schloss Brühl	1656-1972	21
Morschenich	rkKB	Schloss Brühl	1706-1801	2
Moyland	evKB	Koblenz	1696-1950	1
Much	rkKB	Schloss Brühl	1658-1809	3
Muddenhagen	STA	Detmold	1808-1874	1
Müddersheim	STA BA rkKB	Schloss Brühl	1633-1875	10
Muffendorf	rkKB	Schloss Brühl	1627-1798	1
Mülheim	MKB rkKB evKB	Hannover Koblenz Detmold Paderborn Düsseldorf	1650-1945	60
Müngersdorf	rkKB	Schloss Brühl	1781-1805	1
Münster	rkKB STA evKB	Münster Bielefeld Detmold Hannover	1603-1951	92
Münsterbroch	rkKB	Detmold	1808-1874	2
Müntz	rkKB	Schoss Brühl	1662-1798	1
Müsen	evKB	Bielefeld	1649-1913	6
Mussem	rkKB	Detmold	1815-1879	6
Mutscheid	rkKB	Schloss Brühl	1779-1927	1
Mutzenich	rkKB	Schloss Brühl	1637-1798	1
Myhl	BA	Schloss Brühl	1765-1875	11
Nachrodwibling- werde	rkKB evKB	Detmold	1818-1874	6
Nammen	evKB	Detmold Bielefeld	1809-1911	6

Location	Nature of Material	Where Filmed	Dates Covered	No. of Rolls
Natingen	rkKB evKB	Detmold	1815-1874	3
Natzungen	rkKB	Detmold	1808-1874	1
Neersen	evKB BA STA	Schloss Brühl Detmold	1799-1875	19
Neheim	rkKB evKB	Detmold	1779-1874	8
Neidenstein	rkKB	Freiburg	1810-1900	1
Neiheim	evKB	Bielefeld	1855-1951	1
Neinborg	rkKB	Münster	1644-1876	2
Nemmenich	rkKB	Schloss Brühl	1657-1806	1
Neorastrum	rkKB		1750	1
Netphen	evKB rkKB	Mainz Bielefeld	1621-1939	20
Nettelstädt	rkKB evKB	Paderborn Detmold	1666-1879	7
Nettesheim	rkKB BA STA	Schloss Brühl	1665-1875	38
Nettetal	STA	Schloss Brühl	1798-1975	11
Neuahlen	rkKB	Detmold	1803-1874	6
Neuastenberg	rkKB	Detmold	1810-1874	1
Neuenbeken	rkKB	Detmold Paderborn	1776-1874	3
Neuengeseke -Soest-	evKB	Bielefeld	1724-1966	5
Neuenheerse	evKB rkKB	Detmold	1808-1874	5
Neuenkirchen	rkKB	Detmold Münster	1675-1875	10
Neuenknick	evKB	Detmold	1808-1874	2
Neuenrade	evKB STA	Detmold	1810-1874	3
Neuhaus -Paderborn-	evKB rkKB	Detmold Paderborn	1621-1874	7

Location	Nature of Material	Where Filmed	Dates Covered	No. of Rolls
Neukirchen -Bonn-	rkKB	Schloss Brühl	1666-1798	2
Neukirchen -Grevenbroich-	rkKB BA STA	Schloss Brühl	1712-1875	21
Neukirchen -Vluyn-	evKB STA	Düsseldorf Schloss Brühl	1632-1875	26
Neunkirchen -Siegen-	evKB rkKB	Bielefeld Detmold	1680-1912	15
Neurath	rkKB	Schloss Brühl	1688-1798	1
Neuss	BA STA	Schloss Brühl	1799-1875	53
Neustadt	evKB	Schloss Brühl	1737-1809	1
Neustrelitz	evLutKB	Goslar	1736-1928	8
Neviges	rkKB BA	Schloss Brühl	1633-1875	26
Nidegge	BA rkKB	Schloss Brühl	1769-1875	7
Niederau	rkKB	Schloss Brühl	1770-1798	1
Niederaussen	rkKB	Schloss Brühl	1770-1812	1
Niederbachem	rkKB	Schloss Brühl	1673-1798	1
Niederberg	STA rkKB	Schloss Brühl	1706-1875	8
Niederdollendorf	rkKB	Schloss Brühl	1665-1809	2
Niederdrees	rkKB	Schloss Brühl	1719-1798	1
Niederdresseln- dorf	evKB	Bielefeld	1588-1919	8
Niederembt	evKB	Schloss Brühl	1728-1798	1
Niederkassel	rkKB	Schloss Brühl	1770-1809	2
Niederkastenholz	STA	Schloss Brühl	1800-1875	21
Niederkrüchten	BA rkKB AG	Schloss Brühl	1597-1896	21
Niederlaasphe	evKB	Detmold	1808-1874	4

Location	Nature of Material	Where Filmed	Dates Covered	No. of Rolls
Niedermarsberg	evKB rkKB	Detmold Bielefeld Paderborn	1730-1924	5
Niedermehnen	evKB	Detmold	1808-1874	4
Niedermerz	rkKB	Schloss Brühl	1671-1798	1
Niedermörmter	rkKB	Schloss Brühl Münster	1685-1875	3
Niederntudorf	rkKB	Paderborn Detmold	1643-1874	2
Niederplies	rkKB	Schloss Brühl	1770-1810	1
Niedersfeld	rkKB	Detmold Paderborn	1789-1874	5
Niederwenigern	evKB	Bielefeld	1713-1958	2
Niederzier	BA rkKB	Schloss Brühl	1649-1875	9
Nieheim	evKB rkKB	Detmold Bielefeld	1808-1951	2
Niel	rkKB STA	Münster Schloss Brühl	1702-1879	8
Nienberge	BA rkKB	Münster Detmold	1691-1875	4
Niesen	rkKB	Detmold	1808-1874	1
Nienkerk	rkKB	Schloss Brühl Münster	1611-1875	6
Nierenheim	rkKB BA STA	Schloss Brühl	1744-1875	16
Nordborchen	rkKB	Detmold Paderborn	1628-1874	5
Nörde	rkKB evKB	Detmold	1808-1874	2
Nordkemmern	evKB	Detmold Bielefeld	1661-1946	18
Nordkirchen	rkKB	Detmold Münster	1678-1911	5
Nordrheda	evKB rkKB	Detmold	1808-1874	7

Location	Nature of Material	Where Filmed	Dates Covered	No. of Rolls
Nordwalde	rkKB	Münster	1641-1875	3
Norf	rkKB GA	Schloss Brühl	1696-1875	14
Nörvenich	rkKB BA	Schloss Brühl	1646-1875	18
Notteln	rkKB		1749	1
Nottuln	rkKB STA	Berlin-Dahlem Münster	1647-1880	7
Numbrecht	ev.refKB	Schloss Brühl	1749-1819	3
Nuttlar	rkKB	Paderborn Detmold	1658-1874	6
Ober-Erken- schwick	rkKB	Münster	1671-1899	2
Oberkrüchten	rkKB	Schloss Brühl	1634-1798	2
Oberaussem	rkKB	Schloss Brühl	1634-1796	1
Oberbachem	rkKB	Schloss Brühl	1683-1808	1
Oberbauerschaft	evKB rkKB	Detmold	1809-1874	5
Oberbruch- Dremmen	BA	Schloss Brühl	1799-1875	9
Oberdollendorf	rkKB	Schloss Brühl	1650-1809	2
Oberdrees	rkKB	Schloss Brühl	1719-1798	1
Oberelvenich	rkKB	Schloss Brühl	1677-1837	1
Oberembt	rkKB	Schloss Brühl	1733-1800	1
Oberfischbach	evKB	Bielefeld	1670-1969	5
Obergartzem	rkKB	Schloss Brühl	1776-1799	1
Oberhausen	LDS records evKB	Salt Lake City Düsseldorf	1648-1948	9
Oberhaussem	rkKB	Schloss Brühl	1720-1798	1
Oberholsklau	evKB	Bielefeld	1742-1932	4
Oberkassel	ev.refKB rkKB	Schloss Brühl	1669-1809	2
Oberkirchen	rkKB	Detmold	1807-1874	3
Oberlubbe	evKB	Detmold	1815-1873	4

Location	Nature of Material	Where Filmed	Dates Covered	No. of Rolls
Oberlustadt	evKB	Speyer	1720-1812	1
Obermarsberg	evKB rkKB	Bielefeld Detmold Paderborn	1664-1948	6
Obernbeck	evKB	Detmold	1808-1874	3
Oberntudorf	rkKB	Paderborn	1643-1874	1
Oberpleis	rkKB	Schloss Brühl	1727-1809	2
Oberzier	rkKB	Schloss Brühl	1669-1802	1
Ochtrup	evKB rkKB	Bielefeld Münster	1667-1958	6
Odendorf	rkKB	Schloss Brühl	1699-1798	1
Odental	ev.refKB rkKB	Schloss Brühl	1717-1809	2
Öding	evKB rkKB	Bielefeld Detmold	1749-1874	3
Oedt	rkKB STA	Schloss Brühl	1612-1875	10
Oekoven	rkKB BA STA	Schloss Brühl	1761-1875	19
Oelde	rkKB	Detmold Münster	1651-1947	14
Oer-Erken- schwick	rkKB STA	Detmold	1814-1874	2
Oerlinghause	evKB	Bielefeld Detmold	1674-1962	34
Oesterholz	evKB	Bielefeld	1706-1939	3
Oesterweg	evKB	Bielefeld	1614-1938	1
Oestrich -Iserlohn-	evKB	Bielefeld	1733-1925	4
Oeynhausen	evKB rkKB	Bielefeld Detmold	1808-1930	5
Offelten	evKB	Detmold	1815-1874	3
Oidtweiler	rkKB	Schloss Brühl	1701-1798	1
Ökoven	rkKB	Schloss Brühl	1761-1798	1

Location	Nature of Material	Where Filmed	Dates Covered	No. of Rolls
Oldendorf	rkKB	Detmold	1808-1874	1
Oldinghausen	STA	Detmold	1811-1813	1
Olef	rkKB	Schloss Brühl	1770-1818	1
Olfen	STA rkKB	Münster	1650-1934	8
Ollheim	rkKB	Schloss Brühl	1698-1798	1
Olpe	evKB rkKB	Bielefeld Detmold Schloss Brühl	1652-1957	13
Olsberg	rkKB	Paderborn	1614-1874	4
Opherdicke	evKB	Bielefeld	1635-1900	4
Ophoven	rkKB	Schloss Brühl	1694-1798	1
Opladen	rkKB STA BA	Schloss Brühl	1729-1872	24
Oppendorf	evKB	Detmold	1808-1874	6
Oppenwehe	evKB	Detmold	1808-1874	6
Orsbeck	rkKB	Schloss Brühl	1648-1807	1
Orsoy	STA evKB rkKB	Münster Schloss Brühl	1653-1898	11
Ösdorf	rkKB STA	Paderborn Detmold	1656-1874	10
Osnabrück	evKB MKB	Hannover	1822-1937	1
Öspel	evKB	Bielefeld	1896-1931	2
Ossendorf	rkKB evKB	Detmold Paderborn	1654-1874	3
Ostbarthausen	evKB	Detmold	1814-1839	4
Ostbevern	rkKB	Detmold Münster	1599-1875	6
Ostenfelde	rkKB STA	Detmold	1749-1874	3
Ostenland	rkKB STA	Detmold	1808-1874	3
Östereiden	rkKB	Paderborn	1626-1874	2

Location	Nature of Material	Where Filmed	Dates Covered	No. of Rolls
Osterfelde	rkKB	Münster	1668-1878	3
Osterflierich	evKB	Detmold Bielefeld	1730-1935	5
Österweg	rkKB evKB	Detmold	1808-1874	8
Österweihe	rkKB	Paderborn	1748-1941	19
Osterwick	rkKB	Berlin-Dahlem Münster	1607-1895	5
Österwiehe	rkKB	Detmold	1808-1874	7
Ostkilver	evLutKB	Detmold	1852-1873	1
Ostönnen	evLutKB	Bielefeld	1680-1953	3
Ostwig	rkKB	Paderborn Detmold	1658-1874	6
Ötinghausen	evKB	Detmold	1808-1874	4
Ottbergen	rkKB	Detmold	1808-1874	1
Ottenhausen	rkKB	Detmold	1808-1874	5
Ottenstein	rkKB	Münster Detmold Berlin-Dahlem	1621-1928	5
Ottmarsbocholt	rkKB STA	Detmold Münster	1639-1889	6
Ovenhausen	rkKB	Detmold	1808-1874	1
Ovenstadt	evKB	Detmold Bielefeld	1693-1930	7
Overath	rkKB	Schloss Brühl	1720-1809	1
Overberge	evKB	Detmold	1815-1874	4
Padberg	rkKB evKB	Paderborn Detmold	1653-1874	8
Paderborn	MKB STA rkKB evKB	Detmold Paderborn Bielefeld Hannover	1612-1945	32
Pfaffrath	rkKB	Schloss Brühl	1735-1809	2
Palmersheim	STA	Schloss Brühl	1800-1875	21
Papenhofe	rkKB	Detmold	1808-1874	2

Location	Nature of Material	Where Filmed	Dates Covered	No. of Rolls
Papinghausen	evKB	Detmold	1808-1874	2
Pattern	rkKB	Schloss Brühl	1710-1713	1
Peckeloh	rkKB evKB	Detmold Bielefeld	1614-1938	9
Peckelsheim	evKB rkKB	Detmold Bielefeld	1808-1954	5
Pelkum	evKB	Detmold Bielefeld	1703-1951	8
Petershagen	evKB	Detmold Bielefeld	1648-1925	16
Pfakdorf	ev.refKB rkKB STA	Münster Schloss Brühl	1751-1875	14
Pier	rkKB BA	Schloss Brühl	1621-1878	9
Pingsheim	rkKB	Schloss Brühl	1721-1806	1
Plettenberg	STA evKB rkKB	Bielefeld Detmold	1654-1874	20
Polsum	rkKB STA	Münster Detmold	1641-1875	3
Pömsen	rkKB	Detmold	1808-1874	2
Pont	rkKB STA	Münster Schloss Brühl	1735-1882	8
Porz	rkKB evKB	Schloss Brühl Düsseldorf	1696-1909	11
Preuss-Moresnet	evKB	Koblenz	1855-1942	1
Preuss-Oldendorf	rkKB evKB	Detmold Bielefeld	1702-1963	15
Preuss-Ströhen	rkKB evKB	Detmold Bielefeld	1809-1954	10
Puderbach	evKB	Detmold	1808-1874	4
Puffendorf	BA rkKB	Schloss Brühl	1676-1800	2
Pulheim	rkKB	Schloss Brühl	1770-1798	1

Location	Nature of Material	Where Filmed	Dates Covered	No. of Rolls
Pütz	evKB rkKB	Schloss Brühl	1727-1802	2
Quadrath-Ichendorf	rkKB	Schloss Brühl	1779-1800	1
Quernheim	evKB	Bielefeld Detmold	1714-1961	7
Quetzen	evKB	Detmold	1808-1874	2
Raderhorst	evKB PSA	Detmold	1808-1874	4
Radevormwald	STA ZSR PSA	Brühl	1853-1862	1
Radewormwald	evLutKB ev.refKB PSA	Schloss Brühl Detmold	1707-1857	6
Radewormwald	rkKB	Schloss Brühl	1770-1809	1
Raesfeld	rkKB PSA BA	Detmold Münster	1647-1908	6
Raesfeld	STA ZSR PSA	Detmold	1812-1814	1
Rahden	evKB PSA LKA evLutKB	Detmold Bielefeld	1704-1935	26
Rameshoven	rkKB	Schloss Brühl	1674-1798	1
Ramsbeck	evKB PSA LKA	Detmold Bielefeld	1855-1948	2
Ramsbeck	rkKB PSA EA	Detmold Paderborn	1658-1874	8
Ramsdorf	rkKB PSA BA	Detmold Münster	1618-1899	6
Ramsdorf	ZSR STA PSA	Detmold	1812-1814	1
Randerath	evLutKB evKA	Düsseldorf Schloss Brühl	1611-1798	2

Location	Nature of Material	Where Filmed	Dates Covered	No. of Rolls
Randerath	rkKB	Schloss Brühl	1604-1798	2
Rarbach	rkKB PSA	Detmold	1808-1874	3
Ratingen	ZSR STA BGM PSA	Brühl	1810-1875	43
Ratingen	evLutKB ev.refKB	Schloss Brühl	1708-1809	2
Ratingen	rkKB	Schloss Brühl	1684-1810	2
Raumland	evKB LKA PSA	Bielefeld Detmold	1658-1956	12
Ravensberg		Bielefeld	1630-1722	5
Rebbecke	rkKB PSA	Detmold	1808-1874	3
Recke	evKB LKA PSA	Bielefeld Detmold	1685-1967	10
Recke	rkKB PSA BA	Detmold Münster	1609-1899	9
Recklinghausen	ZSR STA BA PSA	Detmold Münster	1801-1874	31
Recklinghausen	evKB LKA KBA PSA	Bielefeld Hannover Detmold	1844-1948	7
Recklinghausen	rkKB BA PSA	Münster Detmold	1691-1903	8
Reelsen	rkKB PSA	Detmold	1808-1874	2
Rees	evLutKB PSA ev.refKB	Detmold	1808-1874	2
Rees	rkKB BA	Münster	1627-1875	9
Rehme	rkKB PSA	Detmold	1863-1874	1

Location	Nature of Material	Where Filmed	Dates Covered	No. of Rolls
Rehme	evKB LKA PSA	Bielefeld Detmold	1648-1951	17
Reiste	rkKB EA PSA	Paderborn Detmold	1637-1874	5
Remagen	evKB evKA	Düsseldorf	1746-1840	1
Remlinghausen	rkKB EA PSA	Paderborn Detmold		4
Remlingrade	evLutKB	Schloss Brühl	1700-1809	1
Remscheid	evKB evKB evLutKB	Schloss Brühl Düsseldorf	1654-1884	35
Remscheid	rkKB	Schloss Brühl	1658-1809	2
Renderath	ZSR BGM PSA	Brühl	1802-1872	1
Retzen	evKB LKA PSA ev.refKB	Bielefeld Detmold	1850-1905	3
Rhade	rkKB BA PSA	Münster Detmold	1670-1875	3
Rheda	rkKB PSA	Detmold	1808-1874	4
Rheda	evKB rkKB LKA evLutKB PSA	Bielefeld Detmold	1622-1961	18
Rhede	rkKB BA	Münster	1653-1897	5
Rhede	ZSR STA PSA	Detmold	1812-1813	1
Rhede -Kr. Borken-	rkKB	Detmold	1815-1874	2
Rhedebrügge	rkKB PSA	Detmold	1815-1874	4

Location	Nature of Material	Where Filmed	Dates Covered	No. of Rolls
Rhedes	rkKB	Detmold	1808-1874	1
Rheidt -Siegkreis-	rkKB	Schloss Brühl	1770-1809	1
Rhein	rkKB	Schloss Brühl	1726-1800	
Rheinbach	rkKB	Schloss Brühl	1732-1798	1
Rheinberg	ZSR BGM STA PSA	Brühl	1799-1875	20
Rheinberg	rkKB BA	Münster	1629-1875	3
Rheine	ZSR BGM	Münster	1811-1814	2
Rheine	evKB LKA	Bielefeld	1838-1942	8
Rheine	rkKB BA	Münster	1613-1874	10
Rheinhausen	ZSR BGM PSA	Brühl	1799-1875	23
Rheinhausen	evKB evKA evLutKB	Schloss Brühl Düsseldorf	1641-1842	4
Rheinhausen	rkKB	Schloss Brühl	1647-1798	1
Rheinkamp	ZSR STA BGM PSA	Brühl	1798-1875	16
Rheinkamp	evLutKB	Schloss Brühl	1675-1896	8
Rheinlach- Lüftelberg	rkKB	Schloss Brühl	1691-1798	1
Rheurdt	rkKB BA	Schloss Brühl Münster	1642-1894	2
Rheurdt	ZSR STA PSA	Brühl	1798-1875	8
Rheydt	ZSR STA BM PSA	Brühl	1799-1875	76

Location	Nature of Material	Where Filmed	Dates Covered	No. of Rolls
Rheydt	evLutKB evKA	Düsseldorf Schloss Brühl	1611-1879	11
Rheydt	evKB evKA	Düsseldorf	1827-1885	5
Rheydt	evKB MKB KBA	Hannover	1902-1914	1
Rheydt	ev.refKB	Schloss Brühl	1633-1798	2
Rheydt	rkKB	Schloss Brühl	1687-1799	3
Rhode	rkKB PSA	Detmold	1808-1874	2
Rhynern	evKB PSA LKA	Detmold Bielefeld Starch Detmold	1665-1955	7
Rhynern	rkKB PSA	Detmold	1819-1874	2
Rhynern	ZSR STA	Detmold	1810-1814	2
Richterich	ZSR BM PSA	Brühl	1799-1875	19
Richterich	rkKB	Schloss Brühl	1759-1816	1
Riesel	rkKB PSA	Detmold	1815-1874	2
Riesenbeck	rkKB BA	Münster	1610-1873	6
Riesenbeck	ZSR STA PSA	Detmold	1811-1814	1
Rietberg	evKB rkKB	Detmold	1810-1874	4
Rietberg	evKB LKA evLutKB	Bielefeld	1853-1966	2
Rietberg	rkKB PSA BA	Detmold Paderborn	1665-1911	18
Rimbeck	rkKB PSA	Detmold	1808-1874	3
Rimbeck	evKB	Detmold	1826-1874	1

Location	Nature of Material	Where Filmed	Dates Covered	No. of Rolls
Rindern	rkKB	Schloss Brühl	1681-1798	1
Ringenberg	rkKB BA	Münster	1831-1875	1
Rinkerode	rkKB BA PSA	Münster Detmold	1661-1876	5
Ripsdorf	rkKB	Schloss Brühl	1760-1798	1
Rodenbeck	evKB LKA	Bielefeld	1766-1922	7
Rodenkirchen	rkKB	Schloss Brühl	1652-1800	3
Rödgen	evKB LKA	Bielefeld	1652-1964	10
Rödingen	ZSR BGM PSA	Brühl	1799-1875	9
Rödingen	rkKB	Schloss Brühl	1628-1798	3
Rödinghausen	evLutKB PSA LKA	Detmold Bielefeld	1664-1913	9
Roetgen	ZSR BGM PSA	Brühl	1799-1875	8
Roetgen	evLutKB	Schloss Brühl	1696-1802	1
Roetgen	rkKB	Schloss Brühl	1664-1798	2
Rohren	rkKB	Schloss Brühl	1651-1798	1
Roitzheim	rkKB	Schloss Brühl	1731-1798	1
Rolfzen	rkKB PSA	Detmold	1808-1874	4
Rommerskirchen	ZSR BGM PSA	Brühl	1799-1875	15
Rommerskirchen	rkKB	Schloss Brühl	1616-1815	2
Rondorf	rkKB	Schloss Brühl	1691-1809	1
Rönsahe	evLutKB LKA	Bielefeld	1530-1937	3
Rorup	KB BA	Münster	1646-1875	1

Location	Nature of Material	Where Filmed	Dates Covered	No. of Rolls
Rosbach	ZSR STA PSA	Brühl	1810-1875	17
Rosbach	evLutKB	Schloss Brühl	1689-1809	2
Rosbach	rkKB	Schloss Brühl	1769-1809	1
Rösebeck	evKB PSA	Detmold	1826-1874	1
Rosellen	ZSR BGM PSA	Brühl	1799-1875	11
Rosenhagen	evKB PSA	Detmold	1808-1873	2
Rösrath	evKB evKA evLutKB	Schloss Brühl Düsseldorf	1684-1809	3
Rosrath	rkKB	Schloss Brühl	1770-1809	1
Rotenhagen	evKB PSA	Detmold	1808-1874	5
Rötgen	rkKB	Schloss Brühl	1637-1798	1
Rothe	rkKB PSA	Detmold	1808-1874	1
Rothenuffeln	ev.refKB	Detmold	1815-1873	4
Rotingdorf	evKB	Detmold	1808-1874	5
Rott	rkKB	Schloss Brühl	1769-1799	1
Rottum -Kr. Unna-	evKB	Detmold	1815-1874	4
Rövenich	rkKB	Schloss Brühl	1770-1798	1
Roxel	rkKB PSA BA	Detmold Münster	1661-1927	5
Rüggeberg	evKB LKA	Bielefeld	1799-1925	2
Rumbeck	rkKB PSA	Detmold	1859-1874	1
Rumeln- Kaldenhausen	ZSR STA PSA	Brühl	1799-1875	11
Ründeroth	ev.refKB	Schloss Brühl	1736-1816	2

Location	Nature of Material	Where Filmed	Dates Covered	No. of Rolls
Rünthe	KB PSA	Detmold	1818-1874	3
Ruppichteroth	evKB evKA evLutKB	Düsseldorf Schloss Brühl Koblenz	1694-1824	3
Ruppichteroth	rkKB	Schloss Brühl	1663-1809	3
Ruhrberg	ZSR BM PSA	Brühl	1799-1875	5
Ruhrberg	rkKB	Schloss Brühl	1702-1798	1
Rüthen	rkKB EA	Paderborn	1612-1874	6
Rüthen	evKB PSA	Detmold	1839-1843	1
Saerbeck	rkKB BA	Münster	1617-1872	3
Salzkoffen	rkKB EA	Paderborn	1635-1874	3
Sand	rkKB	Schloss Brühl	1657-1810	1
Sandbodium	rkKB PSA prof.KB	Detmold	1818-1874	3
Sandebeck	rkKB	Detmold	1808-1874	2
Sankt Vit	rkKB	Detmold	1808-1874	1
Sankt Hubert	ZSR STA PSA	Brühl	1798-1875	12
Sankt Tönis	ZSR STA	Brühl	1798-1835	24
Sankt Tönis	rkKB	Schloss Brühl	1648-1798	1
Sankt Vit	rkKB PSA	Detmold	1808-1874	3
Sassenberg	rkKB BA	Münster	1673-1851	4
Sassenberg -Warendorf-	rkKB PSA	Detmold	1815-1874	2
Sassenberg	ZSR STA	Detmold	1809-1814	1

Location	Nature of Material	Where Filmed	Dates Covered	No. of Rolls
Sassenhausen	evKB	Detmold	1807-1874	2
Satzvey-Firmenich	rkKB	Schloss Brühl	1771-1798	1
Schaephuysen	rkKB	Schloss Brühl	1710-1896	2
Schaephuysen	ZSR STA PSA	Brühl	1798-1875	5
Schale	evKB PSA LKA	Detmold Bielefeld	1716-1967	7
Schale	rkKB PSA	Detmold	1815-1874	3
Schalkmühle	evKB LKA	Bielefeld	1893-1965	2
Schapdetten	rkKB PSA BA	Detmold Münster	1715-1875	3
Scharfenberg	rkKB PSA	Detmold	1808-1874	1
Scharmede	rkKB PSA EA	Detmold Paderborn	1648-1874	3
Scheiderhöhe	rkKB	Schloss Brühl	1770-1809	1
Scherfede	rkKB PSA	Detmold	1808-1874	3
Scherfede	evKB PSA LKA	Detmold Bielefeld	1888-1965	2
Schermbeck	rkKB PSA BA	Detmold Münster	1681-1874	3
Schieder-Schwalenberg	ev.refKB PSA	Detmold	1840-1875	1
Schieder-Schwalenberg	rkKB	Detmold	1858-1875	1
Schiefbahn	rkKB	Schloss Brühl	1675-1798	1
Schiefbahn	ZSR STA PSA	Brühl	1803-1842	1

Location	Nature of Material	Where Filmed	Dates Covered	No. of Rolls
Schlangen	evKB LKA PSA ev.refKB	Bielefeld Detmold	1697-1939	14
Schleiden	rkKB	Schloss Brühl	1695-1798	2
Schleiden	ZSR BGM STA PSA	Brühl	1796-1875	16
Schlich-D'horn	rkKB	Schloss Brühl	1659-1799	1
Schlüsselburg	evKB PSA LKA evLutKB	Detmold Bielefeld	1728-1956	10
Schmalbroich	ZSR STA PSA	Brühl	1798-1900	3
Schmallenberg	rkKB PSA	Detmold	1807-1874	2
Schmechten	rkKB	Detmold	1808-1874	2
Schmidt	rkKB	Schloss Brühl	1769-1798	1
Schmidt	ZSR BGM STA PSA	Brühl	1799-1875	8
Schnathorst	evKB PSA LKA evLutKB	Detmold Bielefeld	1714-1950	11
Schneppenbaum	ZSR STA PSA	Brühl	1798-1875	10
Schöller	ev.refKB	Schloss Brühl	1716-1810	1
Schönau -Euskirchen-	rkKB	Schloss Brühl	1723-1799	1
Schönenberg -Kr. Höxler-	rkKB PSA	Detmold	1808-1874	2
Schöppingen	rkKB BA PSA	Münster Detmold	1672-1895	6
Schöppingen- Wigbold	rkKB		1750	1

Location	Nature of Material	Where Filmed	Dates Covered	No. of Rolls
Schrötting-hausen -Kr. Halle-	evKB PSA	Detmold	1808-1874	5
Schrötting-hausen -Kr. Lübbecke-	evKB	Detmold	1815-1874	3
Schwalenberg	Court record AG	Detmold	1737-1891	35
Schwalenberg	rkKB PSA	Detmold	1854-1875	1
Schwalenberg	evKB PSA LKA ev.refKB	Detmold Bielefeld	1698-1932	17
Schwalmtal	ZSR BGM PSA	Brühl	1799-1875	16
Schwalmtal	rkKB	Schloss Brühl	1648-1811	3
Schwanenberg	ZSR PSA BGM STA	Brühl	1797-1875	7
Schwaney	evKB PSA	Detmold	1854-1874	1
Schwaney	rkKB PSA EA	Detmold Paderborn	1722-1875	2 2
Schwaiz Rheindorf	rkKB	Schloss Brühl	1779-1800	1
Schwarzenau	evKB LKA PSA	Bielefeld Detmold	1846-1885	2
Schwarzenmoor	evKB PSA evLutKB	Detmold	1808-1874	8
Schweckhausen	rkKB PSA	Detmold	1808-1874	3
Schwefe	evKB LKA	Bielefeld	1637-1953	6
Schweicheln-Bermbeck	evLutKB PSA	Detmold	1815-1874	10

Location	Nature of Material	Where Filmed	Dates Covered	No. of Rolls
Schweicheln-Bermbeck	ZSR STA	Detmold	1811-1813	1
Schweinheim	ZSR STA PSA	Brühl	1800-1875	21
Schweinheim	rkKB	Schloss Brühl	1691-1798	2
Schwelle	rkKB PSA EA	Detmold Paderborn	1641-1875	6
Schwelle	ZSR STA PSA	Detmold	1808-1812	1
Schwelm	evKB PSA LKA ev.refKB evLutKB	Detmold Bielefeld	1652-1909	52
Schwelm	rkKB PSA	Detmold	1828-1874	2
Schwelm	ZSR STA	Detmold	1810-1812	1
Schwenningdorf	evLutKB	Detmold	1852-1873	1
Schwerte	evKB PSA LKA evLutKB ev.refKB	Detmold Bielefeld	1584-1936	20
Schwerte	rkKB PSA	Detmold	1831-1874	1
Schwerte	ZSR STA	Detmold	1810-1812	1
Sechtem	rkKB	Schloss Brühl	1617-1810	4
Seelenfeld	evKB	Detmold	1808-1873	2
Seelscheid	evKB rkKB	Schloss Brühl Düsseldorf	1721-1876	5
Selfkant	BA rkKB	Schloss Brühl	1699-1874	36
Selm	rkKB	Detmold Münster	1661-1957	5
Senden	rkKB	Münster	1650-1944	7

Location	Nature of Material	Where Filmed	Dates Covered	No. of Rolls
Sendenhurst	rkKB STA	Münster Detmold	1659-1876	5
Senne II -Bf-	evKB	Detmold	1843-1874	1
Seppenrade	rkKB	Münster Detmold	1722-1914	5
Setterich	BA STA rkKB	Schloss Brühl	1770-1875	7
Sevelen	STA Wallvon evKB rkKB	Den Haag Münster Düsseldorf Schloss Brühl	1614-1876	16
Sichtigvor	rkKB	Paderborn Detmold	1650-1874	4
Siddersen	rkKB	Detmold	1808-1874	2
Siddinghausen	rkKB	Detmold	1808-1874	1
Siegburg	rkKB	Schloss Brühl	1650-1809	1
Sieglau	rkKB	Freiburg	1788-1900	1
Sieger	rkKB STA evKB MKB	Hannover Bielefeld Detmold Schloss Brühl	1623-1942	49
Sieglar	rkKB	Schloss Brühl	1689-1809	2
Siendorf	BA rkKB	Schloss Brühl	1722-1875	9
Silbach	rkKB	Detmold	1808-1874	1
Silixer	evKB	Bielefeld Detmold	1667-1933	10
Simmerath	STA BA rkKB	Schloss Brühl	1670-1875	10
Sindorf	rkKB	Schloss Brühl	1638-1798	1
Sinnersdorf	rkKB	Schloss Brühl	1804-1808	1
Sinstig	rkKB	Schloss Brühl	1633-1939	4
Sinthern	rkKB	Schloss Brühl	1632-1799	1
Sinsenich	rkKB	Schloss Brühl	1662-1798	1
Slamorth	evKB	Schloss Brühl	1675-1810	1

Location	Nature of Material	Where Filmed	Dates Covered	No. of Rolls
Soest	STA evKB rkKB	Detmold Bielefeld	1648-1966	64
Solingen	LDS records MKB BA evKB rkKB	Eibenstock Hannover Schloss Brühl Düsseldorf	1638-1911	89
Soller	rkKB	Schloss Brühl	1770-1800	1
Sommersell	rkKB	Detmold	1808-1874	1
Sonneborn -Detmold-	evKB	Bielefeld	1792-1905	1
Sonneborn -Lemgo-	evKB	Bielefeld	1719-1969	4
Sonneborn	evKB	Bielefeld Schloss Brühl	1661-1809	3
Sonsbeck	evKB	Düsseldorf	1794-1860	1
Sonsbeck	STA evKB rkKB	Berlin-Dahlem Münster Schloss Brühl	1628-1875	28
Sotenich	rkKB	Schloss Brühl	1763-1822	1
Spenge	evKB	Detmold Bielefeld	1729-1930	17
Spexard	rkKB	Detmold	1808-1874	1
Spork -Borken-	rkKB	Detmold	1815-1874	6
Sprockhövel	evKB	Detmold	1732-1947	18
Stadtlohn	rkKB STA	Münster Berlin Detmold	1624-1907	10
Staelen	rkKB	Münster	1794-1875	5
Stahle	rkKB	Detmold	1808-1874	1
Staumühle	evKB	Hannover	1946-1948	1
Steckenborn	rkKB	Schloss Brühl	1740-1798	1
Stedefreud	evKB STA	Detmold	1811-1874	11
Steinhagen	evKB	Detmold Bielefeld	1663-1935	9

Location	Nature of Material	Where Filmed	Dates Covered	No. of Rolls
Steinhausen	rkKB	Detmold Paderborn	1668-1874	3
Steinheim	evKB	Detmold Bielefeld	1808-1950	6
Steinstrass	BA	Schloss Brühl	1799-1875	7
Stemmer	evKB	Detmold	1808-1874	8
Stenern	rkKB	Detmold	1815-1874	6
Stetternich	rkKB	Schloss Brühl	1770-1800	1
Stieldorf	rkKB	Schloss Brühl	1770-1810	1
Stiepel	evKB	Bielefeld	1725-1949	7
Stirpe	rkKB	Detmold Paderborn	1661-1874	11
Stockum	rkKB	Detmold	1779-1874	4
Stolberg	BA evKB	Schloss Brühl Düsseldorf	1615-1875	35
Stollberg	BA	Schloss Brühl	1802-1872	1
Stommeln	rkKB	Schloss Brühl		
Störmede	rkKB	Detmold	1779-1873	3
Stotzheim	STA rkKB	Schloss Brühl	1627-1875	22
Straelen	STA	Schloss Brühl	1798-1875	18
Strassfeld	rkKB	Schloss Brühl	1666-1798	1
Stromberg	rkKB	Detmold	1749-1874	2
Stromberg -Beckum-	evKB rkKB	Düsseldorf Detmold Münster	1636-1875	8
Stukenbrock	rkKB	Detmold	1808-1874	2
Stünsel	evKB	Detmold	1807-1874	2
Süchteln	rkKB STA	Schloss Brühl	1745-1875	21
Suderwick	rkKB evKB	Detmold Bielefeld Münster	1708-1967	11
Südfelde	evKB	Detmold	1808-1874	3

Location	Nature of Material	Where Filmed	Dates Covered	No. of Rolls
Südhemmern	evKB	Detmold	1808-1874	3
Südkamen	evKB	Detmold	1815-1874	4
Südkirchen	rkKB	Detmold Münster	1614-1874	4
Südlohn	STA rkKB evKB	Münster Detmold Berlin	1661-1925	12
Suggerath	rkKB	Schloss Brühl	1715-1798	1
Sulpich	rkKB	Schloss Brühl	1697-1798	1
Sümmern	rkKB	Schloss Brühl	1805-1874	1
Sundern -Ansberg-	rkKB	Schloss Brühl	1779-1874	6
Sundern -Herford-	evKB STA	Schloss Brühl	1811-1874	11
Sundern -Lübbecke-	evKB	Schloss Brühl	1808-1874	4
Sünninghausen	STA rkKB	Schloss Brühl Münster	1659-1877	5
Suttrop	rkKB	Paderborn Detmold	1727-1913	2
Swisttal	rkKB	Schloss Brühl	1666-1798	1
Sylbach	evKB	Bielefeld	1939-1969	1
Syburg	evKB	Bielefeld	1879-1968	1
Talle	evKB	Detmold Bielefeld	1657-1910	14
Tecklenburg	evKB STA	Detmold Bielefeld	1679-1874	7
Telgte	rkKB STA	Detmold Münster	1656-1871	6
Tengern	evKB	Detmold	1815-1874	3
Tetz	rkKB	Schloss Brühl	1741-1800	1
Teveren	BA rkKB	Schloss Brühl	1631-1875	10
Theenhausen	evKB	Detmold	1808-1874	5
Thier	rkKB	Schloss Brühl	1795-1809	1

Location	Nature of Material	Where Filmed	Dates Covered	No. of Rolls
Thorr	rkKB	Schloss Brühl	1643-1798	1
Thüle	rkKB	Detmold Paderborn	1648-1874	3
Thülen	rkKB	Detmold	1808-1874	2
Tietelsen	rkKB	Detmold	1808-1874	1
Tillmoyland	STA	Schloss Brühl	1798-1875	10
Tits	BA rkKB	Schloss Brühl	1614-1875	13
Todtenhausen	evKB	Detmold Bielefeld	1801-1916	9
Tondorf	BA rkKB	Schloss Brühl	1663-1852	3
Tönisberg	rkKB STA	Schloss Brühl	1651-1900	6
Tönnisheide	BA	Schloss Brühl	1853-1872	2
Troisdorf	rkKB	Schloss Brühl	1727-1809	1
Tüddern	BA rkKB	Schloss Brühl	1652-1872	4
Türnich	rkKB	Schloss Brühl	1676-1800	2
Tweihausen	evKB	Detmold	1808-1874	4
Twisteden	STA rkKB	Schloss Brühl	1705-1875	17
Übach-Palenberg	BA rkKB	Schloss Brühl	1615-1875	19
Übbedissen	ev.refKB	Detmold Bielefeld	1750-1926	9
Uckerath	rkKB	Schloss Brühl	1710-1810	2
Udelhoven	rkKB	Schloss Brühl	1715-1798	1
Udenbreth	rkKB STA	Schloss Brühl	1709-1815	6
Udorf	rkKB	Paderborn	1685-1874	2
Uebach-Palenberg see Übach-Palenberg	BA	Schloss Brühl	1798-1875	9

Location	Nature of Material	Where Filmed	Dates Covered	No. of Rolls
Uedem	STA rkKB evKB	Düsseldorf Münster Schloss Brühl	1666-1876	12
Uedemerbruch	STA	Schloss Brühl	1798-1875	6
Uentrop	rkKB evKB	Paderborn Detmold Bielefeld	1679-1943	12
Uffeln	evKB	Detmold	1808-1874	1
Ülpenich	rkKB	Schloss Brühl	1770-1798	1
Ummingen	evKB	Bielefeld	1681-1890	7
Unna	evKB STA rkKB	Detmold Paderborn	1613-1906	38
Üntrop	STA	Detmold	1810-1813	2
Upsprunge	rkKB	Paderborn	1635-1874	3
Unterbruch	BA	Schloss Brühl	1802-1875	2
Unterlubbe	ev.refKB	Detmold	1815-1873	4
Vahlhausen	evKB	Bielefeld	1886-1969	2
Valbert	BA evKB	Detmold Bielefeld	1714-1859	4
Valdorf	evKB	Detmold Bielefeld	1708-1922	16
Varel	rkKB	Münster	1851-1876	1
Varenholz	AG evKB	Detmold Bielefeld	1697-1912	35
Varensell	rkKB	Detmold	1808-1874	8
Varl	evKB	Detmold	1809-1874	5
Veen	STA	Schloss Brühl	1798-1875	11
Veert	rkKB STA	Schloss Brühl	1798-1875	9
Velbert	evLutKB ev.refKB	Düsseldorf Schloss Brühl	1701-1839	5
Velen	rkKB STA	Detmold Münster	1667-1928	9
Vellern	STA	Detmold Münster	1665-1874	5

Location	Nature of Material	Where Filmed	Dates Covered	No. of Rolls
Vellinghausen	Kirchen	Detmold	1839-1842	4
Velmede	rkKB	Paderborn Detmold	1658-1874	6
Veltheim	evKB	Bielefeld Detmold	1725-1942	4
Venne	rkKB	Münster Detmold	1673-1900	2
Vennebeck	evKB	Detmold	1809-1874	3
Verden	rkKB	Detmold	1815-1874	3
Verlar	rkKB	Detmold	1808-1874	3
Verne	rkKB	Paderborn Detmold	1681-1874	4
Vernich	rkKB	Schloss Brühl	1727-1798	1
Vernum	rkKB STA	Münster Schloss Brühl	1798-1875	11
Versmold	evKB rkKB	Bielefeld Detmold	1614-1962	58
Vettweiss	BA rkKB	Schloss Brühl	1669-1875	19
Viersen	rkKB STA evKB BA	Schloss Brühl	1645-1875	60
Villigst	evKB rkKB	Detmold	1818-1874	5
Villip	rkKB	Schloss Brühl	1690-1798	1
Vinsebeck	rkKB	Detmold	1808-1874	1
Vladorf	evLutKB	Detmold	1808-1874	4
Vlaesheim	rkKB	Detmold	1815-1874	1
Vlatten	rkKB	Schloss Brühl	1665-1798	2
Vlatho	evKB	Bielefeld Detmold	1679-1941	16
Voerde	rkKB	Münster	1651-1887	2
Voerde -Dihslaken-	evKB	Hamborn	1693-1926	2

Location	Nature of Material	Where Filmed	Dates Covered	No. of Rolls
Vohrhelm	rkKB		1749-1750	1
Volkmarsen	rkKB	Detmold	1815-1898	1
Völlinghausen	rkKB	Detmold Paderborn	1661-1874	17
Volmarstein	evKB	Bielefeld	1672-1924	13
Volmerdingsen	rkKB STA evKB	Detmold Bielefeld	1766-1940	13
Vörde	evKB	Bielefeld	1801-1937	11
Vörden	rkKB	Detmold	1814-1874	1
Vorhalle	evKB	Bielefeld	1894-1958	1
Vorheld	rkKB STA	Münster Detmold	1653-1876	3
Vorst	rkKB STA	Schloss Brühl	1659-1875	14
Vossenack	rkKB BA	Schloss Brühl	1721-1875	3
Vossheide	evKB	Bielefeld	1939-1969	1
Vosswinkel	rkKB	Detmold	1806-1874	1
Vrasselt	STA	Münster	1750-1900	3
Vreden	rkKB STA	Detmold Münster	1687-1905	22
Vussem	BA	Schloss Brühl	1799-1875	14
Wachtendonk	rkKB BA	Schloss Brühl Münster	1688-1875	2
Wachtendonk	ZSR STA PSA	Brühl	1798-1875	9
Wadersloh	rkKB evKB PSA	Detmold	1810-1874	4
Wadersloh	rkKB PSA BA	Detmold Münster	1636-1875	15
Wadersloh	ZSR STA BA PSA	Münster Detmold	1749-1813	2

Location	Nature of Material	Where Filmed	Dates Covered	No. of Rolls
Wahlen	ZSR BM PSA	Brühl	1800-1875	10
Wahlen	rkKB	Schloss Brühl	1700-1872	2
Wahlsheid	evLutKB	Schloss Brühl	1646-1809	3
Wahlsheid	rkKB	Schloss Brühl	1770-1809	1
Walbeck	rkKB	Schloss Brühl	1666-1875	2
Walbeck	ZSR STA PSA	Brühl	1798-1875	7
Waldbauer	evKB LKA PSA evLutKB	Bielefeld Detmold	1741-1968	4
Waldbröl	evKB evKA evLutKB	Hamborn Düsseldorf Schloss Brühl	1660-1901	14
Waldbröl	rkKB	Schloss Brühl	1769-1809	1
Waldenrath	ZSR BM PSA	Brühl	1797-1875	12
Waldenrath	rkKB	Schloss Brühl Berlin-Dahlem	1640-1802	2
Waldfendt	ZSR BM PSA	Brühl	1799-1875	12
Waldfendt	rkKB	Schloss Brühl	1616-1800	1
Waldhausen -Arnsberg-	rkKB PSA EA	Detmold Paderborn	1650-1874	4
Waldniel	ev.refKB	Schloss Brühl	1759-1802	1
Waldniel	rkKB	Schloss Brühl	1613-1805	3
Waldniel	ZSR STA PSA	Brühl	1799-1875	8
Waldniel -Kempen- Krefeld-	ZSR BM PSA	Brühl	1799-1875	8

Location	Nature of Material	Where Filmed	Dates Covered	No. of Rolls
Walheim	ZSR BM PSA	Brühl	1799-1875	10
Wallenbrück	evLutKB LKA	Bielefeld	1624-1964	4
Walsum	rkKB BA	Münster	1653-1897	2
Waltringhausen -Kr. Lippstadt-	rkKB EA	Paderborn	1683-1874	3
Waltrop	rkKB PSA BA	Detmold Münster	1611-1874	9
Wandhofen	evLutKB PSA ev.refKB	Detmold	1818-1874	4
Wandhofen	rkKB	Detmold	1831-1874	1
Wankum	rkKB BA	Schloss Brühl Münster	1639-1875	3
Wankum	ZSR STA PSA	Brühl	1798-1875	9
Wanne-Eickel	evKB PSA	Detmold	1815-1875	3
Wanne-Eickel	rkKB PSA EA	Detmold Paderborn	1813-1887	5
Warbeyen	rkKB BA	Schloss Brühl Münster	1656-1875	2
Warburg	evKB PSA	Detmold Bielefeld	1826-1935	3
Warburg	evKB KBA MKB	Hannover	1860-1871	1
Warburg	rkKB PSA	Detmold	1808-1874	4
Wardt	rkKB BA	Münster	1636-1875	1
Wardt	ZSR STA PSA	Brühl	1798-1875	6

Location	Nature of Material	Where Filmed	Dates Covered	No. of Rolls
Wardt	refKB evKA	Düsseldorf	1792-1820	1
Warendorf	ZSR BGM STA PSA BA	Detmold Münster	1801-1874	33
Warendorf	MKB evKB KBA	Eibenstock Hannover	1837-1879	3
Warendorf	evKB LKA PSA ev.refKB	Bielefeld Detmold	1835-1957	3
Warendorf	rkKB BA PSA	Münster Detmold	1643-1906	18
Warstein	evKB PSA LKA evLutKB	Detmold Bielefeld	1829-1949	2
Warstein	rkKB EA	Paderborn	1737-1874	3
Wassenberg	ZSR BM PSA	Brühl	1802-1875	9
Wassenberg	rkKB	Schloss Brühl	1680-1807	1
Wattenscheid	evKB LKA PSA	Bielefeld Detmold	1669-1908	13
Wattenscheid	rkKB PSA	Detmold	1815-1874	4
Wattenscheid	ZSR STA	Detmold	1810-1814	1
Weckinghausen	rkKB PSA EA	Detmold Paderborn	1661-1874	17
Weddinghofen	evKB PSA	Detmold	1815-1874	4
Weeze	evKB evKA	Düsseldorf	1655-1880	1

Location	Nature of Material	Where Filmed	Dates Covered	No. of Rolls
Weeze	rkKB BA	Münster Schloss Brühl	1662-1883	6
Weeze	ZSR STA PSA	Brühl	1789-1875	11
Wegberg	ZSR BGM STA	Brühl	1797-1875	28
Wegberg	rkKB	Schloss Brühl	1619-1815	5
Wehdem	evKB PSA LKA evLutKB	Detmold Bielefeld	1663-1952	19
Wehe	evKB PSA	Detmold	1809-1874	5

Wehr
 -Selfkrant-
  kreis-
  Geilenkirchen-
  Heinsberg
	ZSR
	STA
	PSA
		Brühl	1799-1875	8

Wehrden	rkKB PSA	Detmold	1808-1874	2
Wehrendorf	evKB	Bielefeld	1742-1943	4
Weiberg	rkKB PSA EA	Detmold Paderborn	1752-1874	2
Weickede	rkKB EA	Paderborn	1626-1874	2
Weidenau	evKB LKA	Bielefeld	1874-1955	5
Weidenau	ZSR STA	Bielefeld	1810-1813	2
Weidenhausen	evKB LKA PSA	Bielefeld Detmold	1657-1899	6
Weidesheim	ZSR PSA STA	Brühl	1800-1875	21
Weidesheim	rkKB	Schloss Brühl	1630-1798	1
Weiler am Berge	rkKB	Schloss Brühl	1714-1808	1
Weilerswist	rkKB	Schloss Brühl	1741-1802	1

Location	Nature of Material	Where Filmed	Dates Covered	No. of Rolls
Weine	rkKB PSA	Detmold	1808-1874	1
Weisweiler	ZSR BM PSA	Brühl	1799-1875	9
Weisweiler	rkKB	Schloss Brühl	1671-1798	2
Weitmar	evKB LKA	Bielefeld	1680-1910	8
Welbergen	rkKB BA	Münster	1664-1875	1
Welda	evKB PSA	Detmold	1826-1874	1
Welda	rkKB	Detmold	1808-1874	1
Welver	KB	Detmold	1839-1842	4
Welver	evKB PSA LRA evLutKB	Detmold Bielefeld	1649-1951	28
Welver	rkKB PSA	Detmold	1818-1874	5
Wenau	ZSR BGM PSA	Brühl	1799-1875	12
Wenden -Olpe-	rkKB PSA	Detmold	1807-1874	4
Wengern	evLutKB LRA	Bielefeld	1343-1929	19
Wenholthausen	rkKB EA PSA	Paderborn Detmold	1652-1874	4
Werdohl	evKB PSA LRA ev.refKB	Detmold Bielefeld	1715-1917	6
Werdohl	rkKB PSA	Detmold	1863-1874	1
Were -Soest-	evKB	Detmold	1827-1899	2
Were -Soest-	rkKB PSA	Detmold	1779-1874	12

Location	Nature of Material	Where Filmed	Dates Covered	No. of Rolls
Werleshausen	evKB LRA	Bielefeld	1792-1759	1
Wermelskirchen	ev.refKB	Schloss Brühl	1652-1809	7
Wermelskirchen	KB	Schloss Brühl	1775-1788	1
Wermelskirchen	rkKB	Schloss Brühl	1770-1809	1
Werne	rkKB BA	Münster	1635-1883	7
Werne an der Lippe	ZSR STA PSA	Detmold	1801-1874	28
Werne an der Lippe	rkKB	Detmold	1815-1874	2
Wersen	ZSR STA	Detmold	1811-1814	1
Wersen	evKB LRA PSA ev.refKB	Bielefeld Detmold	1655-1896	5
Werste	rkKB PSA	Detmold	1863-1874	1
Werste	evKB	Detmold	1815-1873	2
Werth	evLutKB	Detmold	1815-1874	1
Werth	rkKB	Detmold	1815-1874	1
Werth -Borken-	ZSR STA	Detmold	1812-1813	1
Werth	rkKB BA	Münster	1719-1911	5
Werth	evKB LRA	Bielefeld	1612-1967	5
Werther	evKB LRA PSA evLutKB	Bielefeld Detmold	1657-1904	18
Werther	rkKB PSA	Detmold	1808-1874	1
Weseke	rkKB PSA BA	Münster Detmold	1640-1903	5

Location	Nature of Material	Where Filmed	Dates Covered	No. of Rolls
Wesel	French Church KB	The Hague	1694-1808	1
Wesel	MKB KBA	Hannover	1741-1920	12
Wesel	rkKB BA	Münster	1620-1875	3
Wesel	Walloon Church KB	The Hague	1694-1755	1
Wesseling	ZSR BM PSA	Brühl	1799-1875	7
Wesseling	rkKB	Schloss Brühl	1666-1799	6
Wessum	rkKB PSA BA	Detmold Münster	1648-1901	6
Westbarthausen	evKB PSA ev.refKB	Detmold	1814-1839	4
Westbevern	rkKB PSA BA	Detmold Münster	1654-1875	5
Westenholz -Kr. Paderborn-	rkKB PSA IA	Paderborn Detmold	1717-1944	10
Westerborken	rkKB PSA	Detmold	1815-1874	3
Westereiden	rkKB EA	Paderborn	1626-1874	2
Westerholt	rkKB PSA BA	Detmold Münster	1624-1892	3
Westerholt	ZSR STA PSA	Detmold	1809-1811	1
Westerkappeln	ev.refKB	Detmold	1815-1874	1
Westerkappeln	ZSR STA	Detmold	1810-1813	2
Westerkappeln -Tecklenburg-	evKB LKA	Bielefeld	1649-1907	12

Location	Nature of Material	Where Filmed	Dates Covered	No. of Rolls
Westerkappeln	ZSR	Bielefeld	1810-1814	2
Westerloh	rkKB PSA	Detmold	1815-1874	2
Westerloh	ZSR STA	Detmold	1808-1813	1
Westernkotten	rkKB EA	Paderborn	1661-1874	8
Westerwiehe	rkKB PSA	Detmold	1808-1874	7
Westerwiehe	ZSR STA	Detmold	1808-1813	1
Westheim	rkKB PSA EA	Detmold Paderborn	1725-1874	2
Westhofen	evLutKB LRA	Bielefeld	1680-1886	4
Westhofen -Iserlohn-	rkKB PSA	Detmold	1831-1874	1
Westhofen -Iserlohn-	evKB	Detmold	1819-1874	2
Westkiever	evLutKB	Detmold	1852-1873	1
Westkirchen	ZSR STA	Detmold	1810-1813	1
Westkirchen	KB	Berlin-Dahlem	1750	1
Westkirchen	rkKB PSA BA	Detmold Münster	1684-1875	4
Westönnen	rkKB PSA	Detmold	1808-1874	2
Westrup	evKB	Detmold	1808-1874	6
Wetten	ZSR STA PSA	Brühl	1798-1875	15
Wetten	rkKB	Schloss Brühl	1699-1807	2
Wettes	evKB PSA LKA evLutKB	Detmold Bielefeld	1638-1944	19

Location	Nature of Material	Where Filmed	Dates Covered	No. of Rolls
Wettringen	rkKB BA	Münster	1644-1875	4
Wevelinghoven	ZSR BM PSA STA	Brühl	1799-1875	13
Wevelinghoven	evLutKB evKA ev.refKB	Düsseldorf Schloss Brühl	1655-1902	6
Wevelinghoven	rkKB	Schloss Brühl	1655-1798	3
Wewelsburg	rkKB PSA	Detmold	1808-1874	1
Wewer	rkKB EA PSA	Paderborn Detmold	1707-1875	3
Wewelsburg	rkKB EA	Paderborn	1684-1875	1
Weyer	ZSR BGM PSA	Brühl	1798-1875	8
Wiblingwerde	ev.refKB LKA	Bielefeld	1691-1903	10
Wichterich	rkKB	Schloss Brühl	1683-1814	1
Wickede	rkKB PSA	Detmold	1806-1874	5
Wickede	evKB PSA LKA evLutKB	Detmold Bielefeld	1815-1880	3
Wickrath	ZSR PSA BGM	Brühl	1799-1816	3
Wickrath	evLutKB evKA	Düsseldorf	1721-1799	2
Wickrath -Grevenbroich-	ZSR BGM PSA	Brühl	1799-1875	24
Wickrath -Grevenbroich-	ev.refKB	Schloss Brühl	1721-1799	1
Wichrath -Grevenbroich-	rkKB	Schloss Brühl	1734-1799	1

Location	Nature of Material	Where Filmed	Dates Covered	No. of Rolls
Wiedenbrück	rkKB PSA	Detmold	1808-1874	4
Wiedenbrück	evKB rkKB	Detmold	1810-1874	4
Wiedenbrück	evKB PSA LKA	Detmold Bielefeld	1866-1952	2
Wiedenbrück	evKB KBA MKB	Hannover	1864-1877	2
Wiehl	ev.refKB	Schloss Brühl	1745-1809	3
Wiescherhöfen	KB PSA	Detmold	1818-1874	3
Wietersheim	evKB PSA	Detmold	1808-1874	2
Wildenrath	rkKB	Schloss Brühl	1691-1798	1
Willebadessen	rkKB PSA	Detmold	1808-1874	2
Willegassen	rkKB PSA	Detmold	1808-1874	4
Willich	ZSR STA BGM PSA	Brühl	1799-1875	30
Wilnsdorf	evKB LKA PSA	Bielefeld Detmold	1579-1968	15
Wilnsdorf	rkKB PSA	Detmold	1818-1874	2
Windheim	evKB PSA LKA evLutKB	Detmold Bielefeld	1669-1948	11
Wingeshausen	evKB PSA LKA	Detmold Bielefeld	1680-1930	8
Winnekendonk	ZSR STA PSA	Brühl	1798-1875	10
Winnekendonk	rkKB BA	Schloss Brühl Münster	1710-1875	3

Location	Nature of Material	Where Filmed	Dates Covered	No. of Rolls
Winterberg -Brilon-	rkKB PSA	Detmold	1808-1874	2
Winterscheid	rkKB	Schloss Brühl	1727-1809	2
Winz	KB PSA	Detmold	1866	1
Wipperfeld	evLutKB	Schloss Brühl	1778-1807	4
Wipperfeld	rkKB	Schloss Brühl	1652-1809	3
Wipperfürth	ev.refKB	Schloss Brühl	1789-1809	1
Wipperfürth	rkKB	Schloss Brühl	1648-1809	4
Wissel	rkKB BA	Münster	1805-1875	1
Wissersheim	rkKB	Schloss Brühl	1703-1803	1
Wisskirchen	rkKB	Schloss Brühl	1760-1803	1
Witten	evKB LKA BA evLutKB	Bielefeld Detmold	1728-1948	42
Witten	rkKB PSA	Detmold	1847-1874	2
Witten	ZSR STA	Detmold	1810-1814	2
Witterschlich	rkKB	Schloss Brühl	1690-1798	1
Wittlaer	rkKB	Schloss Brühl	1634-1809	4
Witzhelden	ZSR BGM PSA	Brühl	1810-1875	9
Witzhelden	evKB evKA evLutKB	Düsseldorf Schloss Brühl	1770-1877	6
Wobbel	evKB LKA PSA ev.refKB	Bielefeld Detmold	1691-1919	10
Wolbeck	rkKB PSA BA	Detmold Münster	1674-1875	4
Wollersheim	ZSR BM PSA	Bruhl	1799-1875	11

Location	Nature of Material	Where Filmed	Dates Covered	No. of Rolls
Wollersheim	rkKB	Schloss Brühl	1666-1799	1
Wormbach	rkKB PSA	Detmold	1808-1874	2
Wormeln	evKB PSA	Detmold	1826-1874	1
Wormeln	rkKB	Detmold	1808-1874	1
Wormersdorf	rkKB	Schloss Brühl	1622-1798	1
Wulfen	ZSR STA PSA	Detmold	1812-1814	1
Wulfen	rkKB PSA BA	Detmold Münster	1649-1900	1
Wulferdingsen	rkKB PSA	Detmold	1863-1874	1
Wulferdingsen	ev.refKB	Detmold	1815-1873	4
Wulferdingsen	ZSR STA	Detmold	1808-1814	2
Wülfrath	evKB evKA evLutKB ev.refKB	Düsseldorf Schloss Brühl	1656-1897	13
Wülfrath	rkKB	Schloss Brühl	1762-1809	1
Wüllen	rkKB PSA BA	Detmold Münster	1669-1938	6
Wulmeringhausen	rkKB PSA EA	Detmold Paderborn	1715-1879	8
Wülpke	evKB PSA	Detmold	1808-1872	1
Wunderthausen	evKB PSA LKA	Detmold Bielefeld	1808-1969	3
Wünnenberg	rkKB PSA	Detmold	1808-1874	3
Wuppertal	LG BA	Schloss Brühl	1802-1872	4
Wuppertal	rkKB	Schloss Brühl	1658-1809	8

Location	Nature of Material	Where Filmed	Dates Covered	No. of Rolls
Wuppertal	evKB evLutKB ev.refKB	Detmold Düsseldorf Schloss Brühl	1584-1884	139
Würgassen	rkKB PSA	Detmold	1808-1874	1
Würm	rkKB	Schloss Brühl	1625-1800	3
Würm	ZSR BGM PSA	Brühl	1799-1875	11
Würselen	ZSR BGM	Brühl	1802-1875	18
Würselen	rkKB	Schloss Brühl	1713-1805	2
Wüschheim	ZSR STA PSA	Brühl	1800-1875	21
Wüsten	evKB LKA PSA ev.refKB	Bielefeld Detmold	1671-1923	10
Wyler	rkKB	Schloss Brühl	1723-1805	1
Xanten	ZSR STA PSA	Brühl	1798-1875	18
Xanten	ev.refKB evKA	Düsseldorf	1693-1810	1
Xanten	rkKB BA	Schloss Brühl Münster	1642-1875	10
Zons	ZSR PSA BGM STA	Brühl	1799-1875	13
Zülpich	ZSR BGM	Brühl	1797-1872	1
Zülpich	rkKB	Schloss Brühl	1682-1799	9
Züschen	rkKB PSA	Detmold	1808-1874	1

RHEINLAND-PFALZ

Location	Nature of Material	Where Filmed	Dates Covered	No. of Rolls
Aach	rkKB	Trier	1685-1805	2
Abtweiler	evKB	Düsseldorf	1681-1905	2
Achtelsbach	evKB	Koblenz	1574-1854	2
Adenau	rkKB	Trier	1668-1886	5
Adenbach	LG LRA evKB	Speyer Kusel	1743-1834	4
Ahrweiler	rkKB	Trier	1600-1960	10
Abersbuch	LG LRA	Speyer Kusel	1799-1870	3
Albersweiler	LG evKB rkKB	Speyer	1607-1941	7
Albessen	LG LRA	Speyer Kusel	1817-1875	3
Albisheim	evKB	Speyer Freiburg	1641-1937	8
Alf	rkKB	Trier	1624-1681	1
Alflen	rkKB	Trier	1688-1935	5
Alken	rkKB	Trier	1616-1941	3
Allenbuch	evKB	Koblenz	1617-1798	1
Allenz	rkKB	Trier	1743-1794	1
Alsdorf	rkKB	Trier	1738-1797	1
Alsenbrück	evKB LG	Speyer Freiburg	1700-1945	3
Alsenz	evKB LG	Speyer	1566-1886	9
Alsheim	rkKB	Speyer	1699-1885	6
Alsterweiler	rkKB	Speyer	1567-1798	2
Altdorf	evKB LG	Speyer	1759-1877	5
Altenahr	rkKB	Trier	1740-1798	1

Location	Nature of Material	Where Filmed	Dates Covered	No. of Rolls
Altenbamberg	evKB LG LKA	Speyer	1751-1868	4
Altenglan	evKB LRA BA	Speyer Kusel	1671-1904	25
Altenkirchen	LRA evKB	Speyer Kusel	1718-1906	17
Alterkülz	evKB	Koblenz	1664-1798	1
Althornbach	STA evKB	Zweibrücken Speyer	1559-1875	8
Altlay	rkKB	Trier Mainz	1743-1968	4
Altleiningen	evKB BA	Speyer	1699-1925	5
Altrich	rkKB	Trier	1695-1899	2
Altrip	rkKB BA	Speyer	1651-1830	2
Altscheid	rkKB	Trier	1720-1919	2
Altweidelbach	rkKB	Koblenz	1786-1797	1
Alzey	rkKB	Mainz Speyer	1685-1909	5
Ammeldingen	rkKB	Trier	1821-1899	1
Andernach	rkKB	Hannover Trier	1795-1913	6
Anhausen	evKB	Düsseldorf	1614-1880	9
Annweiler	LG evKB rkKB	Speyer	1556-1921	14
Antweiler	rkKB	Trier	1718-1888	1
Appenheim	rkKB	Mainz	1746-1798	1
Appenhofen	LG rkKB	Speyer	1708-1881	2
Aremberg	rkKB	Trier	1664-1931	3
Arenberg	rkKB	Trier	1654-1893	2
Arenrath	rkKB	Trier	1657-1912	2

Location	Nature of Material	Where Filmed	Dates Covered	No. of Rolls
Armsheim	rkKB	Mainz	1802-1876	1
Arzfeld	rkKB	Trier	1684-1796	4
Arzheim	rkKB	Trier Speyer Freiburg	1726-1961	15
Aschbach	LRA rkKB	Kusel	1818-1874	3
Aspisheim	rkKB	Mainz	1676-1915	2
Ausbacherhof	evKB	Speyer	1706-1873	1
Auw -Bitburg-	rkKB	Trier	1657-1807	2
Ayl	rkKB	Trier	1841-1939	1
Baalborn	evKB LG LRA	Speyer Kaiserslautern	1721-1900	5
Bacharach	rkKB ObBM LRA	Trier Kaiserslautern Koblenz	1577-1908	10
Bad Bertrich	rkKB	Trier	1739-1907	4
Bad Breisig	rkKB	Trier	1617-1814	1
Bad Dürkheim	LG LRA	Kaiserslautern Speyer	1646-1901	118
Bad Hönningen	rkKB	Trier	1652-1883	3
Bad Kreuznach	MKB rkKB	Mainz Freiburg Hannover Düsseldorf Koblenz	1509-1917	13
Bad Münster am Stein	evKB	Koblenz	1733-1798	1
Bad Neuenahr	rkKB	Trier	1646-1911	4
Bad Salzig	rkKB	Trier	1786-1897	3
Badem	rkKB	Trier	1819-1853	1
Badenhard	evKB	Koblenz	1739-1884	2
Badenheim	rkKB	Mainz	1699-1872	1
Bann	rkKB ZSR	Speyer Kaiserslautern	1723-1957	21

Location	Nature of Material	Where Filmed	Dates Covered	No. of Rolls
Barbelroth	evKB	Speyer	1596-1943	3
Bärweiler	evKB rkKB	Trier Koblenz	1686-1869	2
Barweiler	rkKB	Trier	1731-1950	2
Bassenheim	rkKB	Trier	1660-1889	3
Baltenberg	evKB	Speyer	1585-1868	2
Battweiler	ZSR rkKB	Zweibrücken Bezirksgericht	1683-1875	7
Baumholder	rkKB evKB	Trier Mainz Koblenz	1682-1848	5
Bausendorf	rkKB	Trier	1754-1906	2
Baustert	rkKB	Trier	1720-1897	2
Bayerfeld Steckweiler	LG rkKB	Speyer Mainz	1729-1961	4
Becherbach -BK-	LG LRA evKB evKB	Düsseldorf Kusel Mainz Speyer	1616-1906	19
Bechtheim	rkKB	Mainz	1810-1876	2
Bechtolsheim	rkKB	Mainz	1717-1936	2
Beckingen	rkKB	Trier	1721-1792	1
Beilstein	rkKB	Trier	1637-1900	2
Beindersheim	evKB	Speyer	1683-1839	3
Beinhausen	rkKB	Trier	1658-1900	3
Bekond	rkKB	Trier	1804-1938	1
Bell	evKB rkKB	Düsseldorf Trier Koblenz	1568-1823	5
Bellheim	rkKB	Speyer	1684-1960	9
Beltheim	rkKB	Trier	1715-1900	3
Bendorf	rkKB	Trier	1629-1941	4
Bengen	rkKB	Trier	1770-1968	3

Location	Nature of Material	Where Filmed	Dates Covered	No. of Rolls
Bennhausen	evKB LG	Speyer	1818-1863	2
Bensberg	rkKB	Hannover	1841-1906	1
Berg -Germesheim-	ZSR rkKB	Speyer	1733-1905	4
Bergen -Birkenfeld-	evKB	Düsseldorf	1681-1823	3
Berghausen		Speyer	1778-1960	22
Berglicht	rkKB	Trier	1661-1807	1
Bergweiler	rkKB	Trier Mainz	1711-1881	3
Bergzabern	evKB rkKB	Speyer	1617-1943	4
Berndorf	rkKB	Trier	1724-1929	4
Bernkastel	rkKB	Trier	1603-1904	6
Berschweiler	evKB	Berlin-Dahlem Koblenz	1680-1825	2
Berzweiler	LG	Kusel Speyer	1799-1875	3
Bescheid	rkKB	Trier	1719-1812	1
Besslich	rkKB	Trier	1571-1794	2
Bettenfeld	rkKB	Trier	1677-1910	4
Bettenhausen	ZSR	Kaiserslautern	1818-1875	2
Betzdorf	rkKB	Trier	1871-1886	1
Beulich	rkKB	Trier	1641-1897	4
Beulwadenheim	rkKB	Trier	1784-1798	1
Beuren	rkKB	Trier	1751-1875	4
Bickenbach	rkKB	Trier	1663-1880	3
Bickendorf	rkKB	Trier	1651-1955	4
Biebern	evKB rkKB	Koblenz Mainz Trier	1681-1955	6
Biebernheim	evKB	Koblenz	1706-1799	1

Location	Nature of Material	Where Filmed	Dates Covered	No. of Rolls
Biedershausen			1818-1875	4
Biedesheim	evKB LG	Speyer	1685-1868	2
Biersdorf	rkKB	Trier	1699-1895	2
Billigheim	evKB rkKB ZSR	Speyer	1700-1961	12
Bindersbuch	evKB	Speyer	1785-1789	1
Bingen	rkKB	Mainz	1582-1938	11
Binscheid	rkKB	Trier	1695-1885	2
Binsfeld	rkKB	Trier	1806-1895	2
Birburg Rogh	rkKB	Trier	1718-1797	1
Birkenfeld	evKB	Koblenz Düsseldorf Trier	1568-1876	11
Birkenhördt	rkKB LG	Speyer	1751-1900	7
Birkweiler	evKB LG	Speyer	1685-1961	6
Birresbonn	rkKB	Trier	1833-1933	1
Bischheim	LG ZSR	Speyer	1811-1826	2
Bischofdhron	rkKB	Trier	1583-1906	4
Bissersheim	evKB	Speyer	1717-1897	1
Bisterschied	rkKB evKB ZSR LG	Speyer	1710-1826	5
Bitburg -Auw-	rkKB	Freiburg	1662-1911	6
Blankenborn	rkKB LG	Speyer	1751-1900	5
Blankenrath	rkKB	Trier	1655-1907	5
Blasweiler	rkKB	Trier	1707-1968	2
Blaubach	LG BZG	Speyer Kusel	1818-1875	7

Location	Nature of Material	Where Filmed	Dates Covered	No. of Rolls
Bleckhausen	rkKB	Trier	1793-1908	1
Bledesbach	LG LRA	Speyer Kusel	1818-1875	7
Bleialf	rkKB	Trier	1630-1906	2
Bleiderdingen	rkKB	Trier	1747-1802	2
Bobenheim	evKB rkKB	Speyer	1585-1930	10
Bobenthal	rkKB	Speyer	1722-1961	4
Böbingen	ZSR evKB rkKB	Speyer	1651-1953	4
Bochingen	ZSR rkKB	Speyer Freiburg	1726-1838	4
Bockenau	rkKB	Mainz Trier	1732-1796	2
Bockheim	evKB OBBM	Speyer	1633-1927	7
Bodenbach	rkKB	Trier	1862-1914	1
Bodendorf	rkKB	Trier	1680-1877	3
Bodenheim	rkKB	Mainz	1700-1875	2
Bohl-Iggelheim	rkKB AG evKB	Freiburg Speyer	1694-1960	11
Bolanden	LG	Speyer	1804-1825	2
Böllenborn	rkKB	Speyer	1751-1900	4
Bollendorf	rkKB	Trier	1646-1796	1
Böllenhorn	STA	Speyer	1820-1856	1
Bornbogen	rkKB	Trier	1687-1880	3
Boos	rkKB evKB	Trier Koblenz	1658-1965	3
Boppard	rkKB evKB	Trier Düsseldorf	1571-1891	8
Bornheim	STA rkKB evKB	Speyer Freiburg	1785-1917	4

Location	Nature of Material	Where Filmed	Dates Covered	No. of Rolls
Börrstadt	LG rkKB evKB	Speyer Freiburg	1702-1961	7
Börsborn	LRA STA	Kusel	1799-1875	5
Bosenbach	LG evKB LRA	Speyer Kusel	1637-1906	17
Bottenbach	STA BZG	Zweibrücken	1798-1875	6
Brachbach	rkKB	Trier	1872-1936	2
Brachweilerhof		Speyer	1785-1789	1
Branscheid	rkKB	Trier	1803-1903	1
Brauneberg	rkKB	Trier	1690-1930	3
Braunweiler	rkKB	Trier Mainz	1745-1969	4
Breitenbach	STA rkKB evKB LRA	Kusel Freiburg Speyer	1714-1961	19
Bremm	rkKB	Trier	1609-1781	2
Bretzenheim	evKB rkKB	Mainz Koblenz Trier	1720-1804	6
Breuningweiler	LG evKB	Trier Speyer	1802-1891	6
Briedel	rkKB	Trier	1738-1798	1
Brockscheid	rkKB	Trier	1752-1890	1
Brodenbach	rkKB	Trier	1674-1798	1
Brohl	rkKB	Trier	1617-1942	2
Bruch	rkKB	Trier	1684-1857	3
Bruchmühlbau	rkKB STA	Freiburg Kaiserslautern	1739-1948	31
Bruchweiler	rkKB evKB	Speyer Koblenz	1656-1936	6
Brücken	ZSR rkKB	Freiburg Kusel	1741-1959	15

Location	Nature of Material	Where Filmed	Dates Covered	No. of Rolls
Bruscheich	rkKB	Trier	1730-1880	1
Bruttig	rkKB	Trier	1593-1964	3
Bubach	LG rkKB	Koblenz Speyer	1746-1832	2
Bubenhausen	rkKB	Speyer	1798-1881	1
Bubenheim	LG rkKB	Speyer	1705-1911	4
Buch	rkKB	Trier	1653-1968	3
Büchel	rkKB	Trier Speyer	1729-1964	3
Büchelberg	STA	Speyer	1816-1833	1
Büchenbeuren	evKB	Koblenz	1752-1798	1
Buchholz	rkKB	Trier	1667-1906	3
Budenheim	rkKB	Mainz	1622-1875	2
Büdesheim	rkKB	Trier	1688-1921	2
Büdlich	rkKB	Trier	1666-1798	1
Bullay	rkKB	Trier	1684-1798	1
Bundenbach	rkKB	Trier Mainz	1590-1950	5
Bundenthal	rkKB	Speyer	1755-1936	2
Burbach	rkKB	Trier	1803-1878	1
Burgalben	LRA evKB	Speyer	1640-1961	18
Burgbrohl	rkKB	Trier	1543-1889	2
Burgen	rkKB	Trier	1627-1798	1
Burglichtenberg	ZSR	Kusel	1862	1
Burgsponheim	evKB	Koblenz	1713-1798	1
Burrweiler	rkKB	Kaiserslautern Speyer	1599-1908	6
Busenberg	rkKB		1686-1961	3
Butzweiler	rkKB	Trier	1641-1938	2

Location	Nature of Material	Where Filmed	Dates Covered	No. of Rolls
Callbach	LG evKB	Speyer	1802-1955	2
Carlsberg	BGM evKB rkKB	Speyer	1699-1961	9
Clausen	rkKB	Speyer	1806-1913	2
Cochem	rkKB	Trier Koblenz	1656-1926	8
Cölln	LG	Speyer	1818-1836	1
Commershausen	rkKB	Trier	1789-1797	1
Contwig	STA evKB LRA	Zweibrücken Speyer	1683-1960	28
Cronenberg	LG LRA	Speyer Kusel	1684-1874	4
Dackenheim	rkKB evKB	Speyer	1637-1923	3
Dahlem	rkKB	Trier	1731-1891	2
Dahn	rkKB	Speyer	1685-1897	6
Dahnen	rkKB	Trier	1807-1911	2
Daleiden	rkKB	Trier	1687-1899	3
Dammheim	evKB STA	Speyer	1591-1844	3
Dannenfels	evKB LG	Speyer	1698-1901	6
Dannstadt Schauernheim	AG evKB BA rkKB	Speyer	1652-1958	10
Danzenberg	LG STA	Speyer	1799-1957	8
Darsheid	rkKB	Trier	1803-1934	1
Darstein	STA	Speyer	1818-1875	1
Dattenberg	rkKB	Trier	1789-1876	3
Daun	rkKB	Trier Freiburg	1656-1914	5

Location	Nature of Material	Where Filmed	Dates Covered	No. of Rolls
Daxweiler	evKB	Koblenz	1649-1801	1
Deckenheim	rkKB	Speyer	1637-1797	1
Dellfeld	STA rkKB SRA	Speyer	1683-1875	7
Dernbach	rkKB	Speyer	1556-1889	8
Deidesheim	BA rkKB	Speyer	1670-1958	17
Demerath	rkKB	Trier	1803-1905	1
Dennweiler	LRA evKB LG	Speyer Kusel	1818-1875	5
Densborn	rkKB	Trier	1808-1967	2
Dernau	rkKB	Trier	1703-1901	3
Dernbach	rkKB STA	Speyer	1785-1842	2
Detzem	rkKB	Trier	1656-1896	2
Deudesfeld	rkKB	Trier	1779-1900	1
Dhron	rkKB	Trier	1798-1876	1
Dickenschied	evKB	Koblenz Hamborn	1714-1798	2
Dieblich	rkKB	Trier	1657-1835	2
Diedesfeld	rkKB STA	Speyer Freiburg	1647-1961	8
Dielkirchen	LG evKB STA	Freiburg Speyer	1697-1964	13
Dienheim	rkKB	Mainz	1637-1798	1
Dierbach	evKB STA	Speyer	1596-1943	5
Dierdorf	evKB rkKB	Düsseldorf Trier	1676-1945	11
Dietrichingen	LRA STA	Zweibrücken	1798-1875	5
Dietschweiler	STA	Kusel	1799-1875	4

Location	Nature of Material	Where Filmed	Dates Covered	No. of Rolls
Diez	evKB	Hannover	1868-1918	2
Dill	evKB	Koblenz Hamborn	1643-1798	4
Dimbach	STA	Speyer	1816-1859	1
Dirmstein	rkKB	Speyer	1804-1952	3
Dittelsheim	rkKB	Mainz	1715-1876	1
Dittlingen	rkKB	Trier	1764-1871	2
Dittweiler	LRA	Kusel	1799-1875	6
Dockendorf	rkKB	Trier	1679-1899	2
Dockweiler	rkKB	Trier	1726-1899	2
Dohmlammersdorf	rkKB	Trier	1778-1798	1
Dommershausen	rkKB	Trier	1789-1965	3
Donsieders	rkKB	Speyer	1680-1919	1
Dörnbach	LG	Speyer	1810-1826	2
Dörrebach	evKB rkKB	Koblenz Trier	1717-1898	3
Dörrenbach	evKB STA	Speyer	1689-1961	7
Dörrmoschel	evKB LG	Speyer	1704-1897	2
Dreckenach	rkKB	Trier	1617-1937	2
Dreis	rkKB	Trier	1684-1943	3
Dreisen	rkKB LG evKB	Speyer	1648-1957	13
Dromersheim	rkKB	Mainz	1676-1915	2
Drusweiler	evKB	Speyer	1731-1745	1
Duchroth	evKB	Speyer Kaiserslautern	1488-1876	5
Dudeldorf	rkKB	Trier	1741-1883	2
Dudenhofen	rkKB STA	Speyer	1715-1954	28
Dümpelfeld	rkKB	Trier	1644-1968	3

Location	Nature of Material	Where Filmed	Dates Covered	No. of Rolls
Düngenheim	rkKB	Trier	1662-1950	3
Dunzweiler	LRA rkKB	Kusel Speyer	1714-1880	8
Duppach	rkKB	Trier	1737-1906	2
Dusel	rkKB	Freiburg	1756-1957	4
Duttweiler	evKB rkKB	Speyer	1651-1948	4
Ebernburg	evKB LG rkKB	Speyer Freiburg	1681-1948	6
Ebersheim	rkKB	Mainz	1637-1798	1
Ebertsheim	evKB	Speyer	1694-1891	1
Eck	evKB	Bielefeld	1850-1947	2
Eckendorf	rkKB	Trier	1678-1944	2
Eckweiler	evKB	Koblenz	1568-1798	1
Edenkoben	evKB rkKB AG	Speyer	1666-1955	18
Edesheim	rkKB STA	Speyer	1676-1910	7
Ediger	rkKB	Freiburg Trier	1609-1786	3
Edingen	rkKB	Trier	1705-1899	2
Ehlenz	rkKB	Trier	1671-1916	2
Ehrang	rkKB	Trier	1571-1884	3
Ehweiler	LG LRA	Speyer Kusel	1818-1875	3
Eich	rkKB	Mainz Trier	1638-1968	6
Einod	evKB	Speyer	1798-1839	1
Einöllen	LG LRA AG evKB	Speyer Kusel	1730-1964	9

Location	Nature of Material	Where Filmed	Dates Covered	No. of Rolls
Einselthum	rkKB LG evKB	Speyer	1667-1961	6
Eisenach	rkKB	Trier	1783-1881	1
Eisenbach	LRA LG	Speyer Kusel	1634-1893	6
Eisenberg	rkKB evKB LG	Speyer Freiburg	1674-1957	11
Eisenschmitt	rkKB	Trier	1730-1969	4
Ellenz	rkKB	Trier	1614-1886	3
Eller	rkKB	Trier	1614-1798	2
Ellern	evKB	Koblenz	1743-1798	1
Ellerstadt	evKB rkKB BA	Speyer	1686-1942	9
Elmstein	rkKB BA AG rkKB	Speyer	1713-1959	6
Elschbach	LRA	Kusel	1799-1875	5
Elzweiler	LRA	Kusel	1855-1906	2
Engers	rkKB	Trier	1704-1925	3
Enkenbach	STA evKB rkKB LG	Trier Speyer Kaiserslautern Berlin	1663-1957	56
Enkirch	evKB rkKB	Koblenz Trier	1632-1919	4
Ensch	rkKB	Trier	1765-1911	2
Eppenbrunn	rkKB	Speyer	1716-1953	6
Eppstein	BA evKB rkKB	Freiburg Speyer	1716-1946	8
Erbes-Büdesheim	rkKB	Mainz	1738-1927	1
Erden	rkKB	Trier	1690-1906	2

Location	Nature of Material	Where Filmed	Dates Covered	No. of Rolls
Erdesbach	LG LRA	Speyer Kusel	1818-1875	3
Erfenbach	STA	Kaiserslautern	1643-1798	6
Erfweiler	rkKB	Speyer	1787-1897	3
Erlenbach	LG evKB rkKB STA	Speyer Kaiserslautern	1622-1961	19
Ernst	rkKB	Trier	1625-1880	2
Ernstweiler	evKB	Speyer	1798-1881	2
Ernsen	rkKB	Trier	1803-1899	1
Erpolzheim	evKB rkKB BA	Berlin-Dürkheim Speyer	1644-1947	7
Erzenhausen	LG STA	Kaiserslautern Speyer	1798-1875	4
Eschenau	LRA evKB	Kusel Speyer	1634-1875	4
Esch	rkKB	Trier	1807-1852	1
Eschbach	LG rkKB STA	Speyer	1735-1931	5
Eschfeld	rkKB	Trier	1695-1899	2
Essingen	rkKB STA	Speyer Freiburg	1701-1958	9
Essweiler	STA evKB LG	Speyer Kaiserslautern	1637-1906	16
Esthal	rkKB	Speyer	1713-1959	6
Etschberg	evKB LG LRA	Kusel Speyer	1567-1900	12
Ettringen	rkKB	Trier	1691-1948	5
Eulenbis	STA	Speyer Kaiserslautern	1799-1875	4
Euren	rkKB	Freiburg	1600-1876	3

Location	Nature of Material	Where Filmed	Dates Covered	No. of Rolls
Eussenthal	rkKB LG	Speyer	1709-1961	4
Faid	rkKB	Trier	1799-1904	2
Falkenstein	LG	Speyer	1818-1831	1
Fankel	rkKB	Trier	1797-1964	1
Farschweiler	rkKB	Trier	1703-1880	2
Fehrbach	rkKB	Speyer	1794-1960	2
Feilbingert	evKB rkKB LG	Berlin-Dahlem Speyer	1681-1961	10
Fell	rkKB	Trier	1785-1932	2
Felsberg	evKB	Speyer	1699-1868	2
Felsbergerhof	evKB	Speyer	1706-1873	2
Ferschweiler	rkKB	Trier	1808-1940	2
Filsch	rkKB	Trier	1663-1798	1
Filzen	rkKB	Trier	1681-1964	2
Finkenbach	STA evKB LG	Speyer	1662-1900	4
Finthen	rkKB	Mainz	1676-1900	3
Fisch	rkKB	Trier	1696-1798	1
Fischbach	rkKB	Düsseldorf Kaiserslautern Speyer Trier	1656-1948	12
Flemlingen	rkKB LG	Speyer	1778-1908	3
Fleringen	rkKB	Trier	1683-1939	2
Fliessem	rkKB	Trier	1767-1903	2
Flomersheim	rkKB	Speyer	1716-1882	3
Flonheim	rkKB	Mainz	1756-1908	2
Flörsheim	rkKB	Mainz	1700-1908	1
Föckelberg	LRA LG evKB	Speyer Kusel	1799-1893	6

Location	Nature of Material	Where Filmed	Dates Covered	No. of Rolls
Fohren	rkKB	Trier	1644-1917	3
Forst	rkKB BA	Speyer Trier	1656-1958	8
Frankelbach	LRA LG evKB	Speyer Kusel	1640-1925	7
Frankeneck	rkKB	Speyer	1785-1789	1
Frankenstein	LG STA	Speyer Kaiserslautern	1799-1957	11
Frankenthal	AG rkKB STA	Freiburg Speyer	1565-1946	28
Frankweiler	LG	Speyer	1818-1831	1
Freckenfeld	evKB LG	Speyer	1671-1837	3
Frei-Laubersheim	rkKB	Mainz	1698-1908	1
Freimersheim	rkKB LG	Mainz Speyer	1701-1960	7
Freinsheim	rkKB evKB STA	Speyer	1698-1958	8
Freisbach	evKB LG	Speyer	1665-1869	3
Freudenburg	rkKB STA	Trier Mettlach	1675-1922	16
Friedelhausen	evKB LG LRA	Speyer Kusel	1671-1909	6
Friedelsheim	rkKB evKB	Speyer	1654-1885	6
Friesenheim	rkKB	Mainz	1686-1929	3
Frohnhofen	LRA	Kusel	1799-1875	4
Frutzweiler	LRA evKB LG	Speyer Kusel	1818-1878	5
Fürfeld	rkKB	Mainz	1704-1924	1
Fussgönheim	evKB rkKB	Speyer	1727-1888	8

Location	Nature of Material	Where Filmed	Dates Covered	No. of Rolls
Gabsheim	rkKB	Mainz	1697-1908	2
Gappenach	rkKB	Trier	1679-1798	1
Gau-Algesheim		Mainz	1640-1896	2
Gau-Bickelheim	rkKB	Mainz	1654-1875	3
Gau-Heppenheim	rkKB	Mainz	1808-1876	1
Gau-Odenheim	rkKB	Mainz	1706-1908	2
Gau-Weinheim	rkKB	Mainz	1746-1908	1
Gauersheim	evKB LG	Speyer	1667-1926	5
Gaurehweiler	evKB LG	Speyer	1708-1839	5
Gebhardshain	evKB rkKB	Trier Düsseldorf	1705-1910	12
Gebroth	evKB	Koblenz	1714-1798	1
Gehlweiler	evKB	Koblenz	1662-1803	2
Gehrweiler	LG	Speyer	1818-1833	1
Geichlingen	rkKB	Trier	1779-1877	2
Geinsheim	rkKB	Speyer	1655-1960	7
Geiselberg	evKB LRA	Speyer	1822-1899	3
Geisfeld	rkKB	Trier	1708-1960	2
Gelsdorf	rkKB	Trier	1645-1942	3
Gemünden	rkKB evKB	Trier Koblenz	1662-1931	6
Genheim	evKB	Koblenz	1649-1801	1
Gensingen	rkKB	Mainz Trier	1697-1917	2
Gerbach	rkKB evKB LG	Mainz Freiburg Speyer	1714-1959	7
Gerhardsbrunn	STA	Kaiserslautern	1799-1957	7
Germesheim	LG rkKB AG evKB	Speyer	1685-1888	11

Location	Nature of Material	Where Filmed	Dates Covered	No. of Rolls
Gerolsheim	evKB	Speyer	1786-1839	1
Gerolstein	rkKB	Trier	1708-1912	3
Gevenich	rkKB	Trier	1799-1917	1
Gillenbeuren	rkKB	Trier	1726-1798	1
Gillenfeld	rkKB	Trier	1753-1884	2
Gimbsheim	rkKB	Mainz	1637-1798	1
Gimmeldingen	evKB rkKB	Speyer Freiburg	1678-1957	12
Gimsbach	STA evKB	Kaiserslautern Speyer	1701-1957	11
Gindorf	rkKB	Trier	1779-1812	1
Ginsweiler	LRA evKB LG	Speyer Kusel	1654-1907	11
Gipperath	rkKB	Trier	1748-1798	1
Glaadt	rkKB	Trier	1704-1899	1
Gladbach	rkKB	Trier	1684-1798	2
Glanmünchweiler	rkKB evKB LRA	Kusel Speyer	1664-1959	22
Gleisweiler	LG rkKB	Speyer Freiburg	1686-1961	6
Gleiszellen	rkKB LG evKB	Speyer	1731-1875	5
Göcklingen	rkKB LG STA evKB	Speyer	1652-1961	12
Godelhausen	LRA evKB LG	Speyer Kusel	1567-1906	9
Gödenroth	evKB	Koblenz	1568-1798	1
Godramstein	evKB rkKB	Speyer	1637-1961	10
Göllheim	LG evKB rkKB	Speyer	1653-1957	11

Location	Nature of Material	Where Filmed	Dates Covered	No. of Rolls
Gommesheim	evKB LG	Speyer	1665-1869	4
Gonbach	LG	Speyer	1818-1832	1
Gondelsheim	rkKB	Trier	1803-1918	1
Gondenbrett	rkKB	Trier	1799-1939	1
Gondorf	rkKB	Trier	1790-1959	2
Gönnersdorf	rkKB	Trier	1617-1960	2
Gönnheim	rkKB evKB	Speyer	1654-1885	8
Gonserath	rkKB	Trier	1836-1876	1
Gosserweiler	rkKB LG	Speyer	1732-1961	7
Graach	rkKB	Trier	1564-1939	3
Gräfenhausen	LG evKB rkKB	Speyer	1556-1839	8
Gransdorf	rkKB	Trier	1564-1939	4
Greimerath	rkKB	Trier	1706-1893	2
Grenderich	rkKB	Trier	1768-1798	1
Gries	LRA	Kusel	1799-1906	9
Gross-Winternheim	rkKB	Mainz	1699-1905	3
Grossbundenbach	evKB STA	Speyer	1715-1818	3
Grossfischlingen	LG rkKB	Speyer	1701-1960	7
Grosskampen	rkKB	Trier	1779	1
Grosskampenberg	rkKB	Trier	1721-1875	3
Grosskarlbach	evKB rkKB	Speyer	1707-1888	5
Grosslittgen	rkKB	Trier	1725-1857	2
Grossmaischeid	rkKB	Trier	1733-1817	1
Grossniedesheim	evKB BA	Speyer	1727-1873	3

Location	Nature of Material	Where Filmed	Dates Covered	No. of Rolls
Grosstein-hausen	LRA evKB rkKB	Speyer Zweibrücken	1559-1961	15
Grumbach	evKB	Koblenz	1752-1798	1
Grümstadt	rkKB BA evKB	Speyer	1666-1961	13
Guldental	rkKB	Mainz	1756-1796	1
Güls	rkKB	Trier	1332-1884	3
Gumbsweiler	LG evKB LRA	Speyer Kusel	1701-1880	4
Gundersheim	rkKB	Mainz	1700-1874	3
Gundersweiler	LG evKB	Speyer	1802-1870	4
Gundheim	rkKB	Mainz	1699-1908	2
Guntersblum	rkKB	Mainz	1706-1876	1
Gusenburg	rkKB	Trier	1768-1855	2
Gusterath	rkKB	Trier	1725-1798	1
Gutweiler	rkKB	Trier	1659-1922	2
Haardt	evKB	Speyer Bielefeld	1678-1947	6
Habscheid	rkKB	Trier	1798-1910	1
Hachenbach	LRA LG	Zweibrücken Kusel	1818-1874	5
Hackenheim	rkKB	Mainz	1691-1908	2
Hagenbach	rkKB LG	Speyer	1790-1945	2
Hahenbach	evKB	Koblenz	1701-1839	2
Hainfeld	LG rkKB	Speyer	1704-1961	6
Hallgarten	evKB LG	Speyer	1639-1879	8
Hallschlag	rkKB	Trier	1730-1910	2
Halsenbach	rkKB	Trier	1669-1909	4

Location	Nature of Material	Where Filmed	Dates Covered	No. of Rolls
Hambach	rkKB	Speyer Kaiserslautern	1639-1958	9
Hambuch	rkKB	Trier	1673-1930	4
Hamm	evKB rkKB	Koblenz Trier	1681-1939	3
Hammerstein	rkKB	Trier	1656-1951	2
Hanhofen	rkKB STA	Speyer	1693-1918	16
Hardenburg	STA evKB rkKB	Berlin Speyer Kaiserslautern	1646-1947	67
Harspelt	rkKB	Trier	1665-1878	2
Harthausen	rkKB STA	Speyer	1662-1960	24
Herxheim	rkKB	Bad Dürkheim	1701-1829	1
Harxheim	LG evKB rkKB	Speyer Mainz	1664-1961	8
Haschbach	LRA LG evKB	Speyer Kusel	1701-1877	8
Hassloch	rkKB BA evKB	Speyer	1700-1915	7
Hatzenbühl	rkKB LG	Speyer	1719-1941	7
Hatzenport	rkKB	Trier	1706-1884	2
Hauenstein	STA rkKB	Speyer	1788-1961	6
Hauptstuhl	evKB STA	Speyer Kaiserslautern	1691-1879	7
Hausen	evKB	Koblenz	1663-1738	1
Hayna	rkKB LG	Speyer	1677-1960	4
Heckenbach	rkKB	Trier	1676-1907	2
Heckenmünster	rkKB	Trier	1850-1963	1

Location	Nature of Material	Where Filmed	Dates Covered	No. of Rolls
Heddesheim	evKB rkKB	Trier Koblenz	1657-1879	3
Hefersweiler	LG evKB LRA	Speyer Kusel	1699-1906	11
Heidenburg	rkKB	Trier	1705-1868	2
Heidesheim	rkKB	Mainz	1679-1876	1
Heidweiler	rkKB	Trier	1709-1874	4
Heiligenmoschel	evKB STA	Speyer Kaiserslautern	1699-1957	19
Heiligenstein	rkKB STA	Speyer	1659-1950	23
Heimbach-Weis	rkKB	Trier	1614-1960	6
Heimersheim	rkKB	Mainz	1700-1849	1
Heimkirchen	LG evKB STA	Kaiserslautern Speyer Trier Bielefeld	1665-1937	9
Heinshausen	evKB	Speyer	1596-1839	1
Heinsenhausen	LG LRA	Speyer Kusel	1799-1874	3
Heistert	rkKB		1763-1822	1
Helfant	rkKB	Trier	1794-1897	2
Hellenthal	rkKB	Trier	1700-1964	2
Heltersberg	evKB rkKB	Speyer	1755-1960	7
Hengstbach	STA evKB LRA	Speyer Zweibrücken	1743-1875	8
Hennweiler	evKB rkKB	Koblenz Mainz	1655-1802	2
Henschtal	STA	Speyer	1818-1830	1
Hentern	rkKB	Trier	1860-1963	1
Herborn	evKB	Düsseldorf	1813-1824	1
Herchweiler	LG evKB LRA	Speyer Kusel	1552-1878	9

Location	Nature of Material	Where Filmed	Dates Covered	No. of Rolls
Herdorf	rkKB	Trier	1807-1906	4
Herforst	rkKB	Trier	1808-1943	1
Hergersweiler	LG	Speyer	1809-1875	1
Hermersberg	rkKB evKB LRA	Speyer	1724-1868	8
Hermeskeil	rkKB	Trier	1746-1865	5
Herrensulzbach	evKB	Koblenz	1627-1798	1
Herrstein	evKB	Koblenz Düsseldorf	1520-1798	9
Herschbach	rkKB	Trier	1735-1960	3
Herschberg	evKB	Speyer	1729-1939	5
Herschweiler-Pettersheim	LG LRA	Speyer	1818-1906	14
Herschwiesen	rkKB	Trier	1663-1798	1
Herxheim	evKB rkKB	Speyer	1667-1952	16
Herxheimweyher	rkKB	Speyer	1803-1906	2
Herzogenrath	rkKB	Schlors Brühl Köln	1648-1798	2
Hessheim	BA rkKB	Speyer	1700-1954	3
Hettenleidelheim	BA rkKB	Speyer Kaiserslautern	1707-1961	8
Hetzerath	rkKB	Trier	1787-1942	2
Heuchelheim	evKB LG	Speyer	1683-1879	10
Hilchenbach	rkKB	Mainz	1759-1764	1
Hildebrandseck	rkKB	Speyer	1785-1789	1
Hilgerath		Trier	1739-1802	1
Hillesheim	rkKB	Trier	1639-1889	2
Hilst	STA	Speyer	1795-1827	1
Hinterweidenthal	evKB	Speyer	1713-1874	2

Location	Nature of Material	Where Filmed	Dates Covered	No. of Rolls
Hinserath	rkKB	Trier	1862-1929	1
Hinsert	rkKB	Trier	1751-1798	1
Hinsweiler	LRA rkKB evKB LG	Bielefeld Speyer Kusel Frankfurt	1637-1938	10
Hirschfeld	rkKB	Trier	1686-1968	3
Hirschhorn	evKB	Speyer Kaiserslautern	1640-1957	15
Hirzenach	rkKB	Trier	1650-1916	2
Hochdorf-Assenheim	rkKB evKB	Speyer	1589-1958	6
Hochen	evKB	Speyer	1714-1880	2
Hochpochten	rkKB	Trier	1734-1798	1
Hochspeyer	rkKB STA evKB LG	Speyer Kaiserslautern	1713-1957	43
Hochstätten	evKB	Speyer	1690-1849	2
Hochstein	LG	Speyer	1818-1826	1
Hochstetten	LG	Speyer	1818-1829	1
Hohen-Sülzen	rkKB	Mainz	1753-1876	1
Hohenecken	rkKB STA	Kaiserslautern	1643-1959	5
Hohenöllen	evKB	Speyer Kusel	1640-1925	7
Holzbach	evKB	Koblenz	1667-1798	1
Holzfeld	evKB	Koblenz	1670-1798	2
Holzweiler	rkKB	Trier	1687-1869	2
Hönningen	rkKB	Trier	1714-1800	1
Hontheim	rkKB	Trier	1798-1969	1
Horath	rkKB	Trier	1805-1900	1
Horbach	rkKB	Speyer	1710-1927	5

Location	Nature of Material	Where Filmed	Dates Covered	No. of Rolls
Hördt	LG evKB rkKB	Speyer	1695-1961	12
Horhausen	rkKB	Trier	1678-1920	5
Höringen	LG	Speyer	1818-1827	1
Horn	evKB	Koblenz	1654-1798	1
Hornbach	LRA STA evKB rkKB	Zweibrücken Speyer	1559-1960	23
Horrweiler	rkKB	Mainz	1676-1915	2
Horschbach	LG LRA	Kusel Speyer	1799-1894	7
Hottenbach	evKB	Koblenz	1720-1798	1
Hüffler	LG evKB LRA	Speyer Kusel	1567-	6
Hüffelsheim	rkKB evKB	Koblenz Mainz Freiburg	1623-1798	3
Hümmel	rkKB	Trier	1697-1944	3
Hundheim	LRA LG	Speyer	1799-1906	11
Hundsbach	evKB	Koblenz	1714-1873	1
Hunolstein	rkKB	Trier	1801-1876	1
Hupperath	rkKB	Trier	1725-1940	1
Hülschenhausen	rkKB STA	Kaiserslautern	1799-1957	20
Idar	rkKB evKB	Trier Düsseldorf Mainz	1671-1918	8
Idenheim	rkKB	Trier	1798-1939	1
Igel	rkKB	Trier	1706-1895	2
Iggelheim	rkKB BA evKB	Speyer Bielefeld	1603-1959	11

Location	Nature of Material	Where Filmed	Dates Covered	No. of Rolls
Ilbesheim	rkKB evKB LG	Speyer	1682-1949	9
Ilgesheim	evKB	Koblenz	1723-1798	1
Illerich	rkKB	Trier	1848-1926	2
Immesheim	LG	Speyer	1818-1835	1
Impflingen	evKB LG	Speyer	1652-1859	5
Imsbach	evKB LG	Speyer	1724-1870	5
Imsweiler	rkKB LG	Speyer Frankfurt	1699-1950	5
Ingelheim	rkKB	Mainz	1693-1908	3
Ingenheim	LG evKB rkKB	Speyer Bielefeld	1708-1961	7
Ingweiler	evKB	Speyer	1798-1881	2
Insheim	LG evKB rkKB	Speyer	1652-1913	6
Irlich	rkKB	Trier	1637-1943	4
Irmenach	evKB	Koblenz	1647-1798	1
Irrel	rkKB	Trier	1801-1895	2
Irrhausen	rkKB	Trier	1809-1968	2
Irsch	rkKB	Trier	1673-1912	5
Isenburg	rkKB	Trier	1792-1940	2
Ittel	rkKB	Trier	1689-1879	2
Ixheim	evKB	Zweibrücken	1743-1866	3
Jakobsweiler	evKB LG	Speyer	1698-1901	5
Jammelshofen	rkKB	Trier	1779-1966	1
Jettenbach	LG evKB LRA	Speyer Kusel	1742-1906	15
Jockgrim	rkKB	Speyer	1715-1970	7

Location	Nature of Material	Where Filmed	Dates Covered	No. of Rolls
Kaifenheim	rkKB	Trier	1731-1894	2
Kaimt	rkKB	Trier	1820-1885	1
Kaiseresch	rkKB	Trier	1642-1811	3
Kaiserslautern				
Kalkofen	LG	Speyer	1818-1833	1
Kallstradt	rkKB BA evKB	Speyer Bad Dürkheim	1661-1947	8
Kaltenborn	rkKB	Trier	1678-1960	3
Kandel	LG evKB rkKB	Speyer Bielefeld	1622-1966	14
Kanzem	rkKB	Trier	1752-1914	3
Kappel	rkKB evKB	Koblenz Mainz Trier Hamborn	1721-1954	6
Kappellen-Drusweiter	LG evKB	Speyer	1617-1943	3
Kappeln	evKB rkKB	Speyer Trier Koblenz	1671-1798	3
Kapsweger	LG rkKB	Speyer	1792-1934	3
Karbach	rkKB	Trier	1669-1761	1
Karden	rkKB	Trier	1662-1927	4
Kärlich	rkKB	Trier	1782-1960	4
Kastelaun	rkKB evKB	Koblenz Trier	1568-1817	3
Karlshausen	rkKB	Trier	1779-1901	2
Karweiler	rkKB	Trier	1704-1886	3
Kashofen	evKB	Speyer	1691-1879	2
Kastel	rkKB	Trier	1856-1929	1
Kastel-Staadt	rkKB	Trier	1747-1929	5
Katzenbach	AG LG	Speyer	1762-1830	2

Location	Nature of Material	Where Filmed	Dates Covered	No. of Rolls
Katzweiler	LG evKB STA	Speyer Berlin-Dahlem Kaiserslautern	1640-1957	32
Kaulbach	evKB LRA LG	Speyer Kusel	1640-1925	8
Kehrig	rkKB	Trier	1650-1871	1
Kelberg	rkKB	Trier	1649-1941	4
Kell	rkKB	Trier	1662-1957	2
Kellenbach	evKB	Koblenz	1685-1723	1
Kempernich	rkKB	Trier	1657-1904	4
Kenn	rkKB	Trier	1803-1869	1
Kerben	rkKB	Trier	1712-1797	1
Kerzenheim	evKB rkKB LG	Speyer	1664-1957	10
Kesselheim	rkKB	Trier	1628-1900	3
Kesseling	rkKB	Trier	1681-1798	1
Kesten	rkKB	Trier	1686-1924	3
Kettrig	rkKB	Trier	1688-1798	1
Kindenheim	evKB	Speyer	1633-1899	6
Kinderbeuren	rkKB	Trier	1790-1803	2
Kindsbach	STA	Kaiserslautern	1818-1957	12
Kinheim	rkKB	Trier	1803-1949	2
Kirchberg	evKB rkKB	Trier Koblenz Mainz Hamborn	1643-1798	13
Kirchdaun	rkKB	Trier	1663-1968	3
Kirchen	rkKB	Trier	1645-1927	9
Kirchesch	rkKB	Trier	1726-1855	2
Kirchheim	evKB	Speyer	1768-1947	3
Kirchheimbolan- den	rkKB LG evKB	Speyer	1686-1961	19

Location	Nature of Material	Where Filmed	Dates Covered	No. of Rolls
Kirchhof	rkKB	Trier	1794-1932	1
Kirchsahr	rkKB	Trier	1693-1901	2
Kirchweiler	rkKB	Trier	1567-1920	2
Kirf	rkKB	Trier	1691-1798	1
Kirmutscheid	rkKB	Trier	1627-1955	3
Kirn	rkKB evKB	Mainz Koblenz Trier	1660-1889	4
Kirnsulzbach	rkKB	Trier	1803-1853	1
Kirrweiler	rkKB LG	Speyer	1584-1958	12
Kisselbuch	evKB	Koblenz	1716-1798	1
Kleinwintern- heim	rkKB	Mainz	1206-1973	1
Kleinfischlingen	LG rkKB evKB	Speyer	1689-1960	8
Kleinich	evKB	Koblenz	1696-1743	1
Kleinkarlbach	rkKB evKB BA	Speyer Bad Dürkheim	1585-1868	4
Kleinneidesheim	evKB	Speyer	1727-1873	2
Kleinsteinhausen	LRA	Zweibrücken	1798-1875	7
Klingenmünster	LG evKB rkKB	Speyer	1652-1961	12
Klotten	rkKB	Trier	1613-1849	2
Kludenbach	evKB	Hamborn	1746-1798	1
Klüsserath	rkKB	Trier	1636-1922	2
Knittlesheim	evKB rkKB LG	Speyer	1707-1960	6
Knopp-Labach	rkKB STA BA	Zweibrücken Frankfurt	1785-1961	7

Location	Nature of Material	Where Filmed	Dates Covered	No. of Rolls
Knöringen	rkKB STA LG	Speyer	1682-1917	6
Kobern	rkKB	Trier	1659-1945	5
Koblenz	MKB evKB rkKB	Koblenz Frankfurt Trier Hannover	1215-1943	57
Köllerbach	rkKB	Trier	1710-1787	3
Kollweilen	evKB LRA	Speyer Kusel	1742-1906	5
Kommlingen	rkKB	Trier	1733-1798	1
Könen	rkKB	Trier	1681-1890	2
Köngernheim	rkKB	Mainz	1686-1929	3
Königsbach	rkKB BA	Speyer	1638-1959	6
Königsfeld	rkKB	Trier	1710-1962	3
Konken	LG evKB LRA	Kusel Speyer Bielefeld	1552-1949	15
Konz	rkKB	Trier	1723-1875	1
Körborn	LG LRA	Speyer	1818-1875	3
Kordel	rkKB	Trier	1662-1890	2
Korneshütte	rkKB	Trier	1730-1798	1
Körperich	rkKB	Trier	1698-1903	2
Kottenborn	rkKB	Trier	1718-1802	1
Köttenheim	rkKB	Trier	1672-1929	3
Kottweiler	STA	Kaiserslautern	1818-1957	14
Köwerich	rkKB	Trier	1665-1860	2
Koxhausen	rkKB	Trier	1808-1900	2
Kralenberg		Speyer	1791-1879	2
Kreimbach	LA LRA evKB	Speyer Kusel	1640-1925	12

Location	Nature of Material	Where Filmed	Dates Covered	No. of Rolls
Kramer	rkKB	Trier	1803-1889	1
Krettnach	rkKB	Trier	1778-1940	2
Kreuzweiler	rkKB	Trier	1726-1908	6
Kreweiler	rkKB	Trier	1764-1874	2
Krichenbach	LG STA	Speyer	1799-1957	9
Krigsfeld	LG evKB rkKB	Speyer Mainz Berlin-Dahlem	1656-1954	9
Kronau	evKB	Speyer	1778-1789	1
Krottelbach	evKB LG LRA	Speyer Kusel	1714-1880	4
Kröv	rkKB	Trier	1613-1831	3
Kruchten	rkKB	Trier	1525-1913	2
Kruft	rkKB	Trier	1655-1919	3
Kübelberg	rkKB LRA	Speyer Kusel	1704-1919	20
Kues	rkKB	Trier	1641-1798	1
Kulardt	rkKB	Speyer	1729-1938	2
Kusel	evKB LRA LG	Speyer Kusel Mainz	1507-1957	197
Kyllburg	rkKB	Trier	1685-1928	3
Labach	evKB	Speyer	1669-1887	1
Lachen	evKB rkKB BA	Speyer	1663-1948	11
Lambrecht	rkKB AG BA	Speyer	1699-1958	11
Lamsborn	evKB	Speyer	1691-1879	2
Lamsheim	rkKB BA evKB	Speyer	1794-1960	12
Lampaden	rkKB	Trier	1786-1886	2

Location	Nature of Material	Where Filmed	Dates Covered	No. of Rolls
Landau	evKB LG rkKB STA	Speyer Hannover Bielefeld	1564-1960	98
Landkern	rkKB	Trier	1666-1832	2
Landscheid	rkKB	Trier	1798-1876	2
Landstuhl	evKB STA		1669-1957	83
Langenbach	LRA evKB LG	Speyer Kusel	1552-1878	7
Langenfeld	rkKB	Trier	1681-1968	3
Langenkandel	evKB	Speyer	1757-1927	1
Langenlonsheim	evKB rkKB	Trier Mainz Koblenz	1540-1798	3
Langsur	rkKB	Trier	1758-1900	2
Lasel	rkKB	Trier	1799-1884	1
Laubach	rkKB evKB	Mainz Koblenz Trier	1699-1953	5
Laubenleim	evKB	Koblenz	1667-1798	1
Laufeld	rkKB	Trier	1694-1910	2
Laufersweiler	evKB rkKB	Koblenz Hamborn Mainz	1711-1868	4
Laumersheim	rkKB BA evKB	Speyer	1688-1958	6
Lauschied	evKB rkKB	Koblenz Mainz	1695-1921	5
Lauterecken	AG	Mainz Kaiserslautern Speyer Bielefeld Trier	1596-1958	32
Lautersbach	evKB	Speyer	1694-1891	1
Lauterschwan	rkKB	Speyer	1722-1961	4

Location	Nature of Material	Where Filmed	Dates Covered	No. of Rolls
Lautersheim	evKB LG	Speyer	1694-1878	3
Lay	rkKB	Trier	1694-1852	2
Lehmen	rkKB	Trier	1727-1868	5
Leimen	rkKB	Speyer	1770-1961	4
Leimersdorf	rkKB	Trier	1669-1889	2
Leimersheim	rkKB LF	Speyer	1688-1956	8
Leinsweiler	evKB LG	Speyer	1722-1876	5
Leistadt	STA rkKB evKB	Speyer Bad Dürkheim	1700-1947	10
Leiwen	rkKB	Trier	1705-1964	3
Lemberg	evKB	Speyer	1788-1918	4
Lemburg	LRA	Speyer	1788-1798	1
Lettweiler	evKB LG	Speyer	1640-1839	2
Leubsdorf	rkKB	Trier	1789-1870	1
Leutesdorf	rkKB	Trier	1634-1938	4
Lichtenberg	evKB	Koblenz	1571-1798	3
Lichtenborn	rkKB	Trier	1781-1944	3
Liebsthal	LRA LG evKB	Speyer Kusel	1818-1878	5
Lieg	rkKB	Trier	1870-1968	2
Liersberg	rkKB	Trier	1704-1893	2
Lieser	rkKB	Trier	1589-1919	3
Lind	rkKB	Trier	1758-1906	2
Linden	STA evKB rkKB	Speyer Kaiserslautern	1710-1957	20
Lindenberg	rkKB	Speyer	1785-1798	1
Lindenscheid	evKB	Hamborn	1643-1798	3

Location	Nature of Material	Where Filmed	Dates Covered	No. of Rolls
Lingenfeld	LG evKB rkKB	Speyer	1701-1912	9
Lingerhahn	rkKB	Trier	1806-1927	2
Linz	rkKB	Trier	1641-1918	9
Lissendorf	rkKB	Trier	1704-1942	3
Lobloch	rkKB	Speyer	1785-1789	1
Löf	rkKB	Trier	1674-1966	4
Lohndorf	rkKB	Trier	1675-1967	2
Löhndorf	rkKB	Trier	1675-1798	1
Lohnweiler	LG LRA	Speyer Kusel	1818-1875	3
Löllbuch	evKB	Koblenz Düsseldorf	1666-1795	2
Longkamp	rkKB	Trier	1607-1950	4
Longuich	rkKB	Trier	1732-1911	2
Lonnig	rkKB	Trier	1659-1900	3
Lonsfeld	LG	Speyer	1803-1824	6
Lorscheid	rkKB	Trier	1723-1942	2
Lösnich	rkKB	Trier	1690-1803	2
Lötzbeuren	evKB	Koblenz	1665-1823	1
Ludwigshafen	LDS records	Ludwigshafen	1927-1948	1
Ludwigshafen	evKB	Trier Frankfurt Speyer	1651-1918	14
Ludwigshafen	rkKB	Freiburg Speyer	1657-1961	87
Ludwigshafen	AG STA BA	Speyer	1739-1829	13
Ludwigshöhe	rkKB	Mainz	1637-1876	2
Lug	LG	Speyer	1817-1851	1
Lünebach	rkKB	Trier	1805-1926	2

Location	Nature of Material	Where Filmed	Dates Covered	No. of Rolls
Lustadt	STA LG evKB rkKB	Speyer Trier	1710-1960	16
Luthersbrunn	evKB	Speyer	1640-1905	20
Lütz	rkKB	Trier	1669-1831	2
Lutzerath	rkKB	Trier	1683-1894	3
Lützkampen	rkKB	Trier	1779-1915	2
Macken	rkKB	Trier	1641-1968	2
Mackenbach	STA	Kaiserslautern	1798-1957	17
Maikammer	LG rkKB STA	Speyer	1567-1958	14
Mainz	rkKB	Mainz	1160-1899	51
Mainz	MKB	Hannover Berlin-Dahlem	1834-1918	3
Mainz	rkKB	Mainz	1540-1906	34
Mainz	rkKB	Mainz	1613-1906	22
Malberg	rkKB	Trier	1808-1910	1
Mandel	evKB rkKB	Koblenz Trier	1649-1798	2
Manderscheid	rkKB	Trier	1718-1956	3
Mannebach	rkKB	Trier	1640-1918	2
Mannweiler	LG	Speyer	1818-1832	1
Manubach	evKB	Koblenz	1583-1798	2
Marienborn	rkKB	Mainz	1676-1900	3
Marienthal	evKB LG	Speyer	1694-1869	3
Marnheim	evKB LG	Speyer	1648-1875	9
Martinshöhe	rkKB	Speyer	1778-1929	2
Martinsheim	rkKB	Trier	1766-1968	2
Massburg	rkKB	Trier	1716-1798	1

Location	Nature of Material	Where Filmed	Dates Covered	No. of Rolls
Massweiler	STA LRA rkKB	Speyer Zweibrücken Freiburg	1683-1939	14
Masterhausen	rkKB	Trier	1736-1924	4
Matzenbach	evKB	Speyer	1701-1893	4
Mauchenheim	LG evKB	Kusel Speyer Trier	1578-1935	7
Mauschbach	STA BA	Zweibrücken	1798-1875	7
Maxdorf	evKB	Speyer	1794-1922	4
Maximiliansau	rkKB LG	Speyer	1772-1958	4
Mayen	rkKB	Trier	1662-1965	14
Mayschoss	rkKB	Trier	1632-1865	4
Mechtersheim	STA evKB BA	Speyer	1710-1918	22
Meckel	rkKB	Trier	1632-1903	2
Meckenbach	evKB	Koblenz	1661-1868	1
Meckenheim	AG rkKB	Speyer	1670-1885	11
Medord	evKB	Koblenz	1639-1730	1
Meddersheim	evKB	Koblenz	1702-1735	1
Meerfeld	rkKB	Trier	1779-1956	3
Mehlbach	STA LG evKB	Speyer Kaiserslautern	1640-1957	12
Mehlingen	STA evKB LG	Speyer Kaiserslautern	1721-1900	15
Mehren	rkKB	Trier	1723-1920	4
Mehring	rkKB	Trier	1749-1891	2
Meinbonn	evKB	Düsseldorf	1801-1838	1
Meisburg	rkKB	Trier	1831-1900	1

Location	Nature of Material	Where Filmed	Dates Covered	No. of Rolls
Meisenheim	evKB rkKB	Speyer Trier	1607-1822	8
Merl	rkKB	Trier	1792-1798	1
Merscheid	rkKB	Trier	1723-1959	3
Mertesdorf	rkKB	Trier	1852-1913	1
Mertloch	rkKB	Trier	1656-1798	3
Merxheim	evKB rkKB	Trier Koblenz	1597-1963	2
Merzalben	rkKB	Trier	1770-1961	4
Mesenich	rkKB	Trier	1705-1899	2
Messerich	rkKB	Trier	1720-1912	2
Messerbucherhof	evKB	Speyer	1822-1870	1
Mettendorf	rkKB	Trier	1605-1859	5
Metterich	rkKB	Trier	1661-1903	4
Metternich	rkKB	Trier	1624-1900	3
Mettlach	evKB	Koblenz	1663-1798	1
Metzenhausen	evKB	Hamborn	1746-1798	1
Mickenich	rkKB	Trier	1628-1794	1
Miesan	evKB	Speyer	1718-1798	1
Miesenbach	STA	Kaiserslautern	1876-1957	18
Miesenheim	rkKB	Trier	1657-1949	3
Mimbach	rkKB	Trier	1799-1937	4
Minderslache	evKB	Speyer	1622-1927	4
Minfeld	evKB rkKB LG	Speyer	1571-1961	10
Minheim	rkKB	Trier		2
Mittelbach	STA evKB LRA	Speyer Zweibrücken	1743-1875	12
Mittelbexbach	LRA	Kusel	1876-1881	1
Mittelbrunn	evKB STA	Speyer Kaiserslautern	1669-1957	11

Location	Nature of Material	Where Filmed	Dates Covered	No. of Rolls
Mittelreichen-bach	rkKB	Trier	1755-1919	1
Mittelstrimmig	rkKB	Trier	1588-1908	5
Mölschbach	LRA STA LG	Kaiserslautern Speyer	1798-1957	12
Mölsheim	evKB rkKB	Speyer Mainz	1743-1818	2
Mommenheim	rkKB	Mainz	1685-1909	2
Monreal	rkKB	Trier	1621-1964	2
Monzelfeld	rkKB	Trier	1665-1930	3
Monzingen	evKB	Düsseldorf Koblenz	1570-1798	5
Morbach	LG LRA evKB rkKB	Speyer Trier Kaiserslautern	1593-1923	7
Morlautern	STA LG	Speyer Kaiserslautern	1799-1957	14
Mörschbach	evKB	Koblenz	1713-1738	1
Morscheid	rkKB	Trier	1647-1903	5
Morschheim	evKB LG	Speyer	1710-1869	4
Mörsdorf	rkKB	Trier	1670-1919	3
Morsfeld	rkKB STA	Speyer Mainz	1656-1876	5
Mörsheim	LG rkKB evKB	Trier Speyer	1685-1949	7
Moselkern	rkKB	Trier	1606-1829	2
Müden	rkKB	Trier	1730-1798	1
Mudersbach	rkKB	Trier	1828-1932	3
Muhlbach	LG evKB	Speyer	1701-1877	3
Mühlbach	LRA	Kusel	1799-1875	3
Mülheim	evKB	Speyer	1750-1870	1

Location	Nature of Material	Where Filmed	Dates Covered	No. of Rolls
Mühlhofen	evKB	Speyer	1617-1943	1
Mülheim	evKB	Koblenz	1649-1798	2
Müllenbach	rkKB	Trier	1734-1941	4
Münchweiler	evKB rkKB LG	Speyer Berlin-Dahlem Freiburg	1697-1961	18
Münster am Stein	evKB	Koblenz	1733-1798	1
Münster Sarmsheim	evKB rkKB	Trier Koblenz	1651-1944	4
Münsterappel	LG evKB rkKB	Trier Speyer	1610-1929	6
Münstermanfeld	rkKB	Trier	1633-1774	1
Mürlenbach	rkKB	Trier	1689-1874	2
Mussbach	BA evKB rkKB AG	Speyer Trier	1699-1957	17
Mutterstadt	AG BA evKB rkKB	Speyer	1652-1958	17
Nachtsheim	rkKB	Trier	1698-1798	1
Nackenheim	rkKB	Mainz	1669-1876	2
Nanzdiezweiler	AG STA	Speyer Kaiserslautern	1762-1875	7
Nanzweiler	LRA	Kusel	1799-1875	4
Naumburgerhof	evKB	Speyer	1706-1873	2
Naunheim	rkKB	Trier	1633-1886	3
Neef	rkKB	Trier	1619-1906	3
Nehren	rkKB	Trier	1609-1798	1
Neidenbach	rkKB	Trier	1767-1890	1
Niedenfels	AG	Speyer	1747	1
Neroth	rkKB	Trier	1803-1882	1

Location	Nature of Material	Where Filmed	Dates Covered	No. of Rolls
Nerzweiler	LG LRA	Speyer Kusel	1799-1874	2
Neuburg	evKB LG	Speyer Trier	1707-1957	6
Neuenahr	rkKB	Trier	1784-1891	2
Neuerburg	rkKB	Trier	1778-1939	6
Neuerkirch	evKB	Koblenz	1683-1798	1
Neuhemsbach	evKB LG	Speyer Trier	1702-1892	4
Neuhofen	evKB BA	Speyer	1652-1865	4
Neukirchen	AG	Speyer	1763-1817	2
Neuleiningen	BA STA evKB	Speyer	1584-1961	8
Neunkirchen	evKB LRA LG STA rkKB	Kusel Speyer Trier	1695-1955	21
Neupotz	rkKB	Speyer	1688-1910	3
Neustadt	STA rkKB evKB AG	Speyer Trier	1584-1929	44
Neuwied	rkKB evKB	Weierhof Trier Berlin-Dahlem Düsseldorf	1650-1942	13
Nickenich	rkKB	Trier	1798-1961	3
Niederalben	evKB	Speyer	1634-1798	1
Niederauerbach		Speyer	1683-1839	1
Niederberg	rkKB	Trier	1599-1900	4
Niederbettingen	rkKB	Trier	1661-1894	2
Niederbexbach	LRA	Kusel	1799, 1801	1
Niederbreisig	rkKB	Trier	1650-1913	3
Niederbrombach	evKB	Koblenz	1591-1683	1

Location	Nature of Material	Where Filmed	Dates Covered	No. of Rolls
Niederehe	rkKB	Trier	1655-1922	
Niederfell	rkKB	Trier	1617-1968	3
	evKB	Speyer	1634-1798	1
Niederemmel	rkKB	Trier	1658-1900	1
Niederfischbach	rkKB	Trier	1629-1910	8
Nieder-olm	rkKB	Mainz	1650-1929	3
Niederhausen	LG LRA evKB STA	Koblenz Speyer Düsseldorf Zweibrücken	1653-1875	14
Niederheckenbach	rkKB	Trier	1863-1952	1
Niederheimbach	rkKB	Trier	1691-1933	2
Niederhochstadt	LG evKB rkKB	Speyer	1708-1958	9
Niederhorbach	LG	Speyer	1821-1837	1
Niederhosenbach	evKB	Düsseldorf Koblenz	1698-1818	3
Niederkirchen	STA evKB rkKB	Augsburg Speyer Kaiserslautern	1665-1957	34
Niederlauch	rkKB	Trier	1753-1905	2
Niederlützingen	rkKB	Trier	1654-1932	3
Niedermendig	rkKB	Trier	1669-1920	4
Niedermiesau	evKB LRA	Kusel Speyer	1691-1879	3
Niedermohr	STA rkKB	Speyer Kaiserslautern	1752-1957	19
Niedermoschel	evKB LG	Speyer	1566-1886	6
Niederofflingen	rkKB	Trier	1737-1842	2
Niederprum	rkKB	Trier	1617-1798	1
Niederotterbuch	evKB	Speyer	1671-1672	1
Niederprüm	rkKB	Trier	1795-1839	1

Location	Nature of Material	Where Filmed	Dates Covered	No. of Rolls
Niederscheid-weiler	rkKB	Trier	1699-1964	2
Niederschletten-bach	rkKB	Speyer	1722-1961	4
Niederstadtfeld	rkKB	Trier	1697-1883	1
Niederstaufen-bach	evKB LG LRA	Speyer Kusel	1701-1880	6
Nierstein	rkKB	Mainz	1756-1922	2
Niedersulzbach	evKB	Speyer	1640-1925	4
Niederwambach	evKB	Düsseldorf	1698-1875	9
Niederwörres-bach	evKB	Düsseldorf	1568-1795	5
Niederzissen	rkKB	Trier	1719-1889	2
Niefernheim	LG evKB rkKB	Speyer	1737-1961	5
Nierendorf	rkKB	Trier	1669-1798	1
Nierstein	rkKB	Mainz	1637-1922	2
Nittle	rkKB	Trier	1696-1860	3
Nohen	evKB	Koblenz	1824-1854	2
Nohn	rkKB	Trier	1663-1935	3
Norath	rkKB	Trier	1758-1905	3
Norheim	rkKB	Speyer Trier Koblenz	1681-1953	7
Nothweiler	evKB	Speyer	1780-1874	1
Noviand	rkKB	Trier	1685-1810	2
Nusbaum	rkKB	Trier	1722-1847	2
Nünschweiler	evKB rkKB	Speyer Freiburg	1725-1961	5
Nürburg	rkKB	Trier	1685-1949	2
Nussbach	LRA evKB LG	Speyer	1705-1874	6

Location	Nature of Material	Where Filmed	Dates Covered	No. of Rolls
Nussdorf	STA evKB rkKB	Speyer	1592-1942	10
Ober-Erlenbach	rkKB	Mainz	1756-1819	1
Ober-Flörsheim	rkKB	Mainz	1698-1960	2
Ober-Hilbersheim	rkKB	Mainz	1689-1884	1
Ober-Kostenz	evKB	Hamborn	1746-1798	1
Ober-Olm	rkKB	Mainz	1619-1876	2
Oberalben	LG LRA	Speyer Kusel	1818-1875	3
Oberarnbach	STA	Kaiserslautern	1798-1957	7
Oberauerbach	STA LRA	Zweibrücken	1798-1875	6
Oberbillig	rkKB	Trier	1871-1900	1
Oberbreisig	rkKB	Trier	1650-1876	3
Oberdiebach	evKB	Koblenz	1637-1798	1
Oberehe	rkKB	Trier	1717-1798	1
Obereisenbach	evKB	Speyer	1634-1798	1
Oberemmel	rkKB	Trier	1721-1911	3
Oberfell	rkKB	Trier	1772-1966	2
Obergonders-hausen	rkKB	Trier	1759-1798	1
Oberhausen	rkKB LG evKB	Speyer Trier	1596-1943	5
Oberhausen -Zweibrücken-	STA LRA	Zweibrücken	1798-1875	6
Oberheimbach	rkKB	Trier	1712-1957	3
Obernheim-Kirchenarnbach	rkKB STA	Kaiserslautern	1706-1957	21
Oberhochstadt	evKB rkKB	Speyer	1730-1958	8
Oberhofen	evKB	Speyer	1785-1879	2

Location	Nature of Material	Where Filmed	Dates Covered	No. of Rolls
Obekail	rkKB	Trier	1804-1918	1
Oberkostenz	evKB	Koblenz	1746-1798	1
Oberluststadt	evKB rkKB	Speyer Trier	1710-1960	11
Oberlützingen	rkKB	Trier	1680-1798	1
Obermendig	rkKB	Trier	1656-1798	1
Obermiesau	evKB LRA	Speyer Kusel	1718-1906	15
Obermohr	STA AG	Speyer Kaiserslautern	1584-1875	14
Obermoschel	LG rkKB evKB	Trier Speyer Freiburg	1639-1960	11
Oberndorf	evKB	Speyer Freiburg	1652-1960	3
Oberotterbach	evKB rkKB	Speyer Freiburg	1671-1961	7
Obersulzbach	evKB rkKB	Speyer Kaiserslautern	1640-1875	3
Oberstaufenbach	evKB LRA	Speyer Kusel	1799-1893	4
Obersülen	evKB	Speyer	1742-1888	3
Oberweiler	LRA evKB	Speyer Kusel	1640-1925	8
Oberwies	rkKB	Trier	1744-1937	2
Oberwesel	rkKB	Trier	1597-1925	6
Oberwieser	evKB	Speyer	1710-1869	2
Oberwinter	rkKB evKB	Düsseldorf Trier Koblenz	1649-1963	5
Oblies	rkKB	Trier	1758-1800	1
Obrigheim	evKB BA	Speyer	1666-1876	3
Ochtendung	rkKB	Trier	1642-1935	3
Ockenheim	rkKB	Mainz	1676-1885	1

Location	Nature of Material	Where Filmed	Dates Covered	No. of Rolls
Ockenroth	evKB	Koblenz	1649-1801	1
Odenbach	evKB LRA	Speyer Kusel	1566-1906	16
Odernheim	evKB	Speyer	1661-1880	3
Ödingen	rkKB	Trier	1716-1967	2
Oberkonnefeld- Gierend	evKB	Düsseldorf	1678-1838	4
Offenbach	LG evKB rkKB	Koblenz Trier Speyer	1634-1960	12
Offstein	rkKB	Mainz	1719-1876	1
Ohlenberg	rkKB	Trier	1607-1959	3
Ohlweiler	evKB	Koblenz	1724-1777	1
Ohmbach	evKB LRA	Speyer Kusel	1714-1880	3
Olien	rkKB	Trier	1758-1800	1
Ollmuth	rkKB	Trier	1772-1805	1
Olmscheid	rkKB	Trier	1679-1871	3
Olsbrücken	evKB STA	Speyer Kaiserslautern	1640-1957	19
Olsheim	rkKB	Trier	1736-1900	2
Oppenheim	rkKB	Mainz	1637-1876	4
Orbis	evKB	Speyer	1710-1869	2
Ordorf	rkKB	Trier	1675-1867	2
Orenhofen	rkKB	Trier	1805-1897	1
Ormont	rkKB	Trier	1836-1889	1
Osann	rkKB	Trier	1747-1922	2
Osburg	rkKB	Trier	1798-1877	2
Osthofen	rkKB	Mainz	1721-1881	1
Otterbach	rkKB STA	Freiburg Kaiserslautern	1727-1957	21

Location	Nature of Material	Where Filmed	Dates Covered	No. of Rolls
Otterberg	evKB rkKB STA	Kaiserslautern Freiburg Speyer	1589-1961	55
Ottersheim	rkKB STA	Speyer	1705-1911	14
Otterstadt	STA BA rkKB	Speyer	1683-1928	24
Outscheid	rkKB	Trier	1728-1900	2
Palzem	rkKB	Trier	1685-1899	2
Pellingen	rkKB	Trier	1653-1922	2
Perscheid	rkKB	Trier	1705-1906	2
Peterslahr	rkKB	Trier	1656-1945	2
Pettersheim	evKB	Speyer	1653-1880	5
Pfaffendorf	rkKB	Trier	1720-1952	3
Pfalsel	rkKB	Trier	1605-1925	3
Pfalsfeld	evKB	Koblenz	1738-1884	1
Pfeffelbach	evKB	Koblenz	1571-1798	2
Pferdsfeld	evKB	Koblenz	1721-1820	1
Piesport	rkKB	Trier	1604-1935	2
Pillig	rkKB	Trier	1657-1960	2
Pirmasens	evKB rkKB	Speyer	1640-1948	28
Plaidt	rkKB	Trier	1670-1905	4
Platten	rkKB	Trier	1704-1920	1
Pleisweiler	evKB LG	Speyer	1707-1906	7
Pleitzenhausen	evKB	Koblenz	1666-1928	2
Pluwig	rkKB	Trier	1754-1798	1
Pohlbach	rkKB	Trier	1803-1889	1
Polch	rkKB	Trier	1664-1854	2
Pölich	rkKB	Trier	1847-1884	1
Pommern	rkKB	Trier	1612-1847	4

Location	Nature of Material	Where Filmed	Dates Covered	No. of Rolls
Pörrbach	STA	Kaiserslautern	1798-1875	2
Portz	rkKB	Trier	1764-1874	2
Preischeid	rkKB	Trier	1811-1880	1
Pronsfeld	rkKB	Trier	1653-1904	2
Prüm	evKB rkKB	Trier Düsseldorf	1689-1920	9
Puderbach	evKB	Düsseldorf	1701-1880	5
Punderich	rkKB	Trier	1666-1798	1
Queichhambach	evKB	Speyer	1556-1839	7
Queidersbach	evKB STA	Speyer Kaiserslautern	1791-1857	21
Quirnbach	evKB LRA	Speyer Kusel	1804-1906	12
Quirnheim	rkKB BA	Speyer	1700-1915	3
Rachtig	rkKB	Trier	1648-1898	2
Rahlingen	rkKB	Trier	1748-1900	3
Ramberg	LG evKB rkKB	Speyer	1556-1960	12
Ramersbach	rkKB	Trier	1668-1968	2
Rammelsbach	LRA evKB	Speyer Kusel	1567-1900	9
Ramsen	rkKB	Speyer	1699-1957	4
Ramstein	STA STG rkKB	Speyer Kaiserslautern	1584-1957	49
Ransbach	LG	Speyer	1818-1849	1
Ranschbach	rkKB STA	Speyer	1777-1953	3
Ransweiler	evKB STA	Speyer	1654-1907	6
Rapperath	rkKB	Trier	1853-1917	1
Rascheid	rkKB	Trier	1699-1883	2

Location	Nature of Material	Where Filmed	Dates Covered	No. of Rolls
Rathskirche	evKB LRA	Speyer Kusel	1706-1906	6
Rathsweiler	LRA	Kusel	1818-1875	2
Raubach	evKB	Düsseldorf	1679-1837	2
Raumbach	evKB	Speyer	1607-1822	6
Rhaunen	rkKB evKB	Koblenz Trier	1667-1850	2
Ravengiersburg	rkKB	Trier	1699-1931	2
Ravenbeusen	evKB	Koblenz	1716-1835	1
Rayerschied	rkKB	Trier	1720-1942	4
Rech	rkKB	Trier	1898-	1
Rechtenbach	evKB LG	Speyer	1721-1896	5
Rehbach	rkKB	Trier	1684-1946	3
Rehborn	evKB	Speyer	1640-1839	4
Rehhütte	evKB	Speyer	1652-1865	3
Reiffelbach	evKB	Speyer	1734-1839	1
Reinsfeld	rkKB	Trier	1798-1853	1
Rellingen- Littdorf	rkKB	Trier	1696-1868	2
Rehweiler	evKB LRA	Speyer Kusel	1818-1875	4
Reichbachsteeger	STA	Kaiserslautern	1798-1875	5
Reichenbach -Birkenfeld-	evKB	Koblenz	1695-1801	1
Reichenbach- Kaiserslautern	STA evKB rkKB	Speyer Kaiserslautern	1660-1957	22
Reichsthal	evKB LRA	Speyer Kusel	1699-1875	4
Reichelberg	BA	Zweibrücken	1818-1875	4
Reifenberg	LRA STA rkKB	Zweibrücken Speyer Freiburg	1650-1961	9

Location	Nature of Material	Where Filmed	Dates Covered	No. of Rolls
Reiffelbach	evKB LRA	Speyer Kusel	1607-1874	9
Reiffenberg	rkKB	Speyer	1805-1961	2
Reifferscheid	rkKB	Trier	1653-1798	1
Reil	rkKB	Trier	1632-1800	1
Reimsbach	rkKB	Trier	1725-1807	4
Reinsfeld	rkKB	Trier	1705-1935	2
Reipoltzkirche	LRA evKB rkKB	Speyer Kusel	1680-1893	6
Relsberg	evKB LRA	Speyer Kusel	1699-1875	4
Remagen	evKB rkKB	Düsseldorf Koblenz Trier	1649-1840	4
Rengsdorf	evKB	Hamborn	1671-1760	3
Retterroth	rkKB	Trier	1734-1919	2
Reuschbach	STA	Kaiserslautern	1797-1875	4
Rheinallen	rkKB	Trier	1800-1966	2
Rheinböllen	evKB rkKB	Koblenz Trier	1659-1799	2
Rheinbrohl	rkKB	Trier	1613-1937	7
Rheinzabern	LG rkKB	Speyer	1684-1943	9
Rhens	rkKB	Trier	1578-1889	3
Rhodt	LG	Speyer	1816-1833	2
Rieden	rkKB	Trier	1702-1900	3
Rieschweiler	STA evKB LRA	Speyer Zweibrücken	1683-1875	9
Rievenich	rkKB		1754-1798	1
Rimschweiler	LRA evKB STA	Speyer Zweibrücken	1559-1875	11
Ringen	rkKB	Trier	1650-1945	2

Location	Nature of Material	Where Filmed	Dates Covered	No. of Rolls
Ringhuscheid	rkKB	Trier	1744-1863	2
Rinnthal	evKB STA	Speyer	1818-1870	3
Riol	rkKB	Trier	1727-1880	2
Rittersdorf	rkKB evKB	Speyer Trier	1681-1900	2
Rivenich	rkKB	Trier	1724-1963	2
Rockenau	evKB	Koblenz	1694-1798	1
Rockenhausen	rkKB evKB	Speyer	1620-1961	8
Rockeskyll	rkKB	Trier	1705-1905	2
Rodalben	rkKB	Speyer	1693-1930	9
Rödelhausen	rkKB	Trier	1799-1806	1
Rodenbach	evKB rkKB STA	Speyer Kaiserslautern	1633-1957	14
Rödersheim	rkKB BA	Speyer	1589-1958	9
Rohrbach	rkKB evKB LG	Speyer	1652-1900	13
Rommersheim	rkKB	Trier	1680-1901	2
Rondorf	rkKB	Trier	1617-1814	1
Roschbach	rkKB LG	Speyer	1664-1942	5
Rosenkopf	evKB	Speyer	1691-1879	2
Rossbach	LRA	Kusel	1818-1875	3
Roth	rkKB evKB LRA	Trier Speyer Koblenz Kusel	1571-1890	11
Rothselberg	AG evKB	Speyer Trier	1584-1916	14
Roxheim	evKB BA rkKB	Speyer Trier Koblenz	1691-1895	7
Rübenach	rkKB	Trier	1637-1928	3

Location	Nature of Material	Where Filmed	Dates Covered	No. of Rolls
Ruchheim	BA rkKB evKB	Speyer	1670-1942	13
Rüdesheim	evKB rkKB	Koblenz Trier	1660-1839	3
Rudolphskirche	LRA	Kusel	1799-1906	2
Ruhlkirche	rkKB	Mainz	1861-1952	1
Rülsheim	rkKB LG	Speyer	1687-1837	5
Rumbach	evKB	Speyer	1780-1874	2
Rümmelsheim	rkKB	Trier	1669-1798	1
Ruppertsbery	rkKB	Speyer	1638-1960	6
Rüscheid	evKB	Düsseldorf	1801-1838	1
Rüssinger	evKB rkKB	Speyer	1699-1957	6
Rutsweiler	evKB LRA	Kusel Speyer	1640-1877	7
Ruwer	rkKB	Trier	1672-1842	2
Saalstadt	evKB	Speyer	1674-1888	2
Saarburg	rkKB evKB	Trier Hannover	1581-1939	11
Sabershausen	rkKB	Trier	1751-1939	4
Saffig	rkKB	Trier	1700-1927	3
Salm	rkKB	Trier	1809-1927	1
Salmrohr	rkKB	Trier	1802-1898	1
Salzig	rkKB	Trier	1674-1897	4
Sambach	STA	Kaiserslautern	1798-1875	2
Sand	LRA	Kusel	1818-1875	4
Sangerhof	evKB	Speyer	1827-1873	2
St. Alban	evKB LG	Speyer	1714-1830	2
St. Aldegund	rkKB	Trier	1682-1969	2
St. Goar	evKB rkKB	Trier Koblenz	1650-1934	8

Location	Nature of Material	Where Filmed	Dates Covered	No. of Rolls
St. Johann	rkKB	Trier	1691-1955	2
St. Johannisberg	evKB		1661-1830	1
St. Julian	LRA evKB LG	Speyer Kusel	1634-1906	11
St. Martin	rkKB LG	Speyer Freiburg	1671-1961	12
St. Sebastian	rkKB	Trier	1650-1840	2
Sargenroth	evKB	Koblenz	1730-1798	1
Sarmsheim -Münster-	rkKB	Trier	1693-1814	1
Sarresdorf	rkKB	Trier	1708-1798	1
Saulheim	rkKB	Mainz	1697-1912	4
Sausenheim	BA evKB	Speyer	1584-1896	3
Schaidt	LG rkKB	Speyer	1799-1957	4
Schalkenmehren	rkKB	Trier	1764-1968	3
Schallodenbach	rkKB STA	Kaiserslautern	1683-1961	15
Schankweiler	rkKB	Trier	1798-1939	2
Schauren	evKB	Koblenz	1659-1798	1
Scheibenhardt	LG	Speyer	1816-1836	2
Schellweiler	LRA evKB	Kusel	1597-1900	7
Schiersfeld	evKB	Speyer	1662-1907	5
Schifferstadt	STA BA evKB rkKB	Speyer	1603-1958	63
Schillingen	rkKB	Trier	1686-1798	1
Schleich	rkKB	Trier	1765-1798	1
Schleichweiler	rkKB	Trier	1621-1805	4
Schlierschied	evKB	Koblenz	1695-1806	1
Schmalenberg	evKB	Speyer	1822-1865	2

Location	Nature of Material	Where Filmed	Dates Covered	No. of Rolls
Schmitshausen	LRA rkKB STA	Speyer Zweibrücken	1798-1961	8
Schmittweiler	evKB	Speyer	1734-1839	1
Schmittweiler -Kübelberg-	LRA	Kusel	1818-1875	3
Schmittweiler -Odenbach-	evKB LRA	Speyer Kusel	1607-1874	8
Schneckenhause	evKB STA	Speyer Kaiserslautern	1779-1957	10
Schnorbach	rkKB	Trier	1697-1798	1
Schönau	evKB rkKB	Speyer Freiburg	1764-1798	5
Schonborn	evKB	Speyer	1662-1907	5
Schöndorf	rkKB	Trier	1686-1895	2
Schöneberg	rkKB	Trier	1702-1895	2
Schönecken- Wetteldorf	rkKB	Trier	1792-1920	2
Simmern	evKB	Koblenz	1597-1798	1
Schönenberg	LRA	Kusel	1799-1875	11
Schopp		Kaiserslautern	1752-1791	1
Schornsheim	rkKB	Mainz	1637-1908	2
Schrollbach	STA	Kaiserslautern Speyer	1584-1875	8
Schuld	rkKB	Trier	1702-1738	1
Schuller	rkKB	Trier	1785-1908	1
Schwanheim	rkKB LG	Freiburg Speyer	1732-1961	11
Schwarzen	evKB	Hamborn	1746-1798	1
Schwedelbach	STA	Kaiserslautern	1798-1957	5
Schwegenheim	evKB LG	Speyer	1710-1837	4
Schweich	rkKB	Trier	1669-1910	4
Schweigen	evKB LG	Speyer	1685-1896	6

Location	Nature of Material	Where Filmed	Dates Covered	No. of Rolls
Schweighofen	LG evKB rkKB	Speyer	1803-1961	7
Schweix	rkKB STA	Kaiserslautern Speyer	1716-1961	8
Seelen	LRA	Kusel	1818-1875	2
Seesbach	rkKB evKB	Trier Koblenz	1667-1968	5
Sefern	rkKB	Trier	1702-1883	2
Schlem	rkKB	Trier	1581-1879	2
Seibersbach	evKB	Koblenz	1717-1806	1
Seinsfeld	rkKB	Trier	1659-1902	2
Selchenbach	STA LRA	St. Wendel Kusel	1798-1875	15
Sellerich	rkKB	Trier	1786-1804	1
Selsen	rkKB	Mainz	1686-1929	3
Sembach	evKB	Speyer	1721-1900	3
Senheim	rkKB	Trier	1614-1968	4
Sensweiler	evKB rkKB	Berlin-Dahlem Koblenz	1658-1798	2
Serrig	rkKB	Trier	1804-1893	1
Sevenich	rkKB	Trier	1756-1900	2
Siebeldingen	LG evKB rkKB	Speyer	1637-1961	11
Siegelbach	evKB STA	Speyer Kaiserslautern	1735-1957	13
Sien	evKB rkKB	Koblenz Trier	1685-1869	3
Silz	rkKB LG	Speyer	1732-1961	7
Simmern	MKB rkKB evKB	Eibensboch Koblenz Hannover Trier	1597-1968	9
Sinsig	rkKB	Trier	1627-1968	11

Location	Nature of Material	Where Filmed	Dates Covered	No. of Rolls
Sippersfeld	evKB rkKB	Trier Speyer Augsburg Freiburg	1694-1957	12
Sobernheim	evKB rkKB	Düsseldorf Koblenz Trier	1654-1839	6
Sohren	evKB rkKB	Koblenz Trier	1633-1752	2
Sommerloch	rkKB	Trier	1719-1755	1
Sondernheim	LG evKB rkKB	Speyer	1774-1855	3
Spabrucken	rkKB	Trier	1682-1887	2
Spang	rkKB	Trier	1798-1867	1
Spangdahlem	rkKB	Trier	1798-1867	1
Spay	rkKB	Trier	1724-1794	1
Speicker	rkKB	Trier	1732-1888	4
Spesbach	STA AG evKB	Speyer Kaiserslautern	1727-1957	19
Spiesheim	rkKB	Trier	1692-1798	1
Spirkelbach	LG	Speyer	1819-1850	1
Sponheim	evKB rkKB	Koblenz Trier	1652-1898	4
Sponsheim	evKB rkKB	Koblenz Mainz	1647-1926	4
Sprendlingen	rkKB	Mainz	1692-1934	3
Stadtkyll	rkKB	Trier	1790-1900	1
Stahlberg	evKB	Speyer	1798-1815	1
Stambach	LRA STA	Zweibrücke	1798-1875	6
Standenbühl	evKB	Speyer	1648-1875	5
Starkenburg	evKB	Koblenz	1647-1798	1

Location	Nature of Material	Where Filmed	Dates Covered	No. of Rolls
Staudernheim	evKB rkKB	Düsseldorf Trier	1753-1898	3
Stauf	rkKB	Speyer	1699-1957	4
Steeg St. Goar	evKB	Dinssel Koblenz	1572-1798	2
Steffeln	rkKB	Trier	1678-1797	2
Stein	rkKB	Speyer	1732-1961	6
Steinfeld	rkKB LG	Speyer	1686-1923	9
Steinbach a. Donnesberg	evKB	Speyer	1692-1895	2
Steinbach a. Glan	LRA	Kusel	1818-1875	7
Steinbach	evKB	Speyer	1692-1895	2
Steinweiler	LG evKB rkKB	Speyer	1694-1912	7
Steinvenden	evKB STA	Speyer Kaiserslautern	1684-1957	25
Stelsenberg	STA	Speyer Kaiserslautern	1799-1957	8
Stetten	STA rkKB evKB	Speyer	1667-1961	5
Stipshausen	evKB	Koblenz	1689-1798	1
Strohn	rkKB	Trier	1751-1861	1
Stromberg	evKB	Koblenz Düsseldorf	1649-1801	2
Strotzbüsch	rkKB	Trier	1752-1900	2
Stridernheim	rkKB	Speyer	1716-1882	3
Sulm	rkKB	Trier	1722-1798	2
Sulzbuch	evKB	Koblenz	1702-1799	1
Sulzheim	rkKB	Mainz	1695-1959	1
Taben	rkKB	Trier	1677-1925	3
Tawern	rkKB	Trier	1701-1885	2

Location	Nature of Material	Where Filmed	Dates Covered	No. of Rolls
Tellig	rkKB	Trier	1835-1969	2
Temmels	rkKB	Trier	1656-1936	6
Teschenmoschel	evKB STA	Speyer	1704-1897	5
Thaleischweiler	rkKB evKB	Freiburg Speyer Berlin-Dahlem	1720-1939	11
Thalfang	evKB	Koblenz	1650-1798	3
Thalhausen	evKB	Düsseldorf	1801-1836	1
Theisbergstegen	STA LRA evKB rkKB	Speyer Kaiserslautern Kusel	1701-1961	8
Thomm	rkKB	Trier	1735-1799	1
Thornich	rkKB	Trier	1728-1903	2
Thür	rkKB	Trier	1673-1963	3
Tiefenbach	evKB	Speyer	1640-1925	4
Tiefenthal	evKB LG	Speyer	1699-1882	3
Todenroth	evKB	Hamborn	1746-1798	1
Traben	evKB rkKB	Koblenz Trier	1598-1873	5
Traben- Trabach	rkKB	Trier	1687-1873	3
Trahweiler	evKB LRA	Speyer Kusel	1818-1878	4
Traisen	evKB	Koblenz	1623-1798	1
Trarbach	rkKB evKB	Trier Koblenz	1568-1829	6
Trechtingshausen	rkKB	Trier	1610-1944	3
Treis	rkKB	Trier	1682-1930	2
Trier	rkKB	Hannover Berlin-Dahlem	1746-1944	6
Trier	rkKB	Trier	1569-1951	43
Trier-Bescheid	rkKB	Trier	1719-1812	1

Location	Nature of Material	Where Filmed	Dates Covered	No. of Rolls
Trier-Echingen	rkKB	Trier	1780-1899	1
Trier-Irsch	rkKB	Trier	1798-1928	1
Trier-Kastel	rkKB	Trier	1747-1818	1
Trier-Mesenich	rkKB	Trier	1779-1899	1
Trier-Euren	rkKB	Trier	1600-1876	3
Trierweiler	rkKB	Trier	1665-1938	2
Trimps	rkKB	Trier	1657-1901	3
Trippstadt	STA evKB rkKB	Speyer Kaiserslautern	1643-1961	39
Trittenheim	rkKB	Trier	1583-1824	2
Trulben	rkKB	Speyer	1716-1953	6
Udelfangen	rkKB	Trier	1740-1795	1
Udenheim	rkKB	Mainz	1697-1908	3
Üdersdorf	rkKB	Trier	1814-1869	1
Uhler	evKB	Koblenz	1702-1817	1
Ulmen	rkKB	Trier	1646-1903	2
Ulmet	evKB LRA	Speyer Kaiserslautern	1639-1906	15
Undenheim	rkKB	Mainz	1686-1929	6
Ungstein	LG STA	Bad Dürkheim Speyer	1700-1947	12
Unhelbach	rkKB	Trier	1700-1798	1
Unkenbach	evKB	Speyer	1639-1879	5
Untersulzbach	STA	Kaiserslautern	1798-1957	6
Urmitz	rkKB	Trier	1650-1933	4
Urschmitt	rkKB	Trier	1769-1798	1
Ürsfeld	rkKB	Trier	1742-1798	1
Ursig	rkKB	Trier	1729-1839	2
Üss	rkKB	Trier	1673-1923	3
Uxheim	rkKB	Trier	1803-1898	1

Location	Nature of Material	Where Filmed	Dates Covered	No. of Rolls
Vallendar	rkKB	Trier	1640-1904	5
Valwig	rkKB	Trier	1619-1967	3
Veitsrodt	evKB	Düsseldorf	1702-1824	2
Veldenz	evKB rkKB	Koblenz Trier	1646-1887	3
Vendersheim	rkKB	Mainz	1677-1915	3
Venningen	rkKB LG	Mainz Speyer	1753-1958	5
Vinningen	evKB rkKB	Speyer	1640-1953	24
Vischel	rkKB	Trier	1645-1798	1
Vogelbach	STA rkKB evKB	Freiburg Speyer Kaiserslautern	1691-1948	13
Völkersbach	rkKB LG	Speyer	1732-1961	7
Volkersfeld	rkKB	Trier	1740-1798	1
Vollmersweiler	evKB	Speyer	1671-1672	1
Volxheim	rkKB	Mainz	1694-1821	1
Vorderweiden-thaller	evKB LG	Speyer	1684-1910	3
Wachenheim	LG rkKB evKB	Speyer	1700-1867	11
Wahlholz	rkKB	Trier	1666-1798	1
Wahnwegen	evKB LRA	Speyer Kusel	1567-1900	7
Waldalgesheim	evKB rkKB	Koblenz Trier	1698-1908	3
Waldböckelheim	evKB rkKB	Koblenz Trier	1654-1933	5
Waldbreitbach	rkKB	Trier	1655-1943	7
Wald-Erbach	rkKB	Trier	1723-1798	1
Waldesch	rkKB	Trier	1702-1820	2

Location	Nature of Material	Where Filmed	Dates Covered	No. of Rolls
Waldfischbach	LRA evKB rkKB	Speyer	1680-1961	9
Waldgrehweiler	evKB	Speyer	1654-1907	3
Waldhambach	rkKB	Speyer	1735-1954	3
Waldhilbersheim	rkKB	Trier	1580-1935	3
Waldhof-Falkenstein	rkKB	Trier	1779-1793	1
Waldlaubersheim	evKB	Koblenz	1576-1799	1
Waldleiningen	STA	Kaiserslautern	1798-1875	3
Waldmohr	LRA evKB rkKB	Speyer Kusel	1714-1950	27
Walddorf	rkKB	Trier	1727-1926	2
Waldrach	rkKB	Trier	1681-1927	4
Waldrohrbach	rkKB	Speyer	1735-1959	3
Waldsee	STA rkKB LG	Speyer	1798-1955	34
Walhausen	rkKB	Trier	1760-1858	1
Wallenborn	rkKB	Trier	1715-1798	1
Wallendorf	rkKB	Trier	1744-1884	4
Wallenhorn	rkKB	Trier	1715-1798	1
Wallersheim	rkKB	Trier	1678-1882	2
Wallertheim	rkKB	Mainz	1695-1954	1
Wallhalben	evKB	Speyer	1674-1888	2
Wallhalden	evKB	Speyer	1674-1888	2
Wallhausen	rkKB	Trier	1760-1798	1
Walsdorf	rkKB	Trier	1738-1882	2
Walshausen	evKB STA	Speyer Zweibrücken	1725-1875	9
Walsheim	evKB LG	Speyer	1569-1874	7
Wanderath	rkKB	Trier	1709-1958	4

Location	Nature of Material	Where Filmed	Dates Covered	No. of Rolls
Warmsroth	evKB	Koblenz	1649-1801	1
Wartenberg	evKB	Speyer	1721-1900	3
Wassenach	rkKB	Trier	1662-1966	3
Wasserliesch	rkKB	Trier	1792-1907	2
Wattenheim	LG evKB rkKB	Trier Freiburg Speyer	1699-1961	12
Wattweiler	STA	Zweibrücken	1798-1875	5
Waxweiler	rkKB	Trier	1672-1882	4
Webenheim	evKB	Kaiserslautern	1696-1798	2
Wederath	rkKB	Trier	1862-1969	1
Wehlen	rkKB	Trier	1670-1851	2
Wehr	rkKB	Trier	1662-1906	4
Weibern	rkKB	Trier	1861-1910	1
Weidenbach	rkKB	Trier	1798-1939	1
Weidenthal	LG rkKB evKB	Speyer Trier	1713-1959	7
Weiding	rkKB	Trier	1724-1939	3
Weilerbach	evKB	Kaiserslautern	1643-1798	2
Weierbach	rkKB evKB	Trier Kaiserslautern	1737-1906	4
Weiher	rkKB	Speyer	1781-1791	1
Weiler -B.K.-	rkKB evKB	Trier Koblenz	1667-1903	3
Weiler -Cochen-	rkKB	Trier	1692-1798	1
Weiler -Mayer-	rkKB	Trier	1682-1940	2
Weilerbach	STA evKB rkKB	Freiburg Trier Speyer Kaiserslautern	1736-1961	45
Weinfeld	rkKB	Trier	1764-1798	1

Location	Nature of Material	Where Filmed	Dates Covered	No. of Rolls
Weingarten	LG evKB rkKB	Speyer	1705-1960	12
Weinheim	rkKB	Mainz	1756-1890	2
Weinolsheim	rkKB	Mainz	1740-1876	1
Weinsheim	evKB rkKB	Koblenz Trier	1684-1939	4
Weisenheim	rkKB evKB	Bad Dürkheim Speyer	1701-1906	3
Weisenheim am Sand	evKB rkKB	Speyer	1647-1944	8
Weitersweiler	rkKB	Speyer	1698-1961	3
Welcherath	rkKB	Trier	1706-1906	4
Welchweiler	STA	Kusel	1818-1889	3
Welgesheim	rkKB	Mainz	1760-1821	1
Wellig	rkKB	Trier	1662-1963	3
Welschbillig	rkKB	Trier	1488-1905	4
Weltenbach	STA AG	Kaiserslautern Speyer	1792-1875	5
Werlau	evKB	Koblenz	1670-1798	1
Wernersberg	rkKB LG	Speyer	1688-1961	5
Wershofen	rkKB	Trier	1694-1905	2
Weselberg	rkKB	Speyer Freiburg	1777-1961	10
Westheim	evKB LG	Speyer	1710-1915	5
Westhofen	rkKB	Mainz	1690-1876	1
Westum	rkKB	Trier	1798-1912	1
Wetteldorf	rkKB	Trier	1716-1920	3
Weyer	LG	Speyer	1816-1843	1
Weyher	LG rkKB	Speyer	1628-1926	6
Wickenrodt	evKB	Düsseldorf Koblenz	1650-1821	2

Location	Nature of Material	Where Filmed	Dates Covered	No. of Rolls
Wiesbach	evKB	Speyer	1691-1898	4
Wiesbaden-Kastel	rkKB	Mainz	1738-1890	2
Wiesbach	evKB	Speyer Freiburg	1744-1961	6
Wiesbaum	rkKB	Trier	1683-1942	2
Wilgartswiesen	evKB LG	Speyer	1716-1857	4
Wiltingen	rkKB	Trier	1752-1918	2
Wincheringen	rkKB	Trier	1734-1816	2
Winden-Germersheim	evKB LG	Speyer	1596-1943	8
Winden -Landau-	evKB	Speyer	1596-1839	2
Windesheim	evKB rkKB	Koblenz Trier	1684-1798	3
Windsberg	evKB	Speyer	1725-1821	3
Winningen	evKB	Koblenz	1596-1798	2
Winnweiler	evKB rkKB	Speyer	1698-1961	12
Winsweiler	evKB	Speyer	1596-1839	1
Winterbach	evKB STA	Speyer Zweibrücken	1691-1879	8
Winterburg	evKB	Koblenz	1590-1798	1
Wintersdorf	rkKB	Trier	1794-1919	1
Winterspelt	rkKB	Trier	1722-1939	2
Wintrich	rkKB	Trier	1607-1939	3
Winsenheim	rkKB evKB	Trier Koblenz	1652-1802	2
Wirft	rkKB	Trier	1718-1802	1
Wirschweiler	evKB	Koblenz	1656-1800	1
Wissmannsdorf	rkKB	Trier	1735-1911	3
Wittlich	evKB rkKB	Düsseldorf Trier	1587-1906	6

Location	Nature of Material	Where Filmed	Dates Covered	No. of Rolls
Wittlich Buchholz	rkKB	Trier	1806-1854	1
Wittlich Dreis	rkKB	Trier	1787-1858	1
Wittlich Manderscheid	rkKB	Trier	1763-1860	1
Wolf	evKB	Koblenz	1567-1798	1
Wolfstein	evKB rkKB AG BA	Speyer Kusel Freiburg	1699-1961	19
Wolken	rkKB	Trier	1659-1798	1
Wollmerath	rkKB	Trier	1648-1798	1
Wollmesheim	evKB rkKB	Speyer	1685-1949	4
Wollmersheim	LG	Speyer	1819-1834	1
Wöllstein	rkKB	Mainz	1694-1921	2
Wolsfeld	rkKB	Trier	1797-1939	2
Womrath	evKB	Hamborn	1716-1798	1
Wonsheim	rkKB	Mainz	1694-1924	2
Worms	rkKB	Mainz Speyer	1594-1899	22
Wörsbach	evKB STA	Kaiserslautern Speyer	1665-1875	5
Wörth	LG evKB rkKB	Speyer	1707-1939	7
Würrich	evKB	Koblenz	1746-1798	1
Zeiskam	LG evKB rkKB	Speyer Trier	1682-1961	13
Zell Bernkastel	rkKB	Trier	1798-1961	2
Zell	evKB rkKB	Speyer	1746-1961	3
Zell/Zell	rkKB	Trier	1617-1798	2
Zeselberg	evKB	Speyer	1778-1867	2

Location	Nature of Material	Where Filmed	Dates Covered	No. of Rolls
Zornheim	rkKB	Mainz	1578-1908	3
Züsch	rkKB evKB	Trier Koblenz	1725-1902	2
Zweibrücken	rkKB evKB	Zweibrücken	1525	1
Zweikirchen	evKB	Speyer	1640-1925	4
Zeltingen	rkKB	Trier	1648-1968	4
Zerf	rkKB	Trier	1728-1940	2
Zemmer	rkKB	Trier	1804-1849	1
Zewen	rkKB	Trier	1695-1856	1
Zweibrücken	evKB MKB	Zweibrücken Hannover	1564-1941	23
Zweibrücken	rkKB	Freiburg Speyer Zweibrücken	1685-1956	11
Zweibrücken	LRA STA	Zweibrücken	1798-1875	76
Zweibrücken	Zvsta STA BA AG BZG	Zweibrücken	1719-1875	55
Zweibrücken	LRA STA	Zweibrücken	1807-1830	16

SAARLAND

Location	Nature of Material	Where Filmed	Dates Covered	No. of Rolls
Alsweiler	rkKB STA	Trier St. Wendel	1795-1918	25
Altenkessel	evKB	Düsseldorf	1852-1942	6
Altforweiler	STA	Überherrn	1792-1876	20
Altheim	rkKB	Frankfurt Speyer	1690-1961	5
Appach	rkKB	Trier	1781-1792	1
Assweiler	STA	Saarbrücken	1712-1798	12
Auersmacher	rkKB	Kleinblittersdorf Kleinblittersdorf	1798-1875 1733-1939	6 9
Ballweiler	rkKB	Speyer	1803-1961	2
Bardenbach	STA	Wadern	1800-1875	17
Bebelsheim	rkKB	Frankfurt- Speyer	1683-1961	4
Beckingen	rkKB STA	Trier Beckingen	1540-1888	3
Bedensdorf	rkKB	Trier Wallerfang	1716-1917	11
Berus	rkKB STA	Trier Überherrn	1682-1902	22
Besch	rkKB	Trier Luzembourg	1729-1865	3
Besseringen	rkKB STA	Trier Mettlach	1660-1897	18
Bexbach	LRA rkKB	Kusel Speyer	1687-1920	8
Bierfeld	STA	Nonnweiler	1800-1875	13
Biesingen	rkKB	Kaiserslautern	1793-1961	3
Bietzer	rkKB STA	Trier Mersig	1792-1905	20
Biringen	STA	Rehlingen	1793-1875	12
Bischmisheim	STA	Saarbrücken	1738-1878	12
Bisten	rkKB STA	Trier Überherrn	1681-1876	21

Location	Nature of Material	Where Filmed	Dates Covered	No. of Rolls
Bleialf	rkKB	Trier	1816-1902	1
Blickweiler	rkKB	Frankfurt Kaiserslautern	1720-1940	
Bliedahlheim	rkKB	Koblenz	1899-1961	1
Bliesen	rkKB STA	St. Wendel	1682-1975	22
Blieskastel	rkKB	Freiburg	1798-1961	9
Bliesmengen Bolek	rkKB	Freiburg	1798-1971	9
Bliesransbach	STA rkKB	Saarbrücken	1685-1875	13
Böckweiler	evKB	Speyer	1870-1875	1
Borg	rkKB	Trier	1774-1860	2
Bosen	STA	Nonnweiler Nohfelden	1799-1875	23
Bous	rkKB STA	Trier Schwalbach	1792-1930	11
Braunhausen	STA	Nonnweiler	1800-1875	13
Brebach- Fechingen	STA	Saarbrücken	1712-1875	93
Breitfurt	evKB	Speyer	1850-1875	1
Brenschclbach	evKB	Speyer	1449-1868	4
Britten	STA rkKB	Mettbach	1771-1875	3
Brotdorf	rkKB	Trier	1597-1904	3
Bubach	STA	Kusel St. Wendel	1798-1875	15
Bübingen	STA	Saarbrücken	1798-1875	
Büdlingen	rkKB	Mettlach	1672-1852	3
Büschdorf	STA	Mettlach	1672-1852	3
Büschfeld	STA	Wadern	1800-1875	17
Differten	rkKB STA	Trier Wadgassen	1792-1914	37
Dillingen	rkKB	Trier Saarlouis	1696-1879	30

Location	Nature of Material	Where Filmed	Dates Covered	No. of Rolls
Dorf	rkKB	Schmelz	1624-1799	1
Dorenbach	STA evKB	St. Wendel	1608-1875	11
Dreisbach	STA rkKB	Mettlach	1672-1876	10
Dudweiler	evKB STA	Düseld Dudweiler	1670-1831	27
Düppenweiler	rkKB STA	Trier Beckingen	1757-1875	15
Düren	STA	Wallerfangen	1816-1875	8
Eft-Hellendorf	rkKB STA	Trier Mettlach	1774-1875	11
Eimersdorf	STA	Rehlingen	1793-1875	13
Einöd	evKB	Speyer	1798-1881	2
Eiweiler -St. Wendel-	STA	Nohfelden	1799-1875	10
Eiweiler -Saarbrücken-	rkKB STA	Trier Huchweiler	1731-1915	17
Elen	STA	Schwalbach	1792-1875	9
Emmersweiler	rkKB STA	Trier Volklingen	1798-1915	15
Ensdorf	rkKB STA	Trier Schwalbal	1793-1919	13
Ensheim	STA	Saarbrücken	1777-1875	13
Eppelborn	rkKB	Trier	1808-1906	2
Erbringen	STA	Beckingen	1777-1875	13
Erfweiler	rkKB	Frankfurt	1892-1961	1
Eschringen	STA	Saarbrücken	1712-1875	12
Faha	rkKB	Trier	1857-1901	1
Felsberg	STA		1792-1876	32
Freisen	rkKB	Trier	1726-1876	2
Fremersdorf	STA	Rehingen	1793-1875	12
Friedrichsthal	STA	Dudweiler Friedrichthal	1670-1875	27

Location	Nature of Material	Where Filmed	Dates Covered	No. of Rolls
Fürweiler	STA	Rehlingen	1793-1875	12
Gersheim	rkKB	Speyer	1737-1961	2
Gehweiler	STA	Wadern	1800-1875	17
Gerlfangen	rkKB STA	Trier Sehlingen	1793-1900	26
Gersweiler	STA rkKB	Gersweiler Trier	1798-1900	9
Gisingen	STA rkKB	Wallenfangen	1816-1875	8
Gonnesweiler	STA rkKB	Nohfelden	1799-1875	10
Gresaubach	rkKB	Schmelz	1700-1803	3
Gronig	STA	St. Wendel	1795-1875	20
Grossrosseln	rkKB	Trier	1727-1931	4
Güdesweiler	STA	St. Wendel	1795-1875	22
Güdinger	STA	St. Wendel	1798-1875	69
Habkirchen	rkKB	Saarbrücken	1688-1899	2
Hargarten	STA	Beckingen	1777-1875	13
Harlingen	STA	Mersig	1792-1875	13
Hasborn-Dautweiler	rkKB	Trier	1779-1822	2
Hausbach	STA	Losheim	1821-1847	3
Haustadt	rkKB STA	Trier Beckingen	1746-1918	16
Heckendalheim	STA	Saarbrücken	1712-1798	2
Hemmersdorf	rkKB STA	Trier Rehlingen	1793-1911	13
Herbitzheim	rkKB	Frankfurt Speyer	1690-1950	3
Heusweiler	rkKB STA	Heusweiler Trier	1697-1910	19
Hilbringen	rkKB STA	Trier Mersig Mettlach	1672-1918	16

Location	Nature of Material	Where Filmed	Dates Covered	No. of Rolls
Höchen	rkKB LRA	Frankfurt Speyer Kusel	1803-1961	4
Homburg	LRA rkKB evKB	Frankfurt Kusel Speyer	1798-1875	16
Homsrath	STA	Beckingen	1777-1975	15
Hoof	STA LG LRA	Speyer Kusel St. Wendel	1798-1875	16
Hostenbach	STA	Wadgassen	1792-1875	15
Hülzweiler	rkKB	Schwalbach Trier Saarluis	1695-1909	30
Hütersdorf	rkKB	Trier Schmelz	1660-1905	4
Ihn	rkKB STA	Trier Wallenfangen	1700-1875	10
Illingen	rkKB	Trier	1671-1802	2
Ittersdorf	rkKB STA	Trier Wallenfangen	1672-1927	10
Karlsbrunn	STA	Wölklingen	1798-1875	13
Kastel	STA rkKB	Nonnweiler Trier	1680-1875	16
Kirkel-Neuhäuse	ev.refKB	Speyer	1822-1924	2
Kirrberg	rkKB	Kaiserslautern	1803-1961	3
Klarenthal	STA	Gersweiler	1798-1875	8
Kleinblitters-dorf	rkKB STA	Kleinblittersdorf	1733-1939	15
Köllerbach	STA	Sellerbach	1798-1875	10
Leidingen	STA rkKB	Wallenfangen Trier	1697-1892	10
Limbach	STA evKB rkKB	Speyer Schmelz Trier	1713-1865	5
Lisdorf	rkKB	Trier	1804-1934	4

Location	Nature of Material	Where Filmed	Dates Covered	No. of Rolls
Lockweiler	rkKB STA	Trier Waden	1683-1900	19
Losheim	rkKB STA	Trier Losheim	1737-1942	20
Ludweiler	evKB STA	Düsseld Sölklinger	1737-1942	20
Mainzweiler	STA evKB rkKB	St. Wendel	1697-1875	12
Harpingen	STA rkKB	St. Wendel Trier	1700-1945	29
Marth	LG LRA	Speyer Kusel	1818-1906	11
Marth -St. Wendel-	STA	St. Wendel	1798-1875	13
Madern	STA	Rellingen	1793-1875	13
Medelsheim	rkKB	Frankfurt Speyer	1723-1960	4
Menningen	STA	Mersig	1792-1875	19
Merchingen	STA rkKB	Trier	1776-1891	1
Merzig	rkKB STA	Trier Mersig Mettlach	1672-1915	16
Mettlach	STA rkKB	Mettlach Trier	1672-1915	16
Mettrich	rkKB	Trier	1732-1798	1
Michelbach	STA	Weiskirchen	1798-1875	14
Mondorf	rkKB	Trier	1802-1925	1
Morschol	STA	Wadern	1800-1875	17
Motten- Herrschaft	Stewart	Kaiserslautern	1603	1
Münchweiler	STA	Weiskirchen	1798-1875	14
Nalbach	rkKB STA	Trier Nalbach	1688-1917	12
Nassweiler	STA	Völklingen	1798-1875	13
Nennig	rkKB	Trier	1696-1895	2

Location	Nature of Material	Where Filmed	Dates Covered	No. of Rolls
Neuforweiler	rkKB STA	Trier Überhern	1792-1876	21
Neuenkirchen	rkKB STA	Nohfelder Trier	1799-1901	12
Niederbexbach	LRA	Kaiserslautern	1702-1931	1
Niedergailbach	rkKB	Kaiserslautern	1702-1931	2
Niederkirchen	CRA evKB	Speyer Trier Kusel	1781-1906	9
Niederkirchen -Osterthal-	STA evKB	St. Wendel Koblenz	1697-1875	14
Niederlinx- weiler	rkKB evKB STA	St. Wendel Koblenz	1697-1875	14
Niederlöstern	STA	Wadern	1800-1875	17
Niederwürzbach	rkKB	Kaiserslautern	1863-1961	4
Nohfelden	evKB rkKB	Koblenz	1701-1854	3
Nonnweiler	rkKB STA	Trier Nonnweiler	1722-1909	16
Noswendel	STA	Wadern	1800-1902	17
Nunkirche	rkKB STA	Trier Weiskirch	1675-1902	17
Oberesch	STA	Rehlingen	1793-1875	12
Oberleuken	rkKB	Trier	1720-1941	2
Oberkirchen	rkKB	Trier	1848-1934	2
Ottweiler	rkKB	Trier Kaiserslautern	1680-1899	10
Otzenhausen	STA	Nonnweiler	1800-1875	13
Perl	rkKB	Trier	1705-1944	4
Primstal	rkKB STA	Trier Nohfelden	1723-1875	1
Püttlingen	rkKB STA	Völklinger Trier	1723-1892	8
Quierchied	STA rkKB	Heusweiler Trier	1776-1880	15

Location	Nature of Material	Where Filmed	Dates Covered	No. of Rolls
Rammelfangen	STA	Wallenfangen	1816-1875	8
Rappweiler	STA	Weiskirchen	1798-1875	14
Rehlingen	STA rkKB	Rehlingen Trier	1774-1935	16
Reinsbach	rkKB STA	Trier Beckingen	1692-1889	14
Reinheim	rkKB	Frankfurt Speyer	1681-1960	3
Reisbach	rkKB STA	Trier Lebach	1761-1905	13
Remmesweiler	STA evKB rkKB	St. Wendel	1697-1875	13
Rilchingen-Hanweiler Rohrbad	rkKB STA	Kleinblittersdorf	1733-1939	15
Ruberheim	rkKB	Frankfurt Speyer	1690-1940	3
Saal	STA LRA	St. Wendel Kusel	1798-1875	14
Saarbrücken	evKB UB	Düsseldorf	1714-1870	6
Saarbrücken	evKB MKB	Hannover	1867-1941	2
Saarbrücken	rkKB	Trier	1798-1876	4
Saarbrücken	STA	Saarbrücken	1798-1875	69
Saarbrücken	LDS records	Salt Lake City	-1911	1
Saarbrücken-Lauterbach	rkKB	Trier	1856-1910	1
Saarfels	STA	Beckingen	1789-1819	1
Saarhölzbach	STA rkKB	Mettlach	1672-1875	15
Saarluis	evKB MKB	Hannover Berlin-Dahlem	1817-1907	4
Saarluis	rkKB	Saarluis Trier	1681-1899	75
Saarluis	STA	Wallenfangen Saarluis	1793-1875	24

Location	Nature of Material	Where Filmed	Dates Covered	No. of Rolls
Saarluis Beaumarais	rkKB	Trier	1803-1937	2
Saarluis Linsdorf	rkKB	Trier	1804-1934	4
Saarwellingen	rkKB STA	Trier Libach	1798-1912	13
St. Barbara	STA	Wallenfangen	1793-1875	12
St. Ingbert	rkKB	Kaiserslautern Frankfurt Speyer	1790-1954	19
St. Nikolaus	STA	Völklingen	1798-1875	13
St. Wendel	STA evKB MKB	Hannover St. Wendel	1798-1875	26
Schaffenhausen	STA	Wadgassen	1792-1875	15
Scheicht	STA	Dudweiler Saarbrüch	1670-1875	36
Scheuern	rkKB	Trier	1808-1949	2
Schiffweiler	rkKB	Trier	1801-1927	4
Schmelz	rkKB STA	Trier Schmelz	1700-1814	25
Schwalbach	rkKB STA	Trier Saarluis Schwalbach	1695-1901	38
Schwarzenacher	evKB	Speyer	1798-1881	2
Schwarzenbach	STA rkKB	Lebach Trier	1798-1975	12
Schwemmlingen	rkKB	Mettlach	1672-1842	3
Selbach	STA	Nohfelden	1799-1875	10
Siersburg	STA	Rehlingen Trier	1792-1875	14
Sinz	rkKB	Trier	1702-1792	1
Sitzerath	STA	Nonweiler	1800-1875	13
Sötern	STA evKB	Nohfeld Koblenz	1727-1875	14
Spiesen	rkKB	Trier	1799-1893	2

Location	Nature of Material	Where Filmed	Dates Covered	No. of Rolls
Steinbach	rkKB erSTA	St. Wendel	1697-1875	11
Steinberg	STA	Weiskirchen	1798-1875	14
Sulzbach	STA rkKB	Dudweiler Trier Sulzbach	1670-1909	31
Tettingen	rkKB	Trier	1723-1880	2
Thailen	STA	Weiskirchen	1798-1875	14
Thalexweiler	rkKB	Trier	1693-1904	3
Tholey	rkKB	Trier	1808-1917	2
Tünsdorf	STA rkKB	Mettlach Trier	1718-1875	12
Türkismühle	rkKB	Trier	1802-1901	2
Überherrn	STA	Überherrn	1792-1876	20
Überroth-Niederhofe	STA	Nobfelden	1799-1875	10
Uchtelfangen	rkKB	Trier	1747-1875	2
Urexweiler	STA rkKB	St. Wendel Trier	1697-1901	26
Völklingen	rkKB STA	Trier Völklingen	1798-1893	22
Wadern	rkKB STA	Trier Wadern	1649-1922	21
Wadgassen	STA rkKB	Wadgassen Trier	1792-1909	18
Wadrill	STA rkKB	Waden Trier	1670-1895	20
Wahlem	rkKB STA	Trier Losheim	1674-1898	29
Wallenfangen	rkKB STA	Trier Wallenfangen Robel	1679-1898	29
Walsheim	evKB rkKB	Frankfurt Speyer	1704-1961	6
Wehingen-Bethingen	STA	Mettlach	1830-1875	10
Weirweiler	STA	Weiskirchen	1798-1875	14

Location	Nature of Material	Where Filmed	Dates Covered	No. of Rolls
Weiskirchen	rkKB STA	Trier Weiskirchen	1671-1904	17
Weiten	rkKB STA	Trier Mettlach	1782-1899	12
Werbelm	STA	Wadgarse	1792-1875	15
Werschweiler	evKB STA rkKB	St. Wendel	1697-1875	11
Wetschhausen	evKB STA rkKB	St. Wendel	1697-1875	11
Wiesbach	rkKB	Trier	1807-1899	2
Winterbach	STA rkKB	St. Wendel Trier	1795-1875	24
Wolfersheim	rkKB	Frankfurt Speyer	1690-1950	3
Wolfenweiler	evKB rkKB	Koblenz Trier	1641-1855	8

SCHLESWIG-HOLSTEIN

Location	Nature of Material	Where Filmed	Dates Covered	No. of Rolls
Ahrensbök	evKB	Lübeck	1598-1930	5
Ahrensbök	evKB	Lübeck	1687-1949	10
Bad Oldesloe	MKB	Hannover	1867-1871	1
Bad Schwartau	evKB	Lübeck	1610-1925	6
Bad Schwartau	ZSR	Lübeck	1796-1875	1
Bad Schwartau	evKB	Lübeck	1811-1882	2
Bad Schwartau	evKB	Lübeck	1649-1959	16
Basthorst	evKB	Lübeck	1660-1876	1
Behlendorf	ZSR	Lübeck	1941-1955	1
Behlendorf	evKB	Lübeck	1754-1961	6
Berkenthin	evKB	Lübeck	1672-1875	2
Bosau	evKB	Lübeck	1700-1882	3
Bosau	evKB	Lübeck	1701-1959	11
Breitenfelde	evKB	Lübeck	1807-1875	1
Breitenfelde	KB	Lübeck	1701-1876	3
Brunsdorf	KB	Lübeck	1634-1876	5
Büchen	KB	Lübeck	1693-1876	1
Curau	KB	Speyer	1757-1945	4
Curau	ZSR	Lübeck	1796-1875	1
Curau	KB	Lübeck	1864-1883	1
Curau	KB	Lübeck	1741-1959	10
Curau	Kultus-ministerium	Lübeck	1819-1906	1
Eiderstedt		Lübeck	1535-1714	1
Elmenhorst	KB	Lübeck	1801-1859	2
Eutin	evKB	Lübeck	1883-1889	3
Eutin	evKB	Lübeck	1639	1
Eutin	STA	Lübeck	1854-1898	1

Location	Nature of Material	Where Filmed	Dates Covered	No. of Rolls
Eutin	Finanzamt	Lübeck	1948-1949	2
Eutin	evKB	Lübeck	1633-1950	16
Eutin	KB	Lübeck	1720-1911	1
Eutin	KB	Lübeck	1800-1932	11
Eutin	Landes-Kirche	Lübeck	1837-1942	1
Eutin	STA	Lübeck	1905-1954	28
Flensburg	evKB MKB	Hannover	1867-1939	2
Fuhlenhagen	KB	Lübeck	1801-1859	2
Friedrichstadt	KB	Dahlem	1639-1760	3
Garding	KB	Lübeck	1624-1872	3
Geesthacht	KB	Lübeck	1679-1916	3
Gelting	KB Kiel	Lübeck	1557-1827	1
Gleschendorf	KB	Lübeck	1679-1959	10
Gleschendorf	KB	Lübeck	1763-1939	5
Gnissau	KB	Lübeck	1913-1922	1
Gnissau	KB	Lübeck	1764-1959	14
Gottorf	KB Kiel	Lübeck	1485-1828	1
Gross-Berkenthin	KB	Lübeck	1672-1876	2
Gross-Grönau	evKB	Lübeck	1796-1875	1
Gross-Grönau	KB	Lübeck	1629-1876	3
Gross-Pampau	KB	Lübeck	1801-1859	2
Grube	KB	Dahlem	1844-1869	1
Gudow	KB	Lübeck	1635-1879	2
Gülzow	KB	Lübeck	1628-1875	2
Hamberge	ZSR	Lübeck	1796-1875	1
Hamberge	KB	Lübeck	1727-1962	1
Hamwarde	KB	Lübeck	1663-1876	2
Havetoft	evKB	Dahlem	1628-1753	1

Location	Nature of Material	Where Filmed	Dates Covered	No. of Rolls
Hohenhorn	KB	Lübeck	1646-1876	2
Husum	Schützen-gilde	Lübeck	1586-1832	1
Husum	KB	Lübeck	1605-1800	1
Itzehoe	evKB MKB	Hannover	1867-1927	1
Jörl	KB	Dahlem	1741-1763	1
Kappeln	KB		c. 1650-1761	1
Kappeln	evKB		1656-1764	1
Kiel	MKB	Hannover	1850-1871	1
Klein Wesenberg	evKB	Lübeck	1791-1875	1
Klein Wesenberg	KB	Lübeck	1648-1962	4
Koldenbüttel	KB	Lübeck	c. 1630-1800	1
Kotzenbüll	KB	Lübeck	1646-1901	1
Krummesse	KB	Lübeck	1796-1876	1
Krummesse	KB	Lübeck	1640-1880	2
Kuddewörde	KB	Lübeck	1661-1876	2
Langenhorn				1
Lanken	KB	Lübeck	1801-1859	2
Lassohn	KB	Lübeck	1718-1876	2
Lauenburg	KB	Lübeck	1701-1876	7
Linau	evKB	Lübeck	1812-1813	1
Lübeck	evKB	Lübeck	1898-1955	11
Lübeck	MKB	Lübeck		1
Lübeck	STA	Lübeck	1814-1955	14
Lübeck	evKB	Lübeck	1896-1959	1
Lübeck		Lübeck	14th-17th Jh.	2
Lübeck	ZSR	Lübeck	1811-1875	58
Lübeck	MKB	Lübeck	1939-1945	5

Location	Nature of Material	Where Filmed	Dates Covered	No. of Rolls
Lübeck	STA	Lübeck	1938-1943	4
Lübeck		Lübeck	1898-1955	12
Lübeck	Rathaus	Lübeck	1626-1771	2
Lübeck	MKB	Hannover	1900-1937	1
Lübeck	evKB	Lübeck	1655-1960	20
Lübeck	evKB	Lübeck	1651-1906	10
Lübeck	evKB	Lübeck	1717-1927	9
Lübeck	evKB	Lübeck	1908-1960	7
Lübeck	evKB	Lübeck	1950-1959	3
Lübeck	evKB	Lübeck	1581-1960	35
Lübeck	evKB	Lübeck	1951-1960	2
Lübeck	evKB	Lübeck	1937-1945	1
Lübeck	evKB	Lübeck	1914-1954	5
Lübeck	evKB	Lübeck	1934-1954	5
Lübeck	evKB	Lübeck	1934-1945	1
Lübeck	evKB	Lübeck	1929-1957	2
Lübeck	evKB	Lübeck	1946-1960	2
Lübeck	evKB	Lübeck	1934-1960	6
Lübeck	evKB	Lübeck	1774-1960	11
Lübeck	evKB	Lübeck	1948-1956	3
Lübeck	evKB	Lübeck	1953-1960	2
Lübeck	evKB	Lübeck	1951-1954	2
Lübeck	evKB	Lübeck	1950-1956	3
Lübeck	evKB	Lübeck	1830-1954	11
Lübeck	evKB	Lübeck	1832-1954	6
Lübeck	evKB	Lübeck	1879-1954	12
Lübeck	evKB	Lübeck	1938-1954	2
Lübeck	evKB	Lübeck	1936-1954	5
Lübeck	evKB	Lübeck	1938-1954	2

Location	Nature of Material	Where Filmed	Dates Covered	No. of Rolls
Lübeck	evKB	Lübeck	1927-1958	1
Lübeck	evKB	Lübeck	1752-1811	1
Lübeck	evKB	Lübeck	1955	1
Lübeck	evKB	Lübeck	1692-1960	23
Lübeck	evKB	Lübeck	1599-1960	32
Lübeck	evKB	Lübeck	1896-1960	32
Lübeck	evKB	Lübeck	1955	1
Lübeck	evKB	Lübeck	1616-1955	17
Lübeck	MKB	Lübeck	1937-1958	1
Lübeck	evKB MKB	Lübeck	1939-1945	4
Lübeck	evKB	Lübeck	1633-1960	25
Lübeck	evKB	Lübeck	1625-1960	78
Lübeck	evKB MKB	Lübeck	1939-1945	4
Lübeck	Rathaus	Lübeck	1751-1800	2
Lübeck	Rathaus	Lübeck	1726-1805	2
Lübeck	KB	Lübeck	1693-1875	1
Lübeck	KB	Lübeck	1616-1955	152
Lübeck	STA	Lübeck	1814-1939	3
Lübeck	ZSR	Lübeck	1813-1944	2
Lübeck	ZSR	Lübeck	1924-1954	4
Lübeck	ZSR	Lübeck	1953-1957	1
Lübeck	KB	Lübeck	1535-1800	1
Lütan	evKB	Berlin-Dahlem	1743-1790	1
Lütan	KB	Lübeck	1743-1875	2
Malente	KB	Lübeck	1505-1846	2
Malente	KB	Lübeck	1702-1958	16
Malente	KB	Lübeck	1505, 1788-1816	2

Location	Nature of Material	Where Filmed	Dates Covered	No. of Rolls
Malente	KB	Lübeck	1613-1958	13
Malente	evKB	Lübeck	1702-1882	3
Mildstedt	KB	Lübeck	1642-1804	1
Mölln	Landes-superintendur	Ratzeburg	1548-1671	1
Mölln	evKB MKB	Hannover	1866-1889	1
Mölln	KB	Lübeck	1623-1876	7
Mustin	KB	Lübeck	1528-1877	4
Neumünster	MKB	Hannover	1867-1935	1
Neustadt	evKB	Dahlem	1812-1827	1
Niendorf	KB	Lübeck	1704-1876	1
Niendorf	KB	Lübeck	1912-1959	1
Odenbüll	KB	Lübeck	1657-1803	1
Nusse	KB	Lübeck	1937-1941	4
Nusse	evKB	Lübeck	1614-1941	18
Nusse	ZSR	Lübeck	1939-1945	1
Oldenburg	evKB	Dahlem	1772-1865	3
Oldenswort	KB	Lübeck	1653-1828	1
Ording	KB	Lübeck	1760-1921	1
Osterhever	KB	Lübeck	1671-1913	1
Plön	STA	Lübeck	1626-1628 1674-1700	2
Poppenbüll	KB	Lübeck	1653-1900	1
Pötrau	KB	Lübeck	1697-1876	2
Ratekau	KB	Lübeck	1612-1954	6
Ratekau	evKB	Lübeck	1796-1875	1
Ratekau	KB	Lübeck	1763-1907	11
Ratekau	Kultus-ministerium	Lübeck	1822-1861	1
Ratzeburg	KB	Lübeck	1641-1802	1

Location	Nature of Material	Where Filmed	Dates Covered	No. of Rolls
Ratzeburg	MKB	Hannover	1721-1936	2
Ratzeburg	evKB	Goslar	1641-1902	2
Ratzeburg	evKB	Lübeck	1796-1875	1
Ratzeburg	KB	Lübeck	1849-1876	1
Ratzeburg	KB	Lübeck	1640-1876	5
Ratzeburg	KB	Lübeck	1587-1876	4
Ratzeburg	STA ZSR	Lübeck	1811-1813	1
Rendsburg	Militär	Copenhagen	1716-1740	5
Rendsburg	MKB	Hannover	1865-1910	1
Sahms	KB	Lübeck	1684-1876	2
Sandesneben	KB	Lübeck	1687-1877	6
Sankt Peter	evKB	Lübeck	1649-1820	1
Scharbeutz	KB	Lübeck	1956-1959	1
Schlagsdorf	ZSR	Lübeck	1796-1875	1
Schleswig	evKB MKB	Hannover	1865-1882	1
Schleswig	rkKB	Dahlem	1868-1897	1
Schobull	KB	Lübeck	1620-1800	1
Schwabstadt	KB	Lübeck	1681-1863	1
Schwabstadt	KB	Augsburg	1500-1900	10
Schwarzenbek	KB	Lübeck	1639-1875	2
Seedorf	KB	Lübeck	1679-1876	2
Siebenbaumen	KB	Lübeck	1791-1878	2
Siebeneichen	KB	Lübeck	1639-1876	3
Sterleg	KB	Lübeck	1660-1876	11
Stockelsdorf	KB	Lübeck	1889-1916	1
Stockelsdorf	KB	Lübeck	1799-1958	15
Süsel	KB	Lübeck	1735-1930	1
Süsel	evKB	Lübeck	1597-1959	35

Location	Nature of Material	Where Filmed	Dates Covered	No. of Rolls
Süsel	evKB	Lübeck	1821-1876	8
Süsel	KB	Lübeck	1922-1957	3
Tetenbüll	KB	Lübeck	1606-1900	2
Timmendorfer Strand	KB	Lübeck	1926-1959	2
Tönning	KB	Lübeck	1650-1800	2
Travemünde	evKB	Lübeck	1796-1875	1
Ulvesbüll	KA	Lübeck	1613-1804	1
Vollerwieck	KB	Lübeck	1535-1730	1
Welt	KB	Lübeck	1630-1800	1
Witzwort	KB	Lübeck	1692-1768	1

TERRITORIES NOW PART
OF THE GERMAN DEMOCRATIC REPUBLIC
(EAST GERMANY)

COTTBUS

Location	Nature of Material	Where Filmed	Dates Covered	No. of Rolls
Cottbus	Misc. records	Frankfurt	20th century	10
Cottbus	LDS records	Salt Lake City	-1949	7
Cottbus	MilKB	Eibenstock	1821-1868	1
Cottbus	KB	Berlin-Dahlem	1821-1919	1
Drehna	evKB	Berlin-Dahlem	1670-1754	1
Duben	MilKB	Eibenstock	1834-1882	1
Forst	LDS records	Salt Lake City	1931	2
Gross Jehser	evKB	Berlin-Dahlem	1654-1852	1
Gross Leuthen	evKB	Hannover	1679-1836	1
Gross Lubolz	evKB	Goslar	1747-1927	1
Gross Lubolz	evKB	Hannover	1854-1941	
Klein Lubolz	evKB	Goslar	1646-1927	1
Korssen	MilKB	Hannover	1862-1868	1
Krausnick	evKB	Hannover	1660-1903	3
Krossen	MilKB	Eibenstock	1833-1876	1
Krossen	MilKB	Berlin-Dahlem	1833-1920	1
Lübben	evKB	Hannover	1732-1893	9
Lübben	evKB	Hannover	1854-1892	1
Lübben	MilKB	Berlin-Dahlem	1822-1944	1
Lübben	evKB	Hannover	1646-1925	10
Ruhland	Mortgages Gericht	Berlin-Dahlem	1856-1867	1
Schlepzig	evKB	Hannover	1662-1881	2
Spremberg	MilKB	Eibenstock	1832-1875	1

Location	Nature of Material	Where Filmed	Dates Covered	No. of Rolls
Spremberg	MilKB	Berlin-Dahlem	1832-1875	1
Terpt	evKB	Berlin-Dahlem	1667-1800	1
Wilhelm-Pieck-Stadt	MilKB	Berlin-Dahlem	1832-1919	1
Wittmanns-Dorf	evKB	Hannover	1664-1826	1

DRESDEN

Location	Nature of Material	Where Filmed	Dates Covered	No. of Rolls
Bautzen	LDS records	Salt Lake City	1923-1930	1
Bautzen	MilKB	Hannover	1919-1944	1
Bischofswerda	LDS records	Salt Lake City	1931-1950	1
Dresden	LDS records	Salt Lake City	1890-1951	10
Dresden	Church of England KB	Salt Lake City	1837-1848	1
Dresden	All Saints English KB	Salt Lake City	1843-1846	1
Görlitz	LDS records	Salt Lake City	1927-1935	2
Leutewitz	KB	Berlin-Dahlem	1653-1939	1
Löbau	MilKB	Hannover	1919-1944	1
Meissen	LDS records	Salt Lake City	1928-1930	1
Oberseifersdorf	evKB	Warsaw	1832-1847	1
Paussnitz	MilKB	Berlin-Dahlem	1732-1944	1
Rammenau	LDS records	Salt Lake City	1946-1947	1
Zittau	LDS records	Salt Lake City	1930-1932	1

ERFURT

Location	Nature of Material	Where Filmed	Dates Covered	No. of Rolls
Asbach	Gericht	Marburg	1870-1896	1
Asbach	ZSR Justizamt	Marburg	1800-1875	1
Aschara	evLutKB	Berlin-Dahlem	1700-1808	1
Badra	evLutKB	Berlin-Dahlem	1690-1744	1
Beuernfeld	evLutKB	Berlin-Dahlem	1640-1709	1
Bienstät	evLutKB	Berlin-Dahlem	1715-1765	1
Blankenhain	evLutKB	Berlin-Dahlem	1755-1867	1
Dietzenrode	ZSR Justizamt	Marburg	1809	1
Ehrenstein	evLutKB	Berlin-Dahlem	1627-1754	1
Erfurt	LDS records	Salt Lake City	1923-1930	1
Erfurt	MilKB	Hannover	1803-1806	1
Erfurt	MilKB	Hannover	1890-1896	1
Erfurt	MilKB	Berlin-Dahlem	1870-1871	1
Finsterbergen	evLutKB	Berlin-Dahlem	1662-1721	1
Georgenthal	evLutKB	Berlin-Dahlem	1651-1785	1
Gotha	LDS records	Salt Lake City	1902-1907	1
Gotha	evKB	Berlin-Dahlem	1617-1708	3
Gräfenroda	evLutKB	Berlin-Dahlem	1714-1808	1
Gross Schwabhausen	evLutKB	Berlin-Dahlem	1689-1782	1
Grossburschla	ZSR STA	Marburg	1808-1812	1
Hohenkirchen	evLutKB	Berlin-Dahlem	1656-1774	1
Holzthaleben	evLutKB	Berlin-Dahlem	1745-1803	2
Hörselgau	evLutKB	Berlin-Dahlem	1627-1759	1
Kölleda	MilKB	Eibenstock	1834-1873	1
Kranichborn	evLutKB	Berlin-Dahlem	1664-1812	1
Kranichfeld	evLutKB	Berlin-Dahlem	1638-1746	1

Location	Nature of Material	Where Filmed	Dates Covered	No. of Rolls
Lindewerra	evLutKB	Bielefeld	1668-1907	2
Luisenthal	evLutKB	Berlin-Dahlem	1667-1804	1
Magdala	evLutKB	Berlin-Dahlem	1648-1785	1
Melborn	evLutKB	Berlin-Dahlem	1636-1739	1
Molschleben	evLutKB	Berlin-Dahlem	1628-1757	2
Mühlhausen	LDS records	Salt Lake City	1911	1
Mühlhausen	LDS records	Salt Lake City	1889-1907	1
Nohra	evLutKB	Berlin-Dahlem	1736-1803	1
Obersachwerfen	evLutKB	Berlin-Dahlem	1627-1770	1
Plaue	evLutKB	Berlin-Dahlem	1733-1782	1
Rohnstedt	evLutKB	Berlin-Dahlem	1674-1798	1
Rottdorf	evLutKB	Berlin-Dahlem	1805-1848	1
Saalborn	evLutKB	Berlin-Dahlem	1764-1847	1
Schnellmanns-hausen	ZSR STA	Marburg	1808-1812	1
Schönau	evLutKB	Berlin-Dahlem	1684-1788	1
Schwerborn	evLutKB	Berlin-Dahlem	1740-1848	1
Sollstedt	Probate	Berlin-Dahlem	1585	1
Tambach-Dietharz	evLutKB	Berlin-Dahlem	1603-1808	1
Taubach	evLutKB	Berlin-Dahlem	1725-1860	1
Töttelstädt	evLutKB	Berlin-Dahlem	1725-1779	1
Udestestedt	evLutKB	Berlin-Dahlem	1725-1860	1
Waltershausen	evLutKB	Berlin-Dahlem	1626-1666	1
Warza	evLutKB	Berlin-Dahlem	1633-1724	1
Weimar	LDS records	Salt Lake City	1927-1937	3
Wenigenlupitz	evLutKB	Berlin-Dahlem	1712-1797	1
Wernings-hausen	evLutKB	Berlin-Dahlem	1637-1719	1
Wiedenbach	ZSA AG	Marburg	1809	1

Location	Nature of Material	Where Filmed	Dates Covered	No. of Rolls
Wiedermuth	evLutKB	Berlin-Dahlem	1627-1759	1
Wiegleben	evLutKB	Berlin-Dahlem	1782-1808	1

. FRANKFURT/ODER

Location	Nature of Material	Where Filmed	Dates Covered	No. of Rolls
Angermünde	MilKB	Berlin-Dahlem	1833-1928	1
Beeskow	MilKB	Berlin-Dahlem	1816-1944	1
Beeskow	MilKB	Hannover	1797-1833	1
Eberswalde	MilKB	Berlin-Dahlem	1892-1898	1
Frankfurt	JüdGem	Berlin-Dahlem	1847-1878	2
Frankfurt	MilKB	Berlin-Dahlem	1723-1940	20
Frankfurt	MilKB	Hannover	1860-1866	1
Frankfurt	MilKB	Hannover	1860-1867	2
Frankfurt	MilKB	Berlin-Dahlem	1905-1944	1
Friedersdorf	Family papers	Berlin-Dahlem	1807-1837	1
Fürstenwalde	MilKB	Berlin-Dahlem	1802-1932	2
Gartz	MilKB	Berlin-Dahlem	1833-1884	1
Gross Schönebeck	KB	Berlin-Dahlem	1664-1730	1
Schmiedeberg	MilKB	Eibenstock	1834-1877	1
Schwedt	MilKB	Berlin-Dahlem	1801-1870	3
Strausberg	MilKB	Eibenstock	1860-1872	1
Strausberg	MilKB	Berlin-Dahlem	1802-1872	1
Wriezen	MilKB	Eibenstock	1814-1868	1
Wriezen	MilKB	Eibenstock	1869-1876	1
Wriezen	MilKB	Berlin-Dahlem	1814-1879	1
Zechin	evKB	Berlin	1696-1804	1

GERA

Location	Nature of Material	Where Filmed	Dates Covered	No. of Rolls
Aga	evLutKB	Berlin-Dahlem	1729-1800	1
Burgwitz	evLutKB	Berlin-Dahlem	1551-1679	1
Culmitzsch	evLutKB	Berlin-Dahlem	1579-1768	1
Dornburg	evLutKB	Berlin-Dahlem	1717-1784	1
Dorndorf	evLutKB	Berlin-Dahlem	1612-1693	1
Frössen	rökKB	Berlin-Dahlem	1710-1834	2
Gera	LDS records	Salt Lake City	1930	1
Haufeld	evLutKB	Berlin-Dahlem	1666-1848	1
Heilsberg	MilKB	Hannover	1802-1865	1
Hirschberg	evLutKB	Berlin-Dahlem	1715-1785	1
Meckeroda	evLutKB	Berlin-Dahlem	1753-1805	1
Molbitz	evLutKB	Berlin-Dahlem	1551-1679	1
Oppurg	evLutKB	Berlin-Dahlem	1639-1799	1
Pöllwitz	evLutKB	Berlin-Dahlem	1619-1674	1
Reinsdorf	evLutKB	Berlin-Dahlem	1630-1720	1
Roben	evLutKB	Berlin-Dahlem	1591-1886	1
Röpsen	evLutKB	Berlin-Dahlem	1771-1808	1
Saalburg	evLutKB	Berlin-Dahlem	1753-1781	1
Treppendorf	evLutKB	Berlin-Dahlem	1790-1809	1
Unterwellenborn	evLutKB	Berlin-Dahlem	1643-1754	1

HALLE

Location	Nature of Material	Where Filmed	Dates Covered	No. of Rolls
Aschersleben	MilKB	Berlin-Dahlem	1736-1870	2
Bad Dürrenberg	Civil laws regulations	Berlin	1670-1792	1
Bad Frankenhausen	evLutKB	Berlin-Dahlem	1632-1683	1
Ballenstedt	Property records	Goslar	1550	1
Bernburg	Marriage records Probate records	Goslar	1534-1785	3
Bernburg	evKB	Berlin	1594-1635	1
Bernburg	MilKB	Berlin-Dahlem	1895-1920	1
Dessau	STA	Goslar	1610-1638	1
Dessau	evKB	Berlin-Dahlem	1896-1941	1
Düben	MilKB	Berlin-Dahlem	1813-1851	2
Düben	MilKB	Hannover	1851-1868	1
Eisleben	MilKB	Berlin-Dahlem	1851-1868	1
Eisleben	MilKB	Eibenstock	1834-1876	1
Freckleben	Castle records	Goslar	1600-1700	1
Friedeburg	Family papers	Berlin-Dahlem	1798	1
Gardelegen	MilKB	Hannover	1839-1918	1
Halle	MilKB	Hannover	1766-1801	1
Halle	MilKB	Hannover	1771-1800	1
Harzgerode	STA Tax	Goslar	1600-1737	3
Höhnstedt	evLutKB	Berlin-Dahlem	1578-1767	2
Kemberg	MilKB	Eibenstock	1834-1873	1
Lützen	evLutKB	Berlin-Dahlem	1547-1635	1
Merseburg	MilKB	Eibenstock	1834-1877	1

Location	Nature of Material	Where Filmed	Dates Covered	No. of Rolls
Naumburg	MilKB	Berlin-Dahlem	1834-1905	1
Neinstedt	KB	Berlin-Dahlem	1677-1760	1
Nienburg	STA	Goslar	1602-1660	1
Pretzsch	MilKB	Berlin-Dahlem	1830-1928	1
Quedlinburg	MilKB	Berlin-Dahlem	1735-1928	4
Sangershausen	MilKB	Eibenstock	1834-1903	1
Schmiedeberg	MilKB	Berlin-Dahlem	1813-1851	1
Strassberg	evLutKB	Berlin-Dahlem	1747-1799	1
Timmenrode	ZSR BM	Wolfenbüttel	1808-1814	1
Warnstedt	evLutKB	Berlin-Dahlem	1627-1762	1
Zeitz	MilKB	Berlin-Dahlem	1801-1932	1

KARL-MARX-STADT

Location	Nature of Material	Where Filmed	Dates Covered	No. of Rolls
Karl-Marx-Stadt	LDS records	Salt Lake City	1926	1
Karl-Marx-Stadt	LDS records	Salt Lake City	1907-1921	1
Karl-Marx-Stadt	LDS records	Salt Lake City	1950-1951	1
Annaberg Buchholz	KB	Berlin-Dahlem	1498-1550	1
Arnoldsgrün	KB	Berlin-Dahlem	1692-1788	1
Auerbach	LDS records	Salt Lake City	1930-1931	1
Blauenthal	LDS records	Salt Lake City	1945-1948	1
Karl-Marx-Stadt	LDS records	Salt Lake City	1907-1951	8
Karl-Marx-Stadt	Cemetery records	Salt Lake City		1
Meerane	LDS records	Salt Lake City	1831-1953	1
Mittweida	LDS records	Salt Lake City	1929-1930	1
Niederplanitz	LDS records	Salt Lake City	1927-1930	1
Plauen	LDS records	Salt Lake City	1907-1931	2
Reichenbach	LDS records	Salt Lake City	1930	1
Schwarzenberg	LDS records	Salt Lake City	1926-1930	1
Werdau	LDS records	Salt Lake City	1909-1923 1931-1948	1
Zwickau	LDS records	Salt Lake City	1927-1951	6
Zwickau	MilKB	Berlin-Dahlem	1732-1944	1

LEIPZIG

Location	Nature of Material	Where Filmed	Dates Covered	No. of Rolls
Döbeln	LDS records	Salt Lake City	1928-1929	1
Eilenburg	evKB	Berlin-Dahlem	1548-1657	1
Eilenburg	MilKB	Berlin-Dahlem	1801-1932	1
Kriebitzsch	evLutKB	Berlin-Dahlem	1649-1723	1
Leipzig	LDS records	Salt Lake City	1902-1951	9
Leipzig	Church of England KB	London	1864-1875	1
Leipzig	MilKB	Hannover	1900-1943	1
Mehna	evLutKB	Berlin-Dahlem	1727-1808	1
Molwitz	evLutKB	Berlin-Dahlem	1551-1679	1
Podelwitz	KB	Salt Lake City	1623-1707	1
Torgau	MilKB	Berlin-Dahlem	1812-1934	1
Torgau	MilKB	Berlin-Dahlem	1801-1932	1
Zechau	evLutKB	Berlin-Dahlem	1630-1759	1

MAGDEBURG

Location	Nature of Material	Where Filmed	Dates Covered	No. of Rolls
Arendsee	MilKB		1735-1928	1
Ballerstedt	Gericht	Goslar	1574-1602	1
Blankenburg	ZSR BM		1808-1814	1
Blankenburg	evLutKB MilKB	Berlin-Dahlem	1891-1912	1
Breitenhagen	evLutKB	Berlin-Dahlem	1658-1744	1
Burg	MilKB	Hannover	1904-1920	1
Burg	MilKB	Hannover	1755-1767	1
Burg	MilKB	Berlin-Dahlem	1834-1920	2
Calvörde	ZSR BM	Wolfenbüttel	1808-1813	1
Calvörde	JüdGem	Wolfenbüttel	1738-1889	1
Diesdorf	evLutKB	Berlin-Dahlem	1845-1872	1
Gardelegen	MilKB	Hannover	1839-1918	1
Gardelegen	MilKB	Berlin-Dahlem	1860-1919	1
Gardelegen	MilKB	Eibenstock	1860-1876	1
Gardelegen	MilKB	Eibenstock	1582-1944	1
Gerwisch	evLutKB	Berlin-Dahlem	1671-1770	1
Halberstadt	ev.refKB	Berlin-Dahlem	1815-1869	2
Halberstadt	evLutKB	Berlin-Dahlem	1721-1922	5
Halberstadt	MilKB	Hannover	1864-1868	1
Haldensleben	MilKB	Berlin-Dahlem	1834-1893	1
Havelberg	MilKB	Eibenstock	1819-1887	1
Havelberg	MilKB	Berlin-Dahlem	1819-1887	1
Hessen	ZSR BM	Wolfenbüttel	1808	1
Langenweddinen	evLutKB	Berlin-Dahlem	1662-1689	1
Magdeburg	LDS records	Salt Lake City	1932-1935	1

Location	Nature of Material	Where Filmed	Dates Covered	No. of Rolls
Magdeburg	MilKB	Berlin-Dahlem Hannover	1716-1941	25
Pabstdorf	ZSR BM	Wolfenbüttel	1808-1813	1
Schönebeck	MilKB	Eibenstock	1834-1885	1
Schönebeck	MilKB	Berlin-Dahlem	1834-1885	1
Seehausen	MilKB		1735-1928	1
Stenal	MilKB	Berlin-Dahlem	1729-1932	3
Tangermünde	MilKB	Eibenstock	1860-1876	1
Tangermünde	MilKB	Eibenstock	1735-1928	1
Tangermünde	MilKB	Berlin-Dahlem	1860-1884	1
Trautenstein	ZSR BM	Wolfenbüttel	1809-1814	1
Uthmöden	ZSR BM	Wolfenbüttel	1808-1813	1
Warmsdorf	BM	Goslar	1600	
Weren	MilKB		1735-1928	1
Wust	evLutKB	Berlin-Dahlem	1678-1755	1
Zerbst	Feudal land records	Goslar	1367-1733	1
Zerbst	MilKB	Berlin-Dahlem	1772-1793	1
Zobbenitz	ZSR	Wolfenbüttel	1808-1812	1
Zollchow	evLutKB	Goslar	1845-1944	1

NEUBRANDENBURG

Location	Nature of Material	Where Filmed	Dates Covered	No. of Rolls
Ahrensberg	evLutKB	Goslar	1679-1983	1
Alt Kaebelich	evLutKB	Goslar	1665-1875	1
Alt Panstorf	evLutKB	Goslar	1661-1934	1
Alt Rehse	evLutKB	Goslar	1746-1930	1
Alt Schwerin	evLutKB	Goslar	1655-1877	3
Alt Kalen	evLutKB	Goslar	1728-1875	3
Ankershagen	evLutKB	Goslar	1676-1934	3
Anklam	MilKB	Berlin-Dahlem	1728-1919	1
Anklam	MilKB	Eibenstock	1833-1893	1
Babke	evLutKB	Goslar	1664-1928	1
Badresch	evLutKB	Goslar	1650-1875	3
Ballin	evLutKB	Goslar	1810-1875	1
Ballin	evLutKB	Goslar	1667-1934	1
Ballwitz	evLutKB	Goslar	1699-1875	3
Bargensdorf	evLutKB	Goslar	1756-1875	2
Basedow	evLutKB	Goslar	1766-1876	2
Bassow	evLutKB	Goslar	1704-1933	1
Baumgarten	evKB	Hannover	1674-1832	2
Baumgarten	evKB	Goslar	1674-1944	1
Baumgarten	evLutKB	Goslar	1674-1824	1
Behren-Lübchin	evLutKB	Goslar	1700-1884	2
Belitz	evLutKB	Goslar	1632-1908	4
Beseritz	evLutKB	Goslar	1737-1798	1
Blankenforde	evLutKB	Goslar	1664-1928	1
Blankensee	evLutKB	Goslar	1716-1934	1
Boek	evLutKB	Goslar	1672-1934	1
Boizenburg	evLutKB	Goslar	1657-1920	5

Location	Nature of Material	Where Filmed	Dates Covered	No. of Rolls
Bollewick	evLutKB	Goslar	1672-1934	1
Borgfeld	evLutKB	Goslar	1724-1883	1
Bredenfelde	evLutKB	Goslar	1715-1934	3
Breesen	evLutKB	Goslar	1707-1876	4
Bresewitz	evLutKB	Goslar	1687-1930	1
Briggow	evLutKB	Goslar	1697-1934	1
Brohm	evLutKB	Goslar	1673-1933	1
Bröllin	Kirche	Berlin	1695-1838	1
Brudersdorf	evLutKB	Goslar	1703-1890	1
Brunn	evLutKB	Goslar	1750-1875	1
Brunn	evLutKB	Goslar	1810-1859	1
Buchholz	evLutKB	Goslar	1661-1933	1
Buchholz	evLutKB	Goslar	1675-1800	1
Bukow	Census	Goslar	1819	1
Bülow	evLutKB	Goslar	1652-1934	3
Burg Stargard	evLutKB	Goslar	1756-1875	2
Butow	evLutKB	Goslar	1710-1905	1
Cammin	evLutKB	Goslar	1731-1934	1
Cantnitz	evLutKB	Goslar	1715-1935	1
Canzow	evLutKB	Goslar	1668-1934	1
Carwitz	evLutKB		1720-1925	
Chemnitz	evLutKB	Goslar	1707-1876	1
Colpin	evLutKB		1667-1934	1
Conow	evLutKB		1720-1925	1
Dahlen	evLutKB	Goslar	1745-1934	1
Dalmsdorf	evLutKB	Goslar	1700-1875	1
Dammwolde	evLutKB	Goslar	1747-1885	1
Dargun	Census	Goslar	1819	1
Dargun	evLutKB	Goslar	1704-1920	4

Location	Nature of Material	Where Filmed	Dates Covered	No. of Rolls
Dauer	KB	Goslar	1765-1832	1
Dauer	evKB	Hannover	1674-1832	2
Demmin	LDS records	Salt Lake City	1917-1930	1
Dewitz	evLutKB	Goslar	1667-1934	3
Demmin	evLutKB MilKB	Berlin-Dahlem	1860-1937	11
Diemitz	evLutKB	Goslar	1672-1934	1
Domhof Ratzeburg	evLutKB	Goslar	1641-1902	1
Drosedow	evLutKB	Goslar	1681-1891	1
Eichhorst	evLutKB	Goslar	1725-1934	1
Federow	evLutKB	Goslar	1763-1875	1
Feldberg	evLutKB	Goslar	1720-1934	4
Feldberg	evLutKB	Berlin-Dahlem	1839-1866	1
Fincken	evLutKB	Goslar	1670-1700	1
Fincken	evLutKB	Goslar	1747-1885	1
Friedland	evLutKB	Goslar	1705-1934	7
Friedrichshof	evLutKB	Goslar	1842-1884	1
Fürstenberg	evLutKB	Goslar	1646-1876	1
Fürstensee	evLutKB	Goslar	1637-1934	1
Gaarz	evLutKB	Goslar	1704-1863	1
Gardebehn	evLutKB	Goslar	1723-1934	1
Ganzkow	evLutKB	Goslar	1810-1859	1
Gehren	evLutKB	Goslar	1674-1925	2
Genzkow	evLutKB	Goslar	1676-1797	1
Gielow	evLutKB	Goslar	1765-1881	1
Glienke	evLutKB	Goslar	1693-1909	2
Glocksin	evLutKB	Goslar	1831-1934	1
Gnoien	evLutKB	Goslar	1849-1861	1
Gnoien	evLutKB	Goslar	1654-1898	4

Location	Nature of Material	Where Filmed	Dates Covered	No. of Rolls
Gnoien	Census	Goslar	1819	1
Göhren	evLutKB	Goslar	1745-1934	3
Golm	evLutKB	Goslar	1692-1884	1
Gorschendorf	evLutKB	Goslar	1704-1933	1
Grabow	evLutKB	Goslar	1661-1876	1
Gramelow	evLutKB	Goslar	1733-1933	1
Granzin	evLutKB	Goslar	1700-1875	1
Gross Varchow	evLutKB	Goslar	1677-1934	3
Gross Daberkow	evLutKB	Goslar	1803-1875	1
Gross Gievitz	evLutKB	Goslar	1626-1879	1
Gross Gievitz	evLutKB	Goslar	1718-1934	2
Gross Helle	evLutKB	Goslar	1723-1934	1
Gross Leuthen	evLutKB	Goslar	1679-1836	1
Gross Lubolz	evLutKB	Goslar	1854-1941	1
Gross Lukow	evLutKB	Goslar	1676-1921	1
Gross Methling	evLutKB	Goslar	1652-1875	1
Gross Quassow	evLutKB	Goslar	1637-1934	1
Gross Vielen	evLutKB	Goslar	1697-1934	1
Grünow	evLutKB	Goslar	1680-1937	2
Grüssow	evLutKB	Goslar	1747-1881	1
Gutzkow	evLutKB	Goslar	1737-1821	1
Helpt	evLutKB	Goslar	1746-1926	1
Hinrichshagen	evLutKB	Goslar	1745-1934	1
Hinrichshagen	evLutKB	Goslar	1728-1810	1
Hohen Demzin	evLutKB	Goslar	1652-1934	1
Hohen Mistorf	evLutKB	Goslar	1661-1934	3
Hohen Wangelin	evLutKB	Goslar	1723-1875	2
Hohenzieritz	evLutKB	Goslar	1734-1875	1
Holzendorf	evLutKB	Goslar	1650-1875	1

Location	Nature of Material	Where Filmed	Dates Covered	No. of Rolls
Huttenhof	evLutKB	Goslar	1737-1821	1
Ihlenfeld	evLutKB	Goslar	1801-1934	1
Ihlenfeld	evLutKB	Goslar	1718-1934	2
Ivenack	evLutKB	Goslar	1681-1899	3
Ivenack	Census	Goslae	1819	1
Jabel	evLutKB	Goslar	1640-1864	2
Jaebetz	evLutKB	Goslar	1747-1885	1
Jatzke	evLutKB	Goslar	1676-1797	1
Jördenstorf	evLutKB	Goslar	1647-1934	3
Jürgensdorf	evLutKB	Goslar	1727-1913	1
Kakeldutt	evLutKB	Goslar	1664-1928	1
Kambs	evLutKB	Goslar	1787-1921	1
Karchow	evLutKB	Goslar	1710-1905	1
Kaselin	evLutKB	Goslar	1801-1885	1
Kastorf	evLutKB	Goslar	1704-1898	2
Kieve	evLutKB	Goslar	1661-1933	2
Kittendorf	evLutKB	Goslar	1697-1934	3
Kleindaberkow	evLutKB	Goslar	1650-1875	1
Klein Helle	evLutKB	Goslar	1723-1934	1
Klein Mitzow	evLutKB	Goslar	1650-1875	1
Kleppelshagen	evLutKB	Goslar	1674-1925	1
Klink	evLutKB	Goslar	1718-1934	1
Klink	evLutKB	Goslar	1686-1896	1
Klockow	evLutKB	Goslar	1705-1934	1
Knüppeldamm	evLutKB	Goslar	1801-1885	1
Knüppeldamm	evLutKB	Goslar	1747-1885	1
Kogel	evLutKB	Goslar	1740-1915	1
Kotelow	evLutKB	Goslar	1705-1934	1
Kotelow	evLutKB	Goslar	1786-1833	1

Location	Nature of Material	Where Filmed	Dates Covered	No. of Rolls
Kratzeburg	evLutKB	Goslar	1700-1875	2
Krausnick	evLutKB	Hannover	1660-1903	3
Krausnick	evLutKB	Goslar	1660-1903	2
Kreckow	evLutKB	Goslar	1747-1862	1
Krumbeck	evLutKB	Goslar	1715-1934	1
Krummel	evLutKB	Goslar	1672-1934	1
Kublank	evLutKB	Goslar	1692-1884	1
Kussow	evLutKB	Goslar	1740-1867	1
Lapitz	evLutKB	Goslar	1744-1922	1
Lärz	evLutKB	Goslar	1672-1934	2
Leizen	evLutKB	Goslar	1672-1934	1
Leppin	evLutKB	Goslar	1810-1875	1
Leppin	evLutKB	Goslar	1745-1934	1
Levin	evLutKB	Goslar	1682-1882	1
Levin	evLutKB	Goslar	1787-1882	1
Levitzow	evLutKB	Goslar	1656-1886	1
Lexow	evLutKB	Goslar	1698-1919	1
Lichtenberg	evLutKB	Goslar	1715-1934	1
Liepen	evLutKB	Goslar	1798-1933	1
Lindow	evLutKB	Goslar	1673-1922	1
Linstow	evLutKB	Goslar	1649-1899	2
Loitz	evLutKB	Goslar	1733-1933	1
Lübben	evLutKB	Hannover	1646-1925	10
Lübben	evLutKB	Goslar	1632-1921	9
Lübben	evLutKB	Goslar	1646-1925	8
Lübben	evLutKB	Hannover	1632-1921	9
Lubbersdorf	evLutKB	Goslar	1786-1833	1
Lubbersdorf	evLutKB	Goslar	1705-1934	1
Lübkow	evLutKB	Goslar	1744-1922	1

Location	Nature of Material	Where Filmed	Dates Covered	No. of Rolls
Lüdershof	evLutKB	Goslar	1723-1934	1
Ludorf	evLutKB	Goslar	1672-1934	1
Lühburg	evLutKB	Goslar	1671-1901	2
Lukow	evLutKB	Goslar	1676-1921	3
Luplow	evLutKB	Goslar	1677-1934	1
Lütgendorf	evLutKB	Goslar	1753-1913	1
Luttenhagen	evLutKB	Goslar	1715-1934	1
Malchin	Census	Goslar	1819	1
Malchin	evLutKB	Goslar	1631-1915	5
Malchin	JüdGem	Goslar	1787-1935	1
Malchin	evLutKB	Goslar	1707-1876	1
Malchow	Census	Goslar	1819	1
Malchow	evLutKB	Goslar	1698-1881	1
Malchow	evLutKB	Goslar	1698-1919	4
Malchow	evLutKB	Goslar	1826-1842	1
Massow	evLutKB	Goslar	1670-1885	1
Matzdorf	evLutKB	Goslar	1650-1875	1
Melz	evLutKB	Goslar	1675-1809	1
Mildenitz	evLutKB	Goslar	1803-1875	1
Minzow	evLutKB	Goslar	1711-1904	1
Mirow	evLutKB	Goslar	1690-1922	6
Mollenstorf	evLutKB	Goslar	1697-1934	1
Mölln	evLutKB	Goslar	1723-1934	3
Nätebow	evLutKB	Goslar	1672-1934	1
Neddemin	evLutKB	Goslar	1703-1934	1
Neetzka	evLutKB	Goslar	1692-1884	1
Neu Kaebelich	evLutKB	Goslar	1665-1875	1
Neubrandenburg	LDS records	Salt Lake City	1917-1930	1
Neubrandenburg	evLutKB	Goslar	1700-1875	6

Location	Nature of Material	Where Filmed	Dates Covered	No. of Rolls
Neubrandenburg	evLutKB	Goslar	1611-1880	1
Neuenkirchen	evLutKB	Goslar	1718-1934	2
Neuenkirchen	evLutKB	Goslar	1718-1934	1
Neufeld	evLutKB	Goslar	1664-1928	1
Neugarten	evLutKB	Goslar	1715-1934	1
Neukalen	evLutKB	Goslar	1677-1885	2
Neukalen	JüdGem	Goslar	1787-1935	1
Neukalen	evLutKB	Goslar	1704-1875	2
Neukalen	Census	Goslar	1819	1
Neustrelitz	evLutKB	Goslar	1809-1921	1
Neustrelitz	evLutKB	Goslar	1736-1928	1
Neustrelitz	evLutKB	Goslar	1637-1934	7
Neustrelitz	evLutKB	Goslar	1697-1934	1
Neverin	evLutKB	Goslar	1718-1934	2
Pasenow	evLutKB	Goslar	1668-1934	1
Pasewalk	evLutKB	Berlin-Dahlem	1728-1936	4
Pasewalk	Civil records	Berlin	1717	1
Pasewalk	Minute-book of butchers	Berlin	1734-1765	1
Passentin	evLutKB	Goslar	1746-1930	1
Penzlin	evLutKB	Goslar	1747-1898	6
Penzlin	Census	Goslar	1819	1
Penzlin	JüdGem	Goslar	1787-1935	1
Podewall	evLutKB	Goslar	1703-1934	1
Polzow	Kirche	Berlin	1695-1838	1
Poppentin	evLutKB	Goslar	1686-1896	1
Potzlow	evKB	Berlin	1760-1804	1
Prenzlau	evKB	Hannover	1543, 1577, 1600	1

Location	Nature of Material	Where Filmed	Dates Covered	No. of Rolls
Prenzlau	evKB	Hannover	1319-1560 1617-1922	8
Prenzlau	Civil Guard list	Goslar	1735-1950	10
Prenzlau	Military rolls	Berlin-Dahlem	1880-1889	1
Prenzlau	Military rolls	Berlin-Dahlem	1860-1900	2
Prenzlau	Tax records	Goslar	1548-1840	3
Prenzlau	French RefKB	Hannover	1687-1931	1
Prenzlau	STA	Goslar	1586-1918	3
Prenzlau	Deutsch RefKB	Hannover	1695-1938	2
Prenzlau	evKB	Hannover	1584-1876	7
Prenzlau	evKB	Hannover	1625-1899	7
Prenzlau	evKB	Hannover	1235-1944	9
Prenzlau	evLutKB	Berlin-Dahlem	1766-1914	4
Prenzlau	evLutKB	Goslar	1617-1922	5
Prenzlau	evLutKB	Hannover	1617-1922	8
Prenzlau	evLutKB	Goslar	1625-1899	6
Prenzlau	evLutKB	Goslar	1631-1885	7
Prenzlau	evLutKB	Goslar	1600-1876	5
Prenzlau	French RefKB	Goslar	1687-1931	2
Prenzlau	German RefKB	Goslar	1695-1931	2
Prenzlau	MilKB	Berlin-Dahlem	1721-1765	1
Priborn	evLutKB	Goslar	1705-1909	1
Prillwitz	evLutKB	Goslar	1734-1975	2
Qualzow	evLutKB	Goslar	1664-1928	1
Quastenberg	evLutKB	Goslar	1756-1875	2
Rahnenfelde	evLutKB	Goslar	1744-1922	1

Location	Nature of Material	Where Filmed	Dates Covered	No. of Rolls
Rambow	evLutKB	Goslar	1645-1890	2
Ramelow	evLutKB	Goslar	1650-1935	1
Rattey	evLutKB	Goslar	1650-1875	1
Rechlin	evLutKB	Goslar	1685-1811	1
Rehberg	evLutKB	Goslar	1745-1931	1
Rittermanns-hagen	evLutKB	Goslar	1648-1890	2
Ritzerow	evLutKB	Goslar	1727-1913	1
Röbel	evLutKB	Goslar	1672-1934	3
Röbel	evLutKB	Goslar	1675-1864	5
Röbel	Census	Goslar	1819	1
Röckwitz	evLutKB	Goslar	1737-1875	1
Rödlin	evLutKB	Goslar	1731-1934	3
Roga	evLutKB	Goslar	1704-1933	1
Rogeez	evLutKB	Goslar	1740-1915	1
Roggenhagen	evLutKB	Goslar	1832-1875	1
Roggentin	evLutKB	Goslar	1664-1928	3
Röpersdorf	evLutKB	Goslar	1845-1944	1
Rossow	JüdGem	Goslar	1787-1935	1
Rühlow	evLutKB	Goslar	1693-1909	2
Rumpshagen	evLutKB	Goslar	1676-1934	1
Sadelkow	evLutKB	Goslar	1693-1909	1
Satow	evLutKB	Goslar	1740-1915	2
Schenkenberg	evLutKB	Goslar	1674-1944	1
Schenkenberg	evLutKB	Goslar	1674-1824	1
Schenkenberg	evKB	Hannover	1674-1832	2
Schlepzig	evLutKB	Goslar	1662-1881	2
Schloen	evLutKB	Goslar	1661-1900	2
Schonau	evLutKB	Goslar	1718-1934	1

Location	Nature of Material	Where Filmed	Dates Covered	No. of Rolls
Schönbeck	evLutKB	Goslar	1673-1933	3
Schönhausen	evLutKB	Goslar	1650-1875	1
Schönwerder	evLutKB	Berlin-Dahlem	1668-1735	1
Schwanbeck	evLutKB	Goslar	1650-1934	2
Schwandt	evLutKB	Goslar	1723-1934	1
Schwarz	evLutKB	Goslar	1672-1934	1
Schwarz	evLutKB	Goslar	1688-1875	1
Schwerin	evLutKB	Goslar	1672-1934	1
Schwichtenberg	evLutKB	Goslar	1687-1930	1
Schwinkendorf	evLutKB	Goslar	1673-1934	3
Sietow	evLutKB	Goslar	1686-1896	2
Somerstorf	evLutKB	Goslar	1680-1934	1
Spitzkuhn	evLutKB	Goslar	1672-1934	1
Sponholz	evLutKB	Goslar	1740-1867	1
Stargard	evLutKB	Goslar	1756-1875	1
Staven	evLutKB	Goslar	1710-1875	1
Stavenhagen Reuterstadt	evLutKB	Goslar	1727-1913	5
Strasen	evLutKB	Goslar	1865-1883	1
Stuer	evLutKB	Goslar	1681-1911	2
Sulten	evLutKB	Goslar	1697-1934	1
Teschendorf	evLutKB	Goslar	1733-1933	2
Teterow	evLutKB	Goslar	1661-1885	5
Thürkow	evLutKB	Goslar	1656-1886	2
Thurow	evLutKB	Goslar	1637-1934	1
Triepkendorf	evLutKB	Goslar	1720-1897	2
Trollenhagen	evLutKB	Goslar	1709-1934	1
Uckermünde	evLutKB	Berlin-Dahlem	1820-1824	1
Userin	evLutKB	Berlin-Dahlem	1637-1934	1
Varchentin	evLutKB	Berlin-Dahlem	1681-1875	2

Location	Nature of Material	Where Filmed	Dates Covered	No. of Rolls
Vielist	evLutKB	Berlin-Dahlem	1680-1934	2
Vipperow	evLutKB	Berlin-Dahlem	1705-1909	1
Voigtsdorf	evLutKB	Goslar	1650-1875	1
Walkendorf	evLutKB	Goslar	1677-1920	2
Wanzka	evLutKB	Goslar	1731-1934	1
Wanzka	evLutKB	Goslar	1680-1810	1
Warbende	evLutKB	Goslar	1716-1934	4
Warbende	evLutKB	Berlin-Dahlem	1863-1875	1
Waren	evLutKB	Goslar	1699-1876	4
Warlin	evLutKB	Goslar	1711-1934	1
Warnkenhagen	evLutKB	Goslar	1691-1875	3
Wasdow	evLutKB	Goslar	1704-1871	1
Weitin	evLutKB	Goslar	1699-1875	2
Wesenberg	evLutKB	Goslar	1681-1891	3
Wesenberg	evLutKB	Berlin-Dahlem	1681-1809	1
Wetzenow	Kirche	Berlin	1695-1838	1
Wismar	evLutKB	Berlin-Dahlem	1816-1898	1
Wittenborn	evLutKB	Goslar	1786-1833	1
Wittenborn	evLutKB	Goslar	1674-1925	1
Wittmannsdorf	evLutKB	Goslar	1664-1826	1
Woggersin	evLutKB	Goslar	1707-1876	1
Wokuhl	evLutKB	Goslar	1736-1875	2
Wolde	evLutKB	Goslar	1737-1821	1
Wrechen	evLutKB	Goslar	1745-1934	1
Wredenhagen	evLutKB	Goslar	1661-1876	2
Wrodow	evLutKB	Goslar	1744-1922	1
Wulkenzien	evLutKB	Goslar	1770-1896	2
Wustrow	evLutKB	Goslar	1694-1741	1
Zachow	evLutKB	Goslar	1699-1875	1

Location	Nature of Material	Where Filmed	Dates Covered	No. of Rolls
Zahren	evLutKB	Goslar	1697-1934	1
Zartwitz	evLutKB	Goslar	1664-1928	1
Zepkow	evLutKB	Goslar	1661-1876	1
Zielow	evLutKB	Goslar	1705-1909	1
Ziethen	evLutKB	Goslar	1701-1889	1
Zwiedorf	evLutKB	Goslar	1737-1821 1873-1875	1

POTSDAM

Location	Nature of Material	Where Filmed	Dates Covered	No. of Rolls
Altruppin	MilKB	Hannover	1741-1811	2
Banzendorf	evKB	Berlin-Dahlem	1691-1802	2
Brandenburg	MilKB	Berlin-Dahlem	1740-1913	7
Brandenburg	MilKB	Hannover	1748-1811	1
Braunsberg	MilKB	Eibenstock	1833-1884	1
Cammer	evKB	Berlin-Dahlem	1644-1735	1
Dierberg	evKB	Berlin-Dahlem	1691-1802	2
Döberitz	MilKB	Berlin-Dahlem	1897-1938	1
Döberitz	KB	Berlin	1761-1874	9
Döberitz	evKB	Berlin-Dahlem	1681-1808	1
Falkensee	evKB	Berlin-Dahlem	1659-1804	3
Ferbitz	KB	Berlin	1761-1874	9
Fürstenberg	evKB	Berlin-Dahlem	1769-1876	2
Fahrland	evKB	Berlin-Dahlem	1640-1757	1
Falkenrehde	evKB	Berlin-Dahlem	1626-1712	1
Friedenshorst	evKB	Berlin	1722-1785	1
Fürstenberg	evKB	Goslar	1646-1731	1
Golzow	evKB	Berlin-Dahlem		1
Grosswoltersdorf	KB	Berlin	1772-1803	1
Grosswoltersdorf	evKB	Berlin-Dahlem	1652-1763	2
Hindenberg	evKB	Berlin-Dahlem	1691-1802	2
Jüterborg	MilKB	Berlin-Dahlem	1860-1916	1
Jüterborg	MilKB	Berlin-Dahlem	1832-1882	1
Königs Wusterhausen	MilKB	Berlin-Dahlem	1898	1
Kyritz	MilKB	Eibenstock	1876	1
Kyritz	KB	Berlin-Dahlem	1861-1879	1

Location	Nature of Material	Where Filmed	Dates Covered	No. of Rolls
Kyritz	MilKB	Hannover	1724-1800	1
Kyritz	MilKB	Hannover	1801-1809	1
Liebenwalde	MilKB	Berlin-Dahlem	1869-1871	1
Luckenwalde	MilKB	Berlin-Dahlem	1860-1916	1
Marwitz	Misc.	Berlin-Dahlem	1860-1916	1
Mellnsdorf	See Blonsdorf			
Nauen	MilKB	Berlin-Dahlem	1810-1878	1
Neuruppin	STA	Berlin-Dahlem	1584-1887	1
Neuruppin	MilKB	Eibenstock	1820-1876	1
Neuruppin	MilKB	Berlin-Dahlem	1734-1934	2
Oranienburg	MilKB	Eibenstock	1839-1876	1
Oranienburg	MilKB	Berlin-Dahlem	1810-1878	1
Paretz	evKB	Berlin-Dahlem	1671-1743	1
Phöben	KB	Berlin-Dahlem	1672-1802	1
Potsdam	MilKB	Berlin-Dahlem	1888-1900	3
Potsdam	MilKB	Eibenstock	1839-1877	1
Potsdam	MilKB	Berlin-Dahlem	1662-1944	1
Potsdam	MilKB	Hannover	1918-1921	1
Potsdam	MilKB	Berlin-Dahlem	1662-1715	28
Potsdam	MilKB	Hannover	1790-1804	1
Potsdam	KB	Berlin-Dahlem	1847-1852, 1854	1
Potsdam	evKB	Berlin-Dahlem	1617-1715	1
Rathenow	LDS records	Salt Lake City	1922-1930	1
Rathenow	MilKB	Berlin-Dahlem	1810-1878	1
Rathenow	KB	Berlin-Dahlem	1733-1930	1
Rossow	evKB	Goslar	1707-1875	1
Rossow	evKB	Goslar	1799-1896	1
Satzkorn	evKB	Berlin-Dahlem	1640-1757	1

Location	Nature of Material	Where Filmed	Dates Covered	No. of Rolls
Schonberg	evKB	Goslar	1799-1896	1
Schönebeck	MilKB	Hannover	1774-1806	1
Seddin	evKB	Berlin-Dahlem	1831-1887	1
Teltow	MilKB	Berlin-Dahlem	1870-1900	24
Teltow	MilKB	Berlin-Dahlem	1873-1900	43
Tornow	evKB	Goslar	1671-1877	2
Trebbin	KB	Berlin-Dahlem	1766-1782	1
Treuenbrietzen	MilKB	Eibenstock	1833-1868	1
Treuenbrietzen	MilKB	Berlin-Dahlem	1820-1824	1
Treuenbrietzen	MilKB	Berlin-Dahlem	1834-1876	1
Treuenbrietzen	MilKB	Hannover	1764-1806	1
Treuenbrietzen	evKB	Berlin-Dahlem	1688-1728	1
Wildenbruch	evKB	Berlin-Dahlem	1728-1848	1
Wusterhausen	MilKB	Eibenstock	1869-1872	1
Wusterhausen	MilKB	Berlin-Dahlem	1810-1878	1
Zehdenick	MilKB	Berlin-Dahlem	1801-1870	1
Zossen	MilKB	Berlin-Dahlem	1898	1

ROSTOCK

Location	Nature of Material	Where Filmed	Dates Covered	No. of Rolls
Alt-Bukow	evLutKB	Goslar	1652-1921	2
Alt-Karin	evLutKB	Goslar	1653-1934	2
Babst	evLutKB	Goslar	1693-1934	3
Bad Doberan	evLutKB	Goslar	1675-1884	3
Bad Sülze	evLutKB	Goslar	1672-1934	4
Beidendorf	evLutKB	Goslar	1654-1882	3
Bentwisch	evLutKB	Goslar	1704-1823	3
Berendshagen	evLutKB	Goslar	1652-1866	1
Bergen	evLutKB	Goslar	1280-1618	1
Biendorf	evLutKB	Goslar	1776-1875	1
Blankenhagen	evLutKB	Goslar	1704-1894	2
Börgerende	evLutKB	Goslar	1653-1785	2
Börzow	evLutKB	Goslar	1612-1899	2
Bossow	evLutKB	Goslar	1740-1933	1
Buchholz	evLutKB	Goslar	1745-1926	6
Bukow	evLutKB	Goslar	1687-1875	3
Cammin	evLutKB	Goslar	1665-1933	3
Dambeck	evLutKB	Goslar	1658-1917	2
Damshagen	evLutKB	Goslar	1648-1900	2
Dänschenburg	evLutKB	Goslar	1704-1894	1
Dassow	evLutKB	Goslar	1671-1877	2
Dettmamsdorf	evLutKB	Goslar	1691-1869	3
Diedrichshagen	evLutKB	Goslar	1659-1921	2
Dreveskirchen	evLutKB	Goslar	1653-1921	
Elmenhorst	evLutKB	Goslar	1658-1973	1
Friedrichshagen	evLutKB	Goslar	1651-1937	2
Gägelow	evLutKB	Goslar	1700-1934	4
Garz	evLutKB	Berlin-Dahlem	1677-1790	1

Location	Nature of Material	Where Filmed	Dates Covered	No. of Rolls
Glowitz	evLutKB	Berlin	1951-1957	1
Goldebbe	evLutKB	Goslar	1654-1913	1
Greifswald	evLutKB	Berlin-Dahlem	1821-1935	1
Greifswald	MKB	Berlin-Dahlem	1801-1932	1
Gresenhorst	evLutKB	Goslar	1704-1894	1
Gressow	evLutKB	Goslar	1654-1896	2
Grevesmühlen	evLutKB	Goslar	1688-1905	4
Grevesmühlen	Census	Goslar	1819	
Grevesmühlen	STA evKB	Goslar	1658-1913	1
Grubenhagen	evLutKB	Goslar	1667-1875	2
Hanstorf	evLutKB	Goslar	1661-1891	1
Heiligenhagen	evLutKB	Goslar	1657-1805	1
Herrnburg	STA	Goslar	1645-1934	3
Herrnburg	evLutKB	Goslar	1796-1875	1
Hohen Luckow	evLutKB	Goslar	1660-1934	5
Hohen Viecheln	evLutKB	Goslar	1713-1900	2
Hohenkirchen	evLutKB	Goslar	1706-1900	3
Hornstorf	evLutKB	Goslar	1732-1875	1
Insel Poel	evLutKB	Goslar	1700-1934	4
Kalkhorst	evLutKB	Goslar	1639-1936	2
Karin	evLutKB	Goslar	1653-1934	2
Kavelstorf	evLutKB	Goslar	1689-1934	2
Kessin	evLutKB	Goslar	1709-1925	2
Mulsow	evLutKB	Goslar	1654-1975	2
Kleitz	evLutKB	Berlin-Dahlem	1650-1934	7
Kröpelin	Census	Goslar	1819	1
Kröpelin	JüdGem	Goslar	1787-1935	1
Kropelin	evLutKB	Goslar	1738-1875	3

Location	Nature of Material	Where Filmed	Dates Covered	No. of Rolls
Lambrechtshagen	evLutKB	Goslar	1696-1875	1
Lancken	evLutKB	Goslar	1643-1923	1
Lichtenhagen	evLutKB	Goslar	1675-1930	4
Lübow	evLutKB	Goslar	1654-1875	3
Mandelshagen	evLutKB	Goslar	1704-1894	1
Marlow	Census	Goslar	1819	1
Marlow	JüdGem	Goslar	1787-1935	1
Marlow	evLutKB	Goslar	1665-1933	5
Mecklenburg	evLutKB	Goslar	1725-1905	2
Miekenhagen	Census	Goslar	1819	1
Mummendorf	evLutKB	Goslar	1653-1934	1
Netzeband	evLutKB	Goslar	1708-1798	1
Neubukow	Census	Goslar	1819	1
Neubukow	evLutKB	Goslar	1709-1892	3
Neuburg	evLutKB	Goslar	1653-1911	3
Neukloster	Census	Goslar	1819	1
Neukloster	evLutKB	Goslar	1694-1905	3
Ostseebad Kühlungsborn	evLutKB	Goslar	1666-1875	1
Ostseebad Wustrow	evLutKB	Goslar	1651-1875	1
Parkentin	evLutKB	Goslar	1639-1905	2
Passee	evLutKB	Goslar	1654-1875	1
Petchow	evLutKB	Goslar	1616-1875	2
Polchow	evLutKB	Goslar	1651-1889	2
Proseken	evLutKB	Goslar	1693-1912	2
Reinshagen	evLutKB	Goslar	1653-1875	2
Rethwisch	evLutKB	Goslar	1641-1876	2
Retschow	evLutKB	Berlin-Dahlem	1641-1911	3
Ribnitz-Damgarten	evLutKB	Goslar	1589-1876	13

Location	Nature of Material	Where Filmed	Dates Covered	No. of Rolls
Roggow	evLutKB	Goslar	1731-1917	2
Roggenstorf	evLutKB	Goslar	1640-1876	2
Rostock	LDS records	Salt Lake City	1914-1949	4
Rostock	evLutKB	Goslar	1562-1933	2
Rostock	JüdGem	Goslar	1787-1935	2
Rostock	rkKB	Goslar	1758-1933	1
Rovershagen	evLutKB	Goslar	1703-1910	2
Ruting	Census	Goslar	1819	1
Samtenz	evLutKB	Berlin-Dahlem	1792-1839	1
Sanitz	evLutKB	Goslar	1672-1934	4
Satow	evLutKB	Goslar	1751-1902	2
Schönberg	evLutKB	Goslar	1640-1875	6
Selmsdorf	evLutKB	Goslar	1624-1909	2
Stabelow	evLutKB	Goslar	1639-1905	1
Stralsund	Forsvars Departement	Stockholm	1728-1750	6
Stralsund	Gläser-zunft	Berlin	1570	1
Stralsund	MKB	Berlin-Dahlem	1818-1860	1
Stralsund	Kriegsrats-gerichte	Stockholm	1705-1890	25
Tessin	evLutKB	Goslar	1787-1934	3
Thelkow	evLutKB	Goslar	1646-1912	3
Thulendorf	evLutKB	Goslar	1672-1934	1
Vilz	evLutKB	Goslar	1740-1875	1
Volkenshagen	evLutKB	Goslar	1688-1893	2
Volkshagen	evLutKB	Goslar	1704-1894	1
Wendisch Mulsow	evLutKB	Goslar	1654-1875	1
Westenbrügge	evLutKB	Goslar	1649-1882	1
Willershagen	evLutKB	Goslar	1704-1894	1

Location	Nature of Material	Where Filmed	Dates Covered	No. of Rolls
Wismar	evLutKB	Goslar	1765-1905	12
Wismar	Kriegsrat-sakte	Stockholm	1691-1713	3
Wolgast	evLutKB MKB	Berlin-Dahlem	1801-1932	2
Woldegk	evLutKB	Goslar	1668-1934	7
Zurow	evLutKB	Goslar	1695-1934	1

SCHWERIN

Location	Nature of Material	Where Filmed	Dates Covered	No. of Rolls
Alt Meteln	evKB	Goslar	1685-1875	2
Bad Wilsnach	KB	Dahlem	c. 1500-1830	1
Barkow	evKB	Goslar	1766-1875	3
Baumgarten	evKB	Goslar	1690-1875	2
Bellin	evKB	Goslar	1650-1873	1
Benthen	evKB	Goslar	1672-1875	1
Bernitt	evKB	Goslar	1659-1856	1
Blücher	evKB	Goslar	1700-1874	2
Boddin	evKB	Goslar	1671-1875	3
Boitin	evKB	Goslar	1740-1901	1
Brenz	evKB	Goslar	1787-1875	1
Brüel	evKB	Goslar	1685-1934	3
Brunow	evKB	Goslar	1644-1892	3
Brunow	evKB	Goslar	1787-1891	1
Burow	evKB	Goslar	1660-1876	1
Bützow	evKB	Goslar	1670-1875	6
Bützow	KB	Goslar	1698-1875	1
Camin	evKB	Goslar	1677-1903	1
Carlow	evKB	Goslar	1614-1910	2
Conow	evKB	Goslar	1692-1875	2
Cramon	evKB	Goslar	1701-1881	1
Crivitz	evKB	Dahlem	1664-1764	1
Crivitz	evKB	Goslar	1664-1875	4
Dambeck	evKB	Goslar	1674-1901	1
Damm	evKB	Goslar	1678-1922	1
Damm	evKB	Dahlem	1795-1822	1
Demen	evKB	Goslar	1653-1900	1

Location	Nature of Material	Where Filmed	Dates Covered	No. of Rolls
Demern	evKB	Goslar	1641-1888	2
Döbbersen	evKB	Goslar	1670-1885	2
Dobbertin	evKB	Goslar	1674-1903	2
Dömitz	evKB	Goslar	1635-1896	5
Drefahl	evKB	Dahlem	1787-1891	1
Dreilötzow	evKB	Goslar	1695-1875	1
Eickelberg	evKB	Goslar	1740-1875	1
Eldena	evKB	Dahlem	1780-1830	1
Eldena	evKB	Goslar	1780-1934	2
Frauenmark	evKB	Goslar	1714-1882	2
Gadebasch	evKB	Goslar	1626-1879	6
Gägelow	evKB	Goslar	1651-1891	2
Gammelin	evKB	Goslar	1713-1919	2
Garwitz	evKB	Goslar	1672-1875	3
Garwitz	evKB	Dahlem	1795-1822	1
Gischow	evKB	Goslar	1689-1916	1
Gnersdorf	evKB	Goslar	1759-1891	1
Goldberg	evKB	Goslar	1656-1924	3
Gorlosen	evKB	Goslar	1666-1876	6
Grabow	evKB	Goslar	1640-1910	7
Granzin	evKB	Goslar	1704-1896	2
Grazin	evKB	Goslar	1664-1876	2
Grebbin	evKB	Goslar	1657-1922	2
Gresse	evKB	Goslar	1652-1875	1
Gross Brütz	evKB	Goslar	1707-1914	4
Gross Lasch	evKB	Goslar	1640-1904	5
Gross Pankow	evKB	Goslar	1681-1871	2
Gross Raden	evKB	Goslar	1654-1875	1
Gross Salitz	evKB	Goslar	1645-1929	1

Location	Nature of Material	Where Filmed	Dates Covered	No. of Rolls
Gross Trebow	evKB	Goslar	1707-1890	3
Gross Upahl	evKB	Goslar	1745-1907	1
Gülzow	evKB	Goslar	1691-1902	2
Güstrow	evKB	Goslar	1672-1905	3
Güstrow	evKB	Goslar	1774-1933	3
Güstrow	evKB	Goslar	1634-1876	3
Güstrow	evKB	Goslar	1817-1874	1
Güstrow	evKB MKB	Dahlem	1887-1927	1
Güstrow	evKB	Goslar	1677-1731	10
Hagenow	evKB	Goslar	1689-1927	5
Herzberg	evKB	Goslar	1684-1814	1
Herzfeld	evKB	Goslar	1693-1878	1
Hohen Sprenz	evKB	Goslar	1639-1875	3
Holzendorf	evKB	Goslar	1699-1865	2
Jesendorf	evKB	Goslar	1740-1875	1
Kambs	evKB	Goslar	1701-1929	2
Karbow	evKB	Goslar	1662-1883	1
Kirch-Grambow	evKB	Goslar	1640-1671	2
Kirch Jesar	evKB	Goslar	1834-1934	1
Kirchkogel	evKB	Goslar	1754-1882	1
Kladow	evKB	Goslar	1689-1873	1
Kladrum	evKB	Goslar	1715-1934	3
Klein Belitz	evKB	Goslar	1660-1934	5
Klinken	evKB	Goslar	1706-1934	3
Körchow	evKB	Goslar	1740-1900	1
Krakow	evKB	Goslar	1689-1899	3
Kreien	evKB	Goslar	1667-1857	1
Kritzkow	evKB	Goslar	1750-1885	1
Kuhlrade	evKB	Goslar	1659-1875	2

Location	Nature of Material	Where Filmed	Dates Covered	No. of Rolls
Kuppentin	evKB	Goslar	1680-1875	2
Lagge	evKB	Goslar	1723-1902	3
Leussow	evKB	Goslar	1671-1914	2
Lohmen	evKB	Goslar	1641-1934	2
Lüblow	evKB	Goslar	1712-1875	3
Lüblow	evKB	Goslar	1724-1875	2
Lübsee	evKB	Goslar	1653-1876	1
Lübtheen	evKB	Goslar	1706-1875	3
Lübz	evKB	Goslar	1673-1909	5
Lüdershagen	evKB	Goslar	1779-1896	2
Ludwigslust	evKB	Goslar	1864-1934	1
Ludwigslust	evKB	Goslar	1770-1907	6
Ludwigslust	MKB	Dahlem	1873-1911	1
Lüssow	evKB	Goslar	1653-1876	2
Marnitz	evKB	Goslar	1750-1905	3
Melkof	evKB	Goslar	1870-1875	1
Mestlin	evKB	Goslar	1647-1934	1
Moisall	evKB	Goslar	1683-1889	1
Möllenbeck	evKB	Goslar	1752-1924	1
Muchow	evKB	Goslar	1666-1830	3
Mühlen-Eichsen	evKB	Goslar	1670-1918	2
Neese	evKB	Goslar	1649-1918	2
Neu Poserin	evKB	Goslar	1660-1875	3
NeuenKirchen	evKB	Goslar	1740-1905	2
Neu Gülze	evKB	Goslar	1668-1933	2
Neustadt-Glewe	evKB	Goslar	1675-1864	4
Neustadt-Glewe	evKB	Dahlem	1770-1821	1
Pampow	evKB	Goslar	1677-1919	4
Pampow	evKB	Dahlem	1836-1854	1

Location	Nature of Material	Where Filmed	Dates Covered	No. of Rolls
Parchim	MKB	Dahlem	1867-1940	1
Parchim	evKB	Goslar	1651-1875	6
Parchim	evKB	Dahlem	1708-1786	1
Parchim	evKB	Goslar	1651-1875	3
Parum	evKB	Goslar	1647-1889	2
Passow	evKB	Goslar	1740-1799	1
Passow	evKB	Goslar	1801-1885	1
Peckatel	evKB	Goslar	1697-1934	3
Perleberg	MKB	Dahlem	1860-1938	1
Perleberg	MKB	Hannover	1860-1868	1
Perlin	evKB	Goslar	1668-1899	2
Picher	evKB	Goslar	1673-1936	5
Pinnow	evKB	Goslar	1657-1881	2
Plate	evKB	Goslar	1676-1882	3
Plau	evKB	Goslar	1711-1884	3
Pokrent	evKB	Goslar	1740-1934	2
Prestin	evKB	Goslar	1640-1934	3
Pretin	Guts-archiv	Dahlem	1674-1798	1
Pritzier	evKB	Goslar	1681-1885	2
Prüzen	evKB	Goslar	1745-1907	1
Qualitz	evKB	Goslar	1718-1869	1
Recknitz	evKB	Goslar	1659-1863	3
Redefin	evKB	Goslar	1651-1875	3
Redefin	evKB	Goslar	1847-1934	2
Rehna	evKB	Goslar	1641-1890	5
Retgendorf	evKB	Goslar	1680-1901	2
Roggendorf	evKB	Goslar	1650-1876	1
Rühn	evKB	Goslar	1638-1888	1
Schlagsdorf	evKB	Goslar	1641-1913	3

Location	Nature of Material	Where Filmed	Dates Covered	No. of Rolls
Schwaan	evKB	Goslar	1759-1880	3
Schwerin	evKB	Goslar	1604-1943	14
Schwerin	evKB	Goslar	1870-1875	1
Schwerin	evKB MKB	Dahlem	1873-1942	1
Schwerin	evKB	Goslar	1741-1943	7
Schwerin	evKB	Goslar	1869-1934	3
Schwerin	evKB	Goslar	1695-1927	3
Serrahn	evKB	Goslar	1633-1875	2
Slate	evKB	Goslar	1660-1759	1
Söllentin	evKB	Berlin-Hauptarchiv	1701-1842	1
Spornitz	evKB	Goslar	1648-1896	2
Sternberg	evKB	Goslar	1730-1934	4
Stralendorf	evKB	Goslar	1693-1875	2
Suckow	evKB	Goslar	1695-1870	2
Sülsdorf	evKB	Dahlem	1729-1905	3
Tarnow	evKB	Goslar	1653-1875	2
Techentin	evKB	Goslar	1645-1803	2
Tempzin	evKB	Goslar	1740-1875	1
Uelitz	evKB	Goslar	1786-1898	3
Vellahn	evKB	Goslar	1665-1892	3
Vielank	evKB	Goslar	1651-1875	3
Vielank	evKB	Dahlem	1800-1873	1
Vietlübbe	evKB	Goslar	1740-1875	1
Vietlübbe	evKB	Goslar	1661-1861	1
Wamckow	evKB	Goslar	1630-1763	1
Warin	evKB	Goslar	1679-1875	2
Warin	evKB	Dahlem	1753-1795	1
Warsow	evKB	Goslar	1723-1895	3

Location	Nature of Material	Where Filmed	Dates Covered	No. of Rolls
Wattmannshagen	evKB	Goslar	1643-1875	3
Wittenburg	evKB	Goslar	1651-1890	5
Wittenförden	evKB	Goslar	1645-1895	2
Witzin	evKB	Goslar	1740-1875	1
Woosten	evKB	Goslar	1630-1828	1
Woserin	evKB	Goslar	1702-1907	2
Zapel	evKB	Goslar	1677-1885	1
Zarrentin	evKB	Goslar	1659-1882	4
Zarrentin	evKB	Dahlem	1776-1831	1
Zehna	evKB	Goslar	1740-1871	1
Zernin	evKB	Goslar	1787-1934	1
Ziegendorf	evKB	Goslar	1853-1934	1
Zittow	evKB	Goslar	1660-1891	3
Zweedorf	evKB	Goslar	1704-1903	1

SUHL

Location	Nature of Material	Where Filmed	Dates Covered	No. of Rolls
Asbach	STA	Marburg	1808-1812	2
Bad Liebenstein	evKB	Berlin-Dahlem	1614-1763	1
Barchfeld	STA	Marburg	1808-1812	2
Barchfeld	JüdGem	Marburg	1849-1874	1
Böhlen	evKB	Berlin-Dahlem	1701-1829	2
Breitungen	STA	Marburg	1808-1812	1
Eishausen	evKB	Berlin-Dahlem	1715-1812	1
Elgersburg	Book			
Fambach	STA	Marburg	1809-1813	2
Floh	STA	Marburg	1808-1812	1
Frauensee	Book			
Gehaus	evKB	Berlin-Dahlem	1641-1801	1
Gellershausen	evKB	Berlin-Dahlem	1476-1862	1
Goldlauter	LDS records	Salt Lake City	1600-1858	MF
Goldlauter	KB		1604-1852	5
Hellenberg		Steinbach Hallenberg		
Heidersheim		Goldlauter		
Herrenbreitung-en		Breitungen		
Hilburghausen	Book			
Ilmenau	Book			
Lagewiesen	evKB	Berlin-Dahlem	1627-1749	1
Lengfeld	evKB	Berlin-Dahlem	1574-1810	1
Meiningen	Book			
Neuhof	Book			
Oberstadt	evKB	Berlin-Dahlem	1592-1863	1
Oberweissbach	Book			
Rieth	evKB	Berlin-Dahlem	1622-1751	1

Location	Nature of Material	Where Filmed	Dates Covered	No. of Rolls
Rosa	evKB	Berlin-Dahlem	1725-1792	1
Rossdorf	evKB	Berlin-Dahlem	1560-1767	1
Sachsenbrunn Sachsendorf	evKB	Berlin-Dahlem	1560-1767	1
Schalkau	evKB	Berlin-Dahlem	1573-1809	1
Schleusingen	Book			
Schmalkalden	Justizamt	Marburg	1727-1796	5
Schmalden	JüdGem	Marburg	1849-1874	1
Schmalkalden	STA	Marburg	1808-1812	
Schweina		Bad Liebenstein		
Seidinstadt	evKB	Berlin-Dahlem	1701-1769	1
Seligenthal Floh	STA	Marburg	1808-1812	1
Springstille	STA	Marburg	1808-1812	1
Steinbach Hallenberg	STA	Marburg	1790-1820	3
Streudorf	evKB	Berlin-Dahlem	1606-1678	1
Suhl	Administration	Berlin-Dahlem	1766	1
Tiefenort	evKB	Berlin-Dahlem	1816-1854	1
Trusetal	STA	Marburg	1808-1812	1
Westhausen	evKB	Berlin-Dahlem	1557-1801	1
Zella-Mehlis	evKB	Berlin-Dahlem	1742-1799	1

TERRITORIES FORMERLY PART OF THE GERMAN EMPIRE
NOW WITHIN THE BORDERS
OF FRANCE, POLAND, OR THE SOVIET UNION

<u>BRANDENBURG</u>

Location	Nature of Material	Where Filmed	Dates Covered	No. of Rolls
Arensdorf -Stanica-	evKB	Warsaw	1811-1870	1
Arnswalde -Choszczno-	MilKB	Berlin-Dahlem	1831-1866	1
Arnswalde -Choszczno-	evKB	Warsaw	1835-1841	1
Arnswalde -Choszczno-	JüdGem	Berlin	1847-1853	1
Baudach -Budziechöw-	evKB	Warsaw	1661-1796	1
Berlinchen -Barlinek-	evKB	Warsaw	1839-1870	2
Berlinchen -Barlinek-	JüdGem	Berlin	1847-1853	1
Bernickow -Barnkowo-	evKB	Warsaw	1816-1857	1
Crossen -Krosno Odrzanskie-	evKB	Warsaw	1766-1778	1
Forst -Zasieki-	evKB	Warsaw	1738-1812	1
Frieberg -Neumark-	MilKB	Eibenstock Hannover	1772-1874	2
Strzelle -Krajenskie-	JüdGem	Berlin	1847-1853	1
Gablentz -Jabłoniec-	evKB	Warsaw	1661-1796	1
Gleissen -Glisno-	evKB	Warsaw	1671-1870	2
Güstewiese -Gosdowice-	evKB	Warsaw	1651-1750	1
Hanseberg -Krzymöw-	evKB	Warsaw	1707-1835	2

Location	Nature of Material	Where Filmed	Dates Covered	No. of Rolls
Herzogswalde -Zubröw-	evKB	Warsaw	1741-1870	1
Hohen Kränig -Krajnik Gorny-	evKB	Warsaw	1720-1862	2
Klemzig -Klepsk-	evKB	Goslar	1876-1945	1
Konigsberg Neumark -Chojna-	evKB	Warsaw	1581-1827	7
Kulm -Chełm Zarski-	Rök KB	Berlin	1753-1808	1
Kutschlau -Chociule-	ZSR	Berlin	1874-1881	1
Lansberg -Warthe- -Gorzow-	MilKB Rök KB	Eibenstock Hannover Zielona Gora	1742-1809 1856-1870	3 1
Liebenau -Lubrza-	ZSR STA	Berlin	1874-1937	6
Liebenow -Lubieniow-	evKB	Salt Lake City	1855-1870	1
Lindenhain -Chlebowo-	evKB	Warsaw	1664-1797	1
Lippehne -Lipiany-	evKB	Warsaw	1783-1830	1
Meekow -Miechow-	evKB	Warsaw	1811-1870	1
Moestchen -Mostki-	ZSR STA	Berlin	1874-1937	6
Mosau -Mozow-	ZST STA	Berlin	1874-1889	1
Mühlbock -Ołobok-	Rök KB	Zielona Gora	1728-1871	1
Mühlbock -Ołobok-	ZST STA	Berlin	1874-1937	4
Muschten -Myszecin-	ZSR STA	Berlin	1875-1937	4
Neuhöfchen -Nowy Dworek-	ZST STA	Berlin	1874-1937	5
Nieder Kranig -Krajnik Dolny-	evKB	Warsaw	1720-1862 1673-1693	2 1

Location	Nature of Material	Where Filmed	Dates Covered	No. of Rolls
Niedersaathen -Zaton Dolna-	evKB	Warsaw	1720-1784 1785-1853	1 1
Ojerzyce -Ojeriyce-	ZST STA	Berlin	1874-1882	1
Peetzig -Piasek-	evKB	Warsaw	1804-1837	1
Pommerzig -Pomersko-	ZSR STA	Berlin	1874-1937	8
Raduhn -Radun-	evKB	Warsaw	1683-1803	1
Rehdorf -Stoki-	evKB	Hannover	1677-1750	1
Rehdorf -Stoki-	evKB	Warsaw	1753-1836	1
Reipzig -Rycocice-	evKB	Warsaw	1628-1770	1
Rinnersdorf -Rusinow-	ZSR STA	Berlin	1874-1937	5
Rissen -Rosin-	ZST STA	Berlin	1874-1937	4
Rosenthal -Rozasnko-	evKB	Warsaw	1762-1814	1
Schlagenthin -Sławecin-	evKB	Warsaw	1793-1854	1
Schönrode -Dobrułow-	evKB	Warsaw	1811-1870	1
Schweinert -Swiniary-	evKB	Berlin-Dahlem	1729-1944	3
Sellnow -Zieleniewo-	evKB	Warsaw	1751-1845	1
Sommerfeld -Lubsko-	evKB	Warsaw	1657-1810	1
Sorau -Zary-	evKB	Berlin	1835-1837	1
Sorau -Zary-	evKB	Warsaw	1674-1855	1
Stargard -Stargard Gubinski-	evKB Rök KB	Warsaw Warsaw	1760-1829 1690-1760	1 1

Location	Nature of Material	Where Filmed	Dates Covered	No. of Rolls
W. Pieck Stadt -Gubin-	evKB	Warsaw Berlin	1612-1919	12
Zielenzig -Sulecin-	evKB	Warsaw	1626-1651	1

ELSASS-LOTHRINGEN
Bas-Rhin, France

Location	Nature of Material	Where Filmed	Dates Covered	No. of Rolls
Achenheim	rkKB	Strasbourg	1669-1803	2
	Secretaire de la Mairie	Strasbourg	1792-1862	4
	-Hereafter Secretaire-			
Adamsweiler	evKB	Strasbourg	1704-1792	1
	Secretaire	Strasbourg	1792-1862	4
	rkKB	Strasbourg	1680-1793	1
Albe	rkKB	Strasbourg	1743-1792	37
	Secretaire	Strasbourg	1792-1862	6
Allenwiller	rkKB	Strasbourg	1602-1789	10
	evKB	Strasbourg	1593-1806	5
Alteckendorf	evKB	Strasbourg	1753-1793	2
	Secretaire	Strasbourg	1792-1862	4
Altenheim	rkKB	Strasbourg	1644-1807	4
	Secretaire	Strasbourg	1793-1862	2
Altenstadt	rkKB	Strasbourg	1686-1818	14
	Secretaire	Strasbourg	1793-1862	6
Altdorf	Secretaire	Strasbourg	1793-1862	4
Altwiller	rkKB	Strasbourg	1726-1794	3
	Secretaire	Strasbourg	1792-1862	4
	evKB	Strasbourg	1698-1799	2
Andlau -Haut-Rhin-	rkKB	Colmar	1465-1790	1
	rkKB	Strasbourg	1661-1792	23
	Secretaire	Strasbourg	1792-1862	12
Artolsheim	rkKB	Strasbourg	1660-1792	4
	Secretaire	Strasbourg	1792-1862	7
Aschbach	Secretaire	Strasbourg	1793-1862	6
	rkKB	Strasbourg	1683-1792	2
Asswiller	evKB	Strasbourg	1706-1799	1
	Secretaire	Strasbourg	1793-1862	3
	rkKB	Strasbourg	1680-1793	2
Auenheim	Secretaire	Strasbourg	1793-1870	7
	rkKB	Strasbourg	1763-1855	2
Arenheim	rkKB	Strasbourg	1788-1894	1
	Secretaire	Strasbourg	1793-1880	3
Arolsheim	Secretaire	Strasbourg	1792-1892	4

Location	Nature of Material	Where Filmed	Dates Covered	No. of Rolls
Baerendorf	rkKB	Strasbourg	1681-1793	1
	Secretaire	Strasbourg	1792-1862	4
Baerenthal	Secretaire	Strasbourg	1792-1862	7
Balbronn	rkKB	Strasbourg	1687-1791	1
	evKB	Strasbourg	1721-1792	1
	Secretaire	Strasbourg	1792-1862	6
Baldenheim	rkKB	Strasbourg	1743-1791	15
	evKB	Strasbourg	1684-1792	3
	Secretaire	Strasbourg	1793-1862	5
Barembach	Secretaire	Strasbourg	1793-1862	4
Barr	rkKB -Andlau-	Strasbourg	1687-1791	4
	evKB	Strasbourg	1559-1792	22
	Secretaire	Strasbourg	1792-1862	21
Barr -Seigneurie-	Notariat d'ancien regime	Strasbourg	1585-1666	15
Bassemberg	Secretaire	Strasbourg	1792-1862	5
Batzendorf	Secretaire	Strasbourg	1794-1872	5
Behlenheim	rkKB	Strasbourg	1680-1914	1
	Secretaire	Strasbourg	1792-1872	2
Beinheim -incl. Leutenheim-	rkKB	Strasbourg	1686-1793	3
	Secretaire	Strasbourg	1793-1862	10
Bellefosse	Secretaire	Strasbourg	1793-1862	3
Belmont	Secretaire	Strasbourg	1793-1862	5
Benfeld	rkKB	Strasbourg	1605-1792	24
	Secretaire	Strasbourg	1792-1862	18
Berembach= Schirmeck				
Berg	evKB	Strasbourg	1712-1794	2
	Secretaire	Strasbourg	1792-1862	4
Bergbieten	rkKB	Strasbourg	1686-1792	1
	Secretaire	Strasbourg	1792-1862	5
Bernardswiller	Secretaire	Strasbourg	1793-1862	7
	rkKB	Strasbourg	1685-1792	5

Location	Nature of Material	Where Filmed	Dates Covered	No. of Rolls
Bernolsheim	rkKB	Strasbourg	1685-1797	3
	Secretaire	Strasbourg	1792-1872	3
Berstett	evKB	Strasbourg	1665-1792	3
	Secretaire	Strasbourg	1793-1871	6
Berstheim	rkKB	Strasbourg	1795-1970	1
	Secretaire	Strasbourg	1793-1870	1
Bettwiller	evLutKB	Strasbourg	1788-1789	1
	Secretaire	Strasbourg	1793-1862	2
Biblisheim	rkKB	Strasbourg	1744-1786	1
	Secretaire	Strasbourg	1793-1862	3
Biesert= Harskirchen				
Bietlenheim	Secretaire	Strasbourg	1793-1862	3
	evKB	Strasbourg	1600-1792	3
Bilwisheim	rkKB	Strasbourg	1746-1850	1
	Secretaire	Strasbourg	1792-1870	2
Bindernheim	rkKB	Strasbourg	1680-1792	15
	Secretaire	Strasbourg	1793-1862	3
Birkenwald	rkKB	Strasbourg	1602-1810	12
	Secretaire	Strasbourg	1792-1862	3
Birlenback	evKB	Strasbourg	1616-1793	1
	Secretaire	Strasbourg	1793-1862	3
	rkKB	Secretaire	1719-1792	1
Bischheim	rkKB	Strasbourg	1679-1795	4
	evKB	Strasbourg	1638-1793	3
	Secretaire	Strasbourg	1793-1862	11
Bischholtz	evKB	Strasbourg	1736-1791	1
	Secretaire	Strasbourg	1792-1862	2
Bischoffsheim	rkKB	Strasbourg	1651-1803	10
	Secretaire	Strasbourg	1793-1862	8
Bischtroffen- sur-Sarre	rkKB	Strasbourg	1761-1792	1
	evKB	Strasbourg	1684-1869	2
	Secretaire	Strasbourg	1792-1862	2
Bischwiller	rkKB	Strasbourg	1731-1792	1
	evKB	Strasbourg	1684-1792	3
	ev.refKB	Strasbourg	1645-1792	6
	Secretaire	Strasbourg	1792-1865	37
	evMKB	Hannover	1891-1911	1
Bissert	Secretaire	Strasbourg	1794-1862	2

Location	Nature of Material	Where Filmed	Dates Covered	No. of Rolls
Bitschhoffen	Secretaire	Strasbourg	1808-	1
	rkKB	Strasbourg	1703-1792	2
	Secretaire	Strasbourg	1793-1862	6
Bitschwiller-les-Thann	Secretaire	Colmar -Arc.Dep.-	1792-1862	9
Blaesheim	evKB	Strasbourg	1611-1792	3
	Secretaire	Strasbourg	1792-1862	4
Blancherupt	Secretaire	Strasbourg	1793-1862	2
Blienschwiller =Andlau - 10 cards-	rkKB	Strasbourg	1666-1792	4
	Secretaire	Strasbourg	1793-1862	4
Bockenhemen= Sarre-Union				
Boersch	rkKB	Strasbourg	1685-1792	8
	Secretaire	Strasbourg	1792-1862	12
Bosenbiesen	rkKB	Strasbourg	1685-1797	15
	Secretaire	Strasbourg	1792-1862	2
Bofftzheim= Boftzheim= Boofzheim				
Bolsenheim	rkKB	Strasbourg	1685-1792	20
	Secretaire	Strasbourg	1792-1852	3
Boofzheim	rkKB	Strasbourg	1687-1792	16
	evKB	Strasbourg	1685-1792	3
	Secretaire	Strasbourg	1793-1862	8
Bootzheim	rkKB	Strasbourg	1642-1792	12
	Secretaire	Strasbourg	1793-1862	3
Bosselshausen	rkKB	Strasbourg	1686-1792	5
	evKB	Strasbourg	1622-1787	2
	Secretaire	Strasbourg	1792-1862	4
Bossendorf	rkKB	Strasbourg	1743-1792	3
	Secretaire	Strasbourg	1792-1862	2
Bouquenom= Sarre-Union				
Burbach-Le-Bas	Secretaire	Colmar	1792-1872	5
Bourg-Bruche	Secretaire	Strasbourg	1793-1862	5
Bourgheim =Andlau - 10 cards-	rkKB	Strasbourg	1748-1790	2
	evKB	Strasbourg	1784-1792	1
	Secretaire	Strasbourg	1793-1862	4

Location	Nature of Material	Where Filmed	Dates Covered	No. of Rolls
Bouxwiller	rkKB see	Bosselshausen -above-		
	evKB	Strasbourg	1568-1792	9
	Secretaire	Strasbourg	1793-1862	17
Breitenbach	rkKB	Strasbourg	1680-1792	39
	Secretaire	Strasbourg	1793-1862	10
Bremmelbach	Secretaire	Strasbourg	1793-1862	3
	rkKB	Strasbourg	1719-1792	1
Breuschwickers- heim	evKB	Strasbourg	1685-1792	2
	Secretaire	Strasbourg	1792-1872	3
Broque -La-	rkKB	Strasbourg	1678-1792	4
	Secretaire	Strasbourg	1793-1862	8
Brumath	rkKB	Strasbourg	1790-1792	1
	evKB	Strasbourg	1685-1792	2
	Secretaire	Strasbourg	1793-1862	26
Bühl	evKB	Colmar	1736-1822	1
	Secretaire	Colmar	1813-1862	4
	rkKB	Strasbourg	1683-1792	2
Burbach	evKB	Strasbourg	1684-1869	3
	Secretaire	Strasbourg	1793-1862	2
Bust	evKB	Strasbourg	1779-1843	1
	Secretaire	Strasbourg	1793-1862	2
Buswiller	evKB	Strasbourg	1700-1792	2
	Secretaire	Strasbourg	1792-1862	3
Butten	evKB	Strasbourg	1740-1798	1
	Secretaire	Strasbourg	1792-1862	3
Cambach-da- Ville	rkKB	Strasbourg	1743-1790	36
Charmenmühle= Engenthal				
Chatenois -7 cards as Cambach-	rkKB	Strasbourg	1685-1793	25
	Secretaire	Strasbourg	1792-1862	3
Cleebourg	evKB	Strasbourg	1736-1792	1
	Secretaire	Strasbourg	1793-1862	4

Location	Nature of Material	Where Filmed	Dates Covered	No. of Rolls
Climbach	Secretaire	Strasbourg	1785-1862	4
Colroy-la-Roche	rkKB	Strasbourg	1686-1802	2
	Secretaire	Strasbourg	1736-1802	3
Cosswiller	rkKB	Strasbourg	1712-1738	1
	Secretaire	Strasbourg	1793-1871	3
	evKB	Strasbourg	1593-1792	2
Couvent de Reinacker Reinacker= Reutenbourg				
Crastatt	rkKB	Strasbourg	1685-1792	3
	Secretaire	Strasbourg	1793-1862	3
Croettwiller	Secretaire	Strasbourg	1793-1862	2
Dachstein	rkKB	Strasbourg	1655-1793	2
	Secretaire	Strasbourg	1793-1952	3
Dahlenheim	rkKB	Strasbourg	1685-1803	2
	Secretaire	Strasbourg	1792-1869	5
Dalhunden	Secretaire	Strasbourg	1792-1870	5
Dambach	rkKB	Strasbourg	1788-1791	1
	Secretaire	Strasbourg	1792-1862	5
Dambach-da-Ville	rkKB	Strasbourg	1596-1792	12
	Secretaire	Strasbourg	1792-1862	12
Dangolsheim	rkKB	Strasbourg	1594-1792	3
	Secretaire	Strasbourg	1793-1871	5
Daubensand	evKB	Strasbourg	1724-1791	2
	Secretaire	Strasbourg	1793-1862	3
	rkKB	Strasbourg	1743-1787	14
Dauendorf	rkKB	Strasbourg	1603-1837	3
	Secretaire	Strasbourg	1803-1872	5
Dehlingen	rkKB	Strasbourg	1704-1775	1
	Secretaire	Strasbourg	1792-1862	3
Dettwiller	rkKB	Strasbourg	1690-1793	2
	evKB	Strasbourg	1570-1802	7
	Secretaire	Strasbourg	1792-1862	8
Diebolsheim	rkKB	Strasbourg	1685-1793	2
	Secretaire	Strasbourg	1793-1862	4
Diedendorf	evKB	Strasbourg	1698-1797	2
	Secretaire	Strasbourg	1793-1862	2

Location	Nature of Material	Where Filmed	Dates Covered	No. of Rolls
Diefenbach-am-Jal	rkKB	Strasbourg	1705-1792	3
	Secretaire	Strasbourg	1792-1862	4
Diefenbach-les-Woerth	rkKB	Strasbourg	1572-1803	7
	Secretaire	Strasbourg	1793-1862	3
Dieffenthal	Secretaire	Colmar	1793-1862	3
	rkKB	Strasbourg	1619-1792	5
Diemeringen	evKB	Strasbourg	1588-1794	2
	Secretaire	Strasbourg	1793-1862	4
Dimbsthal	rkKB	Strasbourg	1602-1871	14
	Secretaire	Strasbourg	1793-1862	2
Dingsheim	rkKB	Strasbourg	1644-1808	5
	Secretaire	Strasbourg	1792-1870	8
Dittlen= Duttlenheim				
Domfessel	rkKB	Strasbourg	1603-1792	1
	Secretaire	Strasbourg	1794-1862	2
Donnenheim	rkKB	Strasbourg	1638-1859	8
	Secretaire	Strasbourg	1793-1911	2
Dorlisheim	evKB	Strasbourg	1586-1792	10
	Secretaire	Strasbourg	1792-1862	12
Dossenheim-Kockersberg	rkKB	Strasbourg	1691-1853	1
	Secretaire	Strasbourg	1793-1874	2
Dossenheim-sur-Ziasel	evKB	Strasbourg	1570-1802	4
	Secretaire	Strasbourg	1792-1862	4
	rkKB	Strasbourg	1677-1792	5
Drackenbronn	Secretaire	Strasbourg	1793-1862	3
	evKB	Strasbourg	1595-1793	6
	rkKB	Strasbourg	1719-1792	1
Drulingen	evKB	Strasbourg	1703-1826	1
	Secretaire	Strasbourg	1793-1862	3
	rkKB	Strasbourg	1680-1793	1
Drusenheim	rkKB	Strasbourg	1711-1846	3
	Secretaire	Strasbourg	1792-1879	2
Duntzenheim	evLutKB	Strasbourg	1650-1792	3
	Secretaire	Strasbourg	1792-1862	4
Duppigheim	rkKB	Strasbourg	1617-1798	2
	Secretaire	Strasbourg	1793-1852	5

Location	Nature of Material	Where Filmed	Dates Covered	No. of Rolls
Durningen	rkKB	Strasbourg	1687-1788	2
	Secretaire	Strasbourg	1792-1870	3
Durrenbach	rkKB	Strasbourg	1656-1792	4
	Secretaire	Strasbourg	1793-1932	8
Durstel	evKB	Strasbourg	1695-1862	3
	Secretaire	Strasbourg	1793-1862	4
Dürstel	rkKB	Strasbourg	1680-1793	1
Duttlenheim	rkKB	Strasbourg	1686-1791	1
	Secretaire	Strasbourg	1793-1862	6
Eberbach-Seltz	rkKB	Strasbourg	1735-1810	3
	Secretaire	Strasbourg	1793-1862	3
Eberbach-Woerth	Secretaire	Strasbourg	1813-1862	3
Ebersheim	Secretaire	Strasbourg	1793-1862	9
	rkKB	Strasbourg	1685-1792	
Ebersmünster	rkKB	Strasbourg	1595-1797	23
	Secretaire	Strasbourg	1793-1862	7
Eckartswiller	rkKB	Strasbourg	1685-1792	8
	Secretaire	Strasbourg	1792-1862	6
Eckbolsheim	evKB	Strasbourg	1609-1792	6
	Secretaire	Strasbourg	1793-1882	7
Eckersheim	rkKB	Strasbourg	1718-1792	1
Eckwersheim	evKB	Strasbourg	1597-1795	2
	Secretaire	Strasbourg	1793-1870	4
Eichhoffen	rkKB	Strasbourg	1661-1792	6
	Secretaire	Strasbourg	1792-1862	3
Elsasshausen -also Froeschwiller and Woerth-	rkKB	Strasbourg	1642-1792	14
	Secretaire	Strasbourg	1793-1862	5
Engenthal	Secretaire	Strasbourg	1793-1862	6
Engwiller	evKB	Strasbourg	1662-1792	1
	Secretaire	Strasbourg	1813-1862	3
Entzheim	evKB	Strasbourg	1594-1792	2
	Secretaire	Strasbourg	1792-1882	3
Epfig	rkKB	Strasbourg	1715-1792	4
	Secretaire	Strasbourg	1792-1862	11

Location	Nature of Material	Where Filmed	Dates Covered	No. of Rolls
Ergersheim	rkKB	Strasbourg	1588-1793	10
	Secretaire	Strasbourg	1792-1892	5
Erlenbach= Wissembourg				
Ermingen= Oermingen				
Ernolsheim	evKB	Strasbourg	1630-1792	3
	rkKB	Strasbourg	1677-1792	5
Ernolsheim- Bruche	rkKB	Strasbourg	1648-1846	1
	Secretaire	Strasbourg	1793-1932	4
Ernolsheim-les- Saverne= Ernolsheim	evKB	Strasbourg	1736-1792	1
	Secretaire	Strasbourg	1793-1862	4
	rkKB	Strasbourg	1653-1792	5
Erstein	rkKB	Strasbourg	1608-1798	28
	Secretaire	Strasbourg	1792-1862	20
Eschau	rkKB	Strasbourg	1685-1792	3
	Secretaire	Strasbourg	1792-1852	6
Eschbach	rkKB	Strasbourg	1694-1792	5
	Secretaire	Strasbourg	1793-1862	3
Eschburg	rkKB	Strasbourg	1773-1922	1
	evKB	Strasbourg	1768-1789	1
	Secretaire	Strasbourg	1791-1862	5
Eschwiller	Secretaire	Strasbourg	1792-1862	2
Ettendorf	rkKB	Strasbourg	1672-1793	3
	Secretaire	Strasbourg	1792-1862	5
Egwiller	Secretaire	Strasbourg	1792-1862	3
	rkKB	Strasbourg	1715-1767	1
Fegersheim	rkKB	Strasbourg	1685-1791	2
	Secretaire	Strasbourg	1792-1862	7
Fessenheim-le- Bas	rkKB	Strasbourg	1588-1792	8
	Secretaire	Strasbourg	1793-1932	2
Flexbourg	Secretaire	Strasbourg	1792-1862	3
Forstheim	rkKB	Strasbourg	1686-1793	4
	Secretaire	Strasbourg	1791-1862	7
Fort-Louis= Fort Vauban	rkKB	Strasbourg	1691-1793	6
	Secretaire	Stragbourg	1792-1871	4
Fouchy	Secretaire	Strasbourg	1793-1879	6
Fouday	Secretaire	Strasbourg	1793-1862	2

Location	Nature of Material	Where Filmed	Dates Covered	No. of Rolls
Freudeneck= Wangenbourg				
Friedolsheim	Secretaire	Strasbourg	1793-1862	3
	rkKB	Strasbourg	1686-1850	2
Friesenheim	rkKB	Strasbourg	1751-1793	1
	Secretaire	Strasbourg	1793-1862	9
Froeschwiller	Secretaire	Strasbourg	1791-1812	6
	evKB	Strasbourg	1731-1793	4
	rkKB	Strasbourg	1572-1803	5
Frohmuhl	rkKB	Strasbourg	1743-1787	1
	Secretaire	Strasbourg	1793-1862	3
Fullengarten	evKB	Strasbourg	1630-1742	3
Furchhausen	evKB	Strasbourg	1736-1789	2
	Secretaire	Strasbourg	1793-1862	3
Furdenheim	evKB	Strasbourg	1663-1852	2
	Secretaire	Strasbourg	1792-1869	4
Gambsheim	rkKB	Strasbourg	1651-1793	3
	Secretaire	Strasbourg	1792-1862	6
Geipolsheim	Secretaire	Strasbourg	1802-1862	3
Geispolsheim= Geistpoltzheim	rkKB	Strasbourg	1685-1792	4
	Secretaire	Strasbourg	1792-1862	7
Geiswiller	evKB	Strasbourg	1654-1793	2
	Secretaire	Strasbourg	1792-1862	3
Gerstheim	rkKB	Strasbourg	1682-1792	1
	evKB	Strasbourg	1594-1792	4
	Secretaire	Strasbourg	1793-1862	11
Gertwiller	rkKB	Strasbourg	1686-1792	3
	evKB	Strasbourg	1625-1792	4
	Secretaire	Strasbourg	1793-1892	7
Geudertheim	evKB	Strasbourg	1600-1792	3
	Secretaire	Strasbourg	1793-1862	5
Gimbrett	Secretaire	Strasbourg	1793-1872	17
	evKB	Strasbourg	1572-1862	5
	ev.refKB	Strasbourg	1591-1792	3
Gingsheim	rkKB	Strasbourg	1712-1793	2
	Secretaire	Strasbourg	1792-1862	3
Glashütte= Wangenbourg				
Goerlingen	Secretaire	Strasbourg	1793-1862	3

Location	Nature of Material	Where Filmed	Dates Covered	No. of Rolls
Goersdorf	Secretaire	Strasbourg	1794-1862	5
Gottenhouse	Secretaire	Strasbourg	1793-1862	2
	rkKB	Strasbourg	1684-1844	4
Gottesheim	evKB	Strasbourg	1654-1793	2
	Secretaire	Strasbourg	1793-1862	5
Gougenheim	rkKB	Strasbourg	1712-1793	2
	Secretaire	Strasbourg	1793-1932	4
Goxwiller	rkKB	Strasbourg	1704-1792	1
	evKB	Strasbourg	1589-1814	6
	Secretaire	Strasbourg	1792-1862	7
Grandfontaine	rkKB	Strasbourg	1774-1793	1
	Secretaire	Strasbourg	1793-1862	5
Grassendorf	rkKB	Strasbourg	1679-1833	3
	Secretaire	Strasbourg	1792-1862	2
Graufthal= Eschbourg				
Grendelbruch	rkKB	Strasbourg	1649-1792	3
	Secretaire	Strasbourg	1792-1862	6
Gresswiller	rkKB	Strasbourg	1640-1792	1
	Secretaire	Strasbourg	1792-1932	5
Gries	evKB	Strasbourg	1572-1862	5
	Secretaire	Strasbourg	1792-1862	15
	rkKB	Strasbourg	1693-1791	2
Griesbach-de-Bastberg	evKB	Strasbourg	1630-1792	4
	rkKB	Strasbourg	1677-1792	6
	Secretaire	Strasbourg	1794-1862	6
Griesheim-pres-Molsheim	rkKB	Strasbourg	1624-1862	2
	Secretaire	Strasbourg	1792-1862	4
Griesheim-Sur-Souffel	rkKB	Strasbourg	1644-1808	2
Gumbrechts-hoffen	evKB	Strasbourg	1705-1792	1
	Secretaire	Strasbourg	1792-1862	16
Gundershoffen	rkKB	Strasbourg	1743-1787	2
	evKB	Strasbourg	1682-1791	1
	Secretaire	Strasbourg	1793-1812	6
Gungwiller	evKB	Strasbourg	1788-1789	1
	Secretaire	Strasbourg	1793-1862	3
	rkKB	Strasbourg	1680-1793	1
Gunstett	rkKB	Strasbourg	1657-1792	3
	Secretaire	Strasbourg	1793-1862	5
	evKB	Strasbourg	1572-1803	5

Location	Nature of Material	Where Filmed	Dates Covered	No. of Rolls
Haegen= Hagen	rkKB	Strasbourg	1743-1792	2
	Secretaire	Strasbourg	1792-1862	3
Haguenau	evKB	Strasbourg	1684-1792	3
	rkKB	Strasbourg	1605-1907	20
	Secretaire	Strasbourg	1793-1862	39
	Militar- gemeinde	Hannover	1872-1918	1
Handschuheim	evKB	Strasbourg	1660-1790	1
	Secretaire	Strasbourg	1793-1880	3
Hangbietenheim- Hangenbieten	evKB	Strasbourg	1659-1928	1
	Secretaire	Strasbourg	1793-1932	3
Hardt= Woerth				
Harskirchen	evKB	Strasbourg	1698-1799	2
	Secretaire	Strasbourg	1792-1862	7
Hatten	rkKB	Strasbourg	1720-1797	4
	evKB	Strasbourg	1707-1792	3
	Secretaire	Strasbourg	1793-1862	11
Hattmatt	rkKB	Strasbourg	1743-1793	3
	Secretaire	Strasbourg	1792-1862	3
Hauteville= Rothau				
Hegeney	rkKB	Strasbourg	1788-1807	1
	Secretaire	Strasbourg	1792-1862	3
Heidolsheim	Secretaire	Strasbourg	1793-1802	3
	rkKB	Strasbourg	1642-1792	16
Heiligenberg	rkKB	Strasbourg	1772-1792	1
	Secretaire	Strasbourg	1792-1862	2
Heiligenstein	evKB	Strasbourg	1585-1792	6
	Secretaire	Strasbourg	1793-1802	3
Hengwiller	rkKB	Strasbourg	1691-1789	1
	evKB	Strasbourg	1663-1806	3
	Secretaire	Strasbourg	1793-1862	3
Herbitzheim- Kerkastel	rkKB	Strasbourg	1691-1798	2
	evKB	Strasbourg	1721-1794	1
	Secretaire	Strasbourg	1743-1862	8
Herbsheim	rkKB	Strasbourg	1685-1792	16
	Secretaire	Strasbourg	1793-1862	4

Location	Nature of Material	Where Filmed	Dates Covered	No. of Rolls
Hermerswiller	rkKB	Strasbourg	1683-1792	3
	Secretaire	Strasbourg	1793-1802	3
	evKB	Strasbourg	1595-1792	5
Herlisheim	Secretaire	Strasbourg	1792-1871	7
	rkKB	Strasbourg	1687-1792	4
	evKB	Strasbourg	1669-1687	3
Hersbach= Wisches				
Hessenheim	rkKB	Strasbourg	1671-1914	4
	Secretaire	Strasbourg	1793-1862	4
Hilsenheim	rkKB	Strasbourg	1618-1797	3
	Secretaire	Strasbourg	1793-1862	6
Hindisheim	rkKB	Strasbourg	1671-1792	2
	Secretaire	Strasbourg	1793-1862	7
Hinsbourg	rkKB	Strasbourg	1743-1787	1
	Secretaire	Strasbourg	1793-1862	2
Hinsingen	evKB	Strasbourg	1698-1799	2
	Secretaire	Strasbourg	1794-1862	1
Hipsheim	rkKB	Strasbourg	1686-1792	1
	Secretaire	Strasbourg	1793-1862	3
Hirschland	ev.refKB	Strasbourg	1703-1826	1
	evKB	Strasbourg	1698-1799	1
	Secretaire	Strasbourg	1791-1862	2
Hochfelden	rkKB	Strasbourg	1679-1791	7
	Secretaire	Strasbourg	1793-1862	13
Hochfrankenheim= Hohfrankenheim				
Hochstett	Secretaire	Strasbourg	1798-1880	3
Hoenheim	rkKB	Strasbourg	1685-1792	3
	Secretaire	Strasbourg	1792-1862	7
Hoerdt	evKB	Strasbourg	1649-1793	3
	Secretaire	Strasbourg	1793-1862	15
Hoffen	evKB	Strasbourg	1729-1792	1
	Secretaire	Strasbourg	1793-1862	4
	rkKB	Strasbourg	1683-1792	2
Hohatzenheim	rkKB	Strasbourg	1638-1846	8
	Secretaire	Strasbourg	1794-1862	2
	evKB	Strasbourg	1650-1792	4

Location	Nature of Material	Where Filmed	Dates Covered	No. of Rolls
Hohengoeft	rkKB	Strasbourg	1689-1792	3
	Secretaire	Strasbourg	1793-1862	6
Hohenwarth= St. Pierre-Bois				
Hohfrankenheim	evKB	Strasbourg	1737-1789	1
	Secretaire	Strasbourg	1792-1862	2
Hohwiller	rkKB	Strasbourg	1743-1797	5
	Secretaire	Strasbourg	1793-1862	7
	evKB	Strasbourg	1595-1792	5
Holtzheim	rkKB	Strasbourg	1738-1792	1
	Secretaire	Strasbourg	1793-1862	4
Hugshaffen= St. Martin				
Hunspack	evKB	Strasbourg	1681-1807	2
	Secretaire	Strasbourg	1793-1802	3
	rkKB	Strasbourg	1719-1792	1
Hurtigheim	evKB	Strasbourg	1606-1792	2
	Secretaire	Strasbourg	1793-1880	3
Hüttendorf	rkKB	Strasbourg	1636-1797	1
	Secretaire	Strasbourg	1792-1870	3
Huttenheim	rkKB	Strasbourg	1685-1798	2
	Secretaire	Strasbourg	1793-1862	7
Ichtersheim= Schtratzheim	Secretaire	Strasbourg	1793-1869	2
	rkKB	Strasbourg	1639-1791	2
Illkirch- Graffenstaden	rkKB	Strasbourg	1765-1792	1
	evKB	Strasbourg	1569-1792	7
	Secretaire	Strasbourg	1793-1872	9
Imbsheim	evKB	Strasbourg	1663-1792	2
	Secretaire	Strasbourg	1792-1862	4
Ingenheim	evKB	Strasbourg	1650-1792	1
	Secretaire	Strasbourg	1792-1862	3
	rkKB	Strasbourg	1743-1787	3
Ingolsheim	Secretaire	Strasbourg	1793-1862	9
	rkKB	Strasbourg	1719-1792	1
Ingwiller	Secretaire	Strasbourg	1792-1862	9
	rkKB	Strasbourg	1689-1792	4
	evKB	Strasbourg	1614-1815	3
Innenheim	rkKB	Strasbourg	1685-1795	2
	Secretaire	Strasbourg	1792-1862	4

Location	Nature of Material	Where Filmed	Dates Covered	No. of Rolls
Irmstett	Secretaire	Strasbourg	1793-1870	3
Issenhausen	evKB	Strasbourg	1622-1792	4
	Secretaire	Strasbourg	1793-1862	3
Ittenheim	evKB	Strasbourg	1583-1792	2
	Secretaire	Strasbourg	1792-1871	12
	rkKB	Strasbourg	1689-1792	1
Ittlenheim	Secretaire	Strasbourg	1793-1870	3
Jägerthal= Windstein				
Jettersweiler= Jetterswiller	rkKB	Strasbourg	1685-1845	2
	Secretaire	Strasbourg	1792-1862	3
Kaltenhausen= Kaltenhouse	Secretaire	Strasbourg	1793-1871	6
Kauffenheim	rkKB	Strasbourg	1686-1793	2
	Secretaire	Strasbourg	1792-1862	3
	evKB	Strasbourg	1707-1792	1
Keffenach	rkKB	Strasbourg	1719-1792	1
	Secretaire	Strasbourg	1793-1862	3
Keidenbourg= Siegen				
Kertzfeld	rkKB	Strasbourg	1597-1950	2
	Secretaire	Strasbourg	1793-1862	4
Keskastel -also Herbitzheim-	rkKB	Strasbourg	1650-1793	1
	evKB	Strasbourg	1698-1794	1
	Secretaire	Strasbourg	1794-1862	5
Kesseldorf	rkKB	Strasbourg	1743-1774	2
	Secretaire	Strasbourg	1794-1862	3
Kienheim	Secretaire	Strasbourg	1792-1869	3
Kilstett	Secretaire	Strasbourg	1792-1862	7
Kindwiller	rkKB	Strasbourg	1688-1792	1
	Secretaire	Strasbourg	1792-1862	3
Kintzheim	rkKB	Strasbourg	1670-1792	2
	Secretaire	Strasbourg	1792-1862	7
Kirchheim	rkKB	Strasbourg	1685-1792	1
	Secretaire	Strasbourg	1793-1880	4
Kirrwiller	rkKB	Strasbourg	1627-1793	3
	evKB	Strasbourg	1622-1792	1
	Secretaire	Strasbourg	1792-1862	3

Location	Nature of Material	Where Filmed	Dates Covered	No. of Rolls
Kleinfranken- heim	rkKB	Strasbourg	1694-1793	1
	Secretaire	Strasbourg	1792-1869	2
Kleingoeft	Secretaire	Strasbourg	1793-1862	3
	rkKB	Strasbourg	1685-1820	5
Knoersheim	Secretaire	Strasbourg	1793-1862	2
Koegenheim	rkKB	Strasbourg	1685-1792	2
	Secretaire	Strasbourg	1793-1862	6
Kolbsheim	rkKB	Strasbourg	1698-1846	1
	evKB	Strasbourg	1618-1792	1
	Secretaire	Strasbourg	1792-1870	3
Königsbrück= Leutenheim				
Krautergers- heim	rkKB	Strasbourg	1707-1792	3
	Secretaire	Strasbourg	1793-1862	4
Krautwiller	evKB	Strasbourg	1630-1792	1
	Secretaire	Strasbourg	1789-1862	7
Kriegsheim	Secretaire	Strasbourg	1792-1862	3
Kuhlendorf	rkKB	Strasbourg	1743-1817	3
	Secretaire	Strasbourg	1793-1862	3
	evKB	Strasbourg	1656-1792	4
Kuntzenhousen	evKB	Strasbourg	1744-1793	1
	Secretaire	Strasbourg	1793-1862	3
	rkKB	Strasbourg	1693-1791	2
Kuttolsheim	rkKB	Strasbourg	1689-1887	7
	Secretaire	Strasbourg	1793-1870	5
Kutzenhausen	Secretaire	Strasbourg	1793-1932	4
	rkKB	Strasbourg	1713-1797	2
	evKB	Strasbourg	1714-1792	
Lalaye	Secretaire	Strasbourg	1793-1862	4
Lampertheim	rkKB	Strasbourg	1609-1792	7
	Secretaire	Strasbourg	1792-1872	7
Lampertsloch	Secretaire	Strasbourg	1793-1862	3
Landersheim	rkKB	Strasbourg	1688-1791	2
	Secretaire	Strasbourg	1792-1862	3
Langensoultz- bach	rkKB	Strasbourg	1674-1791	3
	Secretaire	Strasbourg	1792-1862	4
Laubach	Secretaire	Strasbourg	1792-1903	4
	rkKB	Strasbourg	1770-1786	1

Location	Nature of Material	Where Filmed	Dates Covered	No. of Rolls
Laubenen= Grendelbruch				
Lauterbourgh -also Scheibenhard-	Secretaire rkKB	Strasbourg Strasbourg	1793-1862 1663-1793	15 9
Leiterswiller	Secretaire	Strasbourg	1793-1862	3
Lembach	Secretaire rkKB	Strasbourg Strasbourg	1793-1862 1716-1792	6 4
Leutenheim -Haguenau- also Littenheim -Sarerne-	rkKB Secretaire	Strasbourg Strasbourg	1695-1793 1795-1932	1 11
Lichtenberg	rkKB evKB	Strasbourg Strasbourg	1725-1789 1736-1787	3 1
Limersheim	rkKB Secretaire	Strasbourg Strasbourg	1673-1792 1793-1862	2 3
Lingolsheim	rkKB evKB Secretaire	Strasbourg Strasbourg Strasbourg	1742-1792 1619-1792 1793-1822	1 2 7
Lipsheim	rkKB Secretaire	Strasbourg Strasbourg	1685-1792 1792-1862	2 3
Littenheim	rkKB Secretaire	Strasbourg Strasbourg	1687-1829 1793-1862	5 3
Lixhausen	rkKB Secretaire	Strasbourg Strasbourg	1758-1792 1792-1862	2 3
Lobsann	rkKB Secretaire	Strasbourg Strasbourg	1743-1778 1793-1862	1 3
Lobstein= Lubstein				
Lochwiller	rkKB Secretaire	Strasbourg Strasbourg	1680-1792 1793-1862	2 3
Lohr	rkKB Secretaire evKB	Strasbourg Strasbourg Strasbourg	1749-1794 1792-1862 1768-1792	1 4 1
Lorentzen	rkKB Secretaire	Strasbourg Strasbourg	1671-1794 1793-1862	2 4
Lubstein= Lupstein	rkKB Secretaire	Strasbourg Strasbourg	1743-1841 1792-1862	3 4

Location	Nature of Material	Where Filmed	Dates Covered	No. of Rolls
Lütenheim= Littenheim= Leutenheim				
Lutzelhouse	rkKB	Strasbourg	1685-1792	1
	Secretaire	Strasbourg	1792-1862	6
Mackenheim	rkKB		1685-1797	2
	Secretaire		1793-1802	4
Mackwiller	Secretaire	Strasbourg	1792-1862	5
Maennolsheim	rkKB	Strasbourg	1686-1850	2
	Secretaire	Strasbourg	1792-1862	2
Maisongoutte	Secretaire	Strasbourg	1793-1862	5
Marckolsheim	rkKB	Strasbourg	1642-1792	11
	Secretaire	Strasbourg	1793-1862	11
Marlenheim	Secretaire	Colmar	1793-1860	9
Marmoutier	Documents	Strasbourg	16th-17th Cent	1
	rkKB	Strasbourg	1602-1731	8
	Secretaire	Strasbourg	1792-1862	9
Marzenheim= Matzenheim				
Mattstall	evKB	Strasbourg	1639-1793	1
	Secretaire	Strasbourg	1793-1862	3
Matzenheim	rkKB	Strasbourg	1793-1862	3
	Secretaire	Strasbourg	1792-1862	5
Mayssengott= St. Martin				
Meinoldsheim= Maennoldsheim				
Meistratzheim	rkKB	Strasbourg	1640-1792	6
	Secretaire	Strasbourg	1793-1862	8
Melsheim	evKB	Strasbourg	1650-1792	2
	Secretaire	Strasbourg	1792-1862	3
Memmelshoffen	Secretaire	Strasbourg	1793-1872	3
Menchhoffen	Secretaire	Strasbourg	1792-1862	3
Mertzwiller	rkKB	Strasbourg	1696-1792	7
	evKB	Strasbourg	1685-1792	1
	Secretaire	Strasbourg	1793-1862	14
Mietesheim	evKB	Strasbourg	1655-1792	2
	Secretaire	Strasbourg	1793-1862	5

Location	Nature of Material	Where Filmed	Dates Covered	No. of Rolls
Minversheim	rkKB	Strasbourg	1691-1799	3
	Secretaire	Strasbourg	1793-1862	5
Mitschdorf	Secretaire	Strasbourg	1793-1862	4
Mittelbergheim	rkKB	Strasbourg	1685-1792	2
	evKB	Strasbourg	1562-1792	7
	Secretaire	Strasbourg	1793-1862	4
Mittelhaus-bergen	evKB	Strasbourg	1788-1792	1
	rkKB	Strasbourg	1664-1787	1
	Secretaire	Strasbourg	1793-1871	3
Mittelhausen	evKB	Strasbourg	1650-1792	4
	Secretaire	Strasbourg	1792-1862	4
Mittelburg= Rangen				
Mittelschaef-folsheim	rkKB	Strasbourg	1744-1804	1
	Secretaire	Strasbourg	1793-1870	3
Mollkirch	rkKB	Strasbourg	1686-1799	3
	Secretaire	Strasbourg	1792-1862	6
Molsheim	rkKB	Strasbourg	1690-1792	6
	Secretaire	Strasbourg	1792-1862	14
Mommenheim	rkKB	Strasbourg	1685-1795	1
	Secretaire	Strasbourg	1794-1869	6
Monswiller	rkKB	Strasbourg	1685-1793	8
	Secretaire	Strasbourg	1793-1862	5
Morsbronn -les-Bains-	rkKB	Strasbourg	1743-1787	1
	evKB	Strasbourg	1736-1792	1
	Secretaire	Strasbourg	1793-1862	3
Morschwiller	rkKB	Strasbourg	1679-1833	2
	Secretaire	Strasbourg	1793-1962	4
Mothern	rkKB	Strasbourg	1788-1792	1
	Secretaire	Strasbourg	1793-1862	10
Muhlbach-Sur-Bruchs	rkKB	Strasbourg	1734-1796	2
	Secretaire	Strasbourg	1793-1862	4
Muhlhausen	evKB	Strasbourg	1736-1791	1
	Secretaire	Strasbourg	1792-1862	3
	MKB	Hannover	1872-1918	1
Munchhausen	rkKB	Strasbourg	1740-1793	3
	Secretaire	Strasbourg	1793-1862	4

Location	Nature of Material	Where Filmed	Dates Covered	No. of Rolls
Mundolsheim	Misc. documents	Strasbourg	17th-18th Cent	1
	evKB	Strasbourg	1685-1768	1
	Secretaire	Strasbourg	1792-1933	3
Muntzenheim= Marckolsheim				
Mussig	evKB	Strasbourg	1722-1790	1
Muttersholtz	evKB	Strasbourg	1644-1792	4
Mutzenhouse	Secretaire	Strasbourg	1792-1862	4
Mutzig	evKB	Hannover	1898-1918	1
	MKB			
	Secretaire	Strasbourg	1793-1862	11
	rkKB	Strasbourg	1609-1792	5
Natzwiller	rkKB	Strasbourg	1794-1686	2
	Secretaire	Strasbourg	1800-1862	4
Neewiller-Pres- Lauterbourg	rkKB	Strasbourg	1741-1792	2
Nehwiller-Pres- Woerth	Secretaire	Strasbourg	1793-1862	5
Neiderbronn-les- Bains= Wissembourg				
Neubois	Secretaire	Strasbourg	1793-1862	4
Neugartheim	Secretaire	Strasbourg	1793-1879	3
Neuhaeusel	rkKB	Strasbourg	1742-1791	1
	Secretaire	Strasbourg	1794-1870	2
Neunhoffen= Dambach				
Neunkirch= Friesenheim				
Neuve-Eglise	rkKB	Strasbourg	1652-1799	3
	Secretaire	Strasbourg	1792-1862	4
Neuwiller	Secretaire	Strasbourg	1793-1862	3
Neuwiller-les- Saverne	rkKB	Strasbourg	1743-1792	6
	Secretaire	Strasbourg	1792-1862	10
Niederaltdorf	Secretaire	Strasbourg	1793-1852	4

Location	Nature of Material	Where Filmed	Dates Covered	No. of Rolls
Niederbetsch-dorf	rkKB	Strasbourg	1743-1817	3
	Secretaire	Strasbourg	1793-1922	8
	evKB	Strasbourg	1656-1792	4
Niederbronn-les-Bains	Secretaire Canton documents	Strasbourg	1823-1862	4
	rkKB	Strasbourg	1659-1792	8
	evKB	Strasbourg	1710-1792	3
	Secretaire	Strasbourg	1792-1862	16
Niederhalsbach	rkKB	Strasbourg	1711-1792	2
	Secretaire	Strasbourg	1792-1869	5
Niederhaus-bergen	evKB	Strasbourg	1603-1792	2
	Secretaire	Strasbourg	1793-1880	3
Niederlauter-bach	rkKB	Strasbourg	1683-1804	2
	Secretaire	Strasbourg	1793-1862	13
Niedermottern= Niedermodern	Secretaire	Strasbourg	1793-1862	4
Niedernai	rkKB	Strasbourg	1685-1792	8
	Secretaire	Strasbourg	1792-1862	7
Niederroedern	rkKB	Strasbourg	1708-1798	2
	evKB	Strasbourg	1758-1792	2
	Secretaire	Strasbourg	1793-1862	12
Niederschaef-folsheim	Secretaire	Strasbourg	1792-1882	4
Niederseebach	Secretaire	Strasbourg	1794-1862	5
	rkKB	Strasbourg	1731-1825	1
Niedersoultz-bach	evKB	Strasbourg	1779-1792	1
	Secretaire	Strasbourg	1793-1862	4
Niedersteinbach	evKB	Strasbourg	1736-1791	1
	Secretaire	Strasbourg	1793-1862	6
Nordheim	Secretaire	Strasbourg	1793-1870	5
	rkKB	Strasbourg	1685-1824	1
Nordhouse	rkKB	Strasbourg	1685-1792	2
	Secretaire	Strasbourg	1793-1862	4
Nothalten	rkKB	Strasbourg	1666-1792	4
	Secretaire	Strasbourg	1792-1862	6
Obenheim	Secretaire	Strasbourg	1793-1862	5
	evKB	Strasbourg	1656-1792	2
Oberbronn	Secretaire	Strasbourg	1793-1862	16
	documents	Strasbourg	17th-18th Cent	1
	evKB	Strasbourg	1598-1792	6
	rkKB	Strasbourg	1679-1792	7

Location	Nature of Material	Where Filmed	Dates Covered	No. of Rolls
Oberdorf-Spachbach	rkKB	Strasbourg	1744-1786	1
	evKB	Strasbourg	1788-1792	1
	Secretaire	Strasbourg	1793-1862	3
Oberdorff= Issenhausen				
Oberhaslach	Secretaire	Strasbourg	1792-1870	5
Oberhausbergen	evKB	Strasbourg	1615-1848	2
	Secretaire	Strasbourg	1793-1869	3
Oberhoffen-les-Wissembourg	Secretaire	Strasbourg	1793-1862	4
Oberhoffen-Sur-Moder	evKB	Strasbourg	1671-1792	3
	Secretaire	Strasbourg	1792-1862	5
Oberlauterbach	rkKB	Strasbourg	1709-1813	2
	Secretaire	Strasbourg	1795-1862	7
Obermodern	rkKB	Strasbourg	1596-1792	2
	Secretaire	Strasbourg	1792-1862	4
Obernai	rkKB	Strasbourg	1646-1796	14
	evKB	Strasbourg	1589-1814	6
	Secretaire	Strasbourg	1793-1862	23
Oberrathsam-hausen= Baldenheim				
Oberroedern	Secretaire	Strasbourg	1794-1862	7
Oberschaef-folsheim	rkKB	Strasbourg	1618-1808	1
	Secretaire	Strasbourg	1792-1932	5
Oberseebach	rkKB	Strasbourg	1688-1793	3
	Secretaire	Strasbourg	1793-1862	14
Obersoultzbach	evKB	Strasbourg	1612-1792	1
	Secretaire	Strasbourg	1792-1862	3
Obersteigen= Engenthal				
Obersteinbach	rkKB	Strasbourg	1740-1793	3
	evKB	Strasbourg	1788-1848	2
	Secretaire	Strasbourg	1792-1862	7
Ocratzheim	Secretaire	Strasbourg	1793-1869	4
Oermingen	evKB	Strasbourg	1649-1793	1
	Secretaire	Strasbourg	1793-1862	4

Location	Nature of Material	Where Filmed	Dates Covered	No. of Rolls
Offendorf	evKB	Strasbourg	1684-1792	3
	rkKB	Strasbourg	1686-1837	3
	Secretaire	Strasbourg	1792-1872	6
Offenheim	rkKB	Strasbourg	1685-1792	1
	Secretaire	Strasbourg	1790-1869	3
Offwiller	Secretaire	Strasbourg	1793-1862	6
	evKB	Strasbourg	1584-1792	2
Ohlungen	Secretaire	Strasbourg	1796-1882	5
Ohnenheim	rkKB	Strasbourg	1685-1792	4
	Secretaire	Strasbourg	1793-1862	4
Orwisheim	evKB	Strasbourg	1685-1794	2
	Secretaire	Strasbourg	1792-1870	3
Ormingen= Herbitzheim				
Orschwiller	rkKB	Strasbourg	1616-1792	3
	Secretaire	Strasbourg	1793-1862	5
Osthoffen	Secretaire	Strasbourg	1793-1872	5
Osthouse	rkKB	Strasbourg	1685-1793	2
	Secretaire	Strasbourg	1793-1862	8
Ostwald	rkKB	Strasbourg	1688-1791	2
	evKB	Strasbourg	1590-1688	2
	Secretaire	Strasbourg	1793-1862	5
Ottenrott= Ottrot				
Ottersthal	rkKB	Strasbourg	1631-1792	2
	Secretaire	Strasbourg	1793-1862	4
Otterswiller	rkKB	Strasbourg	1684-1844	4
	Secretaire	Strasbourg	1793-1862	4
Ottrot	rkKB	Strasbourg	1652-1792	12
	Secretaire	Strasbourg	1792-1862	12
Ottwiller	Secretaire	Strasbourg	1793-1862	3
Petersbach	evKB	Strasbourg	1768-1789	1
	Secretaire	Strasbourg	1793-1862	3
Petite-Pierre	evKB	Strasbourg	1637-1816	6
	rkKB	Strasbourg	1760-1792	3
	Secretaire	Strasbourg	1792-1862	6
		Strasbourg	1662	
Pfaffenhofen	evKB	Strasbourg	1545-1792	6
	rkKB	Strasbourg	1721-1792	2
	Secretaire	Strasbourg	1738-1862	18

Location	Nature of Material	Where Filmed	Dates Covered	No. of Rolls
Pfalzweyer	Secretaire	Strasbourg	1793-1862	3
Pfettisheim	rkKB	Strasbourg	1684-1787	1
	Secretaire	Strasbourg	1793-1877	4
Pfulgriesheim	ev.refKB	Strasbourg	1581-1792	3
	Secretaire	Strasbourg	1792-1862	3
Pisdorf	evKB	Strasbourg	1684-1869	2
	Secretaire	Strasbourg	1792-1862	2
Plaine	Secretaire	Strasbourg	1793-1862	6
	rkKB	Strasbourg	1693-1792	2
Plobsheim	Secretaire	Strasbourg	1792-1872	11
	rkKB	Strasbourg	1689-1788	2
	evKB	Strasbourg	1588-1733	3
Preuschdorf	rkKB	Strasbourg	1659-1788	1
	evKB	Strasbourg	1736-1792	3
	Secretaire	Strasbourg	1793-1862	3
Printzheim	rkKB	Strasbourg	1701-1787	1
	evKB	Strasbourg	1654-1793	1
	Secretaire	Strasbourg	1792-1862	3
Puberg	evKB	Strasbourg	1780-1792	1
	Secretaire	Strasbourg	1792-1862	3
Quatzenheim	evKB	Strasbourg	1605-1833	2
	Secretaire	Strasbourg	1792-1865	3
Rangen	rkKB	Strasbourg	1689-1792	3
	Secretaire	Strasbourg	1793-1862	2
Ranrupt	rkKB	Strasbourg	1685-1792	3
Ratzwiller	Secretaire	Strasbourg	1792-1862	3
Ranwiller	evKB	Strasbourg	1698-1799	5
Ravel= Rothau				
Reichfeld	rkKB	Strasbourg	1702-1792	1
Reichsfeld	rkKB	Strasbourg	1639-1792	3
	Secretaire	Strasbourg	1787-1792	5
Reichshoffen	rkKB	Strasbourg	1685-1793	3
	Secretaire	Strasbourg	1793-1872	8
Reichstett	rkKB	Strasbourg	1683-1792	1
	Secretaire	Strasbourg	1792-1863	5
Reimerswiller	rkKB	Strasbourg	1743	1
	Secretaire	Strasbourg	1793-1862	5

Location	Nature of Material	Where Filmed	Dates Covered	No. of Rolls
Reinhards-münster	Secretaire	Strasbourg	1792-1862	3
	rkKB	Strasbourg	1758-1787	1
Reipertswiller	evKB	Strasbourg	1736-1790	1
	Secretaire	Strasbourg	1793-1862	6
Reitwiller	ev.refKB	Strasbourg	1591-1792	3
	Secretaire	Strasbourg	1793-1870	3
Retschwiller	rkKB	Strasbourg	1743-1778	1
	Secretaire	Strasbourg	1793-1862	5
Reutenbourg	rkKB	Strasbourg	1687-1789	2
	Secretaire	Strasbourg	1792-1862	5
Rexingen	Secretaire	Strasbourg	1793-1862	2
Rhinau	rkKB	Strasbourg	1621-1742	19
	Secretaire	Strasbourg	1793-1862	11
Riantegontte= Rothau				
Ricktolsheim	Secretaire	Strasbourg	1793-1862	4
Riedheim	Secretaire	Strasbourg	1793-1862	3
Riedseltz	rkKB	Strasbourg	1750-1800	1
	Secretaire	Strasbourg	1793-1862	11
Rimsdorf	evKB	Strasbourg	1777-1801	1
	Secretaire	Strasbourg	1793-1862	3
Ringeldorf	rkKB	Strasbourg	1721-1792	2
	Secretaire	Strasbourg	1796-1862	2
Ringendorf	evKB	Strasbourg	1650-1792	2
	Secretaire	Strasbourg	1792-1862	3
Rittershoffen	rkKB	Strasbourg	1720-1797	5
	evKB	Strasbourg	1664-1790	2
	Secretaire	Strasbourg	1793-1862	4
Roeschwoog= Röschvogen	rkKB	Strasbourg	1688-1792	3
	Secretaire	Strasbourg	1792-1862	6
Rohr	rkKB	Strasbourg	1760-1788	1
	Secretaire	Strasbourg	1792-1862	2
Rohrwiller	rkKB	Strasbourg	1799-1805	1
	Secretaire	Strasbourg	1793-1892	4
Romanswiller= Rommoltzwiller	Secretaire	Strasbourg	1792-1932	5
	evKB	Strasbourg	1593-1792	2

Location	Nature of Material	Where Filmed	Dates Covered	No. of Rolls
Roppenheim	rkKB	Strasbourg	1762-1788	1
	evKB	Strasbourg	1688-1791	2
	Secretaire	Strasbourg	1792-1912	5
Rosenwiller	rkKB	Strasbourg	1685-1792	5
	Secretaire	Strasbourg	1792-1862	5
Rosheim	rkKB	Strasbourg	1647-1792	10
	Secretaire	Strasbourg	1792-1862	17
Rossfeld	rkKB	Strasbourg	1752-1792	1
	Secretaire	Strasbourg	1793-1862	7
Rosteig	Secretaire	Strasbourg	1793-1862	5
Rothau -also Waldersbach-	Secretaire		1803-1862	5
	rkKB		1725-1792	4
	evKB		1640-1792	4
Rothbach	evKB	Strasbourg	1685-1792	2
	Secretaire	Strasbourg	1793-1862	6
Rott	evKB	Strasbourg	1735-1789	1
	Secretaire	Strasbourg	1793-1862	5
Rottelsheim	Secretaire	Strasbourg	1793-1876	3
Routzenheim	rkKB	Strasbourg	1763-1855	2
	Secretaire	Strasbourg	1793-1871	5
Rumersheim	rkKB	Strasbourg	1685-1801	3
	Secretaire	Strasbourg	1793-1870	2
Russ	rkKB	Strasbourg	1716-1792	4
	Secretaire	Strasbourg	1793-1862	4
Saales	Secretaire	Strasbourg	1788-1862	4
Saasenheim	rkKB	Strasbourg	1662-1792	2
	Secretaire	Strasbourg	1793-1862	5
Saessolsheim	rkKB	Strasbourg	1743-1789	2
	Secretaire	Strasbourg	1793-1862	5
Saint-Gall= Thal-Marmoutier				
St. Jean des Choux= St. Jean Saverne	Secretaire	Strasbourg	1793-1862	5
	rkKB	Strasbourg	1653-1792	4
		Strasbourg	1750-1757	1
St. Martin	rkKB	Strasbourg	1677-1792	4
	Secretaire	Strasbourg	1793-1862	5
St. Maurice	rkKB	Strasbourg	1791-1792	1
	Secretaire	Strasbourg	1792-1862	4

Location	Nature of Material	Where Filmed	Dates Covered	No. of Rolls
St. Nabor	rkKB	Strasbourg	1647-1792	2
	Secretaire	Strasbourg	1793-1862	3
St. Pierre	rkKB	Strasbourg	1685-1792	3
	Secretaire	Strasbourg	1793-1862	4
St. Pierre-Bois= St. Peters- holtz	rkKB	Strasbourg	1683-1792	2
	Secretaire	Strasbourg	1792-1862	5
Ste. Blaise-la- Roche	rkKB	Strasbourg	1743-1792	1
Ste. Odile= Ottrot				
Salenthal	rkKB	Strasbourg	1762-1792	2
	Secretaire	Strasbourg	1792-1862	2
Salmbach	rkKB	Strasbourg	1684-1792	2
	Secretaire	Strasbourg	1793-1862	8
Sand	rkKB	Strasbourg	1699-1792	1
	Secretaire	Strasbourg	1792-1862	9
Sarre-Union	Secretaire	Strasbourg	1793-1862	13
	rkKB	Strasbourg	1631-1792	6
	evKB	Strasbourg	1596-1857	7
Sarrewerden	rkKB	Strasbourg	1738-1805	2
	Secretaire	Strasbourg	1793-1862	5
Saulxures	rkKB	Strasbourg	1706-1792	2
	Secretaire	Strasbourg	1793-1862	3
Saverne	rkKB	Strasbourg	1631-1792	18
	Secretaire	Strasbourg	1792-1862	25
	evMKB	Hannover	1871-1915	1
Schoeffersheim	rkKB	Strasbourg	1685-1794	1
	Secretaire	Strasbourg	1793-1862	5
Schaffhouse- sur-Seltz	rkKB	Strasbourg	1743-1774	2
	Secretaire	Strasbourg	1795-1862	7
Schaffhouse- sur-Zorn	rkKB	Strasbourg	1764-1792	1
	Secretaire	Strasbourg	1793-1862	3
Schalkendorf	evKB	Strasbourg	1736-1792	1
	Secretaire	Strasbourg	1792-1862	2
Schallbach= Weyer				
Scharrachberg- heim	evKB	Strasbourg	1598-1832	1
	Secretaire	Strasbourg	1792-1870	4

Location	Nature of Material	Where Filmed	Dates Covered	No. of Rolls
Scheibenhard- -also Lauterbourg-	rkKB Secretaire	Strasbourg Strasbourg	1719-1801 1796-1862	2 10
Schelithal= Schleithal				
Scherlenheim	rkKB	Strasbourg	1788-1792	1
Scherwiller	rkKB Secretaire	Strasbourg Strasbourg	1619-1792 1792-1862	5 11
Schillersdorf	evKB Secretaire	Strasbourg Strasbourg	1672-1792 1792-1862	2 4
Schiltigheim	evKB Secretaire	Strasbourg Strasbourg	1575-1792 1792-1862	9 14
Schirmeck	rkKB Secretaire	Strasbourg Strasbourg	1674-1792 1794-1862	3 4
Schirrheim	Secretaire	Strasbourg	1792-1871	7
Schirrhoffen	Secretaire	Strasbourg	1793-1871	4
Schleithal	rkKB Secretaire	Strasbourg Strasbourg	1695-1793 1793-1862	3 16
Schnersheim	rkKB Secretaire	Strasbourg Strasbourg	1705-1817 1793-1870	2 3
Schoenau	rkKB Secretaire	Strasbourg Strasbourg	1643-1792 1793-1862	2 5
Schoenburg	evKB Secretaire	Strasbourg Strasbourg	1768-1792 1793-1862	1 3
Schoenenbourg	rkKB Secretaire	Strasbourg Strasbourg	1685-1792 1793-1862	2 7
Schopperten	Secretaire	Strasbourg	1793-1862	2
Schwabwiller	rkKB Secretaire	Strasbourg Strasbourg	1743-1824 1793-1862	3 6
Schwarzbach	Secretaire	Strasbourg	1793-1862	4
Schwebwiller= Thal-Marmoutier				
Schweighausen= Schweighausen- sur-Moder	Secretaire	Strasbourg	1792-1862	6

Location	Nature of Material	Where Filmed	Dates Covered	No. of Rolls
Schwenheim	rkKB	Strasbourg	1680-1792	3
	Secretaire	Strasbourg	1793-1862	5
Schwindratzheim	rkKB	Strasbourg	1640-1843	6
	Secretaire	Strasbourg	1792-1862	6
Schwobsheim	rkKB	Strasbourg	1710-1797	2
	Secretaire	Strasbourg	1793-1862	2
Selestadt	Archives	Colmar	1495-1790	1
	rkKB	Strasbourg	1604-1792	63
	MKB	Hannover	1871-1919	1
	Secretaire	Strasbourg	1793-1862	49
Seltz	rkKB	Strasbourg	1694-1792	5
	Secretaire	Strasbourg	1793-1862	19
Semersheim	rkKB	Strasbourg	1685-1792	2
	Secretaire	Strasbourg	1792-1862	7
Sessenheim	rkKB	Strasbourg	1733-1792	1
	evKB	Strasbourg	1626-1792	6
	Secretaire	Strasbourg	1792-1892	5
Siegen	rkKB	Strasbourg	1732-1789	1
	Secretaire	Strasbourg	1793-1862	9
Siewiller	Secretaire	Strasbourg	1793-1862	3
	rkKB	Strasbourg	1724-1793	1
Siltzheim	rkKB	Strasbourg	1687-1793	2
	Secretaire	Strasbourg	1793-1862	1
Singrist	rkKB	Strasbourg	1685-1789	2
	Secretaire	Strasbourg	1792-1862	3
Sirischland= Weyer				
Solbach	Secretaire	Strasbourg	1793-1862	2
Souffelweyer- sheim	Secretaire	Strasbourg	1792-1871	3
Soufflenheim	Secretaire	Strasbourg	1793-1862	10
	rkKB	Strasbourg	1748-1793	1
Soultz-les-Bains	Secretaire	Strasbourg	1792-1862	4
Soultz-sous- Foret	Secretaire	Strasbourg	1793-1862	19
	rkKB	Strasbourg	1743-1778	1
	evKB	Strasbourg	1595-1792	5
Spachbach= Woerth				

Location	Nature of Material	Where Filmed	Dates Covered	No. of Rolls
Sparsbach	evKB	Strasbourg	1736-1792	2
	Secretaire	Strasbourg	1792-1862	2
Stattmatten	Secretaire	Strasbourg	1793-1932	3
Steige	rkKB	Strasbourg	1677-1832	5
	Secretaire	Strasbourg	1793-1862	5
Steinbourg	rkKB	Strasbourg	1685-1797	4
	Secretaire	Strasbourg	1792-1862	6
Steinseltz	evKB	Strasbourg	1685-1792	2
	Secretaire	Strasbourg	1793-1862	3
Still	Secretaire	Strasbourg	1792-1862	6
	rkKB	Strasbourg	1636-1792	2
Stotzheim	rkKB	Strasbourg	1631-1797	6
	Secretaire	Strasbourg	1792-1913	8
Strasburg	rkKB	Strasbourg	1689-1792	70
	evKB	Strasbourg	1544-1792	173
	Secretaire	Strasbourg	1793-1856	172
	MKB	Berlin-Dahlem	1871-1918	8
	ev.refKB	Hannover	1656-1792	3
Struth	rkKB	Strasbourg	1743-1787	1
	Secretaire	Strasbourg	1792-1862	3
Stundwiller	rkKB	Strasbourg	1683-1792	2
	Secretaire	Strasbourg	1793-1862	6
Stutzheim	rkKB	Strasbourg	1613-1792	1
	Secretaire	Strasbourg	1793-1870	3
Sundhouse= Sundhausen	rkKB	Strasbourg	1687-1792	1
	evKB	Strasbourg	1601-1792	3
	Secretaire	Strasbourg	1793-1862	6
Surbourg	rkKB	Strasbourg	1644-1793	4
	Secretaire	Strasbourg	1793-1862	15
Thal-Drulingen	Secretaire	Strasbourg	1792-1862	3
Thal-Marmoutier	rkKB	Strasbourg	1602-1731	11
	Secretaire	Strasbourg	1792-1863	4
Thanville	rkKB	Strasbourg	1719-1792	1
	Secretaire	Strasbourg	1793-1862	3
Tiefenbach	evKB	Strasbourg	1743-1792	1
	rkKB	Strasbourg	1738-1792	1
	Secretaire	Strasbourg	1792-1862	3
Traenheim	evKB	Strasbourg	1737-1792	1
	Secretaire	Strasbourg	1792-1870	3

Location	Nature of Material	Where Filmed	Dates Covered	No. of Rolls
Triembach-au Val	Secretaire	Strasbourg	1793-1862	4
Trimbach	rkKB	Strasbourg	1731-1825	1
	Secretaire	Strasbourg	1793-1862	17
Truchtersheim	rkKB	Strasbourg	1685-1792	1
	Secretaire	Strasbourg	1793-1869	3
Uberach	rkKB	Strasbourg	1788-1789	1
	Secretaire	Strasbourg	1793-1862	5
Uhlwiller	rkKB	Strasbourg	1641-1873	5
	Secretaire	Strasbourg	1793-1852	4
Uhrwiller	rkKB	Strasbourg	1776-1792	2
	evKB	Strasbourg	1685-1792	2
	Secretaire	Strasbourg	1793-1862	8
Urbach= Wildersbach				
Urbeis	rkKB	Strasbourg	1760-1792	1
	Secretaire	Strasbourg	1793-1862	5
Urmatt	Secretaire	Strasbourg	1793-1870	3
Urweiller- Wissembourg				
Uttenheim- Benfeld	rkKB	Strasbourg	1685-1792	2
	Secretaire	Strasbourg	1793-1862	7
Uttenhaffen= Gundershaffen				
Uttwiller	evKB	Strasbourg	1707-1792	2
	Secretaire	Strasbourg	1793-1862	2
Valff	rkKB	Strasbourg	1680-1792	2
	Secretaire	Strasbourg	1792-1862	5
Vendenheim	rkKB	Strasbourg	1718-1792	1
	evKB	Strasbourg	1685-1792	3
	Secretaire	Strasbourg	1792-1872	9
Villars-et- Villenotte	Secretaire	Strasbourg	1793-1856	1
Ville	rkKB	Strasbourg	1601-1791	6
	Secretaire	Strasbourg	1793-1862	6
Voellerdingen	evKB	Strasbourg	1777-1798	1
	rkKB	Strasbourg	1603-1744	1
	Secretaire	Strasbourg	1792-1862	3

Location	Nature of Material	Where Filmed	Dates Covered	No. of Rolls
Volksberg	evKB	Strasbourg	1788-1790	1
	Secretaire	Strasbourg	1792-1862	4
Wockenbach= Schirmeck				
Wahlenheim	Secretaire	Strasbourg	1792-1862	3
Walbourg	rkKB	Strasbourg	1719-1793	2
	Secretaire	Strasbourg	1793-1862	6
Walck	Secretaire	Strasbourg	1738-1792	1
Waldolwisheim	rkKB	Strasbourg	1644-1807	3
	Secretaire	Strasbourg	1793-1862	5
Waltenheim-sur-Zorn	evKB	Strasbourg	1682-1792	2
	Secretaire	Strasbourg	1793-1862	6
Wangen	evKB	Strasbourg	1601-1787	1
	Secretaire	Strasbourg	1792-1912	5
Wangenbourg	Secretaire	Strasbourg	1793-1870	2
Wantzenau	rkKB	Strasbourg	1637-1793	5
	Secretaire	Strasbourg	1793-1852	7
Wasselonne	rkKB	Strasbourg	1686-1792	2
	evKB	Strasbourg	1685-1792	5
	Secretaire	Strasbourg	1792-1862	15
Weinbourg	evKB	Strasbourg	1737-1793	2
	Secretaire	Strasbourg	1793-1862	4
Weislingen	rkKB	Strasbourg	1792-1862	4
	Secretaire			
Weitbruch	evKB	Strasbourg	1736-1792	2
	rkKB	Strasbourg	1693-1791	2
	Secretaire	Strasbourg	1793-1869	15
Weiterswiller	rkKB	Strasbourg	1727-1792	2
	evKB	Strasbourg	1628-1792	2
	Secretaire	Strasbourg	1793-1862	5
Westhoffen	Secretaire	Strasbourg	1793-1870	9
	rkKB	Strasbourg	1762-1792	1
	evKB	Strasbourg	1579-1793	2
Westhouse-Marmoutier	rkKB	Strasbourg	1685-1820	5
	Secretaire	Strasbourg	1792-1862	13
Weyer	evKB	Strasbourg	1745-1870	1
	rkKB	Strasbourg	1680-1793	1
	Secretaire	Strasbourg	1794-1862	4

Location	Nature of Material	Where Filmed	Dates Covered	No. of Rolls
Weihersheim	Secretaire	Strasbourg	1792-1862	8
	rkKB	Strasbourg	1637-1802	3
Wickersheim	evKB	Strasbourg	1651-1856	2
	Secretaire	Strasbourg	1792-1862	3
Wildersbach	Secretaire	Strasbourg	1793-1862	3
Willgottheim	rkKB	Strasbourg	1644-1792	2
	Secretaire	Strasbourg	1792-1862	5
Wilshausen	evKB	Strasbourg	1700-1939	1
	Secretaire	Strasbourg	1792-1862	3
Wilwisheim	rkKB	Strasbourg	1683-1799	3
	Secretaire	Strasbourg	1792-1862	4
Wimmenau	evKB	Strasbourg	1570-1941	2
	Secretaire	Strasbourg	1793-1862	4
Windstein	Secretaire	Strasbourg	1793-1862	8
Wingen	Secretaire	Strasbourg	1793-1862	6
	rkKB	Strasbourg	1714-1792	2
	evKB	Strasbourg	1648-1742	1
Wingen-Sur-Moder	rkKB	Strasbourg	1749-1792	2
	evKB	Strasbourg	1757-1792	1
	Secretaire	Strasbourg	1792-1862	4
Wingersheim	rkKB	Strasbourg	1638-1818	7
	Secretaire	Strasbourg	1792-1862	6
Wintershouse	Secretaire	Strasbourg	1792	2
Wintzenbach	rkKB	Strasbourg	1736-1967	3
	Secretaire	Strasbourg	1794-1862	7
Wintzenheim-Kockersberg	evLutKB	Strasbourg	1650-1792	3
	Secretaire	Strasbourg	1792-1870	3
Wisches	rkKB	Strasbourg	1735-1792	2
	Secretaire	Strasbourg	1791-1862	6
Wissembourg	Secretaire	Strasbourg	1793-1862	47
	rkKB	Strasbourg	1689-1792	6
	evKB	Strasbourg	1596-1792	6
	MKB	Hannover	1870-1913	1
Witternheim	rkKB	Strasbourg	1788-1790	1
	Secretaire	Strasbourg	1793-1862	5
Wittersheim	rkKB	Strasbourg	1658-1874	2
	Secretaire	Strasbourg	1792-1871	4
Wittisheim	rkKB	Strasbourg	1683-1797	2
	Secretaire	Strasbourg	1792-1862	6

Location	Nature of Material	Where Filmed	Dates Covered	No. of Rolls
Wiwersheim	rkKB	Strasbourg	1754-1792	1
	Secretaire	Strasbourg	1792-1869	3
Woellenheim	Secretaire	Strasbourg	1793-1873	2
	rkKB	Strasbourg	1644-1792	2
Woerth	rkKB	Strasbourg	1572-1803	5
	evKB	Strasbourg	1572-1803	5
	Secretaire	Strasbourg	1793-1862	13
Wolfisheim	evKB	Strasbourg	1586-1792	2
	rkKB	Strasbourg	1748-1792	1
	Secretaire	Strasbourg	1792-1952	4
Wolfskirchen	rkKB	Strasbourg	1715-1767	1
	evKB	Strasbourg	1671-1846	2
	Secretaire	Strasbourg	1794-1862	4
Wolschheim	evKB	Strasbourg	1736-1789	2
	rkKB	Strasbourg	1685-1849	4
	Secretaire	Strasbourg	1793-1862	2
Wolxheim	Secretaire	Strasbourg	1792-1912	4
Zehnacker	rkKB	Strasbourg	1689-1792	2
	evKB	Strasbourg	1593-1792	1
	Secretaire	Strasbourg	1793-1862	2
Zeinheim	rkKB	Strasbourg	1644-1792	2
	evKB	Strasbourg	1745-1787	1
	Secretaire	Strasbourg	1793-1862	2
Zellwiller	rkKB	Strasbourg	1685-1809	3
	Secretaire	Strasbourg	1793-1862	5
Zinswiller	rkKB	Strasbourg	1679-1862	4
	evKB	Strasbourg	1763-1791	1
	Secretaire	Strasbourg	1793-1862	8
Zittersheim	evKB	Strasbourg	1719-1783	1
	Secretaire	Strasbourg	1792-1862	3
Zoebersdorf	evKB	Strasbourg	1622-1792	4
	Secretaire	Strasbourg	1792-1861	2
Zollingen	evKB	Strasbourg	1761-1792	1
	Secretaire	Strasbourg	1793-1863	2
Zornhoff	rkKB	Strasbourg	1685-1792	2
Zatsendorf	evKB	Strasbourg	1653-1792	1
	Secretaire	Strasbourg	1793-1862	4

ELSASS-LOTHRINGEN
Haut-Rhin, France

Location	Nature of Material	Where Filmed	Dates Covered	No. of Rolls
Algolsheim	rkKB	Colmar	1788-1792	1
	Secretaire de la Mairie		1793-1862	4
-Hereafter Secretaire-				
Altenach	rkKB	Colmar	1665-1793	1
	Secretaire	Colmar	1792-1872	3
Altenbach	rkKB	Colmar	1696-1792	5
	Secretaire	Colmar	1792-1872	2
Altkirch	Secretaire	Colmar	1115-1790	2
	rkKB	Colmar	1682-1792	5
	Archives	Colmar	1793-1862	11
Ammerschwihr	rkKB	Colmar	1584-1792	4
	Secretaire	Colmar	1793-1872	8
Ammerswiller	rkKB	Colmar	1687-1965	2
	Secretaire	Colmar	1795-1872	4
Andolsheim	rkKB	Colmar	1690-1792	1
	evKB	Colmar	1775-1792	1
	Secretaire	Colmar	1793-1872	5
Appenwihr	Secretaire	Colmar	1793-1872	3
Artzenheim	Secretaire	Colmar	1792-1872	5
	rkKB	Colmar	1659-1797	3
Aspach	rkKB	Colmar	1725-1792	2
	Secretaire	Colmar	1793-1872	4
Aspach-le-Bar	rkKB	Colmar	1738-1792	1
	Secretaire	Colmar	1792-1872	5
Aspach-le-Haut	rkKB	Colmar	1760-1787	1
Attenschwiller	rkKB	Colmar	1661-1774	1
Aubure	rkKB	Colmar	1688-1792	1
	Secretaire	Colmar	1761-1872	5
Badricourt= Ballersdorf	rkKB	Colmar	1702-1792	1
	Secretaire	Colmar	1793-1872	5

Location	Nature of Material	Where Filmed	Dates Covered	No. of Rolls
Baldersheim	rkKB	Colmar	1742-1792	1
	Secretaire	Colmar	1793-1872	5
Balgau	rkKB	Colmar	1662-1792	1
	Secretaire	Colmar	1792-1872	5
Balschwiller= Ueberkumen				
Balschwiller	rkKB	Colmar	1677-1792	1
	Secretaire	Colmar	1792-1872	4
Baltzenheim	rkKB	Colmar	1647-1795	1
	Secretaire	Colmar	1792-1872	4
Bantzenheim	rkKB	Colmar	1714-1791	1
	Secretaire	Colmar	1793-1872	13
Bantzheim	rkKB	Colmar	1715-1789	2
Bartenheim	rkKB	Colmar	1519-1804	3
	Secretaire	Colmar	1793-1872	8
Battenheim	rkKB	Colmar	1731-1792	1
	Secretaire	Colmar	1793-1872	6
Beblenheim	rkKB	Colmar	1688-1792	1
	evKB	Colmar	1562-1792	3
	Secretaire	Colmar	1792-1872	7
Bellemagny	Secretaire	Colmar	1792-1872	3
Bendorf	Secretaire	Colmar	1788-1872	4
Bennwihr	rkKB	Colmar	1729-1812	2
	Secretaire	Colmar	1792-1872	6
Berentzwiller	rkKB	Colmar	1773-1789	1
	Secretaire	Colmar	1793-1872	4
Bergheim	rkKB	Colmar	1594-1792	6
	Secretaire	Colmar	1793-1872	17
Bergholtz	rkKB	Colmar	1640-1792	2
	Secretaire	Colmar	1792-1872	4
Bergholtzzell	Secretaire	Colmar	1792-1872	5
Bernwiller	rkKB	Colmar	1685-1792	2
	Secretaire	Colmar	1792-1872	5
Bernwiller	rkKB	Colmar	1645-1792	2
	Secretaire	Colmar	1793-1875	5
Bettendorf	rkKB	Colmar	1661-1798	1
	Secretaire	Colmar	1793-1872	5

Location	Nature of Material	Where Filmed	Dates Covered	No. of Rolls
Bettlach	Secretaire	Colmar	1793-1862	3
Biederthal	rkKB	Colmar	1774-1784	2
	Secretaire	Colmar	1793-1872	3
Biesheim	rkKB	Colmar	1605-1791	3
	Secretaire	Colmar	1793-1862	10
Bilzheim	rkKB	Colmar	1642-1777	1
	Secretaire	Colmar	1792-1872	3
Bischwihr	Secretaire	Colmar	1792-1872	5
Bisel	Secretaire	Colmar	1792-1872	5
Bitschwiller= Willer-sur-Thur	rkKB			
Blodelsheim	rkKB	Colmar	1661-1787	3
	Secretaire	Colmar	1793-1872	11
Blotzheim	rkKB	Colmar	1584-1806	4
	Secretaire	Colmar	1793-1830	1
Bollwiller	Secretaire	Colmar	1793-1872	6
	rkKB	Colmar	1643-1792	5
Bonhomme	rkKB	Colmar	1718-1792	2
	Secretaire	Colmar	1792-1872	7
Bourbac= Murback				
Bourbach-le-Bas	rkKB	Colmar	1715-1792	1
Bourbach-le-Haut	Secretaire	Colmar	1792-1862	4
Bourgfelden= St. Louis				
Bouxwiller	rkKB	Colmar	1585-1792	2
	Secretaire	Colmar	1793-1872	4
Brechaumont	Secretaire	Colmar	1793-1872	4
Breitenbach	Secretaire	Colmar	1792-1872	5
Bretten	rkKB	Colmar	1660-1788	1
	Secretaire	Colmar	1792-1812	5
Brinckheim	rkKB	Colmar	1788	1
	Secretaire	Colmar	1793-1872	3
Brinighoffen	Secretaire	Colmar	1793-1872	3
Bruebach	rkKB	Colmar	1773-1788	2
	Secretaire	Colmar	1793-1872	6

Location	Nature of Material	Where Filmed	Dates Covered	No. of Rolls
Brunstatt	rkKB	Colmar	1584-1788	2
	Secretaire	Colmar	1793-1872	7
Buel= Buhl				
Buethwiller	rkKB	Colmar	1666-1792	1
	Secretaire	Colmar	1792-1872	4
Buhl	rkKB	Colmar	1666-1793	1
	Secretaire	Colmar	1793-1872	6
Burnhaupt-le-Bas	Secretaire	Colmar	1792-1872	6
	rkKB	Colmar	1590-1792	2
Brunhaupt-le-Haut	rkKB	Colmar	1586-1792	2
	Secretaire	Colmar	1792-1872	7
Buschwiller	rkKB	Colmar	1663-1792	2
	Secretaire	Colmar	1793-1872	5
Carsbach	rkKB	Colmar	1773-1789	1
	Secretaire	Colmar	1792-1872	5
Cernay	rkKB	Colmar	1631-1793	2
	Secretaire	Colmar	1792-1872	14
	Archives	Colmar	1791-1812	8
Chalampé	rkKB	Colmar	1715-1789	2
	Secretaire	Colmar	1793-1872	5
Chaussee= Blotzheim				
Chavannes-sur-l'etang	Secretaire	Colmar	1792-1872	5
	rkKB	Colmar	1768-1788	1
Colmar	rkKB	Colmar	1603-1792	27
	evKB	Colmar	1544-1792	14
	MKB	Hannover	1871-1918	2
	Hopital Civil	Colmar	1723-1791	1
	Secretaire	Colmar	1793-1862	68
	Archives	Colmar	1105-1872	7
Courtavon	rkKB	Colmar	1654-1792	2
	Secretaire	Colmar	1792-1872	5
Dannemarie	rkKB	Colmar	1649-1792	7
	Secretaire	Colmar	1792-1872	5
Dessenheim	rkKB	Colmar	1773-1792	1
	Secretaire	Colmar	1792-1927	6
Didenheim	rkKB	Colmar	1656-1800	1
	Secretaire	Colmar	1793-1872	6

Location	Nature of Material	Where Filmed	Dates Covered	No. of Rolls
Diefmatten	rkKB	Colmar	1730-1791	1
	Secretaire	Colmar	1792-1872	8
Dietwiller	Secretaire	Colmar	1773-1862	5
Dinckhoff= Dinghoff= Jungholtz				
Dolleren	Secretaire	Colmar	1793-1862	5
Durlinsdorf	rkKB	Colmar	1646-1802	1
	Secretaire	Colmar	1793-1862	5
Durmenach	rkKB	Colmar	1585-1792	4
	Secretaire	Colmar	1775-1872	6
Durrenentzen	rkKB	Colmar	1650-1792	4
	Secretaire	Colmar	1792-1872	13
Echerg= Ste. Marie-aux- Mines				
Eglingen	rkKB	Colmar	1646-1803	2
	Secretaire	Colmar	1793-1872	5
Eguisheim	rkKB	Colmar	1585-1792	5
	Secretaire	Colmar	1792-1872	13
Elbach	Secretaire	Colmar	1792-1872	3
Emlingen	Secretaire	Colmar	1793-1872	3
	rkKB	Colmar	1753-1792	1
Enschingen	Secretaire	Colmar	1793-1872	3
Ensisheim	Archives	Colmar	1297-1790	2
	rkKB	Colmar	1582-1792	6
	Secretaire	Colmar	1792-1872	12
Eschbach-au- val	Secretaire	Colmar	1792-1872	3
Escherg= St. Marie aux Mines				
Eschentzwiller	rkKB	Colmar	1581-1793	2
	Secretaire	Colmar	1793-1872	6
Eteimbes	rkKB	Colmar	1773-1788	1
	Secretaire	Colmar	1792-1872	4
Falkwiller·	Secretaire	Colmar	1792-1872	4
Feldbach	rkKB	Colmar	1678-1792	2
	Secretaire	Colmar	1793-1872	4

Location	Nature of Material	Where Filmed	Dates Covered	No. of Rolls
Feldkirch	rkKB	Colmar	1643-1792	5
	Secretaire	Colmar	1793-1872	5
Fellering	Secretaire	Colmar	1792-1872	5
Ferrette	rkKB	Colmar	1582-1792	2
	Secretaire	Colmar	1793-1872	4
Fessenheim	rkKB	Colmar	1663-1792	1
	Secretaire	Colmar	1793-1872	6
Fislis	Secretaire	Colmar	1793-1872	3
Flaxlanden	rkKB	Colmar	1664-1812	2
	Secretaire	Colmar	1793-1872	6
Folgensbourg	rkKB	Colmar	1722-1798	2
	Secretaire	Colmar	1793-1872	6
Fortschwihr	rkKB	Colmar	1667-1792	2
	Secretaire	Colmar	1792-1872	5
Franken	rkKB	Colmar	1648-1792	3
	Secretaire	Colmar	1793-1872	7
Freland	Secretaire	Colmar	1792-1872	11
	rkKB	Colmar	1676-1792	3
Freudstein= Willer-Sur- Thur				
Friessen	rkKB	Colmar	1698-1802	2
	Secretaire	Colmar	1793-1872	5
Froeningen	rkKB	Colmar	1685-1789	2
	Secretaire	Colmar	1786-1872	10
Fulleren	Secretaire	Colmar	1793-1872	5
Galfingue	rkKB	Colmar	1745-1792	2
	Secretaire	Colmar	1793-1872	6
Geishouse	Secretaire	Colmar	1792-1872	5
	rkKB	Colmar	1627-1792	5
Geispitzen	Secretaire	Colmar	1793-1872	7
Geiswasser	Secretaire	Colmar	1793-1872	4
Gemarcourt= Gommersdorf				
Giersberg= Ribeauville				
Gildwille	rkKB	Colmar	1738-1787	1
	Secretaire	Colmar	1792-1872	4

Location	Nature of Material	Where Filmed	Dates Covered	No. of Rolls
Golbach	rkKB	Colmar	1777-1792	1
Goldbach	Secretaire	Colmar	1792-1872	5
Gommersdorf	rkKB	Colmar	1790-1791	1
	Secretaire	Colmar	1792-1892	3
Grentzingen	rkKB	Colmar	1673-1792	2
	Secretaire	Colmar	1793-1872	5
Griesbach-au-Val	Archives	Colmar	1760-1770	1
	Secretaire	Colmar	1792-1872	5
Grussenheim	Secretaire	Colmar	1793-1872	5
	rkKB	Colmar	1685-1792	3
Gueberschwihr	Archives	Colmar	1200-1795	1
	rkKB	Colmar	1657-1792	4
	Secretaire	Colmar	1792-1872	10
Guebwiller	Archives	Colmar	1465-1790	1
	Secretaire	Colmar	1792-1872	19
	rkKB	Colmar	1582-1792	9
Guémar	rkKB	Colmar	1653-1792	3
	Secretaire	Colmar	1792-1872	9
Guerenatten	rkKB	Colmar	1773-1792	1
	Secretaire	Colmar	1792-1872	4
Guewenheim	rkKB	Colmar	1773-1790	1
	Secretaire	Colmar	1792-1872	6
Gundolsheim	rkKB	Colmar	1773-1792	1
	Secretaire	Colmar	1792-1872	6
Gunsbach	rkKB	Colmar	1751-1792	2
	evKB	Colmar	1755-1792	2
	Secretaire	Colmar	1792-1872	7
Habsheim	Secretaire	Colmar	1793-1872	10
	rkKB	Colmar	1581-1792	2
Hagenbach	rkKB	Colmar	1682-1808	2
	Secretaire	Colmar	1792-1872	4
Hagenthal-le-Bas	Secretaire	Colmar	1792-1872	6
	rkKB	Colmar	1749-1792	2
Hagenthal-le-Haut	Secretaire	Colmar	1793-1872	5
Hartmannswiller	rkKB	Colmar	1712-1792	2
	Secretaire	Colmar	1792-1872	6
Hattstatt	Secretaire	Colmar	1715-1927	10
	rkKB	Colmar	1722-1792	2

Location	Nature of Material	Where Filmed	Dates Covered	No. of Rolls
Hausgauen	rkKB	Colmar	1685-1792	1
	Secretaire	Colmar	1793-1872	5
Hecken	Secretaire	Colmar	1792-1872	3
Hegenheim	rkKB	Colmar	1599-1787	4
	Secretaire	Colmar	1793-1872	9
Heidwiller	rkKB	Colmar	1660-1803	2
	Secretaire	Colmar	1793-1862	3
Heimersdorf	Secretaire	Colmar	1793-1872	5
Heimsbrunn	rkKB	Colmar	1584-1792	1
	Secretaire	Colmar	1793-1872	4
Heiteren	Archives	Colmar		3
	Secretaire	Colmar	15th-17th Cent	2
Heiteren	rkKB	Colmar	1667-1801	3
	Secretaire	Colmar	1793-1872	4
Heiwiller	Secretaire	Colmar	1793-1872	3
	rkKB	Colmar	1685-1792	2
Helfrantzkirch	rkKB	Colmar	1718-1791	1
	Secretaire	Colmar	1803-1872	5
Henflingen	Secretaire	Colmar	1793-1872	3
Herrlisheim	rkKB	Colmar	1587-1792	2
	Secretaire	Colmar	1792-1872	7
Hesingue	rkKB	Colmar	1746-1792	1
	Secretaire	Colmar	1793-1872	6
Hettenschlag	Secretaire	Colmar	1794-1872	3
Hindlingen	Secretaire	Colmar	1802-1872	5
Hirsingue	Secretaire	Colmar	1793-1862	6
	rkKB	Colmar	1773-1792	1
Hirtzbach	rkKB		1793-1872	4
	Secretaire		1580-1789	1
Hirtzfelden	Secretaire	Colmar	1792-1872	5
	rkKB	Colmar	1665-1812	2
Hochstatt	rkKB	Colmar	1665-1793	3
	Secretaire	Colmar	1792-1872	6

Hohlandsbourg=
 Wintzenheim

Location	Nature of Material	Where Filmed	Dates Covered	No. of Rolls
Hohrod	Secretaire	Colmar	1792-1852	4
Holtzwihr	rkKB	Colmar	1685-1792	2
	Secretaire	Colmar	1792-1872	4
Hombourg	rkKB	Colmar	1677-1794	2
	Secretaire	Colmar	1793-1872	5
Horbourg= Wihr-en- Plaine	Archives	Colmar		4
	evKB	Colmar	1560-1792	4
	Secretaire	Colmar	1792-1872	9
Houssen	Archives	Colmar		1
	rkKB	Colmar	1639-1792	1
	Secretaire	Colmar	1792-1872	5
Hunawihr	evKB	Colmar	1560-1791	5
	rkKB	Colmar	1689-1791	1
	Secretaire	Colmar	1792-1872	21
Hundsbach	rkKB	Colmar	1685-1792	2
	Secretaire	Colmar	1793-1872	3
Hunnigue	rkKB	Colmar	1685-1791	5
	Secretaire	Colmar	1792-1872	8
Husseren-les- Chateaux	rkKB	Colmar	1648-1800	2
	Secretaire	Colmar	1792-1862	6
Husseren- Wesserling	Secretaire	Colmar	1792-1872	5
Illfurth	rkKB	Colmar	1792-1872	2
	Secretaire	Colmar	1792-1872	6
Illhaeusern	Secretaire	Colmar	1793-1872	5
Illzach	evKB	Colmar	1560-1790	1
	Secretaire	Colmar	1798-1872	6
Ingersheim	Secretaire	Colmar	1792-1872	9
	rkKB	Colmar	1656-1792	2
Issenheim	Archives	Colmar		1
	rkKB	Colmar	1587-1792	3
	Secretaire	Colmar	1793-1872	7
Jebsheim	evKB	Colmar	1670-1792	3
	Secretaire	Colmar	1792-1872	7
Jettingen	rkKB	Colmar	1773-1789	1
	Secretaire	Colmar	1792-1872	5
Jungholtz	Secretaire	Colmar	1793-1808	3
Kappelen	rkKB	Colmar	1589-1792	2
	Secretaire	Colmar	1793-1872	5

Location	Nature of Material	Where Filmed	Dates Covered	No. of Rolls
Katzenthal	rkKB	Colmar	1687-1792	2
	Secretaire	Colmar	1792-1872	7
Kayersberg	rkKB	Colmar	1655-1792	4
	Secretaire	Colmar	1793-1872	14
Kembs	Secretaire	Colmar	1793-1872	7
	rkKB	Colmar	1639-1793	3
Kientzheim	rkKB	Colmar	1773-1791	1
	Secretaire	Colmar	1793-1872	9
Kiffis	rkKB	Colmar	1788-1789	1
	Secretaire	Colmar	1793-1872	3
Kingersheim	Secretaire	Colmar	1792-1872	5
Kirchberg	rkKB	Colmar	1591-1793	6
	Secretaire	Colmar	1792-1872	5
Kirchheim= Turckheim				
Knoeringue	rkKB	Colmar	1586-1789	2
	Secretaire	Colmar	1793-1872	4
Koestlach	rkKB	Colmar	1705-1792	2
	Secretaire	Colmar	1793-1872	5
Koetzingen	rkKB	Colmar	1519-1789	1
	Secretaire	Colmar	1793-1892	5
Kruth	Secretaire	Colmar	1795-1872	6
Kunheim	evKB	Colmar	1792-1872	2
	Secretaire	Colmar	1792-1872	5
Labaroche	rkKB	Colmar	1683-1799	4
	Secretaire	Colmar	1793-1872	9
Haut-Landsberg= Wintzenheim				
Landser	rkKB	Colmar	1588-1792	3
	Secretaire	Colmar	1793-1872	7
Landskron	Secretaire	Colmar	1792-1872	6
Lapoutroie	rkKB	Colmar	1650-1792	4
	Secretaire	Colmar	1792-1872	10
Largitzen	Secretaire	Colmar	1793-1872	4
Lautenbach- Schweighouse	rkKB	Colmar	1643-1792	5
	Secretaire	Colmar	1792-1872	5

Location	Nature of Material	Where Filmed	Dates Covered	No. of Rolls
Lautenbachzell	rkKB	Colmar	1653-1869	4
	Secretaire	Colmar	1792-1872	6
Lauw	Secretaire	Colmar	1792-1872	5
Lecelle or Lucelle	rkKB	Colmar	1777-1872	1
	Secretaire	Colmar	1793-1872	3
Leimbach	rkKB	Colmar	1737-1792	3
	Secretaire	Colmar	1792-1872	6
Levoncourt	rkKB	Colmar	1773-1792	1
	Secretaire	Colmar	1793-1872	3
Leymen	rkKB	Colmar	1635-1792	2
	Secretaire	Colmar	1792-1872	7
Liebenswiller	rkKB	Colmar	1774-1780	3
	Secretaire	Colmar	1793-1862	4
Liebsdorf	Secretaire	Colmar	1793-1872	3
Liepvre	rkKB	Colmar	1690-1792	4
	Secretaire	Colmar	1793-1872	9
Ligsdorf	rkKB	Colmar	1661-1794	2
	Secretaire	Colmar	1793-1872	5
Linnsdorf	Secretaire	Colmar	1792-1872	4
Linthal	Secretaire	Colmar	1794-1872	6
Logelheim-Logelnheim	rkKB	Colmar	1644-1792	2
	Secretaire	Colmar	1793-1872	5
Luemschwiller	rkKB	Colmar	1543-1811	2
	Secretaire	Colmar	1793-1872	6
Lutran	rkKB	Colmar	1777-1788	1
	Secretaire	Colmar	1793-1872	4
Luttenbach	Secretaire	Colmar	1793-1872	5
Lutter	rkKB	Colmar	1658-1802	2
	Secretaire	Colmar	1793-1872	3
Lutterbach	Minutes de greffier	Colmar	1578-1821	43
		Colmar	1608-1792	1
	rkKB	Colmar	1793-1872	7
	Secretaire			
Magny	Secretaire	Colmar	1792-1872	4
Magstatt	rkKB	Colmar	1586-1792	2
	Secretaire	Colmar	1793-1862	4

Location	Nature of Material	Where Filmed	Dates Covered	No. of Rolls
Magstatt-le-Haut	rkKB	Colmar	1586-1792	3
	Secretaire	Colmar	1792-1872	7
Malmersprach	Secretaire	Colmar	1742-1872	4
	rkKB	Colmar	1627-1792	5
Manspach	rkKB	Colmar	1627-1792	7
	Secretaire	Colmar	1792-1872	5
Marbach	Archives	Colmar	1070-1793	1
			1757-1760	1
Masevaux= Masmünster	Archives	Colmar	1465-1790	3
	rkKB	Colmar	1584-1792	5
	Secretaire	Colmar	1792-1872	12
Mertzen	rkKB	Colmar	1640-1792	3
	Secretaire	Colmar	1793-1872	4
Merxheim	rkKB	Colmar	1649-1792	2
	Secretaire	Colmar	1792-1872	6
Metzeral	Secretaire	Colmar	1792-1872	7
Meyenheim	rkKB	Colmar	1642-1792	1
	Secretaire	Colmar	1793-1872	5
Michel-le-Bas	rkKB	Colmar	1781-	1
Michelbach	rkKB	Colmar	1773-1790	1
	Secretaire	Colmar	1793-1872	3
Michelbach-le-Bas	rkKB	Colmar	1781-	1
	Secretaire	Colmar	1793-1872	3
Michelbach-le-Haut	rkKB	Colmar	1661-1829	2
	Secretaire	Colmar	1793-1872	4
Mittelwihr	rkKB	Colmar	1559-1793	2
	Secretaire	Colmar	1792-1872	4
Mitzach	Secretaire	Colmar	1792-1872	3
Moernach	Secretaire	Colmar	1793-1872	6
Mollau	rkKB	Colmar	1669-1792	2
	Secretaire	Colmar	1792-1872	5
Montreux-Jeune	rkKB	Colmar	1650-1792	2
	Secretaire	Colmar	1792-1872	5
Montreux-Vieux	rkKB	Colmar	1774-1792	1
	Secretaire	Colmar	1792-1872	4
Moos	Secretaire	Colmar	1793-1872	3
Moosch= Mooschbach	Secretaire	Colmar	1792-1872	6

Location	Nature of Material	Where Filmed	Dates Covered	No. of Rolls
Morschwiller	rkKB	Colmar	1773-1789	1
Morschwiller-le-Bas	rkKB	Colmar	1663-1789	1
	Secretaire	Colmar	1793-1872	6
Mortzwiller	Secretaire	Colmar	1792-1872	5
Moyen-Muespach	rkKB	Colmar	1773-1789	1
	Secretaire	Colmar	1793-1872	3
Muespach-le-Bas	rkKB	Colmar	1585-1797	2
	Secretaire	Colmar	1793-1872	4
Muespach-le-Haut	Secretaire	Colmar	1863-1872	1
Muhlbach-Sur-Münster	rkKB	Colmar	1739-1792	1
	evKB	Colmar	1574-1792	7
	Secretaire	Colmar	1792-1872	4
Mulhouse	Archives	Colmar Strasbourg		
	LDS records	Colmar	1948 and earlier	
Mulhouse	rkKB	Colmar	1620-1788	1
	Secretaire	Colmar	1798-1872	90
	MKB	Eibenstock	1871-1876	1
Mulhouse-Dornach	rkKB	Colmar	1773-1789	1
	Secretaire	Colmar	1793-1872	7
Mulhuse	rkKB	Colmar	1620-1788	1
Munchhouse	rkKB	Colmar	1690-1792	1
	Secretaire	Colmar	1793-1872	4
Münster	Archives	Colmar	1235-1790	2
	rkKB	Colmar	1603-1789	4
	Secretaire	Colmar	1793-1872	15
Muntzheim	rkKB	Colmar	1561-1792	3
	Secretaire	Colmar	1792-1862	5
Munwiller	rkKB	Colmar	1718-1834	1
	Secretaire	Colmar	1792-1872	3
Murbach	Archives	Colmar	8th -18th Cent	
	rkKB	Colmar Paderborn	1771-1793	2
	Secretaire	Colmar	1793-1872	3
Nambsheim	rkKB	Colmar	1662-1793	2
	Secretaire	Colmar	1792-1872	4
Neuenweeg= Blotzheim				

Location	Nature of Material	Where Filmed	Dates Covered	No. of Rolls
Neuf-Brisach	Archives	Colmar	1684-1698	1
	MKB	Hannover	1871-1918	1
	rkKB	Colmar	1699-1792	7
	Hopital Militaire	Colmar	1733-1792	1
	Secretaire	Colmar	1792-1872	11
Neuwiller	rkKB	Colmar	1781-1788	1
Niederbruck	Secretaire	Colmar	1792-1872	3
Niederentzen	rkKB	Colmar	1658-1792	1
	Secretaire	Colmar	1792-1872	4
Niederhergheim	rkKB	Colmar	1773-1792	1
	Secretaire	Colmar	1792-1872	5
Niederlarg	Secretaire	Colmar	1793-1862	3
Niedermorschwihr	rkKB	Colmar	1688-1792	2
	Secretaire	Colmar	1792-1872	6
Niffer	rkKB	Colmar	1740-1790	1
	Secretaire	Colmar	1792-1872	4
Nuewiller	Secretaire	Colmar	1793-1872	4
Oberbruck	Secretaire	Colmar	1591-1793	4
	rkKB	Colmar	1793-1872	4
Oberdorf	Secretaire	Colmar	1793-1872	4
Oberentzen	rkKB	Colmar	1660-1788	1
	Secretaire	Colmar	1792-1872	4
Oberhergheim	rkKB	Colmar	1598-1792	2
	Secretaire	Colmar	1792-1872	6
Oberlarg	rkKB	Colmar	1722-1789	1
	Secretaire	Colmar	1793-1872	3
Obermorschwihr	rkKB	Colmar	1651-1792	1
	Secretaire	Colmar	1792-1872	5
Obermorsch- willer	rkKB	Colmar	1773-1789	1
	Secretaire	Colmar	1793-1872	4
Obersaasheim	rkKB	Colmar	1633-1792	2
	Secretaire	Colmar	1792-1872	4
Oderen	rkKB	Colmar	1618-1791	3
	Secretaire	Colmar	1792-1872	6
Ollwiller	rkKB	Colmar	1712-1792	2
Oltingue -en-	rkKB	Colmar	1606-1792	1
	Secretaire	Colmar	1793-1872	4

Location	Nature of Material	Where Filmed	Dates Covered	No. of Rolls
Orbey	rkKB	Colmar	1647-1792	5
	Secretaire	Colmar	1792-1926	22
Orschwihr	rkKB	Colmar	1666-1792	2
	Secretaire	Colmar	1792-1927	6
Osenbach	rkKB	Colmar	1773-1822	2
	Secretaire	Colmar	1792-1872	4
Ostheim	rkKB	Colmar	1737-1791	1
	Secretaire	Colmar	1792-1872	7
Ottmarsheim	rkKB	Colmar	1584-1791	1
	Secretaire	Colmar	1793-1872	4
Pairis/ Orbey	Secretaire	Colmar	1792-1872	19
Petit-Landau	rkKB	Colmar	1755-1790	1
	Secretaire	Colmar	1792-1872	5
Pfaffenheim	rkKB	Colmar	1660-1824	4
	Secretaire	Colmar	1792-1872	9
Pfastatt	rkKB	Colmar	1774-1789	1
	Secretaire	Colmar	1793-1872	5
Pfetterhouse	rkKB	Colmar	1668-1789	1
	Secretaire	Colmar	1793-1872	3
Pulversheim	rkKB	Colmar	1773-1792	1
	Secretaire	Colmar	1793-1872	3
Raedersdorf	rkKB	Colmar	1754-1792	1
	Secretaire	Colmar	1793-1872	4
Raedersheim	rkKB	Colmar	1639-1792	1
	Secretaire	Colmar	1793-1927	3
Rammersmatt	Secretaire	Colmar	1792-1872	8
	rkKB	Colmar	1737-1827	1
Ranspach	rkKB	Colmar	1627-1792	6
	Secretaire	Colmar	1792-1872	4
Ranspach-le-Bas	rkKB	Colmar	1686-1792	2
	Secretaire	Colmar	1793-1872	4
Ranspach-le-Haut	rkKB	Colmar	1737-1789	1
	Secretaire	Colmar	1793-1872	3
Rantzwiller	rkKB	Colmar	1645-1790	1
	Secretaire	Colmar	1793-1872	3
Reguisheim	rkKB	Colmar	1664-1792	1
	Secretaire	Colmar	1792-1872	9

Location	Nature of Material	Where Filmed	Dates Covered	No. of Rolls
Reininque	rkKB	Colmar	1640-1792	2
	Secretaire	Colmar	1793-1872	4
Rhann, Roderen	Secretaire	Colmar	1792-1872	4
Ribeauville	Archives	Colmar	1115-18th Cent	5
	Secretaire	Colmar	1792-1872	22
Rickwiller	rkKB	Colmar	1782-1789	1
	Secretaire	Colmar	1793-1872	4
Riedisheim	rkKB	Colmar	1740-1789	1
	Secretaire	Colmar	1793-1872	5
Riedwihr	rkKB	Colmar	1777-1792	1
	Secretaire	Colmar	1792-1872	3
Riespach	rkKB	Colmar	1585-1793	3
	Secretaire	Colmar	1793-1872	3
Rimpach-pres-Gruebwiller	Secretaire	Colmar	1725-1872	6
Rimpach-pres-Maseraux	Secretaire	Colmar	1792-1872	4
	rkKB	Colmar	1591-1793	4
Rimbachzell	rkKB	Colmar	1784-1790	1
	Secretaire	Colmar	1793-1872	4
Riquewihr	Archives	Colmar	1297-1693	5
	rkKB	Colmar	1685-1792	2
	evKB	Colmar	1631-1792	4
Rixheim	rkKB	Colmar	1656-1793	3
	Secretaire	Colmar	1793-1872	9
Roderen	Secretaire	Colmar	1792-1872	5
Rodern	Secretaire	Colmar	1793-1872	3
	rkKB	Colmar	1643-1791	2
Roggenburg	rkKB	Colmar	1788-1789	1
Roggenhouse	rkKB	Colmar	1773-1792	1
Romagny	Secretaire	Colmar	1792-1872	3
Rombach-le-Franc	rkKB	Colmar	1786-1792	1
	Secretaire	Colmar	1793-1927	9
Roppentzwiller	rkKB	Colmar	1682-1792	1
	Secretaire	Colmar	1793-1872	4
Rorschwihr	rkKB	Colmar	1741-1792	1
	Secretaire	Colmar	1793-1872	4
Rosenau	Secretaire	Colmar	1794-1872	5

Location	Nature of Material	Where Filmed	Dates Covered	No. of Rolls
Rouffach	Archives	Colmar	1393-1786	1
	rkKB	Colmar	1580-1792	9
	Secretaire	Colmar	1793-1872	13
Ruederbach	Secretaire	Colmar	1793-1872	3
Ruelisheim	rkKB	Colmar	1666-1791	1
	Secretaire	Colmar	1793-1872	6
Rummersheim-le-Haut	rkKB	Colmar	1773-1803	1
	Secretaire	Colmar	1792-1872	5
Rustenhardt	rkKB	Colmar	1692-1803	1
	Secretaire	Colmar	1793-1872	4
St. Amarien	rkKB	Colmar	1627-1792	7
	Secretaire	Colmar	1752-1862	10
St. Cosme	rkKB	Colmar	1644-1792	1
	Secretaire	Colmar	1792-1872	2
St. Didier-au-Mont-d'or	Secretaire	Colmar	1792-1902	6
St. Hippolyte	rkKB	Colmar	1642-1792	44
	Secretaire	Colmar	1792-1872	12
St. Louis	Secretaire	Colmar	1792-1872	11
St. Ulrich	Secretaire	Colmar	1793-1872	3
Ste. Crois-aux-Mines	rkKB	Colmar	1712-1792	39
	Secretaire	Colmar	1792-1927	22
Ste. Crois-en-Plaine	rkKB	Colmar	1587-1792	2
	Secretaire	Colmar	1793-1872	8
Ste. Marie-aux-Mines	Archives	Colmar		8
	rkKB	Colmar	1634-1792	25
	refKB	Colmar	1562-1792	11
	evLutKB	Colmar	1614-1792	7
	Secretaire	Colmar	1792-1812	39
Sausheim	rkKB	Colmar	1644-1792	1
	Secretaire	Colmar	1793-1872	4
Schlienbach	rkKB	Colmar	1584-1792	1
Schlierbach	Secretaire	Colmar	1793-1872	4
Schoppenwihr	Archives	Colmar	-18th Cent	1
Schweighouse	rkKB	Colmar	1773-1791	1
	Secretaire	Colmar	1792-1872	3
Schwoben	rkKB	Colmar	1685-1792	2
	Secretaire	Colmar	1793-1872	2

Location	Nature of Material	Where Filmed	Dates Covered	No. of Rolls
Sentheim	rkKB	Colmar	1674-1792	1
	Secretaire	Colmar	1792-1872	5
Seppois-le-Bas	rkKB	Colmar	1773-1789	1
	Secretaire	Colmar	1793-1872	5
Seppois-le-Haut	Secretaire	Colmar	1793-1872	3
	rkKB	Colmar	1793-1872	2
Sewen	rkKB	Colmar	1591-1793	4
	Secretaire	Colmar	1792-1872	4
Sickert	Secretaire	Colmar	1792-1872	3
Sierentz	rkKB	Colmar	1694-1792	3
	Secretaire	Colmar	1793-1872	8
Sigolsheim	rkKB	Colmar	1664-1794	2
	Secretaire	Colmar	1792-1872	6
Sondernach	Secretaire	Colmar	1792-1872	4
Sondersdorf	rkKB	Colmar	1585-1792	3
	Secretaire	Colmar	1793-1872	3
Soppe-le-Bas	rkKB	Colmar	1662-1792	2
	Secretaire	Colmar	1792-1872	4
Soppe-le-Haut	rkKB	Colmar	1690-1792	2
	Secretaire	Colmar	1792-1872	4
Soultz-Haut-Rhin	Archives	Colmar	1686-1932	5
	rkKB	Colmar	1582-1792	8
	Secretaire	Colmar	1792-1872	20
Soultzbach-les-Bains	rkKB	Colmar	1692-1792	2
	Secretaire	Colmar	1792-1872	6
Soultzeren	evKB	Colmar	1755-1792	1
	Secretaire	Colmar	1792-1872	5
Soultzmatt	rkKB	Colmar	1587-1792	4
	Secretaire	Colmar	1792-1872	9
Spechbach-le-Bas	rkKB	Colmar	1639-1852	1
	Secretaire	Colmar	1793-1872	5
Spechbach-le-Haut	Secretaire	Colmar	1792-1872	8
	rkKB	Colmar	1640-1803	2
Staffelfelden	Secretaire	Colmar	1785-1808	6
	rkKB	Colmar	1737-1792	1
Steinbach	rkKB	Colmar	1773-1788	1
	Secretaire	Colmar	1792-1872	4

Location	Nature of Material	Where Filmed	Dates Covered	No. of Rolls
Steinbrunn-le-Bas	rkKB Secretaire	Colmar Colmar	1640-1792 1793-1872	1 4
Steinbrunn-le-Haut	rkKB Secretaire	Colmar Colmar	1584-1789 1787-1872	1 5
Steinsoultz	rkKB Secretaire	Colmar Colmar	1682-1792 1793-1872	1 5
Sternenberg	rkKB Secretaire	Colmar Colmar	1738-1791 1792-1872	1 8
Stetten	Secretaire	Colmar	1793-1872	7
Storckensohn	Secretaire	Colmar	1792-1872	5
Stosswihr	Secretaire	Colmar	1793-1872	6
Strueth	Secretaire	Colmar	1793-1872	6
Sundhoffen	evKB Secretaire	Colmar Colmar	1563-1792 1793-1872	 7
Tagolsheim	rkKB Secretaire	Colmar Colmar	1716-1789 1792-1872	1 4
Tagsdorf	rkKB Secretaire	Colmar Colmar	1685-1792 1792-1944	2 5
Thann -Roderen-	rkKB Archives Secretaire	Colmar Colmar Colmar	1587-1794 1216-1790 1792-1872	2 1 75
Thannenkirch	Secretaire	Colmar	1792-1872	12
Traubach-le-Bas	rkKB Secretaire	Colmar Colmar	1660-1790 1792-1872	3 8
Traubach-le-Haut	rkKB Secretaire	Colmar Colmar	1660-1790 1792-1872	3 8
Turckheim	Archives rkKB Secretaire	Colmar Colmar Colmar	1340-1790 1498-1792 1793-1872	1 5 22
Ueberkumen	rkKB Secretaire	Colmar Colmar	1677-1792 1792-1872	1 5
Ueberstrass	Secretaire	Colmar	1796-1872	5
Uffheim	rkKB Secretaire	Colmar Colmar	1747-1789 1793-1872	2 7
Uffholtz	rkKB Secretaire	Colmar Colmar	1773-1793 1784-1872	2 12

Location	Nature of Material	Where Filmed	Dates Covered	No. of Rolls
Ungersheim	rkKB	Colmar	1584-1800	2
	Secretaire	Colmar	1793-1927	10
Urbes	Secretaire	Colmar	1792-1872	7
Urschenheim	Secretaire	Colmar	1650-1792	4
	rkKB	Colmar	1792-1872	15
Valdieu	Secretaire	Colmar	1792-1872	6
Vieux-Ferrette	rkKB	Colmar	1788-1789	2
Village-Neuf	rkKB	Colmar	1665-1792	3
	Secretaire	Colmar	1793-1872	11
Voegtlinshoffen	rkKB	Colmar	1737-1791	2
	Secretaire	Colmar	1792-1872	8
Vogelgrun	Secretaire	Colmar	1792-1872	5
Walbach	Archives	Colmar	16th-18th Cent	1
	Secretaire	Colmar	1792-1872	26
	rkKB	Colmar	1686-1796	4
Walck	Secretaire	Colmar	1848-1862	1
Waldersbach	Secretaire	Colmar	1793-1862	2
Waldhambach	evKB	Colmar	1683-1790	2
	Secretaire	Colmar	1792-1862	4
Waldinghofen	rkKB	Colmar	1745-1800	2
	Secretaire	Colmar	1793-1872	7
Walheim	rkKB	Colmar	1660-1793	2
	Secretaire	Colmar	1793-1872	8
Waltenheim	rkKB	Colmar	1694-1792	4
	Secretaire	Colmar	1793-1872	6
Wasserbourg	Archives	Colmar	16th-18th Cent	1
	rkKB	Colmar	1688-1792	1
	Secretaire	Colmar	1792-1872	5
Wattwiller	rkKB	Colmar	1712-1792	4
	Secretaire	Colmar	1792-1872	18
Weckolsheim	rkKB	Colmar	1772-1832	2
	Secretaire	Colmar	1792-1872	7
Wegscheidt	rkKB	Colmar	1591-1793	4
	Secretaire	Colmar	1792-1872	5
Wentzwiller	rkKB	Colmar	1749-1792	4
	Secretaire	Colmar	1793-1872	6
Werentzhouse	rkKB	Colmar	1585-1792	2
	Secretaire	Colmar	1793-1872	6

Location	Nature of Material	Where Filmed	Dates Covered	No. of Rolls
Westhalten	rkKB	Colmar	1653-1792	3
	Secretaire	Colmar	1792-1872	7
Wettolsheim	Secretaire	Colmar	1719-1872	11
	rkKB	Colmar	1648-1792	2
Wickerschweier	rkKB	Colmar	1685-1792	2
Wickerschwihr	Secretaire	Colmar	1793-1927	8
Widensolen	rkKB	Colmar	1650-1792	4
	Secretaire	Colmar	1792-1872	8
Wihr-au-Val	Archives	Colmar	16th-18th Cent	1
	rkKB	Colmar	1773-1792	2
	Secretaire	Colmar	1793-1872	13
Wihr-en-Plaine	Secretaire	Colmar	1793-1872	7
Wildenstein	Secretaire	Colmar	1797-1875	4
Willer	rkKB	Colmar	1773-1789	1
	Secretaire	Colmar	1793-1872	4
Willer-Altkirch	rkKB	Colmar	1686-1786	1
	Secretaire	Colmar	1793-1872	4
Willer-Sur-Thur	rkKB	Colmar	1696-1792	5
	Secretaire	Colmar	1793-1872	9
Winckel	rkKB	Colmar	1733-1792	2
	Secretaire	Colmar	1793-1869	8
Wintzenheim	Archives	Colmar	1435-1789	1
	rkKB	Colmar	1793-1872	19
		Colmar	1584-1793	4
Wittelsheim	Archives	Colmar	1542-1821	44
	rkKB	Colmar	1773-1803	1
	Secretaire	Colmar	1792-1872	6
Wittenheim	Archives	Colmar	1465-1790	2
	rkKB	Colmar	1685-1797	3
	Secretaire	Colmar	1793-1872	6
Wittersdorf	rkKB	Colmar	1753-1792	1
	Secretaire	Colmar	1793-1872	4
Wolfersdorf	Secretaire	Colmar	1793-1872	3
Wolfgantzen	rkKB	Colmar	1733-1792	1
	Secretaire	Colmar	1792-1872	3
Wolschwiller	rkKB	Colmar	1693-1789	1
	Secretaire	Colmar	1793-1862	4
Wuenheim	rkKB	Colmar	1698-1789	3
	Secretaire	Colmar	1793-1872	9

Location	Nature of Material	Where Filmed	Dates Covered	No. of Rolls
Zaessingen	rkKB	Colmar	1722-1808	1
	Secretaire	Colmar	1793-1862	11
Zellenberg	Archives	Colmar	1574-1685	1
	rkKB	Colmar	1667-1792	2
	Secretaire	Colmar	1793-1872	12
Zillisheim	rkKB	Colmar	1679-1792	2
	Secretaire	Colmar	1793-1872	6
Zimmerbach	rkKB	Colmar	1588-1792	2
	Secretaire	Colmar	1793-1872	8
Zimmersheim	rkKB	Colmar	1690-1792	1
	Secretaire	Colmar	1793-1872	2

OSTPREUSSEN[1]

Location	Nature of Material	Where Filmed	Dates Covered	No. of Rolls
Allenstein	evLutKB	Berlin-Dahlem	1779-1944	7
-Olsztyn-	evMilGem	Hannover	1909-1911	1
	evKB	Berlin-Charlottenburg	1779-1911	1
	rkKB	Berlin-Dahlem	1659-1807	1
Alt Passarge -Stara Pasłęka-	evLutKB	Berlin-Dahlem	1807-1944	1
Alt Schöneberg -Wrzesina-	rkKB	Berlin-Dahlem	1659-1807	1
Angerburg	evKB	Warsaw	1811-1830	1
-Wegorzewo-	evKB	Berlin-Dahlem	1729-1763	1
Arnau -Ornowo-	evKB	Warsaw	1815-1870	3
Arnswald -Grabowo-	evKB	Berlin-Charlottenburg	1917-1941	1
	evKB	Salt Lake City	1761-1937	4
Arys	evKB	Berlin-Dahlem	1700-1944	10
-Orzysz-	evKB	Berlin-Charlottenburg	1938-1944	1
Aweyden	evKB	Warsaw	1814-1822	1
-Nawiady-	evKB	Warsaw	1764-1846	4
Baranowen -Baranowo-	evKB	Berlin	1851-1944	2
Barten	evKB	Salt Lake City	1531-1944	14
-Barciany-	evKB	Berlin-Charlottenburg	1743-1906	1
	STA	Berlin-Dahlem	1938-1943	1
Bartenstein	evKB	Warsaw	1852-1874	1
-Bartoszyce-	evKB	Berlin-Dahlem	1644-1944	20
	rkKB	Berlin-Dahlem	1875-1888	1
	evKB	Berlin-Charlottenburg	1726-1942	2
	MilKB	Hannover	1746-1797	1
	MilKB	Hannover	1763-1827	1
	MilKB	Hannover	1777-1817	1
	MilKB	Hannover	1784-1811	1
	MilKB	Hannover	1798-1807	1
	MilKB	Eibenstock		

[1]This portion of Ostpreussen went to Poland after World War II and is now part of the provinces of Olsztyn and Białystok.

Location	Nature of Material	Where Filmed	Dates Covered	No. of Rolls
Bäslack -Bezławki-	evKB STA	Salt Lake City Salt Lake City	1851-1944 1915-1943	2 1
Benern -Bieniowo-	rkKB rkKB rkKB rkKB	Berlin-Dahlem Berlin-Dahlem Salt Lake City Salt Lake City	1567-1891 1567-1889 1567-1875 1567-1874	3 4 1 1
Benkheim -Banie Mazurskie-	STA	Berlin-Dahlem	1874-1937	10
Bischofsburg -Biskupiec-	rkKB evKB rkKB evKB	Berlin-Dahlem Hannover Berlin-Dahlem Salt Lake City	1643-1900 1899-1917 1643-1897 1792-1944	8 1 10 5
Bischofstein -Bisztynek-	evKB	Salt Lake City	1794-1944	3
Blandau -Bludowo-	rkKB	Berlin-Dahlem	1565-1846	2
Borkenwalde -Moź Dzany-	Geburts reg.	Berlin	1914, 1931-1938	1
Brosymmen -Borsymy-	evKB	Berlin-Dahlem	1803-1875	1
Brassendorf -Kleszczewo-	evKB	Berlin- Charlottenburg	1937-1943	1
Braunsberg -Braniewo-	evLutKB rkKB rkKB rkKB	Berlin-Dahlem Berlin-Dahlem Berlin-Dahlem Warsaw	1851-1944 1565-1896 1567-1938 1774-1870	4 33 3 1
Briesen -Wąbrzezno-	evKB rkKB	Berlin-Dahlem Berlin-Dahlem	1831-1911 1845-1846	3 1
Brosowen -Brzozowo-	STA	Berlin-Dahlem	1874-1889	1
Buchholz -Bukowiec-	evKB	Warsaw	1852-1874	1
Buddern -Budry-	STA	Berlin-Dahlem	1874-1938	11
Camionken -Kamionki-	STA	Berlin	1874-1921	7
Czychen -Cichy-	evKB	Warsaw	1800-1865	2
Deutsch-Krone -Wałcz-	evKB	Berlin	1869-1930	1

Location	Nature of Material	Where Filmed	Dates Covered	No. of Rolls
Deutsch Wilten -Wielochy-	evKB	Berlin-Charlottenburg	1767-1944	1
Deutschendorf -Wilczęta-	evKB	Warsaw	1799-1870	1
Dietrichswalde -Gietrzwald-	rkKB	Berlin	1676-1825	1
Doben -Doba-	STA	Berlin	1874-1883	1
Dönhofstädt -Drogosze-	STA	Berlin	1938-1952	1
Drengfurth -Srokowo-	evKB MilKB	Berlin-Dahlem Hannover	1800-1942 1773-1810	11 1
Drigelsdorf -Drygały-	evKB	Berlin	1781-1875	3
Dubeningken -Dubeninki-	evKB	Berlin	1830-1944	3
Eckersberg -Florczaki-	evKB	Berlin-Dahlem	1914-1944	1
Eichendorf -Dąbrówka-	evKB	Warsaw	1767-1876	1
Eichhorn -Wiewiórki-	evKB	Berlin-Dahlem	1767-1876	6
Eichmedien -Nakomiady-	evKB	Warsaw	1665-1766	1
Elditten -Ełdyty Wielkie-	rkKB rkKB	Berlin Berlin-Dahlem	1792-1882 1807-1882	1 1
Engelstein -Wegielsztyn-	STA	Berlin	1874-1938	9
Falkenau -Sokolica-	evKB	Berlin	1670-1892	1
Frankenau -Franknowo-	rkKB	Berlin	1609-1744	1
Frauenburg -Frombork-	rkKB	Berlin	1631-1891	4
Frauendorf -Babiak-	rkKB rkKB	Berlin-Dahlem Berlin	1772-1892 1772-1892	3 2

Location	Nature of Material	Where Filmed	Dates Covered	No. of Rolls
Friedrichshof -Rozogi-	evKB	Warsaw	1765-1838	3
Gallingen -Galiny-	evKB	Warsaw	1836-1838	1
Gehlenburg -Biala Piska-	evKB	Berlin-Dahlem	1839-1850	1
Gehsen -Jeźe-	evKB	Berlin	1846-1876	1
Geierswalde -Gierzwałd-	evKB evKB	Berlin-Dahlem Warsaw	1553-1944 1830-1870	3 1
Gilgenburg -Dabrówno-	evKB rkKB	Berlin-Dahlem Berlin-Dahlem	1694-1944 1733-1766	3 1
Glottau -Głotowo-	rkKB evKB MilKB	Berlin-Dahlem Berlin-Charlottenburg Hannover	1766-1889 1747-1941 1778-1868	2 5 1
Goldap -Gołdap-	evKB evKB	Berlin-Charlottenburg Berlin	1747-1941 1711-1944	5 13
Gonsken -Gaski-	evLutKB Gov't rec.	Berlin-Dahlem Goslar	1800-1874 1825	1 1
Grabowen -Grabowo-	evKB evKB rkKB	Berlin-Charlottenburg Salt Lake City Warsaw	1917-1941 1761-1937 1629-1870	1 4 9
Grodzisko -Grodzisko-	STA	Berlin	1874-1889	2
Gross Bössau -Biesowo-	rkKB	Berlin-Dahlem	1690-1873	4
Gross Czymochen -Cimochy-	evKB	Berlin-Dahlem	1773-1944	2
Gross Gardienen -Gardyny-	evLutKB	Berlin-Dahlem	1814-1830	1
Gross Kirsteinsdorf -Kiersztanowo-	evKB	Berlin-Dahlem	1812-1944	1
Gross Kleeberg -Klebark Wielki-	rkKB	Berlin	1716-1754	1
Gross Köllen -Kolno-	rkKB	Berlin-Dahlem	1603-1892	3

Location	Nature of Material	Where Filmed	Dates Covered	No. of Rolls
Gross Lemkendorf -Lamkowo-	rkKB	Warsaw	1628-1847	2
Gross Peisten -Piasty Wielkie-	evKB	Berlin-Dahlem	1610-1944	2
Gross Pötzdorf -Pacółtowo-	evKB	Berlin-Dahlem	1784-1944	1
Gross Rautenberg -Wierzno Wielkie-	rkKB	Berlin-Dahlem	1637-1847	4
Gross Rohdau -Rodowo-	evKB	Lübeck	1755-1944	3
Gross Rosinsko -Rozynsk Wielki-	rkKB	Berlin-Dahlem	1767-1784	1
Gross Schläfken -Sławka Wielka-	evKB evKB	Berlin Berlin	1749-1935 1802-1831	4 1
Gross Stürlack -Sterlawki Wielkie-	evKB	Berlin	1734-1779	2
Gross & Klein Sunkeln Sąkiety Wielkie & Małe	STA	Berlin	1874-1889	1
Gross Thierbach -Grądki-	evKB	Berlin-Dahlem	1683-1944	2
Gudnick -Gudniki-	evKB	Berlin	1692-1828	1
Guja -Guja-	STA	Berlin	1874-1828	1
Gurnen -Górne-	evKB evKB	Berlin Berlin-Charlottenburg	1749-1944 1915-1944	4 1
Guttstadt -Dobre Miasto-	rkKB rkKB	Berlin-Dahlem Berlin-Dahlem	1635-1876 1633-1892	3 9
Haarzen -Harsz-	STA	Berlin	1874-1890	1
Hanshagen -Janikowo-	evKB	Berlin-Dahlem	1776-1944	1

Location	Nature of Material	Where Filmed	Dates Covered	No. of Rolls
Heeselicht -Leszcz-	evKB	Berlin-Dahlem	1764-1944	1
Heiligelinde -Swięta Lipka-	rkKB	Berlin	1636-1895	5
Heiligenthal -Swiatka-	rkKB	Berlin	1689-1888	2
Heilsberg -Lidzbark Warmiński-	evKB rkKB evKB	Berlin-Dahlem Berlin-Dahlem Berlin-Charlottenburg	1776-1930 1588-1868 1831-1861	3 9 1
Heinrikau -Henrykowo-	rkKB	Berlin	1681-1832	1
Herrndorf -Mylnarska Wola-	evKB	Warsaw	1859-1870	1
Herzogswalde -Kriąsnik-	evKB evKB	Warsaw Berlin-Dahlem	1858 1943-1945	1 1
Hirschfeld -Jelonki-	evLutKB	Berlin-Dahlem	1658-1944	9
Jesziorowsken/ Seehausen -Jeziorowskie-	STA	Berlin	1874-1938	4
Johannisburg -Pisz-	evKB	Berlin	1766-1892	5
Kalkstein -Wapnik-	rkKB	Warsaw	1675-1870	2
Kandien -Kanigowo-	evLutKB	Berlin-Dahlem	1768-1944	1
Kiwitten -Kiwity-	rkKB	Berlin	1654-1884	10
Klaussen -Klusy-	evLutKB	Berlin-Dahlem	1773-1944	2
Klein Jerutten -Jerutki-	evKB	Berlin	1754-1875	5
Klein Koslau -Kozłówko-	evKB	Berlin	1749-1935	4
Kleszowen -Kleszczewo-	evKB	Berlin-Charlottenburg	1937-1943	1
Klingenberg -Ostre Bardo-	evKB	Berlin	1712-1944	1

Location	Nature of Material	Where Filmed	Dates Covered	No. of Rolls
Kölmersdorf -Wisniowo Ełckie-	evLutKB	Berlin-Dahlem	1773-1944	2
Königlich Queetz -Kwiecewo-	rkKB	Berlin	1683-1882	3
Korschen -Korsze-	STA	Berlin	1938-1943	2
Kraplau -Kraplewo-	evKB	Warsaw	1811-1870	2
Krekollen -Krekole-	rkKB	Berlin-Dahlem	1733-1944	2
Kruglanken -Kruklanki-	STA	Berlin	1874-1938	6
Kurken -Kurki-	evKB	Berlin-Dahlem	1799-1944	2
	evKB	Warsaw	1860-1869	1
Kutten -Kuty-	evKB	Berlin-Charlottenburg	1691-1903	3
	STA	Berlin	1874-1938	11
Lamgarben -Garbno-	evKB	Berlin-Dahlem	1567-1944	5
Langenau -Łęgowo-	evKB	Lübeck	1736-1944	1
Langheim -Łankiejmy-	STA	Berlin	1938-1943	1
Langwalde -Dlugobór-	rkKB	Augsburg	1847-1882	1
	rkKB	Berlin	1566-1806	1
Lauck -Ławki-	evKB	Warsaw	1799-1870	1
Lautern -Lutry-	rkKB	Berlin	1708-1878	5
Lenzen -Łęcze-	evKB	Warsaw	1630-1811	2
Lichtenau -Lechowo-	rkKB	Berlin	1599-1847	1
Liebemühl -Miłomłyn-	evKB	Warsaw	1815-1870	3
Liebstadt -Miłakowo-	evKB	Berlin-Dahlem	1851-1868	1

Location	Nature of Material	Where Filmed	Dates Covered	No. of Rolls
Lippinken -Lipinki-	rkKB	Berlin	1716-1888	4
Lissen -Lisy-	STA	Berlin	1874-1938	7
Lötzen -Giżycko-	rkKB	Augsburg	1910-1944	1
	STA	Berlin	1847-1937	24
Lyck -Ełk-	rkKB	Kirchheim	1900-1944	1
	evKB	Berlin	1742-1870	1
	evLutKB	Berlin-Dahlem	1890-1941	2
Marggrabowa -Olecko-	evLutKB	Salt Lake City	1708-1824	1
	evLutKB	Berlin-Dahlem	1703-1731	1
	evLutKB	Berlin-Dahlem	1684-1943	15
Marienfelde -Glaznoty-	evKB	Warsaw	1823-1846	1
Mehlsack -Pieniężno-	evKB	Berlin-Dahlem	1688-1806	1
	rkKB	München	1688-1806	1
Mierunsken -Mieruniszki-	evKB	Berlin-Dahlem	1919-1925	1
Mitschullen -Miczuly-	STA	Berlin	1880	1
Mittenheide -Turosl-	rkKB	Berlin	1848-1874	1
Morag -Milakowo-	evKB	Berlin-Dahlem	1836-1945	10
Moschen -Mroczno-	rkKB	Berlin	1644-1875	1
Mragowo -Mikolajki-	evKB	Berlin-Dahlem	1693-1944	30
	evKB	Berlin	1693-1767	1
Mühlen -Mielno-	evKB	Warsaw	1823-1870	1
	evLutKB	Berlin-Dahlem	1704-1944	4
	evKB	Warsaw	1823-1870	1
Muhlhausen Kreis -Mlynary-	JüdGem	Koblenz	1873-1938	1
Münsterberg -Cerkiewnik-	rkKB	Berlin	1684-1776	2
Muschaken -Muszaki-	evKB	Berlin	1768-1875	5
Neidenburg -Nidzica-	evKB	Berlin-Dahlem	1704-1944	6

Location	Nature of Material	Where Filmed	Dates Covered	No. of Rolls
Neu Bartelsdorf -Nowa Wieś-	evKB	Berlin	1856-1944	1
Nidzica -Sarnowo-	rkKB	Warsaw	1765-1848	2
Nikolajken -Mikołajki-	STA evKB	Berlin Berlin-Dahlem	1693-1802 1693-1944	1 15
Nossberg -Orzechowo-	rkKB rkKB	Berlin Berlin	1568-1906 1568-1881	2 3
Ostrowit -Ostrowite-	rkKB	Berlin	1729-1874	3
Paaris -Parys-	STA	Berlin	1938-1943	1
Paulswalde -Pawłowo-	STA rkKB rkKB	Berlin-Dahlem Salt Lake City Berlin	1874-1938 1567-1870 1567-1897	4 1 2
Petersberg -Piotrówko-	STA	Berlin	1874-1938	4
Peterswalde -Piotraszewo-	rkKB	Salt Lake City	1567-1846	1
Plasswich -Płoskinia-	rkKB	Berlin	1788-1891	4
Olschöwen -Olszewo-	STA	Berlin	1874-1938	4
Open -Opin-	rkKB	Warsaw	1640-1798	1
Orlen -Orło-	STA	Berlin	1876-1881	1
Osterode -Ostróda-	evKB rkKB	Warsaw Warsaw	1815-1870 1854-1870	3 1
Polnisch Dombrowken -Dąbrówka-	evKB	Warsaw	1767-1876	1
Popiollen -Popioły-	STA	Berlin		
Possessern -Pozezdrze-	STA	Berlin	1874-1938	7
Potzdorf -Pacółtowo-	evKB	Warsaw	1830-1870	1
Prassen -Prosna-	STA	Berlin	1938-1943	1

Location	Nature of Material	Where Filmed	Dates Covered	No. of Rolls
Preussisch Holland -Pasłęk-	MilKB	Eibenstock	1746-1800	1
	MilKB	Eibenstock	1833-1887	1
	evKB	Berlin-Dahlem	1594-1944	1
	evKB	Berlin-Dahlem	1875-1924	1
	ZSR	Koblenz	1825-1907	1
	evKB	Berlin-Dahlem	1594-1944	21
Pülz -Pilec-	STA	Berlin	1938-1943	1
Queetz -Kwiecewo-	rkKB	Berlin	1683-1890	5
Radomo -Radomno-	rkKB	Berlin	1724-1874	3
Rastenburg -Kętrzyn-	evKB	Berlin	1909-1934	1
	STA	Berlin-Dahlem	1939-1943	8
	evKB	Berlin-Dahlem	1650-1944	33
	evKB	Berlin-Dahlem	1724-1944	4
	MilGem	Hannover	1719-1832	3
Regulowken -Regulówka-	STA	Berlin	1872-1930	2
Reichenau -Rychnowo-	evKB	Berlin-Dahlem	1784-1944	1
Reichau -Boguchwały-	evKB	Warsaw	1837-1848	1
Reichenbach -Rychliki-	evKB	Berlin-Dahlem	1649-1944	12
Reichenberg -Kraszewo-	rkKB	Berlin	1651-1884	2
	rkKB	Berlin	1614-1884	2
Reimersdorf -Ignalin-	rkKB	Berlin	1566-1822	4
Reuss -Cimochy-	evKB	Berlin-Dahlem	1773-1944	2
Richtenberg -Skarzyn-	evKB	Berlin-Dahlem	1902-1944	1
Riesenburg -Prabuty-	rkKB	Warsaw	1864-1870	1
Rogehnen -Rogajny-	evKB	Berlin-Dahlem	1638-1944	4
Roggenhausen -Rogóż-	rkKB	Warsaw	1574-1764	1
	rkKB	Berlin	1608-1843	1

Location	Nature of Material	Where Filmed	Dates Covered	No. of Rolls
Rosengarten -Radzieje-	evKB	Berlin	1700-1944	6
	STA	Berlin	1874-1938	7
	evKB	Berlin-Charlottenburg	1921-1944	1
	evKB	Berlin-Charlottenburg	1802-1890	1
Rosenthal -Rożenthal-	rkKB	Berlin	1665-1874	2
	rkKB	Berlin	1728-1874	2
	rkKB	Berlin	1663-1874	2
Rössel -Reszel-	rkKB	Berlin	1579-1848	4
Rothfliess -Czerwonka-	evLutKB	Berlin-Dahlem	1842-1892	1
Samrodt -Sambród-	evKB	Warsaw	1823-1870	2
Schalmey -Szalmia-	rkKB	Berlin	1746-1881	2
Schimonken -Szymonka-	evKB	Berlin-Dahlem	1702-1944	4
	evKB	Berlin-Dahlem	1840-1881	1
Schippenbeil -Sepol-	evKB	Berlin	1654-1944	13
	evKB	Berlin-Charlottenburg	1929-1944	1
Schlitt -Skolity-	rkKB	Berlin	1639-1939	2
	rkKB	Berlin	1708-1893	2
Schmauch -Skowrony-	evKB	Warsaw	1858-1869	1
Schmückwalde -Smykow-	evKB	Warsaw	1823-1870	1
Schönau -Surowe-	evKB	Berlin-Dahlem	1783-1944	1
Schönbruch -Szczurkowo-	evKB	Warsaw	1823-1867	1
Schönfliess -Kraskowo-	STA	Berlin	1881-1943	1
Schwarzenau -Szwarcenowo-	rkKB	Berlin	1772-1910	3
Schwarzstein -Czerniki-	evLutKB	Berlin-Dahlem	1713-1944	6
Schwentainen -Swietajno-	evKB	Warsaw	1800-1839	1

Location	Nature of Material	Where Filmed	Dates Covered	No. of Rolls
Seeburg -Jeziorany-	evKB	Berlin-Dahlem	1824-1944	1
Seehausen -Jeziorowskie-	STA	Berlin	1874-1938	4
Selbongen -Zelwągi-	LDS records	Salt Lake City	1931-1957	1
	LDS records	Salt Lake City	1950-1951	1
Sensburg -Mrągowo-	evKB	Berlin	1693-1802	1
	evKB	Berlin-Dahlem	1843-1886	1
	evKB	Berlin-Dahlem	1659-1944	13
	rkKB	Berlin-Dahlem	1862-1889	1
Siewken -Żiwki-	STA	Berlin	1874-1938	4
Simnau -Szymonowo-	evKB	Warsaw	1849-1870	1
Skottau -Szkotowo-	evKB	Berlin-Dahlem	1737-1875	3
Sobiechen -Sobiechy-	STA	Berlin	1874-1888	1
Soldau -Działdowo-	evKB	Warsaw	1860-1870	1
Soltmahnen -Soltmany-	STA	Berlin	1913-1934	1
Sonnenborn -Słonecznik-	evKB	Warsaw	1823-1874	2
Sperling -Wróbel-	STA	Berlin	1874-1889	1
Steinort -Sztynort-	STA	Berlin	1874-1938	4
Stolzhagen -Kochanowka-	rkKB	Berlin	1653-1875	2
Sturnhübel -Grzęda-	rkKB	Berlin	1754-1810	1
	rkKB	Berlin	1778-1826	1
Sulimmen -Sulimy-	STA	Berlin	1874-1920	11
Surminnen -Surminy-	STA	Berlin-Dahlem	1874-1889	2
Süssenthal -Sętal-	rkKB	Berlin	1750-1854	1
	rkKB	Berlin	1750-1879	2
	rkKB	Berlin	1750-1874	1

Location	Nature of Material	Where Filmed	Dates Covered	No. of Rolls
Talheim -Dąbrówka-	evKB	Berlin	1813-1842	1
Tannenberg -Stebark-	evKB	Berlin-Dahlem	1761-1944	3
Thurau -Turowo-	rkKB	Berlin	1806-1930	1
Tillitz -Tylice-	rkKB	Berlin	1806-1930	1
Tolksdorf -Tolkowiec- -Tołkiny-	STA rkKB	Berlin Berlin	1881-1943 1576-1888	1 5
Treuburg -Olecko-	evKB evKB evKB Grundbücher	Berlin-Dahlem Salt Lake City Salt Lake City Goslar	1684-1943 1708-1824 1812-1835 1825	15 1 1 1
Turoscheln -Turośl-	rkKB	Berlin	1848-1874	1
Venedien -Wenecja-	evKB	Warsaw	1823-1874	2
Waldhof -Orlen- -Orlo-	STA	Berlin	1876-1881	1
Wartenburg -Barczewo-	evKB evKB	Berlin Berlin-Charlottenburg	1791-1944 1833-1944	2 1
Wehlack -Skierki-	STA	Berlin	1881-1943	1
Wenden -Winda-	evKB STA	Berlin Berlin	1917-1944 1938-1943	1 1
Wenzken -Więcki-	STA	Berlin	1874-1938	2
Wernegitten -Kłębowo-	rkKB	Berlin	1717-1860	1
Wielitzken -Wieliczki-	evKB evKB Grundbücher evKB evKB	Berlin Berlin-Charlottenburg Goslar Berlin-Dahlem Warsaw	1800-1874 1899-1917 1825 1911-1944 1738-1850	5 1 1 1 2
Wiesenthal -Przerwanki-	STA	Berlin	1874-1890	2

Location	Nature of Material	Where Filmed	Dates Covered	No. of Rolls
Wischniewen	evKB	Berlin-Dahlem	1773-1944	2
-Kölmersdorf-	evLutKB	Berlin-Dahlem	1890-1941	2
-Wisniowo				
Ełckie-				
Wolfsdorf	evKB	Warsaw	1832-1870	2
-Wilczkowo-	rkKB	Berlin	1630-1883	1
Wormditt	rkKB	Warsaw	1636-1734	1
-Orneta-	evKB	Berlin	1873-1944	1
	evKB	Berlin-Charlottenburg	1836-1912	1
	rkKB	Berlin	1491-1890	4
	rkKB	München	1569-1739	1
Wusen -Osetnik-	rkKB	Berlin	1815	1
Wuslack -Wozławki-	rkKB	Berlin	1696-1896	3
Wuttrienen -Butryny-	rkKB	Berlin	1686-1809	1
Zallenfelde -Sałkowice-	evKB	Berlin-Dahlem	1838-1944	1

OSTPREUSSEN[1]

Location	Nature of Material	Where Filmed	Dates Covered	No. of Rolls
Allenau	evKB	Berlin	1750-1799	1
-Porechye-	evLutKB	Berlin-Dahlem	1629-1939	1
Alt Pillau	evLutKB	Berlin-Dahlem	1663-1944	5
-Baltiysk-	evKB	Berlin-Dahlem	1645-1945	14
	MilKB	Hannover Eibenstock	1639-1944	6
	LDS records	Salt Lake City	1901-1931	1
Alt Rossgarten	evKB	Berlin-Dahlem	1898-1933	1
Arnau	evLutKB	Berlin-Dahlem	1817-1874	2
	evKB	Berlin-Dahlem	1818-1874	2
Auglitten -Pravdinsk Dist.-	evLutKB	Berlin-Dahlem	1636-1865	2
Bilderweitschen	evKB	Berlin-Dahlem	1715-1874	6
-Lugovoye-	evKB	Berlin	1755-1913	1
Birkenmühle -Kalimino-	evKB	Berlin-Dahlem	1830-1923	5
Borchersdorf	evKB	Berlin-Dahlem	1841-1874	2
-Zelenopolye-	evLutKB	Berlin-Dahlem	1800-1944	5
Brandenburg -Ushakowo-	evKB	Berlin-Dahlem	1621-1742	1
Breitenstein	evKB	Berlin-Dahlem	1736-1944	12
-Ulyanovo-	evKB	Berlin-Dahlem	1800-1905	2
Budwethen -Malomozhyz- skoye-	evKB	Berlin	1746-1772	1
Darkehmen	ZSR	Goslar	1597-1924	1
-Ozersk-	AG	Goslar	1763-1850	1
	MKB	Berlin-Dahlem	1732-1944	1
	evKB	Berlin-Dahlem	1652-1923	4
Didlacken	evKB	Berlin-Dahlem	1721-1770	1
Deutsch Wilten	evKB	Berlin	1668-1944	2
Ebenrode -Nesterov-	evKB	Berlin-Dahlem	1725-1856	7

---

[1]This portion of Ostpreussen went to the Soviet Union after World War II and is now called Kaliningrad Oblast.

Location	Nature of Material	Where Filmed	Dates Covered	No. of Rolls
Eydtkuhnen -Chernyshev- skoye-	evLutKB	Berlin-Dahlem	1882-1944	5
Fischhausen -Primorsk-	evKB ZSR evKB evKB	Berlin-Dahlem Goslar Berlin Berlin- Charlottenburg	1822-1874 1526-1863 1648-1944 1864-1924	2 1 13 1
Friedland -Prawdjinsk-	ZSR Heer ZSR AG MKB evKB	Goslar Goslar Goslar Eibenstock Berlin-Dahlem Berlin	1198-1897 1526-1863 1763-1850 1732-1944 1640-1888	2 1 1 2 6
Gawaiten -Gavrilovo-	evKB	Berlin	1767-1898	5
Georgenau	evKB	Berlin	1671-1944	1
Gerdauen -Schelsnodoro- schnu-	ZSR ZSR ZSR	Goslar Goslar Goslar	1198-1897 1526-1863 1763-1850	3 1 1
Germau -Russkoye-	evKB	Berlin	1622-1944	8
Gilge -Matrosovo-	evKB	Berlin-Dahlem	1853-1904	1
Goeritten -Pushkino-	evLutKB	Berlin	1811-1892	2
Goldbach -Slawinski-	evLutKB	Berlin-Dahlem	1801-1872	1
Gross Heydekrug -Vzmorye-	evKB	Berlin	1896-1944	3
Gross Lenkening- en= Grosslenken= Lenkenau -Lesnoje-	evLutKB	Berlin-Dahlem	1896-1944	2
Gross Ottenhagen	evLutKB	Berlin-Dahlem	1800-1874	2
Gross Warning- ken -Zablotnoye-	evKB	Hannover Berlin-Dahlem	1893-1944	2
Grumbkowkeiten -Pravdino-	Heer AG ZSR	Goslar	1526-1863	1

Location	Nature of Material	Where Filmed	Dates Covered	No. of Rolls
Gumbinnen -Gusev-	evKB	Berlin	1733-1919	7
	rkKB	Augsburg	1901-1944	1
	evKB	Berlin-Charlottenburg	1765-1798	1
Heiligenthal -Mamonowo-	Heer			
	AG			
	ZSR	Goslar	1520-1883	1
	ZSR	Goslar	1763-1850	1
	ZSR	Goslar	1597-1924	1
	MKB	Berlin-Dahlem	1732-1944	1
Heiligenwalde -Ushakovo-	evKB	Berlin-Dahlem	1805-1874	4
Heinrichswalde -Slavak-	AG	Goslar	1763-1850	1
Insterburg -Chernyak- hovsk-	MKB	Berlin-Dahlem Hannover	1770-1944	2
	evKB	Berlin-Charlottenburg Berlin Berlin-Dahlem	1752-1944	5
	ev.refKB	Berlin-Charlottenburg	1790-1921	6
	Burgher rolls	Hamburg	1935-1939	1
	ZSR	Koblenz	1857-1862	1
	LDS records	Salt Lake City	1901-1930	1
	Heer			
	AG			
	ZSR	Goslar	1526-1863	1
	ZSR	Goslar	1198-1897	1
	ZSR	Goslar	1763-1850	1
	ZSR	Goslar	1597-1924	1
Jodlauken -Meschdurat- schj-	ZSR	Goslar	1763-1850	1
Juditten	evLutKB	Berlin-Dahlem	1681-1946	4
	evKB	Berlin-Dahlem	1805-1874	3
Jurgaitschen or Königskirch -Kanash-	evKB	Berlin-Dahlem Hannover	1845-1944	14
Kreuzburg -Slavskoye-	Heer			
	AG			
	ZSR	Goslar	1526-1863	1
	ZSR	Goslar	1597-1924	1
	ZSR	Goslar	1198-1897	1
Kallningken -Prokhladnoye-	evKB	Berlin-Dahlem Hannover	1775-1944	3
Kaukehmen -Yasnoye-	AG	Goslar	1763-1850	1

Location	Nature of Material	Where Filmed	Dates Covered	No. of Rolls
Klein Gnie -Mozyr-	evKB		1897-1944	1
Klein Shönau	evKB	Berlin-Dahlem	1558-1920	2
Kleszowen -Bagrationovo-	evKB	Berlin-Dahlem	1858-1944	3
Kobbelbude -Svetioye-	Heer AG ZSR	Goslar	1526-1863	1
Königsberg -Kaliningrad-	LDS records	Salt Lake City	1907-1949	7
	KG	Berlin-Dahlem	1848-1874	1
	Royal Orphanage	Berlin		1
	rkKB -various-	Berlin-Dahlem Augsburg	1604-1945	18
	evKB -various-	Berlin- Charlottenburg Berlin-Dahlem Berlin Salt Lake City Warsaw	1579-1944	194
	StGer ZSA	Berlin Berlin-Dahlem Koblenz	1837-1866 1847-1877 1809-1880	24
	MKB	Berlin-Dahlem Eibenstock Hannover	1704-1944	59
	KB -Mennonite-	Berlin-Dahlem Berlin	1766-1875 1848	27
Königsberg- Haberberg -Kaliningrad-	evKB	Berlin-Dahlem	1618-1826	2
Königsberg- Haffstrom -Kaliningrad-	evLutKB evKB	Berlin-Dahlem Berlin-Dahlem	1816-1873 1817-1873	2 4
Königsberg- Lobenich -Kaliningrad-	evKB	Berlin-Dahlem Berlin- Charlottenburg Berlin	1675-1936	5
Königsberg- Neurossgraten -Kaliningrad-	evKB	Berlin-Dahlem	1650-1873	1
Königsberg- Sackheim -Kaliningrad-	evKB	Berlin-Dahlem	1820,1873	1
Königsberg- Steindamm -Kaliningrad-	evKB	Berlin-Dahlem	1708-1833	1

Location	Nature of Material	Where Filmed	Dates Covered	No. of Rolls
Königsberg-Tragheim -Kaliningrad-	evKB	Berlin-Dahlem	1636-1800	1
Korrehnen -Guryevsk-	rkKB	Berlin	1684,1703	1
Kucherneese -Yasnoye-	AG	Goslar	1763-1850	1
Laukischken -Saranskoje-	Heer AG ZSR	Goslar	1526-1863	1
Labiau -Polessk-	ZSR evKB	Goslar Berlin-Dahlem	1526-1924 1853-1945	3 1
Laptau -Muromskoe-	evKB	Berlin	1813-1874	2
Lasdehnen -Krasnosnamensk-	AG	Goslar	1763-1850	1
Lichtenhagen -Jablonovoye-	evKB evLutKB	Berlin-Dahlem Berlin-Dahlem	1800-1944 1800-1945	3 2
Lochstadt -Primorsk-	evLutKB	Berlin-Dahlem	1663-1944	5
Löwenhagen -Komsomolsk-	evKB	Berlin-Charlottenburg Berlin-Dahlem	1627-1944	13
Ludwigswalde	evKB	Berlin-Dahlem	1799-1874	6
Mahnsfeld	evLutKB	Berlin-Dahlem Berlin	1800-1944	5
Mallwischken or Malwe -Majskoje-	Grundbuch AG	Goslar Goslar	1823,1835 1763-1850	1 1
Medenau -Logvino-	evKB	Berlin-Charlottenburg Berlin Berlin-Dahlem	1796-1874	7
Neuendorf	evLutKB	Berlin-Dahlem	1800-1944	3
Neuhausen -Gurjewsk-	evLutKB	Berlin-Dahlem	1822-1874	2
Neuischken -Neunischken-	evKB	Berlin Berlin-Charlottenburg	1767-1943	3
Neukirch -Timirjasowo-	AG	Goslar	1763-1850	1

Location	Nature of Material	Where Filmed	Dates Covered	No. of Rolls
Norkitten	AG	Goslar	1763-1850	1
Palmnicken -Yartarny-	evKB	Berlin Berlin-Dahlem	1894-1944	4
Pelleningken -Sagorsk-	AG	Goslar	1763-1850	1
Petersdorf	evKB	Berlin-Dahlem	1844-1944	6
Pillkallen -Dobrovolsk-	evKB	Warsaw	1742-1817	1
Pobethen -Romanovo-	evKB	Berlin-Dahlem	1807-1874	8
Posen	ZSR	Berlin-Dahlem	1824-1944	1
Postnicken -Zaliwnojo-	evLutKB	Berlin-Dahlem	1800-1874	2
Powunden -Chrabrowo-	evLutKB	Berlin-Dahlem	1813-1874	5
Preussisch Eylau -Bagrationovsk-	MKB	Eibenstock	1847-1870	1
Quednau -Kwednau-	evLutKB evKB	Berlin-Dahlem Berlin-Dahlem	1801-1874 1802-1874	2 3
Ragnit -Neman-	Heer AG ZSR ZSR ZSR MKB evKB Grundbuch	Goslar Goslar Goslar Eibenstock Berlin-Dahlem Berlin-Dahlem Goslar	1526-1863 1198-1897 1763-1850 1732-1944 1767-1775 1823	1 1 1 3 1 1
Rauschen -Svetlogorsk-	evKB	Berlin-Dahlem	1901-1944	1
Rositten -Rybachyi-	evKB	Berlin-Dahlem	1809-1874	3
Rudau -Guryevsk-	evKB rkKB	Berlin-Dahlem Berlin	1811-1874 1684,1703	2 1
Sadweitschen -Zadvaytschen-	LDS records	Salt Lake City	1714-1735	1
Sarkau -Zarkau-	evKB	Berlin-Dahlem Salt Lake City	1664-1874	3
Schaacken	evKB evLutKB	Berlin-Dahlem Berlin-Dahlem	1800-1874 1799-1874	3 2

Location	Nature of Material	Where Filmed	Dates Covered	No. of Rolls
Schestocken -Peterstal-	Grundbuch	Berlin-Dahlem	1934-1942	1
Schillehnen -Pobedino-	Grundbuch AG	Goslar Goslar	1823,1835 1763-1850	1 1
Schirwindt -Kutusowo-	Grundbuch	Goslar	1823,1835	1
Schlossbach -Nevskoye-	AG	Berlin	1874-1944	1
Schlossberg -Dobrovolsk-	evKB Grundbuch	Warsaw Goslar	1742-1817 1823,1835	1 1
Schönbruch -Shirokoye-	evKB	Warsaw	1823-1867	1
Schönwalde -Jaroslawskoje- -Pravdinsk Dist.-	evLutKB evLutKB	Berlin-Dahlem Berlin-Dahlem	1805-1874 1636-1865	2 2
Seeligenfeld	evKB	Berlin-Dahlem	1800-1874	2
Stallüponen or Ebenrode -Nesterov-	Grundbuch AG evLutKB	Goslar Goslar Berlin Berlin-Charlottenburg	1823,1835 1783-1850 1817-1877 1801-1854	1 1 4 1
Starkenberg	evLutKB	Berlin-Dahlem	1766-1887	2
Steinbeck	evLutKB evKB	Berlin-Dahlem Berlin-Dahlem	1800-1944 1800-1874	3 2
Taplacken -Taplaki-	Heer AG ZSR	Goslar	1526-1863	1
Thierenberg	evKB	Berlin-Dahlem	1841-1944	3
Tilsit -Sovetsk-	KB-Mennonite LDS records ZSR AG evLutKB rkKB evKB	Berlin-Dahlem Salt Lake City Goslar Hamburg Goslar Berlin-Dahlem Berlin-Dahlem Berlin-Dahlem	1775-1827 1901-1923 1198-1897 1763-1850 1624-1944 1692-1878 1700-1847	1 1 4 1 3 4 4
Trempen -Nowostrojewo-	AG	Goslar	1763-1850	1
Wargen	evKB	Berlin-Dahlem	1804-1874	7

Location	Nature of Material	Where Filmed	Dates Covered	No. of Rolls
Wehlau -Znamensk-	evLutKB MKB	Berlin-Dahlem Eibenstock	1833-1944 1832-1893	10 1
Wilhelmsberg -Ozersk-	evKB	Berlin-Dahlem	1736-1944	4
Wittenberg -Nivenskoye-	Heer AG ZSR	Goslar	1526-1863	1

OSTPREUSSEN
-Memel-[1]

Location	Material	Where Filmed	Covered	Rolls
Buddelkehmel -Budelkiemis-	evKB	Berlin	1727-1739	1
Collaten -Kalote-	STA	Berlin	1897-1938	4
Crottingen -Kretinga-	STA	Berlin-Dahlem	1872-1938	7
Dawillen -Dovilai-	STA	Berlin	1874-1938	11
Didlaken -Didlauke-	evKB	Berlin	1727-1739	1
Gelsinnen -Gelsiniai-	STA	Berlin	1854-1890	2
Goldap -Virbalis-	MilKB	Hannover	1778-1868	1
Götzenhofen -Kleipeda-	STA	Berlin	1874-1928	3
Gross-Jagschen -Selinai-	STA	Berlin	1874-1938	6
Kairinn -Kairiai-	STA	Berlin	1911-1938	2
Kakelbeck -Karklinkai-	STA	Berlin	1885-1938	2
Klausmühlen -Dirvupiai-	STA	Berlin	1874-1938	5
Kolatten -Normantai-	STA	Berlin	1874-1897	5
Mehlneraggen -Melnrage-	STA	Berlin-Dahlem	1934-1938	1
Memel -Klaipeda-	evKB	Berlin-Dahlem	1772-1944	31

---

[1]The Memel territory, part of Ostpreussen, went to Lithuania
after World War I and to the USSR -Lithuanian SSR- after
World War II. These localities are located in the catalog
under Lithuania.

Location	Nature of Material	Where Filmed	Dates Covered	No. of Rolls
Memel -Klaipeda-	STA	Berlin-Dahlem	1874-1925	3
Memel -Kleipeda-	Heer AG ZSR	Goslar	1526-1863	1
Memel -Kleipeda-	Guild records	Goslar	1597-1924	1
Memel -Kleipeda-	Misc. records	Goslar	1198-1897	1
Memel -Kleipeda-	MilKB	Berlin-Dahlem	1732-1944	1
Memel -Kleipeda-	LDS records	Salt Lake City	1903-1929	1
Nidden -Nida-	STA	Berlin-Dahlem	1874-1938	4
Paul-Narmund -Normantai-	STA	Berlin	1874-1897	5
Plaschken -Plaskiai-	evKB	Berlin-Dahlem	1911-1944	1
Prökuls -Priekule-	STA	Berlin	1874-1938	66
Prökuls -Priekule-	evKB	Berlin-Dahlem	1732-1892	10
Prökuls -Priekule-	Heer AG STA	Goslar	1526-1892	1
Schillgallen -Silgaliai-	rkKB	Berlin-Dahlem	1822-1877	1
Schwarzort -Juodkrante-	STA	Berlin	1874-1938	2
Truschellen -Truseliai-	STA	Berlin	1874-1938	6
Wischwill -Viesvile-	evKB	Berlin-Dahlem	1862-1900	1
Wittauten -Vyautai-	STA	Berlin	1874-1938	7

POMMERN

Location	Nature of Material	Where Filmed	Dates Covered	No. of Rolls
Albrechsdorf -Karszno-	evKB	Hannover	1900	1
Alt Storkow -Storkowo-	evKB	Warsaw	1813-1860	1
Altdamm=Stettin -Szczecin-				
Arnswalde -Choszczno-	evKB	Warsaw	1835-1841	1
Belgard -Białogard-	evKB MilKB KB	Berlin-Dahlem Hannover Salt Lake City	1842-1849 1866-1868 1802-1870	1 1 2
Berlinchen -Barlinek-	evKB	Warsaw	1839-1870	2
Bernickow -Barnkovo-	evKB	Warsaw	1816-1857	1
Bewerdick -Biebrówek-	evKB	Warsaw	1766-1870	5
Blankenfelde -Kłosowice-	KB evKB	Salt Lake City Warsaw	1840-1859 1840-1870	1 2
Bosenthin -Bodzecin-	KB evKB	Salt Lake City Warsaw	1850-1870 1809-1842	1 1
Braschendorf -Brudzeń-	evKB	Warsaw	1766-1870	5
Bredow=Stettin -Szczecin-				
Bromberg -Bydgoszcz-	MKB	Berlin-Dahlem	1831-1866	1
Buckow -Buczkowo-	evKB KB	Frankfurt Salt Lake City	1658-1958 1836-1870	4 1
Buddendorf -Budno-	evKB	Warsaw	1786-1855	1
Burzlaff -Borysław-	evKB	Warsaw	1799-1835	1

Location	Nature of Material	Where Filmed	Dates Covered	No. of Rolls
Daarz -Darż-	evKB	Warsaw	1758-1837	1
Damerfitz -Dąbrowice-	evKB	Warsaw	1758-1837	1
Dischenhagen -Dzisna-	evKB	Warsaw	1766-1870	5
Dramburg -Drawsko Pomorskie-	MilKB	Hannover	1763-1838	5
Falkeburg -Złocieniec-	evKB	Warsaw	1809-1835	1
Falkenwalde -Tanowa-	evKB	Hannover	1651-1775	1
Frauendorf -Szczecin Golęcino-	evKB	Berlin- Charlottenberg	1678-1931	7
Freiheide -Godowo-	evKB	Warsaw	1700-1858	1
	evKB	Warsaw	1859-1870	1
Friedeberg -Strzelce Krajeńskie-	Justizamt	Berlin	1847-1853	1
Geritz -Jarzyce-	evKB	Warsaw	1798-1838	1
Gollnow -Goleniów-	evKB	Warsaw	1798-1838	1
Grabow -Grabowo-	evKB	Warsaw	1763-1773	2
	evKB	Warsaw	1774-1835	1
Greifenberg -Gryfice-	evKB	Berlin-Dahlem	1742-1917	1
Gross Brüskow -Bruskowo Wielkie-	evKB	Berlin	1780-1870	1
Gross Christinenberg -Kuniska Wielkie-	KB	Salt Lake City	1840-1870	1
	KB	Salt Lake City	1840-1857	1
	evKB	Warsaw	1840-1876	1
Gross Duebsow -Dobieszewo-	evKB	Berlin- Charlottenberg	1831-1945	3
	KB	Salt Lake City	1831-1875	1
Gross Tychow -Tychowo-	evKB	Warsaw	1799-1835	1

Location	Nature of Material	Where Filmed	Dates Covered	No. of Rolls
Grossenhagen -Tarnowo-	evKB	Warsaw	1653-1832	1
Gross Ziegenort -Trzebież-	evKB	Berlin	1633-1769	1
Hackenwalde -Krępsko-	evKB evKB	Warsaw Warsaw	1766-1870 1837-1870	4 2
Hagen -Randow- -Tatynia-	evKB evKB	Berlin Berlin	1651-1765 1801-1929	1 1
Hammer -Babigoszcz-	evKB	Warsaw	1766-1870	5
Harmsdorf -Niewiadowo-	evKB KB	Warsaw Salt Lake City	1809-1870 1850-1870	2 1
Hermelsdorf -Nastazin-	KB evKB	Salt Lake City Warsaw	1792-1879 1795-1870	2 3
Hohen Kränig -Krajnik Górny-	evKB	Warsaw	1720-1862	2
Jasenitz -Jasienica-	evKB	Warsaw	1641-1776	1
Kannenberg -Kania-	evKB	Warsaw	1795-1867	3
Kantrek -Łożnica-	evKB	Warsaw	1766-1870	5
Karnkewitz -Karnieszewice-	KB evKB	Salt Lake City Warsaw	1835-1870 1836-1870	2 1
Karwitz -Karwice-	evKB KB	Warsaw Salt Lake City	1714-1847 1801-1821	1 1
Kattenhof -Kąty-	evKB	Warsaw	1766-1870	4
Kolberg -Kolobrzeg-	evKB	Warsaw	1633-1834	8
Korkenhagen -Budzieszowce-	evKB KB	Warsaw Salt Lake City	1777-1879 1802-1879	2 1
Köslin -Koszalin-	JüdGem MilKB	Warsaw Hannover- Fibersock	1812-1846 1740-1892	1 2
Kratzig -Krasnik Łobeski-	evKB evKB	Salt Lake City Warsaw	1752-1860 1752-1865	1 1

Location	Nature of Material	Where Filmed	Dates Covered	No. of Rolls
Langerose -Pogorzelice-	evKB	Warsaw	1862-1870	1
Langenberg -Święta-	KB	Salt Lake City	1783-1839	1
Lenz -Łeczyca-	evKB	Warsaw	1835-1870	1
Liebenow -Lubieniów-	evKB	Warsaw	1829-1870	1
Linde -Sulinowo-	evKB evKB	Salt Lake City Warsaw	1837-1870 1837-1879	1 1
Lippehne -Lipiany-	evKB	Warsaw	1793-1830	1
Lubchow -Lubiechowo-	evKB	Hannover	1922-1957	1
Lubzin -Lubczyna-	evKB	Warsaw	1703-1816	2
Luisenhof -Ciołkowo-	evKB	Warsaw	1766-1870	5
Lupow -Łupawa-	evKB	Warsaw	1743-1870	1
Malchow -Malechowo-	KB evKB	Salt Lake City Warsaw	1713-1811 1714-1826	2 1
Massow -Maszewko-	KB evKB	Salt Lake City Warsaw	1766-1869 1651-1870	2 1
Massow -Maszewo-	evKB	Warsaw	1651-1870	4
Mützenow -Możdzanowo-	KB evKB	Salt Lake City Warsaw Berlin	1831-1871 1622-1916	4 5
Nahausen -Grabowo-	evKB	Warsaw	1673-1773	2
Nahausen -Nawodna-	evKB	Warsaw	1673-1693 1774-1843	1
Naugard -Nowogard-	evKB	Warsaw	1768-1855	1
Nemitz -Niemica-	KB evKB	Salt Lake City Warsaw	1647-1709 1647-1708	1 1
Neu Massow -Maszewko-	evKB	Warsaw	1758-1870	1

Location	Nature of Material	Where Filmed	Dates Covered	No. of Rolls
Neuendorf -Ogorzele- -Budzieszowce-	evKB	Warsaw	1777-1879	2
Neuenkirchen -Dołuje-	evKB	Warsaw	1603-1749	1
Neuwarp -Nowe Warpno-	evKB KB	Hannover Salt Lake City	1896-1900 1832-1875	1 1
Niedersaathen -Zatoń Dolna-	evKB	Warsaw	1720-1784	1
Nörenberg -Ińsko-	evKB	Warsaw	1831-1870	2
Pagenkopf -Bagna-	evKB	Warsaw	1760-1822	1
Parlin -Parlino-	evKB	Warsaw	1742-1870	2
Peetzig -Piasek-	evKB	Warsaw	1804-1837	1
Persanzig -Pasecko-	evKB	Warsaw	1836-1870	1
Pielburg -Pile-	KB evKB	Salt Lake City Warsaw	1837-1871 1716-1870	1 2
Pluggentin -Samtens-	evKB	Berlin	1792-1839	1
Politz -Police-	evKB	Warsaw	1800-1835	1
Priemhausen -Przemocze-	evKB	Warsaw	1816-1852 1858-1870	1 1
Puddenzig -Podańsko-	evKB	Warsaw	1786-1870	2
Putzig -Jędrzejewo-	evKB	Warsaw	1808-1865	1
Pyritz -Pyrzyce-	MilKB evKB	Berlin-Dahlem Warsaw	1834-1870 1783-1830	1 1
Raduhn -Raduń-	evKB	Warsaw	1683-1803	1
Rehdorf -Stoki-	evKB evKB	Hannover Warsaw	1677-1750 1753-1836	1 1
Reichenbach -Radaczewo-	evKB	Warsaw	1678-1875	2

Location	Nature of Material	Where Filmed	Dates Covered	No. of Rolls
Reichenfelde	evKB	Warsaw	1673-1693	1
-Grabowo-	evKB	Warsaw	1673-1693	1
-Nawodna-			1774-1843	
Rendow	evKB	Warsaw	1783-1816	1
-Święta-				
Rensedow	evKB	Warsaw	1833-1860	1
-Rzeskowo-				
Resehl	evKB	Warsaw	1777-1879	2
-Radzanek-			1845-1870	1
-Budzieszowce-	evKB	Salt Lake City	1845-1863	1
Rogow	evKB	Warsaw	1744-1767	1
-Rogowo-				
Rörchen	evKB	Warsaw	1856-1870	1
-Rurka-				
Rosenow	evKB	Warsaw	1758-1837	1
-Rożnowo-				
Rosenthal	evKB	Warsaw	1762-1814	1
-Rożańsko-				
Rügenwalde	evKB	Warsaw	1672-1805	1
-Darłowo-				
Schmolsin	evKB	Warsaw	1655-1800	1
-Smoldzino-			1818-1865	1
Schurow	evKB	Warsaw	1862-1870	1
-Skorowo-				
Schwanteshagen	KB	Salt Lake City	1849-1870	1
-Swiętoszewo-			1850-1870	1
Sellnow	evKB	Warsaw	1751-1845	1
-Zieleniewo-				
Siebuckow See: Buckow				
-Rukow Murskie-				
Siegelkow	evKB	Warsaw	1766-1870	5
-Zychlikowo-				
Soldekow	evKB	Warsaw	1647-1708	1
-Solechowo-				
Sophiental	evKB	Warsaw	1766-1870	5
-Nowogard-				
-Dobroszyn-				
Speck	evKB	Warsaw	1766-1870	5
-Mosty-				

Location	Nature of Material	Where Filmed	Dates Covered	No. of Rolls
Stargard	MilKB	Berlin-Dahlem	1831-1866	1
-Stargard	KB	Salt Lake City	1805-1870	1
Szczeciński-	evKB	Warsaw	1694-1852	1
	evKB	Warsaw	1719-1870	4
Stettin	ZSR	Berlin	1874-1945	2711
-Szczecin-	Stadt-Register	Berlin	1700	1
	Regierungs-amt	Berlin	1660-1747	2
	JüdGem	Berlin	1848-1850	1
	LDS records	Salt Lake City	1923-1949	6
	Birth rec. Hospital	Berlin	1902-1945	15
	Heer	Berlin	1797-1935	1
	KB	Hannover	1860-1866	1
	Heer	Stockholm	1706	1
	rkKB	Berlin	1849-1944	1
	KB	Kirchheim	1809-1944	8
	evKB	Berlin	1603-1945	195
	evKB	Salt Lake City	1750-1945	752
	rkKB	Salt Lake City	1823-1875	1
Stolp -Słupsk-	LDS records	Salt Lake City	1932-1938	3
Stolzenhagen -Ognica-	evKB	Berlin	1672-1885	2
Treptow -Trzebiatów-	evKB	Warsaw	1605-1668	1
Triegkaff -Trzygłow-	evKB	Warsaw	1640-1779	1
Völschendorff -Wołczkowo-	ZSR	Berlin-Dahlem	1874-1975	14
Wahrlang -Warnołęka-	evKB	Hannover	1900	1
Wendisch Buckow See: Buckow -Bukowo-				
Wildenbruch	evKB	Salt Lake City	1817-1830	1
-Swobnica-	evKB	Warsaw	1786-1830	1
Winterhagen -Grabno-	evKB	Warsaw	1655-1821	1
Wittenfelde -Bielice-	evKB	Warsaw	1760-1822	1
-Bagna-	evKB	Warsaw	1760-1922	1
Wrechow -Orzechów-	evKB	Hannover	1699-1875	1

Location	Nature of Material	Where Filmed	Dates Covered	No. of Rolls
Zachow -Czachów-	evKB	Hannover	1699-1750	1
Zahden -Siadło Górne-	ZSR	Berlin-Dahlem	1874-1945	15
Zartzig -Stracholin- -Łęczyca-	evKB	Warsaw	1835-1870	1
Zarnekow -Czarnkowo-	evKB	Warsaw	1794-1835	1
Ziegenort -Trzebiez-	evKB	Hannover Berlin	1633-1769 1633-1769	1 1
Zizow -Cisowo-	evKB	Warsaw	1724-1784	1
Züllchow -Zelechowa-	evKB	Berlin	1889-1926	3

POSEN

Location	Nature of Material	Where Filmed	Dates Covered	No. of Rolls
Adelnau -Odolanow-	rkKB	Poznan	1808-1865	2
Adelnau -Odolanow-	evKB	Poznan	1770-1865	6
Alt Bialtsch -Kosten- -Bialcz-	evKB	Poznan	1836-1865	1
Alt Bialtsch -Kosten- -Bialcz-	Zivilreg.	Poznan	1810-1817	1
Alt Bialtsch -Paraeczewo	Zivilreg.	Poznan	1808-1858	1
Alt Bialtsch -Wielichowo-	rkKB	Poznan	1818-1829	1
Alt Bialtsch -Wielkie-	rkKB	Poznan	1808-1829	1
Alt Bialtsch -Wilkowo- -Polskie-	rkKB	Poznan	1812-1865	2
Alt Bialtsch -Wonieść-	rkKB	Poznan	1809-1865	2
Alt Bialtsch -Wyskoc-	rkKB	Poznan	1808-1865	2
Alt Bialtsch -Zielecin-	rkKB	Poznan	1818-1829	1
Alt Kloster -Wolstein- -Kaszczor-	rkKB	Poznan	1818-1854	2
Alt Laube -Długie Stare-	rkKB	Poznan	1818-1829	1
Alt Kirch -Krosno- -Alt Tomischel- -Str. Tomysl-	evKB STA	Poznan Berlin-Dahlem	1776-1855 1874-1885	8 4
Bartschin -Batcin-	rkKB	Poznan	1824-1830	1
Bauchwitz -Bukowiec- -Zielona-	STA		1874-1938	6

Location	Nature of Material	Where Filmed	Dates Covered	No. of Rolls
Bentschen -Zbaszyn-	STA	Berlin	1934-1938	1
Betsche -Pszczew-	rkKB	Poznan	1632-1870	7
Bersche -Pszczew-	STA	Berlin	1874-1938	7
Birnbaum -Miedzychod-	evKB	Poznan	1645-1794	2
Boschmin -Kozmin-	rkKB JüdGem	Poznan	1811-1812	1
Blesen -Bledzew- -Ziel-	STA	Berlin	1874-1925	4
Bojanowo	MKB	Eibenstock	1867-1890	1
Bojanowo	evKB	Poznan	1670-1865	13
Bojanowo	ZSR	Poznan	1832-1865	1
Borni -Wollstein-	rkKB	Poznan	1643-1865	6
Wolsztyn	rkKB	Poznan	1809-1854	2
Borug -Boruja- -Wosztyn-	evKB	Poznan	1818-1872	3
Bromberg	Lawyer files	Berlin-Dahlem		4
Bromberg	Geheime Staatsakten	Berlin-Dahlem	1852-1872	4
Bromberg	evKB	Poznan	1773-1865	28
Bromberg	MKB	Hannover	1774-1920	11
Bromberg	JüdGem	Poznan	1823-1865	1
Bromberg	rkKB	Poznan Münster Augsburg	1645-1865	20
Bromberg	LDS records	Salt Lake City	1837-1857	1
Bukowiec -Neutomischel-	STA	Poznan Berlin-Dahlem	1812-1936	10
Choyna -Chojna-	STA	Berlin	1874-1935	15

Location	Nature of Material	Where Filmed	Dates Covered	No. of Rolls
Chica Göra -Neutomischel-	STA	Berlin	1878-1886	1
Cielle	evKB	Lübeck	1867-1910	2
Crone -Koronowo-	evKB	Lübeck	1795-1943	11
Crone -Koronowo-	rkKB	Berlin	1744-1852	1
Crone -Koronowo-	JüdGem	Poznan	1847-1874	1
Culm -Chelmno-	Mennoniten	Berlin-Dahlem	1824-1855	3
Czarnikau -Czarnków-	ZSR	Poznan	1815-1855	22
Czerlin -Czerlin-	STA	Berlin	1888-1940	20
Debenke -Debno- -Wyrzysk-	evKB	Lübeck	1863-1898	1
Deutsch Wilke -Wilkowo Leszczyńskie-	evKB	Poznan	1818-1829	1
Deutsch Wilke -Wilkowo Leszczyńskie-	ZSR	Poznan	1812-1865	2
Deutschdorf -Strzyzew	evKB	Poznan	1854-1865	1
	rkKB	Poznan	1854-1865	1
Dobsch -Dobrcz-	rkKB	München Berlin	1775-1934	5
Dobsch -Dobrcz-	ZSR	Berlin	1775-1839	1
Dreidorf -Gross- -Klein- -Wielkie- -Wirrsitz-	rkKB	Berlin-Dahlem München	1773-1953	5
Eberspark -Chlebno-	evKB	Lübeck	1821-1839	1
Eichberg -Debagora-	ZSR	Poznan	1815-1865	1
Eichenried -Debno-	rkKB	Poznan	1818-1839	1

Location	Nature of Material	Where Filmed	Dates Covered	No. of Rolls
Exin -Schubin- -Keynia-	evKB	Poznan	1819-1867	4
Exin -Schubin- -Keynia- -Szubin-	rkKB	Poznan	1835-1874	2
Falkenwalde -Sokola Dabrowa-	rkKB	Poznan	1716-1870	2
Falkenwalde -Sokola Dabrowa-	STA	Berlin	1874-1937	7
Feldkirch -Ruchocice-	rkKB	Poznan	1808-1856	2
Fordon	rkKB	Poznan Augsburg	1774-1874	5
Fordon	evKB	Posnan	1817-1896	10
Fordon	JüdGem	Poznan	1820-1852	3
Fraustadt -Wschowa-	STA	Berlin	1890-1919	1
Fraustadt -Wschowa-	evKB	Berlin	1798-1920	3
Fraustadt -Wschowa-	JüdGem	Poznan	1838	1
Freimark -Krostkowo-	rkKB	Berlin-Dahlem München	1652-1939	5
Friedendorf -Spokojna-	rkKB	Poznan	1818-1854	2
Friedheim -Miasteczko-	evKB	Lübeck	1796-1943	2
Friedenhorst -Jastrzebsko Stare-	STA	Berlin-Dahlem	1874-1935	10
Friedenhorst -Jastrzebsko Stare-	evKB		1854-1865	1
FriedrichsHohe -Kosztowo-	rkKB	München	1841-1907	1
Gnesen -Gniezno-	MKB	Eibenstock Hannover	1834-1868	3

Location	Nature of Material	Where Filmed	Dates Covered	No. of Rolls
Gnesen -Gniezno-	MKB	Poznan	1497-1840	26
Gnesen -Gniezno-	evKB	Poznan	1818-1865	5
Gnesen -Gniezno-	JüdGem	Posnan	1840-1847	1
Goerchen -Miejska Gorka-	evKB	Poznan	1776-1865	4
Goerchen -Miejska Gorka-	rkKB	Poznan	1818-1819	1
Goglin -Goglin-	evKB	Hannover	1872-1935	1
Golmitz -Chełmsko-	rkKB	Poznan	1775-1863	2
Gollantsch	STA	Berlin	1874-1940	35
Gollantsch	STA	Berlin	1874-1940	35
Golancz	rkKB	Poznan	1614-1826	2
Grätz -Grodzisk-	evKB	Poznan	1818-1865	2
Grätz -Grodzisk-	rkKB	Poznan	1818-1865	3
Grenzendorf -Krzyzowniki-	rkKB	Poznan	1829-1855	4
Grodzisk -Grodzisko-	rkKB	Poznan	1778-1853	2
Gromaden -Gromadno-	rkKB	Berlin-Dahlem Kirchheim	1750-1876	3
Gross Golle -Gołaszewo-	evKB	Poznan	1846-1865	1
Gross Neudorf	evKB	Lübeck	1861-1904	3
Gowawieś Wielka	rkKB	Poznan	1817-1867	2
Gross Wudschin -Wudzyn-	rkKB	Berlin Augsburg	1782-1874	3
Hanner-Boruy -Boruja-	evKB	Poznan	1818-1872	3
Hermannsdorf -Radzicz-	evKB	Lübeck	1863-1927	1

Location	Nature of Material	Where Filmed	Dates Covered	No. of Rolls
Hohensalza	evKB	Hannover	1799-1929	6
Jnowroclaw	MKB	Eibenstock	1834-1868	2
Jlgen -Lgiń-	rkKB	Poznan	1720-1870	3
Kaltzig -Kalsko-	rkKB	Poznan	1775-1863	2
Karge -Kargowa Wies-	MKB	Eibenstock	1849-1865	1
Kolmar -Chodziez-	rkKB	Poznan	1819-1867	3
Kolmar -Chodziez-	evKB	Poznan	1809-1865	5
Kolmar -Chodziez-	STA	Berlin	1815-1945	33
Königlich Wiershütten	rkKB	Berlin	1773-1859	2
Königlich Wiershütten	STA	Berlin	1766-1889	1
Koschmin -Kozmin-	ZSR	Poznan	1811-1812	1
Koschmin -Kozmin-	evKB	Poznan	1818-1865	4
Kotten -Kocien Wielkiev-	KB	Poznan	1735-1891	1
Koschmin -Kozmin-	rkKB JüdGem	Poznan	1811-1812	1
Krotoschin -Krotoszyn-	rkKB	Poznan	1818-1865	3
Krotoschin -Krotoszyn-	evKB	Poznan	1790-1865	5
Krotoschin -Krotoszyn-	JüdGem	Poznan	1825-1847	2
Kruschin -Kruszyny-	rkKB	Berlin	1773-1831	1
Kurheim -Powidz-	rkKB	Poznan	1818-1865	2
Kurnatowitze	STA	Berlin	1877-1935	8

Location	Nature of Material	Where Filmed	Dates Covered	No. of Rolls
Kursdorf -Konradowo-	rkKB		1655-1885	9
Kutschkau -Chociszewo-	rkKB		1700-1870	1
Kwiltsch -Kwilcz-	STA	Berlin-Dahlem Poznan	1808-1939	3
Lasswitz -Lasocice	evKB	Poznan	1635-1865	3
Latowitz -Latowice-	evKB	Poznan	1853-1865	1
Leiperode -Lipno-	STA	Berlin	1936-1938	1
Lindenwald -Wawelno-	rkKB	Berlin	1745-1869	1
Lindenwerder -Lipiagora-	evKB	Poznan	1839-1865	1
Lissa	MKB	Eibenstock	1833-1919	1
Leszno	evKB	Poznan	1818-1865	14
Lissen -Łysiny-	rkKB	Poznan	1683-1871	1
Libsens -Łobzenica	rkKB	Münster Augsburg	1622-1939	7
Lobsens -Łobzenica	evKB	Lübeck	1773-1925	13
Lubosch	rkKB	Poznan	1808-1824	1
Lubosz	STA	Berlin	1874-1935	11
Lupitze -Łupice-	rkKB	Poznan	1818-1854	2
Malchow Slawe	ZSR	Poznan	1808-1865	2
Mauche -Mochy-	rkKB	Poznan	1818-1854	2
Meseritz -Miedzyrzecz-	evKB	Berlin-Dahlem	1840-	1
Meseritz -Miedzyrzecz-	JüdGem	Berlin-Dahlem	1848-1903	1
Meseritz	rkKB	Poznan	1645-1870	2

Location	Nature of Material	Where Filmed	Dates Covered	No. of Rolls
Mixstadt -Mikstat-	rkKB	Poznan	1818-1854	2
Mixstadt -Mikstat-	STA	Poznan	1836-1846	1
Mönkenwerth -Makowarsko-	rkKB	Augsburg Berlin	1763-1862	3
Moschin -Mosina-	JüdGem	Poznan	1835-1836	1
Mrotschen -Mrocza-	rkKB	Augsburg	1725-1880	4
Mrotschen -Mrocza-	evKB	Lübeck	1786-1944	8
Muhlental Izbica Kugawska	rkKB	Poznan	1769-1865	12
Muhlental Izbica Kujawska	ZSR	Poznan	1810-1865	3
Murke -Lissa- Murkowo -Leszno-	STA	Berlin-Dahlem	1906-1920	3
Murke -Schmiegel- Morkowo	rkKB	Poznan	1818-1829	1
Murkingen Murkowo	rkKB	Poznan	1818-1829	1
New-Siedel -Siedlemin-	rkKB	Poznan	1820-1832	1
Neudorf -Nowawies-	rkKB	Poznan	1716-1870	2
Neuheim -Strzelewo	rkKB	Augsburg Berlin	1775-1897	3
Neustadt -Lwowek-	rkKB	Poznan	1808-1865	7
Neustadt -Lowowek-	rkKB	Poznan	1809-1865	3
Nitsche -Nietaszkowo-	evKB	Poznan	1790-1798	1
Obersitz -Obrzycko-	evKB	Poznan	1660-1865	8

Location	Nature of Material	Where Filmed	Dates Covered	No. of Rolls
Obersitz -Obrzycko-	rkKB	Poznan	1811-1860	2
Obrawalde -Obrzyce-	STA	Berlin	1926-1937	5
Orzeschkowo -Orzeszkowo-	rkKB	Poznan	1818-1839	1
Orzeschkowo -Orzeszkowo-	evKB	Poznan	1665-1836	1
Oscht -Osiecko-	rkKB	Poznan	1716-1870	2
Öseln -Osielsko-	rkKB	Berlin Augsburg	1784-1925	4
Öseln -Osielsko-	ZSR	Berlin Poznan	1784-1925	1
Osielsk -Osielsko-	ZSR	Berlin Poznan	1784-1925	1
Ostrowo -Ostrow-	MKB	Eibenstock	1833-1846	1
Ostrow -Ostrow-	evKB	Poznan	1775-1865	7
Ostrowo -Ostrow-	ZSR	Poznan	1808-1865	4
Otteraue -Otorowo-	evKB	Lübeck	1869-1899	1
Paradies -Goscikowo-	STA	Berlin	1874-1938	3
Peteraue -Piotrowo-	evKB	Poznan	1660-1865	3
Pleszew -Pleschen-	MKB	Eiberstock Berlin-Dahlem	1833-1918	2
Pleschen -Pleszew-	evKB	Poznan	1819-1854	4
Pleschen -Pleszew-	rkKB	Poznan	1819-1854	3
Pleschen -Pleszew-	ZSR	Poznan	1835-1845	1
Pogorzelle -Pogorzela-	evKB	Poznan	1853-1865	
Prittisch -Przytoczna-	evKB	Poznan	1840-1851	1

Location	Nature of Material	Where Filmed	Dates Covered	No. of Rolls
Prittisch -Przytoczna-	rkKB	Poznan	1754-1870	1
Prittisch -Przytoczna-	STA	Berlin	1874-1937	1
Pudewitz -Pobiedziska-	evKB	Poznan	1787-1865	7
Pudewitz -Pobiedziska-	rkKB	Poznan	1688-1865	4
Punitz -Poniec-	evKB	Poznan	1678-1865	5
Putzig -Jedrzejewo-	evKB	Poznan	1808-1865	1
Putzig -Jedrzejewo-	evKB	Poznan	1808-1865	
Rakwitz -Rakoniewice-	evKB	Poznan	1662-1859	5
Rakwitz -Rakoniewice-	rkKB	Poznan	1818-1854	1
Rawitsch -Rawicz-	MKB	Eibenstock Hannover	1834-1918	2
Rawitsch -Rawicz-	evKB	Poznan	1701-1865	14
Rawitsch -Rawicz-	rkKB	Poznan	1837-1865	2
Reisen -Rydzyna-	evKB	Poznan	1776-1865	1
Reisen -Rydzyna-	rkKB	Poznan	1817-1830	5
Revier -Rejowiec-	evKB	Poznan	1776-1865	3
Rogasen -Rogozno-	Magistrat	Poznan	1817-1847	2
Rogsen -Rogoziniec-	STA	Berlin	1874-1940	9
Rokitten -Rokitno-	rkKB	Poznan	1775-1863	2
Rokitten -Rokitno-	STA	Berlin	1875-1937	5

Location	Nature of Material	Where Filmed	Dates Covered	No. of Rolls
Rokitten -Rokotno-	STA	Berlin	1875-1937	5
Rosterschütz -Władyslawow-	evKB	Hannover	1826-1945	2
Rosterschütz	evKB	Hannover	1836-1945	2
Rosterschütz -Władyslawow-	ZSR	Poznan	1776-1865	12
Rothenburg -Rostarzewo-	evKB	Poznan	1818-1854	2
Runau -Runowo-	evKB	Poznan	1821-1865	1
Sandberg -Piaski-	evKB	Poznan	1776-1865	4
Sarne -Sarnowa-	evKB	Poznan	1787-1865	2
Sarne -Sarnowa-	rkKB	Poznan	1818-1865	2
Scherlin -Czerlin-	STA	Berlin	1888-1940	20
Schildberg	evKB	Poznan	1806-1865	4
Schildberg	rkKB	Poznan	1818-1855	3
Schlemsdorf -Szemzdrowo-	evKB	Poznan	1659-1794	1
Schlossberg -Sadkowiec-	rkKB	Berlin-Dahlem	1721-1830	1
Schlossberg -Sadki-	rkKB	Berlin Kirchheim	1721-1898	3
Schlossberg -Gora-	rkKB	Poznan	1820-1829	1
Schmückert -Bojanowo-	evKB	Poznan	1670-1865	13
Schneidemühle -Pila-	STA	Berlin-Dahlem Poznan	1815-1945	187
Schneidemühle -Pila-	LDS records	Salt Lake City	1927-1949	4
Schneidemühle -Pila-	MKB	Hannover	1841-1868	2

Location	Nature of Material	Where Filmed	Dates Covered	No. of Rolls
Schoken -Skoki-	evKB	Poznan	1688-1865	10
Schoken -Skoki-	ZSR	Poznan	1808-1819	1
Schönlanke -Trzcianka-	ZSR	Poznan	1815-1870	25
Schrimm -Śrem-	MKB	Berlin-Dahlem	1833-1918	1
Schrimm -Śrem-	evKB	Poznan	1841-1865	2
Schrimm -Śrem-	Magistrat	Poznan	1817-1847	1
Schrimm -Śrem-	ZSR	Poznan	1814-1815	1
Schulitz -Soleckujawski-	evKB	Lübeck	1833-1900	5
Schulitz -Solelkujawski-	rkKB	Berlin Kirchheim	1663-1925	10
Schulitz -Soleckujawski-	STA	Poznan	1823-1847	1
Schussenze -Ciosaniec-	rkKB	Poznan	1714-1870	2
Schwabensee -Gromadno-	rkKB	Berlin Kirchheim	1741-1874	2
Schwarzau -Błaszki-	ZSR	Berlin-Dahlem	1807-1940	34
Schwarzwald -Czarnylas-	evKB	Poznan	1847-1865	1
Schwersenz -Swarzedz-	LDS records	Salt Lake City	1820-1871	1
Schwersenz -Swarzedz-	evKB	Poznan	1702-1871	7
Schwersenz -Swarzedz-	rkKB	Poznan	1818-1861	3
Schwetzkau -Swieschiechowo-	rkKB	Poznan	1816-1829	1
Słesin	rkKB	Poznan	1741-1866	1

Location	Nature of Material	Where Filmed	Dates Covered	No. of Rolls
Sontop -Satopy-	STA	Berlin-Dahlem	1907-1935	2
Storchnest -Osieczna-	evKB	Poznan	1775-1865	4
Strelno -Strzelno-	rkKB	Augsburg Berlin	1775-1897	3
Tiefenbach -Ksiazwiel- kopolski-	evKB	Poznan	1803-1863	6
Tillendorf -Tylewice-	rkKB	Poznan	1683-1871	1
Trembatschau -Trebaczow-	evKB	Poznan	1765-1865	3
Wahlstatt -Wojnowo-	MKB	Eibenstock	1838-1878	1
Weisseck -Wysoka-	evKB	Lübeck	1864-1914	1
Weisseck -Wysoka-	rkKB	Berlin-Dahlem Kirchheim	1745-1892	3
Weisseck -Wysoka-	ZSR	Berlin	1745-1892	2
Wessenhöhe	evKB	Lübeck	1853-1920	1
Weichselhorst -Włoki-	rkKB	Berlin-Dahlem Berlin	1782-1878	3
Wiershütten	rkKB	Berlin	1760-1889	3
Wiershütten	ZSR	Poznan	1817-1834	1
Wilhelmsort	evKB	Lübeck	1856-1944	2
Wirsitz	evKB	Lübeck	1797-1937	5
Wirsitz	rkKB	Berlin Kirchheim	1745-1892	3
Wirsitz	ZSR	Berlin	1796-1876	1
Wissek	evKB	Lübeck	1797-1937	5
Wissek	rkKB	Berlin Kirchheim	1745-1892	3
Wissek	ZSR	Berlin	1745-1892	2
Wluki	rkKB	Berlin	1782-1883	3

Location	Nature of Material	Where Filmed	Dates Covered	No. of Rolls
Wolfskirch -Wilkowo-	evKB	Poznan	1818-1829	1
Wongrowitz -Wagrowiec-	STA	Berlin	1874-1945	46
Wongrowitz -Wagrowiec-	rkKB	Poznan	1636-1839	2
Woynowo -Wojnowo-	MKB	Eibenstock	1838-1878	1
Wreschen -Wrzesnia-	KG	Berlin	1837-1865	10
Wreschen -Wrzesnia-	MKB	Eibenstock	1833-1848	1
Wreschen -Wrzesnia-	evKB	Berlin-Dahlem	1833-1918	1
Wreschen -Wrzesnia-	rkKB	Poznan	1700-1831	2
Wrotzk -Wrocki-	rkKB	Berlin Kirchheim	1739-1936	3
Wtelno -Wtelno-	rkKB	Berlin-Dahlem	1746-1866	3
Wtelno	ZSR	Berlin	1745-1857	1
Zaborowo	evKB	Poznan	1644-1870	5
Zduny	evKB	Berlin-Dahlem Eibenstock	1834-1925	2
Zduny	ZSR	Poznan	1713-1865	13
Zedlitz -Siedlnica-	rkKB	Poznan	1693-1805	1
Zinsdorf -Ciezkowo-	evKB	Berlin	1908-1961	1
Zirke -Sierakow-	evKB	Hannover Poznan	1388-1856	4
Zlotnik -Złotniczki-	ZSR	Berlin	1874-1935	8

SCHLESIEN[1]

Location	Nature of Material	Where Filmed	Dates Covered	No. of Rolls
Adelsdorf -Zagrodno-	evKB	Warsaw	1701-1853	1
Agnetendorf -Jagniątków-	evKB	Warsaw	1742-1870	6
Albendorf -Wambierzyce-	rkKB	Warsaw	1701-1870	6
Albendorf	rkKB	Breslau	1727-1756	1
Alt Altmannsdorf -Starczów-	rkKB	Breslau	1711-1812	2
Alt Kosel -Stare Koźle-	rkKB	Warsaw	1765-1870	5
Alt Lomnitz -Stare Łomnica-	rkKB	Warsaw	1766-1870	3
Alt Röhrsdorf -Stare Rochowice-	evKB	Warsaw	1766-1835	1
Alt Schalken- dorf -Stare Stiołkowice-	rkKB	Warsaw	1751-1870	7
Alt Schalkowitz= Alt Schalkendorf -Stare Siołkowice-				
Alt Waltersdorf -Stary Waliszów-	rkKB	Warsaw	1614-1870	6
Alt Wette -Swiętów-	rkKB	Warsaw	1765-1870	4
Altenwalde -Stary Las-	rkKB	Warsaw	1766-1870	1

---

[1]There is another collection of Silesian materials in the archives of the Genealogical Society which dovetails nicely with this one. Compiled before World War II and preserved on microfiche, it is now being cataloged for use.

Location	Nature of Material	Where Filmed	Dates Covered	No. of Rolls
Altheinrichau -Stary Henryków-	rkKB	Breslau	1651-1798	3
Altkemnitz -Stara Kamenica-	evKB	Warsaw	1794-1852	4
Alstett -Nowa Cerekwia-	rkKB	Warsaw	1714-1870	2
Arnsdorf -Hirschberg- Miłków	rkKB	Warsaw	1766-1870	3
Arnsdorf in Riesengebirge -Miłków-	rkKB	Breslau	1628-1725	2
Arnsdorf -Karnków-	Chronicle	Hannover	1395-1909	1
Autischkau -Ucieszków-	rkKB	Warsaw	1738-1870	2
Babitz -Babice-	rkKB	Warsaw	1718-1870	2
Bad Pleinerz -Duszniki Zdrój-	MKB rkKB	Warsaw Warsaw	1839-1870 1765-1870	1 10
Baedorf -Niedźwiedź-	rkKB	Breslau	1699-1784	1
Baerwalde -Niedźwiednik	rkKB	Breslau Warsaw	1652-1850	5
Bankwitz -Bąkowice-	rkKB	Breslau Berlin	1679-1800	3
Baranowitz -Baranowice-	Court records Gerichtsamt evKB	Warsaw Warsaw	1810-1874 1812-1858	3 2
Bartschdorf -Bartków-	Published Book 1939			
Bärwalde -Niedźwiednik-	rkKB	Breslau Warsaw	1652-1870	5
Baudmannsdorf -Budziwojów-	rkKB	Warsaw	1798-1865	4

Location	Nature of Material	Where Filmed	Dates Covered	No. of Rolls
Benkowitz -Bieńkowice-	rkKB	Breslau Warsaw	1683-1870	7
Berbisdorf -Dziwiszów-	evKB	Warsaw	1822-1840	1
Berendorf= Benkowitz -Bieńkowice-				
Bertelsdorf -Uniegoszcz-	rkKB	Warsaw	1794-1865	1
Berthelsdorf -Barcinek-	evKB	Warsaw	1790-1822	1
Berzdorf -Boznowice-	rkKB	Berlin Warsaw	1650-1870	2
Berun -Bieruń Stary-	rkKB	Warsaw	1820-1871	2
Bielitz -Bielice-	rkKB	Breslau Warsaw	1582-1874	7
Bienowitz -Bieniowice-	KB	Warsaw	1815-1842	1
Bierdzan -Bierdzany-	rkKB	Warsaw	1820-1870	1
Bilchengurno -Pilchowice-	rkKB	Warsaw	1823-1870	2
Birkenbrück -Brzeznik-	rkKB	Warsaw	1708-1864	1
Birngrütz -Grudza-	rkKB	Breslau Warsaw	1672-1880	3
Bischofstal -Ujazd	MKB rkKB	Hannover Berlin	1801-1809 1622-1675	1 1
Bladen -Włodzienin-	rkKB	Warsaw	1715-1870	4
Bleischwitz -Bliszczyce-	rkKB	Warsaw	1820-1870	1
Blüchertal -Zawonia-	evKB	Warsaw	1708-1800	1

Location	Nature of Material	Where Filmed	Dates Covered	No. of Rolls
Boberröhrsdorf -Siedlecin-	evKB	Warsaw	1748-1873	10
Bobersberg -Bobrowice-	evKB	Warsaw	1813-1870	1
Boberullersdorf -Wrzeszczyn-	evKB	Warsaw	1787-1870	2
Boguschowitz -Boguszowice-	rkKB	Warsaw	1848-1870	1
Bohmischweigs- dorf -Czechoslovakia, Viśnova-	evKB	Warsaw	1832-1847	1
Bolkenhain -Bolków-	evKB rkKB	Warsaw Breslau	1615-1816	3
Borckendorf -Brochocin-	rkKB	Warsaw	1798-1865	4
Borkendorf -Burgrabice-	rkKB	Warsaw	1695-1870	5
Bösdorf -Pakosławice-	rkKB	Warsaw Berlin	1738-1848	2
Boyadel -Bojadla-	evKB	Warsaw	1765-1846	1
Branitz -Branice-	rkKB	Warsaw	1700-1870	3
Bratsch -Braciszów-	rkKB	Warsaw	1795-1865	1
Breitenfeld -Makowice-	rkKB	Warsaw	1765-1870	6
Breslau -Wrocław-	LDS records	Salt Lake City	1907-1938	7
Breslau -Wrocław-	MKB	Hannover Eibenstock Dahlem	1729-1942 1759-1801 1741-1945	13 1 17
Breslau -Wrocław-	Prison KB	Warsaw	1862-1868	1
Breslau -Wrocław-	evKB	Warsaw	1788-1870	147
Breslau -Wrocław-	rkKB	Berlin Warsaw	1701-1874	17

Location	Nature of Material	Where Filmed	Dates Covered	No. of Rolls
Brieg -Brzeg-	MKB evKB evKB	Berlin-Dahlem Warsaw Warsaw	1723-1944 1594-1859 1712-1902	3 18 12
Briesnitz -Brzeznica-	rkKB	Breslau	1638-1728	1
Brinnitz -Brynica-	rkKB	Breslau	1657-1731	1
Broschütz -Brożec-	rkKB	Warsaw	1789-1870	4
Broslawitz -Zbroslawice-	rkKB	Breslau	1765-1796	1
Brostau -Brzostów-	rkKB evKB	Zielona Góra Zielona Góra	1824-1870 1714-1815	1 1
Brückenberg -Bierutowice-	evKB	Warsaw	1845-1870	1
Brunberg -Zielona Góra-	MKB	Berlin=Dahlem	1741-1806	1
Brunberg -Zielona Góra-	rkKB	Warsaw	1825-1870	2
Brunberg -Zielona Góra-	rkKB evKB	Berlin	1652-1816	6
Brunberg -Zielona Góra-	evKB	Warsaw	1798-1870	2
Brunne=Brinnitz -Brynica-				
Brunzelwaldau -Broniszów-	rkKB	Breslau Warsaw	1668-1970	5
Brzeg=Brieg -Brzeg-				
Brzestz -Brzezce-	rkKB	Warsaw	1820-1870	2
Buchelsdorf -Niemysłowice-	rkKB	Warsaw	1794-1867	3
Buchendam -Buczyna-	evKB	Warsaw	1741-1870	1
Buchwald -Bukowiec-	evKB rkKB	Warsaw	1749-1870	3
Buchwald=Budiendamm -Buczyna-				

Location	Nature of Material	Where Filmed	Dates Covered	No. of Rolls
Bujakow -Bujaków-	rkKB	Warsaw	1800-1865	6
Burkardsdorf -Bierdzany-	rkKB	Warsaw	1820-1870	1
Canth -Kąty Wrocławskie-	rkKB	Warsaw	1765-1870	4
Casimir -Kazimierz-	rkKB	Warsaw	1796-1870	2
Christianstadt -Krzystkowice-	rkKB	Salt Lake City	1690-1743	1
Chrosczinna -Chróścina Opolska-	rkKB	Warsaw	1742-1870	3
Chrosczütz -Chrościce-	rkKB	Warsaw	1818-1870	1
Chrzumczütz -Chrzaszczyce-	rkKB	Warsaw	1715-1870	5
Corsenz -Korzeńsko-	evKB	Warsaw	1840, 1861-1870	2
	rkKB	Warsaw	1810-1870	2
Czarnowanz -Czarnowąsy-	rkKB	Warsaw	1811-1870	3
Dambrau -Dąbrowa-	rkKB	Warsaw	1767-1870	6
Dembio -Dębie-	rkKB	Warsaw	1827-1870	2
Deutsch Kamitz -Kępnica-	rkKB	Warsaw	1830-1870	3
Deutsch Leippe -Lipowa-	rkKB	Warsaw	1765-1870	4
Deutsch Müllmen -Wierzch-	rkKB	Warsaw	1804-1870	4
Deutsch Neukirch= Altstett -Nowa Cerekwia-				

Location	Nature of Material	Where Filmed	Dates Covered	No. of Rolls
Deutsch Probnitz -Nowy Browiniec-	rkKB	Warsaw	1817-1870	2
Deutsch Rasselwitz -Racławice Sląskie-	rkKB	Warsaw	1658-1870	6
Deutsch Wartenberg -Olyn-	evKB rkKB	Warsaw Warsaw	1805-1860 1655-1885	1 10
Deutsch Wette -Nowy Swietów-	rkKB	Warsaw	1651-1870	5
Dietzdorf -Ciechów-	rkKB	Warsaw	1799-1870	1
Dittersdorf -Dytmarów-	rkKB	Warsaw	1765-1870	3
Döberle -Dobra-	evKB	Warsaw	1725-1765	2
Dohms -Luboszów-	evKB	Warsaw	1848	1
Dollna -Dolna-	rkKB	Warsaw	1689-1870	3
Domnowitz -Domanowice-	rkKB	Warsaw	1810-1870	1
Domslau -Domasław-	evKB	Warsaw	1825-1870	7
Dramatal=Brosawitz -Zbrosławice-				
Dromsdorf -Drogomiłowice-	evKB	Warsaw	1819-1836	1
Dürr Arnsdorf -Jarnoltów-	rkKB	Warsaw	1855-1870	1
Ebersdorf -Domaszków-	rkKB	Warsaw	1735-1875	6

Location	Nature of Material	Where Filmed	Dates Covered	No. of Rolls
Eckersdorf -Kącik-	rkKB	Warsaw	1794-1839	1
Eichenau -Wojcice-	rkKB	Warsaw	1766-1870	3
Eisemost -Żelazny Most-	rkKB	Warsaw	1839-1870	1
Ellguth Turawa -Ligota Turawa-	rkKB	Warsaw	1813-1870	4
Erdmannsdorf -Myslakowice-	evKB	Warsaw	1841, 1854	1
Ernsdorf=Reichenbach -Dzierżoniów-				
Falkenau -Chróścina Nyska-	rkKB	Warsaw	1788-1870	4
Falkenberg -Niemodlin-	evKB rkKB	Berlin Warsaw	1802-1810 1689-1870	1 3
Falkenberg -Sokola-	evKB	Warsaw	1825-1849	1
Falkendorf -Fałkowice-	rkKB	Warsaw	1765-1870	6
Falkenhain -Sokołowiec-	rkKB evKB	Warsaw	1794-1874 1794-1870	2 3
Falkowitz=Falkendorf -Fałkowice-				
Fischbach -Karpniki-	evKB	Warsaw	1742-1840	6
Fraustadt -Wschowa-	JüdGem evKB	Dahlem-Berlin	1890-1919 1798-1920	1 2
Freiburg -Swiebodzice-	Property record rkKB ZSR	Hauptarchiv Berlin-Dahlem Warsaw Warsaw	18th-19th Cent 1734-1872 1784-1870	1 4 2
Freiwalde -Lesica-	rkKB	Warsaw	1591-1870	7
Freyhanstadt -Cieszków-	rkKB	Warsaw	1794-1870	1

Location	Nature of Material	Where Filmed	Dates Covered	No. of Rolls
Freystadt -Kożuchów-	evKB	Warsaw Hannover Berlin	1706-1893	19
Freystadt -Kożuchów-	JüdGem	Warsaw	1849-1873	1
Freystadt -Kożuchów-	rkKB	Warsaw	1794-1870	2
Friedersdorf -Biedrzychowice-	evKB	Warsaw	1800-1865	3
Friedersdorf -Neustadt- -Biedrzychowice-	rkKB	Warsaw	1719-1870	5
Friedland -Korfantów-	rkKB	Warsaw	1838-1870	3
Friedewalde -Skoroszyce-	rkKB	Warsaw	1765-1871	7
Fuchshübel -Strzeganowice-	rkKB	Warsaw	1766-1870	1
Fürstenau -Kziąż Śląski-	evKB rkKB	Warsaw Berlin	1820-1840 1666-1743	1 1
Fürstenau -Milin-	rkKB	Warsaw	1824-1848	1
Fürsteneich -Zabor-	evKB	Warsaw	1742-1840	8
Gaablau -Jablów-	evKB	Warsaw	1810-1852	1
Gammau -Gamów-	rkKB	Warsaw	1856-1870	1
Gauers -Goworowice-	rkKB	Warsaw	1766-1870	1
Gaulau -Gulów-	evKB	Warsaw	1766-1863	1
Geibsdorf -Siekierczyn-	evKB	Warsaw	1839-1865	3
Gemelwitz -Jemielnice-	rkKB	Warsaw	1733-1870	5
Geroldsdorf -Gierałtowice-	rkKB	Warsaw	1737-1870	2

Location	Nature of Material	Where Filmed	Dates Covered	No. of Rolls
Gesess -Ujezdziec-	rkKB	Warsaw	1765-1793	4
Gieraltowitz=Geroldsdorf -Gierałtowice-				
Giersdorf -Opolnica-	evKB	Warsaw	1700-1795	1
Giesmannsdorf -Gostków-	evKB	Warsaw	1817-1820	1
Gimmelwitz=Gemelwitz -Jemielnica-				
Gleinig -Glinka-	rkKB	Warsaw	1792-1870	1
Gleiwitz -Gliwice-	LDS records	Salt Lake City	1931-1957	1
Gleiwitz -Gliwice-	MKB	Eibenstock	1835-1876	1
Gleiwitz -Gliwice-	evKB	Warsaw	1840-1861	1
Gleiwitz -Gliwice-	JüdGem	Warsaw	1858-1861	1
Glogau -Glogów-	evKB MKB	Warsaw Eibenstock Hannover	1706-1831 1795-1934	2 8
Gnadenfeld -Pawlowiczki-	rkKB	Warsaw	1724-1870	4
Golasowice -Golasowice-	evKB	Warsaw	1812-1858	2
Gontkowitz -Gadkowice-	evKB	Warsaw	1832-1870	5
Görlitz -Zgorzelec-	evKB rkKB	Warsaw Warsaw	1617-1847 1785-1870	3 3
Goschütz -Goszcz-	rkKB	Warsaw	1798-1870	5
Gräditz -Grodziszcze-	rkKB	Warsaw	1743-1870	11

Location	Nature of Material	Where Filmed	Dates Covered	No. of Rolls
Grafenort -Gorzanów-	rkKB	Warsaw	1766-1866	3
Gramschütz -Grębocice- e	rkKB evKB	Warsaw	1585-1741	3
Greibnig -Grzybiany-	evKB	Warsaw	1842-1864	2
Gremsdorf -Gromadka-	evKB	Hannover	1945-1950	1
Greulich -Grodzanowice-	evKB	Hannover	1945-1950	1
Gröbing -Grobniki-	rkKB	Warsaw	1742-1870	3
Grögersdorf -Grzegorzów-	evKB	Warsaw	1721-1794	1
Groschowitz -Groszowice-	rkKB	Warsaw	1835-1870	1
Gross Baudiss -Budziszów Wielki-	evKB	Warsaw	1819-1836	1
Gross Döbern -Dobrzeń Wielki-	rkKB	Warsaw	1765-1865	4
Gross Grauden -Grudynia Wielka-	rkKB	Warsaw	1732-1870	4
Gross Karlowitz -Karlowice Wielkie-	rkKB	Warsaw	1779-1862	3
Gross Kottorz -Kotorz Wielki-	rkKB	Warsaw	1692-1870	7
Gross Logisch -Lagoszów Wielki-	rkKB	Zielona Góra	1793-1870	1
Gross Mahlendorf -Malerzowice Wielkie-	rkKB	Warsaw Breslau	1582-1870	4

Gross Merzdorf=Schmellwitz
-Marcinowice-

Location	Nature of Material	Where Filmed	Dates Covered	No. of Rolls
Gross Mohnau -Maniów Wielki-	rkKB	Warsaw	1720-1870	3
Gross Nädlitz -Nadolice Wielkie-	evKB	Warsaw	1849-1870	2
Gross Neukirch -Polska Cerekiew-	rkKB	Warsaw	1723-1870	5
Gross Neundorf -Złologłowice-	rkKB	Warsaw	1825-1870	1
Gross Nimsdorf -Naczęsławice-	rkKB	Warsaw	1719-1870	4
Gross Petrowitz -Pietrowice Wielkie-	rkKB	Warsaw	1717-1870	5
Gross Rudau -Rudy-	rkKB	Warsaw	1663-1870	5
Gross Stanisch -Staniszcze Wielkie-	rkKB	Warsaw	1805-1870	3
Gross Stein -Kamień Śląski-	rkKB	Warsaw	1766-1870	4
Gross Strehlitz -Strzelce Opolskie-	MKB rkKB	Eibenstock Warsaw	1834-1868 1765-1870	1 7
Gross Tinz -Tyniec Legnicky-	evKB	Warsaw	1818-1846	1
Gross & Klein Bargen -Babkowo-	evKB rkKB	Warsaw	1810-1870	4
Gross Wartenberg -Syców-	evKB	Warsaw	1766-1808	1
Gross Ziedel -Staniszcze Wielkie-	rkKB	Warsaw	1805-1870	3
Gross Zyglin -Żyglin-	rkKB	Warsaw	1800-1870	3
Grossbriesen -Brzeziny-	rkKB	Warsaw	1765-1871	7

Location	Nature of Material	Where Filmed	Dates Covered	No. of Rolls
Grossenbohrau -Borów-	rkKB	Warsaw	1794-1870	2
Grosspeterwitz=Gross Petrowitz -Pietrowice Wielkie-				
Grosswandriss -Wądroże Wielkie-	evKB	Warsaw	1808-1820	1
Grottkau -Grodków-	rkKB	Warsaw	1740-1870	11
Grüben -Grabin-	rkKB	Warsaw	1735-1870	6
Grün Hartau -Zielenice-	evKB	Warsaw	1700-1857	1
Grüssau -Krzeszów-	rkKB	Warsaw	1694-1870	18
Grzendzin -Grzędzin-	rkKB	Warsaw	1765-1870	7
Gumpersdorf -Komprachcice-	rkKB	Warsaw	1747-1870	2
Habelswerdt -Bystrzyca Kłodzka-	rkKB MKB	Warsaw Eibenstock	1691-1870 1832-1879	17 1
Halbau -Iłowa-	evKB	Warsaw	1860-1865	1
Halbendorf -Półwsie-	rkKB	Breslau	1615-1685	1
Hammer -Młoty-	rkKB	Warsaw	1691-1870	17
Hammer -Kuźnia Raciborska-	rkKB	Warsaw	1800-1870	3
Hartau -Borowina-	rkKB	Warsaw	1794-1870	2
Hartenau -Twardawa-	rkKB	Warsaw	1715-1870	6

Location	Nature of Material	Where Filmed	Dates Covered	No. of Rolls
Hartmannsdorf	rkKB	Warsaw	1839-1970	2
-Jarogniewice-	evKB	Warsaw	1794-1870	3
Haselbach -Leszczyniec-	rkKB	Warsaw	1834-1870	1
Haunau	evKB	Warsaw	1711-1870	12
-Chojnów-	rkKB	Warsaw	1762-1870	2
	ZSR	Frankfurt	1945-1946	1
	STA			
Hausdorf -Jugowa-	evKB	Warsaw	1794-1865	4
Haynau=Haunau -Chojnów-				
Hedwigstein -Kościeliska-	rkKB	Warsaw Berlin	1738-1870	5
Heidau -Gać-	evKB	Warsaw	1846-1870	2
Heidersdorf -Łagiewniki-	rkKB	Warsaw	1801-1870	1
Heinersdorf -Dziewietlice-	rkKB	Warsaw	1780-1870	3
Heinrichau -Henryków-	rkKB	Warsaw	1666-1870	13
Heinzendorf -Bagno-	rkKB	Warsaw	1745-1870	3
Hennersdorf -Henryków Lubański-	rkKB	Warsaw	1837-1865	3
Hennersdorf	evKB	Warsaw	1835-1863	2
-Osiek	rkKB	Warsaw	1852-1860	1
Hermsdorf	evKB	Warsaw	1742-1870	5
-Sobieszów-	rkKB	Warsaw	1822-1870	1
Hermsdorf -Jerzmanice- Zdrój-	evKB	Warsaw	1794-1870	1
Hermannsdorf -Jerzmanowo-	evKB	Warsaw	1842-1849	1
Herrmannsdorf -Męcinka-	rkKB	Warsaw	1765-1846	2

Location	Nature of Material	Where Filmed	Dates Covered	No. of Rolls
Herrnstadt -Wąsosz-	MKB	Eibenstock Hannover	1802-1868	2
Hertwigswaldau -Cholków-	evKB	Warsaw	1806-1870	2
Herzogwaldau -Mirocin-	rkKB	Warsaw	1788-1870	1
Himmelwitz= Gemelwitz -Jemielnica-				
Hindenburg -Zabrze-	LDS records rkKB	Salt Lake City Warsaw	1927-1937 1800-1870	8 12
Hirschberg -Jelenia Góra-	evKB rkKB MKB	Berlin Warsaw Hannover	1709-1957 1745-1870 1835-1950	58 7 3
Hochkirch -Wysoka Cerekiew-	rkKB	Warsaw	1821-1870	3
Hochkirch -Koscielec-	evKB	Warsaw	1697-1870	5
Hohenfriedeberg -Dobromierz-	evKB rkKB	Warsaw Warsaw	1794-1865 1845-1870	4 1
Hohenliebentahl -Lubiechowa-	evKB	Warsaw	1794-1870	4
Holzkirch -Kościelnik-	evKB	Warsaw	1857-1865	2
Hummelstadt -Lewin Kłodzki-	rkKB	Warsaw	1766-1870	9
Hünern=Heidau -Psary-	evKB			
Hüttenguth= Habelswerdt -Huta-				
Jakobskirch -Jakubów-	rkKB	Warsaw Berlin	1663-1870	2

Location	Nature of Material	Where Filmed	Dates Covered	No. of Rolls
Janowitz -Janowice Wielkie-	evKB rkKB	Warsaw Warsaw	1794-1814 1794-1870	1 2
Janowitz -Cyprzanów-	rkKB	Warsaw	1766-1870	2
Jätschau -Jaczów-	evKB rkKB	Warsaw Zielona Góra	1714-1815 1825-1870	1 1
Jauer -Jawor-	evKB	Warsaw Berlin	1692-1851	3
Jauer -Jawor-	rkKB	Berlin	1567-1766	3
Jauer -Jawor-	MKB	Hannover Eibenstock	1790-1866	2
Jauer -Jawor-	Land and Property	Dahlem	18th-19th Cent	1
Jeschona -Jasiona-	rkKB	Warsaw	1720-1870	5
Kalkau -Kalków-	rkKB	Warsaw	1797-1870	3
Kammerswaldau -Komarno-	evKB rkKB	Warsaw Warsaw	1794-1848 1794-1870	3 3
Kamnig -Kamiennik-	rkKB	Warsaw	1751-1870	4
Kanig -Kaniów-	evKB	Warsaw	1676-1870	2
Kanth -Kąty Wrocławskie-	rkKB	Warsaw	1765-1870	4
Karlsburg -Dobra-	evKB	Warsaw	1725-1765	2
Karzen -Karczyn-	evKB	Warsaw Berlin	1700-1717 1832-1845	1 1
Kasimir -Kazimierz-	rkKB	Warsaw	1796-1870	2
Katscher -Kietrz-	rkKB	Warsaw	1656-1870	13
Kauffung -Wojcieszów	rkKB evKB	Warsaw Warsaw	1767-1870 1800-1870	4 4

Location	Nature of Material	Where Filmed	Dates Covered	No. of Rolls
Keilerswalde -Kielcza-	rkKB	Warsaw	1765-1870	3
Keltsch=Keilerswalde -Kielcza-				
Ketschdorf -Kaczorów-	evKB	Warsaw	1794-1870	5
Keulendorf -Kulin-	rkKB	Warsaw	1728-1870	1
Klein Strehlitz -Strzeleczki-	rkKB	Warsaw	1765-1870	4
Klosterbrück -Czarnowąsy-	rkKB	Warsaw	1811-1870	3
Klutschau -Klucz-	rkKB	Warsaw	1739-1867	2
Knispel -Księże Pole-	rkKB	Warsaw	1662-1870	1
Knobelsdorf -Czartkowice-	rkKB	Warsaw	1798-1865	4
Koischwitz -Koskowice-	evKB	Warsaw	1827-1865	2
Kolbnitz -Chelmiec-	rkKB	Warsaw	1771-1870	1
Komprachczütz -Komprachcice-	rkKB	Warsaw	1747-1870	2
Königshain -Wojciechowice-	rkKB	Warsaw	1587-1870	2
Konradswaldau -Kondratów-	evKB	Warsaw	1793-1870	2
Konradswaldau -Grzędy-	evKB	Warsaw	1794-1852	1
Konradswaldau -Mrowiny-	evKB	Warsaw	1777-1809	1
Konradswaldau -Górowo-	evKB	Warsaw	1821-1870	2
Koppendorf -Pniewie-	rkKB	Warsaw	1765-1870	1

Location	Nature of Material	Where Filmed	Dates Covered	No. of Rolls
Köppernig -Koperniki-	rkKB	Warsaw	1857-1870	1
Koppitz -Kopice-	rkKB	Warsaw	1766-1870	6
Korsenz -Korzeńsko-	evKB	Warsaw	1840, 1861-1870	2
	rkKB	Warsaw	1810-1870	2
Kosel -Koźle-	rkKB	Warsaw	1673-1870	15
	MKB	Hannover	1765-1806	1
Kostelitz -Kościeliska-	rkKB	Warsaw	1765-1870	4
		Berlin	1738-1765	1
Kostenthal -Gościęcin-	rkKB	Warsaw	1725-1870	7
Kottwitz -Kotowice-	rkKB	Berlin	1716-1766	1
	evKB	Warsaw	1836-1860	1
Krampe -Krępa-	rkKB	Berlin	1666-1737	1
Krappitz -Krąpkowice-	evKB	Warsaw	1812-1852	1
	rkKB	Warsaw	1765-1870	8
Kraschen -Chrościna-	rkKB	Warsaw	1816-1870	1
Krascheow -Krasiejów-	rkKB	Warsaw	1805-1870	1
Kreuzburg -Kluczbork-	MKB	Eibenstock	1798-1918	1
		Hannover	1789-1807	1
	JüdGem	Warsaw	1813-1815	1
Kreuzendorf -Goluszowice-	rkKB	Warsaw	1702-1870	2
Krummhübel -Karpacz-	rkKB	Breslau	1628-1725	2
Kühschmalz -Kobiela-	rkKB	Warsaw Berlin Salt Lake City	1658-1870	5
Kunersdorf -Brzezia Łąka-	rkKB	Warsaw	1847-1870	1
Kunzendorf -Sieroszowice-	evKB	Warsaw	1741-1870	3

Location	Nature of Material	Where Filmed	Dates Covered	No. of Rolls
Kunzendorf -Trzebina-	rkKB	Warsaw	1765-1870	4
Kunzendorf- Grosshau -Pastewnik-	evKB	Warsaw	1818-1838	2
Kupferberg -Miedzianka-	evKB rkKB	Warsaw Warsaw	1794-1856 1794-1870	6 2
La̎hn -Wleń-	rkKB	Warsaw	1720-1870	2
Lammsdorf -Łambinowice-	rkKB	Warsaw	1740-1870	4
Landeshut -Kamienna Góra-	evKB	Warsaw	1828-1870	1
Landsberg -Gorzów Sląski-	rkKB	Warsaw	1801-1870	7
Lang Neundorf -Dlużec	rkKB evKB	Salt Lake City Warsaw	1668-1747 1794-1870	1 3
Langeh -e- Lwigsdorf -Pogwizdów-	evKB	Warsaw	1794-1849	1
Langendorf -Bodzanów-	rkKB	Warsaw	1734-1870	12
Langenöls -Olszyna-	evKB	Warsaw	1856-1865	3
Langhermsdorf -Urzuty-	rkKB	Warsaw	1839-1970	2
Langlieben -Długomilowice-	rkKB	Warsaw	1729-1870	4
Langwasser -Chmieleń-	rkKB	Warsaw	1712-1874	1
Lansitz -Łężyca-	evKB rkKB	Salt Lake City	1701-1736	1
Laskowitz -Laskowice-	evKB	Warsaw	1837-1871	2
Laskowitz -Laskowice-	rkKB	Warsaw	1778-1870	1

Location	Nature of Material	Where Filmed	Dates Covered	No. of Rolls
Lassoth -Lasocice-	rkKB	Warsaw	1766-1859	2
Lauban -Lubań-	evKB Kloster MKB	Warsaw Warsaw Hannover	1822-1865 1654-1858 1916-1920	7 3 1
Leipe -Lipa-	rkKB	Salt Lake City	1607-1761	2
Leisersdorf -Uniejowice-	evKB	Warsaw	1794-1853	1
Leisnitz -Lisieice-	rkKB	Warsaw	1717-1870	2
Leobschütz -Głubczyze-	rkKB	Warsaw	1648-1870	10
Leschnig -Leśnik-	rkKB	Warsaw	1853-1870	1
Leschnitz -Leśnica-	rkKB	Warsaw	1808-1870	5
Lesten -Czernina-	evKB	Warsaw	1866	1
Leuber -Lubrza-	rkKB	Warsaw	1766-1870	3
Leuthen -Lutynia-	evKB	Warsaw	1839-1870	4
Lewin -Lewin Kłodski-	rkKB	Warsaw	1766-1870	9
Lichtenwaldau -Krzyżowa-	evKB	Warsaw	1858-1870	1
Liebanthal -Lubomierz-	rkKB	Warsaw	1859-1870	1
Liebenau -Lubnów-	rkKB	Warsaw	1765-1874	1
Liegnitz -Legnica-	evKB rkKB	Warsaw Berlin-Dahlem Warsaw	1574-1871 1937-1957 1845-1846	74 2 3
Lindewiese -Lipowa-	rkKB	Warsaw	1696-1870	4
Lipschau Dohms -Luboszów-	evKB	Warsaw	1848	1

Location	Nature of Material	Where Filmed	Dates Covered	No. of Rolls
Lissek -Lyski-	rkKB	Warsaw	1828-1870	1
Lobendau -Lubiatów-	evKB	Warsaw	1805-1864	3
Lobris -Luboradz-	rkKB	Warsaw	1662-1870	1
Lohnau -Łany-	rkKB	Warsaw	1680-1870	3
Lohnig -Łagiewniki Sredzkie-	evKB	Warsaw	1819-1836	1
Lomnitz -Lomnica-	evKB	Warsaw	1794-1854	5
Londzin -Lędziny-	rkKB	Warsaw	1820-1870	2
Lonkau -Łąka-	rkKB	Warsaw	1820-1870	1
Löwen -Lewin Brzeski-	evKB	Warsaw	1712-1902	12
Löwenberg -Lwówek Śląski-	MKB	Eibenstock	1834-1887	1
Löwitz -Lewice-	rkKB	Warsaw	1820-1870	1
Lüben -Lubin-	rkKB	Warsaw	1775-1870	3
Lublinitz -Lubliniec-	MKB rkKB evKB	Hannover Warsaw Warsaw	1914-1919 1831-1864 1830-1866	1 1 1
Lubowitz -Lubowice-	rkKB	Warsaw	1766-1870	4
Ludwigsdorf -Chrośnica	evKB rkKB	Warsaw Warsaw	1794-1870 1816-1870	2 1
Ludwigsdorf -Charbielin-	rkKB	Warsaw	1730-1862	4

Location	Nature of Material	Where Filmed	Dates Covered	No. of Rolls
Lugnian -Lubniany-	rkKB	Warsaw	1773-1870	3
Maiwaldau -Maciejowa-	evKB rkKB	Warsaw Warsaw	1794-1846 1794-1863	4 1
Makau -Maków-	rkKB	Berlin Warsaw	1688-1870	4
Malitsch -Maluszów-	evKB	Warsaw	1747-1809	1
Maltsch -Malczyce-	Publications only			
Margareth -Gajków-	rkKB	Warsaw	1860-1861	1
Marienthal -Niemojów-	rkKB	Warsaw	1591-1870	7
Markowitz -Markowice-	rkKB	Warsaw	1732-1870	5
Markt Bohrau -Borów-	evKB rkKB	Warsaw Breslau	1784-1796 1588-1815	1 4
Marschwitz -Marszowice-	evKB	Hannover	1923-1946	1
Matzkirch -Maciowakrze-	rkKB	Warsaw	1766-1870	2
Mechnitz -Mechnica-	rkKB	Warsaw	1790-1870	3
Mechwitz -Miechowice Oławskie-	evKB	Warsaw	1766-1853	1
Melling -Mielnik-	rkKB	Warsaw	1766-1866	3
Merzdorf -Marcinowice-	rkKB	Warsaw	1817-1872	1
Miedzna -Miedzna-	rkKB	Warsaw	1817-1870	1
Milzig -Milsko-	evKB rkKB	Warsaw	1696-1860	3

Location	Nature of Material	Where Filmed	Dates Covered	No. of Rolls
Mittel Arnsdorf -Karnków-	evKB Chronik	Hannover	1395-1909	1
Modlau -Modla-	evKB	Hannover	1945-1950	1
Mogwitz -Mąkowice-	rkKB	Warsaw	1765-1870	6
Mühlwirtz -Milowice-	evKB	Warsaw	1756-1870	1
Münsterberg -Ziębice-	evKB rkKB	Warsaw Warsaw Berlin	1742-1870 1629-1870	9 26
Myslowitz -Mysłowice-	evKB rkKB Court record	Warsaw Warsaw Warsaw	1857-1865 1800-1865 1847-1870	3 8 4
Nädlingen=Gross Nädlingen -Nadolice Wielkie-				
Nassiedel -Nasiedle-	rkKB	Warsaw	1690-1870	8
Naumburg -Nowogrodziec-	rkKB	Warsaw	1802-1871	2
Nechlau -Niechlów-	evKB	Warsaw	1645-1870	10
Neisse -Nysa-	MKB rkKB	Hannover Warsaw	1850-1868 1765-1870	1 24
Neudorf -Nowizna-	rkKB	Warsaw	1811-1870	7
Neudorf am Gröditzberge -Nowa Wieś Grodziska-	evKB	Warsaw	1794-1799	1
Neudorf -Nowa Wieś Kącka-	rkKB	Warsaw	1767-1870	1
Neuen -Krzeszów-	rkKB	Warsaw	1694-1870	18
Neukemnitz -Nowa Kamienica-	rkKB	Warsaw	1794-1874	1

Location	Nature of Material	Where Filmed	Dates Covered	No. of Rolls
Neukirch -Nowy Kościół	evKB rkKB	Warsaw Warsaw	1794-1870 1794-1843	7 1
Neumarkt -Środa Śląska-	MKB evKB	Eibenstock Warsaw	1802-1810 1742-1877	1 20
Neunz -Niwnica-	rkKB	Warsaw	1765-1870	4
Neusalz -Nowa Sól-	evKB rkKB	Warsaw Zielona Góra	1804-1870 1769-1871	6 2
Neustadt -Prudnik-	MKB rkKB	Hannover Warsaw	1732-1810 1822-1870	2 7
Neustädtel -Nowe Miasteczko-	rkKB	Warsaw	1764-1870	2
Neuwalde -Nowy Las-	rkKB	Warsaw	1669-1870	4
Neuweistritz -Nowa Bystrzyca-	rkKB	Warsaw	1691-1870	17
Niebusch -Niwiska-	evKB	Warsaw	1830-1870	3
Nieder Arnsdorf= Mittel Arnsdorf -Karnków-				
Nieder Harpersdorf -Twardocice-	rkKB	Warsaw	1794-1870	3
Nieder Hermsdorf -Jasienica Dolna-	rkKB	Warsaw	1765-1870	7
Nieder Salzbrunn -Szczawienko-	rkKB	Warsaw	1752-1870	1
Niederhannsdorf -Jaszkowa Dolna-	rkKB	Warsaw	1673-1870	8
Niedersteine -Ścinawka Dolna-	rkKB	Warsaw	1704-1887	9
Nilbau -Nielubia-	rkKB	Warsaw	1847-1870	4

Location	Nature of Material	Where Filmed	Dates Covered	No. of Rolls
Nimbsch= Niebusch -Niemcza-				
Nimmersath -Plonina-	evKB	Warsaw	1818-1838	2
Nimptsch -Niemcza-	rkKB	Berlin Warsaw	1707-1870	4
	evKB	Warsaw	1559-1839	13
Ober Arnsdorf= Mittel Arnsdorf -Karnków-				
Ober Glasersdorf -Szklary Górne-	rkKB	Warsaw	1775-1870	1
Ober Glauche -Głuchów Górny-	evKB	Warsaw	1790-1814	1
Ober Glogau -Glogówek-	rkKB	Warsaw	1869-1870	1
Ober Harpersdorf= Nieder Harpersdorf -Twardocice-				
Ober Jastrzemb -Jastrzębie Górne-	rkKB	Warsaw	1842-1846	1
Ludwigsthal -Piaske P. Lubsza-	evKB	Warsaw	1830-1866	1
Ober Schwedelsdorf -Szalejów Górny-	rkKB	Warsaw	1626-1880	11

Location	Nature of Material	Where Filmed	Dates Covered	No. of Rolls
Obraberg -Podlegórz-	rkKB	Warsaw	1666-1754	1
Ochelhermsdorf -Ochla-	evKB	Warsaw	1794-1860	1
Oderwalde -Dziergowice-	rkKB	Warsaw	1830-1870	4
Oels -Oleśnica	rkKB	Warsaw	1858-1870	1
Ohlau -Oława-	MKB	Hannover	1852-1856	1
Öls=Oels -Oleśnica-				
Oppersdorf -Wierzbiecice-	rkKB	Warsaw	1765-1870	4
Oppeln -Opole-	evKB rkKB	Warsaw Warsaw	1828-1835 1724-1870	1 15
Ostrosnitz -Ostrożnica-	rkKB	Warsaw	1766-1870	3
Ostwalde -Polomia-	rkKB	Warsaw	1840-1848	1
Ottmachau -Otmuchów-	rkKB	Warsaw	1786-1870	6
Ottmuth -Otmęt-	rkKB	Warsaw	1811-1870	4
Padligar -Podlegórz-	rkKB	Warsaw	1666-1754	1
Pahlowitz -Pawlowice Male-	evKB	Warsaw	1824-1872	1
Parchwitz -Prochowice-	rkKB	Warsaw	1769-1870	3
Patschkau -Paczków-	MKB	Eibenstock Berlin-Dahlem	1835-1846 1830-1850	1 1

Location	Nature of Material	Where Filmed	Dates Covered	No. of Rolls
Pawlau -Pawlow-	rkKB	Warsaw	1714-1870	1
Pawlowitzke= Gnadenfeld -Pawlowiczki-				
Petersdorf -Piechowice-	Publications only			
Peterwitz -Piotrowice-	rkKB	Warsaw	1771-1870	1
Peucker -Poniatów-	rkKB	Warsaw	1624-1870	5
Pfaffendorf -Rudzica-	rkKB	Warsaw	1771-1799	1
Pilgramsdorf -Pielgrzymka-	evKB	Warsaw	1793-1870	3
Piltsch -Pilszcz-	rkKB	Warsaw	1629-1870	4
Pless -Pszczyna-	MKB evKB rkKB	Berlin-Dahlem Warsaw Warsaw	1831-1919 1794-1870 1821-1870	1 5 3
Plothow -Płoty-	evKB	Hannover	1655-1944	8
Podrosche -Żary-	evKB	Berlin Warsaw	1674-1855	2
Pohlom -Połomia-	rkKB	Warsaw	1840-1848	1
Pohlschildern -Szczytniki n. Kaczawa-	evKB	Warsaw	1815-1842	1
Polnisch Krawarn -Krowiarki-	rkKB	Berlin Warsaw	1766-1870	3
Polnisch Nettkow -Nietków-	evKB	Warsaw	1813-1860	1
Polnisch Neudorf -Polska Nowa Wieś-	rkKB	Warsaw	1747-1870	2
Polnisch Neukirch -Polska Cerekiew-	rkKB	Warsaw	1723-1870	5

Location	Nature of Material	Where Filmed	Dates Covered	No. of Rolls
Polnish Wette=Alt Wette -Swiętów-				
Polsnitz -Pelcznica-	rkKB	Warsaw	1859-1870	1
Pommerswitz -Pomorzowice-	rkKB	Warsaw	1767-1870	1
Pontwitz -Poniatowice-	evKB	Warsaw	1806-1870	3
Pontwirtz=Pontwitz -Poniatowice-				
Poselwitz -Postolice-	evKB	Warsaw	1808-1848	1
Powitzko -Powidzko-	rkKB	Warsaw	1810-1870	5
Prausnitz -Prusice-	evKB	Warsaw	1765-1838	7
Prauss -Prusy-	evKB	Warsaw	1777-1870	1
Prieswitz -Rrzyszowice-	rkKB	Warsaw	1800-1870	3
Priebus -Przewoz	evKB rkKB	Warsaw Warsaw	1843,1854,1858 1860-1870	1 1
Probsthain -Proboszów-	evKB	Warsaw	1794-1864	2
Profen -Msciwojów-	rkKB	Warsaw	1662-1870	2
Proskau -Proszków-	rkKB	Warsaw	1757-1870	4
Pschow -Pszów-	rkKB	Warsaw	1852-1870	2
Pstrzonsna -Pstrążna-	rkKB	Warsaw	1839-1870	1
Psychod -Przechód-	rkKB	Warsaw	1722-1870	6
Pürben -Pierzwin-	rkKB	Warsaw	1839-1970	2

Location	Nature of Material	Where Filmed	Dates Covered	No. of Rolls
Quaritz -Gaworzyce-	KB		1801-1805	2
Radoschau -Radoszowy-	rkKB	Warsaw	1738-1870	2
Radzionkau -Radzionków- -Tarnowskie Góry-	rkKB	Warsaw	1800-1870	5
Radziunz -Radziądz-	rkKB	Warsaw	1810-1870	3
Rasselwitz -Racławiczki-	rkKB	Warsaw	1658-1870	10
Rathmansdorf -Ratnowice-	rkKB	Warsaw	1810-1870	1
Ratibor -Racibórz	MKB rkKB	Hannover Warsaw	1787-1806 1723-1870	1 12
Reesewitz -Radzowice-	evKB	Warsaw	1834-1870	2
Reggenfelde -Rzeczyca-	rkKB	Warsaw	1781-1870	1
Reibnitz -Rybnica-	evKB	Warsaw	1778-1830	2
Reichenau -Bogaczewice-	rkKB	Warsaw	1720-1870	9
Reichenau -Niwa-	rkKB	Warsaw	1849-1870	1
Reichenau -Bogatynia-	evKB	Warsaw	1617-1819	2
Reichenbach -Dzierżoniów-	rkKB MKB	Warsaw Eibenstock	1811-1870 1860-1882	7 1
Reindersdorf -Komorzno-	evKB	Berlin-Dahlem Hannover	1800-1908 1800-1908	5 6
Reinschdorf -Reńska Wieś-	rkKB	Warsaw	1781-1870	3
Reisern -Chróścina Opolska-	rkKB	Warsaw	1742-1870	3
Regersdorf -Stanów-	rkKB	Breslau	1638-1728	1

Location	Nature of Material	Where Filmed	Dates Covered	No. of Rolls
Rengersdorf -Krosnowice-	rkKB	Warsaw	1720-1870	5
Reppersdorf -Godziszową-	evKB	Warsaw	1747-1809	1
Richterstal -Zdziechowice-	rkKB	Warsaw	1806-1870	1
Riegersdorf -Rudziczka-	rkKB	Warsaw	1782-1870	3
Riemertscheide -Rusocin-	rkKB	Warsaw	1766-1870	3
Rietschütz=Reggenfelde -Rzeczyca-				
Roben -Rowne-	rkKB	Warsaw	1768-1870	1
Rosengrund -Zakrzów-	rkKB	Warsaw	1765-1870	3
Rosenthal -Różanka-	rkKB	Warsaw	1624-1870	4
Rosmierz -Rozmierz-	rkKB	Warsaw	1766-1870	7
Rosnochau -Rozkochów-	rkKB	Warsaw	1730-1870	3
Rosstal -Racławiczki-	rkKB	Warsaw	1765-1870	4
Rossweide=Rossnochau -Rozkochów-				
Rothbrünnig -Brennik-	rkKB	Warsaw	1813-1870	1
Rothenburg -Czerwieńsk-	evKB	Hannover	1655-1944	8
Rothkirch -Kościelec-	evKB	Warsaw	1697-1872	5
Rückers -Szczytna Śląska-	rkKB	Warsaw	1741-1870	5
Rudnik -Rudnik-	rkKB	Warsaw	1739-1868	3

Location	Nature of Material	Where Filmed	Dates Covered	No. of Rolls
Ruhbank -Sędzisław-	evKB	Warsaw	1817-1820	1
Saabor -Zabor-	evKB	Warsaw	1742-1870	8
Saalberg -Zachelmie-	evKB	Warsaw	1742-1870	6
Sabschütz -Zawiszyce-	rkKB	Warsaw	1724-1870	1
Sächsisch Haugsdorf -Nawojów Łużicki-	evKB	Warsaw	1654-1870	7
Sakrau -Zakrzów-	rkKB	Warsaw	1765-1870	3
Salesche -Zalesie Śląskie-	rkKB	Warsaw	1725-1870	4
Sauerwitz -Zubrzyce-	rkKB	Warsaw	1802-1870	1
Schäferberg -Wysokie-	rkKB	Berlin	1702-1740	1
Schawoine -Zawonia-	evKB	Warsaw	1708-1800	1
Schertendorf -Przylep-	evKB rkKB	Hannover Berlin	1655-1944	10
Schiedlawe -Szydlów-	rkKB evKB	Warsaw	1810-1870	4
Schierau -Zerów-	rkKB	Warsaw	1798-1865	4
Schlaup -Słup-	evKB	Warsaw	1857-1871	1
Schlawentzitz -Slawiecice-	rkKB	Warsaw	1737-1870	10
Schlegel -Słupiec-	rkKB	Warsaw	1741, 1870	6

Location	Nature of Material	Where Filmed	Dates Covered	No. of Rolls
Schlichtings- heim -Szlichtyngowa-	School Rec. evKB ZSR JüdGem	Berlin-Dahlem Warsaw Warsaw	1886-1890 1645-1870 1835-1847	1 10 1
Schlüsselgrund -Klucz-	rkKB	Warsaw	1739-1867	2
Schmellwitz -Śmiałowice-	rkKB	Warsaw	1782-1870	4
Schmiedeberg -Kowary-	rkKB	Warsaw	1671-1870	5
Schmietsch -Smicz-	rkKB	Warsaw	1740-1870	5
Schmottseifen -Pławna-	rkKB	Warsaw	1755-1870	8
Schnellewalde -Szybowice-	rkKB	Warsaw	1862-1870	1
Schobersfeld -Brożec-	rkKB	Warsaw	1789-1870	4
Schömberg -Chełmsko-	rkKB	Warsaw	1766-1870	11
Schönbrunn -Studniska Górne-	evKB	Warsaw	1725-1844	2
Schönbrunn -Jabłonów-	rkKB	Warsaw	1814-1816	1
Schönfeld -Podolany-	rkKB	Warsaw	1798-1865	4
Schönfeld -Krzywiczyny-	evKB	Berlin-Dahlem	1800-1908	5
Schönhorst -Krasiejów-	rkKB	Warsaw	1805-1870	1
Schönkirch=Gontkowitz -Gądkowice-				
Schönkirch -Chrzaszczyce-	rkKB	Warsaw	1715-1870	5
Schönwaldau -Rzasnik-	evKB	Warsaw	1794-1870	2
Schosnitz -Sośnica	rkKB	Warsaw	1801-1825 1851-1870	1

Location	Nature of Material	Where Filmed	Dates Covered	No. of Rolls
Schreiberhau -Szklarska Poręba-	rkKB	Warsaw Berlin	1741-1870 1682-1780	3 1
Schreibersdorf -Pisarzowice-	evKB	Warsaw	1831-1860	1
Schurgast -Skorogoszcz-	rkKB	Warsaw	1766-1870	5
Schwammelwitz -Trzeboszowice-	rkKB	Warsaw	1694-1870	5
Schwartzengrund -Kopice-	rkKB	Warsaw	1766-1870	6
Schweidnitz -Świdnica-	rkKB	Warsaw	1834-1870	1
Schweinitz -Świdnica-	evKB rkKB	Warsaw Warsaw	1816-1840 1794-1860	1 1
Sczedrzik -Szczedrzyk-	rkKB	Warsaw	1765-1870	8
Seichau -Sichów-	rkKB	Warsaw	1766-1870	1
Seifersdorf -Lukaszów-	evKB	Warsaw	1794-1853	1
Seifersdorf -Msciczów-	evKB	Warsaw	1800-1857	2
Seiffersdorf -Radwanów-	rkKB	Warsaw	1839-1970	2
Seiffersdorf -Radomierz-	rkKB	Warsaw	1794-1870	2
Seiffersdorf bei Grottkau -Przylesie Dolne-	rkKB	Warsaw	1781-1870	1
Seitendorf -Zatonie-	rkKB	Warsaw	1785-1870	3
Seitendorf -Schönau- -Mysłów-	evKB	Warsaw	1794-1870	2
Seitendorf -Gniewoszów-	rkKB	Warsaw	1624-1870	5
Seitendorf -Poniatów-	rkKB	Salt Lake City	1626-1842	2

Location	Nature of Material	Where Filmed	Dates Covered	No. of Rolls
Seitendorf=Seitendorf -Schönau- -Mysłów- -Jauer-				
Simsdorf -Szymanów-	evKB	Warsaw	1794-1865	4
Sohrau -Żory-	evKB	Warsaw	1851-1870	1
	rkKB	Warsaw	1838-1870	2
Soppau -Zopowy-	rkKB	Warsaw	1811-1870	1
Spätenwalde -Zalesie-	rkKB	Warsaw	1691-1870	17
Spiller -Pasiecznik-	evKB	Warsaw	1850-1870	1
Sprottau -Szprotawa-	rkKB	Berlin	1650-1799	3
Steinborn -Kamionka-	rkKB	Warsaw	1839-1970	2
Steinkirche -Biały Kościoł-	evKB	Warsaw	1842-1859	2
Steinsdorf -Osetnica-	evKB	Warsaw	1794-1810	1
Stephansdorf -Radzikowice-	Mis. rec.	Salt Lake City	1414-1936	1
Sternalice -Sternalice-	rkKB	Warsaw	1765-1870	4
Straupitz -Strupica-	evKB	Warsaw	1836-1844	1
	rkKB	Warsaw	1798-1865	4
Strebitzko -Trzebicko-	rkKB	Warsaw	1839-1861	1
Strehlen -Strzelin-	evKB	Warsaw	1634-1699	1
	rkKB	Warsaw	1766-1870	6
Stubendorf -Izbicko-	rkKB	Warsaw	1705-1870	3
Stuhlseiffen -Rudawa-	rkKB	Warsaw	1712-1870	3

Location	Nature of Material	Where Filmed	Dates Covered	No. of Rolls
Sulau -Sulów-	evKB	Warsaw	1835-1892	4
Tarnau -Tarnów Opolski-	rkKB	Warsaw	1766-1870	2
Tempelfeld -Owczary-	rkKB	Warsaw	1835-1870	2
Theimendorf -Radostów-	evKB	Warsaw	1794-1865	4
Thule -Tuły-	rkKB	Warsaw	1857-1870	1
Tiefenfurt -Parowa-	evKB	Warsaw	1766-1799	1
Tiefhartmanns- dorf -Podgórki-	evKB	Warsaw	1848-1870	2
Trachenberg -Żmigród-	Court rec. evKB rkKB	Berlin Warsaw Warsaw	17th-20th Cent 1810-1869 1810-1870	1 11 4
Trebnitz -Trzebnica-	evKB rkKB	Warsaw Warsaw	1766-1827 1650-1821	2 4
Tribelwitz -Przybyłowice-	evKB	Warsaw	1747-1809	1
Troppolwitz -Opawica-	rkKB	Warsaw	1662-1870	6
Tscheschen- hammer -Kuźnica Czeszycka-	rkKB	Warsaw	1855-1870	1
Tschirnau -Czernina-	evKB	Warsaw	1866	1
Tschischdorf -Strzyżowiec-	evKB	Warsaw	1787-1870	2

Location	Nature of Material	Where Filmed	Dates Covered	No. of Rolls
Twardawa -Twardawa-	rkKB	Warsaw	1715-1870	6
Tworkau -Tworków-	rkKB	Warsaw	1795-1871	4
Ulbersdorf -Wojcieszyn-	evKB	Warsaw	1794-1852	2
Ullersdorf -Ołdrzychowice Kłodzkie-	rkKB	Warsaw	1695-1870	6
Ullersdorf -Ulanowice-	evKB	Hannover	1922-1947	1
Ullersdorf Liebenthal -Wojciechów-	rkKB	Warsaw	1819-1870	1
Uschütz -Uszyce-	rkKB	Warsaw	1812-1870	1
Voigtsdorf Habelschwerdt -Wójtówka-	rkKB	Warsaw	1691-1870	17
Volkmannsdorf -Włodary-	rkKB	Warsaw	1734-1871	6
Wahlstatt -Legnickie Pole-	MKB	Eibenstock	1838-1876	1
Waldau -Ulesie-	evKB	Warsaw	1809,1813	1
Waltdorf -Prusinowice-	rkKB	Warsaw	1765-1870	6
Waltersdorf -Niegosławice-	rkKB evKB	Salt Lake City	1667-1729	1
Walzen -Walce-	rkKB	Warsaw	1703-1870	5
Wandwitz -Wojnowice-	rkKB	Warsaw	1685-1870	4
Warmbrunn -Cieplice Śląskie-Zdrój-	rkKB	Warsaw	1833-1870	1
Wederau -Wiadrów-	evKB	Warsaw	1825-1849	1

Location	Nature of Material	Where Filmed	Dates Covered	No. of Rolls
Weichau -Wichów-	evKB	Warsaw	1794-1870	4
Weigsdorf -Wigancice Żytawskie-	evKB	Warsaw	1832-1847	1
Weihendorf -Wojnowice-	rkKB	Warsaw	1738-1871	3
Wiesau -Łąka-	rkKB	Warsaw	1842-1870	1
Wilhelmsbruch -Unisławice-	Publications only			
Wilkau -Wilków-	evKB	Warsaw	1645-1870	10
Wiltschau -Wilczków-	evKB	Warsaw	1820-1850	1
Winzig -Winsko-	MKB MKB	Eibenstock Hannover	1834-1886 1802-1834	1 1
Wittenau -Uszyce-	rkKB	Warsaw	1821-1870	1
Wittenau -Zdziechowice-	rkKB	Warsaw	1806-1870	1
Wohlau -Wołów-	MKB	Eibenstock Berlin-Dahlem Hannover	1861-1869 1833-1918 1802-1832	1 1 1
Woinowitz=Weihendorf -Wojnowice-				
Woitscheke -Wysokie-	rkKB	Berlin	1702-1740	1
Woitz -Wojcice-	rkKB	Warsaw	1766-1870	3
Wojnowitz=Weihendorf -Wojnowice-				
Wolfau -Wilków-	evKB	Warsaw	1645-1870	10
Würgsdorf -Wierzchosława wice-	evKB rkKB	Warsaw Breslau	1856-1857 1615-1702	1 1

Location	Nature of Material	Where Filmed	Dates Covered	No. of Rolls
Wüsteröhrsdorf -Redziny-	evKB rkKB	Warsaw Warsaw	1794-1849 1794-1870	1 2
Wyssoka -Wysoka-	rkKB	Warsaw	1765-1870	5
Zabelkau -Zabełków-	rkKB	Warsaw	1864-1870	1
Zabrze -Zabrze-	LDS records rkKB	Salt Lake City Warsaw	1927-1957 1800-1870	9 12
Zedlitz -Siedlce-	evKB	Warsaw	1750-1870	1
Zellin -Zielina-	rkKB	Warsaw	1742-1870	5
Ziegenhals -Głuchołazy-	MKB rkKB	Eibenstock Warsaw	1875-1889 1734-1870	1 11
Zirkwitz -Cerekwica-	rkKB	Warsaw	1800-1870	3
Zölling -Solniki-	rkKB	Warsaw	1794-1870	3

WESTPREUSSEN

Location	Nature of Material	Where Filmed	Dates Covered	No. of Rolls
Adlig Liebenau	rkKB	Berlin	1826-1854	1
-Lignowy Szlacheckie-	rkKB		1826-1856	1
Alt Grabau	rkKB	Augsburg	1835-1879	1
-Grabowo-	rkKB	Muttlich	1842-1913	1
Alt Fietz -Stary Wiec-	Meldeamt	Berlin-Dahlem	1918-1932	1
Alt Kischau	rkKB	Augsburg	1838-1849	1
-Stara	rkKB	Munich	1838-1925	2
Kyszewa-	rkKB	Berlin	1732-1849	3
	rkKB	Warsaw	1789-1816	1
Altfelde	evKB	Lübeck	1670-1892	1
-Stare Pole-	evKB	Warsaw	1831-1849	1
Althausen	rkKB	Berlin-Dahlem	1677-1879	1
-Olszowka Kwidzyń-	rkKB	Munich	1836-1874	1
Alt Mark -Stary Targ-	rkKB	Berlin	1784-1896	2
Baarenhof -Dworek-	evKB	Lübeck	1721-192-	5
Bahrendorf -Niedźwiedź-	rkKB	Berlin-Dahlem	1816-1817	1
Baldenburg	Heer	Berlin-Dahlem	1816-1877	4
-Biaty Bor-	Grundbuchamt		1773-1858	13
Boręty -Palczewo-	rkKB	München	1749-1909	2
Barloschno -Barłoźno-	rkKB	Berlin-Dahlem	1691-1811	
Barkoschin -Barkoschin-	evKB	Lübeck	1787-1944	5
Bartschin -Barcin-	rkKB	Warsaw	1824-1830	1
Berent		Hannover	1813-1892	1
-Kościerzyna-	ZSR	Lübeck		
	evKB	Lübeck	1781-1944	7
	rkKB	Berlin-Dahlem	1642-1849	3
	rkKB	Munich	1834-1896	4
	rkKB	Berlin-Dahlem	1642-1906	5
	ZSR	Warsaw	1847-1865	1

Location	Nature of Material	Where Filmed	Dates Covered	No. of Rolls
Bergfriede	rkKB	Berlin-Dahlem	1754-1845	4
-Borzyskowy-	rkKB	Berlin-Dahlem	1756-1845	3
	rkKB	Berlin-Dahlem	1835-1837	1
	rkKB	Warsaw	1703-1767	1
	rkKB	München	1894-1945	1
	rkKB	München	1835-1932	4
Blandau	rkKB		1694-1877	1
-Błędowo-	rkKB	Berlin	1764-1866	1
	rkKB	Warsaw	1885-1877	1
	rkKB	Münster	1841-1932	3
Bobau	rkKB	Muenster	1833-1854	1
-Bobowo-	rkKB	Berlin-Dahlem	1670-1832	2
Bohlschau	evKB	Warsaw	1823-1849	1
-Bolszewo-	evKB	Lübeck	1774-1929	1
Bohnsack	evKB	Lübeck	1659-1904	7
-Sobieszewo-				
Bordzichow	evKB	Lübeck	1833-1883	3
-Borzechowo-				
Braunsfelde	rkKB	Berlin-Dahlem	1867-1939	1
-Łopatki-				
Briesen	evKB	Berlin-Dahlem	1831-1911	3
-Wąbrzeżno-	rkKB	Berlin-Dahlem	1845-1846	1
	evKB	Lübeck	1875-1930	3
	rkKB	Muenster	1685-1875	4
Briesen Adlig	rkKB	Berlin-Dahlem	1828-1901	1
-Brzeźno-				
Bruss	rkKB	Berlin-Dahlem	1665-1841	2
-Brusy-	rkKB	Muenster	1833-1866	2
Bukowitz	evKB	Lübeck	1855-1943	3
-Bukowiec-				
Burgfelde	rkKB	Augsburg Muenster	1836-1900	2
-Osiek-	rkKB	Munich	1865-1939	1
Cammin	AG	Berlin-Dahlem	1571-1820	1
-Kamień-	evKB	Lübeck	1865-1943	1
Christburg	rkKB	Warsaw	1808-1865	1
-Dzierzgoń-	rkKB	Berlin	1714-1783	1
	rkKB	Berlin	1714-1826	2
	rkKB	Munich	1814-1895	2
	evKB	Lübeck	1671-1931	9
	rkKB	Munich	1846-1867	1
	evKB	Warsaw	1850-1865	1
Chrostkowo	ZSR	Warsaw	1808-1865	4
-Chrostkowo-	rkKB	Munich	1841-1889	4

Location	Nature of Material	Where Filmed	Dates Covered	No. of Rolls
Colmannsfeld	rkKB	Frankfurt	1749-1874	2
-Chełmoniec-	rkKB	Frankfurt	1837-1874	1
	rkKB	Augsburg	1837-1874	1
	rkKB	Munich	1749-1874	1
Czattkau -Czatkowy-	KB	Warsaw	1809-1812	
Czernikow	rkKB	Munich	1850-1888	4
-Czernikowo-	ZSR	Warsaw	1808-1865	5
Czersk	rkKB	Munich	1821-1854	1
-Czersk-	rkKB	Augsburg	1855-1879	2
	rkKB	Berlin	1733-1863	2
Danziger	rkKB	Augsburg	1852-1939	2
Heisternest	ZSR	Warsaw	1809-1812	1
-Jastarnia-	rkKB	Berlin	1796-1852	1
	rkKB	Berlin	1796-1852	1
Darsen -Dźwierzno-	evKB		1767-1800	1
Dembowo -Dębowo-	rkKB	Munich	1829-1939	3
Deutsch Damerau	rkKB	Berlin	1688-1736	1
-Dąbrówka	rkKB	Munich	1779-1936	3
Malborska-	rkKB	Berlin	1688-1725	1
Dirschau Tczew	rkKB	Berlin-Dahlem	1721-1903	1
-Gardschau-	rkKB	Munich	1831-1886	1
-Godziszewo-	rkKB	Berlin-Dahlem	1727-1913	2
	evKB	Warsaw	1797-1865	5
	evKB	Lübeck	1637-1944	9
	evKB	Lübeck	1808-1919	4
	KB	Warsaw	1828-1848	1
	rkKB	Berlin	1732-1852	2
	rkKB	Munich	1852-1902	3
Dobrzejewice	rkKB	Munich	1821-1889	2
-Dobrzejewice-	ZSR	Warsaw	1713-1859	4
Dobrzyn	rkKB	Munich	1846-1888	5
-Dobrzyń n.	ZSR	Warsaw	1808-1865	10
Wislą-	ZSR	Warsaw	1838-1865	2
Dombrowken -Dąbrówka Królewska-	rkKB	Berlin	1772-1909	1
Dreidorf -Dzwierszno-	rkKB	Munich	1848-1943	3
Dretz also	rkKB	Berlin	1695-1859	2
Dritschmin	ZSR	Warsaw	1774-1795	1
-Drzyeim-				

Location	Nature of Material	Where Filmed	Dates Covered	No. of Rolls
Dulsk	rkKB	Munich	1863-1886	3
-Dulsk-	ZSR	Warsaw	1808-1865	5
Dzierondzno	rkKB	Kirchheim	1765-1900	2
-Dzierzgzno-				
Eberspark	evKB	Lübeck	1821-1839	1
-Chlebno-				
Ellerwald	KB	Weierhof	1744-1940	3
-Adamowo-				
-Janowo-				
-Jozefowo-				
-Kazimierzewo-	KB	Berlin-Dahlem	1820-1847	1
-Władyslawowo-	KB	Weierhof	1744-1940	
Falkenburg	rkKB	Augsburg	1838-1882	1
-Żolędowo-	rkKB	Munich	1838-1939	1
Fischau	KB	Lübeck	1653-1907	4
-Fiszewo-				
Flatow	evKB	Warsaw	1658-1675	1
-Złotów-	Innere Verwaltung	Berlin-Dahlem	1821-1831	3
Frankenhagen	rkKB	Berlin	1719-1752	1
-Silno-				
Friedrichsbruch	AG	Berlin-Dahlem	1801	1
-Plosków-				
Friedrichshöhe	rkKB	Munich	1841-1907	1
-Kosztowo-	rkKB	Berlin	1768-1840	2
Fürstenau	evKB	Lübeck	1680-1940	6
-Kmiecin-				
Fürstenwerder	evKB	Munich	1714-1940	1
-Żulawki-	rkKB	Munich	1701-1944	2
Gardschau=Dirschau				
-Godziszewo-				
Garnsee	evKB	Lübeck	1634-1939	12
-Gardeja-				
Garschin	rkKB	Berlin-Dahlem	1937	1
-Garczyn-	rkKB	Berlin-Dahlem	1768-1939	1
	rkKB	Berlin-Dahlem	1769-1844	1
	rkKB	Munich	1813-1936	2
Gemlitz	evKB	Warsaw	1814-1865	1
-Giemlice-	rkKB	Munich	1647-1944	4
Gischkau	evKB	Lübeck	1649-1944	3
-Juszkowo-	evKB	Warsaw	1814-1865	2

Location	Nature of Material	Where Filmed	Dates Covered	No. of Rolls
Glessen	rkKB	Berlin	1770-1853	1
-Glesno-	rkKB	Munich	1854-1930	1
Gnojau	rkKB	Munich	1708-1828	1
-Gnojewo-	evKB	Lübeck	1762-1876	4
Göbeln	rkKB	Munich	1866-1940	1
-Gowidlino-				
Gohra	rkKB	Berlin-Dahlem	1738-1925	1
-Góra-	rkKB	Warsaw	1824	1
is a part of	rkKB	Augsburg	1844-1859	1
Neustadt	rkKB	Warsaw	1738-1825	1
-Wejherowo-	rkKB	Munich	1853-1914	1
Gollub	Innere	Berlin-Dahlem	1819-1839	1
-Golub-	Verwoltung	Berlin-Dahlem	1772-1773	2
	Katasteramt			
Görren	rkKB	Warsaw	1782-1785	1
-Gorrenschin-	rkKB	Berlin-Dahlem	1747-1900	1
-Goręczyno-	rkKB	Munich	1867-1917	1
Gorzberg	rkKB	Munich	1830-1896	3
-Gorzno-				
Gosslershausen	rkKB	Berlin	1734-1914	1
-Jabłowowo-				
Gramtschen	evKB	Warsaw	1696-1865	3
-Grębocin-				
Graudenz	Innere	Berlin-Dahlem	1827-1845	11
-Grudziadz-	Verwoltung			
	evKB	Warsaw	1865-1866	1
	evKB	Berlin-Dahlem	1622-1919	40
	rkKB	Berlin-Dahlem	1661-1900	8
	KB	Berlin-Dahlem	1805-1892	5
	evKB	Berlin	1848-1853	1
	evMKB	Hannover	1774-1920	2
	MKB	Hannover	1774-1823	
	Innere	Berlin	1811-1835	2
	Verwoltung			
Griebenau	rkKB	Augsburg	1833-1875	1
-Grzybno-	rkKB	Munich	1846-1882	1
Griewenhof	evKB	Lübeck	1898-1915	1
-Grzywno-				
Grochowalsk	rkKB	Munich	1840-1894	2
-Grochowalsk-	ZSR	Warsaw	1808-1865	2

Location	Nature of Material	Where Filmed	Dates Covered	No. of Rolls
Gromaden -Gromadno-	rkKB	Kirchheim	1835-1876	1
Grondzau -Grążawy-	rkKB rkKB	Munich Berlin-Dahlem	1852-1888 1792-1859	1 1
Gross Bislaw -Bysław-	rkKB rkKB	Munich Berlin	1824-1877 1776-1852	3 1
Gross Chelm -Wielkie Chełmy-	ZSR	Berlin	1838-1841	1
Gross Czyste -Wielkie Czyste-	rkKB rkKB	Berlin Munich	1688-1851 1778-1822	1 1
Gross Falkenau -Wielkie Walichnowy-	rkKB	Munich	1763-1927	3
Gross Gartz -Wielki Garo-	rkKB rkKB	Berlin Munich	1704-1858 1832-1899	1 1
Gross Katz -Wielki Kack-	rkKB	Berlin	1825-1847	1
Gross Kommorsk -Wielki Komorsk-	rkKB	Munich	1798-1817	1
Gross Konarczyn -Konarzyny-	rkKB rkKB	Berlin Munich	1727-1868 1787-1868	2 1
Gross Könnern -Komorsk-	rkKB	Munich	1843-1891	2
Gross Kornlage -Konarzyny-	rkKB	Munich	1855-1892	1
Gross Krebs -Rakowiec-	evKB	Lübeck	1744-1893	5
Gross Lesewitz -Lasowice Wielkie-	evKB KB	Lübeck Lübeck	1825-1869 1814-1938	1 1
Gross Leistenau -Lisnowo-	evKB	Berlin-Dahlem	1766-1912	15
Gross Lichtenau -Lichnowy-	evKB KB rkKB rkKB	Lübeck Lübeck Munich Augsburg	1704-1926 1800-1874 1744-1886 1764-1826	3 1 2 1
Gross Liniewo -Liniewo-	ZSR	Berlin	1883-1885	1

Location	Nature of Material	Where Filmed	Dates Covered	No. of Rolls
Gross Lipschin -Lubieszyn-	ZSR	Berlin	1904-1919	1
Gross Lunau -Wielkie Łunawy-	evKB KB	Lübeck Berlin-Dahlem	1845-1937 1848-1852	9 1
Gross Mousdorf -Myszewo-	evKB evKB	Lübeck Warsaw	1690-1925 1728-1811	6 1
Gross Montau -Matowy Wielkie-	rkKB	Munich	1749-1868	2
Gross Nebrau -Nebrowo Wielkie-	evKB	Lübeck	1624-1921	7
Gross Plochot-schin -Plochocin-	rkKB	Berlin	1768-1821	1
Gross Plowenz -Płoweż-	rkKB rkKB	Berlin-Dahlem Berlin-Dahlem	1695-1831 1686-1831	1 1
Gross Radowisk -Wielkie Radowiska-	rkKB	Kirchheim	1858-1936	1
Gross Radziki -Radziki Duże-	ZSR rkKB ZSR rkKB	Warsaw Augsburg Warsaw Augsburg	1807-1817 1855-1875 1808-1865 1855-1870	1 1 6 1
Gross Schliewitz -Słiwice-	rkKB rkKB rkKB	Warsaw Berlin Berlin	1821-1842 1663-1826 1618-1826	1 1 1
Gross Sibsau -Bzowo-	rkKB rkKB	Berlin Augsburg	1756-1833 1833-1944	1 2
Gross Starsin -Starzyno-	rkKB rkKB rkKB	Berlin Munich Augsburg	1687-1845 1825-1845 1827-1858	1 1 1
Gross Trampken -Trąbki Wielkie-	rkKB	Augsburg	1766-1917	2
Gross Tromnau -Trumieje-	evKB	Lübeck	1661-1934	10
Gross Turse -Turze-	evKB	Lübeck	1908-1944	1
Grünkirch -Rojewice-	evKB	Lübeck	1913-1929	1

Location	Nature of Material	Where Filmed	Dates Covered	No. of Rolls
Grutta -Gruta-	rkKB	Berlin-Dahlem	1690-1893	3
Grützen -Gruczno-	rkKB	Augsburg	1863-1944	1
	evKB	Lübeck	1877-1917	1
	rkKB	Berlin-Dahlem	1733-1867	1
	rkKB	Warsaw	1820-1874	1
Gruppe -Grupa-	evKB	Lübeck	1854-1905	7
Guettland -Güttland- -Koźliny-	evKB	Lübeck	1662-1936	3
	ZSR	Warsaw	1809-1812	1
Gurschno -Gorzno-	rkKB	Berlin-Dahlem	1772-1831	1
	rkKB	Augsburg	1869-1874	1
Hammerstein -Czarne-	Grundbuchamt	Berlin-Dahlem	1773	1
	Katasteramt	Berlin-Dahlem	1772-1773	1
	rkKB	Berlin	1752-1789	1
Heiderode -Czersk-	rkKB	Berlin	1773-1863	2
	rkKB	Augsburg	1855-1879	2
	rkKB	Munich	1821-1854	1
	ZSR	Berlin-Dahlem	1939	2
	ZSR	Warsaw	1832-1848	1
Heimscot -Przeczno-	rkKB	Kirchheim	1752-1777	1
Heinrichsdorf -Przysiersk-	ZSR	Berlin	1671-1841	1
Hela -Hel-	evKB	Lübeck	1786-1943	2
	STA	Warsaw	1810-1811	1
	evKB	Warsaw	1633-1693	1
Hermannsbad -Ciechocinek-	rkKB	Munich	1810-1878	4
	ZSR	Warsaw	1757-1868	6
	rkKB	Augsburg	1918-1940	4
Hermannsruhe -Kowki-	evKB	Lübeck	1867-1936	2
Herrengreben -Grabiny Zameczek-	evKB	Warsaw	1814-1838	1
	STA	Warsaw	1809-1812	1
Heubude -Stogi-	KB	Lübeck	1896-1926	3
	KB	Weierhof	1772-1900	1
Hoch Stüblau -Zblewo-	rkKB	Berlin	1726-1835	1
	rkKB	Augsburg	1826-1892	3
Hohenkirch -Książki-	evKB	Berlin-Dahlem	1773-1938	7

Location	Nature of Material	Where Filmed	Dates Covered	No. of Rolls
Hoppendorf -Hopowo-	evKB	Lübeck	1895-1944	1
Iwitz -Iwiec-	evKB	Lübeck	1889-1911	1
Jablau -Jabłowo-	rkKB	Augsburg	1854-1871	1
Jastrow -Jastrowie-	evKB	Warsaw	1773-1778	1
Jastrze-m-bie -Jastrzębie-	rkKB rkKB	Berlin Augsburg	1794-1919 1844-1926	1 1
Jeschewo -Jeżewo-	evKB rkKB rkKB	Lübeck Berlin Augsburg	1891-1899 1752-1847 1842-1910	1 1 3
Janowa -Janowa-	rkKB	Augsburg	1833-1944	1
Jungfer -Marzęcino-	evKB	Lübeck	1798-1911	7
Kae-ä-semark -Kiezmark-	evKB ZSR	Lübeck Warsaw	1687-1904 1809-1811	4 1
Kalwe -Kalwa-	rkKB	Berlin	1680-1885	2
Kamin -Kamień-	rkKB	Augsburg	1675-1911	3
Karnkewitz -Karnieszewice-	evKB	Warsaw	1836-1870	1
Karnkowo -Karnkowo-	KB ZSR	Augsburg Warsaw	1844-1875 1770-1865	2 6
Karthaus -Kartuzy-	evKB evKB	Warsaw Lübeck	1852-1865 1852-1944	1 2
Kaschorek -Kaszczorek-	rkKB	Berlin	1802-1803	1
Katznase -Kaczynos-	evKB evKB	Lübeck Warsaw	1639-1944 1794-1865	3 1
Kiewo -Kijewo Krolewskie-	rkKB	Berlin	1787-1931	1
Kikol -Kikol-	rkKB ZSR	Augsburg Warsaw	1849-1901 1782-1865	3 7

Location	Nature of Material	Where Filmed	Dates Covered	No. of Rolls
Kierchenjahn	rkKB	Berlin	1731-1842	1
-Kościelna	rkKB	Berlin-Dahlem	1798-1842	1
Jania-	rkKB	Augsburg	1843-1920	2
Kirchlindau	rkKB	Berlin	1782-1859	1
-Wudzyn-	rkKB	Augsburg	1853-1874	1
Kladau -Kłodawa-	rkKB	Augsburg	1714-1940	2
Klein Bolumin	rkKB	Augsburg	1700-1907	5
-Bolumin-	rkKB	Berlin-Dahlem	1667-1830	2
Klein Katz	evKB	Lübeck	1661-1943	5
-Mały Kack-	evKB	Warsaw	1823-1848	1
Kleinplotzen -Plochocinek-	rkKB	Augsburg	1730-1832	1
Klonowken	rkKB	Berlin	1739-1799	1
-Klonówka-	rkKB	Augsburg	1782-1843	2
	rkKB	Augsburg	1800-1929	2
Kölln	rkKB	Warsaw	1732-1843	1
-Kielno-	rkKB	Warsaw	1823-1865	1
	rkKB	Berlin	1746-1819	1
	rkKB	Augsburg	1842-1901	2
Kokoschken	rkKB	Augsburg	1818-1927	2
-Kokoskowy-	rkKB	Berlin	1757-1825	1
Kökschufer -Kokocko-	rkKB	Augsburg	1800-1840	1
Konigsdorf	rkKB	Berlin	1593-1781	1
-Krolewo-	rkKB	Warsaw	1806-1865	1
	rkKB	Augsburg	1775-1876	3
Konitz	rkKB	Warsaw	1810-1849	1
-Chojnice-	evMKB	Hannover	1833-1842	1
	evKB	Lübeck	1632-1917	16
	rkKB	Berlin	1651-1844	2
	rkKB	Augsburg	1845-1878	3
Konojad -Konojady-	evKB	Lübeck	1891-1942	1
Kossabude -Kosobudy-	evKB	Lübeck	1863-1943	1
Krangen -Krąg-	evKB	Lübeck	1907-1912	1

Location	Nature of Material	Where Filmed	Dates Covered	No. of Rolls
Krockow	evKB	Warsaw	1718-1763	1
-Krokowa-	evKB	Lübeck	1617-1944	6
	evKB	Berlin	1718-1823	1
Krojanke -Krajenka-	Katasteramt	Berlin-Dahlem	1773	1
Kruschin -Kruszyn-	rkKB	Augsburg	1832-1905	2
Kulm	evMKB	Hannover	1826-1919	2
-Chełmo-	evKB	Berlin-Dahlem	1767-1940	25
	rkKB	Berlin-Dahlem	1667-1850	5
	KB	Berlin-Dahlem	1824-1855	3
	rkKB	Warsaw	1777-1782	1
	rkKB	Berlin	1776-1830	5
	rkKB	Augsburg	1818-1899	7
	MKB	Eibenstock	1830-1891	1
Kulmsee -Chełmża-	evKB	Warsaw	1803-1865	4
Kunzendorf	evKB	Lübeck	1783-1922	2
-Kończewice-	rkKB	Augsburg	1664-1899	2
Ladekopp	evKB	Lübeck	1783-1922	4
-Lubieszewo-	KB	Weierhof	1775-1873	1
	Amtsregister	Berlin-Dahlem	1753-1785	1
Lalkau -Lalkowy-	rkKB	Berlin Augsburg	1800-1934	3
Langebose -Pogorzelice-	evKB	Warsaw	1862-1870	1
Langenau -Łęgowo-	rkKB	Augsburg	1661-1924	4
Langfuhr -Wrzesziz-	evKB	Lübeck	1896-1937	6
Lebehnke -Stara Lubianka-	AG	Berlin-Dahlem	1776-1806	
Leibschau -Lubiszewo Tczewskie-	rkKB	Berlin	1704-1856	1
Lemberg	rkKB	Berlin	1678-1896	1
-Lembarg-	rkKB	Augsburg	1841-1898	1

Location	Nature of Material	Where Filmed	Dates Covered	No. of Rolls
Lenzen -Lecze-	evKB	Warsaw	1630-1811	1
Lesno -Leśno-	rkKB	Warsaw	1824-1849	2
	rkKB	Berlin	1736-1861	1
Lessen -Łasin-	evKB	Lübeck	1860-1939	4
	rkKB	Berlin	1710-1887	7
	rkKB	Warsaw	1820-1843	1
Lessnau -Leśniewo-	rkKB	Augsburg	1844-1908	3
Lesno -Leśno-	rkKB	Berlin	1736-1861	1
Letzkau -Leszkowy-	KB	Lübeck	1643-1944	4
	ZSR	Warsaw	1809-1811	1
Lichnau -Lichnowy-	rkKB	Berlin	1653-1830	1
	rkKB	Augsburg	1831-1944	2
Lichtfelde -Jasna-	evKB	Warsaw	1664-1750	1
	evKB	Lübeck	1751-1887	3
	rkKB	Berlin-Dahlem	1650-1892	1
	rkKB	Berlin	1756-1892	1
	rkKB	Warsaw	1794-1865	1
Liebenau -Gostycyn-	rkKB	Berkub	1797-1879	1
	rkKB	Warsaw	1791-1895	1
Liebichau -Lubichowo-	rkKB	Augsburg	1824-1925	2
Lienfelde -Liniewo- See - Gross Liniewo	ZSR	Berlin	1883-1885	1
Liessau -Lisewo- See - Kunzendorf	evKB	Lübeck	1789-1841	1
Lindenau -Linowo Królewskie-	rkKB	Berlin	1613-1933	1
	rkKB	Augsburg	1901-1939	1
Linsk -Lińsk-	rkKB	Berlin	1678-1787	1
Lintzau -Luzino-	rkKB	Augsburg	1839-1910	2
	rkKB	Berlin	1670-1839	1
Lipno -Lipno-	rkKB	Berlin-Dahlem	1810-1825	1
	rkKB	Augsburg	1865-1874	1
	ZSR	Warsaw	1824-1865	9
	ZSR	Warsaw	1808-1865	11
	ZSR	Augsburg	1880-1886	1

Location	Nature of Material	Where Filmed	Dates Covered	No. of Rolls
Lippusch	evKB	Lübeck	1869-1944	1
-Lipusz-	rkKB	Berlin	1806-1840	1
	rkKB	Berlin	1813-1840	1
	rkKB	Augsburg	1838-1913	2
Lissewo	rkKB	Munich	1800-1856	1
-Lisewo-	ZSR	Warsaw	1818-1842	1
Lobedau	rkKB	Augsburg	1773-1913	2
-Lobdowo-				
Lobfelde	rkKB	Berlin	1824-1840	1
-Lubiewo-	rkKB	Munich	1824-1840	1
Lobsens	rkKB	Augsburg	1622-1939	4
-Lobźenica-	rkKB	Muenster	1936-1939	1
	rkKB	Augsburg	1766-1808	1
	rkKB	Augsburg	1809-1824	1
Löblau	ZSR	Warsaw	1809-1812	1
-Lublewo-	evKB	Warsaw	1796-1814	1
	evKB	Lübeck	1689-1943	8
Loebsch	rkKB	Augsburg	1875-1912	1
-Łebcz-				
Long	rkKB	Kirchheim	1848-1877	1
-Ląg-				
Lonzin	rkKB	Augsburg	1842-1902	5
-Łążyn-	ZSR	Warsaw	1808-1859	4
	ZSR	Augsburg	1867-1878	1
Losendorf	evKB	Lübeck	1633-1923	2
-Łoża-				
Lubau	evKB	Lübeck	1903-1944	1
-Lubiewo-	rkKB	Berlin	1824-1840	1
	rkKB	Warsaw	1820-1846	1
	rkKB	Augsburg	1847-1911	2
Lusin	rkKB	Augsburg	1839-1910	2
-Luzino-	rkKB	Berlin	1670-1839	1
Marienau	evKB	Berlin	1925-1944	1
-Marynowy-	rkKB	Augsburg	1693-1944	3
	evKB	Lübeck	1773-1925	2
Mariensee	evKB	Warsaw	1832-1865	2
-Przywidz-	evKB	Lübeck	1832-1922	5
	rkKB	Warsaw	1841-1847	1
Marienwerder	evKB	Lübeck	1643-1944	30
-Kwidzyń-	evKB	Lübeck	1801-1905	1
	evKB	Berlin-Dahlem	1854-1864	1

Location	Nature of Material	Where Filmed	Dates Covered	No. of Rolls
Markushof -Markusy-	KB	Berlin	1754-1892	2
Marzdorf -Walcz-	Innere Verwaltung	Berlin-Dahlem	1820-1877	17
	Grundbuchamt	Berlin-Dahlem	1701-1839	7
	Katasteramt	Berlin-Dahlem	1772-1773	2
	evKB	Berlin	1869-1930	1
Mattern -Matarnia-	rkKB	Augsburg	1870-1898	1
	rkKB		1630-1849	1
	rkKB	Augsburg	1756-1899	2
Mechau -Mechowo-	rkKB	Berlin	1627-1845	1
	rkKB	Warsaw	1827-1830	1
	rkKB	Warsaw	1766-1774,1805	1
	rkKB	Berlin	1626-1843	1
Meisterwalde -Mierzeszyn-	rkKB	Augsburg	1716-1855	2
	evKB	Lübeck	1891-1905	1
	rkKB	Warsaw	1841-1865	1
Mewe -Gniew-	AG	Berlin-Dahlem	1773-1842	4
	evKB	Lübeck	1681-1944	7
	rkKB	Augsburg	1780-1902	4
Mielenz -Miłoradz-	rkKB	Augsburg	1639-1912	2
Mirchau -Mirachowo-	evKB	Lübeck	1854-1944	1
Mockrau -Mokre-	evKB	Lübeck	1830-1936	3
	rkKB	Berlin	1761-1933	1
Mönkenwerth -Mąkowarsko-	rkKB	Augsburg	1834-1862	1
	rkKB	Berlin	1763-1833	1
	rkKB	Berlin	1767-1833	1
Montau -Matwy-	KB	Berlin	1661-1874	1
	KB	Salt Lake City	1782-1944	2
Mszanno -Mszano-	rkKB	Berlin	1695-1874	1
	rkKB	Augsburg	1858-1864	1
Müggenhal -Rokitnica-	evKB	Lübeck	1650-1882	3
	ZSR	Warsaw	1809-1812	1
Mühlbanz -Miłobądż-	rkKB	Berlin-Dahlem	1750-1874	3
	rkKB	Warsaw	1785-1801	1
	rkKB	Warsaw	1838-1865	1
	rkKB	Berlin	1750-1874	1
Münsterwalde -Opalenie-	evKB	Lübeck	1900-1944	1
	rkKB	Augsburg	1710-1879	1

Location	Nature of Material	Where Filmed	Dates Covered	No. of Rolls
Nassenhuben -Mokry Dwór-	evKB ZSR	Lübeck Warsaw	1727-1816 1809-1812	1 1
Neu Barkoschin -Barkoczyn-	evKB	Lübeck	1787-1944	5
Neubraa -Nowa Brade-	evKB	Warsaw	1843-1856	1
Neudorf -Gross- -Nowa Wieś Wlk.-	evKB	Lübeck	1861-1904	3
Neudorf -Nowa Wieś Królewska-	rkKB	Berlin	1725-1897	1
Neudörfchen -Nowa Wioska-	evKB evKB	Lübeck Warsaw	1711-1944 1624-1770	5 1
Neuenburg -Nowe-	KB evKB	Salt Lake City Berlin	1782-1944 1773-1940	2 9
Neufahrwasser -Nowy Port-	evKB evKB evKB	Warsaw Warsaw Lübeck	1804-1865 1839-1854 1833-1943	2 1 6
Neugolz -Golce-	evKB	Warsaw	1860-1870	1
Neuheim -Dąbrówka Nowa-	rkKB	Augsburg	1844-1897	2
Neuhof -Garbek-	Katasteramt	Berlin-Dahlem	1772-1773	1
Neukirch -Nowa Cerkiew-	rkKB evKB rkKB rkKB	Augsburg Lübeck Augsburg Augsburg	1729-1906 1642-1880 1830-1871 1729-1889	4 2 1 4
Neukirch Höhe -Pogrodzie-	rkKB	Augsburg	1760-1935	2
Neukrug -Nowa Karczma-	evKB	Lübeck	1815-1901	1
Neu Palaschken -Nowe Polaszki-	evKB	Lübeck	1727-1944	8
Neustadt -Wejherowo-	rkKB	Augsburg	1845-1898	1
Neuteich -Nowy Staw-	evKB rkKB	Lübeck Augsburg	1700-1924 1684-1899	5 3

Location	Nature of Material	Where Filmed	Dates Covered	No. of Rolls
Neuzippnow -Sypniewko-	evKB	Warsaw	1835-1870	1
Niederzehren -Czarne Dolne-	evKB	Lübeck	1801-1944	3
Niezywienc -Nieżywiec-	rkKB	Berlin	1751-1831	1
	rkKB	Kirchheim	1832-1897	2
Notzendorf -Krzyżanowo-	rkKB	Berlin	1696-1859	1
	rkKB	Warsaw	1850-1865	1
Ohra -Orunia-	evKB	Lübeck	1761-1928	14
Okonin -Orunia-	rkKB	Berlin	1707-1939	2
	rkKB	Berlin	1707-1940	2
Orle -Orunia-	rkKB	Augsburg	1808-1940	6
	ZSR	Warsaw	1822-1854	2
	ZSR	Augsburg	1811-1925	1
Orlofferfelde -Orłowo-	KB	Weierhof	1562-1899	1
Osche -Osie-	evKB	Lübeck	1853-1912	5
	rkKB	Augsburg	1845-1896	1
	ZSR	Berlin	1640-1882	1
	rkKB	Augsburg	1854-1912	1
Osiek -Osiek n. Wisła-	rkKB	Augsburg	1856-1893	2
	rkKB	Augsburg	1840-1882	2
	ZSR	Augsburg	1869-1885	1
	ZSR	Warsaw	1808-1865	5
Ossenholz -Osieciny-	ZSR	Augsburg	1869-1925	3
	ZSR	Augsburg	1826-1934	3
	ZSR	Warsaw	1869-1925	3
	ZSR	Warsaw	1826-1855	2
Osterwick -Ostrowite-	evKB	Lübeck	1647-1921	4
	evKB	Warsaw	1809-1812	1
Osterwick -Ostrowite- Silno-	rkKB	Berlin	1759-1851	1
	rkKB	Augsburg	1851-1940	3
	ZSR	Berlin	1760-1851	1
Ostrometzko -Ostromecko-	rkKB	Augsburg	1700-1907	5
	evKB	Lübeck	1837-1944	3
	rkKB	Berlin	1762-1834	1
Oxhöft -Oskwie-	rkKB	Augsburg	1799-1899	4
Pappeln -Topolno-	rkKB	Berlin	1695-1867	1
	rkKB	Kirchheim	1863-1930	1
	rkKB	Augsburg	1843-1881	1

Location	Nature of Material	Where Filmed	Dates Covered	No. of Rolls
Parchau	rkKB	Augsburg	1831-1905	2
-Parchowo-	rkKB	Berlin	1808-1845	1
Pehsken	rkKB	Augsburg	1782-1879	3
-Piaseczno-		Augsburg	1640-1757	1
Pelplin	evKB	Berlin-Dahlem	1733-1833	1
-Pelplin-	evKB	Augsburg	1833-1874	2
Postlin	rkKB	Berlin	1679-1883	5
-Postlin-	rkKB	Berlin	1679-1882	3
-Postolin-				
Petershagen	KB	Göttingen	1775-1841	1
-Żelichowo-				
Pfeilsdorf	rkKB	Berlin-Dahlem	1796-1876	1
-Płużnica-	rkKB	Augsburg	1863-1920	1
Pflugsdorf	rkKB	Augsburg	1795-1940	1
-Płuskowęsy-				
Piasken	ZSR	Berlin	1841-1871	1
-Piaski-				
Pfennigsdorf	rkKB	Augsburg	1851-1908	1
or	rkKB	Berlin	1768-1855	1
Pienonskowo				
-Pieniążkowo-				
Pinschin	rkKB	Augsburg	1780-1883	1
-Pinczyn-	rkKB	Berlin	1710-1769	1
Pluskowenz	rkKB	Augsburg	1795-1940	1
-Pluskowęsy-				
Podwitz	rkKB	Augsburg	1770-1835	1
-Podwiesk-	rkKB	Augsburg	1818-1865	1
Pogutken	evKB	Lübeck	1890-1911	1
-Pogódki-	rkKB	Augsburg	1853-1905	2
	rkKB	Berlin	1748-1852	1
	rkKB	Berlin	1757-1852	1
Pokrzydowo	rkKB	Berlin	1804-1857	1
-Pokrzydowo-	rkKB	Augsburg	1837-1908	1
Polnisch Brzozie	rkKB	Augsburg	1833-1930	1
-Brzozie-	rkKB	Berlin	1722-1832	1
Polnisch Cekzin	rkKB	Augsburg	1833-1930	1
-Cekcyn-	rkKB	Berlin	1722-1832	1
Polnisch Cekzin	rkKB	Berlin	1803-1834	1
-Cekcyn-	rkKB	Kirchheim	1830-1909	2
	rkKB	Warsaw	1802-1834	1

Location	Nature of Material	Where Filmed	Dates Covered	No. of Rolls
Pomehrendorf	evKB	Lübeck	1786-1819	1
-Pomorska	evKB	Hannover	1774-1937	5
Wieś-	evKB	Lübeck	1774-1937	4
Ponschau -Paczewo-	evKB	Berlin	1770-1819	1
Poppau -Popowo-	KB	Warsaw	1809-1811	1
Posilge	rkKB	Berlin	1674-1909	2
-Żuławka Sztumska-	rkKB		1674-1912	2
Postlin -Postolin-	rkKB	Berlin	1679-1882	12
Pragenau	rkKB	Augsburg	1665-1887	6
-Pręgowo-	evKB	Warsaw	1620-1738	1
Praust	evKB	Warsaw	1814-1865	2
-Pruszcz	evKB	Lübeck	1622-1900	5
Gdański-	ZSR	Warsaw	1809-1811	1
Preussisch Mark	evKB	Lübeck	1690-1941	8
-Przezmark-	evKB	Lübeck	1838-1939	6
Preussisch	ZSR		1812-1939	1
Stargard	MKB	Eibenstock	1771-1869	1
-Starogard	evKB	Lübeck	1658-1940	14
Gdański-	rkKB	Warsaw	1719-1730	1
	evMKB	Hannover	1869-1920	1
	KB	Lübeck	1812-1939	2
	MKB	Hannover	1777-1869	1
	rkKB	Augsburg	1832-1895	5
	rkKB	Kirchheim	1666-1701	1
Pröbbernau	evKB	Warsaw	1660-1845	1
-Przebino-	evKB	Lübeck	1824-1888	1
Prust	rkKB	Berlin	1756-1847	1
-Pruszcz-	rkKB	Berlin	1756-1848	1
Pulsnitz	rkKB	Berlin-Dahlem	1796-1876	1
-Płużnica-	rkKB	Augsburg	1863-1920	1
Quaschin	evKB	Warsaw	1823-1846	1
-Chwaszczyno-	rkKB	Kirchheim	1848-1929	1
	rkKB	Berlin	1744-1835	1
Quiram -Chwiram-	Grundbuch	Berlin-Dahlem	1828	
Radebusch	rkKB	Berlin	1770-1869	1
-Radoszki-	rkKB	Kirchheim	1834-1896	1

Location	Nature of Material	Where Filmed	Dates Covered	No. of Rolls
Radensburg -Raciążek-	rkKB	Kirchheim	1894-1940	8
	ZSR	Augsburg	1913-1924	1
	ZSR	Warsaw	1809-1859	1
Radomin -Radomin-	rkKB	Kirchheim	1843-1890	1
Radosk -Radoszki-	rkKB	Kirchheim	1834-1896	1
	ZSR	Warsaw	1808-1815	1
	rkKB	Berlin	1770-1969	1
Radziki= Gross Radziki -Radziki Duże-				
Rahmel -Rumia-	evKB	Lübeck	1859-1939	2
	evKB	Warsaw	1859-1865	1
	rkKB	Warsaw	1713-1766	1
	rkKB	Berlin	1761-1856	1
	rkKB	Kirchheim	1852-1940	1
Raikau -Rajkowy-	rkKB	Berlin	1719-1909	3
	rkKB	Berlin	1719-1852	2
Rambeltsch -Rebielcz-	evKB	Lübeck	1649-1943	4
	evKB	Warsaw	1853-1865	1
Rasmushausen -Niewieścin-	rkKB	Berlin	1738-1856	1
	rkKB	Kirchheim	1843-1874	1
	ZSR	Warsaw	1774-1816	1
Rauden -Rudno-	evKB	Lübeck	1690-1944	6
Rederitz -Nadarzyce-	LDS records		1835-1870	1
	evKB	Warsaw	1835-1870	1
Reetz -Raciąż-	rkKB	Warsaw	1800-1851	1
	rkKB	Kirchheim	1793-1895	1
	rkKB	Berlin	1757-1829	1
Rehden -Radzyń Chełmiński-	evKB	Berlin-Dahlem	1772-1941	24
	rkKB	Berlin-Dahlem	1674-1942	7
Rehwalde -Rywald-	rkKB	Berlin	1788-1938	2
	rkKB	Berlin	1847-1938	1
Reichenberg -Bogatka-	evKB	Lübeck	1613-1916	3
	evKB	Warsaw	1814-1857	2
	ZSR	Warsaw	1809-1812	1
Rentschkau -Rzeczkowo-	evKB	Hannover	1929-1944	1

Location	Nature of Material	Where Filmed	Dates Covered	No. of Rolls
Rheda	rkKB	Warsaw	1823-1846	1
-Reda-	rkKB	Kirchheim	1743-1918	2
	rkKB	Berlin	1826-1854	1
Rheinfeld -Przyjaźń-	evKB	Lübeck	1681-1941	7
Rheinsberg	evKB	Lübeck	1898-1941	1
-Ryńsk-	rkKB	Berlin	1677-1874	1
	rkKB	Kirchheim	1850-1875	1
	rkKB	Berlin	1677-1875	1
Roggenhausen	rkKB	Berlin-Dahlem	1574-1891	5
-Rogożno-	rkKB	Berlin	1574-1885	4
Roneck -Rojewo-	evKB	Lübeck	1913-1929	1
Runowo	rkKB	Kirchheim	1819-1835	1
-Runowo-	evKB	Hannover Berlin	1889-1944	1
Rudak -Rudak-	evKB	Berlin	1820-1878	1
Ruze	rkKB	Munich	1840	1
-Róże-	ZSR	Warsaw	1808-1858	8
Rosenort -Jurandowo-	KB	Weierhof	1858-1942	1
Ruthenberg -Raciniew-	evKB	Warsaw	1775-1830	1
Sarnau	rkKB	Kirchheim	1838-1910	2
-Sarnowo-	ZSR	Berlin	1631-1837	2
Sartowitz or Dolne -Górne Sartowice-	rkKB	Kirchheim	1860-1940	1
Schadwalde -Szawałd-	evKB	Lübeck	1698-1881	2
Scharnese	rkKB	Berlin	1683-1800	1
-Czarze-	rkKB	Kirchheim	1840-1874	1
Schidlowitz -Szydłowiec-	evKB	Warsaw	1853-1863	1
Schirotzken	evKB	Lübeck	1773-1944	7
-Serock-	rkKB	Kirchheim	1831-1892	3
Schloppe -Człopa-	evKB	Warsaw	1773-1834	1

Location	Nature of Material	Where Filmed	Dates Covered	No. of Rolls
Schlössen -Slesin-	rkKB	Kirchheim	1841-1939	2
Schmellen -Chmielno-	rkKB rkKB	Berlin Kirchheim	1644-1874 1860-1925	3 2
Schmentou -Smętowo Graniczne-	evKB	Berlin	1843-1897	1
Schoenwalde -Szemud/ Szynwald-	rkKB	Berlin	1757-1874	2
Schönbaum -Drzewnica-	evKB evKB ZSR	Berlin Warsaw Warsaw	1650-1941 1814-1865 1809-1811	5 3 1
Schön-e-berg -Ostaszewo-	evKB KB rkKB	Lübeck Lübeck Kirchheim	1698-1879 1800-1874 1749-1915	2 1 2
Schönberg -Szymbark-	rkKB	Lübeck	1694-1944	15
Schönbrück -Szembruk-	rkKB	Berlin	1795-1917	1
Schöneck -Skarszewy-	evKB rkKB rkKB	Lübeck Berlin Kirchheim	1636-1929 1814-1853 1837-1913	23 1 1
Schöneich -Szynych-	rkKB rkKB	Berlin Kirchheim	1741-1830 1800-1876	1 1
Schönhaim -Łąg-	rkKB	Kirchheim	1848-1877	1
Schönsee -Kowalewo Pom.-	rkKB evKB rkKB	Augsburg Berlin-Dahlem Kirchheim	1773-1929 1820-1933 1722-1930	1 8 3
Schönwalde -Szynwald-	rkKB	Berlin	1757-1874	2
Schönwalde -Szemud-	rkKB	Kirchheim	1870-1939	2
Schounwiese -Krasna Łąka-	rkKB rkKB	Berlin Berlin	1780-1870 1780-1899	2 2
Schrotten -Serock-	evKB rkKB	Lübeck Kirchheim	1773-1944 1831-1892	7 3
Schrotz -Skrzatusz-	Grundbuchamt	Berlin-Dahlem	1804-1806	2

Location	Nature of Material	Where Filmed	Dates Covered	No. of Rolls
Schulitz	rkKB	Berlin	1663-1891	4
-Solec Kujawski-	rkKB	Berlin	1663-1844	2
Schurow -Skorowo-	evKB	Warsaw	1862-1870	1
Schwanau	rkKB	Berlin	1711-1857	1
-Sianowo-	rkKB	Kirchheim	1843-1922	1
Schwabensee -Gromadno-	rkKB	Kirchheim	1835-1876	1
Schwartau -Zwartowo-	evKB	Warsaw	1677-1796	1
Schwarzau	rkKB	Berlin	1779-1852	1
-Swarzewo-	rkKB	Berlin	1772-1852	1
Schwarzau -Swarzewo-	rkKB	Kirchheim	1781-1935	3
Schwarzwald	rkKB	Kirchheim	1771-1915	7
-Czarnylas-	rkKB	Augsburg	1820-1844	1
Schweike	rkKB	Berlin	1785-1876	1
-Świekatowo-	rkKB	Berlin	1802-1858	2
Schwenten -Święte-	ZSR	Berlin	1733-1929	2
Schwetz	evKB	Lübeck	1855-1943	3
-Świecie-	rkKB	Berlin	1792-1860	2
Seefeld	rkKB	Kirchheim	1824-1919	4
-Przodkowo-	ZSR	Berlin	1785-1830	1
Seeheim	rkKB	Kirchheim	1832-1847	2
-Osieczek-	rkKB	Berlin	1751-1831	1
Seehof -Bługowo-	rkKB	Berlin-Dahlem	1773-1869	1
Sierakowitz	evKB	Lübeck	1888-1902	1
-Sierakowice-	rkKB	Berlin	1750-1835	1
	rkKB	Kirchheim	1836-1875	4
Skempen	rkKB	Kirchheim	1851-1867	2
-Skępe-	ZSR	Augsburg	1870-1875	1
Skurz	evKB	Lübeck	1847-1944	3
-Skorcz-	rkKB	Berlin	1715-1821	1
	rkKB	Kirchheim	1771-1939	4
Sobbowitz	evKB	Lübeck	1789-1925	8
-Sobowidz-	evKB	Warsaw	1821-1865	2

Location	Nature of Material	Where Filmed	Dates Covered	No. of Rolls
Spethal -Szpetal Górny-	rkKB	Kirchheim	1847-1891	2
Stalle -Stalewo-	evKB evKB	Lübeck Warsaw	1665-1887 1806-1865	5 1
Steegen -Stegna-	evKB	Warsaw	1814-1865	5
Steinforth -Trzyniec-	evKB	Warsaw	1843-1856	1
Stendsitz -Stężyca Szlachecka-	rkKB rkKB evKB	Berlin Kirchheim Lübeck	1692-1860 1835-1933 1907-1944	1 2 1
Stolzenberg -Chełm-	rkKB KB	München Lübeck	1683-1900 1784-1808	9 1
Strasburg -Brodnica-	evKB rkKB rkKB rkKB rkKB ZSR ZSR	Lübeck Berlin-Dahlem Kirchheim Berlin-Dahlem Berlin Warsaw Warsaw	1630-1944 1638-1847 1801-1897 1801-1834 1693-1847 1840-1847 1808-1853	6 3 4 1 2 1 4
Streep -Strzepz-	rkKB rkKB	Augsburg Warsaw	1845-1898 1713-1745	1 1
Strellin -Strzelno-	rkKB rkKB	Kirchheim Berlin	1849-1918 1812-1825	1 1
Strepsch -Strzepcz-	rkKB rkKB	Berlin Augsburg	1810-1846 1846-1892	1 1
Stüblau -Steblewo-	evKB evKB ZSR	Lübeck Warsaw Warsaw	1741-1921 1660-1865 1809-1812	3 2 1
Stuhm -Sztum-	evKB rkKB	Lübeck Kirchheim	1691-1920 1670-1907	9 6
Subkau -Subkowy-	rkKB rkKB rkKB rkKB	Warsaw Berlin Kirchheim Berlin	1780-1865 1687-1865 1843-1926 1686-1840	1 1 3 1
Sullenschin -Sulęczyno-	evKB rkKB rkKB	Lübeck Augsburg Berlin-Dahlem	1863-1877 1856-1938 1706-1866	1 1 2
Swaroschin -Swarożyn-	evKB	Lübeck	1889-1944	1
Tansee -Swierki-	evKB	Lübeck	1661-1891	2

Location	Nature of Material	Where Filmed	Dates Covered	No. of Rolls
Tarnowke -Tarnówka-	evKB	Warsaw	1845-1870	1
Thiensdorf -Jezioro-	evKB	Lübeck	1637-1891	8
	KB	Weierhof	1782-1943	1
	KB	Lübeck	1801-1874	1
	KB	Berlin	1835-1890	1
	KB	Berlin	1754-1892	2
Thiergart -Zwierzno-	rkKB	Berlin	1688-1922	2
Thorn -Toruń-	Innere Verwaltung	Berlin-Dahlem	1846-1879	1
	evKB	Warsaw	1605-1865	12
	evKB	Berlin	1800-1880	1
	evKB	Lübeck	1800-1944	24
	evMKB	Hannover	1815-1920	6
	evMKB	Hannover	1773-1808	1
Thymau -Tymawa-	rkKB	Kirchheim	1849-1872	1
Tiefenau -Tychnowy-	rkKB	Berlin	1709-1857	3
Tiege -Marynowy-	rkKB	Augsburg	1693-1944	3
Tiegenhagen -Tujce-	rkKB	Augsburg	1873-1944	1
Tiegenhof -Nowy Dwór Gdański-	evKB	Lübeck	1784-1922	8
	KB	Lübeck	1820-1874	1
	rkKB	Kirchheim	1870-1883	1
Tiegenort -Tujsk-	KB	Lübeck	1745-1912	8
Tillau -Tyłowo-	rkKB	Berlin	1803-1874	1
	rkKB	Warsaw	1753-1805	1
Tolkemit -Tolkemick-	rkKB	Kirchheim	1698-1889	6
Tragheim -Trogamin- or -Tragamin-	KB	Göttingen	1766-1944	1
Tragheimerweide -Barcice-	KB	Weierhof	1766-1944	1
Trombin -Trąbin-	rkKB	Kirchheim	1846-1889	2
	ZSR	Warsaw	1808-1865	5

Location	Nature of Material	Where Filmed	Dates Covered	No. of Rolls
Trutenau -Trutnowy-	evKB evKB	Warsaw Lübeck	1814-1838 1661-1925	1 3
Trunz -Milejewo-	evKB evKB	Lübeck Lübeck	1680-1796 1796-1899	6 4
Tuchel -Tuchola-	Grundbuchamt Innere Verwaltung evKB rkKB evKB	Berlin-Dahlem Berlin-Dahlem Lübeck Berlin-Dahlem Warsaw	1828 1809-1839 1774-1910 1799-1832 1790-1830	1 3 7 1 1
Unislaw -Unisław-	rkKB rkKB	Lübeck Augsburg	1659-1800 1782-1913	1 3
Vandsburg -Więcbork-	evKB rkKB	Lübeck Augsburg	1770-1874 1836-1920	8 1
Villigass -Wieldządz-	evKB	Lübeck	1889-1914	3
Wabsch -Wąbcz-	rkKB rkKB ZSR	Berlin Kirchheim Berlin	1760-1841 1843-1876 1760-1887	1 1 2
Waldau -Wałdowo-	rkKB	Kirchheim	1610-1865	3
Waldau -Wałdowo-	rkKB	Berlin-Dahlem	1774-1816	1
Weichselhorst -Włoki-	rkKB	Berlin	1782-1908	1
Weichselmünde -Wisłoujście-	KB	Lübeck	1630-1938	6
Weisseck -Wysoka-	rkKB	Kirchheim	1858-1891	1
Wernersdorf -Pogorzała Wieś-	evKB KB rkKB	Lübeck Lübeck Kirchheim	1770-1928 1852-1872 1716-1944	3 1 3
Wielle -Wiele-	rkKB ZSR	Kirchheim Berlin	1839-1883 1768-1858	2 1
Wilckenwalde -Sypniewo-	rkKB	Kirchheim	1730-1877	1
Wilhelmshuld -Mirachowo-	rkKB	Augsburg	1639-1912	2

Location	Nature of Material	Where Filmed	Dates Covered	No. of Rolls
Wirsitz	rkKB	Munich	1841-1907	1
-Wyrzyńsk-	ZSR	Berlin	1769-1879	1
Wittenburg	evKB	Lübeck	1893-1914	1
-Dębowa Łąka-	ZSR	Berlin	1915-1929	1
Wollenthal	evKB	Lübeck	1847-1944	3
-Wolental-	rkKB	Berlin	1715-1821	1
	rkKB	Kirchheim	1771-1939	2
Wonneberg	evKB	Lübeck	1648-1936	7
-Ujeścisko-	evKB	Warsaw	1814-1853	1
Wossitz	evKB	Lübeck	1660-1944	3
-Osice-	ZSR	Warsaw	1809-1811	1
	evKB	Warsaw	1814-1847	1
Wotzlaff	evKB	Lübeck	1612-1928	6
-Wocławy-	rkKB	Kirchheim	1867-1923	1
Wrotzk	rkKB	Berlin	1739-1851	1
-Wrocki-	rkKB	Berlin	1739-1841	1
	rkKB	Kirchheim	1842-1936	2
Wyschin	evKB	Augsburg	1854-1939	1
-Wrocki-	rkKB	Kirchheim	1831-1901	1
Zabartowo	rkKB	Kirchheim	1773-1826	1
-Zabartowo-				
Zarnowitz	rkKB	Berlin	1720-1839	1
-Żarnowiec-				
Zempelburg	evKB	Lübeck		14
-Sępolno	rkKB	Kirchheim	1751-1901	3
Krajeńskie-	evKB	Lübeck	1781-1927	11
Zeyer	evKB	Lübeck	1774-1904	9
-Kępki-				
Zippnow	evKB	Warsaw	1780-1870	1
-Sypniewo-				
Zlotterie	rkKB	Berlin	1796-1803	1
-Złotoryja-				
Zoppot	evKB	Lübeck	1821-1929	4
-Sopot-				
Zuckau	rkKB	Munich	1705-1830	1
-Żukowo-	rkKB	Kirchheim	1831-1890	2
	rkKB	Berlin	1618-1845	2